BETWEEN FORM AND EVENT

D1332721

COMMONALITIES

Timothy C. Campbell, *series editor*

MIGUEL VATTER

BETWEEN FORM AND EVENT
Machiavelli's Theory of Political Freedom

FORDHAM UNIVERSITY PRESS
New York   2014

Between Form and Event: Machiavelli's Theory of Political Freedom was originally published in hardcover by Kluwer Academic Publishers, 2000.

First Fordham University Press edition, 2014

Library of Congress Control Number: 2013954280

Printed in the United States of America

16 15 14   5 4 3 2 1

For Vanessa, Lou, Esteban, and Alize

TABLE OF CONTENTS

PART 2: MACHIAVELLI'S THEORY OF HISTORY: MODES OF ENCOUNTER BETWEEN ACTION AND TIME

PART 3: THE EVENT OF THE REPUBLIC
– THE RETURN TO BEGINNINGS

ACKNOWLEDGMENTS TO THE PAPERBACK EDITION (2014)

I am grateful to Fordham University Press and to Helen Tartar in particular for bringing out a paperback edition of the original text, for it is not evident that a book which thematizes the innovative and emancipatory function of historical repetition would get a second chance at finding its public. As every repetition is also the occasion for an innovation, I have decided to cut the original Conclusion, which was a forward-looking, programmatic text that has now been rendered superfluous by my posterior writings, and replace it with the Afterword, in which I propose to restate my position in *Between Form and Event* in dialogue with subsequent work done in the area of republicanism and Machiavelli studies. I also briefly indicate in which directions my thinking on these questions has since developed. Apart from a new index, the main text remains unchanged.

THE PRIORITY OF EVENT OVER FORM
IN MACHIAVELLI'S DISCOURSE

"How to govern was, I believe, one of the fundamental questions about what was happening in the 15th and 16th centuries.... Facing them head on and as compensation, or rather, as both partner and adversary to the arts of governing, as an act of defiance, as a challenge, as a way of limiting these arts of governing and sizing them up, transforming them, of finding a way to escape from them, or, in any case, a way to displace them, with a basic distrust, but also and by the same token, as a line of development of the arts of governing, there would have been something born in Europe at that time, a kind of general cultural form... which I would very simply call the art of not being governed or better, the art of not being governed like that and at that cost. I would therefore propose, as a very first definition of critique, this general characterization: the art of not being governed quite so much."

Michel Foucault, *What is Critique?*

"The so-called problem of contemporary democracy... is that any conception of democracy grounded in the citizen-as-actor and politics-as-episodic is incompatible with the modern choice of the state as the fixed center of political life and the corollary conception of politics as continuous activity organized around a single dominating objective, control of or influence over the state apparatus.... Democracy needs to be reconceived as something other than a form of government.... The experience of which democracy is the witness is the realization that the political mode of existence is such that it can be, and is, periodically lost.... Democracy is a political moment... a rebellious moment that may assume revolutionary, destructive proportions, or may not."

Sheldon Wolin, *Fugitive Democracy*

*MI È PARSO PIÚ CONVENIENTE ANDARE DIETRO ALLA VERITÀ
EFFETTUALE DELLA COSA*

The history of political philosophy leading to Machiavelli is the history of reasons why human praxis ought to comply with pre-established orders or forms. With Machiavelli human praxis discovered its freedom in the antagonism to the sphere of form, in the experience that orders previously regarded as fixed and unchange-able could be overthrown, in the suspicion that this world of ours does not provide secure foundations to any possible order or form. After Machiavelli, political thinking is confronted with an alternative: either it seeks another foundation for its orders in this difficult new freedom, or it questions the need for free human praxis to depend on the primacy of order. This book reconstructs the reasoning that leads from Machiavelli's discourse to this alternative; it takes the position, on the basis of this discourse, that the first alternative is impracticable or aporetic, and tries to sketch, from this discourse, some lines of flight for political thought to follow, should it wish to embark, certainly not for the first time, in the second, no less arduous alternative.

The argument of the book can be stated simply. Machiavelli's perspective on political life as a whole turns around the question of whether political freedom can be founded in a given political form. Political freedom, in turn, is constituted by its internal relation to the historicity of the world of human affairs. This reciprocal entailment of freedom and history means that, under one aspect of the relation, free human action is responsible for historical, as opposed to natural, change. Conversely, under the other aspect of the relation, free human action is enabled by its rootedness in the historical situation. To designate this situatedness I shall speak of the event-character of political freedom. The concept of event, as introduced here, stands in opposition to the concept of form and to its cognate concept of a well-founded order. The double sense in which political freedom is historical, then, serves to articulate the dualism between strategies of foundation and events of subversion that I find in Machiavelli's discourse. This dualism seals the aporetic nature of the foundation of political freedom, of the project of *constitutio libertatis*. Since I take this project to be one of the defining traits of politics in modernity, the argument carries the further consequence that Machiavelli, in virtue of the ways in which he unites a new consciousness of history with a new conception of politics, provides one of the originary elaborations of the situation of modernity as a site of conflict between foundationalist and emancipatory claims.

I propose a reading of Machiavelli that is philosophical, though not exclusively so. Although there exist several precedents for such an approach, from Spinoza, Vico and Rousseau to contemporary interpreters like Leo Strauss, Isaiah Berlin, Claude Lefort and Gennaro Sasso, Machiavelli is far from receiving the philosophically informed treatment ordinarily reserved for other canonical figures in the Western tradition of political thought. True enough, Machiavelli does not present what the ancients would call a doctrine and the moderns a system. A literary corpus composed of a political manifesto for princes, a commentary on several books by a Roman historian, a treatise on war, a history of Florence written on commission, a few plays, smaller and mostly occasional political and cultural writings, diplomatic briefs, and letters to friends does not seem to contain many texts that can be unproblematically classed as works of philosophy.[1] Undoubtedly there are other, deeper reasons for the disregard with which Machiavelli has been treated as a philosophical thinker. The fact remains that his discourse rarely has been portrayed in the kind of "solitude" that a philosophical approach usually provides without further ado to its subjects.[2]

My interpretation of Machiavelli's discourse attempts to be faithful to its discontinuity, singularity and solitude. It presents this discourse as an originary

---

[1] For Machiavelli's role as theorist and "teacher," see the views of Gennaro Sasso, *Niccolò Machiavelli* (Bologna: Il Mulino, 1993); Leo Strauss, *Thoughts on Machiavelli* (Chicago: University of Chicago Press, 1978); and Sebastian de Grazia, *Machiavelli in Hell* (Princeton: Princeton University Press, 1989).

[2] On the "solitude" of Machiavelli, see the considerations expressed in Louis Althusser, "Machiavel et nous," *Écrits philosophiques et politiques*, vol. 2 (Paris: Stock/Imec, 1995).

moment of modern thought as such.[3] The problems posed by discursive discontinuities to the task of interpretation and to its undeniable dependence on what
counts as tradition are well known.[4] I confront these problems through an
interpretation that is impure or hybrid. I read Machiavelli philosophically in the
sense of paying attention to the construction of concepts and the innovation of
vocabularies as a function of the performance of his arguments. For instance, the
concept of state (*stato*) by the end of *The Prince* will not have the same sense that
a reader attributes to it at the beginning of the text, nor for that matter will the
concept have the same sense that it does in other, roughly contemporary political
discourses, for example in the *Consulte e Pratiche* of the Florentine Republic or
in the political treatises of Guicciardini, unless, of course, one wishes to deny that
The Prince contains a unique set of arguments. The reconstruction of these
arguments, in turn, is invariably informed by my understanding of the pertinent
contemporary philosophical conversations, both because such understanding is
hermeneutically productive and because I wish to add Machiavelli's voice to such
conversations.

My approach to Machiavelli takes into account the work of historians of ideas
and linguistic practices.[5] I differ from them to the extent that I do not grant

---

[3] Particularly strong statements of the "originality" of Machiavelli are found in Isaiah Berlin, for
whom a "unifying monistic pattern is at the very heart of traditional rationalism, religious and
atheistic, metaphysical and scientific, transcendental and naturalistic, that has been characteristic of
western civilisation. It is this rock, upon which western beliefs and lives have been founded, that
Machiavelli seems, in effect, to have split open" ("The Originality of Machiavelli," in *Against the
Current. Essays in the History of Ideas* [London: Hogarth Press, 1979], 68); and in Leo Strauss, for
whom "in his teaching concerning morality and politics Machiavelli challenges not only the religious
teaching but the whole philosophic tradition as well" (*Thoughts on Machiavelli*, 232). Other traditions
of interpretation tend to downplay this "originality." For instance, Quentin Skinner has recently
argued for the existence of a "neo-roman theory of free states" which has been "a prominent feature
of Roman legal and moral argument, and had subsequently been revived and adapted by the defenders
of republican *libertà* in the Italian Renaissance, above all by Machiavelli in his *Discorsi* on Livy's
history of Rome." (*Liberty Before Liberalism*, [New York: Cambridge University Press, 1998],10).
There are other, intermediary positions, for example that of Mark Hulliung who on the one hand
argues that Machiavelli is "the first and one of the greatest subversives of the humanist tradition,"
and, on the other hand, maintains that this subversion consists in a simple return to "the ancient model
he admired and hoped to reproduce in modern times... none other than that singularly expansionary,
singularly successful Roman republic whose way of life had been the fulfilment of *virtus*, and ethic
of glory, grandeur, and heroism.... Machiavelli, then, is admittedly not the prophet of a life 'beyond
good and evil' – he is not an amoralist; rather, he is one possible fulfilment of pagan morality."
(*Citizen Machiavelli* [Princeton: Princeton University Press, 1983], ix and 6).
[4] For the primacy of discursive discontinuities see the programmatic texts of Michel Foucault,
L'ordre du discours (Paris: Gallimard, 1971); and Walter Benjamin, "Erkenntniskritische Vorrede,"
Ursprung des deutschen Trauerspiels, in *Gesammelte Schriften* I,1 (Frankfurt: Suhrkamp, 1974). On
questions of philosophical historiography and the historiography of philosophy, see Paul Veyne,
Comment on ecrit l'histoire, suivi de Foucault revolutionne l'histoire (Paris: Seuil, 1978); and
Richard Rorty, Jerome B. Schneewind, Quentin Skinner, eds. *Philosophy in History: Essays on the
Historiography of Philosophy* (Cambridge: Cambridge University Press, 1984).
[5] For studies on the language of politics at the time of Machiavelli, not all of which always manage
to avoid the confusion between homonymy and synonymy, see Felix Gilbert, *Machiavelli and
Guicciardini. Politics and History in Sixteenth Century Florence* (Princeton: Princeton University
Press, 1965); Nicolai Rubinstein, "Notes on the word stato in Florence before Machiavelli," in
Florilegium historiale: essays presented to Wallace K. Ferguson (Toronto: Toronto University Press,
1971); idem., "Stato and regime in 15th century Florence," in *Per Federico Chabod*, Annali della
Facoltà di Scienza Politiche (Perugia: Olschki, 1980-1); Rudolf von Albertini, *Firenze dalla*

objective reality to the contexts of tradition in which a given text finds itself
embedded. The reason is that only the text, but never the context, of a discourse
has the capacity to construct new concepts and in so doing can function historically, i.e., can make (intellectual) history. Therefore the contexts of tradition and
the historical continuities that I reconstruct or adopt from others are employed
strategically, in view of isolating the moments of rupture effected by the given
discourse under analysis.[6] In short, I have tried to write about Machiavelli in a
way that "meets needs that neither unphilosophical history nor unhistorical
philosophy is likely to fulfill."[7]

Giving priority to the discussion of the ways in which Machiavelli's discourse
effects discontinuities over the reconstruction of its contexts of tradition carries
a price: the selective approach to the texts that are chosen from this discourse.
This book does not aspire to present the entire Machiavellian corpus in order to
avoid the practice that such presentations tend to adopt, namely, stringing brief
citations from disparate locations in Machiavelli's discourse and fashioning more
or less haphazard connections at the expense of the inner logic of the discourse's
arguments. Because these arguments exist and need to be followed closely, often
through lengthy textual passages, I found it equally unfruitful to hope to accomplish this kind of interpretative work with even one of Machiavelli's central texts,
in the fashion of an exhaustive commentary. Therefore the interpretation offered
here centers itself on selected parts of *The Prince* and the *Discourses on Livy*
because these two texts arguably contain the essence of the discourse's discontinuity.[8] I concentrate on the latter text because it alone explains its own relation
and the relation held by its more famous counterpart with respect to the discourse
as a whole, while neither taken in themselves exhausts it.

THE INTERPRETATION IN THREE THESES

Each of the three main parts of the interpretation investigates an aspect of the
internal relation between freedom and history in Machiavelli's discourse and
works out its consequences for the modern vision of political life. In the conclusion I propose a new reconstruction of Machiavelli's disputed legacy to modernity.

Part one is dedicated to the new conception of political freedom found in
Machiavelli's discourse and its consequences for his theory of the state or political

---

repubblica al principato (Turin: Einaudi, 1995); and Maurizio Viroli, *From Politics to Reason of
State* (New York: Cambridge University Press, 1992).

[6] In the interminable list of works dedicated to Machiavelli, two model interpretations stand out in
their adoption of the hybrid approach I advocate: Claude Lefort, *Le Travail de l'oeuvre: Machiavel*
(Paris: Gallimard, 1986), and Gennaro Sasso, *Machiavelli e gli antichi e altri saggi*, 3 vols. (Milan:
Ricciardi, 1987).

[7] Richard Rorty, *Truth and Progress. Philosophical Papers 3* (New York: Cambridge University
Press, 1998), 258. Rorty understands this third genre of historiography as *Geistesgeschichte* and gives
a very wide sense to the term.

[8] Niccolò Machiavelli, *Discourses on Livy*, trans. and ed. Harvey C. Mansfield and Nathan Tarcov
(Chicago: University of Chicago Press, 1996); Niccolò Machiavelli, *The Prince*, trans. Harvey C.
Mansfield (Chicago: University of Chicago Press, 1998); idem, *The Prince*, trans. Robert M. Adams
(New York: W.W. Norton and Co., 1992). For the most part I employ these translations, although I
have made changes when appropiate.

form. The central concern of classical political thought turns around the question of who should rule.[9] From this concern emerges the goal of determining the best form of government or regime (*politeia*), since the desired solution to the question is always refracted through a theory of justice: those should rule whose rule is the "best." Machiavelli rejects the primacy of the question of who should rule, and, along with it, of the ideal of a best or just way of ruling, in order to think political life from the standpoint of political freedom as no-rule, as the suspension of domination.[10] In Machiavelli, rule and no-rule, domination and freedom, are fundamental and irreducible factical traits of political life. But they are not equiprimordial at the level of reflection on political life: freedom alone is index of itself and of its opposite. Against the received tradition that holds Machiavelli to be the thinker of stable rule, the first thesis of my interpretation is that Machiavelli relativizes the question of what form ought to be assumed by the activity of ruling in order to pose the question of the situation or event of no-rule, from which all forms of government and every legal order are to emerge and into which they may be revoked if political life is to remain free.

Such priority of the event over the form means, first of all, that the question of how to change the political form overtakes the question of what is the right political form. Machiavelli can relativize the problem of political form because he introduces a new task in political life: to articulate the changes of political form and legal order in relation to the demands for freedom as absence of domination becomes more important than securing the permanence and stability of any given political form of domination. This perspectival shift decenters the state or political form so that political life, as a whole, comes to be seen as revolutionary, both in the events that constitute the state as well as in those that deconstitute it.[11]

---

[9] As Sheldon Wolin says, "Greek political theory developed a political science that was notable for its rule-centeredness. Its preoccupations were with who should rule and how rule by the best or better sort might be assured." (Sheldon Wolin, "Norm and Form: The Constitutionalizing of Democracy," in J. Peter Euben, John R. Wallach, Josiah Ober eds. *Athenian Political Thought and the Reconstruction of American Democracy* [Ithaca: Cornell University Press, 1994], 44). Yet, contrary to what Wolin seems to suggest, this rule-centeredness seems to be present also in "the movement toward democracy in fifth-century Athens": if "its ideology of equality (*isonomia*) can be seen as a protest by the demos against that [aristocratic] conception of rule," it is no less the case that "the push toward democracy... was not, as it was and still is represented to be, a simple demand for 'equality before the law.' It was an attempt to redefine the terms of ruling and being ruled by insisting on a share of power." (Ibid., 46). In other words, the demos sought to participate in ruling, not to abolish it.

[10] In the words of Hannah Arendt, political freedom means that political actors are living "under conditions of no-rule, without a division between ruler and ruled." (Hannah Arendt, *On Revolution* [New York: Penguin, 1977], 30). I discuss this idea of political freedom below, in relation to Arendt, Michel Foucault, Claude Lefort, Quentin Skinner and Philip Pettit.

[11] The shift from form to event in thinking about politics has lately been the subject of Sheldon Wolin's work in democratic theory. See Sheldon Wolin, "Norm and Form;" and "Fugitive Democracy," in S. Benhabib, ed. *Democracy and Difference. Contesting the Boundaries of the Political* (Princeton: Princeton University Press, 1996), 31-45. Wolin states that "instead of a conception of democracy as indistinguishable from its constitution, I propose accepting the familiar charges that democracy is inherently unstable, inclined toward anarchy, and identified with revolution and using these traits as the basis for a different, *a*constitutional conception of democracy.... I try here to account for the mostly abortive efforts at democratic constitutionalism and for the stubborn reemergence of democratic movements by proposing a theory in which democratic constitutionalism is representative of a moment rather than a teleologically completed form." (Wolin, "Norm and Form," 37-39). From the perspective that I develop in this book, Wolin's theory has two significant shortcomings: it lacks a philosophical development of the concept of "moment" or, in my

One advantage of this reading is that it resolves the traditional opposition between those interpretations that see the Florentine thinker as the forerunner of liberalism and/or reason of state and/or power politics,[12] and those that see in him the transmission link from ancient to modern civic republicanism.[13] Retrospectively, it is possible to identify both liberal and republican elements in Machiavelli, and my interpretation shows how his discourse can function as their genealogical origin.[14] By showing that the primary end of political life cannot be that of providing secure foundations for the state, Machiavelli traces the modern political space as a force field whose antithetical poles are the form of the state and the event of the republic. These polarities correspond to two basic modern political practices: the "liberal" process of securing rule (in a dual sense: securing the subjects with respect to the state, and making it secure for the state to rule its subjects), and the "republican" or revolutionary events of no-rule in which the exercise of legitimate domination is suspended in order to give a voice to those who desire not to be dominated, and to amend the political form or constitutional framework in the direction expressed by this desire.

If my thesis is correct, then the sense of Machiavelli's republicanism is paradoxical: the republic, as a political form, does not exist and will never exist because the *res publica* is not a political form (*res*) at all but denotes an iterable event in which forms of legitimate domination are changed in a revolutionary fashion. Republican events reveal the necessity of a given social and political order in its contingent origin and thereby opens this order to the possibility of its radical change. The modern republic is an event of political freedom that exists "beyond the state," that discloses for political life a modality of action which does not fall under the process of securing political forms of domination.[15]

---

terminology, of "event;" and it never explicitly distinguishes between democracy, defined as popular rule, and republic, defined as no-rule.

[12] For Machiavelli as a proto-liberal, see Strauss, *Thoughts on Machiavelli*; and Max Horkheimer, *Anfänge der bürgerlichen Geschichtsphilosophie* (Frankfurt: Fischer, 1970). For Machiavelli as founder of reason of state, see Friedrich Meinecke, *Machiavellism: the doctrine of raison d'etat and its place in modern history* (New Brunswick: Transaction Publishers, 1998); and Michel Senellart, *Machiavélisme et raison d'état XIIe-XVIIIe siècle* (Paris: PUF, 1989). For Machiavelli as thinker of power politics, see Hulliung's thesis that Machiavelli's "constant principle is that the greatest triumphs of power politics are the monopoly of free, republican communities." (Hulliung, *Citizen Machiavelli*, 5).

[13] On Machiavelli as civic republican, see J.G.A Pocock, *The Machiavellian Moment. Florentine Political Thought and the Atlantic Republican Tradition* (Princeton: Princeton University Press, 1975); and G. Bock, Q. Skinner, and M. Viroli, eds. *Machiavelli and Republicanism* (Cambridge: Cambridge University Press, 1990).

[14] This aspect of my work broadly converges on the claim, lately made both by Quentin Skinner in *Liberty Before Liberalism*, ch.2, and Philip Pettit in *Republicanism. A Theory of Freedom and Government* (New York: Oxford University Press, 1997), ch.1, that liberal negative liberty emerges as an attempt to neutralize, in favor of the interests of the monarchical state (*raison d'état*), the theory of freedom present in early modern republicanism. My interpretation shows how both the republican conception of freedom and its liberal neutralization or cooptation are essential moments of modern political life as this is represented in Machiavelli.

[15] Miguel Abensour has recently formulated a similar position: "Just like a disorder that is not destined to be an other order, democracy has an irreducible sense as the refusal of synthesis, refusal of order, as the invention in time of the political relation that overflows and transcends the state. If democracy can oppose itself to the state, this is because politics never ceases to struggle against it." (Miguel Abensour, *La démocratie contre l'État. Marx et le moment machiavélien* [Paris: PUF, 1997],

Part two offers a new interpretation of Machiavelli's theory of history. The prevailing accounts of ancient and modern historical consciousness attribute their difference to the distinction between a circular and a linear conception of historical becoming.[16] I argue that the essential difference between ancients and moderns in respect to conceptions of history is that for the former the end of human praxis consists in corresponding to what the times or circumstances demand, whereas for the latter the freedom of human praxis is evinced in its power to change, rather than to correspond to, the times. This shift in the ways of thinking about the relation between action and circumstances is first articulated by Machiavelli conceiving of history as an effect of free action.

The second thesis I defend is that the new concept of political freedom can be formulated in terms of the power of human praxis to change the times or circumstances. More specifically, political freedom is indissoluble from that type of action which can revoke the contingent into the necessary and the necessary into the contingent. The revocability of modal status is what defines an action that has the power to "change the times." It is only in virtue of this capacity to change its circumstances that the action is called "free" in a strictly political sense. Previous interpretations of Machiavelli's theory of history missed this simple yet decisive thesis because they failed to situate his famous elaboration of the relation between virtù and fortuna in a wider context, both within the discourse itself and in relation to the relevant contexts of tradition regarding the relation between action and time in the ancients. In Machiavelli, the discussion of virtù and fortuna must be decoded starting from his theory of encounter (*riscontro*), first found in the fragment of the *Ghiribizzi al Soderino*, and then elaborated in more detail both in *The Prince* and in the *Discourses on Livy*.[17] According to this theory, the essence of historical becoming lies in the collision or polemical encounter (*riscontro*) between human action and its circumstances, such that as a result of this meeting the times themselves undergo a change.

The relevant contexts of tradition have to do with the theory of modalities in the ancients, and in particular with the traditional problem posed by the Master Argument. In my discussion of this context, the break which Machiavelli effects with the ancients at the cosmological and ontological level comes most clearly to light. Machiavelli's theory of the *riscontro* between action and times presupposes a momentous revolution in the metaphysical order of priority between the

---

115). But Abensour does not provide his own theory of the "Machiavellian moment" with a new reading of Machiavelli, choosing to adopt Pocock's understanding of the same.

[16] On this difference in the "shapes" of ancient and modern history, which owes much of its force to the prejudice that modern historicity essentially takes the form of "linear" progress, there is broad agreement, in spite of their major differences, among thinkers like R.G. Collingwood, *The Idea of History* (London: Oxford University Press, 1973); Karl Löwith, *Meaning in History* (Chicago: University of Chicago Press, 1949); and Hans Blumenberg, *Die Genesis der kopernikanischen Welt* (Frankfurt: Suhrkamp, 1975). The use of the distinction between linear and circular shapes of history to mark the difference between ancient and modern historical consciousness has been severly criticized by Arnaldo Momigliano, *Essays in Ancient and Modern Historiography* (Oxford: Oxford University Press, 1977); ibid, *The Classical Foundations of Modern Historiography* (Berkeley: University of California Press, 1990); and by Santo Mazzarino, *Il pensiero storico classico*, 2 vols. (Bari: Laterza, 1983).

[17] The work of Gennaro Sasso on the theory of the *riscontro* formulated in the *Ghiribizzi al Soderino* is the only important exception in the secondary literature.

dimension of the form and that of the event. For the relation established between the freedom of human action and historical becoming presupposes that the dimension of the event, or what I have called the dimension of the encounter between action and circumstances, is taken out of the realm of the contingent, defined in terms of the determinate negation or simple opposition to the realm of the necessary, and posited as the origin of the difference between necessity and contingency. In other words, whereas the ancients grounded the opposition between necessity and contingency in the dimension of form or substance, which is itself defined as necessary, Machiavelli uproots this opposition from that dimension and displaces it onto the dimension of the event, where the opposition can be sollicited through action that changes the times. This dis-location of the modal difference into the dimension of the event means that one can no longer speak of an absolute "necessity" of events, of an extra-historical determination of the encounters between human praxis and its circumstances, but, on the contrary, everything that is "necessary" is endowed with an event-character: things become necessary in and through the encounter of practices and times, not outside of them, and therefore they can cease to be necessary in time; likewise for all forms and substances.

The advantage of this reading is that it offers a new way of thinking about what Meinecke called "the triad of naturalism, voluntarism and rationalism" that characterizes Machiavelli's "system."[18] Meinecke sees a contradiction between these terms which he resolves by expanding the range of naturalism: "the same force which impelled princes to refrain from being good under certain circumstances, also impelled men to behave morally; for it is only from necessity that men perform good actions. Necessity was therefore the spear which at the same time both wounded and healed."[19] In this way, the priority assigned by Machiavelli to the circumstances, and above all to the possibility of changing the circumstances through action, is missed. Rather than acknowledging that what is necessary varies according to the circumstances, and therefore is itself a contingent determination, the argument of naturalism always resolves the contingency of human action into the scheme of necessity thereby denying, in one stroke, both freedom and historicity to the human condition.

Machiavelli's purported naturalism is the main justification for denying an important role to his discourse in the constitution of modern historical consciousness. One should distinguish between two kinds of interpretations of this naturalism. Some interpreters ascribe to Machiavelli a "mythical" naturalism according to which historical becoming is dependent on a premodern conception of the cosmos and its natural motions, be these construed in terms of a natural teleology or an astral theology.[20] Other interpreters ascribe to the Florentine an equally ahistorical "scientific" naturalism according to which his conception of historical becoming is a result of the application of the modern "scientific"

---

[18] Meinecke, *Machiavellism*, 38.

[19] Ibid., 40.

[20] See Eugenio Garin, *Medioevo e Rinascimento* (Rome: Laterza, 1973); idem, *Rinascite e Rivoluzioni* (Rome: Laterza, 1976); and Anthony Parel, *The Machiavellian Cosmos* (New Haven: Yale University Press, 1992).

approach to natural phenomena onto the sphere of human affairs.[21] My interpretation rejects both versions of naturalism in Machiavelli by showing the relative role played by necessity in the reconstruction of the conditions of human praxis. Turning around Meinecke's famous formulation, one can say that it is not the sword of necessity that both wounds and heals but rather that what appears as necessary emerges from a certain employment of symbolic and political violence on the part of orders that in this way prevent the contingent and revocable character of their origins to appear in the light of day.

Part three brings to a close my discussion of the reciprocal relation between political freedom and history in Machiavelli by examining the sense in which the freedom to change the times is itself enabled by its historical situatedness. Political freedom has an historical apriori that accounts for its unfoundable character, its lack of a metaphysical origin, of an extra-historical, substantial ground. The mutual dependency of freedom and history allows Machiavelli to offer an immanent account of historical becoming. The constitution of history is no longer dependent on historically-transcendent factors like nature or divine providence, as is the case for the ancients. As a consequence one can say that in Machiavelli not only politics, but also history, attains a certain "autonomy," and indeed neither can do so without the other achieving it as well.[22]

The third thesis is that the historical apriori of political freedom takes the shape of historical repetition. The theory of historical repetition is explicitly found in the third book of the *Discourses on Livy*, where Machiavelli argues that political freedom always happens in a "return to beginnings": political freedom has the character of an event in which innovation and repetition coincide. The return to beginnings, far from being the moment in which political freedom flows back to its presumed origin or principle, instead denotes the experience of a discontinuity and a caesura from origins and principles that bind back and predetermine the possibilities of action. Here repetition is originary: there is simultaneously a

---

[21] For Machiavelli as technician of politics, see Cassirer's judgment: "*The Prince* is neither a moral nor an immoral book: it is simply a technical book….[Machiavelli] never blames or praises political actions; he simply gives a descriptive analysis of them…. Machiavelli studied political actions in the same way as a chemist studies chemical reactions" (Ernst Cassirer, *The Myth of State* [New Haven: Yale University Press, 1974], 154-155); Horkheimer, *Geschichtsphilosophie*, passim.; and lately Roger D. Masters, *Machiavelli, Leonardo and the science of power* (Notre Dame: University of Notre Dame Press, 1996). Under the rubric of "scientific" naturalism I also include interpreters who believe that Machiavelli's concept of history is a result of his application of modern psychological naturalism to human affairs. For the most articulate version of this position, see Gennaro Sasso, *Studi su Machiavelli* (Naples: Morano, 1967).

[22] In this sense, my interpretation moves against the widely held prejudice that Machiavelli does not represent a significant moment in the development of modern historical sense, as shown by his "absence" in the canonical representations of the rise of modern historical consciousness found, among others, in Benedetto Croce, *Teoria e storia della storiografia* (Milan: Adelphi, 1989); Friedrich Meinecke, *Historism: the Rise of a New Historical Outlook* (London: Routledge, 1972); Frank Manuel, *Shapes of Philosophical History* (Stanford: Stanford University Press, 1965); and Reinhard Koselleck, *Futures Past. On the Semantics of Historical Time* (Cambridge: MIT Press, 1985).

radical withdrawal of principle (*arche*) and a resurgence of freedom (*an-arche*) as the spontaneity of unconditioned beginning.[23]

The theory of the return to beginnings has been either ignored or misinterpreted by the tradition of Machiavelli interpretation.[24] More often than not, it is adduced as yet another example of Machiavelli's dependency on classical thought because the problematic of the return to beginnings, or of historical repetition, is mistakenly identified with the circular conception of history of the ancients. In reality, if properly understood, the discourse on historical repetition constitutes yet another major break with antiquity on the part of Machiavelli. If repetition is understood actively, as the practical negation of origins and originality, rather than passively, as the imitation of a pregiven original or model, then the possibility of historical repetition becomes a thoroughly modern possibility that corresponds to the modern experience of revolutionary events. In these events, in fact, the necessity of a given legal and political order is revoked ("reduced to its beginning" as Machiavelli says) to the contingency of its emergence, and therefore lets itself be overthrown; while, conversely, the contingency of new orders are given the appearance of necessity. Without this possibility of "repeating" the necessary as the contingent, and the contingent as the necessary, there would be no radical political change.

My interpretation of historical repetition, and the cognate problem of what Machiavelli intends by "imitation of the ancients," leads directly to the reconstruction of the theory of political change in his discourse. In revolutionary events the discrepancy between political freedom and the foundation of political forms of domination is experienced at its most intense. Machiavelli shows that the practices of political foundation based on tradition, authority and religion, all draw their normative force from their attachment to pure origins, that is, to founding instances that are withdrawn from the active practice of historical repetition, from the active subversion of origins. It stands to reason that his theory of political change would be based on the primacy of historical repetition, which alone promises to undermine the above sources of legitimacy for political domination.

Following this argument, I identify in Machiavelli a theory of citizenship, based on the active practice of historical repetition, that is capable of expressing the revolutionary potential of political freedom as no-rule. Furthermore, it is only from within such a theory of citizenship that one can best understand the critique of the uses of morality in politics for which the Machiavellian discourse has always been chastised. My claim is that the critique of morality and religion found in Machiavelli can only be understood as a function of his theory of political freedom. In spite of innumerable treatments of the question of the "autonomy" of

---

[23] On the concept of originary repetition see the work of Jacques Derrida from *De la Grammatologie* (Paris: Editions de Minuit, 1967) to *Specters of Marx* (New York: Routledge, 1994); and Gilles Deleuze, *Difference and Repetition* (New York: Columbia University Press, 1994).

[24] For instance, neither Sasso nor Mansfield, author of the only commentary on the *Discourses on Livy* in English (*Machiavelli's New Modes and Orders* [Ithaca: Cornell University Press, 1979]), discuss in detail, or assign particular significance to, the theory of return to beginnings and the problem of historical repetition. Hannah Pitkin, in *Fortune is a Woman* (Berkeley: University of California Press, 1984) and Claude Lefort, in *Le Travail de l'oeuvre*, both attempt to discuss this problem, but fail to see in the structure of historical repetition an enabling condition for political freedom.

politics from morality in Machiavelli, the prevailing sensation is that the debate has not moved beyond two ideal-typical positions: the one which bluntly asserts, and finds ample textual evidence for, "the evil character of his thought;"[25] the other which claims, on considerably less textual evidence, that "Machiavelli regards the rule of law as the basic feature of civil and political life…. When he speaks of rule of law, Machiavelli always means rule of just laws – that is, laws and statutes that aim at the common good."[26] Both positions fail to see that at the basis of Machiavelli's conception of political life stands a theory of political freedom that casts into question the very ideal of a good or just form of rule. In its practice, this theory of political freedom calls for finite events of subversion or suspension of those practices of domination that find their underpinnings in morality, and to this extent the practice of the free political life entails that one "learn how not to be good."[27] Conversely, if there is no doubt that Machiavelli has a transgressive conception of political life (and in particular, transgressive of the so-called "rule of law"), it is equally certain that his goal remains, always and only, the free political life and his thought, therefore, is not "evil" if by this one intends that it advocates the reduction of political and human life to a life of domination and oppression. My interpretation in part three of the debate on Machiavelli's "immoralism" brings up a last question which I develop in the conclusion of the work: is the discourse of political freedom incommensurable with that of morality or legitimacy in the political situation of modernity? If so, can this incommensurability account for the conflict between politics and morality in modernity?

MACHIAVELLI'S THEORY OF POLITICAL FREEDOM AND THE QUESTION OF LEGITIMACY

Pocock remarks that Machiavelli's "great originality is that of a student of delegitimized politics."[28] This is correct if one takes it to mean that Machiavelli discloses a discursive site that lies outside of the discourse on legitimacy (and thus also outside the absence of legitimacy, which as mere negation falls within that sphere), and that prompts its self-questioning, its crisis. This site marks the caesura between the classical dogmatism about legitimacy, which presupposes that either in the heavens or on earth there exists something that guarantees legitimacy, and the modern critical approach to legitimacy for which something can be criticized only by raising the question of its legitimacy, while, at the same time, every attempt to legitimate something is in turn viewed critically, suspiciously.[29] Machiavelli's discourse generates the anxiety that feeds the modern

---

[25] Strauss, *Thoughts on Machiavelli*, 12.

[26] Maurizio Viroli, *Machiavelli* (New York: Oxford University Press, 1998), 122-3.

[27] Machiavelli, *The Prince*, XV.

[28] Pocock, *Machiavellian Moment*, 163.

[29] Recent versions of the "philosophical discourse of modernity," from Koselleck to Blumenberg and Habermas, have identified in modernity a characteristic anxiety with respect to its own legitimacy. Modernity as a whole is seen as stamped by the crisis of legitimacy, both in the sense that it evinces a deep uncertainty about its legitimacy, and in the sense that it can pursue its *krisis* or critique only by raising the question of legitimacy. See Reinhard Koselleck, *Critique and Crisis: Enlightenment and the Parthogenesis of Modern Society* (New York: Berg, 1988); Hans Blumenberg, *The*

discourse on legitimacy because, in advance of and as a condition for deploying its critique, it raises the suspicion that nothing, neither on earth nor in the heavens, is legitimate in itself, unconditionally.

If one could be certain that there exists something that is in itself or unconditionally legitimate, then raising the question of legitimacy would in principle be a legitimate practice and critique would be a safe and ultimately reassuring endeavor. There would be no reason for the uneasiness of modernity. But if "nothing is legitimate" then whoever raises the question of legitimacy necessarily becomes engaged in a subversive practice. The experience of modernity with the project of critique seems more congruent with this second scenario. The anxiety associated to the question of legitimacy turns out to be directly connected to its nihilism: if anything, under the appropiate critical scrutiny, will inevitably reveal its illegitimacy, and if it should turn out that this critique itself cannot but be illegitimate, then the Machiavellian suspicion that nothing (neither what is criticized, nor what criticizes) is absolutely legitimate would be confirmed. Machiavelli's discourse, like a black hole, exerts a gravitational pull on the whole of modern political philosophy, calling it back to this uncanny of legitimation which it tends all too easily to forget or repress.

The connection between nihilism and the question of legitimacy is embodied in the modern phenomenon of revolution. For as both Burke and Sièyes point out from opposite sides of the barricade, the mainspring of any revolution is precisely the radical lack, the nothingness of legitimacy on the part of those who raise the question of the legitimacy of the given order, of the Ancien Règime.[30] There is a degree-zero of legitimacy that at once drives revolution and modernity: for both, "an extreme pressure toward self-assertion gives rise to the idea of the epoch as self-foundation... *that emerges from nothing.*"[31] The decisive problem for any account of modernity consists in determining the traits of this "nothing" that calls forth the project of self-foundation by employing the weapon of critique, while it simultaneously induces into a further "turn of the screw" whereby every order that emerges from critique and from revolution is in turn inexorably called into question.

In her analysis of revolutions in modernity, Hannah Arendt points out that the nihilism conjured by the question of legitimacy corresponds to the "abyss of

---

Legitimacy of the Modern Age (Cambridge: MIT Press, 1983); and Jürgen Habermas, *The Philosophical Discourse of Modernity* (Cambridge: MIT Press, 1987).

[30] In this context, Arendt speaks about "Sièyes's vicious circle: those who get together to constitute a new government are themselves unconstitutional, that is, they have no authority to do what they set out to achieve." (Arendt, *On Revolution*,184).

[31] Blumenberg, *Legitimacy of the Modern Age*, 97. Emphasis mine. Where Blumenberg and I disagree is in his failure to appreciate the political condition of the "zero point of the disappearance of order," of the "revolutionary reduction of historical positivity to elementary anarchism," (ibid., 221) that Blumenberg first locates in the Hobbesian construct of the "state of nature," and which I have identified in Machiavelli's employment of the idea of freedom as no-rule (literally, an-archy). For another argument in favor of Machiavelli's foundational role in modernity based on Blumenberg's hypothesis on the modern epoch, see Robert Hariman, "Composing Modernity in Machiavelli's *Prince*," *Journal of the History of Ideas* L,1 (1989): 3-29. I agree with Hariman that "just as Skinner and J.G.A. Pocock have done for modern political thought, Blumenberg has raised the stakes for the study of all early modern thought. Machiavelli lies in a blind spot of his epochal perspective, however." (Ibid., 24).

freedom" that poses an enormous problem to the modern revolutionary project of founding new worldly orders (*novus ordo saeclorum*). For how can freedom as "the spontaneity of beginning something new" out of nothing at the same time be "a stable, tangible reality," a foundation of the new order?[32]

My interpretation of Machiavelli suggests that there is no positive answer to Arendt's question because there is an irreconcilable antagonism between political freedom and political foundation. Political freedom can neither serve as a foundation for political order, nor can it be founded itself in a political form, without negating itself. From this abyssal structure of political freedom it follows that revolutions are both possible and necessary (because no political form can find a stable support in political freedom), and yet take place in a situation that transcends and relativizes the sphere of legitimacy (because political freedom cannot offer itself as a normative foundation, neither for the political form nor for its revolution).[33] The nihilism that enables the question of legitimacy to take the form of critique corresponds to the unfoundable character of modern political freedom.

The anti-foundationalist claims I make on behalf of Machiavelli's discourse depend on my interpretation of his idea of political freedom. I contend that the idea of political freedom as the practice of no-rule or of not being governed is central to Machiavelli's understanding of politics. Once political life is viewed from the perspective offered by this idea of freedom, the fact of rule or government loses its veneer of inevitability. One can then raise the question of legitimacy with respect to forms of rule in the most radical way, namely, from a standpoint of no-rule, as the moderns in fact have raised it, both theoretically in the question of critique, and practically throughout their revolutionary tradition.

Furthermore, since political freedom as no-rule is also unworkable for the purposes of imposing rule, it itself does not need to, nor can it be legitimized. Indeed, the very incommensurability of this idea of freedom with respect to the discourse of legitimacy determines the nihilistic undertow experienced by the question of legitimacy, according to which no one who raises this question can hope to find a definitive answer, a final solution, in a new worldly order, whichever this may be. Freedom as no-rule turns the modern revolutionary project of *constitutio libertatis* into an aporia because a form of rule cannot be founded on no-rule without contradiction. As a consequence what falls to the wayside are the twin ideas of an irrevocable order of things and of a final revolution. The revolutionary origin of order in modernity is therefore both unavoidable and contingent, finite. The expression of this paradox is simply that revolutions (the emergence of the new) are essentially iterable: either they repeat themselves or they are not.

---

[32] Hannah Arendt, *The Life of the Mind* (New York: Harcourt Brace, 1978), 203.

[33] Perhaps it is the impossibility of separating these antinomical, yet enabling, conditions of modern political life that has permitted the adoption of Machiavelli's name both by revolutionary and conservative projects since the earliest reception of his work. For the classical presentation of the problem of Machiavelli's "two faces," see Hans Baron, "Machiavelli the Republican Citizen and Author of *The Prince*," in *In Search of Florentine Civic Humanism. Essays on the Transition from Medieval to Modern Thought*, 2 vols. (Princeton: Princeton University Press, 1988): II, 101-151; and Raymond Aron, *Machiavel et les tyrannies modernes* (Paris: Éditions de Fallois, 1993).

The merit of recovering the idea of political freedom as no-rule in our times goes to Hannah Arendt.[34] But Arendt does not apply this idea to her readings of Machiavelli. On the contrary, she attributes this idea of freedom to classical political thought and employs this belief to criticize the kind of revolutionary trajectory that Machiavelli, on her account, gives to modern political thought. In his last, unfortunately programmatic texts on the genealogy of the Enlightenment, Michel Foucault corrects the situation by locating in the Renaissance the "multiplication of all the arts of governing" as well as the simultaneous emergence of the question "how not to be governed" which covers the sense of political freedom as no-rule.[35]

Most recently, Philip Pettit (following the lead of Quentin Skinner) has also identified Machiavelli as a central source of the "language of freedom as non-domination."[36] But Pettit's definition of domination as being "subject to the arbitrary power of another"[37] is much too narrow to do justice to Machiavelli's intuitions. For on the basis of Pettit's definition, the idea of freedom as non-domination cannot be used to criticize the exercise of "non-arbitrary power" or legitimate domination. Indeed, Pettit holds the view that *"the laws of a suitable state*, in particular the laws of a republic, *create the freedom* enjoyed by citizens."[38] On the contrary, I shall argue that the belief that any framework of legal

---

[34] For Arendt, freedom as no-rule "was coeval with the rise of the Greek city-states. Since Herodotus, it was understood as a form of political organization in which the citizens lived under conditions of no-rule, without a division between ruler and ruled. This notion of no-rule was expressed by the notion of isonomy, whose outstanding characteristic among the forms of government, as the ancients had enumerated them, was that the notion of rule (the 'archy' from *archein* in monarchy and oligarchy, or the 'cracy' from *kratein* in democracy) was entirely absent from it." (Arendt, *On Revolution*, 30). Arendt refers to Herodotus III, 80-2 as the source for her concept of isonomy or no-rule: "There the spokesman for Athenian democracy, which, however, is called isonomy, declines the kingdom which is offered him and gives as his reason: 'I want neither to rule nor to be ruled.'" (Ibid., 285) Arendt also speaks of a "political body in which rulers and ruled would be equal, that is, were actually the whole principle of rulership no longer applied." (Ibid., 172). On Arendt's understanding of freedom as an-archy and its importance for the critique of foundationalism in political philosophy, see the important indications offered in Reiner Schürmann, *Heidegger on Being and Acting: From Principles to Anarchy* (Bloomington: Indiana University Press, 1987).

[35] See Michel Foucault, "What is Critique?" and "What is Revolution?" in Sylvère Lotringer, ed., *The Politics of Truth* (New York: Semiotext(e), 1997). Although Foucault does not identify which Renaissance thinkers theorized the desire "not to want to be governed." The presence of this idea of freedom outside of the Western tradition is documented by Pierre Clastres in his analyses of "the Indian world," where he identifies "a vast constellation of societies in which the holders of what elsewhere would be called power are actually without power; where the political is determined as a domain beyond coercion and violence, beyond hierarchical subordinations; where, in a word, no relationship of command-obedience is in force." (Pierre Clastres, *Society Against the State* [New York: Zone Books, 1987], 11-12).

[36] Pettit has tried to articulate this idea of freedom by showing "that this language of domination and freedom – this language of freedom as non-domination – connects with the long, republican tradition of thought that shaped many of the most important institutions and constitutions that we associate with democracy." (Pettit, *Republicanism*, 4).

[37] Ibid., 31. See also the following definition: "Being unfree does not consist in being restrained; on the contrary, the restraint of a fair system of law – a non-arbitrary regime – does not make you unfree. Being unfree consists in being subject to arbitrary sway: being subject to the potentially capricious will or the potentially idiosyncratic judgment of another. Freedom involves emancipation from any such subordination, liberation from any such dependency. It requires the capacity to stand eye to eye with your fellow citizens, in a shared awareness that none of you has a power of arbitrary interference over another." (Ibid., 5).

[38] Ibid., 36. Emphasis mine.

domination actually "creates" political freedom stands at the antipodes of the modern republicanism born with Machiavelli. As I read him, Machiavelli constantly calls into question what in Pettit remains mere prejudice, namely, that freedom as no-rule or non-domination is apriori reconcilable with the legal domination of the state. If Machiavelli is a theorist of critique and revolution it is because of his investigation of the antagonism between political freedom and political form.

The antagonism between political freedom and political form has to date passed unperceived by those interpreters, like Claude Lefort and Quentin Skinner, who read Machiavelli primarily as a thinker of political freedom.[39] For Skinner "any understanding of what it means for an individual citizen to possess or lose their liberty must be embedded within an account of what it means for a civil association to be free."[40] Here the idea of political freedom, which as such need not exhibit a necessary connection to the political forms adopted by civil association, is already wholly compromised in the project of the state, of its freedom or unfreedom. In a second moment, the freedom of the state is analyzed on the basis of a specific and unquestioned analogy with the human body according to which freedom coincides with the unity of a will that commands over the body that incarnates it: "Free states, like free persons, are thus defined by their capacity for self-government. A free state is a community in which the actions of the body politic are determined by the will of the members as a whole."[41] But Skinner's conception of political freedom as self-government is clearly not the same as the idea of political freedom as no-rule. Whereas the latter stands in contradiction with the very idea of domination, the former does not, for a state can be free in Skinner's sense while dominating some, if not all, of its members. For this to be the case, it is enough that "the will of the members as a whole" is a will to dominate others or to dominate themselves, even without recognizing to themselves this desire.[42] Furthermore, Skinner draws a problematic identity between the freedom of a body and the unity of the will that commands the body. This identity excludes on principle the articulation of freedom in terms of resistance and contrast to the exercise of command that is central to Machiavelli's account of political freedom. Equally central to this account are the traits of plurality and self-differentiation, which are also excluded on principle by Skinner's reduction of freedom to the function of unity.

That even "the best republic not only is unable to, but also does not tend to suppress ruling [le commandement], which always hides oppression," does not

---

[39] See Lefort's claim that "supposing that Machiavelli maintains the concept of end, this concept acquires a completely new meaning. What the city strives toward is the preservation of freedom." (Claude Lefort, "Machiavel et la verità effettuale," in Écrire à l'épreuve du politique [Paris: Calmann-Lévy, 1992], 171). See also Skinner's claim that "the basic value in the Discourses is that of liberty." (Quentin Skinner, The Renaissance, vol.1 of The Foundations of Modern Political Thought [Cambridge: Cambridge University Press, 1978], 157).

[40] Skinner, Liberty Before Liberalism, 23.

[41] Ibid., 26-7.

[42] For example, by virtue of participating in the legal system of the state (even of a "free" state in Skinner's sense), which may very well preserve certain of my liberties or rights, I am nonetheless imposing on myself and others a given form of legal domination as well as a whole series of infra-legal practices of domination that are shielded by the legal system.

escape Lefort.[43] It does not do so because, in contrast to Skinner's unitarian model of the political body, Lefort emphasizes that "the audacity of Machiavelli… can best be ascertained in his conception of social division and of political freedom," that is, in the unity of these two terms.[44] Lefort is one of the few readers who systematically supports his interpretation on the fundamental division in Machiavelli's discourse between the desire to rule and the desire for no-rule. But the identification of political freedom and political form reemerges in Lefort as soon as he reduces the republic to "the rule of law… the principle of the equality before the law,"[45] and equates freedom as no-rule with this form of legal rule, republican freedom with the kind of civil liberty that the state can provide its citizens.[46] In this respect, Lefort's reading differs from Skinner's only to the extent that for Lefort "the fecundity of the law depends on the intensity of their [the two basic desires] opposition."[47] Rather than see in the irreconcilable conflict between rule and no-rule the sole condition that permits one to articulate an effective critique of legal domination, i.e., of that domination that is exercised in and through the rule of law, Lefort seems to sublate Machiavelli's intuition of the conflictual basis of political life under the chimeric unity of "the free institution."[48]

If Machiavelli undoubtedly carries out "a destructive critique of the best regime, as this was conceived by the classical authors,"[49] he is no less critical of the idea of a "free regime" of domination. For in Machiavelli no regime, form or institution of rule is capable of integrating political freedom as no-rule without suffering some sort of disintegration. Machiavelli makes the crucial distinction between a form of rule that is "free," in the sense that it is "constitutional" (for example, as the rule of law, or the rule of the majority, etc.), and the kind of political freedom that is freedom from rule. This distinction opens a theoretical space from which to question the claim, fundamental to modern republican constitutionalism, that "the democratic principle cannot be implemented except in the form of law."[50] In the end, the "audacity" of Machiavelli consists in importing the idea of freedom as no-rule as an essential aspect of political life, such that the ideal of a "free state" or "free form of government" is compromised, and with that the possibility of expanding political life outside of, and counter to, the practices of legitimate domination is disclosed.

---

[43] Lefort, *Écrire à l'épreuve du politique*, 173.

[44] Ibid., 172.

[45] Ibid., 170.

[46] "On what depends the vitality of a city? To its attachment to freedom. And what is the distinctive trait of a free city? There, man does not depend on man, but he obeys the law. The Republic is the regime in which the equality of citizens before the law is recognized." (Ibid., 168).

[47] Ibid., 174.

[48] Ibid., 174. Wolin, on the other hand, points out that "institutionalization depends on the ritualization of the behavior of both rulers and ruled to enable the formal functions of the state – coercion, revenue collection, policy, mobilization of the population for war, law making, punishment, and enforcement of the laws – to be conducted on a continuing basis." (Wolin, "Norm and Form," 36).

[49] Lefort, *Écrire à l'épreuve du politique*, 143.

[50] Jürgen Habermas, *Between Facts and Norms* (Cambridge: MIT Press, 1996), 94. Emphasis mine.

MACHIAVELLI AND MODERN HISTORICAL SENSE

Machiavelli belongs to modernity not just because he raises the question of legitimacy so as to place legitimacy in question. Equally important is the fact that his discourse makes a decisive intervention in the *Querelle des anciens et modernes* on the side of the moderns.[51] Machiavelli operates a massive discontinuity with respect to the classical and Christian political and philosophical traditions.[52] The whole question consists in identifying the hypothesis that accounts for this break with the ancients. The hypothesis I put forward is that Machiavelli's discourse is an originary site for both the modern historical sense and the modern concept of politics. More specifically, his theories of politics and history are inseparable because of the internal relation that he establishes between political freedom and the historical essence of political forms.[53] As I argue at length, the historicity of political freedom accounts for the modernity of his concept of politics, while the idea that history is an effect of political freedom accounts for the modernity of his concept of history.

Few of Machiavelli's contemporary interpreters doubt that his political ideas belong among the moderns, and most would argue that they initiate the modern tradition of political thought.[54] But with respect to his thinking about history

---

[51] For the best argument in favor of a Renaissance origin of the *Querelle* see Hans Baron, "The *Querelle* of the Ancients and the Moderns as a Problem for Present Renaissance Scholarship," in *Search of Florentine Civic Humanism*, II: 72-100. See also Charles Trinkaus, "*Antiquitas* Versus *Modernitas*: an Italian Humanist Polemic and its Resonance," *Journal of the History of Ideas* XLVIII, 1 (1987): 11-21.

[52] On this point there is a surprising convergence between two interpreters of Machiavelli, Lefort and Strauss, who otherwise find themselves at opposite sides of the spectrum. As Lefort says, "one must render due homage to Leo Strauss. He was the first to have shown that the *Discourses* contained the same principles as *The Prince*, but that the praise of the Roman republic and of the virtue of its citizens is at the service of a philosophical project that breaks with the teachings of the Tradition." (Lefort, *Écrire à l'épreuve du politique*, 143). Against a consolidated interpretative tradition that wishes to number Machiavelli among the moderns, those thinkers who furthered the reception of classical political thought in the movement that Baron called "civic humanism," Strauss speaks of "Machiavelli's revolt against classical political philosophy" (Strauss, *Thoughts on Machiavelli*, 233). On the idea of "civic humanism," see Hans Baron, *In Search of Florentine Civic Humanism*, passim.

[53] For some views on Renaissance historical consciousness, none of which pursue the internal link between the development of historical consciousness and the development of a new idea of politics, both in general and in reference to Machiavelli, see Peter Bondanella, *Machiavelli and the Art of Renaissance History* (Detroit: Wayne State University Press, 1973); August Buck, "Des Geschichts-denken der Renaissance," in *Schriften und Vorträge des Petrarca-Instituts Köln* IX (Krefeld: Sherpe, 1957); Peter Burke, *The Renaissance Sense of the Past* (New York: St. Martin's Press, 1970); Eric Cochrane, *Historians and Historiography in the Italian Renaissance* (Chicago: University of Chicago Press, 1981); Nancy Struever, *The Language of History in the Renaissance: Rhetoric and Historical Consciousness in Florentine Humanism* (Princeton: Princeton University Press, 1970); and H. Weisinger, "Ideas of History During the Renaissance," *The Journal of History of Ideas* 6 (1945).

[54] As Felix Gilbert puts it, referring to the *Prince* and the *Discourses*: "These two treatises signify the beginning of a new stage – one might say, of the modern stage – in the development of political thought." (Gilbert, *Machiavelli and Guicciardini*, 153). More radical still, Harvey Mansfield states that "Machiavelli is not often given credit for the revolutionary change he initiated and in time accomplished. He began a project, later picked up and developed by other modern philosophers, for a permanent, irreversible improvement in human affairs establishing a new political regime. The project is often called 'modernity,' though modernity is understood no longer as a project but rather as a historical force – one that may now have come to an end." (Harvey C. Mansfield, *Machiavelli's Virtue* [Chicago: University of Chicago Press, 1996], 109). The most notable exception is probably represented by Parel's *The Machiavellian Cosmos* who argues that Machiavelli's mindset is thoroughly impregnated by medieval astrology. But see also the position of Maurizio Viroli,

Machiavelli is still generally classed among the ancients. It is not difficult to find passages in Machiavelli that appear to endorse the uniformity of human nature throughout history, the uncritical adoption of Polybius's cycle of constitutions, the naïve return to the ancients through imitation of their ways, and the belief in the cyclical pattern of human events, to name but a few.[55] Garin best summarizes the case for Machiavelli's pre-modern historical sense: "we find ourselves confronted to the *topos* of *historia magistra*, or to the 'postulate of uniformity,' but also, and above all, to the emergence of the consequences of the fatal 'circle' dear to several positions held by the more or less radical Aristotelianism that was condemned in Paris in 1277, positions that pertain both to physics and astrology."[56] The belief that Machiavelli's writings, in particular the *Discourses on Livy*, combine, more or less confusedly, an ancient philosophy of history with a modern theory of politics, in the best of cases, leads to the formulation of a "dramatic antinomy between the immutable course of history and the exhortation to apply the knowledge of ancient history to impress a more reasonable course to the government of states."[57] In reality there is no such antinomy or contradiction because Machiavelli does not uphold an ancient philosophy of history at all. To speak of antinomy here is merely to hide the fact that this sort of reading proposes a double-headed approach to Machiavelli's thought that produces interpretative impasses.[58]

A more promising line of interpretation assigns a far more central role to the question of history in Machiavelli's thought, and even sees in him a central figure in the emergence of modern historicism, but it places his political thought in a misconstrued continuity with the classical political tradition, thereby weakening, if not denying, the force of the intuitions regarding the modernity of his historical thought. This line of interpretation is the one that argues for Machiavelli as a

---

according to which "the claim that we should regard him as one of the founders of the spirit of modernity must be reconsidered.... Instead of continuing to study Machiavelli as the initiator of the modern science of politics and a forerunner of modernity, we should study his works as the highest point of the tradition of Roman *scientia civilis*.... The very lines which, we have been endlessly told, mark the birth of modern politics are, in content and method, a brilliant essay of deliberative rhetoric as taught by Roman masters." (Viroli, *Machiavelli*, 3-4).

[55] Respectively in Machiavelli, *Discourses on Livy*, I, 39; I, 2; I, preface; and *Florentine Histories*, V, 1.

[56] Eugenio Garin, *Machiavelli fra politica e storia* (Turin: Einaudi, 1993), 4.

[57] Ibid., 19.

[58] The best attempt to articulate Machiavelli's thinking about history as falling under a cyclical conception of history is found in Herfried Münckler, *Machiavelli. Die Begründung des politischen Denkens der Neuzeit aus der Krise der Republik Florenz* (Frankfurt: Fischer, 1990). This work is a rare attempt to understand "Machiavelli's unification of philosophy of history and political ways of acting." (Ibid., 241). In my judgment this attempt fails because Münckler commits two errors. First, he divides the possible conceptions of history into a cyclical and a linear model, assigning to modernity the latter, whereas modern historical consciousness evades this dualism. (Ibid., 39-63). Second, he assigns to Machiavelli the cyclical idea of history present in Polybius, but claims that Machiavelli gives a modern application of this historical model. "The eternal up and down of states and peoples and the cycle of constitutions... in his theory prove to be the necessary presuppositions for the successful mastery of history by men.... The analysis of cyclical laws of history, for Machiavelli, is the presupposition for the capacity of states to evade their *fatum*." (Ibid., 45). In this interpretation one has another "mixed" picture of Machiavelli's thought: the goal of "mastering history" or, as he puts it following Blumenberg, "the fact that man himself has to take care of his own self-assertion" belongs to the "program of modernity" (ibid., 103-4); while the employment of the cyclical model of history is admittedly a borrowing from ancient theories. (Ibid.,106-127; 344-5).

continuation of "civic humanism," best represented by the works of Baron and Pocock.

From the very beginning of his influential reconstruction of the tradition of Florentine "civic humanism," dating back to work begun in the 1930s, Baron insists that a "wholly original conception of history became the model for Florentine thinking in the Renaissance."[59] The idea that Renaissance thought finds its deepest source in a change of historical conceptions is a thesis that has not lost its boldness, and for which my interpretation hopes to provide other, more convincing reasons.[60] Despite Baron's claim that "for the history of historical thinking, something like a Copernican revolution was achieved through Bruni's work,"[61] one is bound to be disappointed if one interrogates Baron's thesis further. Indeed, if Leonardo Bruni's historiography breaks with an "astrology of history" as much as with a "theology of history," it does so in favor of the systematic application of "the fundamentals of humanistic psychology"[62] that unlock "the immutable causes and laws of history."[63] For Baron the "Copernican turn" in modern historical thinking amounts to a psychologically filtered naturalistic approach to history, as opposed to the "medieval view of supernaturally ordained agencies."[64] It is difficult to see how such a reduction of history to nature can figure the promised origin of modern historical consciousness.

In *The Machiavellian Moment* Pocock follows Baron in as much as he intends to depict "early modern republican theory in the context of an emerging historicism."[65] But where Baron embarks on the path of a psychologistic and naturalistic reduction of history, Pocock wants to arrive to modern historicism through the analysis of political thought.[66] Pocock's contribution to contemporary political theory consists in having brought to light the problem of the relation between the theory of political form (in this case, republics) and historical becoming that lies at the heart of modern republican theory:

The one thing most clearly known about republics was that they came to an end in time, whereas a theocentric universe perpetually affirmed monarchy, irrespective of the fate of particular monarchies. It was not even certain that the republic was the consequence of a principle. *To affirm the republic, then, was to break up the timeless continuity of the hierarchic universe into particular moments:*

---

[59] Hans Baron, "The Changed Perspective of the Past in Bruni's *Histories of the Florentine People*," in *In Search of Florentine Civic Humanism*, I: 44.

[60] It is no coincidence that Blumenberg's *The Legitimacy of the Modern Age* concludes with a comparative analysis of the epochal shift between the Cusan and the Nolan philosophies of history. See also Agnes Heller, *Renaissance Man* (London: Routledge, 1978) for an approach to Renaissance thought which argues for the fundamental importance of the shift in conceptions of historicity.

[61] Baron, *In Search of Florentine Civic Humanism*, I: 52.

[62] Hans Baron, "Bruni's *Histories* as an Expression of Modern Thought," ibid., 69-71.

[63] Ibid., 92.

[64] Ibid.

[65] Pocock, *Machiavellian Moment*, 3.

[66] "A vital component of republican theory – and, once this had come upon the scene, if no earlier, of all political theory – consisted of ideas about time, about the occurrence of contingent events of which time was the dimension, and about the intelligibility of the sequences (it is as yet too soon to say processes) of particular happenings that made up what we should call history. It is this which makes it possible to call republican theory an early form of historicism." (Ibid.) Pocock's formulation of what he calls a "republican vision of history" culminates in his analysis of Machiavelli's discourse as a "sociology of liberty." (Ibid., 83 and 211).

those periods of history at which republics had existed and which were worthy of attention, and those
at which they had not and which consequently afforded nothing of value or authority to the present....
The particularity and historicity of the republic involved the particularization of history and its
secularization.... Thought was approaching the threshold of modern historical explanation, and the
central discovery of the historical intellect that "generations are equidistant from eternity" – that each
of the phenomena of history existed in its own time, in its own right, and in its own way.[67]

Pocock sketches the idea that republics have an internal relation to historical
"moments" in which the "hierarchic universe" and its "timeless continuity" is
questioned. In my terminology, this means that republics, far from being stable
political forms of domination, are rather best understood as events in which pre-
established orders of domination (what Pocock refers to as hierarchies) are cast
into question and, it is but one and the same thing, historical change is effected.
Such change is an historical discontinuity, an event that explodes the "timeless"
continuum of tradition by reducing its "value and authority" to "nothing," and in
this sense attains its autonomy and right to be "equidistant from eternity."[68] What
Pocock calls "Machiavellian moments" are, in reality, these republican events in
which the unity of politics and history verifies itself in the experience that all
political forms can and must find their beginning and end in revolutionary events.

Yet Pocock never formulates the philosophical claim that forms the backbone
of my interpretation: the priority of these moments or events of delegitimatization
over all forms of domination (or hierarchies) such that political forms can be said
to have anarchic origins, that is, beginnings in events that are characterized by the
suspension of the division between rulers and ruled. The anarchic chararacter of
the republican event, for which he nevertheless gives, en passant, a negative
formulation ("it was not even certain that the republic was the consequence of a
principle") remains uninvestigated. No positive formulation is given because in
Pocock there seems to be no awareness of the internal relation that obtains
between political freedom and historical discontinuities or revolutionary moments.
The *Machiavellian Moment*, paradoxically, misses the event-character of
republican political freedom.

Pocock's central thesis that "the political thought stemming from the restoration of the *vivere civile* in 1494 is therefore profoundly Aristotelian, and consists
largely in efforts to define how the essentials of the Aristotelian *politeia* may be
established under Florentine conditions"[69] is presented as if it were a simple fact
in the history of ideas. This is far from being the case. In reality, Pocock reads
Aristotle into Machiavelli (and into the modern republicanism stemming from
Machiavelli) because Aristotle's discourse presents a solution to the central
question invoked at every turn by *The Machiavellian Moment*, namely, "asking

---

[67] Ibid., 54. Emphasis mine.

[68] Pocock here is paraphrasing L. von Ranke's famous dictum "Jede Epoche ist unmittelbar zu Gott."
(L. von Ranke, *Über die Epoche der neueren Geschichte. Vorträge dem Könige Maximilian II. Von
Bayern gehalten* [Darmstadt: 1982], 7). The sense I wish to give to Pocock's term "Machiavellian
moment" is analogous to Walter Benjamin's subversive appropiation of Ranke's saying: "Every
moment is the final judgment for what happened in some preceding moment. If every epoch is
immediately in relation to God, it is such only as the messianic time of a preceding epoch." (Walter
Benjamin, *Gesammelte Schriften* [Frankfurt: Suhrkamp, 1979-89], I:1174-5).

[69] Pocock, *Machiavellian Moment*, 116.

whether the *vivere civile* and its values could indeed be held stable in time."[70] It is the preoccupation with the stability of political form and with the values that legitimate the practice of domination, functioning as the basic hermeneutical prejudice, that leads Pocock to Aristotle without allowing him to question whether it is the case that this "stability" and these "values" have an essential relation to the existence of modern political freedom, to that "sociology of liberty" that Pocock identifies in Machiavelli. Pocock gives up from the start, and without argumentation, on the possibility that modern political freedom might have a positive relation to the contingency of political forms.

Pocock's reconstruction of modern republicanism thus offers the inverted mirror image of Garin's thesis: if Garin claims that Machiavelli belongs to the ancients thanks to his theory of history and to the moderns thanks to his political theory, Pocock tries to show that in Machiavelli the discourse on historical becoming is modern, but the problems that it poses for politics are both formulated and resolved through a return to classical political theory. Pocock's project founders on the assumption that Machiavelli is a representative, even if in a time of crisis for the ideals of citizenship, of Aristotelian civic virtues.[71] This representation of the origins of modern republicanism as returning to the tradition of civic republicanism blocks from view a whole other possible reconstruction of modern republicanism that turns on its revolutionary impetus. The republicanism of Machiavelli, like that of his admirers from Spinoza and Milton, through Rousseau, Fichte and Jefferson, to Marx and Sorel is fundamentally distinct from ancient republicanism because of its revolutionary pathos.[72]

This pathos informs those interpreters who have tried to follow the guiding thread of the internal relation between political and historical theories in Machiavelli, fully aware of the modernity of both. Chief among these stands Lefort's *Le Travail de l'oeuvre: Machiavel*, with which my interpretation shares a great affinity. Lefort shows his awareness of the constitutive role played by history in Machiavelli's theory of political form by arguing that this theory operates with "the difference between a transcendental history and an empirical history – between an operative history and represented history, and as a consequence between the politics that is instituted in the form of factual regimes and the instituting politics from which derives all factual regimes."[73] The idea that history exercises a transcendental function in Machiavelli is correct if understood to mean that historicity is a condition of possibility of (modern) politics. But for Lefort

---

[70] Ibid., 83.

[71] A large and varied series of interpreters who have criticized the thesis of Machiavelli's continuity with the Aristotelian and Ciceronian roots of civic humanism has shown this assumption to be untenable. For a sample of these varied critiques to Pocock's continuistic thesis see Sasso, *Niccolò Machiavelli*; Lefort, *Le Travail de l'oeuvre: Machiavel*; Hulliung, *Citizen Machiavelli*; Mansfield, *Machiavelli's Virtue*; Vickie Sullivan, "Machiavelli's Momentary 'Machiavellian Moment': A Reconsideration of Pocock's Treatment of the *Discourses*." *Political Theory* 20 (1992): 309-18; and Marco Geuna, "La tradizione repubblicana e i suoi interpreti: famiglie teoriche e discontinuità concettuali," *Filosofia Politica* XII,1 (1998): 101-32.

[72] For one such possible narrative of the revolutionary tradition of modern political thought emerging out of Machiavelli, see Antonio Negri, *Le pouvoir constituante. Essai sur les alternatives de la modernité* (Paris: PUF, 1995).

[73] Lefort, *Le Travail de l'oeuvre*, 586.

historical becoming is a function of the transcendental act of giving oneself the pure form of the law that allows for action to transcend its given conditions and change them. From my perspective, on the contrary, the rule of law, whether autonomous or heteronomous, transcendental or empirical, cannot actually effect radical historical change, for this depends on the power of political freedom as no-rule. Whereas the latter coincides with the happening of history in those revolutionary events denoted by Lefort when he speaks of "the instituting politics from which derives all factual regimes," the former simply falls into the scope of these events and therefore can neither account for them nor regulate them from its so-called "transcendental" standpoint.

Althusser is the other significant interpreter of Machiavelli to read his discourse as a revolutionary one, more precisely, following Gramsci, as a "utopian revolutionary manifesto."[74] Unlike Lefort, Althusser avoids the trap of fashioning a transcendental conception of history in which, in the last instance, the form still claims its priority over the event. For Althusser, "it is not an exaggeration to claim that Machiavelli is... the first thinker who has... constantly, insistingly and profoundly thought in the conjuncture, that is, in its concept of the singular contingent case [*pensé dans la conjoncture, c'est-à-dire dans son concept de cas singulier aléatoire*]."[75] What Althusser calls the "conjuncture" I term the event. In this sense, my thesis that in Machiavelli political life is thought from the priority assigned to the dimension of the event rather than of the form overlaps with Althusser's basic intuition. Where I differ with Althusser is in his reductive, and in many respects inconsistent, belief that for Machiavelli the decisive "conjuncture" consists in the establishment of a lasting political form: "Machiavelli is interested only in one form of government: the one that allows a state to last."[76]

Althusser is nearly unique, among the readers of Machiavelli, to have noticed the purely dialectical employment of the cyclical view of history: "the position of Machiavelli on the duration of the state contradicts the thesis of the infinite circle of constitutions. What Machiavelli wants, in fact, is not a government that passes, but a state that lasts."[77] Yet this does not mean that Machiavelli's discourse can be reduced to a theory of lasting institutions. The "state that lasts" is also a stage that is passed over in Machiavelli's attempt to render an account of the thoroughly historical nature of the state: the historicity of the political form entails also the moment or event in which the "state that lasts" comes to its end, and this occurs in the revolutionary or republican events in which the state-form is suspended. Indeed, if there is a single trait that characterizes modern republicanism as it emerges out of Machiavelli, this would be the thought that the state-form cannot be thought outside of the immanent and imminent possibility of its "end."

Althusser claims that Machiavelli's constant attempt to think "the conjunctural case of the matter [*le cas conjonctuel de la chose*]" makes him "the greatest materialist philosopher of history, at the same rank of Spinoza who declared him

[74] Althusser, *Écrits philosophiques et politiques*, II, 66.
[75] Ibid., 59.
[76] Ibid., 85.
[77] Ibid., 86.

acutissimus, extremely acute."[78] In one of those ironies with which intellectual history abounds, Althusser's judgment happens to coincide with that of Leo Strauss, who not only considers Spinoza to be "the hard-headed, not to say hard-hearted, pupil of Machiavelli,"[79] but also remains the strongest proponent of the thesis that Machiavelli's theory of chance lies at the origin of modern historical consciousness.[80] Strauss levels two central charges against Machiavelli's thought which in a sense contain the essential terms of the disputed legacy that Machiavelli leaves to modernity. The first charge is that Machiavelli no longer respects the absolute distinction between validity and facticity, thereby initiating the conflict between politics and morality; the second charge is that Machiavelli claims for human action the power to dominate chance, thereby at once founding modern philosophy of history and reducing politics to a technique. Although Strauss brings up these charges from the standpoint of an interpretation of Machiavelli that is untenable, nontheless the charges reflect the knot of problems that are raised by the Machiavellian legacy, and whose high stakes for contemporary political thinking are undeniable. But in order to address them I first need to present anew Machiavelli's discourse in its *verità effettuale*.

---

[78] Ibid., 162.

[79] Leo Strauss, "Preface to the English Translation," in *Spinoza's Critique of Religion* (Schocken Books, New York: 1965), 15.

[80] See Leo Strauss, "The Three Waves of Modernity," in *An Introduction to Political Philosophy* (detroit: Wayne State University Press, 1989), 87; idem., *On Tyranny* (New York: Free Press, 1991), 106.

PART I

THE FORM OF THE STATE – ON BEGINNINGS

"Form and event are categories and only as categories can they be distinct. In lived experience their relation is unstable and fluid and at every moment reversible. We live in an existence that continuously closes itself into essence and in an essence that at every instant breaks open into existence. However, the relation between form and event is not always the same. There are cultures in which the form dominates over the event, others in which the event dominates the form."

Carlo Diano, *Forma ed Evento*

"Je n'ai jamais mordu dans la miche de pain des casernes sans m'émerveiller que cette conction lourde et grossière sut se changer en sang, chaleur, peut-etre en courage. Ah, pourquoi, mon esprit, dans ses meilleurs jours, ne possède-t-il jamais qu'une partie des pouvoirs assimilateurs d'un corps?"

Marguerite Yourcenar, *Memoires d'Hadrien*

"Scipio gives a brief definition of the state, or republic, as the property of the people [*res publica est res populi*]. Now if this is a true definition then the Roman republic was never a reality, because the Roman state was never the property of the people."

Augustine *City of God* XIX, 21

THE STATE AS HISTORICAL CONSTRUCTION IN MACHIAVELLI

Machiavelli argues for the essence of the state as a historical construction. *The Prince* demonstrates that the historicity of political form provides the unsurpassable horizon within which the modern state must construct its unity and struggle for its permanence in time. The *Discourses on Livy* shows that the change of political forms, in revolutionary political events, is the site of the happening of history. Since for Machiavelli historical becoming is parsed by changes in political constitutions it is more exact to assert that the historical construction of the state, rather than allowing the state to accede to its essence, betrays the impossibility of conceiving the state as a natural substance or kind. The desubstantialization of the state opens onto a vision of political life as a situation for the construction and destruction, appearance and disappearance, of "new modes and orders."[1]

By way of contrast, classical political thought understands the political form (*politeia*) as a natural form, conceiving it as having a foundation in nature (the cosmos) rather than a situation in history.[2] As Aristotle asserts in paradigmatic fashion: "it is evident that the state is a creation of nature, and that man is by nature a political animal."[3] In the *History of the Peloponnesian War* the state or polis is already at its akme when it steps out into history and engages in war with other states. For Thucydides this history is inevitably tragic and spells the downfall of the state: the war highlights the "natures" or "characters" of the states because these flare up in the war, at once shedding light and extinguishing themselves.[4] In Plato's dialogues, from the *Republic* to the *Laws*, the separation of political form and history is exceedingly marked, to the extent that the true or best *politeia* can only be rendered in dialogue, after recognizing the corrupt nature of all actually existing states. For Plato, though less tragically than in Thucydides,

---

[1] Machiavelli, *Discourses on Livy*, I, preface.

[2] On the attempt by classical political thought to "insure the nullity of history" in the constitution of human political order, see John G. Gunnell, *Political Philosophy and Time* (Middletown, CT: Wesleyan University Press, 1968), ch.4, passim. On the "naturalness" of the classical polis as "an institution designed, within limits conditioned by the potentialities of the material, to secure mankind from accident or spontaneity," see Charles N. Cochrane, *Christianity and Classical Culture* (New York: Oxford University Press, 1980), ch.3, passim.

[3] Aristotle *Politics* 1253a1-3. Aristotle voices a general belief among the ancients, irrespective of their specific conceptions of nature which need not have been teleological, when he argues that "the proof that the state is a creation of nature and prior to the individual is that the individual, when isolated, is not self-sufficing; and therefore he is like a part in relation to the whole." (Ibid.). For a non-teleological conception of the state, which is nonetheless considered as a "creation of nature," see the myth of Protagoras in Plato's *Protagoras*.

[4] Thucydides does not consider that the "history" he narrates and that gives "eternal" value to the actors of the drama, is constitutive of the process that gives the states their form or constitution. Such a process is termed by him an "archeology" and qualifies as pre-historical. Athens and Sparta step into the historical stage already fully formed and at their most powerful, only to engage in a bitter and tragic war that leaves them both weak and spent.

history is virtually synonymous with the corruption of political form.[5] Even Polybius, who tries to understand the novelty that the Roman Republic represents in the history of political constructions, in the end fails to perceive the historicity of Rome since the greatness achieved by this state during its history is primarily a result of its unique constitutional form.[6] In general, one can say that for classical thought history is the series of events that happen to the state from the outside (even if these events are matters of domestic politics), once it has already acquired its constitution or political form.[7] History occurs when the political form enters into motion (*kinesis, metabole*) and seeks to assert its actuality in extraneous material or circumstances. In the first chapter I discuss the priority of form over event in classical political thought as providing the central conceptual framework against which Machiavelli's break is best understood.

In Machiavelli's understanding of politics and history, the priority of form over event is reversed. The fundamental role played by history in the understanding of political form stands out in the preface to the first book of the *Discourses on Livy*. Machiavelli's claim to embark on "a path as yet untrodden by anyone" in search for "new modes and orders" is predicated on his having acquired "a true knowledge of histories [*vera cognizione delle storie*]."[8] He attributes the incapacity of his contemporaries to have "recourse to the examples of the ancients" in questions of politics "not so much from the weakness into which the present religion has led the world, or from the evil that an ambitious idleness has done to many Christian provinces and cities, as from not having a true knowledge of histories."[9] His contemporaries lack, above all else, the innovative or modern understanding of history whose principles and results the *Discourses on Livy* prides itself with discovering.[10]

---

[5] On these points one may profitably consult Konrad Gaiser, *Platon und die Geschichte* (Stuttgart: Frommann Verlag, 1961). Both Gaiser and Gunnell employ Plato's myth of Saturn in the *Statesman* as paradigmatic for the classical belief that history, if considered apart from natural or divine order, is harbinger of decadence. In Gunnell's terms, "political time or history is a movement that inevitably degenerates into the original 'dissimilarity' of chaos. The salvation of the state is possible only if, like the cosmos, it is endowed at its foundation with an element which can impart to it the quality of everlastingness by assimilating it to the time of the universe at large." (Gunnell, *Political Philosophy and Time*, 195). For Gaiser, historical corruption is ultimately not tragic because in it "die Entwicklung gleichzeitig zum allgemein Zerfall und zu immer hoherer Erkenntnis hin fortschreitet." (Ibid., 12).

[6] "The principal factor which makes for success or failure is the form of a state's constitution [*politeia*]: it is from this source [*arche*], as if from a fountain-head, that all designs and plans of action not only originate but reach their fulfilment." (Polybius *Histories* VI,2).

[7] Confirmation of this general thesis is found in Christian Meier, *The Greek Discovery of Politics* (Cambridge: Harvard University Press, 1990), ch.7 and 8, passim. Meier argues that the consolidation of political form over political life (which he terms "politicization") in Greek political experience, starting from the fifth century, is combined with a lack of historical consciousness (which he terms "temporalization"). (Ibid., 176-179).

[8] Machiavelli, *Discourses on Livy,* I, preface.

[9] Ibid.

[10] In his commentary of these texts, Mansfield curiously downplays the importance of the new historical sense that Machiavelli wishes to introduce and instead claims that the principal culprit for the misunderstanding of the ancients is to be found with Christian teachings, indeed, with the belief that "the world has been transformed by the coming of Christ" such that people "do not believe that the ancients are imitable today." (Mansfield, *Machiavelli's New Modes and Orders*, 27). This understanding of Christianity as harbinger of a new idea of history simply confirms my point that what is of primary importance for Machiavelli is the change in historical sense, such that a

The inadequate historical sense of his times is responsible for the fact that "the infinite number who read them [the histories of the ancients] take pleasure in hearing of the variety of accidents contained in them without thinking of imitating them, judging that imitation is not only difficult but impossible – as if heaven, sun, elements, men had varied in motion, order, and power from what they were in antiquity."[11] By which Machiavelli does not mean that the political life of the ancients is ruled by the same natural regularity as the political life of the moderns because if this were the case then a problem of imitation could not arise at all. The possibility of imitating the ancients logically presupposes the sense of historical distance between the models and their potential imitators that would be lacking if both the ancients and the moderns would act, always already, in the same ways because they obey the same natural laws, in analogy with the ahistorical motions of "heaven, sun, elements."

Furthermore, the existence of historical distance is an irreducible phenomenon, as is reiterated by the preface to the second book of the *Discourses on Livy* where Machiavelli, after having criticized those who "always praise ancient times... and accuse the present" for bad reasons, proceeds to expound what "I may understand of the former [ancient] and of the latter [present] times, so that the spirits of youths who may read these writings of mine can flee the latter and prepare themselves to imitate the former at whatever time fortune may give them opportunity for it."[12] The distance between ancient and present times is a primordial given for Machiavelli; it is the condition of possibility for the development of the historical sense that allows his discourse to read the histories of the ancients in such a way as to bring their past back to life for the present.[13]

The only way in which the past can be reborn for the present without denying the effective reality of historical distance is by showing how the "modes and orders" of the ancients were just as historically constituted as those found in the present.[14] What such a historical constitution of form entails will become

---

comparison between ancients and Christians with regard to their conceptions of history and nature becomes at all possible for him. Indeed, this new or modern historical sense provides the basis from which Machiavelli carries out his critique of Christianity. The lack of importance given to the problem of history in Machiavelli's thought is evident also in Mansfield's recent interpretations. In the essay "Machiavelli and the idea of progress," for instance, Mansfield admits that Machiavelli's historical sense is a result of his overcoming both classical and Christian ideas of history, but he does not attempt to establish the bases of Machiavelli's modern historical consciousness and is content to reduce the latter merely to the break with "the cyclical change of sects or civilizations" that according to him characterizes the ancient concept of history. (Mansfield, *Machiavelli's Virtue*, 121).

[11] Machiavelli, *Discourses on Livy*, I, preface.

[12] Ibid., II, preface.

[13] In general, Machiavelli never refers to history as *historia gestarum* without interposing the difference of "ancient" and "modern." For example, in the first preface of the *Discourses on Livy* he says that his interpretation of Livy will be done "according to knowledge of ancient and modern things" (ibid., I, preface); and in the dedication to *The Prince* he speaks of "the knowledge of great men, which I have learned through a long experience of modern things and a continuous study of ancient ones [*la cognizione delli uomini grandi, imparata da me con una lunga esperienza delle cose moderne e una continua lezione delle antiche*]." (Machiavelli, *The Prince*, dedication).

[14] In contrast, Lefort argues that in Machiavelli's discourse historical distance or temporal difference is pure illusion and needs to be reduced to the "natural" laws of society, all of which turn on the class struggle between the people and the nobles. In turn, these "natural" laws stand at the basis of the historical character of political orders: they are natural laws of history, so to speak. (Lefort, *Travail de l'oeuvre*, 462). There is a problematic naturalization of history in Lefort's interpretation: the social

progressively clear throughout my interpretation. For the moment, the relevant point made by the two prefaces of the *Discourses on Livy* is that there is nothing "original" about the ancients in the sense that they do not stand at the origin of history and thus beyond its reach. In other words, only because the ancients are not original can they be imitated and, as I will show, surpassed. To point out the absence of an authentic origin or ahistorical foundation Machiavelli retrieves, in the first preface, the old saw that there is nothing new under the sun.[15]

The analogy with natural objects found in the first preface can easily mislead the reader into assuming that the Florentine thinker holds to an essentialist understanding of the uniformity of human nature throughout history which, along with his call to imitate the ancients, would seem to imply the adoption on his part of a cyclical conception of history, generally associated with the ancients. This impression is all the stronger given that such a conception presupposes an isomorphism between the circular motions of nature and the motions of human actions, and Machiavelli's analogy seems to lend itself to such a reading.

But this analogy can receive a wholly different sense, more complicated and more paradoxical, if attention is paid to the context in which it appears. The context is a discussion of the spell cast by aesthetical objects that are considered to be originals: "Considering how much honor is awarded to antiquity, and how many times – letting pass infinite other examples – a fragment of an ancient statue has been bought at a high price because someone wants to have it near oneself, to honor his house with it, and to be able to have it imitated by those who delight in that art...."[16] Machiavelli compares the experience felt by the reader toward the ancients conjured up by their histories to the aesthetic feeling of the Renaissance collector and patron of the arts. The lack of historical sense in these readers is caused by their transferring onto the deeds of the ancients the "aura" projected by

---

constitution of every political order is identical and historically invariant; it corresponds to the class struggle. Temporal difference is merely an illusion that covers this constitution and in so doing allows for the "real repetition of scandals. The destruction of the illusion gives the power to break the cycle of repetition.... Whereas those who mistake the identity turn out to be the agents of repetition, those who unveil it become the agents of historical creation." (Ibid., 516). Lefort's account of historical creation suffers from the basic aporia present in all structuralist accounts of history: the structure that accounts for the synchronic and identical ground of a given diachronic series (in this case: class struggle) cannot be at the same time responsible for marking the difference, for generating the event, that breaks with all synchronic dimensions in order to open up a new diachronic series.

[15] In the words of the second preface, "the world has always been in the same way and has always had as much good as wicked in it. But the wicked and the good vary from province to province, as is seen by one who has knowledge of those ancient kingdoms, which varied from one to another because of the variation of customs, though the world remained the same." (Machiavelli, *Discourses on Livy*, II, preface). Sasso attempts to reconcile Machiavelli's apparent "doctrine of the uniformity of human history through the times" with the equally undeniable insistence on historical variation in his discourse by arguing as follows: "Situations are always the same (and history is therefore uniform) when one cosniders them from the point of view of the 'quality' of human sentiments and passions. But they are always different (and history is therefore not uniform) when considered from the more concrete and material point of view of effective results: because what dissolves an identity of this kind is precisely the initial diversity of the 'provinces,' of habits, of religion, of everything that, in Machiavelli's political thought, characterizes the internal life of states." (Sasso, *Studi su Machiavelli*, 209). Sasso's solution suffers from the same structuralist bias I identified above in Lefort that downplays the fundamental historical situatedness of all naturalistic determinants in Machiavelli's discourse, as I argue at length in part 2.

[16] Machiavelli, *Discourses on Livy*, I, preface.

their aesthetical objects. This "aura" is defined as "the unique phenomenon of a distance, however close it may be. If, while resting on a summer afternoon, you follow with your eyes a mountain range on the horizon or a branch which casts its shadow over you, you experience the aura of those mountains, of that branch."[17] The *Discourses on Livy* is written in order to destroy the aura of the ancients. Aura is destroyed by the "sense of the universal equality of things,"[18] or, what is the same, by the rejection of the normative distinction between original and copy. Machiavelli's analogy with the motion of natural objects ("as if heaven, sun, elements men had varied in motion, order, and power from what they were in antiquity") employs the "universal equality" of this motion, i.e., the fact that the sun moved in the same way for the ancients as it does for the moderns, in order to destroy that aura, that sense of originality, that unbridgeable distance caused by naturalizing the historical situatedness of the ancients that so captivates and paralyzes his contemporaries. In the second chapter I illustrate a particularly important instance of Machiavelli's rejection of the reduction of history to nature: his critique of the "natural cycle of political constitutions" found in Polybius. This cycle is representative of the generalized denial in classical political thought of the historical construction of the state.[19]

The Prince features another famous formula for the break with classical and Christian thought: Machiavelli claims that his discourse is oriented toward the "effective truth of the matter rather than the imagination of it [*la verità effettuale della cosa che alla immaginazione di essa*]."[20] This phrase is generally understood as a rejection of idealism in politics in favor of a more realistic approach:

Many have imagined republics and principalities that no one has ever seen or known in reality; for there is such a difference between how one lives and how one ought to live that he who neglects what is done for the sake of what ought to be done learns his own ruin rather than preservation: because

---

[17] Walter Benjamin, "The Work of Art in the Age of Mechanical Reproduction," in *Illuminations* (New York: Schocken, 1968), 222.

[18] Ibid., 223.

[19] In the "Dedicatory Letter" to *The Prince* Machiavelli writes: "I hope it will not be thought presumptuous if a man of low social rank undertakes to discuss the rule of princes and lay down instructions for them. When painters want to represent landscapes, they stand on low ground to get a true view of the mountains and hills; they climb to the tops of the mountains to get a panorama over the valleys. Similarly, to know the people well one must be a prince, and to know princes well one must be, oneself, of the people." (Machiavelli, *The Prince*, dedication). The terrain of politics can be surveyed from two opposing perspectives, that of the prince and that of the people. Only the people can know the effects of a prince and conversely only a prince can know those of the people. It follows that an effective politics, whether from the side of the prince or of the people, requires knowledge of the effects of actions and consequently requires the political actor to change its perspective. Effective political knowledge is only gained by an actor who, like the painter in the analogy, traverses the distance from one position to another. In this sense, the dedicatory letter to *The Prince* announces its intention to destroy the "aura" of the prince and of its state. For in this text Machiavelli makes power a function of knowledge, and knowledge a function of viewing matters from the positions of opposite subjects, thereby dispelling the illusion of an irreducible distance between the positions of the prince and the people. By opening up any given position of power to any given political subject, Machiavelli's theory allows whoever applies its knowledge to take over the opposite position or perspective from where they find themselves. That the destruction of the aura of the prince is brought about by introducing, as I will discuss below, the people's perspective as an essential element of modern politics, also corresponds to Benjamin's thesis that such destruction is an effect of the process of "the adjustment of reality to the masses and of the masses to reality." (Benjamin, "Work of Art," 223).

[20] Machiavelli, *The Prince*, XV.

a man who wants to profess his goodness in everything is bound to come to ruin among so many who are not good.[21]

The claim that the normative understanding of politics belongs to its imaginary or ideological construction, rather than to its effective truth, has led some interpreters to the belief that Machiavelli's innovation consists in the application of instrumental and strategic rationality to politics with the result being that politics is reduced to the activity of providing secure foundations to the state.[22]

This line of interpretation is misleading, for the pursuit of the "effective truth" of politics cannot be separated from the attempt to gain a "true knowledge" of history. Together, these two formulae reveal that Machiavelli's project consists in delineating an effective history of politics, or an analysis of political life in terms of the real forces at play in history. The first consequence of this analysis is that the project of giving an unquestionable and irrevocable foundation to political form, to the state, is the essential concern of a normative understanding of politics. Only such an understanding attempts to model political life in accordance with standards (forms) that are separated from historical becoming. The project of securing the political form from the effects of historical becoming can only derive its condition of possibility from the application to politics of the presupposition that there is a radical transcendence between fact and norm, between real and ideal. The former is by definition submitted to historical contingency whereas the latter claims to stand above history, and for that reason alone can serve as the source of stability with respect to the play of historical forces.

As I show in the third chapter, Machiavelli reveals that the problem of the foundation of the state, the search after an absolute beginning for the state that can serve as a perpetual source of command in political life, is always articulated by the grammar of normative language: authority in opposition to force, religion in opposition to transgression, common good and concord in opposition to strategic gain and discord. In short, the project of establishing an unequivocal beginning of the state, which is equivalent to the project of encasing and subjecting political life once and for all to a political form, is identical to the project of constituting a system of political authority. Breaking with this view of politics, the *Discourses on Livy* argues that the effective truth of political form is historical. There is nothing original or natural, that is, ahistorical about the political form. The attempt to protect the political form of rule from the process of historical becoming is only a way of securing rule in a system of authority. Conversely, by showing that political form is historically constructed Machiavelli shows that extra-constitutional, revolutionary changes of political forms function as their conditions of possibility.

In political life, the change of form is primordial with respect to the project of securing form. To demonstrate this fundamental thesis, Machiavelli introduces a new perspective into the analysis of historical becoming: the end of *vita activa* is no longer the "good life" but the "free life." Aristotle's belief that "all communi-

---

[21] Ibid.
[22] I refer to the bibliographical indications found in the Introduction.

ties aim at some good, the state or political community, which is the most authoritative [*kuriotate*] of all, and which embraces all the rest, aims at good in a greater degree than any other, and at the highest good,"[23] reflects the internal relation between the question of the highest good and the question of rule (of what is authoritative), characteristic of classical political thought.[24] For the ancients it is senseless to distinguish between the question of "the purpose of the state" and the question of "how many forms of rule [*arche eide*]" there are, and which one is the best.[25] Therefore Aristotle can say that the purpose of the state is not just that of allowing individuals to "live together" but more crucially "that they are also brought together by their common interests in so far as they each attain to any measure of good life."[26] And this entails that "the true forms of government are those in which the one, or the few, or the many, govern with a view to the common interest."[27] Individuals come together and constitute a *politeia* because of a "common interest" that is satisfied, in an immediate rather than representative sense, by a "true" form of government. One can say that for classical political philosophy what is truly held in common is the desire to rule, and, conversely, participation in the activity of ruling and being ruled allows for the emergence of the common interest, that is, allows for the emergence of justice. This dialectical relation between ethics and politics, between the practice of virtue and the practice of rule, that defines the classical idea of the state as an "ethical substance" is expressed by Aristotle in the belief that "excellence [*arete*] must be the care of a state which is truly so called."[28]

But the internal relation between rule and justice merely discloses the decisive problem of classical political thought: who ought to rule? The answer cannot simply be "whoever is most just" or "whoever secures the common interest," precisely because it is impossible to determine what is the common interest independently of the exercise of rule.

Then ought the just [*epieikis*] to rule and have supreme power [*to kurion*]? But in that case everbody else, being excluded from power, will be dishonored. For the offices of the state are posts of honour; and if one set of men always holds them, the rest must be deprived of them. Then will it be good that

---

[23] Aristotle *Politics* 1252a3-5.

[24] Mansfield is one of the few interpreters to have perceived the importance of this point. According to Mansfield, "the classical notion of the regime… is the rule of the whole of any society by a part of that society, which by its rule, gives that society its particular character…. Thus the most important question to ask about any society is: who rules? When that question is answered, one has learned the ordering principle of the society, for rulers make laws that conform to their rule." (Mansfield, *Machiavelli's Virtue*, 236). Mansfield then proceeds to argue that Machiavelli breaks with this classical understanding of regime. Here our interpretations on the nature of this break diverge considerably as will appear evident in what follows.

[25] That is why Aristotle joins them together: "let us consider what is the purpose of a state, and how many forms of rule there are." (Aristotle *Politics* 1278b15-17).

[26] Ibid., 1278b2-25.

[27] Ibid., 1279a28-30. The internal relation between the good life and the political life is brought out directly in Aristotle's definition of the citizen: "He who has the power to take part in the deliberative or judicial administration of any state is said by us to be a citizen of that state; and, speaking generally, a state is a body of citizens sufficing for the purposes of life." (Ibid., 1275b17-22).

[28] Ibid., 1280b7-8. For the concept of ethical substance, see Joachim Ritter, *Metaphysik und Politik: Studien zu Aristoteles und Hegel* (Frankfurt: Suhrkamp, 1977).

the one best man should rule? That is still more oligarchical, for the number of those who are dishonoured is thereby increased.[29]

It is only on the assumption that the struggle for the "good life" is at the same time a struggle for rule that the solution to the problem of who should rule assumes as its most basic criterion the establishment of political friendship (*philia*) and concord (*homonoia*). A good constitution both needs and fosters political concord: it must work towards the ideal of the exclusion of political conflict, which at best will be replaced by the innocuous *agon* of citizens who recognize each other as equals in ruling and being ruled in order to mark their inequality through virtuous or noble actions.[30]

In the fourth chapter I argue that Machiavelli denies the primacy of the classical question of who ought to rule in order to show that political life must open itself to the demands for no-rule, for political freedom as absence of domination. Machiavelli rejects the telos of the "good life" that the ancients assign to political life, and along with that he rejects the primacy of concord. Instead, he argues that political life must express the "free life," and as a consequence it must understand itself in terms of the irreducible discord between the process of securing rule (*arche*) and the affirmation of no-rule (*an-arche*) as a common political existence characterized by the absence of domination.

Machiavelli relativizes the question of rule and decenters the instance of form within political life. The consolidation of political rule can only occur from within a situation that is animated by the desire for political no-rule. Forms of government and legal orders emerge from and can be revoked into such a situation. The situation of no-rule is by definition formless: it can only be referred to through the grammar of events. The priority of the situation over the norm, of the event over the form, articulates one of the fundamental aspects in which Machiavelli breaks with classical political thought and inaugurates political modernity: the question of how to change the political form has overtaken the question of what is the right form.

The historical construction of the state means that the primacy of political discord situates the political form in a process of historical becoming that predicates the possibility of the permanence and stability of the political form always already on the basis of the change of political form. In other words, the historical character of the political form is so radical and thoroughgoing that the very meaning of political life as free life coincides with a revolutionary process. For Machiavelli the free state coincides with the dynamic whereby the state establishes its essence only if it can produce and reproduce itself through its own negation. The free state is radically anti-natural. The fifth chapter illustrates this thesis through a discussion of Machiavelli's reconstruction of the constitutional changes and the institutional innovations that characterize the genesis of the Roman republic.

---

[29] Aristotle *Politics*, 1281a29-34.
[30] On the relation between friendship and the good life, see Aristotle *Politics* 1280b35-1281a5.

In the sixth chapter the revolutionary process that constitutes political life as free life is shown to be an equivocal rather than univocal process. In Machiavelli the expression "free state" contains an antinomical relation. For the irreducible character of the discord between freedom as the praxis of no-rule and legitimate domination as the practice of rule sunders political life into an oppositional field whose antithetical poles receive the names of republic and state. The revolutionary process that constitutes the state attempts to provide a foundation for the free life, or, more exactly, to give political freedom its reality in the form of the state. This process requires the neutralization of the fundamental discord between rule and freedom. Machiavelli refers to it as the process of corruption. Therefore the life of the state, the process whereby it acquires its foundation, is equivalent to the process of corruption of free life. Conversely, the revolutionary process that constitutes the republic restores the virtual or anti-realist character of political freedom by subverting the foundations of the state, by suspending the given order of legal domination and allowing political life to break out of its current form. It turns out that the republic (*res publica*) is not a political form or substance (*res*) at all: there exist republican events in which the necessity of given social and political orders is revealed in its contingency and these orders are opened to revolutionary change.

CHAPTER 1

THE PRIORITY OF FORM OVER EVENT IN THE ANCIENTS

All terms that compose a basic vocabulary[1] draw their meaning from their capacity to function as hinges or primary articulations of discursive totalities. Their meaning is completely dependent on the degree of articulateness, or flexibility, with which they manage to endow the given discourse that hinges on them. So it is with my use of the terms "form" and "event," which are intended, at first, to articulate what I understand to be the basic discontinuity between classical and modern political thought, as this discontinuity is staged in Machiavelli's discourse. My claim is that classical political thought understands the relation between political forms and historical becoming in and through the privilege accorded to the former, hence the priority of form over event in the ancients. Conversely, in modern political thought, beginning with Machiavelli, political form is historicized and there emerges a priority of the event over the form.

In order for this kind of narrative to be persuasive, the vocabulary of form and event not only should be rooted in classical thought but it should also serve to bridge the ancients with the moderns. I borrow the vocabulary of form and event from the work of Carlo Diano, who systematically employs these concepts as basic "phenomenological principles" for a holistic interpretation of the ancient Greek world.[2] What makes Diano's interpretation so pertinent for a study of Machiavelli is its emphasis on the history of the concept of chance (*Tyche*) in classical thought, for this history can be stretched out all the way to the Renaissance and, indeed, beyond. Additionally, Diano shows how the approaches to chance in classical thought are symptomatic of the kinds of relation established between the domain of the event (to which chance belongs) and that of the form, thereby providing a basis from which to discern the new relationship established between these domains through the analysis of the role of chance in Machiavelli's discourse.

For Diano, "what distinguishes the Greek is the sense of reality as form: a great eye which opens onto the world and projects its images into the eternal."[3] For the highest representatives of the theory of forms, Plato and Aristotle, the form is ultimately detached, to a greater or lesser degree, from the individual which instantiates it, and is hypostasized into the necessity of the genus or essence. For example, Socrates is conceived as a unity of matter and form qua human being.

---

[1] I refer to the discussion of the concept of vocabulary in Richard Rorty, *Contingency, Irony, and Solidarity* (Cambridge: Cambridge University Press, 1995), ch.1.
[2] For a general statement of this interpretation, see Carlo Diano, *Forma ed Evento. Principi per una interpretazione del mondo greco* (Venice: Marsilio, 1993).
[3] Ibid., 50.

The individual therefore remains contingent and, like Oedipus, the son of *tyche*. And, just like individuals compose history, so history is the reign of *tyche*.... Because, if the thing is the "thing that is seen" [Diano translates in this way the Platonic *eidos* or *idea*], i.e., if it is form, then the accidents inevitably fall outside of the substance, and for the event there remains nothing but the mere necessity of the fact, which is expressed by *tyche*.[4]

I believe that this exteriority of the event with respect to the form, this non-essentiality of history with respect to being in classical thought, provides the best general formulation of the philosophical and political position that Machiavelli subverts in the most radical way. For this reason, it is essential to begin the discussion of his discourse by reconstructing the political meaning of the priority of form over event in classical thought.

Whether Diano's thesis concerning the relation between form and event in the Greeks, and my reconstruction of their political thought on its basis, are in themselves correct would require, at the very least, another book to demonstrate. But what the ancients are "in themselves" (if this question makes sense at all in the end) is not a decisive issue for my interpretation: what matters is only how they need to be in order for Machiavelli's discourse to be what it is. To the objection that such use of the ancients is an abuse of them, I can only reply that this is the form in which they have been transmitted and betrayed by Machiavelli himself, and, perhaps, by all of modernity after him.

According to Diano, the concept of chance (*tyche, fortuna*) refers to the domain of events. An event is not just something that happens (*quicquid evenit*) but that which happens to someone (*id quod cuique evenit*). Since the event happens to a determinate subject it is said to happen here and now (*hic et nunc*). But also every event is felt to come from somewhere that lies outside of the subject and surrounds it: these are its circumstances, and they are indefinite.[5] The event is understood as a relation between two terms: one is the "*cuique* as pure existentiality that is punctualized in the *hic et nunc*, the other is the spatial-temporal periphery from which the *evenit* is felt to come.... The first term is finite, the second infinite and as *ubique et semper* comprehends all space and all time: it is in it that the 'divine' is found."[6]

In contradistinction to the domain of events stands the domain of forms. The form results from the attempt to give a closure to the domain of the event.

The reaction of man to this rupture of time and opening of space created inside and around him by the event is to give to these events a structure and, by enclosing them, to give a norm to the event. What differentiates human cultures, just as individual lives, is the different closure that they give to the space and the time of the *periechon*, and the history of humankind, just as the history of each of us, is the history of these closures.[7]

---

[4] Ibid., 51-56. On this point, see the analogous remarks found in Cochrane, *Christianity and Classical Culture*, 97.

[5] The first name given to the indefiniteness of what surrounds the subject is Anaximander's *apeiron periechon*; the latest versions of this *periechon*, according to Diano, are Heidegger's *In-der-Welt-sein* and Jaspers's *Umgreifende*. With these names, Diano also reveals some of the sources for his own hermeneutical prejudices.

[6] Diano, *Forma ed Evento*, 71.

[7] Ibid., 74.

Diano distinguishes between two kinds of forms or closures corresponding to the theoretical and practical faculties. On the one hand, the pure forms (*eide*) express the thing considered as it is in and for itself, exclusive of any relation to other: the thing that "exhausts its essence in its capacity to be contemplated." On the other, practical forms (*symbola*) or "forms of the event," refer to the capacity of human action to shape the circumstances in which it finds itself.[8]

From the perspective offered by this vocabulary, the topic of chance in the history of political thought offers a privileged site for treating the problem of how human beings are affected by, and are capable of changing, their circumstances through the kind of forms that they give to their actions. The variety of treatments of chance in political discourses express the possibilities envisaged by human beings to (cor-)respond, in their actions, to circumstances. Two basic strategies of response seem to emerge in the main tradition of Western political philosophy, depending on the relation of predominance established between the *vita contemplativa* and the *vita activa*. Either action models itself on pure and necessary forms that remain unaffected by events, and access to these forms is available only through contemplation and theory, or action chooses to engage the circumstances, the events, in view of changing them, in order to win a space for human freedom in which necessity does not enter. In the first case, political practice will seek to impose orders and laws that make human life as impregnable to the disruption of circumstances as possible, but this also entails the establishment of political forms of domination that are resistant to contestation and change. In the second case, political practice requires an appreciation for the contingency of all political forms and therefore for the necessity of their change. In what follows I suggest that the classical tradition of political thought, in spite of important differences among its discourses, generally tends towards the articulation of the first strategy, that is, tends to assign a privilege to the contemplative attitude towards the problem of the event, thus viewing the task of politics in terms of the purification of the political form from the danger of its immanent and imminent contingency.[9]

CHANCE, PROVIDENCE AND POLITICAL FORM AS ETHICAL SUBSTANCE

Hesiod first introduces the term *tyche* in association with the event of divine manifestation (*tyche theoun*). This association remains constant in Greek thought until Anaxagoras, the teacher of Pericles, separates its concept from the religious

---

[8] Diano understands the hero of the *Iliad*, the "poem of force" to use the expression of Simone Weil, as the hero of form: "because between form and form there can only be relationships of force: the form is an absolute that excludes mediation.... this is the force of action which has its end in itself, the force which is proper to the form." Conversely, the hero of the *Odyssey* is the hero of the event; the hero of practical intelligence (*metis*) and mediation. "Achilles dies young, because the form, being unable to change or bend itself, breaks upon clashing with the event: Ulysses, changeable and flexible, follows the spirals of the event, and death catches up to him in old age." (Ibid., 64). On *metis* and its opposition to the theoretical access to forms through *phronesis* and *nous*, see M. Detienne, J.-P. Vernant, *Les Ruses de l'Intelligence. La Métis des Grecs* (Paris: Flammarion, 1974).

[9] That some aspects of Greek thought, both in philosophy and literature, argue that this danger is ineluctible, and that, as a consequence, the priority of form over event is ultimately "tragic," clearly does not invalidate this priority itself. For an interpretation of the problem of chance in the Greeks along these "tragic" lines, see Martha Nussbaum, *The Fragility of Goodness: Luck and Ethics in Greek Tragedy and Philosophy* (Cambridge: Cambridge University Press, 1986).

association with the divine.[10] This separation opens the dilemma that Euripides would later formulate in the *Hyppolitus*: one must choose between the gods and *tyche*. Either those events that happen to humans have some transcendent purpose or meaning and so depend on the gods (idea of fate as *Heimarmene*), or they are without purpose and so depend upon *tyche*. In the case of Anaxagoras, once *tyche* is desacralized the space is left open for *nous* (intellect), which in nature is expressed by mechanical or efficient causation and in human beings by their *techne*.[11]

The concept of *tyche* finds its first significant political treatment with Thucydides. The historian posits the opposition between *gnome* (practical intelligence, but also steadfast conviction as regards what is to be done) and *tyche* in order to account for the ways of human action.[12] In Pericles's first speech one finds the Anaxagorean definition of *tyche* as what happens in an unexpected way, contrary to plan or calculation (*para logon*).[13] There is in this definition an important trivialization of the power of chance, which is no longer seen as an objective force impervious to reason[14] but as a result of human error, and therefore as something subjective.

Pericles's conception of chance allows for the legitimation of the office of the military and political leader (*strategos*) as a means to control *tyche*. Holders of this office were not elected by lot, but rather with regard to *arete* (excellence). This is why Thucydides can say that the Athenian polis is a democratic constitution only in name, being effectively guided by Pericles through a policy based on the belief of the supremacy of *gnome* over *tyche*.[15] As Pericles explains in the "Funeral Oration," the belief that *gnome*, and thus political *techne*, can defeat chance requires that the city be open to constant change and innovation to meet any unforeseen circumstance with new plans and resources.[16]

Yet Pericles also defends the belief that his guidance of the city is not tyrannical because it reflects the "spirit" or "ethical substance" (*ethos*) of the Athenian polis and of its citizen body.[17] The Athenian *ethos* voiced in Pericles's speech reflects the two principal traits of ancient political freedom. First, the citizen places the preservation of the city and of its values higher than its own self-preservation, and this grants the citizen a degree of immortality and freedom from chance because, should the citizen die for the city, it would be its own

---

[10] Diano, *Forma ed Evento*, 40. Diano gives a detailed analysis of Anaxagoras's crucial vocabulary shift with respect to the concept of *tyche* in an important essay, "Edipo figlio della *Tyche*," in *Saggezza e poetiche degli antichi* (Vicenza: Neri Pozza, 1968).

[11] Diano, *Saggezza e poetiche,* 143-148. On Anaxagoras and the conception of technical progress that his desacralization of chance makes possible, see Ludwig Edelstein, *The Idea of Progress in Classical Antiquity* (Baltimore: Johns Hopkins Presss, 1967), ch. 2.

[12] In the following discussion of chance in Thucydides I rely on Lowell Edmunds, *Chance and Intelligence in Thucydides* (Cambridge: Harvard University Press, 1975).

[13] Thucydides *Peloponnesian War* 1.140.

[14] See Archidamus's view, according to which "it is impossible to calculate accurately events that are determined by chance." (Ibid., 1.84).

[15] Edmunds, *Chance and Intelligence,* 53. See Thucydides *Peloponnesian War* 2.37 and 2.65.

[16] On the sense of technical progress in Thucydides and his contemporaries, see Meier, *The Greek Discovery of Politics*, 201-206.

[17] For the extended discussion of this point, see Edmunds, *Chance and Intelligence,* 56-71.

character or *ethos* that is preserved by the city in virtue of this sacrifice.[18] For Pericles, chance can only really affect the individual, not the city as a whole.[19] Second, it is the spirit of the Athenian citizen that assures Pericles that chance will be defeated, according to the presupposition of his own policy: the patriotism of the citizen is shown in its restless activity that incurrs risks; only by running risks does one acquire experience; lastly, the systematization of experience becomes *techne* which allows one to eliminate the unforeseen and thus to provide security and stability to the polis.[20]

But there is a decisive tension present in Pericles's account of the role of chance in politics. The control of chance through politics understood as a *techne* requires the constant innovation and change of the city; yet the city cannot be so changed that it loses its proper character (*ethos*) and thereby forsakes the adherence to the common good by the citizens that gives the city its consistency as an ethical substance, in virtue of which it can withstand the change of circumstances. In the end, the "Funeral Oration" recognizes that the possibility to control chance rests more on the "nature" of the human being as a citizen and a mortal than on its capacity as a technician and a planner. The human being dedicates its life to the city, and thus lives politically as a citizen, for the sake of a political immortality and a political transcendence of its individual limitations that make it prey to chance and misfortune.[21]

Plato's understanding of the role played by chance in politics is in many senses the reverse of that found in Thucydides, but it takes its point of departure from a similar meditation on the lesson of Periclean politics. Just as Thucydides gives voice to the Periclean belief that Athens should be a school for virtue, so too Plato argues in the *Laws* that the goal of the city is not the mere preservation of the citizen's life, but its becoming as excellent as possible.[22] It is for this reason that giving laws to a city counts as "the most perfect of all tests of manly virtue."[23] But unlike Thucydides, Plato makes the strong claim that "chances and accidents of every sort, occurring in all kinds of ways, legislate everything for us…. almost all human affairs are matters of chance. With regard to the sailing art, the pilot's art, the art of medicine, and the art of the general it seems good to say all this."[24] Whereas the Sophist teaching that lies behind Thucydides's analyses holds that careful planning and constant innovation in the face of changing circumstances, features which characterize the art of politics (*techne politike*) modelled on the art of sailing or on the art of the general, can minimize the role played by chance in human affairs, Plato suggests that these arts will always depend on chance and cannot master it. Plato, as it were, reads Agathon's saying that " *techne* loves *tyche* [chance] and *tyche* [success] loves *techne*" to mean that chance alone gives

---

[18] See the discussion of political immortality in the Greek polis found in Hannah Arendt, "The Concept of History – Ancient and Modern," in *Between Past and Future* (New York: Penguin, 1977), 46-48.

[19] Thucydides *Peloponnesian War* 2.60-64.

[20] Ibid., 1.70; 1.18; 1.71; 6.18; and Edmunds, *Chance and Intelligence*, 88.

[21] Thucydides *Peloponnesian War* 1.64.

[22] Plato *Laws* 707d.

[23] Ibid., 708d.

[24] Ibid., 709a.

the occasion for the emergence of the kind of experience that leads to those arts that serve as model for Pericles's understanding of politics. Therefore this art is always dependent on chance as a condition of possibility of finding its success against chance.

Not human craftiness (*metis*) but only "god – and together with god, chance and opportunity – pilots all human things."[25] The coordination of god and chance in guiding the course of human affairs is better known as "providence." The *Laws* is perhaps the first text in the Western tradition of political thought to provide a providential account of politics, or a political understanding of providence. In other words, with the *Laws* the first form of political theology is born.[26]

Plato's high regard for the power of chance over and against the possibilities inherent in political craft is matched by his low regard for the political freedom of democratic Athens. In the same text, he argues that in order to give laws to a city with the purpose of educating to excellence the citizens living under them, the lawgiver requires a "tyrannized city... and let the tyrant be young, possessed of an able memory, a good learner, courageous and magnificent by nature."[27] But only "some chance" could bring together a "good" tyrant and a "praiseworthy lawgiver," and "if this should happen, then the god has done almost all the things that he does when he wants some city to fare especially well."[28] The best regime, should it come into existence, will be a function of providence.

The "best city emerges out of tyranny, with an eminent lawgiver and an orderly tyrant,"[29] for two reasons. The first is eminently practical: it is much easier to give a completely new code of law to a tyrannized city than to cities with a democratic or oligarchical constitution because these are divided into many, antagonistic centers of power that would never agree to accept this new code of law as being in the interest of everybody.[30] The second and decisive reason is illustrated by Plato's use of the myth of Kronos (Saturn) and the Golden Age.[31] It is well known that this myth exerted an enormous influence in antiquity and in the Renaissance, but a proper interpretation of its significance still eludes us.[32] According to the version of the myth in the *Laws*,

Kronos understood that, as we have explained, human nature is not at all capable of regulating the human things when it possesses autocratic authority over everything, without becoming swollen with insolence and injustice. So, reflecting on these things, he set up at that time kings and rulers within our cities – not human beings, but demons, members of a more divine and better species. He did just what we do now with sheep and the other tame herd animals. We do not make cattle themselves

---

[25] Ibid., 709b-c.

[26] Before Plato, Greek thought treats events either as a more or less immediate manifestation of the divine (e.g., Hesiod) or as a matter of chance (e.g., Anaxagoras). In the first case, providence is strictly a religious affair; in the latter case, chance is strictly a political affair (and is used to bring forth a critique of religion). There is no attempt to unite religion and politics into a political theology or a theologically founded politics as one finds in Plato's *Laws*.

[27] Ibid., 710a. This passage will play a significant role in the Renaissance Neoplatonic vindication of enlightened tyranny, as I discuss in part 2, ch. 3.

[28] Ibid., 710d.

[29] Ibid., 710d-e.

[30] Ibid., 710e-711a.

[31] This myth also appears in Plato's *Statesman*, 271d-274e.

[32] I discuss the general significance of the myth of Kronos for Machiavelli in part 3, ch.2.

rulers over cattle... instead, we exercise despotic dominion over them, because our species is better than theirs. The same was done by the god who was a friend of humanity: he set over us the better species of demons, who supervised us in a way that provided much ease for them and for us. They provided peace and awe and good laws and justice without a stint. Thus they made it so that the races of men were without civil strife, and happy. What this present argument is saying... is that there can be no rest from evils and toils for those cities in which some mortal rules rather than a god.[33]

The myth of Kronos serves Plato to illustrate his solution to the classical question of whether it is better for laws or for individuals to rule over human beings. This question arises from the tension between the universal validity of the law and the justice or fitness of its application in diverse situations: because the law cannot govern its own application in every situation, another possibility to decide the question of who should rule is to find an individual who would know how to do the right thing in every situation, and would thus need no law. Such an individual is a demonic or divine agent.

Plato's solution to this problem consists in giving the name of "law" to what is "godly" or "demonic" in the sense specified by the myth of Kronos.[34] Only where laws will rule over citizens in the same way that the demons ruled over men in the age of Kronos can there be a city at peace.[35] Plato's interpretation inaugurates a fundamental theme in the history of political ideas: only divine or demonic providence (*pronoia*) can lead to political concord (*homonoia*). Only the divine piloting of chance such that a tyrannized city encounters the right lawgiver and establishes laws that will be respected as if they were divine, can lead to the elimination of power-struggles, of social conflicts, and as a consequence can establish true concord.

According to the *Laws*, humans have only two available political options. The first option is to give those citizens who are in power the right to make laws. This case envisions all the classical regimes in which the power to make laws rests either with the one, the few, or the many (monarchy, aristocracy, democracy). But in this case Plato argues that "the laws exist for the sake of some [and] we declare the inhabitants to be 'partisans' rather than citizens, and declare that when they assert their ordinances to be the just things they have spoken in vain."[36] For Plato any regime in which citizens are allowed to make and unmake laws in order to govern themselves contains the potential for civil strife. By way of contrast, the Sophists, from Anaxagoras to Thucydides, argue that the political art exists precisely in order to control the innumerable contingencies to which humans open themselves up once they choose to govern themselves. In the *Laws* Plato enhances the power of chance in order to be able to depreciate the capacity ascribed to political art to deal with such contingencies, precisely because his intention is to

---

[33] Plato *Laws* 713c-714a.
[34] "In public life and in private life... we should obey whatever within us partakes of immortality, giving the name 'law' to the distribution ordained by intelligence." (Ibid., 714a).
[35] In the *Statesman*, 297d-301a Plato makes explicit the idea behind his employment of the myth of Kronos: the knowledge required to do the right thing at the right time is not available to humans, but only to superior intellects, to demonic intelligences. If humans pretend that they can be demonic, then the result will be a city at war with itself. Therefore the best way to confront the problem of justice for humans is to grant a demonic status to human law.
[36] Plato *Laws* 715b.

dissuade humans from the option of self-government itself, what the Greeks called the option of *isonomia*.

The second option, favored by Plato, is an ironic variation on the ideal of *isonomia*: humans are "equal before the law" because they can never aspire to make or unmake laws. Citizens will all be simply the "servants of the laws." As the Athenian says:

> Where the law is itself ruled over and lacks sovereign authority, I see destruction at hand for such a place. But where it is despot over rulers and the rulers are slaves of the law, there I foresee safety and all the good things which the gods have given to cities.[37]

At this point, the requirement of a tyrannized city is clear: for only under such a regime have all citizens lost the possibility of becoming rulers, and therefore may be persuaded into accepting a system of laws that will replace the tyrant. But, of course, the function of this system of laws remains tyrannical because it will not broach any attempt on the part of the citizens to transcend or surpass the laws in order to make and unmake them in accord with the needs of the citizen body as determined by themselves through political deliberation and choice.

To sum up, the inordinate power of chance over against the capacity of political action reflects Plato's belief that laws should be superior to human political activity and should rule over such activity in a despotic or tyrannical way. Likewise, this desire for the stability and fixity of law and order expresses the inner meaning of the idea of divine providence in Plato's *Laws*. Divine providence is the mythical representation given to that ideological schema which assigns to chance its omnipotent role in order to limit the claims of human practical intelligence, but which does so only for the sake of establishing an integral political order, a divinization of the legal system such that it may stand above politics and protect human beings from the risks of political conflict and discord. For Plato, providence is the historico-philosophical pendant to a concept of political concord and harmony that denies to human beings the capacity to govern themselves by making and unmaking their laws in accordance to their desire not to be dominated by their contingent circumstances, by chance. Since Plato asserts that giving laws to a city counts as "the most perfect of all tests of manly virtue,"[38] it follows that his concept of divine providence introduces the reconciliation between "manly virtue" and chance as the seal for the project of founding an unchangeable system of law and order.

In contrast to Plato, Aristotle's appreciation of chance and contingency is linked to the project of rehabilitating human practical activity and bringing back, within human instead of demonic limits, the goal of mastering the situation by acting as the situation demands.

> Hence it is hard work to be excellent, since in each case it is hard work to find what is intermediate; e.g., not everyone, but only one who knows, finds the midpoint in a circle. So also getting angry, or giving and spending money, is easy and anyone can do it; but doing it to the right person, in the right

---

[37] Ibid.
[38] Ibid., 708d.

amount, at the right time; for the right end, and in the right way is no longer easy, nor can everyone do it.[39]

For Aristotle the moral virtues as practical dispositions to choose the intermediate, or mean, have an internal relation to the contingency of situations over which these virtues do not have control. Aristotle defines moral virtue in reference to the dianoetic virtue of prudence because this faculty orients the individual within the horizon of the contingent as such, of that which can be otherwise than it is, and coupled with the moral virtues allows the individual to determine how to do the right thing in the given situation, i.e., at the right time.[40]

The relation of dependency in which the right action stands to the situation allows Aristotle, in the *Nicomachean Ethics*, to reject providence as a factor in his explanation of human action. Happiness, the state of acting virtuously, requires external goods, namely, the situations in which to act with virtue (e.g., one cannot be generous if one has no wealth), that are not dependent on the actor alone but on chance. This partial dependence of virtue on chance signals a separation in Aristotle between the divine and human life that cannot be bridged by providence. If virtue were its own reward, i.e., if virtue did not depend on chance to some degree, as Plato and the Stoics argue on the assumption that the good is absolute and not just the good "for us," then the divine would have to intervene in the human world in order for individuals to attain such good. But Aristotle's theology asserts the opposite: the divine is indifferent to the human world and impotent with respect to what happens in it.[41] In Aristotle there is no Platonic *daimon* or Stoic *pronoia* to steer the circumstances in relation to the right actions. Indeed, the distance of the divine, as source of necessity, from the sublunary world is precisely what lies at the basis of the Aristotelian account of the sphere of contingency. But, in compensation for the withdrawal of the divine, the individual gains a margin of freedom with respect to the circumstances, such that occasions (*kairos*) arise, some of the times and only for some time, to master them.[42]

The separation that Aristotle effects between chance and providence allows him to avoid the "tyrannical" solution to the problem of establishing law and order that is found in Plato. Aristotle does not attempt to model the constitution of the city on a conception of the form which is immune to circumstances, and consequently he never allows the law to rule over citizens in a despotic fashion, that is, by taking away from citizens the possibility of making and unmaking their laws, and thus to be engaged in the practice of ruling. On the contrary, the citizen is defined precisely in terms of its capacity to legislate and judge.[43] This definition of the

---

[39] Aristotle *Nicomachean Ethics* 1109a25-30.

[40] "Virtue is a state that decides [*hexis proairetike*], [consisting] in a mean, the mean relative to us, which is defined by reference to the right rule [*logos*], i.e., to the rule such as the prudent individual [*phronimos*] would define it." (Ibid., 1106b36). "Phronesis is about human concerns, about what is open to deliberation. For we say that deliberating well is the function of the prudent person [*phronimos*] more than anyone else; but no one deliberates about what cannot be otherwise, or about what lacks a goal that is a good achievable in action." (Ibid., 1141b10-13).

[41] Aristotle *Metaphysics* 1074b27-32.

[42] I return to these themes throughout part 2, chs.1-3.

[43] "He who has the power to take part in the deliberative or judicial administration of any state is said by us to be a citizen of that state." (Aristotle *Politics* 1275b17-20).

citizen entails the internalization of chance in the process that determines the just way of ruling. The distance between chance, at one extreme, and the divine, at the other, in the cosmological discourse finds its analogy in the political discourse with the distance between the citizen "who shares in governing and being governed" and the demonic individual

whose excellence is so pre-eminent that the excellence or political capacity of all the rest admit of no comparison with his or theirs, he or they can no longer be regarded as part of a state; for justice will not be done to the superior, if he is reckoned only as the equal of those who are so far inferior to him in excellence and in political capacity. Such a man may truly be deemed a god among men. Hence we see that legislation is necessarily concerned only with those who are equal in birth and capacity; and that for men of pre-eminent excellence there is no law – they are themselves a law.[44]

In this case, Aristotle explicitly justifies ostracism with regard to such demonic individuals in the name of the possibility of human and political justice.

Although Aristotelian prudence is premised on the idea that there is an internal relation between contingency and justice because the form (the good) is not completely separate from the matter (the situation, the event), nevertheless in Aristotle, as in Plato, there persists a priority of the form over the event. This priority is visible in Aristotle's definition of the political form (*politeia*) as a form of "revolution of offices." Aristotle internalizes the revolution of government (*metabole politeion*) into the political form so that the potential for civil strife present in every constitution (of which he was as acutely aware as Plato) can be given a form and neutralized. In the *Laws* Plato denounces the claims raised by the different parts of the political community to participate in citizenship as the source of all civil strife and lack of concord; he settles these claims extra-politically, at once tyrannically and philosophically. Aristotle sees in the capacity of the political form to give political expression to these aspirations the very "salvation of the state":

This is why the principle of reciprocity, as I have already remarked in the *Ethics*, is the salvation of states. Even among freemen and equals this is a principle which must be maintained, for they cannot all rule together, but must change at the end of the year or some other period of time or in some order of succession. The result is that upon this plan they all govern; just as if shoemakers and carpenters were to exchange their occupations, and the same persons did not always continue as shoemakers and carpenters.[45]

In opposition to Plato, Aristotle internalizes chance into the sphere of the political form by advocating the circulation of rule among citizens. But this kind of internalization of the revolution or rotation of government into the form of government is the way in which Aristotle manages to preserve, at the limit, the classical priority of the form over the event. This priority is clearly stated by Aristotle when he says that the rotation of rule is itself the expression of a law (of a form): "That is why it is thought to be just that among equals everyone be ruled as well as rule, and therefore that all should have their turn. We thus arrive at law;

---

[44] Ibid., 1284a1-15.
[45] Ibid., 1261a30-37.

for an order of succession implies law."[46] The step that still remains inconceivable for Aristotle (just as it is inconceivable for the Aristotelian-Ciceronian tradition of civic humanism) is the one from a position that advocates the internalization of revolution into the political form with a view to circulate the rule between man and man, to a position that thinks the possibility of an external revolution of political forms with a view to interrupt the rule of man over man. This is the step taken by Machiavelli, as I show below.

The Polybian discourse on chance attempts a synthesis of Platonic and Aristotelian motifs in order to account for the unique phenomenon of the historical constitution of the Roman republic. Polybius's application of the priority of form over event to this historical phenomenon provides an ideal contrast for the reversal of priorities effected by Machiavelli. The *Discourses on Livy* begins with a discussion of Polybius's analysis of Roman constitutional history in part because this analysis recapitulates and synthesizes the decisive acquisitions of Plato and Aristotle while translating them into a context, the historical genesis of the Roman republic, that favors Machiavelli's goal of demonstrating the historicity of political form.

Polybius shows himself as the transitional figure from Greek to Roman political thought nowhere more evidently than in his treatment of chance which is thematized through what would become a classic topic all the way to Montesquieu and Gibbon: did the Roman empire owe its prodigious growth to virtue or fortune?[47] Polybius's account of chance has perplexed a number of commentators, not the least because it seems contradictory.[48] At times Polybius speaks as if the emergence of the empire was due to a providential fortune.[49] In these cases, his concept of *Tyche* is already overdetermined by the Hellenistic mythological construct of chance as a goddess that traverses Latin literature up to the early Renaissance. At other times, the Roman conquest is explained in terms of rational calculation on the part of the Roman people.[50] Here chance preserves the disenchanted meaning that is found in Thucydides, i.e., as a name for those events "of which it is difficult or impossible for mortal men to grasp the causes" and that

---

[46] Ibid., 1287a15-20.

[47] For the best discussion of this topic see Santo Mazzarino, *La Fine del Mondo Antico* (Milan: Rizzoli, 1995).

[48] See Kurt von Fritz, *The Theory of Mixed Constitutions in Antiquity* (New York: Columbia University Press, 1954); and F.W. Walbank, *A Historical Commentary on Polybius* (Oxford: Clarendon Press, 1970). In what follows I am indebted to both treatments of the concept of *tyche* in Polybius, although my solution to the apparent contradictions differ markedly from those of both authors.

[49] "Just as *Tyche* has steered almost all the affairs of the world in one direction and forced them to converge upon one and the same goal, so it is the task of the historian to present to his readers under one synoptical view the process by which she has accomplished this general design.... *Tyche* is for ever producing something new and for ever playing a part in the lives of men, but in no single instance has she ever put on such a show-piece as in our times." (Polybius, *Histories* I,4).

[50] "The supremacy of the Romans did not come about, as certain Greek writers have supposed, either by chance or without the victors knowing what they were doing. On the contrary, since the Romans deliberately chose to school themselves in such great enterprises, it is quite natural that they should not only have boldly embarked upon their pursuit of universal dominion, but that they should actually have achieved their purpose." (Ibid., I,63).

"one may justifiably refer them, in one's difficulty, to the work of a god or of chance."[51]

Yet Polybius is not contradicting himself by explaining Roman success in terms of rational calculation and at the same time in terms of the providential meaning of chance. Rather, he is giving voice to a deeply ingrained *forma mentis* in classical thought, whose main features have already been presented in the previous discussions. There is an underlying argument in Polybius divergent claims and it can be reconstructed as follows. There exists such a thing as fickle chance:

> By a slight shift of the scale she brings about changes of the greatest moment to either side... she sports with mankind as if her victims were little children.... Remember this change of *Tyche*, I beg you, and do not be over-proud, but keep your thoughts at this moment upon the human scale of things, in other words, follow that course which will produce the most good and the fewest evil consequences.[52]

These words (which Hannibal addresses to Scipio after his defeat and before the destruction of Carthage) reflect Polybius's opinion that the best response to the fickleness of chance consists in following the way of moderation and prudence, remembering human limitations. But Polybius's point is deeper: he believes that this counsel is just what gets put into practice in the political constitution of Rome, which he identifies as the rational cause of Rome's greatness. In fact, "the principal factor which makes for success or failure is the form of a state's constitution: it is from this source, as if from a fountainhead, that all designs and plans of action not only originate but reach their fulfilment."[53] Polybius opposes, therefore, the fickleness of *Tyche* as source of unexpected changes in the course of events to the virtue and strength of the political form or constitution.[54] This virtue itself depends on the principle of moderation that the Roman constitution embodies.

In order to explain the specificity of the Roman constitution, Polybius gives six possible forms of government and describes "the process whereby the different forms of government are naturally transformed into one another." This process he calls "the cycle of political revolution (*anakuklosis*), the law of nature (*physeus oikonomia*) according to which constitutions change, are transformed, and finally revert to their original form."[55] The law of political forms is "natural" and therefore unchangeable. According to Polybius it will apply also to the Roman state.[56] But the cycle can also be slowed down or resisted through political virtue

---

[51] Ibid., XXXVI,17.

[52] Ibid., XV,6-7.

[53] Ibid., VI,2.

[54] "The test of true virtue in a man surely resides in his capacity to bear with spirit and dignity the most complete transformations of fortune, and the same principle should apply to our judgments of states. And so, since I could find no greater or more violent changes of fortune in our time than those which befell the Romans, I have reserved this place in my history for my study of their constitution." (Ibid., VI,2).

[55] Ibid., VI,5 and VI,9, respectively. For a detailed account of the constitutional cycle in Polybius, see von Fritz, *Theory of Mixed Constitution*, ch. 4. I discuss Polybius's theory of constitutional change and Machiavelli's critique thereof in the next chapter.

[56] Ibid., VI,57.

by counteracting the tendencies of all the forms of government to exceed their limits, and this can be done only by setting up a mixed constitution, "so that no one principle (*arche*) should become preponderant... but that the power of each element should be counterbalanced by the others.... The constitution should remain for a long while in equilibrium thanks to the principle of reciprocity."[57] It is this kind of political moderation that accounts for the stability of the Roman constitution and for the greatness of the Roman state.

In this way, Polybius offers a synthesis between Plato's belief in the capacity of concord to stabilize the political form against both internal and external causes of unrest and change, and Aristotle's belief that such political moderation, far from being imposed despotically, requires the prudent circulation of rule between the parts of the political body that is achieved with a mixed constitution. But where Plato thought that only providence could bring together a tyrant and a lawgiver that would achieve concord, for Polybius, who had before him the experience of Roman political intelligence which arrived at the mixed constitution not "by means of abstract reasoning (*dia logos*), but rather through the lessons learned from many struggles and difficulties (*dia pollon agonon*); and finally by always choosing the better course in the light of the experience acquired from disasters,"[58] it is the political concord (*homonoia*) achieved by moderation and virtue that is rewarded by the providence (*pronoia*) of Rome's successes against fickle fortune.

The synthesis of virtue and fortune in a providential scheme is a motif that dominates Roman political thought.[59] What is not explicit in Polybius appears clearly in later Roman authors: the unity of virtue and fortune that expresses providence depends on interpreting virtuous actions as those that bring about the concord of the parts of the city; these virtues are ascribed to the aristocratic components of the city, which employ their authority (*auctoritas*) in order to keep political conflict, stemming from the demands of the plebeians for wider political participation and land reform, within the bounds of "moderation."[60]

The foregoing analysis of the political understanding of chance in the classical political tradition shows that a fundamental presupposition of this tradition is the belief that political action can match its circumstances (can correspond to the events) only when it is directed towards the goal of transforming the political regime into an ethical substance (i.e., when it is pursuing the foundation of political form as a good). The state becomes an ethical substance in the sense that the more "ethical" one makes political rule (i.e., the more political rule is moderate and directed towards the maintenance of concord), the more "substantial" (i.e., stable and integral) does the regime become, leaving it less vulnerable to (demands for) changes of circumstances, and therefore the more providential does its path in the world seem. Providence denotes the priority of form over event, of theory over practice, in classical political philosophy. Put another way,

---

[57] Ibid., VI,10.

[58] Ibid.

[59] This synthesis has also been identified by Cochrane's discussion of *Romanitas*, although he gives a different genesis and context for it. (Cochrane, *Christianity and Classical Culture*, 158-160).

[60] See part 2, ch. 4 for a detailed discussion of Roman conceptions of providence and their political significance.

the classical idea of the state as ethical substance has an internal relation to a providential conception of history because the more "prudent" or "moderate" political rule becomes, the more does the encounter between action and circumstances take the appearance of a predetermined match or fit between the two, i.e., the more the encounter appears "providential" in nature. Providence is merely the name given to the dialectical relation between ethical or prudential action and political form, between the good and the practice of ruling: when the good rules (in the sense that action is moderate), then the rule is good (in the sense that the regime acquires the stable character of a substance and expands its dominion in a seemingly providential fashion). This politico-philosophical schema applies, *grosso modo*, to Plato as to Aristotle, to Polybius as to Cicero. The following chapters discuss the strategies and motivations behind Machiavelli's destruction of this fundamental schema of classical political thought in the *Discourses on Livy*.

CHAPTER 2

THE NATURAL ORIGIN OF POLITICAL FORM:
THE CIRCLE OF CONSTITUTIONS

THE PROBLEM OF THE BEGINNINGS OF POLITICAL FORMS

The *Discourses on Livy* carries out a massive critique of the claim that political life can be reduced to the practice of giving a political form, a legal and legitimate order, to the existence in common of individuals. Machiavelli calls into question the classical belief that the instance of form rules over political life, that the form is the foundation or *arche* (beginning and principle) of politics. His goal consists in the thoroughgoing critique of a foundationalist conception of political life.[1] Present throughout classical political thought, the belief that political form lies at the foundation of politics is radicalized by Polybius, who claims that "in all political situations we must understand that the principal factor which makes for success or failure is the form of a state's constitution (*politeia*): it is from this beginning (*arche*), as if from a fountain-head, that all designs and plans of action not only originate but reach their fulfilment."[2] The political form (constitution) is said to lie at the beginning of all political action, and also rules over the meaning of this action by guiding it to its end or fulfilment. It is no doubt due to Polybius's belief that the appropiately moderate, or mixed, political form could master not only the internal contingencies of political life, but above all the external vagaries of historical becoming that his work acquires a tremendous importance both in the history of modern constitutionalism and in the the history of modern historiography.[3]

---

[1] In the secondary literature it is not uncommon to find the thesis that Machiavelli's discourse turns on the privilege assigned to "foundations." For instance: "[Machiavelli] saw that the whole of Roman history and mentality depended upon the experience of foundation, and he believed it should be possible to repeat the Roman experience through the foundation of a unified Italy which was to become the same sacred cornerstone for an 'eternal' body politic for the Italian nation as the founding of the Eternal City had been for the Italic people" (Arendt, *Between Past and Future*, 138); "[Machiavelli's] concern with history and change was not so much to find meaning in the course of events or to explicate a theory of change as to determine how to create a permanent order.... The foundation was the determinative act, and the sustenance of political order depended on a periodic reaffirmation of the foundation for a renewal of its vitality.... The perpetuation of order was grounded in the abolition of history" (Gunnell, *Political Philosophy and Time*, 245); "for Machiavelli, the state and its values are founded on nothing else than the act of foundation" (Bernard Guillemain, *Machiavel. L'anthropologie politique* [Geneva: Libraire Droz, 1977], 285).

[2] Polybius, *Histories* VI,2.

[3] For Polybius's influence on modern constitutionalism, see the classical works of Charles McIlwain, *Constitutionalism : Ancient and Modern* (Ithaca, NY: Great Seal Books, 1961); Arendt, *On Revolution*; Wilfried Nippel, *Mischverfassungstheorie und Verfassungsrealität in Antike und Früher Neuzeit* (Stuttgart: Klett-Cotta, 1980), and Pocock, *Machiavellian Moment*. For Polybius and modern historiography, see Arnaldo Momigliano, *The Classical Foundations of Modern Historiography* (Berkeley: University of California Press, 1990).

But the connection between the two senses of *arche* (beginning and principle) that Polybius attaches to political form in his fundamental formula is not immediately evident. What Polybius means is that the political form or constitution determines who rules in the sense of who commands or initiates the action. In this function, the political form is an *arche* because it lies at the "beginning" of political action. Additionally, the political form rules over the meaning of the action that it has commanded (*"from this beginning (arche)*, as if from a fountain-head, *all designs and plans of action* not only originate but *reach their fulfilment"*). In this second function, the political form is an *arche* because it assigns to political action a "principle" of rule: the political form, as principle, imposes the form of ruling over the action, i.e., it reduces all political action into actions of ruling and being ruled, commanding and obeying. In this sense, to speak of the political constitution as a "form of government" is redundant: the political form imposes the practice of ruling or governing and, vice versa, ruling is a question of imposing political form.[4] Finally, there is a third meaning to the Polybian idea of political form as *arche*, which is not explicitly stated in the above formula, but emerges as soon as one inquires into what particular kind of political form manages to fulfill the promise withheld by positing political form as *arche*, i.e., the promise of internal and external stability of rule. For Polybius, as pointed out above, the only political form that fulfills its promise is the mixed constitution. As a mixed form, the political form not only imposes on political action the principle of rule, but does so in a way that rule is itself "principled," becoming a rule of laws.[5] The perfected meaning of political form as *arche* of political life, then, is the rule of laws, the principled version of the principle of rule.

The triple sense in which the political form functions as *arche* or foundation of political life poses three distinct but related tasks for Machiavelli's attempt to map out a non-foundationalist, an-archic understanding of political life. The first of these consists in investigating the "beginnings" of political form. The *Discourses on Livy* starts with an extended discussion of Polybius's theory of political form and its application to the case of Roman constitutional history. Machiavelli's approach to Polybius's text is genealogical: his question is whether it is "true," in the sense of "historically effective," that the political form lies at the "beginning" of political life, as Polybius claims. Machiavelli is persuaded of the opposite: political form has more than one beginning or origin because it is inherently a historical construction. This being the case, determining the "beginning" of the political form reveals itself, always already, as a matter of politics, in a number of related senses. First, every political form is the expression of a specific politics that is pursued prior to the form and, as it were, under its cover. Politics has a history before it acquires a form. Second, those discourses that reconstruct the beginnings of political forms are themselves political and betray specific ideological investments. The history of a political form is always a theoretical

---

[4] For a wide-ranging discussion of the dual meaning (as beginning and principle) of the Greek and Latin terms for foundation (*arche, principium*), see Schürmann, *Heidegger on Being and Acting*, 97-112.

[5] For a brief overview of the development of constitutional terms related to *nomos*, including the expression "rule of laws" in classical political thought, see Meier, *The Greek Discovery of Politics*, ch.7, passim.

reconstruction that serves a political purpose. In this chapter I show how both of these claims are brought out by Machiavelli's reading of Polybius's account of the "beginnings" of political form.

Only once the political form has been decentered from its place at the "beginning" of political life is it possible to engage in the second task: refuting the Polybian claim that the political form rules over the historical becoming of political life. In order to achieve this task Machiavelli analyzes the dynamic whereby the primacy of form resolves itself in the reduction of political life to the practice of ruling, and, conversely, how the practice of ruling becomes identical with the process of imposing the political form on political life, i.e., identical with the process of securing the permanence of the political form. This is the dynamic that establishes the system of authority and the rule of laws, which I discuss in chapter three. The third and last task involved in Machiavelli's destruction of the classical priority of form consists in rejecting the assumption that political life turns on the question of legitimating rule by the establishment of the rule of laws. To accomplish this task Machiavelli identifies another, anti-authoritarian source of political life that effectively challenges the predominance of the form as *arche* of political life. The discussion of this source of political freedom is given in chapter four, and with it Machiavelli's first major confrontation with the political foundationalism of classical political thought comes to an end.

NATURAL POLITICAL FORMS AND THE CYCLE OF CONSTITUTIONS

The first chapters of the *Discourses on Livy* (I, 1-4) feature a discussion of the classical topic regarding the different kinds of constitutions or political forms that human beings can adopt. Under cover of an apparently neutral, atemporal review of these forms, of their advantages and disadvantages, a historical discriminant is at work in Machiavelli's discourse such that from the presentation of the different forms emerges a typology of possible historical beginnings of political forms, thereby initiating the argument as to the historical construction of the state. There are three historical beginnings which I call the "natural," "religious," and "free" origins of political form; each corresponds to a different stage of historicity achieved by the political form.[6]

---

[6] The historical character of the beginnings of political form has not been properly commented upon by the secondary literature on the *Discourses on Livy*. In his essay "Necessity in the Beginnings of Cities" Mansfield supports the contention that "for Machiavelli there is just one beginning – necessity" (Mansfield, *Machiavelli's Virtue*, 55) by offering a detailed reading of *Discourses on Livy* I,1 that fails to situate this text in the context of the other initial chapters. In this way, the general problem of beginnings and political form is not properly focused, and Mansfield misses Machiavelli's central point regarding the historicity of political forms and their systems of legitimacy. It is not enough to say that "Machiavelli conceives of many beginnings, not just one. A state must periodically return toward its beginning; its first beginning does not simply determine its course of life," if no argument is provided to explain why the "first beginning" is not enough to determine the state or political form. (Ibid., 55). Indeed, Mansfield's formulation already obscures Machiavelli's discovery that "the state" or the political form is not a simple construct that has a beginning towards which one must, "periodically," return to: political form is a thoroughly historical construct and therefore it is inherently not simple and cannot have a beginning as such. Or, stated otherwise, if "a beginning" of the political form is distinguished, it is always already from within a historical process that precedes it and surpasses it, as I show below in detail. Furthermore, the logic of "necessity" that Mansfield

The way Machiavelli proceeds in the first chapters of the *Discourses on Livy* is itself an illustration or performance of the central thesis that political forms have historical origins. Machiavelli begins by accepting Polybius's fundamental presupposition that the political form coincides with the beginning (*arche*) of political life. He assumes as valid Polybius's belief that political forms are given "by nature."

I say that some who have written on republics say that in them is one of three states – called by them principality, aristocrats, and popular – and that those who order a city should turn to one of these according as it appears to them more to the purpose. Some others, wiser according to the opinion of the many, have the opinion that there are six types of government, of which three are the worst; that three others are good in themselves but so easily corrupted that they too come to be pernicious. For the principality easily becomes tyrannical; the aristocrats with ease become a state of the few; the popular is without difficulty converted into licentiousness…. So, constrained by necessity, or by the suggestion of some good man, or to escape such license, they [the multitude] returned anew to the principality; and from that, degree by degree, they came back toward license, in the modes and for the causes said. It is while revolving in this cycle that all republics are governed and govern themselves.[7]

As commentators have noticed, Machiavelli follows very closely the classification of forms offered by Polybius in the sixth book of the *Histories*, which refers in turn to the classifications found in Plato's *Republic* and *Laws*.[8] The Polybian classification asserts that there are six kinds of political forms given by nature: kingship (*basileus*), aristocracy, democracy are the "good" forms, to which correspond one-man rule (*monarchia*), minority rule, and mob rule as their corrupt or "bad" versions.[9] Polybius argues that these forms are related to each other in

---

provides to explain the multiplicity of beginnings of political forms is philosophically confused, and cannot possibly account for the complexities of Machiavelli's thesis regarding the historicity of political form. Mansfield argues that in Machiavelli "necessity refers to what is humanly necessary, as opposed to what is necessary to the fulfillment of human nature" (ibid., 55). This is correct as far as it goes, but if necessity is always "relative" to human beings one is under obligation to expound the human capacity that can relativize necessity and provide a theory of human freedom. Although he claims that "necessity abstractly understood seems irresistible; it would put human freedom in as much danger as came from Christian divinity," Mansfield never treats explicitly and at length Machiavelli's theory of freedom. (Ibid., 55). Furthermore, if necessity is always already relative necessity, then it is logically impossible for it to function as the "one beginning," contrary to Mansfield's initial thesis. For a detailed discussion of the role played by necessity in Machiavelli see the arguments in parts 2 and 3 of this book.

Lefort for his part claims, correctly, that "the order of the City cannot be distinguished from a style of becoming," and that "Machiavelli does not let one think that the first order is the good one, because he makes the Roman *ordine* the product of a history," only to remain very generic with respect to the concrete steps and arguments that lead to Machiavelli's thesis regarding the historicity of Rome and of all political forms. These steps pass through a complicated and wide-ranging critique of the political and philosophical assumptions of Polybius and, behind him, of all classical political tradition that are left unanalysed in Lefort's interpretation.

[7] Machiavelli, *Discourses on Livy*, I, 2.

[8] Polybius, *Histories* VI,3 and VI,5. For a detailed discussion of the cycle in Polybius and its relation to other versions in Plato and Aristotle, see von Fritz, *Theory of the Mixed Constitution*, 60-75. The best comparative work on Machiavelli and Polybius is found in Gennaro Sasso, "La teoria dell'anacyclosis," and "Polibio e Machiavelli: costituzione, potenza, conquista," in *Studi su Machiavelli*. The first article in particular features a careful study of the similarities and differences between the Polybian and Machiavellian versions of the constitutional cycle. See also Mansfield, *Machiavelli's New Modes and Orders*, 35-38.

[9] Polybius, *Histories* VI,4.

a cycle (*anakuklosis*) whereby there is a continuous and irresistible transition from a "good" form into its "bad" or "corrupt" version, and then from this one to a different "good" form, which decays into its "bad" version, and so on. I discuss the logic of these transitions below. For the moment, my concern is to determine the domain over which the cycle of constitutions applies in Polybius's and Machiavelli's discourses.

For Polybius, the existence of this cycle of constitutions is evident to anyone who makes "a careful study of the beginnings, origins and changes which are natural to each of these forms of government" because the "life" of each form of government follows a "natural law." In reality, Polybius's discourse features two "natural laws": one which links the transition from one political form to another (the *anacyclosis* of constitutions), the other which applies to each of the constitutions and refers to their "growth [*auxesis*], perfection [*akme*] and decay [*phthisis*]."[10] Polybius's unique claim is that the *anakuklosis* of constitutions, the "cycle of political revolutions," is the "law of nature [*phuseus oikonomia*] according to which constitutions change, are transformed, and finally revert to their original form." The cycle prescribes the "natural economy" of political revolutions, consequently it predetermines all possible historical changes and, if one can identify at which stage any given state finds itself, it allows one to know its future, although not to predict exactly when the given changes are going to happen. For Polybius, even the Roman political form, as every other form, will follow this "natural economy": "for this state, if any ever did... takes its foundation and its growth from natural causes, and will pass through a natural evolution to its decay."[11]

The capital difference between Machiavelli's understanding of the cycle and Polybius's is that for the Florentine the cycle is undoubtedly "natural" but it is not sempiternal: it does not control the historical existence of the states. "It is by turning in this cycle that all republics governed and govern themselves: but rarely do they return to the same governments, for almost no republic can have so long a life as to be able to pass many times through these changes and remain on its feet."[12] For Machiavelli no state is strong enough to resist more than a few passages through the cycle: the cycle leads to the certain death of the state that is locked in it. Therefore the cycle of constitutions cannot possibly reflect the "natural economy" of political life just because its economy is incapable of accounting for the very process of life (growth, acme, decay) that Polybius thought it could. Polybius believes that the unique growth and success of the Roman state falls under the *anakuklosis*, while Machiavelli claims exactly the opposite: any state that remains locked in its spiral will perish in a brief period of time, "becoming subject to a neighboring state that is ordered better than it."[13] The Polybian coincidence of political form with the beginning (*arche*) of political life, i.e., the assumption that political form is given "by nature," and therefore follows

---

[10] Ibid. On the potential contradiction between these two natural laws, see Sasso, *Studi su Machiavelli*, 187-196.
[11] Polybius, *Histories* VI,9. On this point and the problem it poses for the internal coherence of Polybius's discourse, see von Fritz, *Theory of Mixed Constitution*, 84-89.
[12] Machiavelli, *Discourses on Livy*, I,2.
[13] Ibid., I,2.

its "laws," leads directly to the contradiction that on the basis of such an assumption political life could barely get started.[14]

Two clear textual indications show that Machiavelli rejects in a thorough fashion the Polybian claim that the "natural law" of the *anakuklosis* constitutes the *arche* or foundation of political life. The first indication is that, in direct contrast to Polybius, the cycle of constitutions is a product of chance: "These variations of government arise by chance among men."[15] Therefore, on purely logical grounds, its status cannot be that of a "principle" (*arche*) of the *physeus oikonomia*, the "law of nature," which for Polybius determines the inevitable destiny of all political forms in time.[16] As Sasso elegantly phrases the difference: for Polybius the cycle contains time so that time cannot consume it, whereas the opposite is the case for Machiavelli.[17]

But if the cycle of constitutions does not constitute the *arche* of political life, then what does it describe? My hypothesis is that this cycle spells out the fate of any state whose origin is merely natural. The kind of political form which has a naturalistic origin, which is not capable of breaking with those natural determinants of action that lead into the cycle of constitutions, of which I speak below, is fated to enter the cycle and be destroyed by it. Machiavelli simply reverses the domain over which Polybius's *anakuklosis* applies: rather than legislating over the historical trajectory of states, the cycle describes the existence of all states that have not had an effective historical existence; it describes the pre-historical fate of states.

One can say that the cycle of constitutions plays the part that the "state of nature" does in the subsequent tradition of modern natural right. For this tradition, just as for Machiavelli, political existence (*status civilis*) begins when the *status naturalis* is left behind. In the "state of nature," just as in Machiavelli's "cycle of constitutions," the life of the state is "poore, nasty, brutish, and short" to cite Hobbes. Those interpreters who deny that Machiavelli has a modern conception of history on the grounds that they understand him to be in agreement with Polybius concerning the supra-historical validity of the cycle of constitutions have not perceived that for Machiavelli the cycle has an infra-historical validity, i.e., a validity which is limited to those states that are incapable of breaking with their

---

[14] Mansfield is aware that Machiavelli's description of what happens to a state that remains in the natural cycle of constitutions, "casts doubt on the very notion of a cycle." (Mansfield, *Machiavelli's New Modes and Orders*, 38). But he does not see the performative contradiction that Machiavelli ascribes to this naturalistic theory of political form, and, on the contrary, proceeds to defend classical naturalism as an "equivocal support from nature for human actions" because the "greater power of extrahuman forces… can be understood as support for human responsibility not only because they do not destroy man completely but also because they do override all human force and thereby allow human worth to be asserted." (Ibid., 38-39). Sasso thinks that for Machiavelli the cycle of constitutions does not have the status of a natural law but is "a simple inclination of things that the careful virtù of the legislator can interrupt and modify." (Sasso, *Studi su Machiavelli*, 199). This position does not quite do justice to Machiavelli's point, which is far stronger: a natural political form is a self-contradictory entity.

[15] Machiavelli, *Discourses on Livy*, I, 2.

[16] Sasso, *Studi su Machiavelli*, 199-200.

[17] Ibid., 171-2.

natural conditions of existence, and thus are incapable of attaining, at once, a historical and a political existence.[18]

There exists a second textual indication that supports the hypothesis that the cycle of constitutions in Machiavelli describes a natural and unsustainable state of political life rather than the whole span of its historical existence, as Polybius asserts. In *Discourses on Livy* I,2 Machiavelli twice speaks of a "straight road" that leads the state to its "perfect and true end."

So that republic can be called happy whose lot is to get one man so prudent that he gives it laws ordered so that it can live securely under them without needing to correct them. One sees that Sparta observed them for more than eight hundred years without corrupting them.... That city has some degree of unhappiness that, by not having fallen upon a prudent orderer, is forced of necessity to reorder itself. Of these still more unhappy is that which is farthest from order, and *that one is farthest from it that by its orders is altogether off the straight road [diritto cammino] that might lead it to the* perfect and true end.[19]

The "straight road" refers to the historical and political trajectories apparently assumed by states like Sparta and Rome. The image conveys the mutual exclusion that holds between a circle and a straight line; it strongly suggests that Sparta and Rome are states that have managed to break away from the natural cycle of constitutions.

There is no mention of such a "straight road" in Polybius's *Histories*, and this is perfectly consistent with his belief that it is impossible to break away from the cycle of constitutions to which even Sparta and Rome are subject. Indeed, the metaphor of a "straight road" is absent from Greek and Roman discussions on constitutional cycles. Machiavelli is citing from, and playing off, an image that first appears in Augustine's *City of God*.[20]

---

[18] It is highly significant that the *Discourses on Livy* never returns to Polybius's cycle of constitutions nor makes any attempt to read historical events on the basis of its model. In any case, my reading of Machiavelli's use of the cycle stands in strong opposition to those interpretations that see the state as a non- or anti-historical phenomenon. For a radical version of such an interpretation see Guillemain who argues that "the violence of the legislator is completely natural... there is no creation of force, all energy at the disposal of the state is borrowed from the animal spontaneity which it determines as impure and which it cannot destroy. The founder orders powers that preexist him.... States are more virtuous [*gaillards*] the closer they are to their beginning, that is, to the natural source from where they have emerged; they are more corrupted the further they are are from this source and the more the virtù of the founder effaces itself. Time gives birth to degenerate forms; it is the great master of decadence." (Guillemain, *Machiavel. L'anthropologie politique*, 276). Likewise, the purely negative value that I assign to the cycle of constitutions in Machiavelli contrasts with all the attempts to give a positive, even decisive, value to it and in so doing fit his complex theory of political form into its procrustean bed. See for example Hulliung, who conflates Machiavelli and Polybius completely, claiming that "crucial to their procedure for linking theory and practice was the subsumption of history under the category of nature, specifically through the notion of cyclical history.... Machiavelli, taking his cue from Polybius, sought in nature the foundation of a theory of action." (Hulliung, *Citizen Machiavelli*, 154).

[19] Machiavelli, *Discourses on Livy*, I, 2. Emphasis mine. Machiavelli also says of Rome that "if its first orders were defective, nonetheless they did not deviate from the straight path [*diritta via*] that could lead them to perfection." (Ibid.).

[20] Sasso's careful commentary of Machiavelli's divergences from Polybius's account of the cycle does not mention this striking image but is preoccupied to point out that Rome's purported "perfection" does not mean its "eternity." (Sasso, *Studi su Machiavelli*, 202). Mansfield also misses the reference to Augustine and therefore lacks the proper historico-philosophical frame of reference for Machiavelli's subsequent discussion of how historical contingency or "accidents... can not only

Such are the arguments with which the ungodly try to turn our simple piety from the straight road, and to make us join them in "walking in circles." But faith ought to laugh at these theories, even if reason could not refute them. In fact we can do more than that. With the help of the Lord our God, reason, and cogent reason, breaks up those revolving circles which speculative theory has devised. [21]

In this text, Augustine opposes the "straight road" of Divine Providence to the "revolving circles" in accordance with which pagan philosophers thought of natural motion.[22]

The Augustinian reference does not signify at all that Machiavelli's conception of history is a linear one, analogous to that ascribed to Augustine by certain interpreters.[23] For one, the "road" that Roman history takes, in Machiavelli's reconstruction, is far from being "straight," nor does it promise to lead the soul to its eternal salvation (that is part of Machiavelli's irony in citing Augustine against Polybius). The concept of history found in Machiavelli is neither circular nor linear. The *Discourses on Livy* does provide a new paradigm of historical becoming, but the attempts by previous interpreters to reduce it either to "providential," "naturalistic" or "progressivist" schemas have failed in part because they did not recognize in Machiavelli's discourse the transcendence of history over nature and its political conditions of possibility.

Augustine's image of the "straight road" breaking through the "voluble circles" of natural motion simply serves to establish Machiavelli's rejection of the validity of Polybius's natural cycle in the domain of political history. A state can have an effective historical existence only on condition that it breaks out of the vicious, because natural, cycle of constitutions. For Machiavelli, history begins with a break from nature. This history will not be the providential one of the city of God. Instead, it will be determined in its basic traits from a comparative analysis of the history of Rome, which Machiavelli claims to have finally cognized in its *verità effettuale*, moving beyond the horizons provided by Polybius and Augustine, disclosing the new horizon of modern historical consciousness.

---

help but make perfect" a political form. (Mansfield, *Machiavelli's New Modes and Orders*, 34). Indeed, this reference argues against Mansfield's one-sided claim that Machiavelli uses "the non-Christian classical notion of a cycle of civilization rising and falling by nature" in his polemic against Christianity. One can say that the opposite is equally the case. Which is not to say that I disagree with Mansfield's final point that Machiavelli's discourse attempts to transcend both Christian and classical teachings. (Ibid., 36).

[21] Augustine *City of God* XII,18.

[22] Another reference to the Augustinian motif of the "straight road" to salvation appears in Machiavelli's discussion of Christianity in *Discourses on Livy*, II, 2.

[23] Among these, the best known examples are Karl Löwith, *Meaning in History* (Chicago: University of Chicago Press, 1949); and Oscar Cullman, *Christus und die Zeit* (Zollikon-Zürich: Evangelischer Verlag, 1946). On the distinction between linear and circular shapes of history, see also Henri-Charles Puech, *En quête de la Gnose* (Paris: Gallimard, 1978), I, 1-23. The debate on the circular versus linear conceptions of history held by the ancients and moderns, respectively, has proven in large measure a false debate, certainly in regard to the complexity of classical historiography, but also in regard to the claim that modern conceptions of history are merely secularized versions of the linearity of Christian *Heilsgeschichte*. For an accurate description and refutation of the above debate, see Arnaldo Momigliano, "Il Tempo nella Storiografia Antica," in *La Storiografia Greca* (Turin: Einaudi, 1982), 64-94; and Santo Mazzarino, *Il Pensiero Storico Classico* (Bari: Laterza, 1966), 2: 412-461. For the critique of the secularization theory, see Blumenberg, *The Legitimacy of the Modern Age*, passim.

The first result of Machiavelli's confrontation with Polybius is the thesis that any political form that wishes to enjoy a historical existence must break from its natural beginnings. Since the natural beginning of political life means the adoption of one of the simple constitutional forms, a state accedes to history in and through through a break with all pure forms:

[because] if an orderer of a republic [*ordinatore di una republica*] orders one of those three states [*stati*] in a city [i.e., one of the three "good" political forms], he orders it there for a short time; for no remedy can be applied there to prevent it from slipping into its contrary because of the likeness that the virtue and the vice have in this case.[24]

From the start, the attempt to generate an adequate (historically effective) conception of political life calls for the progressive relativization of political form. Indeed, it is the purity or simplicity of political form that keeps political life in its natural condition; a condition that is, in the short run, destructive of the very possibility of political life.

If the naturalization of political form destroys political life, it follows that such life can maintain itself only if its political form is not given by nature but historically constructed. The *Discourses on Livy* presents two possibilities for the historical construction of the state, which I call, respectively, the "religious" and the "free" origins of political life. In turn, each of these historical modes of construction marks a further degree of relativization of political form: the religious origin leads away from the conflation of political life with a pure political form in order to introduce the state as a "mixed form." The free origin decenters the state as "mixed form" in favor of what Machiavelli terms a "mixed body" that makes place for a wholly other dimension of political life deprived of form.

THE MONARCHICAL SYSTEM OF RULE

To grasp the logic of the discontinuities between the natural and the historical origins of the state it is necessary to describe the natural determinants of political action that determine the cyclical movement of simple forms and the "likeness which in such case virtue has to vice."[25] Polybius's discussion of the cycle of constitutions is at the same time a narrative about the origins of normative concepts: the distinction between "good" and "bad" political forms turns on whether the respective form is imposed by "reason" or by "force," whether the respective rulers "serve the common interest" or merely "indulge their own appetites."[26] Machiavelli follows the main lines of Polybius's narrative of the origins of the grammar of justice, but concludes that in the "natural economy" of political life there is no clear difference or separation between virtue and vice, reason and force. This conclusion does not reflect Machiavelli's own theses

---

[24] Machiavelli, *Discourses on Livy,* I, 2.
[25] The main commentaries on this part of *Discourses on Livy* I,2 either give a philosophically empoverished paraphrase of the text (as in Mansfield, *Machiavelli's New Modes and Orders*, 36-37; and Sasso, *Studi su Machiavelli*,171-173) or ignore it (as in Lefort, *Le Travail de l'oeuvre*, 467-470).
[26] Polybius *Histories* VI, 6-8.

concerning virtue and vice. The aitiology of "justice" presented in *Discourses on Livy* I,2 in order to account for the corrupt character of the entire cycle of constitutions is a strategic discourse that has only a negative, critical function.[27] Its purpose is to expose the pernicious effects of the conception of justice in classical natural right, as this appears in Polybius's narrative, for the development of political life.[28] Just like with the theory of the *anakuklosis*, it is misleading to think that the validity of Machiavelli's aitiology of justice extends beyond the limits in which it can be used to illustrate the performative contradictions of the classical naturalistic conception of political life.[29] For Machiavelli, the "natural" origin of justice undermines a legitimate or principled distinction between virtue and vice as much as the "natural" origin of the political form undermines the possibility of political life.

Machiavelli's aitiology of justice is briefly stated:

since the inhabitants were sparse in the beginning of the world, they lived dispersed for a time like beasts; then, as generations multiplied, they gathered together, and to be able to defend themselves better, they began to look to whoever among them was more robust and of greater heart, and they made him a head, as it were, and obeyed him [*e fecionlo come capo e lo ubedivano*]. From this arose the knowledge of things honest and good, differing from the pernicious and bad. For, seeing that if one individual hurt his benefactor, hatred and compassion among men came from it, and as they blamed the ungrateful and honored those who were grateful, and thought too that those same injuries could be done to them, to escape like evil they were reduced to making laws and punishments for whoever acted against them: hence came the knowledge of justice.[30]

The criterion for the choice of the "natural" leader is simply might or force, for the first concern is that of protection. In the natural condition, the difference between "good" and "bad," the normative criterion, is based on might: what is harmful to the leader, who is charged with the protection of everyone, is hated by everyone and seen as a peril to everyone. As a consequence the law is established

---

[27] This point is frequently missed in the secondary literature. Mansfield, for example, seems to understand the aitiology as if it has universal validity: "Polybius gives a realistic account of the 'first notion' of justice, implying a higher and more complete understanding, but Machiavelli allows the realistic origin of justice to determine '*the* knowledge of justice' (italics added)" (Mansfield, *Machiavelli's New Modes and Orders*, 37); Hulliung believes that Machiavelli "uncritically reproduced" Polybius's theory (Hulliung, *Citizen Machiavelli*, 140-143); whereas Sullivan takes Machiavelli to task for giving a reductive version of "Polybius's intricate account of the origin of the understanding of justice" (Vickie Sullivan, *Machiavelli's Three Romes* [Ithaca: Cornell University Press, 1997], 92).

[28] Which is not to say that the doctrines of classical natural right can be reduced to Polybius's narrative on justice. I pursue Machiavelli's critique of other aspects of these doctrines in part 2, chs.1-2 and throughout part 3.

[29] In this sense, Machiavelli's aitiology of justice shows remarkable affinities with a peculiar practice found in classical historiography: "This genealogical literature... was a narration of *aitia*, of origins.... Its purpose is to tell the story of where a man, a custom or a city draw their existence. Once it is born, the city lives its own historical existence, which no longer belongs to the aitiology." (Paul Veyne, *Les Grecs ont-ils cru a leurs mythes?* [Paris: Seuil,1983], 125). Aitiologies refer to the natural or pre-historical origins of a practice or institution. According to Veyne's analysis, their function is purely strategic, allowing politicians to legitimate or break alliances, demand services from other cities, etc. Similarly, the aitiology in Machiavelli's text exposes the ideological element of Polybius's discourse on natural origins; it does not apply to the effective historical origins of political life.

[30] Machiavelli, *Discourses on Livy,* I, 2.

in order to mark and distinguish those things that cause such harm and that have to be disallowed: "hence came the knowledge of justice."

In Machiavelli's narrative, the naturalistic origin of justice is a system of rule whereby might makes right. Following Polybius's distinction between a monarch (*monarchos*) and a king (*basileus*),[31] Machiavelli refers to the first simple or pure form of rule with the "name of one single head/leader [*nome d'uno solo capo*]," in other words, with the name of a mon-arch. For this reason, the system in which might makes right, in which obligation to the ruler is based on the ruler's capacity to protect the subjects, should be called the monarchical system of rule. The term of monarchy is particularly adequate to describe the natural political form because it expresses its principle: a univocity of rule (*mono-archein*) is the result of a system in which laws are made to identify and exclude every source of negativity directed at whoever is in power, i.e., at whoever holds the greatest might. The origin of the simple form of constitution is "natural" because it is decisively characterized by its inability to internalize negativity or opposition. All simple political forms are mon-archical in this sense, that is, in them law and order emerge from absolute might or irresistible force.[32]

Once the monarchical system of rule is in place, the cycle of simple political forms begins. The first "natural" transition occurs between monarchy and kingship: the egoistic impulse for common protection turns against the bearer of the irresistible force that protects and threatens at the same time, and replaces this totemic leader by an elected king, this time "not the most hardy but the one who would be more prudent and more just."[33] With this transition, whose "natural" character is due to the logic of obligation based on force and protection, the only natural givens featured in Machiavelli's narrative, the *anakuklosis* is off on its course that will lead to the early and necessary death of the natural state.

Machiavelli attributes the transition from "good" to "bad" political forms in the cycle to "the likeness which in such a case virtue has to vice." This expression acquires its meaning only in the context of the monarchical system of rule. Based on the principle that might makes right, this system requires such "likeness" because it demands that whatever part of the community has more might at any given time ("vice") occupy the place or function of the monarch for the sake of the protection of the whole community ("virtue"). The political form or state thereby has a "right" to pass into the hands of those parts that, turn by turn, are most irresistible: first one, then the few, finally the many. The cycle of simple constitutions is inevitable once the imposition of political form originates from the place of the monarch which can only be occupied by the bearer(s) of irresistible

---

[31] Polybius defines a *monarchia* as one-man rule based on force, to be distinguished from kingship or *basileia*, a system of rule in which "reason becomes more powerful than ferocity or force" because the force of the leader supports the judgments of the majority in matters of conduct, i.e., in determining what is just or noble, and rewards and punishes "each according to his deserts." (Polybius *Histories* VI, 6).

[32] It is no coincidence that Hobbes's deduction of justice from the state of nature also applies the logic of *protego ergo obligo*, and finds the source of law in irresistible force. The difference between Hobbes and Polybius turns on the description of the "natural state" of humankind: for Hobbes it is a state characterized by the absolute status of individual freedom. The monarchical system in Hobbes is therefore set up to protect the negative liberty of individuals.

[33] Machiavelli, *Discourses on Livy,* I, 2.

force, of domination. Machiavelli's aitiology of justice suggests that the ideal of political form ruling over all of political life found in Polybius's theory is itself parasitic on the principle that might makes right, i.e., on that principle which supports the mon-archical conceit that the grammar of rule should be the only grammar of political life.

The cycle of constitutions constitutes a vicious circle because there is an absence of opposition or resistance to the principle of might within the political form or state. In its simplicity, the state cannot internalize a principle counter to that of domination and force, for whatever threatens dominion is immediately outlawed. In this way, the simple political form excludes the principle of the rule of laws. The state undermines its possibility to achieve stability and permanence because its laws repeatedly exclude their own principle, namely, the principle or rule of law and order, in virtue of their identification and expulsion of what is counter to pure might, i.e., the "force" of law itself. This is the profound reason for the radical instability of every simple political form, for the "natural" necessity that simply replaces one order by another until the whole political body exhausts itself in license and disintegrates. In the end, the Polybian cycle of constitutions reveals that the natural condition of political life is simply the state of human affairs in which force is the principle or law.

Machiavelli's discourse indicates the logic of the next step in the effective genesis of political form: in order to break from the natural origin of political form, the law must be put in a position to rule, such that it can counter the rule of force. Instead of any possible bearer of force, it is the law that must now take the place of the monarch. The result of this substitution is that force is no longer monarchical in its structure: the monarchical system of rule fissures itself and gives rise to a political form that allows for a plurality of forces to express themselves at any given time. The political form undergoes a profound transition from "simple" to "mixed form." The substitution of law for force in the place of the monarch calls for the constitution of a new source of "force" for the law other than natural might. This source is found in a political employment of religion. Therefore, the first break with the natural origin of political form, the first instance of its historical origin, occurs when law has a religious origin and the simple political form fissures itself into a "mixed" or "composite" form that gives expression to a plurality of forces.[34] The monarchical system of rule is thereby replaced by what can be called the authoritarian system of rule.

---

[34] Unlike Polybius, Machiavelli does not seek to match the transition from monarchy to kingship and then to tyranny, aristocracy, etc. in the natural cycle of constitutions of political forms with the historical transition between Romulus and Numa, or between Romulus and the Senate thematized later in the *Discourses on Livy*. As I discuss below, there are at least two indications why the *anakuklosis* does not apply to the history of the Roman state as reconstructed by Machiavelli: first, Romulus breaks up the monarchic principle by creating the Senate; second, the transition from Romulus to Numa brings about the decisive break with the "natural" origin of law because with Numa the law finds its foundation in authority and religion, not in force.

CHAPTER 3

THE RELIGIOUS ORIGIN OF POLITICAL FORM: THE SYSTEM OF AUTHORITY

THE FOUNDER AND THE SYSTEM OF AUTHORITY

"At the heart of Roman politics… stands the conviction of the sacredness of foundation."[1] In "What is authority?" Arendt offers a still unsurpassed philosophical analysis of the religious origin of political form exhibited by the Roman system of authority. In the Roman political experience, the foundation of the state is "sacred" because it is understood to be an absolute beginning: "the central, decisive, unrepeatable beginning of their whole history, a unique event."[2] What makes this beginning absolute is the attitude or ethos of those who follow it. Arendt argues that for the Romans this attitude is prescribed in their religion which "literally meant re-ligare: to be tied back, obligated, to the enormous, almost superhuman and hence always legendary effort to lay the foundations, to build the cornerstone, to found for eternity."[3] From this religious constitution of the act of foundation emerges the system of rule that turns on authority:

the word auctoritas derives from augere, augment, and what authority or those in authority constantly augment is the foundation. Those endowed with authority were the elders, the Senate or the patres, who had obtained it by descent and by transmission (tradition) from those who had laid the foundations for all things to come, the ancestors, whom the Romans therefore called the maiores.[4]

Arendt concludes that "the strength of the Roman trinity of religion, tradition and authority lay in the binding force of an authoritative beginning to which 'religious' bonds tied men back through tradition."[5]

Arendt's description of the Roman system of authority corresponds remarkably well to the three senses in which Polybius understands political form to be the *arche* of political life. According to the first sense of *arche*, the political form stands at the beginning of political life and designates who will command. This sense corresponds, in Arendt's account, to the legendary *auctores* who "inspired the whole enterprise… he is the actual 'author' of the building, namely, its founder; with it he has become an 'augmenter' of the city."[6] The second sense of political form as *arche* refers to the imposition on all political action of the form of rule, of the division between those who command and those who obey. This sense corresponds to the authoritarian practice of rule proper, whence all citizens who are politically active must obey or carry out [*gerere*] the command of

---

[1] Arendt, *Between Past and Future*, 120.
[2] Ibid., 121.
[3] Ibid.
[4] Ibid., 122.
[5] Ibid., 125.
[6] Ibid., 122.

augmentation [*augere*] transmitted by those who maintain the founder's legacy alive, namely, the *patres* of the Senate.[7] Through this system of authority, the few rule over the many. The last sense of political form as *arche* refers to the sole form that can actually rule over all political life: this form is the mixed constitution, which features a rule of law that draws its "force" from what Arendt calls the "authoritative beginning."[8]

The first chapters of the *Discourses on Livy* offer an alternative reading of the system of authority that seeks to displace it from the center of Roman political life. Machiavelli aims at a vision of political life that is free from the foundational role assigned to political form in the Polybian and Arendtian reconstructions of the Roman political experience. The very idea of the "sacredness of foundation," and with it the religious origin of political form, comes under criticism. Working through the senses of *arche* found in Polybius, Machiavelli first dismantles the absoluteness of foundation through a reading of the political function of the founder in the authoritarian project of imposing the division between rulers and ruled (the principle of rule) over all of political life. In a second moment, the transition from the principle of rule to the rule of laws made through the constitution of a mixed political form comes under critical scrutiny. To analyse this transition, Machiavelli employs the Spartan model of mixed constitution as the pure type of authoritarian and foundational rule of law in order to compare it against his reconstruction of the Roman model, which features an expanded sense of political life. The point of the comparison is to show that political life in republican Rome cannot be reduced to the "experience of foundation" and the system of authority that emerges from it.

That Machiavelli connects the figure of the founder to the religious origin of political form is evident from the contiguity of his discussion of these themes (*Discourses on Livy*, I, 9-10 and I, 11-15, respectively). The more difficult problem is which of these, founder or religion, has a relative priority, and what such a priority means for the proper understanding of the system of authority. The

---

[7] Arendt offers a suggestive genealogical account of the dualism between command [*augere*] and obey [*gerere*] that I adopt throughout: "To the two Greek verbs *archein* ('to begin', 'to lead', finally 'to rule') and *prattein* ('to pass through', 'to achieve', 'to finish') correspond the two Latin verbs *agere* ('to set in motion', 'to lead') and *gerere* (whose original meaning is 'to bear'). Here it seems as though each action were divided into two parts, the beginning made by a single person and the achievement in which many join by 'bearing' and 'finishing' the enterprise, by seeing it through. Not only are the words interrelated in a similar manner, the history of their usage is very similar too. In both cases the word that originally designated only the second part of the action, its achievement - *prattein* and *gerere* - became the accepted word for action in general, whereas the words designating the beginning of action became specialized in meaning, at least in political language. *Archein* came to mean chiefly 'to rule' and 'to lead' when it was specifically used, and *agere* came to mean 'to lead' rather than 'to set in motion'. Thus the role of the beginner and leader, who was a *primus inter pares* (in the case of Homer, a king among kings), changed into that of a ruler; the original interdependence of action, the dependence of the beginner and the leader upon others for help and the dependence of his followers upon him for an occasion to act themselves, split into two altogether different functions: the function of giving commands, which became the prerogative of the ruler, and the function of executing them, which became the duty of his subjects." (Hannah Arendt, *The Human Condition* [Chicago: University of Chicago Press, 1958], 189).

[8] "Of the definitely formulated foundations of the political power of the Senate, the most important was the rule that bills accepted by a majority vote in the popular assembly did not acquire the force of law until they had been approved by the Senate and the latter had officially given its *auctoritas*." (von Fritz, *Theory of the Mixed Constitution*, 195).

problem is clearly visible in Arendt's treatment of authority where, on the basis of the religious piety (*pietas*) of the Roman citizen who was continuously bound "back to the beginning of Roman history, the foundation of the eternal city," she surmises that the "stability and authority of any given body politic [must derive] from its beginning.... One is tempted to conclude that it was the authority which the act of foundation carried within itself... that assured stability for the new republic."[9] Seeking a purely immanent, political interpretation of the phenomenon of foundation, Arendt proceeds to argue that "it is futile to search for an absolute to break the vicious circle in which all beginning is inevitably caught, because this 'absolute' lies in the very act of beginning itself."[10] The key to the system of authority consists in positing the beginning of political form as an absolute, which at one and the same time ab-solves this beginning from all historical becoming and sets it up as a foundation that commands the subsequent history of the form. The mythical status of the founder derives from such an ab-solute position of the founding act.

But the real question remains open: who or what posits the beginning as absolute? Depending on the answer that is given, two possible readings of the figure of the founder emerge. On one account, the founder posits the beginning as absolute. This entails that the founder who is charged with beginning not only is "the initial cause of the institution... [but] in addition he is the origin, the basic principle... of the order he founds. Thus he lives on in what he has created, attaining a secular immortality.... The founder, then, is an unmoved mover, a source of change not the product of earlier changes."[11] In Weberian terminology one can say that on this account the authority of the political form derives from the founder's charisma.[12]

On another account, the beginning is posited as an absolute by the system of authority, and the founder is reduced to being a function of this system. The beginning is authoritative because of the religious institution which takes it upon itself to bind back (*re-ligio*) all political action to that beginning and in so doing rehearse the moment of form-giving tied to the founding act.[13] The internal relation between authority and act of foundation is surmised from the fact that authority keeps that act "present" through history by increasing its significance.

The very concept of Roman authority suggests that the act of foundation inevitably develops its own stability and permanence, and authority in this context is nothing more or less than a kind of necessary "augmentation" by virtue of which innovations and changes remain tied back to the foundation which, at the same time, they augment and increase. Thus the amendments to the Constitution augment and increase the original foundations of the American republic; needless to say,

---

[9] Arendt, *On Revolution,* 198-199.

[10] Ibid., 204.

[11] Pitkin, *Fortune is a Woman,* 54.

[12] I refer to the typology of legitimate domination given in Max Weber, *Economy and society,* eds. G. Roth and C. Wittich (Berkeley: University of California Press, 1978), 215-246.

[13] Arendt speaks of the Roman senate as an institution in which one finds a "presence" of the founders "and with them the spirit of foundation was present, the beginning, the *principium* and principle, of those *res gestae* which from then on formed the history of the people of Rome." (Arendt, *On Revolution,* 200).

the very authority of the American Constitution resides in its inherent capacity to be amended and augmented.[14]

This text suggests that for the repetition of the beginning to have authoritative effects, the relation between repetition and beginning must be an external one. The beginning is said to function as a principle, is posited as absolute, because it causes or conditions the repetition of "itself." The repetition itself, though, does not begin anything radically new.[15] That is why the repeated beginning, or what Arendt calls the "augmentation," is recognizable as falling under the same political form given at the foundation, i.e., as being "more of the same." This "sameness" is what Arendt means when she says that the retrieval or repetition of the revolutionary beginning amounts to "*a coincidence* of foundation and preservation by virtue of augmentation."[16] In short, the beginning is absolute because it is ab-solved from being "just another beginning" and can thus be posited as the "first beginning." In this way, "its" repetition by "other" beginnings simply reinforces its primacy, which effectively grants it authority. Augmentation amounts to a process of "continuous founding by many men, and even by classes in interaction" whose very continuity disallows new beginnings, other beginnings.[17] In Weberian terminology one can say that it is the "routinization of charisma" that retroactively posits a charismatic origin for its own use.[18]

For the most part, commentators think that Machiavelli holds the first account of founders, in keeping with the prejudice that political form is given "in the beginning" rather than historically.[19] More subtle interpretations of the problem of foundation in Machiavelli, while questioning the mythical character of the first account of founders, endorse a vision of political life that falls within the second account of founders, within the system of authority. These readings seem to be

---

[14] Ibid., 203.

[15] For this to occur, an internal relation between beginning and repetition needs to obtain. Such a concept of originary repetition does not belong to the system of authority but to the critique thereof. I discuss this idea of historical repetition as originary repetition in part 3.

[16] Ibid., 203. Emphasis mine.

[17] Pitkin, *Fortune is a Woman*, 100.

[18] On the routinization of charisma, see Weber, *Economy and Society*, 1121-22. In these passages Weber suggests that, in spite of their opposition, charisma and the process of its routinization are essentially connected by a common "religious" character: "The two *basically antagonistic* forces of charisma and tradition *regularly merge with one another*.... Both charisma and tradition rest on a sense of loyalty and obligation which always has a religious aura." (Ibid., emphasis mine).

[19] For the paradigmatic expression of this position, see Meinecke: "But the virtù which the founder and ruler of a State had to possess counted for Machiavelli as virtù of a higher order. For in his opinion this kind of virtù was able, by means of appropiate 'regulations,' to distill out of the thoroughly bad and wretched material of average specimens of humanity the other kind of virtù in the sense of civic virtue; to a certain extent the latter was virtù of a secondary quality, and could only be durable if it was rooted in a people whose spirit was naturally fresh and unspoilt. This separation of virtù into two types, one original and the other derived, is of exceptional significance for a complete understanding of the political aims of Machiavelli." (Meinecke, *Machiavellism*, 32). Other treatments of the figure of the founder, from those of Skinner (*Machiavelli* [Oxford: Oxford University Press, 1981], 55-58) to Pitkin, *Fortune is a Woman*, ch. 3, while attempting to provide other solutions to Meinecke's dilemma, do not escape its terms. For the most recent version of this interpretive trend, see Sullivan, for whom "the lone ruler plays a prominent role in the story that unfolds in the *Discourses*. A single man must found a republic or reorder a corrupt one and a thriving republic owes its very existence to him." (Sullivan, *Machiavelli's Three Romes*, 160).

unaware that Machiavelli puts forward this second account of founders in order to overcome the system of rule congenital to it.[20]

In Machiavelli the figure of the founder is completely internal or functional to the system of authority and to the primacy that this system assigns to the maintenance of political form within political life. A strong indication in favor of this interpretation comes from the fact that Machiavelli rarely discusses the founder "in itself," as an origin that stands in ab-solute isolation.[21] Put in Weberian terminology, Machiavelli's focus is generally on how the charisma of the founder gets routinized and, more subversively, on how the routinization itself posits this charisma. What counts is the possible role that the founder can have in the establishment of the priority of form in political life. This role is ultimately secondary because, in the end, it is the routinization of charisma that effectively establishes political form and not the charismatic agent itself, for whom any and every form is always provisional, a mere expression of its power, and hence always potentially revocable.[22]

In discussing the beginnings of cities (*Discourses on Livy* I,1) Machiavelli seems to ascribe the greatest possible importance to the founder. The text quickly moves to the case of the foundation of cities by foreigners who owe nothing to their "fatherland" (*paese patrio*) so as to be able to consider the founder as the effective *principio* (beginning and principle) of the city. "In this case one can recognize the virtue of the builder and the fortune of what is built, which is more or less marvelous as the one who was the beginning [*principio*] of it was more or less virtuous."[23] The virtue of the founder is determined by two factors: the choice of site and the ordering of laws. Yet in both respects the role given to the founder as *principio* is quickly subverted and becomes a secondary matter.

Because men work either by necessity or by choice, and because there is greater virtue to be seen where choice has less authority, it should be considered whether it is better to choose sterile places for the building of cities so that men, constrained to be industrious and less seized by idleness, live more united, having less cause for discord, because of the poverty of the site.... This choice would without doubt be wiser and more useful if men were content to live off their own and did not wish to command others. Therefore, since men cannot secure themselves except with power, it is necessary to avoid this sterility in a country and to settle in the most fertile places, where, since [the city] can expand because of the abundance of the site, it can both defend itself from whoever might assault it

---

[20] This is the case of Pitkin's interpretation of founders that stresses the incompatibility of the visions of politics represented by founders and citizens, "the one repressive and stressing uniformity, the other requiring plurality and conflict; the one hierarchical, the other equalitarian." (Pitkin, *Fortune is a Woman*, 97). Pitkin does not consider the possibility that these dualisms fall under the ideology of citizenship developed by the system of authority that I am outlining, for which the founder is undoubtedly a mythical, yet necessary element. Evidence to this effect lies with Pitkin's discussion of the possibility of augmentation as one of the crucial marks of a purportedly "non-authoritarian" citizen-based vision of politics, when this possibility lies at the heart of the authoritarian system that Machiavelli critiques. (Ibid.,100). An effective anti-authoritarian political life requires a far more radical vision of politics, as I discuss below.

[21] In chapter 5 below I discuss at some length one of the few exceptions to this rule, where Machiavelli considers the founder in its ideal-typical purity.

[22] This point is made by Weber in his analysis of the "revolutionary nature of charisma" where he argues that "genuine charismatic domination knows no abstract laws and regulations and no formal adjudication.... In a revolutionary and sovereign manner, charismatic domination transforms all values and breaks all traditional and rational norms." (Weber, *Economy and Society*, 1115-6).

[23] Machiavelli, *Discourses on Livy*, I,1.

and crush anyone who might oppose its greatness. As to the idleness that the site might bring, the laws should be ordered to constrain it by imposing such necessities as the site does not provide.[24]

If things really depended on the founder alone then the choice of the sterile site would seem to be "wiser" and grant greater virtù to the city. But from the start Machiavelli places the city in a context that negates the isolation sought by the founder and takes away the force of its choice: for in this context men are not "content to live off their own" and seek to rule over others, making the only proper response that of expansion. In turn, the founder lacks the capacity to assure this expansion because it depends on the "necessity ordered by laws" [*necessità ordinata dalle leggi*] that emerge progressively in the history of the city: the "many necessities the laws made by Romulus, Numa, and the others imposed," as Machiavelli adds, suddenly multiplying the founders of Rome.[25]

The relative position of the founder becomes explicit later in this first chapter when Machiavelli, inverting the initial attempt to isolate the figure of the founder, manifests a surprising and complete indifference to the question of who actually founded Rome: "So if whoever examines the building of Rome takes Aeneas for its first progenitor, it will be of those cities built by foreigners, while if he takes Romulus it will be of those built by men native to the place; and in whichever mode, he will see that it had a free beginning, without depending on anyone."[26] The role of the founder is not unique and therefore the founder cannot stand as the effective *arche* or *principio* of political form. On the contrary, the founder is purely functional to the "necessities" of the political form: since the form needs to have a free beginning, it will be founded by Aeneas; since it needs laws that will make it powerful, it will be founded by Romulus (and Numa and others). The founder is constructed a posteriori as the one who fulfills some of the "objective" conditions of political form. The initial thesis that the virtù of the city depends on the virtù of the founder is reversed.

That the founder is a function of the process of foundation rather than its first, ab-solute cause is reiterated in the discussion of Romulus. According to Machiavelli's presentation of the founding legend, Romulus "killed his brother, then consented to the death of Titus Tatius the Sabine, chosen by him as partner in the kingdom," in order to remain alone at the moment of founding.

So a prudent orderer of a republic, who has the intent to wish to help not himself but the common good, not for his own succession but for the common fatherland, should contrive to have authority alone; nor will a wise understanding ever reprove anyone for any extraordinary action that he uses to order a kingdom or constitute a republic. It is very suitable that when the deed accuses him, the effect excuses him; and when the effect is good, as was that of Romulus, it will always excuse the deed.[27]

The isolation of the founder ("to have authority alone") is only relative: it is a moment in the process of constituting "the common good" and "the common

---

[24] Ibid.

[25] Ibid. On the multiplication of Roman foundations, see the discussion in Michel Serres, *Rome: the Book of Foundations* (Stanford: Stanford University Press, 1991).

[26] Machiavelli, *Discourses on Livy*, I,1.

[27] Machiavelli, *Discourses on Livy*, I,9. Emphasis mine.

fatherland." In this context, these expressions refer to the idea of the state as ethical substance: the kind of political form that is constructed by the system of authority, as I show below.

In particular, the oneness of the founder is relative to the multiplicity of the citizens: together they compose the binary formula of authority: one to found (*agere*) and many to maintain (*gerere*). For "if one individual is capable of ordering, *the thing itself is ordered to last long* not if it remains on the shoulders of one individual but rather *if it remains in the care of many and its maintenance stays with many.*"[28] If "the common good" designates a political form that lasts in time, then its duration is achieved only if "many" are set on supporting this form. But such support requires, by definition, that the "many" be deprived, from the beginning, of the possibility of beginning something radically new, of breaking with the first beginning, with the foundation, which, on the contrary, they can only "augment." Consequently, the isolation of the founder is solely a logical requirement for placing the "many" in the political position of the "maintainers" of a given political form of domination over which they exercise control in an authoritative way. By cutting themselves off from the possibility of being founders, the "many" in question cut themselves off from the violence inherent in the first establishment of political form in order to accede to the standpoint of authority, of a non-violent legal and routinized form of domination or rule.

But who are these "many" for the sake of whose authority the founder needs to "have authority alone"? Machiavelli identifies them as the potential members of the Senate, the patricians, the few, whose reiterated attempts to rule over the people, the plebeians, (a political actor which has yet to be introduced theoretically) marks the history of the Roman republic:

That Romulus was one of those ["who has the intent to wish to help not himself but the common good"], that he deserves excuse in the deaths of his brother and his partner, and that what he did was for the common good and not for his own ambition, is demonstrated by *his having at once ordered a Senate with which he took counsel and by whose opinion he decided.*[29]

The founder is "one" always already in conjunction with the "many" to whom the founder's isolation allows to accede to a position of authority, an authority that is followed by the founder itself. It is difficult to find a clearer formulation of Machiavelli's belief that the system of authority fashions for itself a founder and not vice versa. One could say that in Machiavelli's Romulus, the routinization of charisma is at work in the charismatic agent itself. Indeed, the effect of Romulus's "extraordinary action" is deemed to be "good" only because "he does not leave the authority he took as an inheritance to another; for since men are more prone to evil than to good, his successor could use ambitiously that which had been used virtuously by him."[30] In other words, Romulus's access to sole authority is only justified because he immediately employs this position to break with the

---

[28] Ibid., emphasis mine.
[29] Ibid., emphasis mine.
[30] Ibid.

simplicity of the political form and institutes, along with kingship, the Senate. The institution of the Senate is intended to preclude any future individual from having, ever again, "authority alone" in the absolute and isolated manner of the founder: henceforth authority would be shared and exercised by those who are not-one, namely, by the few who compose the Senate.

The new system of rule, which breaks with the simple political form and aims toward the ideal of an ethical substance, of a lasting "common good," establishes its authority through religion.

Since the heavens judged that the orders of Romulus would not suffice for such an empire, they inspired in the breast of the Roman Senate the choosing of Numa Pompilius as successor to Romulus so that those things omitted by him might be ordered by Numa. As he found a very ferocious people and wished to reduce it to civil obedience with the arts of peace, he turned to religion as a thing altogether necessary if he wished to maintain a civilization; and he constituted it so that for many centuries there was never so much fear of God as in that republic, which made easier whatever enterprise the Senate or the great men of Rome might plan to make.[31]

This is not the place to discuss Machiavelli's theory of religion, pagan or Christian.[32] My intention is merely to show how Machiavelli understands the religious essence of the system of authority and of its sole purpose: steering political life toward the establishment of a stable political form.[33] The first piece of evidence is obviously that Roman religion is presented as an invention of the Senate that produces, for the purpose of instituting it, a charismatic founder, Numa.[34] The secondariness of the founder reveals the priority of the system of authority (represented by the Senate) over the founder (Numa) in a political form that desires to gain "empire" and "civilization" through the institution of religion,

---

[31] Ibid., I,11.

[32] For such a discussion, see part 3, ch. 4.

[33] In her analysis of Machiavelli's portrayal of Roman religion, Sullivan argues against the received view that Machiavelli favors religion as an instrument of state. "Machiavelli's embrace of the pagan religion represents an important step to a very different destination - one that regards all appeals to divine entities as dangerous to a state." (Sullivan, *Machiavelli's Three Romes*, 103). I find myself in agreement with Sullivan's basic thesis that Machiavelli is a critic of the political employment of religion but for different reasons than her. According to my reading, religion is the basis of an authoritarian system of rule that seeks the stability of political form. It fails to achieve this stability because both the freedom and the power of political life calls for the possibility of radical changes of political form that are, by definition, rejected by the system of authority. These changes are effected by a political agent that Machiavelli calls "the people." Machiavelli's analysis of Roman religion is designed to show how Roman religion is constantly used against the "people" in favor of the "nobles." This is the fundamental reason why religion is problematic for a free and powerful political life. In short, whereas Sullivan argues that religion is dangerous to the stability of political form, to the state, I argue that religion is efficacious in stabilizing political form, but that this very stability is what endangers the freedom and power of political life.

[34] According to Weber "the genuinely charismatic ruler… is responsible to the ruled – responsible, that is, to prove that he himself is indeed the master willed by God." (Weber, *Economy and Society*, 1114). Analogously, Machiavelli insists on the fact that "the authority of God… was quite necessary to Numa, who pretended to be intimate with a nymph who counseled him on what he had to counsel the people. It all arose because he wished to put new and unaccustomed orders in the city and doubted that his authority would suffice. And truly there was never any orderer of extraordinary laws for a people who did not have recourse to God, because otherwise they would not have been accepted." (Machiavelli, *Discourses on Livy*, I,11).

and in that way effectively break from the pre-historical, natural cycle of simple political forms and accede to a historical existence.[35]

The second piece of evidence is that religion is explicitly introduced as a means through which the few (the Senate) can rule over the many (the "very ferocious people") by "reducing it to civil obedience with the arts of peace," i.e., through authority rooted in "the fear of God" rather than in violence.[36] Religion is instrumental in imposing, at one and the same time, the form of rule, i.e., the division between ruler and ruled, and the primacy of political form over political life.

Marveling, thus, at his [Numa's] goodness and prudence, the Roman people yielded to his every decision. Indeed it is true that since those times were full of religion and the men with whom he had to labor were crude, they *made much easier the carrying out of his plans, since he could easily impress any new form whatever on them.*[37]

Machiavelli identifies the political effect of religion, namely, placing the people in a position of obedience to the orders of the nobility and Senate ("carrying out his plans"), with the imposition of form over the nonresisting "matter" of the people.

Religion does not assure the "goodness" of specific laws and orders as much as it determines that what is "good" is the stability of rule itself, of political form as such. It is no coincidence that Machiavelli offers his most significant illustration of the political use of religion on the part of the nobles by citing an episode from the early history of the conflict between patricians and plebeians over agrarian redistribution:

Very many tumults had arisen in Rome caused by the tribune Terentillus when he wished to propose a certain law [the first Agrarian law].... Among the first remedies that the nobility used against him was religion, which they made to serve in two modes. In the first, they had the Sybilline books seen and made to respond that through civil sedition, dangers of losing its freedom hung over the city that year – a thing that, though exposed by the tribunes, nonetheless put such terror in the breasts of the plebs that it was cooled off in following them.[38]

---

[35] The secondary or relative character of the founder is reiterated by Machiavelli when he states that "if one had to dispute over which prince Rome was more obligated to, Romulus or Numa, I believe rather that Numa would obtain first rank." (Ibid.).

[36] In "What is authority?" Arendt offers one of the best discussions of the political employment of religion (understood as "fear of God") for the purposes of ruling the many by the few. This political use of religion begins with Plato and runs throughout Christianity. "Nothing, indeed, is more suggestive in this context than that it was Plato who coined the word 'theology,' for the passage in which the new word is used occurs again in a strictly political discussion, namely in *The Republic*, when the dialogue deals with the founding of cities. This new theological god is neither a living God nor the god of the philosopher nor a pagan divinity; he is a political device, 'the measurement of measurements,' that is, the standard according to which cities may be founded and rules of behavior laid down for the multitude.... Theology to him was part and parcel of 'political science,' and specifically that part which taught the few how to rule the many." (Arendt, *Between Past and Future*, 131).

[37] Machiavelli, *Discourses on Livy*, I,11. Emphasis mine.

[38] Ibid., I,13.

Religion stands in an antithetical relation to political conflicts, like the one around the Agrarian laws, that imperil the stability of rule desired by the patricians and vouched for by the authority of their political organ, the Senate.

The coincidence of religion and the interest in the stability of rule is reiterated by Machiavelli's analysis of the fact that "the Gentile religion was founded on the responses of the oracles and on the sect of the diviners and augurs."[39] When these oracles and augurs

> began to speak in the mode of the powerful, and as that falsity was exposed among peoples, men became incredulous and apt to disturb every good order. Thus, princes of a republic or of a kingdom should maintain the foundations of the religion they hold; and if this is done, it will be an easy thing for them to maintain their republic religious and, in consequence, good and united.[40]

Machiavelli's employment of "good" in texts such as these refers to the essential relation between religion as a moral force that serves to "keep men good, to bring shame to the wicked,"[41] and religion as a political instrument that preserves the orders established by the nobility, by the *aristoi* (the good as in "the best"). For this reason Machiavelli says that religion should remain in the hands of "the princes of a republic or of a kingdom" who in principle are averse to any political conflict, disturbance, or change brought about by the people that might imperil their rule. To maintain a "republic religious and, in consequence, good and united" is identical to maintaining a political form in which to rule (as the few and good) and to be ruled (as the many and bad) are the only political options.

The religious goal of maintaining a political form "good and united" is nothing other than a restatement of the classical ideal of the state as ethical substance that I discussed in the first chapter. Machiavelli exposes how religion works in the system of authority that underlies such an ideal: it permits one to draw an identity between "every good order" and the good of all order. A strong indication that his critique of Roman religion envisages the whole ideal of classical ethical substance is that religion is praised by paraphrasing the providential formulation of the ideal of ethical substance that I showed to be common to classical political thought from Plato to Cicero: "the religion introduced by Numa was among the first causes of the happiness of that city... for it caused good orders; good orders make good fortune; and from good fortune arose the happy successes of enterprises."[42] It is now a question of discussing the logic behind the system of authority and its belief that political concord leads to the providential path of a political form through history. In other words, it is a question of examining the sense in which the religious origin of political form, while allowing the state to accede to history, still does not allow one to think the historicity of political form to its fullest extent.

---

[39] Ibid., I,12.
[40] Ibid.
[41] Ibid., I,11.
[42] Ibid.

THE MIXED CONSTITUTION AND THE RULE OF LAWS

In order for a state to exist in history it needs to break away from the natural cycle of constitutions, into which it falls due to the simplicity of its political form, and attain a mixed constitution. Two paths are available for breaking with the cycle of simple constitutions, symbolized by the political experiences of Sparta and Rome. Speaking of cities that "were at once governed by their own will," Machiavelli refers to those which "were given laws by one alone and at a stroke, either in their beginning or after not much time, like those that were given by Lycurgus to the Spartans; some had them by chance and at many different times, and according to accidents, as had Rome."[43] Sparta and Rome are employed as ideal types through which to study the kinds of historical origins of political form as well as the kinds of political freedoms that states can obtain.

On the surface, the paths of Sparta and Rome lead to the same end: the mixed political constitution. In fact this is not the case: Machiavelli pits these two models against each other, staging the conflict between the ancients and moderns through the kind of historical dialectic it establishes between these ideal types. Specifically, Sparta represents the model for the "ancient" state, whereas Rome represents the model for the "modern" state. An "ancient" state is one that is constituted with historical becoming in mind, so to speak, but whose form is intended to resist historical becoming, both externally and internally. The religious origin of political form corresponds to the moment of "antiquity" in any given political life. Conversely, a "modern" state is constituted in and through historical becoming: it is a state which emerges in a political life that exists by historicizing its political form.[44] What I call the free origin of political form corresponds to the moment of "modernity" in political life.

Furthermore, "modern" and "ancient" states are not simply mutually exclusive. The "modern" state incorporates in its political life the modes of the "ancient" state, but also surpasses them in the range of possibilities disclosed by its wider political life. The political life of the "ancient" state is determined by an authoritarian system of rule that, in its ideal form, is identical to a system of rule in which law represents the highest authority. The political life of the "modern" state, as constructed in the argument of the *Discourses on Livy*, does not turn on any given system of rule at all, rather it is predicated on the possibility of overturning every attempt to systematize or totalize the instance of legitimate domination or legal

---

[43] Ibid., I,2.

[44] My reading is very close to the one proposed by Lefort: "the same necessity commands the history of Florence as that of Rome, as it commanded that of Sparta... the three cities merely provide three different answers to the same problem, and these responses each contain a developmental schema." (Lefort, *Le Travail de l'oeuvre*, 486). For Lefort, Sparta refuses itself to history whereas Rome "assumes the risks of history and its effective history remains closely associated to the principle of the genesis of the state.... In speaking about Rome, the author advances a theory of a historical society." (Ibid., 487) My objection to Lefort is simply that in Machiavelli's discourse history is not "commanded" by any "necessity," and that political conflict, in all its senses, does not constitute such a "necessity" but rather offers the matrix for its transcendence. Furthermore, as I have shown, the state does not have one "principle of genesis" but a plurality of them. Finally, Machiavelli's interpretation of the history of Rome certainly "advances a theory of a historical society," but this theory makes room for the possibility of transcending the form of the state rather than coinciding with its highest expression.

rule. In this sense, "modern" political life as Machiavelli conceives has an essential anti-authoritarian component.

Nominally, Sparta and Rome are both mixed constitutions because their political forms share in the three "good" forms of government:

So those who prudently order laws having recognized this defect [of simple constitutions], avoiding each of these modes by itself, chose one that shared in all, judging it firmer and more stable; for the one guards the other, since in one and the same city there are the principality, the aristocrats, and the popular government.[45]

In the case of Sparta, though, the mixed constitution is arrived at through the "prudence" of the founder-legislator, Lycurgus; whereas in the case of Rome,

notwithstanding that it did not have a Lycurgus to order it in the beginning in a mode that would enable it to live free a long time, nonetheless *so many accidents arose in it through the disunion between the plebs and the Senate that what an orderer had not done, chance did.*[46]

From the start the opposition at stake between the models of Sparta and Rome is starkly defined: the prudence of the founder-legislator who determines the foundational role of political form, on the one side, against the chance of political conflict that signifies the anti-foundational role of revolutionary changes of form, on the other.

Machiavelli's analysis of the origin and finality of the Spartan constitution contains a critique of the prudential *logos* of the founder-legislator,[47] symbolized throughout classical political thought by the figure of Lycurgus.[48] For Machiavelli the historical construction of political form cannot be reduced to the prudence of a founder-legislator. The critique of such prudence only makes sense on my hypothesis that Machiavelli assigns a priority to the domain of the event over that of form in political life: if prudence constitutes a historical origin of political form in the minimal sense of breaking with the natural origin of form, still prudence is itself a faculty that, in the widest sense, attempts to anticipate events and neutralize their effects. A prudential foundation of political form seeks to immunize the form from the contingency of its own origin. But from what else does the prudential foundation of political form immunize political life? At what price is the stability of the Spartan order maintained?

The prudence of Lycurgus consists in giving a place to the three good forms of rule in the Spartan constitution so that their forces can check each other. The simplicity of the political form is fissured into a multiplicity of political forms.

---

[45] Machiavelli, *Discourses on Livy*, I,2.

[46] Ibid. Emphasis mine.

[47] Polybius first makes the distinction between constitutions that originate *dia logon* (through the prudence of the legislator) or *dia pollon agonon* (through the plurality of conflicts). (Polybius *Histories* VI,10).

[48] Lycurgus is mentioned both in the discussion of political foundation (Romulus) and in that of religious foundation (Numa), condensing in one figure the whole problem of foundation. (Machiavelli, *Discourses on Livy*, I,9 and I,11). He is not mentioned in the discussion of mythical founders in *The Prince*, VI. The reason for this absence is that Lycurgus stands for the founder as relative to a system of authority whereas the mythical founders cited in *The Prince* are absolute founders. Their logico-political function is clarified below in ch. 5.

But, as Machiavelli points out, this division produces a greater unity of the state, an increased stability and solidity of the political form itself: the perpetual conflict between forces found in the cycle of constitutions is checked. This kind of political unity, instituting itself by giving rise to a multiplicity over which it rules, is only possible if the instance of the law occupies the place of the monarch that Machiavelli introduced in his discussion of the cycle of constitutions. The place of the monarch lies outside of the three "good" forms of government: when it is occupied by any one of the forces in the city that seek to rule, that is, when it coincides with an instance of might, then the "rule of might" obtains. But when the place of the monarch is occupied by the instance of the law, and no longer by any of the parts of the city, then the "rule of laws," in its most primitive yet fundamental shape, results.

In other words, the discussion of the founder-legislator in the *Discourses on Livy* should be read as Machiavelli's main intervention in the debate on the classical ideal of *nomos basileus*, the sovereignty of law.[49] Machiavelli approaches the debate by asking under what conditions the law can assume its sovereign status, thereby taking the place of violence or force. The analysis of the founder-legislator explores the revolution that causes the "principle of might" (or the "law of the strong") to convert itself into the "might of principle" (or the "rule of laws"). Already Plato's *Gorgias* had in view such a revolution: when Callicles voices the ideal of *nomos basileus* he expresses a version of the "law of the strongest" or of the principle that "might makes right" common among the old Greek aristocracy sung by Pindar.[50] One can say that Callicles enunciates the ideal of *nomos monarchos*, since the monarch, in Plato as in Polybius, is at first simply the strongest. Socrates's subsequent argument that veritable strength belongs only to those who do right with others (those who live in accordance to justice) reverses Callicles's principle into that of "right gives might." In the *Gorgias*, Socrates enunciates the shift from the "monarchy" of force to the "kingship" of law, and thus inaugurates the historically-effective sense of the expression *nomos basileus* in later classical thought.

In the political arrangement that constitutes the system of authority, the desire for domination voiced by Plato's Callicles (and which, not coincidentally, is said to belong to the "nobility"), falls under the command of the law. The law has command over the division between those that command and those that obey. In order to achieve this command the law must appeal to a force which is not might: this force of the law has a religious origin, and it consists in authority.[51] Although

---

[49] On the formula *nomos basileus*, see Marcello Gigante, *Nomos basileus* (Naples: Bibliopolis, 1993); on the origin of the rule of laws in classical political thought and practice, see Martin Ostwald, *From Popular Sovereignty to the Sovereignty of Law: Law, Society and Politics in Fifth-Century Athens* (Berkeley: University of California Press, 1986); and Christian Meier, *The Greek Discovery of Politics*.

[50] Plato *Gorgias* 484b-c.

[51] Arendt shows how the revolution in the meaning of *nomos basileus* started in Plato's *Gorgias* consists in the establishment of authority as a system of rule in which the few can dominate the many without violence. Arendt remarks that in the *Gorgias* Plato first discovers that the law can acquire its "force" to counterbalance and keep in check the force of might only by appealing to religion: in this case, to the idea of punishments and rewards granted to the immortal soul in the afterlife. (Arendt, *Between Past and Future*, 129, fn.44). It is also clear from the *Gorgias* that the rule of laws

there are a number of ways in which one can think the religious foundation of political form in the ancients, it is Machiavelli's analysis that poses the basic question: under what conditions do the forces of the city bind to each other (*re-lego*), both in the sense of constituting the unity of the state and in the sense of being pledged to each other, as opposed to being bent on their mutual destruction?

AUTHORITY AND CONCORD

Authority can be defined as that force pertaining to a command which demands obedience without coercion, without the use of violence.[52] The prudential nature of the arrangement conceived by the founder-legislator consists in setting against each other the forces of domination so that the might of each part is moderated by that of the others. This arrangement is accepted by all the forces at issue, by all the parts of the city, in what amounts to a fundamental instance of unanimity or concord (*homonoia, concordia*). The law given by Lycurgus expresses the shared belief of who should rule in the city. Its authority, therefore, depends on its capacity to engender this concord or shared belief as to who is to rule: only in this sense does the law command the distribution of rule, that is, the division between those who rule and those who obey, without having to appeal to force.

The relation between prudence and concord is one of two ways in which the religious foundation of the sovereignty of the law manifests itself. The other way consists in the use of the act of foundation by "one" in order to place the "many" in a position of shared authority discussed previously. But how does the prudence of the founder-legislator achieve concord among the forces or parts of the city? What is the relation between the founder's prudential foresight (*pronoia*) and the shared belief in the justice of the laws expressed by civic concord (*homonoia*)? My thesis is that the shared belief in the rule of laws binds together or pledges the parts of the city in a religious sense because this rule is prudential in nature, and prudence, in classical antiquity, is closely associated to the divine. Cicero frequently remarks that *prudentia* (prudence) is a contracted form of *providentia* (providence).[53] Machiavelli, for his part, insists on the religious foundation of laws when he points out that "whoever reviews infinite actions, both of the people of Rome all together and of many Romans by themselves, will see that the citizens feared to break a pledge much more than the laws."[54] From Cicero through Machiavelli to modern scholarship the institution of the auspices has always been

---

is functional to the imposition and stabilization of form over matter. The stability of political form, therefore, requires religion.

[52] I follow Arendt's definition of authority which has set the basis for most contemporary discussions of the idea: "Authority precludes the use of external means of coercion; where force is used, authority itself has failed. Authority, on the other hand, is incompatible with persuasion, which presupposes equality and works through a process of argumentation. Where arguments are used, authority is left in abeyance. Against the egalitarian order of persuasion stands the authoritarian order, which is always hierarchical." (Arendt, *Between Past and Future*, 93). On the contemporary debate, see Joseph Raz, ed., *Authority* (Oxford: Blackwell, 1990); and J. Pennock, J. Roland, John W. Chapman, eds., *Authority Revisited* (New York: New York University Press, 1987).

[53] Cicero *De re publica* VI,1; idem, *De natura deorum* II,22,58; idem, *De legibus* I,23,60.

[54] Machiavelli, *Discourses on Livy*, I,11.

understood to lie at the core of Roman religion.[55] In order to explain the sense in which political prudence has a providential or religious ground Ortega y Gasset suggests a brilliant interpretation of this institution which sheds light on the political logic both of Roman concord and of Spartan rule of laws, supporting my claim that in the *Discourses on Livy* these two political phenomena illustrate one and the same system of authority that lies at the basis of the "ancient" conception of political form.

According to Ortega y Gasset, the institution of the auspices manifests a belief in divine providence which signifies that the individual, far from being alone in the world, understands itself to be surrounded by "absolute realities that have more power than it does and on which it is necessary to count on. Instead of just letting oneself go in the action proposed by one's mind, one must detain oneself and submit oneself to the judgment of these gods," which is the originary sense of *pro-videntia*.[56] "This conduct, by which one does not live lightly," but rather exhibits what the Romans called *gravitas*, by which one "comports oneself with prudence in regard to the transcendent reality," is one of the basic meanings that the word *religio* has for the Romans.[57] Indeed, Ortega y Gasset argues that r*e-lego* should be understood as the contrary of *nec-lego*: the religious ethos is the contrary of a "negligent" behavior. Ortega concludes his analysis by explaining that "auspice [*auspicium*]" came to signify "command [*imperium*]," so that to be under the auspices of someone was to be at their orders.

These elements help to explain, in turn, the religious foundation of the authority constitutive of the rule or force of law. The law gains its authority from the fact that it expresses the shared belief by all parts of the city that their forces are surrounded by other forces which count for them as "absolute realities," and which can be neglected only at the highest cost. Religion, therefore, expresses the deepest form of recognition of the absoluteness of violence or might. But the very fact that religion recognizes such absoluteness allows it to raise this consciousness of violence above violence and might: one can say that it allows this conscious-ness to receive the auspices of violence, and thereby to gain "command" (*imperium*) over and above it. What defines the authority of the law is this non-violent command of the law over and against the forces of domination on the basis of the recognition of the absolute reality of domination, and consequently of the need for these forces not to neglect each other but instead to mutually recognize their interdependency, to pledge each to the other.

Lycurgus in Sparta and Numa in Rome give laws that bind those that live under them religiously. Machiavelli discerns the political meaning of this religiosity in the idea that no part or force in the city will be able to do what it wants before

---

[55] Machiavelli's whole analysis of "Gentile religion" is an interpretation of the political function of "the responses of the oracles and the sect of diviners and augurs." (Machiavelli, *Discourses on Livy* I,12). The institution of augury is prominently featured in *Discourses on Livy*, I,13-15. Arendt, for her part, follows Theodor Mommsen's *Römisches Staatsrecht* (Tübingen: Wissenschaftliche Buchgemeinschaft, 1952), in relating the binding force of authority to the institution of the auspices. The close connection between authority and auspices is also attested in Émile Benveniste, *Le vocabulaire des institutions indo-européennes*, vol. 2 (Paris: Minuit, 1969).
[56] José Ortega y Gasset, *Del Imperio Romano* (Madrid: Alianza, 1985), 155.
[57] Ibid.

consulting the other parts, the other forces that lie beyond it, that transcend it, and upon whose providence it must count. The theologico-political origin of the rule of laws, the prudent replacement of force by the law as the sole, monarchical criterion for government of the city, is what allows for the mixture of forms of rule. The system of authority that attempts to apply the principle of rule over all political life therefore finds finds its completed political expression in the uncontested rule of laws that characterizes the mixed constitution.

THE SHORTCOMINGS OF THE STATE AS ETHICAL SUBSTANCE

The religious underpinning of the classical system of rule based on the prudence of the founder-legislator and on the authority of the rule of laws reconfirms the internal relation that obtains between the ideal of the common good and the practice of ruling in the ancient state. This state has been called, at least since Hegel, an "ethical substance" on the basis of the immediate relation between ethics and politics that one finds therein. Machiavelli's analysis of the ideal type of ethical substance, namely, the Spartan model of the state, provides the first extra-moral (or value-free) description of the political dynamic that produces ethical substance: the more political rule becomes ethical, in the sense that it prudently moderates its rule in the mixed constitution, the more the concord sustaining the regime gives substance to its rule. This consolidation of the political form, this moulding of political life into a fixed and unchangeable form, is intended to leave the state less vulnerable to unexpected changes of circumstances, to the effects of chance. For this reason, in classical historiography and political thought, the mixed constitution tends to be seen as a providential entity, and this in at least two senses. First, because of the belief that the mixed constitution would not have emerged were it not for the figure of the founder-legislator whose prudence and foresight excludes both the necessity of natural processes and the contingency of mere chance events. Second, the mixed constitution is deemed providential because of the belief that the integrity of the political form, i.e., the well-foundedness of legal domination, renders it immune to historical becoming: the domain of the event would seem not to be able to pierce through the armor of the integral state.

Machiavelli offers a concerted critique of the providential origin of the state as mixed government. The main argument developed in *Discourses on Livy*, I,3-8 is that restricting political life to an authoritarian system of rule, to a system in which the rule of laws is politically uncontestable, while it produces an immediate link between justice ("ethics") and domination ("politics"), nonetheless does so at the expense of the freedom and power of the political life in question. Machiavelli does not deny that the classical ideal of ethical substance achieves its goal of constructing an integral political form or state. The state is integral in the double sense of the term: it is self-enclosed, united in concord, wholesome (the very characteristics that compelled Hegel to call the classical *Sittlichkeit* a "beautiful" totality); and the state is integral in the sense that its domination is well-founded, i.e., morally grounded in the authority of the rule of laws. Rather, Machiavelli's point is that the integrity of the state falls short of the possibilities intrinsic in political life, namely, falls short of attaining political freedom and political power. Since these are the characteristics of the republican modality of political life, the conclusion is that the authoritarian and integral state falls short of the republic. The *Discourses on Livy* advances the thesis that there is a qualitative leap from the integrity of the state defined by the internal relation between justice and domination, to the republican modality of political life, which is defined by the internal relation between freedom and power.

By identifying ethical substance as a shortcoming of political life, Machiavelli can employ the comparison between Sparta and republican Rome to separate these two models in favor of the latter, in turn exposing the ideological character of the system of authority represented by the former. The first result is that, when compared to Rome, the Spartan constitution is mixed only in name. In reality it is a system of rule whose parts are only noble (aristocratic and kingly) because constituted by those who are mighty.

Sparta, as I said, was governed by a king and by a narrow Senate. It could maintain itself for so long a time because they could live united a long time: there were few inhabitants in Sparta, for they blocked the way to those who might come and inhabit it, and the laws of Lycurgus were held in repute.... For Lycurgus with his laws made more equality of belongings in Sparta and less equality of rank; for there was an equal poverty and the plebeians were less ambitious because the ranks of the city were spread among few citizens and were kept at a distance from the plebs; nor did the nobles, by treating them badly, ever give them the desire to hold rank. This was because the Spartan kings, placed in that principality and set down in the middle of the nobility, had not greater remedy for upholding their dignity than to keep the plebs defended from every injury, which made the plebs not fear and not desire rule.[58]

In other words, the mixed constitution of the Spartans is able to maintain political concord exclusively on the basis of the systematic exclusion from political life of the "plebeians" or the "not nobles" (*ignobili*), as Machiavelli calls them.

Ethical substance is possible only on condition that the "people" be excluded from political life. The reason for this exclusion is due to their fundamental political character:

if one considers the end of the nobles [*nobili*] and the not-nobles [*ignobili*], one will see in the former a great desire to dominate and in the latter only the desire not to be dominated [*solo desiderio di non essere dominati*], and thus a greater will to live freely [*maggiore volontà di vivere liberi*].[59]

The desire not to be dominated[60] is the only factical, political trait of the "people" or not-nobles. To avoid misunderstandings, with the term "the people [*il popolo*]" Machiavelli does not refer to a unitary substance; the people is everyone who finds a motive for action in the sole desire not to be dominated. Conversely, the nobility is everyone who finds a motive for action in the sole desire to dominate. Clearly one and the same individual or group can take both subject-positions in different circumstances. Given this definition of the people as bearers of a desire not to be dominated it becomes clear that the effective condition for the rule of

---

[58] Machiavelli, *Discourses on Livy*, I,6.

[59] Ibid., I, 5.

[60] I discuss at length this desire for freedom as non-domination in the next chapter.

laws in the system of authority, i.e., for placing the law in the place of the monarch, is the exclusion of the people and their desire for freedom from domination. The law can take the place of the monarch and command over the division between rulers and ruled because there is unanimity (*homonoia*, *concordia*) between the parts of the city about the fact that only the desire to dominate of the nobles will be recognized and regulated, but there will be no political recognition of the not-nobles and their desire not to be ruled.

If one assumes, along with Arendt, that the minimal definition of a republic is "a form of government... where the rule of law, resting on the power of the people, would put an end to the rule of man over man,"[61] then the exclusion of the people as the fundamental condition for the institution of the sovereignty of law and the mixed constitution in the system of authority rules out that "ancient" ethical substance can qualify as a republic.[62] By emphasising that without giving power to the people's desire for no-rule, all rule of laws ceases to be "republican" and becomes "princely," Machiavelli invents a "modern" sense of republicanism.

The second objection to the ideal of the state as ethical substance consists in denying that the integrity of the state, what Machiavelli refers to as its closed off character, effectively immunizes the state from historical becoming and contingency. The exclusion of the people from political life, although it is the condition for the presence of political concord, is at the same time the source of the powerlessness of the state.

Considering thus all these things, one sees that it was necessary for the legislators of Rome to do one of two things if they wished Rome to stay quiet [in concord] like the above-mentioned republics: either not employ the plebs in war, as did the Venetians, or not open the way to foreigners, as did the Spartans. They did both, which gave the plebs strength and increase and infinite opportunities for tumult [discord]. But if the Roman state had come to be quieter... it would also have been weaker because it cut off the way by which it could come to the greatness it achieved.... if you wish to make a people numerous and armed so as to be able to make a great empire, you make it of such a quality that you cannot then manage it as you please [*non lo puoi maneggiare a tuo modo*]; if you maintain it either small or unarmed so as to be able to manage it, then if you acquire dominion you cannot hold it or it becomes so cowardly that you are the prey of whoever assaults you.[63]

Here the internal relation between freedom and power is directly opposed to the relation between concord and domination. The passage does not pronounce itself on whether founding the political form on the power of the people is ultimately motivated by the need to achieve empire or by the desire for political freedom. I treat the question of the relative priority of freedom or conquest in the next

---

[61] Hannah Arendt, "On Violence," in *Power*, ed. Steven Lukes (New York: Blackwell, 1986), 60.

[62] Strikingly, Machiavelli also denies that Venice is a republic by giving a detailed analysis of the process by which its state constituted itself by excluding the "people": "Venice did not divide the government by names, but under one appellation all those who can hold administration are called gentlemen.... As they [the original inhabitants of the site] joined together often in councils to decide about the city, when it appeared to them that there were as many as would be sufficient for a political way of life, they closed to all others who might come newly to inhabit there the way enabling them to join in government. In time, when enough inhabitants found themselves in that place outside the government so as to give reputation to those who governed, they called [the latter] gentlemen and the other the populace." (Machiavelli, *Discourses on Livy*, I,6).

[63] Ibid.

chapters. For the moment what counts is the ultimate powerlessness of the authoritarian state with respect to historical becoming due to the impossibility of integrating into its political form the desire for freedom of the people. The authoritarian state effects the exclusion of the people in order to achieve as substantial or static a form as possible in the hope of resisting the negative effects of a change of circumstances, both internally (in the shape of political conflicts intending to bring about revolutionary changes) and externally (in the shape of conflicts with other states). The resistance to change which is characteristic of ethical substance is intimately tied to the prudential practice of ruling that constitutes it. Prudence is always directed to an "outside," to an exteriority that holds some danger and against which one must protect oneself. Machiavelli shows that the exteriority from which political form is to be kept closed off has, as its metaphysical referents, chance and matter, while it has the people and their disruptive desire for freedom as its political referents. The prudential ideal forgets that the gravest dangers for a political body, as Machiavelli says, come from inside the political form, in fact, they arise out of the naturalization and sacralization of such form.

The prudential ideal of classical political thought can be formulated as acting in the right way at the right time. This ideal translates itself into the belief that the encounters of the ethical substance (or of the political actions which issue from it) with the exteriority of circumstances will reveal a providential match between the two.[64] Machiavelli's critique of ethical substance denies the presuppositions of this prudential ideal, at bottom, the very concept that forms can resist the domain of events. Far from the achievement of ethical substance being able to grant the political form a providential character in its encounters with the times, with the domain of events, the achieved integrity of the state cuts short the historical existence of political life.[65] Historical becoming decides the issue between the ideal of the ethical substance and the republican modality of political life:

But since all things of men are in motion and cannot stay steady, they must either rise or fall; and to many things that reason does not bring you, necessity brings you. So when a republic that has been ordered so as to be capable of maintaining itself by not expanding, and necessity leads it to expand, this would come to take away its foundations and make it come to ruin sooner. So, on the other hand, if heaven were so kind that it did not have to make war, from that would arise idleness which would make it either effeminate or divided; these two things together, or each by itself, would be the cause of its ruin. Therefore, since one cannot, I believe, balance this thing, nor maintain the middle way exactly, in ordering a republic there is need to think of the more honorable part and to order it so that if indeed necessity brings it to expand, it can conserve what it has seized. To return to the first

---

[64] I discuss in detail the prudential ideal and its relation to the temporality of action in part 2.

[65] Hence Machiavelli's remarks on the ease with which the integrity of the political form perishes at the hands of "accidents" or "events": "The first of these [Sparta], after it had subjected almost all of Greece to itself, showed its weak foundation upon one slightest accident; for when other cities rebelled, following the rebellion of Thebes, caused by Pelipodas, that republic was altogether ruined. Similarly, having seized a great part of Italy - and the greater part not with war but with money and astuteness - when it had to put its forces to the proof, Venice lost everything in one day." (Machiavelli, *Discourses on Livy*, I,6).

reasoning, I believe that it is necessary to follow the Roman order and not that of the other republics.[66]

What trumps the ideal prudential conception of political form and action is the domain of events themselves: the facticity of events that happen without a cause simply cannot be foreseen by the rational capacity, by the *logos*, of any founder-legislator. There is no predetermined harmony between human action and its circumstances: the effective truth of "all things of man" is not in accord with reason, and it has more force than reason. This is why historical becoming, the domain of events, at first appears under the aegis of necessity.

But "necessity" is only the first word, not the last. In texts like the one cited above, necessity refers to the aspect of historical becoming that is mismatched with the form-giving capacities of human action. Necessity means that events happen in ways that are not predetermined, that there is an exteriority that resists, always already, the imposition of form. This is the sense of necessity that Machiavelli opposes to the providential understanding of events that requires the con-formity of action and times. But this opposition merely serves to open another possibility. Precisely because the prudential action that establishes the integral, and thus static, character of political form is undermined by the necessity of historical becoming, so it is possible that by breaking with the providential presupposition of a conformity between action and times, the necessity of historical becoming will change its value into that of freedom. In this way Machiavelli opens a possibility that effectively breaks with the classical tradition of political thought: only the political life that dedicates itself to the experience of the contingency of political forms of domination, in the name of political freedom from domination, can find in the affirmation of historical becoming its full existence. Machiavelli thereby brings to completion the part of his discourse that intends to illustrate, on the terrain of historical becoming, the dialectical over-coming of the "ancient" ideal of the integral state (Sparta, Venice), with its exclusion of the event from its form, by the "modern" practice of political life (Machiavelli's redescription of republican Rome), which founds itself on the possibility of displacing the monarchical role assumed by political form through revolutionary events where political actions change the times and bring into existence new modes and orders.

---

[66] Ibid.

CHAPTER 4

THE FREE ORIGIN OF POLITICAL FORM:
FROM THE PRINCIPLE OF LAW TO THE DISCORD OF
PRINCIPLES

THE CONCEPT OF FREEDOM IN CIVIC REPUBLICANISM

The single most important factor that blocks Machiavelli's thesis of the historical construction of political form from view is the misunderstanding of his concept of political freedom. Machiavelli expounds a conception of political freedom that is anti-foundational and anti-authoritarian. The historicity of the political form is but a consequence of such a conception of freedom. For Machiavelli, political freedom is defined by its power or capacity to transcend the domain of political form: freedom cannot be realized, without thereby losing itself, by the sovereign rule of laws, by the integral state, or by the well-founded order. As a consequence, the transcendence of political freedom expresses itself in the de-realization of political form, or in the withdrawal of its foundations. But the de-realization of form can only belong to the domain of the event. The transcendence of political freedom with respect to political form expresses the priority of the event over the form. By positing the origin of political form in the transcendence of political freedom, Machiavelli establishes at the same time the radical historicity of political form.

An important interpretative trend attempts to situate Machiavelli's discourse in continuity with the "civic republican" tradition of politics, in part as a reaction to the previously hegemonic interpretative trend that identified Machiavelli as the precursor of modern "reason of state."[1] Perhaps the fundamental tenet of the republicanism developed by the discourse of civic humanism is the identification of political freedom with the rule of laws, interpreted in accordance to the recovered ideals of classical ethical substance.[2] Referring to the civic republican tradition, a recent interpreter says (echoing the terms of classical ethical substance that Machiavelli, as I just showed, exposes in all of their ideological commitments): "the fundamental requirement of political life is the rule of law…. To live politically or civilly means to live under the rules of civil law or justice. Indeed, the very aim of civil justice is to make individuals live the life of the *civitas* or *polis*."[3] The belief that Machiavelli's republicanism is of the civic humanist sort

---

[1] On the history of the opposition between politics as "the art of the republic" and politics as "reason of state," see Viroli, *From Politics to Reason of State*, ch.1 and 2, passim.

[2] For a concise formulation of this tenet, see Viroli, *Machiavelli*, 116-121.

[3] Ibid., 116. The terms of classical ethical substance are also clearly expressed in the following remarks: "Quattrocento republican theorists equated political and civil life with republican government or with mixed government - that is, a form of government which wisely combines the virtues of monarchy, aristocracy, and popular government. This latter interpretation, whose importance can hardly be overestimated, was endorsed by the theorists who were looking at the Republic of Venice as the model political constitution. The Venetian Lorenzo de' Monaci

because it "regards the rule of law as the basic feature of civil and political life;" because it advocates "legal order as the fundamental basis of civil life;" in sum, because "political liberty exists only where the law is sovereign,"[4] stands in complete contrast to my thesis that Machiavelli's theory of political freedom is irreducible to the grammar of the rule of laws and of the ideal of the state as ethical substance. For this reason before presenting the features of this theory, it is incumbent on me to address the philosophical arguments and textual interpretations behind the version of the civic republican concept of freedom that is currently hegemonic in the debate on the meaning of modern republicanism.

For nearly two decades Quentin Skinner has dedicated much of his work[5] to the exposition and philosophical defense of what he calls the "republican ideal of political liberty,"[6] with which he wants to overcome the dichotomy between negative and positive freedom introduced by Isaiah Berlin.[7] Negative freedom is defined as "the absence of some element of constraint which inhibits the agent from being able to pursue different options,"[8] or, as in Hobbes, simply the "absence of opposition." This is the notion of freedom that is associated with modern liberalism; the kind of personal liberty whose safeguard and enlargment is understood by modern natural right theories to be the end of political association. Positive freedom, in contrast, is associated with the Aristotelian-Thomist tradition of political thought. According to this communitarian tradition, to be free is to be actually engaged in the pursuit of those ends that lead to *eudaimonia* or "human flourishing." These ends, at least since Aquinas, have been thought of in terms of the duties that natural law prescribes to every human being in virtue of

---

summarized the conventional understanding, saying that a true political constitution is one 'where the laws rule' and the best way to ensure the rule of law is to imitate the mixed government as exemplified by Venice." (Ibid., 117) As I showed above, Venice together with Sparta are precisely the models of "ancient" states based on a system of authority that Machiavelli seeks to displace on the ground that their adherence to "civil justice" and the "rule of law" covers a system of legal domination in which the few (nobility) rule over the many (people) such that political life is deprived both of freedom and of power.

[4] Ibid., 121, 135, 119, respectively.

[5] See Quentin Skinner, "Machiavelli on the Maintenance of Liberty," *Politics. Journal of the Australasian Political Studies Association* 18, no.2 (1983): 3-15; idem, "The Idea of Negative Liberty: Philosophical and Historical Perspectives," in *Philosophy in History*, ed. R. Rorty, J.B. Schneewind, and Q. Skinner (Cambridge: Cambridge University Press, 1984), 193-221; idem, "The Paradoxes of Political Liberty," in *The Idea of Freedom*, ed. A. Ryan (Oxford: Oxford University Press, 1979), 183-205; idem, "The Republican Ideal of Political Liberty," in *Machiavelli and Republicanism*; idem, *Liberty Before Liberalism*.

[6] In the more recent *Liberty Before Liberalism*, Skinner speaks of a "neo-roman theory of free states." But his interpretation of Machiavelli's theory of freedom, which he considers one the greatest exponents of the "neo-roman theory," (ibid., 10) has not changed substantially from his previous work.

[7] Isaiah Berlin, "Two Concepts of Liberty," in *Four Essays on Liberty* (Oxford: Oxford University Press, 1982). The literature on the dichotomy introduced by Berlin is enormous. For a representative series of essays on the topic, which include Quentin Skinner's "The Paradoxes of Political Liberty," and Charles Taylor's "What's Wrong with Negative Liberty," see A. Ryan, *Idea of Freedom*. For some of the best formulations of the contemporary debate on political freedom, see Norberto Bobbio, *Liberalism and Democracy* (London: Verso, 1990); John Rawls, "The Priority of Right and Ideas of the Good," in *Political Liberalism* (New York: Columbia University Press, 1993); Habermas, *Between Facts and Norms*, ch.7, passim; Raymond Geuss, "Auffassungen der Freiheit," *Zeitschrift für philosophische Forschung*, 49, no.1 (1995): 1-14; and Jean-Fabien Spitz, *La Liberté politique* (Paris: PUF, 1995).

[8] Skinner, "Republican Ideal of Political Liberty," 293.

being a social and political animal. In short, the positive conception of freedom defines freedom as the exercise of certain social and political virtues that make up "the good life."

Skinner's republican ideal of freedom falls midway between the liberal and the communitarian conceptions. He believes, along with liberal thought, that negative freedom has priority over positive freedom; but, akin to communitarian thought, he argues that negative freedom cannot stand on its own nor can it be adequately protected by relying solely on a liberal system of rights. Negative freedom requires political freedom, which he defines through the following two criteria: political freedom involves self-government, and therefore also public service, that is, the cultivation of so-called civic virtues.[9] Secondly, political freedom may require individuals "to be forced to be free" because the performance of "public duties is indispensable to the maintenance of our liberty." If it happens that individuals "may sometimes fail to remember this," it follows that they "may have to be coerced into [civic] virtue and thereby constrained into upholding a liberty" which, left to themselves, they would have undermined.[10]

Skinner interprets Machiavelli's theory of freedom as containing the following argument (one that he employs to support the claims I just stated above). There is no personal (negative) freedom unless one has public freedom, unless one lives in a free state. The freedom of the state is understood in terms of autarchy: freedom from external as well as internal servitude. Autarchy presupposes citizens willing to govern themselves, and thus in possession of civic virtues. But human beings are also "naturally corrupt." They have "a natural tendency to ignore the claims of their community as soon as they seem to conflict with the pursuit of their own immediate advantage."[11] Given the above assumptions, the following problem poses itself: "how can naturally self-interested citizens be persuaded to act virtuously, such that they can hope to maximise a freedom which, left to themselves, they will infallibly throw away?"[12] The answer that Skinner finds in his interpretation of Machiavelli's republicanism is that faith must be placed "in the coercive powers of the law."[13]

Unlike the liberal persuasion which views the coercion of laws as a necessary evil in order for individuals to enjoy their personal liberties without infringing on the liberties of others, and unlike the Rousseauian and Kantian conviction that true freedom consists in obeying the moral law, that is, consists in autonomy (as opposed to autarchy), Skinner believes that "*by coercing people into acting in such a way as to uphold the institutions of a free state, the law creates and preserves a degree of individual liberty* which, in its absence, would promptly collapse into absolute servitude."[14] In short, the kernel of Skinner's position is the

---

[9] This position is reiterated, in more historical terms, by Skinner in *Liberty Before Liberalism*, 82-87.
[10] Skinner, "Republican Ideal of Political Liberty," 295.
[11] Ibid., 304.
[12] Ibid., 305.
[13] Ibid. In *Liberty Before Liberalism* Skinner repeats that "the people incline to *corruzione*, not *virtù*.... If civic virtue is to be encouraged (and public liberty thereby upheld), *there will have to be laws designed to coerce the people out of their natural and self-defeating tendency to undermine the conditions necessary for sustaining their own liberty*." (Ibid., 33, fn.103; emphasis mine). He then proceeds to refer the reader to the article I am analysing.
[14] Ibid., 305. Emphasis mine.

positive, essential relation established between freedom and the coercion of the law on the basis of certain assumptions regarding the idea of corruption.

Skinner's fundamental assumption is that corruption "is simply a failure of rationality, an inability to recognise that our own liberty depends on committing ourselves to a life of virtue and public service."[15] The root of this failure lies with the supposedly "natural" tendency of individuals to favor their self-interest. Machiavelli is saddled with the view that people are naturally corrupt because, as Skinner paraphrases, people only want freedom as a means, either to satisfy their ambition or to consolidate their security of possession. Skinner bases his view of corruption on a passage in *Discourses on Livy*, I,16: "as Machiavelli explains, some people place a high value on the pursuit of honor, glory and power: 'they will want their liberty in order to be able to dominate others'. But other people merely want to be left to their own devices, free to pursue their own family and professional lives: 'they want liberty in order to be able to live in security'."[16] I claim that this nodal point in Skinner's argument is based on a crucial misreading of Machiavelli's discourse. For the two possibilities mentioned above, which undoubtedly characterize freedom as a means, do not exhaust the concept of freedom applicable to "the people."

Granted the point, which I do not concede, that people only desire freedom as a means or negative liberty, Skinner can proceed to find a source for civic virtue outside of and above the people of the political community, since their desires are only a source of corruption. Not surprisingly, Skinner finds the source of civic virtue in the coercion of the laws, and therefore concludes that political liberty must come from "founders" (charismatic leaders),[17] or from "religion" which is "capable of harnessing the self-interested motivations of the religious in such a way as to enable the fear of God to be turned to public account,"[18] or finally from constitutional mechanisms that allow for a manipulation of social and political conflict between the parts of the body politic in order to bring about the "rule and order" that is "able to preserve the city's liberty." [19] In short, for Skinner, Machiavelli's theory of political freedom is characterized by all the salient features of the system of authority. With such a conception of political freedom Skinner makes a religion out of participation in civic and political life, or, what is the same, he reduces political life to the establishment and preservation of the state as ethical susbtance.[20]

Skinner's misreading consists in the failure to distinguish between negative liberty and the desire not to be dominated. For Machiavelli only the latter is a factical and political trait of the political subject he calls "the people." The popular

[15] Ibid., 304.

[16] Ibid., 302.

[17] Skinner states that "no community has the least hope of avoiding corruption [*corruzione*]... unless it happens to be blessed with two large and wholly gratuitous pieces of luck.... A leader and lawgiver of outstanding virtù... and a succession of later leaders in whom the natural tendency of mankind towards *corruzione* is similarly and almost miraculously replaced by a willing and *virtuoso* commitment to the promotion of public interest at all costs." (Skinner, "Maintenance of Liberty," 7).

[18] Ibid., 12.

[19] Ibid.

[20] Thereby confirming the suspicions against proponents of modern republican freedom upheld by Rawls and Habermas in the works cited above.

desire for freedom as non-domination constitutes the condition of possibility for constructing the concept of the republic. The desire not to be dominated refers to the desire for the absence of a division between rulers and ruled, not to a desire for "self-government" or autarchy, as Skinner interpolates.[21] I argue that for Machiavelli a republic can exist only if political life integrates this desire for no-rule, if by republic one understands that modality of political life in which "the rule of law, resting on *the power of the people*, would put *an end to the rule of man over man*," to cite Arendt's definition once again. In a republican political life, power has an internal relation to the desire not to be dominated, and hence it must be understood in antithesis to coercion. The people are powerful when they disclose spaces of no-rule in which no member commands and none obeys because all their speech and action is moved by the desire not to be dominated. The "rule of law" stands under such a power to contest command in the name of the people's desire for no-rule, even in the case that the command of the laws claims to lead the people to autarchy (as in Skinner) or to autonomy (as in Rousseau and Kant).[22]

The distinction between negative freedom and the desire not to be dominated found in Machiavelli reveals how misleading Skinner's conception of the nature of corruption is. Corruption is not a "natural" endowment of the people, linked to their negative freedom, that must be kept in check by laws that impose civic virtues on them. On the contrary, in the following chapters I argue that for Machiavelli the corruption of political life is a result of the project of establishing the priority, and securing the integrity, of political form through an authoritarian understanding of the rule of law and order. This project closes the public space of contestation of command, the space of conflict between the desire not to be dominated and the desire to command, and so generates laws and orders that are not founded on the power of the people but rather on the ambition of the ruling parts of the political body, whatever these may be.

At this point I can analyse the "free" origin of political form, which corresponds, in Machiavelli's ideal-typical reconstruction in the *Discourses on Livy* to the historical constitution of the Roman republic. The thesis I attribute to Machiavelli is that a republic remains in existence only while its political life is animated by the people's desire not to be dominated, by the capacity of its citizens to contest and renew any legal and political order, and by the consciousness that corruption lies with the oppressive illusion of the stability of political form.

---

[21] Skinner, *Liberty Before Liberalism*, 25-26. By way of contrast, Arendt defines political freedom in terms of the concept of isonomy, "as a form of political organization in which the citizens *lived together under conditions of no-rule, without a division between rulers and ruled.... This notion of no-rule was expressed by the word isonomy, whose outstanding characteristic among the forms of government... was that the notion of rule (the 'archy' from archein in monarchy and oligarchy, or the 'cracy' from kratein in democracy) was entirely absent from it.*" (Arendt, *On Revolution*, 30; emphasis mine). See my discussion of isonomy, and in general of the problem of "equality before the law," in part 3, chs.3 and 4.

[22] The distinction between freedom as no-rule and freedom as autonomy is worked out in the conclusion, where I offer a comparison between the Machiavellian and Kantian understanding of political freedom.

THE ANTI-FOUNDATIONAL BEGINNING OF THE REPUBLIC

In radical contrast to the historical origin of the system of authority, represented ideal-typically by Sparta and Venice, the historical process through which the Roman republic constitutes itself as a mixed body is a revolutionary one that breaks with the prudential logic of the founder-legislator. As Machiavelli says, Rome receives its laws and orders not "by one alone and at a stroke... [but] *by chance and at many different times, and according to accidents.*"[23] The "chance" and the "accidents" refer, respectively, to the two distinct events that mark the emergence of free political life in Rome. The first event is the expulsion of the kings by Brutus. The second event occurred when "the people rose up against" the Roman nobility by withdrawing to the Aventine hill in what amounts to the first recorded act of civil disobedience. "So as not to lose the whole," the nobility "was constrained to yield the people its part," and in this way "a place to the popular government" was given in the constitution through the institution of the "tribunes of the plebs."[24] In Machiavelli's reconstruction of the republic's historical origin these two events symbolize the salient features of republican freedom. Throughout its history, and as a condition for its survival, the Roman republic would return to the symbolic content of these originary events.

Machiavelli's apparently simple assertion that in Rome the mixed constitution was a result of chance and accidents entails a series of important considerations. First, it entails that the constitution given to Rome by its founders, Romulus and Numa, the constitution based on the prudent union of the authority of the Senate with the command of the king, counts as a mixture of forms of rule but not yet as a mixed body (*corpo misto*), which for Machiavelli is the only type of political body that is truly characterized by a free life (*vivere libero*) and that deserves the name of republic. The mixture of forms of government is a necessary but not sufficient condition for a free life:

Romulus and all the other kings made many and good laws that conform still to a free life [*conformi ancora al vivere libero*]; but because their end was to found a kingdom and not a republic, when that city was left free [*rimase libera*], many things that were necessary to order in favor of freedom [*ordinare in favore della libertà*] were lacking, not having been ordered by those kings.[25]

The clear separation that Machiavelli makes between the kingdom instituted by Romulus and the republic that began when Rome "was left free" of kings indicates that a free political life is unattainable by the system of authority alone. This claim is supported by the fact that Machiavelli calls Brutus, and not Romulus or Numa, the "father of freedom" in Rome.[26] Furthermore, in *Discourses on Livy*, I,2 Machiavelli is still echoing the Polybian understanding of political mixture and speaks of the "republic" as being "mixed" (*mista*) because it integrates three forms of rule (*governo*) corresponding to the "principality," the "aristocracy," and the "people." But he never identifies explicitly the *vivere libero* with the establish-

---

[23] Machiavelli, *Discourses on Livy,* I,2. Emphasis mine.
[24] Ibid.
[25] Machiavelli, *Discourses on Livy*, I,2.
[26] Ibid., III,1.

ment of the mixed political form.[27] Rather, this mixed form simply allows "the state of that republic to be more stabilized [*più stabilito lo stato di quella republica*]."[28] And, as Machiavelli shows immediately after with his praise of political conflict, a "stable state" is by no means identical to a "free life."

The discontinuity between monarchical and republican Rome is marked by the irruption of "chance," which refers to the event of Brutus's expulsion of the kings. Chance here stands for the kind of revolutionary event that the prudence of the founder-legislator (be it Romulus or Lycurgus) cannot possibly foresee since its goal is to found a stable political order, impervious to radical change. In this sense, the event designated by Brutus amounts to an anti-foundational beginning of political life. The action of Brutus does not even count as the origin of a political form because its goal is not the establishment of a particular institution but simply the expulsion of a previous political form, hence Machiavelli's locution that Rome "was left free" by this event. One can say that the event of Brutus is both anti- and non-foundational: it sets itself in opposition to the logic of the founder-legislator, and it marks the absence of the principle of rule (*archein*, in its double sense of foundation and rule) with the expulsion of the political form of monarchy. To point out the lack of foundational force in the event of Brutus Machiavelli refers to its character of "chance," for chance is what has no ground.[29]

That the event of Brutus is an event of "chance" entails that nothing, in the preceding order of things, called for it or caused it. Machiavelli in this way emphasizes the discontinuity between the period of Roman history in which political life turns on the system of authority set up by the nobles through the Senate, and the republican period initiated by the institution of the Tribunate, in which political life "remained mixed, and made a perfect republic, to which perfection it came through the disunion of the plebs and the Senate."[30] There is a double irony in calling "perfect" the republic divided by political conflict.[31] The

---

[27] These careful and necessary distinctions between mixed political form and free political life, between the classical understanding of the mixed constitution and Machiavelli's radical innovation of this idea are often disregarded by interpreters. Witness the following passage: "Machiavelli's republicanism is a commitment to a well-ordered popular government. By a well-ordered, or moderated, republic he means, in accordance with Cicero's concept of orderliness or moderation, a republic in which each component of the city has its proper place. As examples he cites Sparta... and Rome." (Viroli, *Machiavelli*, 125). Viroli here joins political models and ideals (e.g., the "moderation" of aristocratic Sparta to the unruliness of conflict in republican Rome) that Machiavelli keeps distinct and whose opposition defines the sense of his discourse.

[28] Ibid, I,2. The joining of the locutions *corpo misto* and *vivere libero* occurs later, in *Discourses on Livy*, III,1.

[29] This point is missed by Pitkin's otherwise rich discussion of the figure of Brutus. Pitkin sees Brutus as the "ultimate" founder figure and brings together what Machiavelli carefully tries to separate, namely, "the two Roman Founders, Romulus and Brutus." (Pitkin, *Fortune is a Woman*, 58-59).

[30] Machiavelli, *Discourses on Livy*, I,2.

[31] The ironical employment of the term "perfection" in this text is equally missed by Mansfield and Tarcov who claim that "in giving preference to Rome's accidental perfection because it is more flexible than that of Sparta's one-time classical legislator Lycurgus, he shows again that tyranny - the rule of *uno solo* - works well, or best, in the context of a republic" (Machiavelli, *Discourses on Livy*, ed. Harvey C. Mansfield and Nathan Tarcov, Introduction, xxviii); and by Viroli who responds to the above claim by saying that "it is obvious that, for Machiavelli, Rome was not perfect because it allowed room for tyranny, but became perfect only when it gave itself a constitution in which 'all three kinds of government there had a part'." (Viroli, *Machiavelli*, 214). In fact, Machiavelli's text

irony is directed, first of all, against the classical belief that perfection in politics entails, in principle, the integrity of the political form maintained through concord. Which is to say that for Machiavelli the perfect or wholesome state, in the classical sense, is not a republic, and, conversely, the "perfect" republic, in Machiavelli's sense, requires the non-integrity of the state or political form. Republican political life exceeds the strictures imposed by the integrity of political form, it transcends the instance of form.

Machiavelli's locution is also ironical when compared to his initial statement that it takes a founder-legislator to set political life on the "straight road" to the "perfect republic" by giving it "laws ordered so that it can live securely under them without needing to correct them."[32] Rome did not become the "perfect" republic through a linear historical process: on the contrary, it is only by effecting repeated breaks and discontinuities with the linearity imposed by the system of authority that the republic emerges. By "linearity" I refer to the authoritarian ideal of an origin (*arche*) of political life coinciding with a political form that rules over an indefinite stretch of time, taking account, always already, of any possible circumstance, in such a way as to exclude the emergence of a radical novelty that would disrupt the continuity of rule as much as the rule of continuity.

If the historical construction of political form in Machiavelli's discourse is not often recognized, or done justice to, perhaps this is because the existence and character of the discontinuity between the religious origin of the Roman state as a system of authority and the free origin of the Roman republic usually passes unperceived. Even a careful reader like Sasso overlooks the ironical use of the locutions "perfect republic" and "straight road" in Machiavelli's text in order to claim that the process of giving Rome a mixed constitution

terminates under the sign of completeness and coherence. Under the sign of completeness because what was added later [i.e., after Romulus's initial act of foundation], in time, made "perfect" a framework which up to that point had been "defective": under the sign of coherence, because the addition was actually made possible by what had been ordered and realized by the laws that were already in existence.[33]

For Sasso the historical construction of the republic is a "complementary" process that builds on the foundations established by Romulus and Numa. As I show below, Machiavelli understands the republic more as the result of a "supplementary" process that calls into question these foundations as a condition of possibility for the emergence of republican freedom.[34]

---

indicates quite clearly the political conflict between the nobility and the people as the source of Roman "perfection": the meaning of both the mixed participation to government and the presence of tyrannical moments in the free political life of republican Rome can be determined only in reference to this conflict, not vice versa.

[32] Machiavelli, *Discourses on Livy*, I,2. Incidentally, in *Discourses on Livy*, I,9 Machiavelli takes this characterization of Spartan constitutional history back and points out the various attempts to "renew" the Lycurgan order made by the Spartan kings Agis and then Cleomenes.

[33] Sasso, "Machiavelli e Romolo," in *Machiavelli e gli antichi* I: 127.

[34] On the Derridean distinction between "complement" and "supplement" see my discussion of historical repetition in part 3, ch.2.

Just as Machiavelli remarks in the first preface to the *Discourses on Livy*, without the historical sense that his text intends to foster in the readers it is all too easy to be captivated by the ideological linearity and continuity of Roman history as this is presented by classical historiography. For Machiavelli, this imaginary history reflects the wishes and interests of the "nobility" and the "Senate," of those who want to rule in history rather than historicize, and render contingent, the process of ruling.[35] The discontinuity effected first by Brutus and then by the institution of the Tribunate with respect to the system of authority, i.e., to the "uninterrupted continuity" of augmentation of the foundation through the administration of political life by the "unbroken line of successors" provided by the Senate and the nobility,[36] means that the emergence of the republic has a revolutionary origin. Machiavelli reads Roman historians as if to rub their history "against the grain" in order to show that political freedom emerges and survives only to the extent that it is possible to break with what Arendt calls the "coincidence of authority, tradition, and religion, all three simultaneously springing from the act of foundation"[37] that constitutes a foundational understanding of politics, that is, an understanding of politics geared toward the establishment of a stable and integral system of legal domination. If it is the case that "by virtue of *auctoritas*, permanence and change were tied together, whereby, for better and worse, throughout Roman history, change could only mean increase and enlargement of the old,"[38] then Machiavelli's reconstruction of Roman history brings out, as a counterpoint, an anti-foundational vision of political life in which the primacy of political freedom over legitimate domination is internally related to a conception of history that privileges an analysis of discontinuities and ruptures.

THE REPUBLICAN SUPPLEMENT: THE PLACE OF DISCORD

According to Machiavelli's account, the expulsion of the kings by Brutus replaces prudence by chance as the "principle" guiding the historical constitution of political order.[39] This replacement needs to be analyzed with care. To begin with, it is not exact to say that chance is the new principle guiding the determination of who is to rule the city. Chance cannot replace prudence in a literal sense because it cannot serve as principle. The expression of a replacement of prudence by chance therefore signals a lack of principle. By saying that in republican political life chance lies at the origin of order, Machiavelli means that after Brutus there is no longer one principle that overlooks and guides the historical becoming of the republic: the "place of the monarch," occupied first by violence, and then by law, has been dis-placed in order to make room for another "place" which remains, after Brutus, unoccupied. Since, in the system of authority the law occupies the

---

[35] I discuss Machiavelli's critique of Roman historiography in more detail in part 2, ch.4.
[36] Arendt, *On Revolution*, 201.
[37] Ibid.
[38] Ibid.
[39] Machiavelli points out that Brutus had to "play crazy" in order to get rid of the tyrant probably to bring attention to just this substitution of chance for prudence as criterion for constitution of order, which could be seen as a sort of "madness." (Machiavelli, *Discourses on Livy*, III,2).

"place of the monarch" before the advent of Brutus, the action of Brutus directly calls into question the idea that the rule of laws is the sole principle of political life. The irruption of chance as a political factor thus expresses a new historical situation in which the law is no longer sovereign or mon-archical, in which it no longer has sole control over the practice of rule and the exercise of domination. In a word, after Brutus the authority of the law is not everything; if it were, there would be no place for chance.

In order to understand the significance of the empty place that the action of Brutus brings to the constitutional arrangement of political life, one needs to return to the basic shortcoming of the system of authority and its principle of *nomos basileus*. The sovereign status given to law in this system entails that the law cannot possibly command itself not to command; the law cannot serve as the ground for an interruption of its command. By taking the "place of the monarch," the law regulates force and makes domination legitimate, but it does not and cannot call into question either force or domination. The law cannot recognize a situation in which there is no domination, and thus a situation to which it cannot apply. And the reverse is equally true: not only does the "force of the law" presuppose the existence of force that it can regulate, but only where force dominates the situation can the law apply to it. The law, therefore, is always "forcing the situation," so to speak, by reflecting the situation of the dominant forces. The sovereignty of the law literally leaves no place for the practice of political freedom as no-rule. It is, as a matter of principle, incapable of accepting a situation in which there would be no domination because that situation would fall outside of its purview, would prove an exception to the law. The expulsion of the kings is symbolic of the expulsion of this sovereignty of the law. The republican concept of freedom emerges when obligation to the law, to the instance of order and command, is no longer the pre-eminent (mon-archic) or authoritative factor in political life.

Since the value of concord depends on the pre-eminence of the rule of laws in political life, by dis-placing the sovereignty of the law Brutus's action adds to political life a place for discord, without which this political life cannot be said to be free or powerful.

I say that to me it appears that those who damn the tumults between the nobles and the plebs blame those things that were the first cause of keeping Rome free.... *They do not consider that in every republic are two diverse humors, that of the people and that of the great, and that all the laws that are made in favor of freedom arise from their disunion, as can easily be seen to have occurred in Rome....* Nor can one in any mode, with reason, call a republic disordered where there are so many examples of virtue; for good examples arise from good education, good education from good laws, and good laws from those tumults that many inconsiderately damn. For whoever examines their end well will find that they have engendered not any exile or violence unfavorable to the common good but laws and orders in benefit of public freedom.[40]

---

[40] Ibid., I,4. Emphasis mine.

In this justly famous passage, Machiavelli rejects once and for all the ideal of the state as ethical substance, whose highest value is political concord.[41] Machiavelli presents for the first time in the history of political thought "the concept of the productivity of social conflict for political development."[42] Yet the thesis that free political life originates from political discord, that "all the laws that are made in favor of freedom arise from their ["the people" and "the great"] disunion," is all too often interpreted as if political conflict has as its inner purpose the construction of a better political form. The finality of the law to rule over the whole field of political life remains unquestioned because it is assumed that Machiavelli only meant that such finality is better achieved by giving legal expression to the conflicts between social forces than by using the law to repress or exclude these conflicts. In short, Machiavelli would still favor the sovereignty of the law, the classical ideal of the common good, but the means through which to impose this sovereignty or arrive at an expression of this good would have changed, involving conflict rather than concord.[43]

I consider this line of interpretation of the topic of discord in Machiavelli to be misguided. It ignores completely the significance of the action of Brutus: the addition of place that accounts for political discord, which is made possible by the dis-placement of the sovereignty of the law, means, first and foremost, that political discord invests the law itself and therefore cannot be expressed or pacified or unified by the form of legal order. By positing discord as the origin of political freedom Machiavelli does not mean that in the "modern" republic, instead of the concord and unanimity about who should rule characteristic of the "ancient" state, there will be the possibility of disagreeing and competing over who should rule. Far more radically, the action of Brutus defines a political life in which the unanimity and univocity of rule itself is expelled. Traditionally the republic is defined as a political without kings. Machiavelli departs from tradition by construing the abolition of monarchy symbolized by Brutus as a rejection of

---

[41] For Lefort, Machiavelli's defense of discord "destroys the beautiful image of the state.... [He] does not allow one to think that the first order is the good one, because he makes of the Roman *ordine* the product of a history; he does not allow one to think that the law imposes this order, by the sovereign intervention of a wise man, because he roots this order in social conflict; and he suggests that the praise of *unione* entails the misrecognition of class divisions, and one destroys freedom by masking them." (Lefort, *Travail de l'oeuvre*, 475).

[42] Roberto Esposito, *La Politica e la Storia. Machiavelli e Vico* (Naples: Liguori, 1980), 59.

[43] For instance, the importance of political conflict is minimized by Viroli's claim that "the squabbles and conflicts that a Roman-like constitution is likely to produce should be considered inconveniences which are necessary to keep the city free and able, if needed, to expand." (Viroli, *From Politics to Reason of State*, 161). Here the instance of conflict is completely subsumed under the political form. By asserting that the mixed constitution produces political conflict rather than being one possible response to it, Viroli actually reverses what Machiavelli says. Furthermore, conflict is not seen as the origin of free political life, but merely as something that "keeps the city free," as something that must be added to an already existing political freedom: "In recommending the tumultous but powerful Roman republic... Machiavelli was not dismissing the republican ideal of politics [of civic humanism] as the art of establishing and preserving a free city. He was simply pointing out to his contemporaries that politics must face *the additional task of handling civic discord as a fact of life in the city*." (Ibid., emphasis mine). For Viroli, political conflict is a secondary matter for political freedom whereas the rule of laws lies at its origin. Again, Machiavelli states exactly the opposite: "all the laws that are made in favor of freedom arise from their ["the people" and "the great"] disunion." For Machiavelli, laws that are not made in favor of "public freedom" can constitute the "common good" only in an ideological sense, the sense he attributes to the ancient ideal of ethical substance.

the belief that ruling (*archy*) be the sole (*mono*) issue of politics. Political freedom henceforth depends on inscribing the antagonism between practices of rule and practices of no-rule into the legal and political form.

The discord for which Brutus prepares the way is not a social conflict between forces with homogeneous desires of domination, but a political conflict between the form of rule and the desire for freedom as no-rule which belongs with "the people that desires not to be commanded or oppressed," as Machiavelli reiterates in *The Prince*.[44] Machiavelli's republicanism focuses on how freedom as no-rule can enter into political life as an effective force. Political life transcends the limitations of political form the moment that the latter owes its origin to a discord that takes place between an instance of rule and a demand for no-rule. The security and stability of the state or political form, in this situation, cannot possibly be the final end of a political life animated by the discord between the desire for domination and the desire not to be commanded or oppressed.[45]

The desire for freedom that belongs to the people is identical to the desire for a suspension of relations of domination, that is, for the interruption of command-obey relations.

Without doubt, if one considers the end of the nobles and of the ignobles, one will see great *desire to dominate* in the former, and in the latter *only desire not to be dominated.... So when those who are popular are posted as the guard of freedom, it is reasonable that they have more care for it, and since they are not able to seize it, they do not permit others to seize it.*[46]

Machiavelli defines the desire for freedom belonging to the people in negative terms. The kind of negativity ascribed to it is determined solely by the fact that this desire takes the place left empty by Brutus, that is, the place or situation

---

[44] "Il populo [che] desidera non essere commandato né oppresso." (Machiavelli, *The Prince*, IX).

[45] The great merit of Lefort's interpretation consists in emphasising that the dissymmetry between the desires of the people and those of the nobles lies at the basis of political freedom. (Lefort, *Le Travail de l'oeuvre*, 472-477). Where I disagree with Lefort is in the belief that "the foundation of the law and of freedom is the desire of the people" (ibid., 476), since the transcendence of the desire for freedom with respect to the rule of law passes unperceived. A recent interpretation that does justice to the intuition regarding the heterogeneity of desires is found in Gérald Sfez, "Machiavel: la raison des humeurs," *Rue Descartes*, nos.12-13 (May 1995): 11-37. Following and radicalizing the intuitions of Lefort, Sfez speaks of the conflict between political desires in terms of a "logic of the heterogeneous" that stands in contrast to the "logic of common interest." (Ibid., 16). Sfez correctly argues that "to speak of a common good presupposes that there is at least one predominant desire that everyone shares: not a desire that all can satisfy, but a desire that all can desire.... The direct regime of general interest, irrespective of its formula, finds its transcription in an indirect regime which is that of the sharing between all of a same aspiration (of a same desire and a same fear). Now, Machiavelli's thought breaks with this figurability of the good." (Ibid., 20). Where I disagree with Sfez is in his belief that the conflict between desires ultimately plays into the hands of the stability of the state rather than expands the horizons of political life beyond the form of the state: "the political relation between forces, placed under the good auspices of the differend [between the desires]... finds its legitimacy and its consistency due to its capacity to limit what is without measure by relating two heterogeneous dismeasures, such that the limit, of which the law is the fundamental support, finds itself at the meeting point of the dismeasures.... It is the differend that grants consistency and mobility to the political relation, without this relation having to incorporate itself. It is what assures the stability of the State." (Ibid., 19). For another important contribution to the recent literature on political discord, see Jacques Rancière, *Dis-agreement: Politics and Philosophy* (Minneapolis: University of Minnesota Press, 1999).

[46] Machiavelli, *Discourses on Livy*, I,5. Emphasis mine.

which lies outside of the domain of legal domination. It is only because it emerges from the exteriority to the domain of rule that the desire not to be dominated refers to a concept of political freedom that negates precisely the instance of rule. The people's desire for freedom is the desire for no-rule.

By giving a place in political life to the people's desire for freedom as no-rule, Machiavelli defines the essential trait of political freedom in terms of the possibility of discord with respect to legal domination in its dimensions of facticity and validity. The desire for freedom as no-rule transcends every given social and political form that imposes a distinction between who commands and who obeys. In a literal sense, the people's desire not to be commanded or oppressed is an extra-constitutional desire that can never be integrally realized in any form of government or stabilized by any legal order of domination. This means that the place of this desire cannot be occupied by any of the constituted parts of the state: it is the place from which those who are excluded from participating in, and being-part of, the process of rule can speak and act. This place is the position of the political subject which Machiavelli designates as the not-nobles (*ignobili*), the people as the subject (*materia*) without form or formation. The place taken by the desire for freedom which is essentially discordant with the desire for domination must lie outside of the political form as such: it corresponds to that materiality of the political body prior to its being constituted into parts that are functional to the interest of the state. The place of the desire for freedom is the origin of a multiplicity or plurality that cannot be organized by the law in the specific sense that it resists being-part of the process of domination and therefore cannot be regulated by the law. But it is precisely by virtue of this resistance to the process of rule that the discord born from the desire for freedom can interrupt this rule and demand or cause the re-ordering of the state. The discord between the desire for domination and the desire not to be oppressed or commanded thus constitutes the revolutionary origin of political form that defines a republican political life.[47]

THE FREE OR REVOLUTIONARY ORIGIN OF POLITICAL FORM

The discord that results from decentering the "place of the monarch" (i.e., all instances of rule) and adding a place for the desire for no-rule withdraws from the state its capacity to generate concord and thereby strips the political form of its

---

[47] Mansfield's reading of the political role of the people in Machiavelli's discourse is vitiated by a basic mistake: the belief that the desire for no-rule is non-political. Mansfield speaks about "the division of human beings into political and nonpolitical men, princes and peoples;" and proceeds to claim that "for Machiavelli, only some few men are political, and they rule in every regime, whatever it is called. The people do not wish to rule, and when they rule, they are being managed by their leaders. They are matter without form, body without head. Since they cannot rule, the regime is always the rule of a prince or princes." (Mansfield, *Machiavelli's Virtue*, 237). As I show below, the idea that the popular desire for freedom as no-rule is "nonpolitical," turns the people into a completely passive subject on which any form of rule can be imposed, is incorrect. Furthermore, it spoils Mansfield basically correct intuition that "the modern impartial regime" depends on the people becoming "the judge of all government. They do not form a government themselves; the people do not rule." (Ibid., 115). Machiavelli's point is precisely that the people can "judge" the form of government because they stand "outside" it in virtue of their desire for no-rule which, when activated, forms the revolutionary ground of all modern regimes, as I demonstrate in chapters 5 and 6 below.

providential character, i.e., destroys the belief in the sacrality of the command of the state over political life as a whole. The political and legal order of the state is revealed to be radically contingent. The contingency of order, as Machiavelli understands it, means that the condition of possibility of political order is the re-ordering or change of orders. The possibility of instituting political form presupposes the possibility of de-instituting, of radically changing, this form. The free or political life is essentially revolutionary, that is, it entails *metabole politeion* as a necessary moment of the *politeia*. Modern politics, according to Machiavelli, turns on the belief that any political order, if it is to be constituted and legitimated, must also be open to its deconstitution and delegitimation. The only legitimate order is the one that can be made to suffer its own radical contingency.

That the contingency of political form entails the necessity of the political change of form can be understood to mean that all instances of form and order in a free political life emerge from an event-like interruption of a prior form and order, from the suspension of the command-obey relation. Every political form is always already a possible response to a previous questioning of order brought forward by the desire for freedom as no-rule. There is no a priori necessity of political form because the discord between the desire to rule and the desire for no-rule has taken away the presumptive necessity of rule. One sense of the event-like emergence of political form, one possible response given to the a priori putting into question of order, consists in giving the political form an a posteriori foundation or legitimacy by making it necessary to the realization of political freedom as no-rule. In this case, political form is said to presuppose its change because the contingency of the form is changed into its necessity. Another sense of the event-like emergence of form becomes apparent if one considers that every realization of freedom as no-rule is also its reification, that is, any given form is bound, in the course of time, to stop counting as an acceptable response to the question posed by the desire for freedom as no-rule. As a consequence, the necessity of this form can be revoked into contingency and the form itself can be overthrown. In this case, political form is said to presuppose its change because the necessity of the order is changed into its contingency.

Machiavelli advances the thesis that only a political life which is constituted by such moments of negativity, which rejects the naturalization of political form and shows its essence to be completely invested by historical becoming, can be said to manifest a "free life" (*vivere libero, vivere politico*). The political body that is "politically alive" (*viva politicamente*) in this sense alone can be properly called a republic.[48] For Machiavelli a free political life requires the survival of the

---

[48] Viroli claims that "the word '*politico*' is always joined with the familiar vocabulary of the *civitas* and never used in a different sense." (Viroli, *From Politics to Reason of State*, 154). If it is undoubtedly the case that at least since Aquinas up to and including the civic humanists, the Aristotelian term *bios politikos* (political life) is rendered by the expression "civil and political life" (*vita civile e politica*), in Machiavelli there is a distinct separation between what a "civil life" (*vivere civile*) and a "political life" (*vivere politico*) designate. The first term corresponds roughly to the requirements for a "good life" in classical political thought; whereas the second term corresponds to Machiavelli's new requirements for a "free life." As the glossary provided by the Mansfield and Tarcov edition of the *Discourses on Livy* helps to show, the terms *vivere civile* and *vivere politico* or *vivere libero* never coincide, with two exceptions (*Discourses on Livy*, I,55 and I,9, respectively). I

discord between political freedom and rule of laws. Political freedom can never be completely realized by any factical political and legal order. As Lefort says: "disorder… is the operation of the desire for freedom that keeps open the question of the unity of the state and, in unveiling it, forces those who direct it to put into play once again its destiny."[49] One can say that Machiavelli's idea of republican freedom is animated by a "savage" or "unprincipled" counter-principle that contradicts the "civil life" based on legal domination because it expresses a desire for no-rule that is unbound from the interests of the state and allows for a radical contestation of its orders.[50] The desire for freedom as no-rule is literally a counter-principle of political life because it motivates act and speech that go counter to the *princeps/principium* of domination. Only the de-centering of the sovereign principle of law and the emergence of the discordant counter-principle of freedom as desire not to be dominated, allows for the entrance of the people (the bearers of this desire) into the state, thus giving way to a republican "free life" (*vivere libero*). But, at the same time, the participation of the people in the state 'participates' the integrity of the political form, lacerates the unity of the state, and dissolves its ethical substance. The state or political form is thereby exposed to the effective history that emerges from the collision of two antithetical dynamics, constitutive of modern political life, which I discuss in what follows.

---

develop the theoretical grounds for the distinction between "civil" and "political" life in part 3, ch. 3 and 4.

[49] Lefort, *Travail de l'oeuvre*, 477.

[50] I employ the term "savage" in order to evoke the senses that Montaigne, Spinoza, and Rousseau were to give to this concept, and which were given new life in the works of Claude Lévi-Strauss, Pierre Clastres, Claude Lefort, Gilles Deleuze and Félix Guattari. For a stimulating discussion of the "savage" character of free political life, with which my work shares a great affinity, see Miguel Abensour, "Démocratie sauvage et principe d'anarchie," *Cahiers de philosophie* (Lille) 18, *Les choses politiques* (Winter 1994-5): 125-149. I discuss the meaning of this savage and political counter-principle in Machiavelli's discourse throughout part 3.

CHAPTER 5

THE TOPOLOGY OF POLITICAL FREEDOM

POLITICAL TOPOLOGY, OR THE SITUATED CHARACTER OF THE LAW

By adding the place of discord to the topology of the state found in classical political thought, Machiavelli maps out a new conception of the political body. This new concept of the political body is illustrated by the "mixed body" (*corpo misto*) of the Roman republic that emerges with the entrance of the people into the constitution through the institution of the Tribunate. Just like political life, after the event of Brutus, cannot be reduced to the activity of establishing and securing rule but must include the practice of no-rule, so too the political body that supports this expanded conception of political life cannot be reduced, after the Tribunate, to the organic or purposive totality of the state. In Machiavelli the mixed political body is irreducible to the form of the state: the republic is not a kind of state; it exceeds the limits imposed by political form as such. Machiavelli's analysis of the process through which the people's desire for no-rule becomes instituted demonstrates the irreducible character of the political body with respect to the form of the state because it shows that the state can only occupy the totality of the political space, and thus also the place of discord, if it can suspend its very force as state. In order to impose its form over the political body, the state must internalize into its form the negation of itself as form. In other words, the people enter political life through special institutions, like that of the Tribunate, that contrast the proper activity of the state, i.e., the administration of rule. These institutions of political contrast, or counter-institutions, carve up the state so as to clear a space in which to voice and act out the demands of no-rule.

In this chapter the transcendence of political freedom with respect to the form of the state is examined topologically. So far I have shown that one of the central novelties advanced by Machiavelli's *Discourses on Livy* consists in decentering the instance of political form in political life. By way of contrast, in classical political thought the topology of politics is dependent on the form: the place of politics coincides with that of the form.[1] For example, in Aristotle the achievement of the polity or constitutional government (*politeia*), by which he means that best form of government by the many whose perversion is democracy, "may be described generally as a fusion of oligarchy and democracy."[2] This fusion or "union of these two modes is a common or middle term between them." As it turns out, for Aristotle there is a political class that corresponds to this mean, which he calls the "middle class" (*mesois*):

---

[1] See Wolin, "Norm and Form," passim.
[2] Aristotle *Politics* 1293b35.

Those who have too much goods of fortune, strength, wealth, friends and the like are neither willing nor able to submit to authority.... On the other hand, the very poor, who are in the opposite extreme, are too degraded. So that the one class cannot obey, and can rule only despotically; the other knows not how to command and must be ruled like slaves. Thus arises a city, not of freemen, but of masters and slaves, the one despising, the other envying; and nothing can be more fatal to friendship and good fellowship in states than this.... A city ought to be composed, as far as possible, of equals and similars; and these are generally the middle classes. Wherefore the city which is composed of middle-class citizens is necessarily best constituted in respect of the elements of which we say the fabric of the state naturally consists.... Thus it is manifest that the best political community is formed by citizens of the middle class, and that those states are likely to be well-administered in which the middle class is large, and stronger if possible than both the other classes... for the addition of the middle class turns the scale, and prevents either of the extremes from being dominant.[3]

For Aristotle the addition of a place which stands in the "middle" between the two extreme classes of the wealthy and the poor is the condition of possibility of imposing a stable form to the political life, such that it does not degenerate into the pre-political relation of domination between masters and slaves, but rather permits for the shared exercise of rule characteristic of a political life in which the rule of laws is "supreme over all."[4] The topology of the political body follows the requirements of the state.

For Machiavelli, instead, the institution of the Tribunate represents the possibility of a "middle" that, far from securing the supremacy of the rule of laws, decenters the instance of such a rule. In this way, Machiavelli inaugurates what I take to be a fundamental motif of modern political thought: free political life is possible only on condition that the normative domain as such is politically situated. The integrity of the state no longer emerges out of the just distribution of functions; the law is no longer what assigns to each political actor its own or proper place, as in the classical arguments in favor of a rule of laws over a rule of men. On the contrary, the law and the state are both "put in their place," in the sense that they emerge from a situation of conflict (between the demands for rule and those for no-rule) that neither the state nor the law can control and predetermine. A free political life entails the situatedness of the question of justice, and thereby the non-integrity of the state as instance of legitimate rule.

The concept of a topology of politics, or, what is the same, of the situation of politics, can be explained in two contiguous registers: through the distinction between matter and form, and through the distinction between event and form. Indeed, by speaking of the topology or situation of politics my hope is to direct attention to what can be called the materiality of events. In this chapter, I concentrate on the distinction between matter and form by showing that Machiavelli's groundbreaking attempt to situate the normative domain in political life is articulated through a massive reversal of the classical priority assigned to form over matter in politico-philosophical discourse. In the next chapter, I discuss the other facet of Machiavelli's political topology, namely, his articulation of the priority of the event over the form in political life.[5]

---

[3] Ibid., 1295b15-1296b39.
[4] Ibid., 1292a33.
[5] The discussion of the relation between matter and event, situation and history in Machiavelli is pursued in parts 2 and 3.

THE GUARD OF FREEDOM, OR WHAT IS BEYOND THE STATE IN THE STATE

Machiavelli's interpretation of the Roman republic as a mixed political body highlights the role of what I call counter-institutions. A mixed political body obtains in Rome only with the entrance of the people into the constitution by way of the institution of the tribunes of the people, which begins the history of political discord in the city. Most interpreters share the assumption that political discord is functional to the unification or integration of the state. In other words, they follow the tradition of classical political thought in reading the creation of the Tribunate as an instance of the ideal of mixed government.[6] Sasso offers a paradigmatic formulation of this assumption: discord is the "premise and the first principle of reality - the permanent and conflictual given (permanent in its conflictuality) on which the legislators and the men of state have to work on, not in order to extinguish it, but to order its free, vital power into a rational form."[7] For Sasso, Machiavelli's analysis of the Tribunate exemplifies the way in which social conflict gets expressed by the political form such that there obtains "the participation of the basic forces of the 'city' to its government."[8] I argue that a mixed political body cannot be reduced to a "mixed form of government" because the mixture does not refer to the purported capacity of the constitution of the state to give political expression to the desire to rule of the different parts of the political body as a way in which the state can achieve its unity. The state cannot count as such an expressive unity because what is mixed in the political body are not homogeneous political desires that happen to be in conflict about who should rule, but two heterogeneous political desires (the desire to dominate and the desire not to be dominated) that cannot be subsumed under a common term. The mixed body politic of a republic is an inherently unstable mixture that cannot assume the definite and fixed form of the state, even if the latter exhibits a mixed constitution.

---

[6] On this ideal, see James M. Blythe, *Ideal Government and the Mixed Constitution in the Middle Ages* (Princeton: Princeton University Press, 1992).

[7] Sasso, *Niccolò Machiavelli*, 503.

[8] Ibid., 510. Sasso does not think that political discord places into question the integrity of the state, or that Machiavelli displaces the state from its centrality in political life. On the contrary, he claims that for Machiavelli what counts is that "the state be assured of the harmonious functioning of its constitutive organs; that its existence be protected from the attacks of particularistic violence; that the uneliminable conflictuality which, in every state, follows from the 'natural' presence of opposed 'humors'... be put in the service of reason and, in the last instance, of the expansive force of conquest.... Machiavelli looks to the rights of citizens... and to the submission of the sovereign to the empire of the law from the perspective of the strength and functioning of the state." (Ibid., 511). Other examples of this functionalist understanding of political discord which subsumes it under the logic of the integrity of the state can be found in Esposito, for whom Machiavelli's point is that "union, true union, not only does not exclude separation, division, and conflict, but is not realizable outside of it." (Esposito, *Politica e la Storia,* 59). Esposito argues that "political unification realizes itself and flows along the channels of social division, originating in a form of reproduction that separates economy and politics and functionalizes the first to the dominion of the second.... [Politics for Machiavelli] is nothing other than the organization of social war.... The social division is precisely the content of the bourgeois political form." (Ibid., 64-67). See also Münckler, *Machiavelli*, chs. 6 and 9, whose titles ("Machiavelli's highest political goal: the foundation and stabilization of the state" and "the mixed constitution as guarantee of political stability," respectively) make clear the position of the author.

Two corollaries follow from the non-identity of the state with the mixed political body. First, the mixture that constitutes the political body of the republic can never be the result of the prudent political art of the founder-legislator that imposes a political form onto the passive material of the people. Second, the political body of the republic is not an organic totality, composed of parts which are always already functional to the life of the state, because the desire for freedom as no-rule is precisely what resists any functional reduction in the interest of the totality of the state. These two characteristics of the mixed political body are condensed in the striking metaphor found in Machiavelli's text: by expelling the kings from Rome Brutus cuts the "head" of the monarchical political body and leaves open a place for discord in political life; by occupying this place of discord and instituting the tribunes, the people give Rome another "heart" (Lat. *cor, cordis*) that beats, always dis-cordantly and never in unison, with the remaining heart of the Senate.[9] These two hearts are the metaphors for the two desires that are at play in the political body of a republic and that account for the non-univocity of its political life, i.e., for the fact that republican political life does not have the good of the state (the "common good") as its inner purpose, but rather consists in the practice of effective "public freedom" (*pubblica libertà*).

That the mixed political body is irreducible to the form of the state becomes apparent in the analysis of the institution of the Tribunate (*Discourses on Livy,* I, 4-5).

And if the tumults were the cause of the creation of the tribunes, they deserve the highest praise; for besides giving popular administration its part [*oltre al dare la parte sua all'amministrazione popolare*], they were constituted as a guard of Roman freedom [*per guardia della libertà romana*].[10]

The Tribunate allows the people to participate in the process of ruling. In and through the institution of the Tribunate, the political form seems to colonize the place of discord, that is, seems to pacify the conflict between patricians and plebeians by giving this conflict a formal expression. But Machiavelli explicitly states that the Tribunate has another role besides that of allowing the internal colonization of the space of the political body (the public space). Indeed, he claims that the state's occupation of the place of discord fails because the Tribunate as "organ" of the state does not pacify the discord between plebs and nobles, nor does it unify the disunion between the people and the Senate, which lasted "from the Tarquins to the Gracchi, which was more than three hundred years... [and] engendered not any exile or violence unfavorable to the common good but laws and orders in benefit of public freedom."[11]

Machiavelli clearly distinguishes the constitutional role of the Tribunate from its properly political, and extra-constitutional, role. Seen from the perspective of

---

[9] The reference to the "head" of the mon-archical political body is found in *Discourses on Livy,* I,2 (I cite the passage above in ch. 2); the reference to the people as "heart" of the republic is found in *Discourses on Livy,* II,30 (I comment on this text in part 2, ch.4).

[10] Ibid., I,4.

[11] Machiavelli, *Discourses on Livy,* I,4. The phrase subtly distinguishes the "common good" from "public freedom": whereas political discord is "not unfavorable" to the former, it is simply "in benefit of" the latter.

the state, the Tribunate gives "popular administration its part." The state expands its constitution by "adding the part" of the people to the administration of rule. But seen from the perspective of the people, the Tribunate "takes apart" the state's machinery of legal rule in order to safeguard political freedom as no-rule. It is in this latter position that the Tribunate assumes a truly political role, one that maintains the political life a free life.[12] And this political role coincides with the part-icipation, with the laceration, of the integrity of the state. Machiavelli defines this other role of the Tribunate by saying that it was capable of "being ever after the intermediaries [*mezzi*] between the plebs and the Senate and prevent the insolence of the nobles."[13] The Tribunate cuts the state "down the middle" (Ital. *nel mezzo*), turns the state against itself, as the only way in which to defend the people's desire for freedom as no-rule.

In its political and extra-constitutional role the Tribunate does not represent at all the interests of the people considered as an integral part of the political body, as the homogeneous counter-point to the Senate and the nobles. Machiavelli does not deny that, as a constituted part of the political body, the people share a certain homogeneity with the nobles: the latter are characterized by the humor which "desires to maintain honor already acquired," while the people "desires to acquire what it does not have."[14] But the Tribunate serves the interest of "those who are popular [*i popolari*]," those who are distinguished by the desire for freedom as no-rule, those who are not yet integrated into the state. The operative difference is between the people considered as political subjects who "since they are not able to seize" freedom, also "do not permit others to seize it," and the people considered as a political subject "which desires to acquire what it does not have" and so is in competition with those who "desire to maintain the honor already acquired."[15] In fact, the desire not to be dominated does not belong to any part of the political body as such, but to the materiality of the body considered prior to its formation and organization into the parts that will be totalized by the constitution of the state. Only in giving voice to the unarticulated desire for freedom as no-rule that belongs to the political body *qua* body does the Tribunate serve as "guard of freedom [*guardia della libertà*]," while by its strangely "inoperative" functioning it reflects the absence of organization of the political body precisely by interrupting the purposive functioning of the totality of the state.

The concept of a "guard of freedom" represents an important innovation in political language. It cannot be found in the Greek and Roman political vocabulary, nor in that of medieval civic humanism.[16] The main feature of the counter-

---

[12] "For those who have prudently constituted a republic, among the most necessary things ordered by them has been to constitute a guard for freedom, and according as this is well placed, that free life [*vivere libero*] lasts more or less." (Ibid., I,5).

[13] Ibid., I,3.

[14] Machiavelli, *Discourses on Livy,* I,5. I discuss the presence of the "acquisitive" desire in the people in the next chapter, in the context of the discussion of corruption.

[15] Ibid., I,5. Sfez is one of the few commentators who clearly perceives the difference between the "desire for possession," with its logic of "interest" and "appropiation," and the "desire for freedom," with its distinct logic. (Sfez, "Machiavel: la raison des humeurs," 13-16).

[16] Perhaps one of the notable exceptions is Leonardo Bruni who, in his *Laudatio of the City of Florence,* seems to give an anticipation of Machiavelli's employment of the concept of "guard of freedom" when he speaks of the need to have "safeguards" against the very "defenders of the law,"

institutions that are intended to safeguard public freedom is that they incorporate a *sui generis* authority that is antagonistic to the authority which constitutes the "force" of the law. The guard of freedom only acts in and through its capacity to suspend the command-obey relation presupposed by any legal or political command whatsoever. The "force" of the guard of freedom consists essentially in the power to veto the claim to rule of a law or magistracy, that is, of the *imperium* of the state. The guard of freedom is the pure negativity of the constitution: one can say that it is located at the limits of constitutionality and serves to redefine these limits.[17]

As example of the negativity characteristic of the safeguard of freedom Machiavelli adduces another counter-institution: that of the "public accusation."

To those who are posted in a city as guard of its freedom one cannot give a more useful and necessary authority than that of being able to accuse citizens to the people, or to some magistrate or council, when they sin in anything against the free state.[18]

The accusation, as Machiavelli understands it, refers most properly to a political employment of free speech that preserves the desire for freedom as no-rule by "accusing" before the people any individual or group that desires to gain

---

against those who assure that "no one's power in the city will be above the law." (Leonardo Bruni, *Laudatio*, IV, in *The Humanism of Leonardo Bruni*, ed., Gordon Griffiths, James Hankins, David Thompson [Binghamton: Medieval & Renaissance Texts & Studies in conjunction with the Renaissance Society of America, 1987], 117).

[17] It is interesting to note that historians of Roman constitutional history concurr with Machiavelli's politico-philosophical interpretation of the tribunes and their relation to the people as bearers of a desire for freedom as no-rule. For instance, von Fritz points out the extra-constitutional, anti-functional and "negative" political role played by the people: "There may have been a certain balance of power between the patricians and plebeians, but *this was anything but a balance of positive functional powers, the latter remaining almost completely in the hands of the patrician Senate and the patrician magistrates. The powers of the people, on the other hand, were mostly negative,* consisting of the power of rejecting proposals for laws made by consuls in the Comitia Centuriata, the power of the tribunes to protect individual plebeians from the coercive power of the curule magistrates, and the semipositive power of making official demands for legislation and of making trouble if such demands were not met. It is not certain whether... *the tribunes of the plebs in that early period possessed the very far-reaching power of intercession which appears to have developed in the course of time from their ius auxilii, and by virtue of which the tribunes, by their simple veto, could not only forbid any individual intended action of a magistrate within Rome, but in addition could forbid generally, and in advance, any action which any magistrate might undertake in execution of a senatus consultum.*" (von Fritz, *Theory of the Mixed Constitution*, 206-7; emphasis mine.) More generally, von Fritz speaks about the "increase in the veto powers of the tribunes... [that] left the community with *an excess of negative powers the like of which can hardly be found in any other state in history*;" (ibid., 209) and concludes by saying that the "political order of the Roman Republic.... [has as] its most distinctive characteristic *the superabundance of negative powers* to prevent action which it developed in the course of the struggle of the plebeians against the patrician aristocracy." (Ibid., 219; emphasis mine). On the post-Machiavellian understanding of the institution of tribunes as "instruments of lawful resistance" and, more generally, as connected to the idea of republican revolution, see Wilfried Nippel, "Ancient and Modern Republicanism: 'Mixed Constitutions' and 'Ephors'," in Biancamaria Fontana, ed. *The Invention of the Modern Republic* (Cambridge: Cambridge University Press, 1994): 6-26.

[18] Machiavelli, *Discourses on Livy*, I,7.

possession of the public space.[19] This institution publicizes the on-going processes of domination in the private sphere, and it does so by resisting the privatization of the public space at the hands of the state. In short, the public accusation institutes the voice of the people (*vox populi*) qua those who desire not to be oppressed.[20] It is an anti-authoritarian voice because it can contra-dict or speak against the authority of the Senate, where the voice of law and order resonates.

Like the Tribunate, the institution of the accusation has a purely negative import: that of suspending command in order to open the possibility of publicly questioning the desire for domination that lies behind it. Both the Tribunate and the public accusation are institutions that occupy the place of discord opened by Brutus's expulsion of the kings. By virtue of occupying this place, they are institutions of the state which are turned against the state. Through the Tribunate and the public accusation the political form effectively internalizes its own negation. In the powerful expression of Emanuel Levinas, one can say that for Machiavelli republican counter-institutions are "beyond the state in the state [*au-delà de l'état dans l'état*]."[21] They express the fundamental discord between the voice of the rule of laws and the voice of freedom as no-rule which is constitutive of the republican political body. The discord of voices and of authorities constitutes the effective break of the republic with the unanimity or univocity (*homo-noia, con-cordia*) that characterizes the state in the system of authority.[22]

---

[19] Machiavelli's republican concept of freedom of speech corresponds neither to the modern, liberal right to free speech nor to what the Greeks called *parrhesia*, the freedom to speak frankly to those in positions of power that one also finds as the topic of many meditations in the work of Tacitus. Machiavelli speaks of this latter Roman freedom of speech while making a distinction between the "good emperors" and the "bad" ones. "For in those governed by the good he will see a secure prince in the midst of secure citizens, and the world full of peace and justice; he will see the Senate with its authority, the magistrates with their honors, the rich citizens enjoying their riches, nobility and virtue exalted; he will see all quiet and all good and, on the other side, all rancor, all license, corruption and ambition eliminated. He will see golden times when each can hold and defend the opinion he wishes." (Machiavelli, *Discourses on Livy,* I,10). One must take this praise of the "good emperors" and of the Augustean "golden age" of peace with a grain of salt: it is part of a rhetorical strategy intended to discredit Caesar's elimination of the Republic. In any case, Machiavelli is aware that the republican conception of free speech was already dead by the time of the Empire.

[20] See Machiavelli's discussion of the dictum *vox populi, vox Dei*: "Not without cause may the voice of the people be likened to that of God; for one sees a universal opinion produce marvelous effects in its forecasts, so that it appear to foresee its ill and its good by a hidden virtue." (Machiavelli, *Discourses on Livy,* I,58). This discussion occurs in the midst of the chapter entitled "The multitude is wiser and more constant than a prince."

[21] The expression comes from Emanuel Levinas, *Nouvelles lectures talmudiques* (Paris: Minuit, 1996).

[22] Another example of counter-institution is the (question of the) Agrarian law during the Roman republic. When Machiavelli gives a positive reading of the Agrarian laws (discussed below) he does so in virtue of their power to redistribute wealth at the level of classes rather than of individuals. In this sense, the conflict around the Agrarian laws can be interpreted as yet another resistance to the privatization of the public, in this case, a resistance to the unlimited institution of the right to private property.

THE ACEPHALIC POLITICAL BODY AND THE POWER OF THE PEOPLE

The opening of the state to what is excluded by the facticity of its political and legal order, namely, the people and their desire for freedom as no-rule, accounts not only for the freedom of political life, but also for the power of the political body. The question of who is a better safeguard of public freedom, the people or the nobles, permits Machiavelli to address the origin and inner logic of the political formula of the Roman Republic: *auctoritas* in the Senate, *potestas* in the people. If the element of authority (*auctoritas*) corresponds to the desire to sacralize the state, to give ethical substance to the legal order, and in general to maintain the hegemony of the law over political life as a whole, then the element of power (*potestas*) obtains only when the desire for freedom of the people is armed. But an armed desire for freedom is just what allows Rome to increase its dominion and acquire an empire.

The discussion of political freedom leads Machiavelli to posit an internal relation between freedom and conquest:

If someone wished, therefore, to order a republic anew, he would have to examine whether he wished it to expand like Rome in dominion and in power or truly to remain within narrow limits. In the first case it is necessary to order it like Rome and make a place for tumults and universal dissensions, as best one can; for without a great number of men, and well armed, a republic can never grow, or, if it grows, maintain itself.[23]

In the end, the question of whether to conquer or not to conquer is not something that can be decided theoretically, by a founder who "wished to order a republic anew": "to many things that reason does not bring you, necessity brings you."[24] In this case it is the inescapability of historical becoming that leads to the need for conquest. The phenomenon of political conquest touches directly on the problem of the relation between power and freedom, and it is no doubt for this reason that Sasso remarks that "the question of conquest... reveals itself as the center which generates the most delicate problems found in the political 'philosophy' of Machiavelli."[25]

The problem of the relation between freedom and power consists in determining which of these terms has a relative priority, granted Machiavelli's thesis that their relation is an internal or essential one. Sasso argues forcibly that power constitutes the *terminus ad quem* and freedom the *terminus a quo* of Machiavelli's discussion of republican political life:

What counts, for Machiavelli, is not that the citizens be "free," but that the state be effectively master of its political and social content - and therefore be capable of lasting. Or, if one prefers: in order for the state to master its content and thus to last, the citizens must be free.... [Machiavelli] is a theorist of the state, which must be free because freedom means power.... In the last instance the content of freedom is, for Machiavelli, power which freedom stimulates and heightens.... Just like freedom refers back to power, so does power refer back... to the "popular" and "democractic" choice. In order

---

[23] Machiavelli, *Discourses on Livy*, I,6.
[24] Ibid.
[25] Sasso, *Niccolò Machiavelli*, 527.

to be "free," the state must be strong; in order to be free and strong, the state must be "popular" and "democratic."[26]

My reading of the *Discourses on Livy* calls for the inversion of this relation between freedom and power: it is the drive to political freedom that makes the drive to conquest inevitable. There are two basic reasons for this claim. First, the free political life is possible only if the "safeguard of freedom" is put in the hands of the people, considered as the unformed material composing the political body. This material is absorbed in the process of conquest. Or, stated otherwise, there is a need for conquest because there is a need for the state to open itself to the people, thus allowing for a free political life. Conquest results from the prior requirement of the free political body that the "matter" constituted by the people remain irreducible to the "form" of the state, and this un-formed "matter" can only be provided through the conquest and assimilation of foreign peoples. Second, Machiavelli argues that the cause of conquest lies with the impotence of the political form to resist historical becoming, with the unavoidable condition in which "all things of men are in motion and cannot stay steady." But here again, what leads to the reification of the political form is the lack of political freedom as no-rule. Only the latter decenters the political form and allows for a political life that gives priority to the change of form over its stability.

The argument designed to show that the desire for freedom as no-rule lies at the basis of the people's *potestas*, and thus at the basis of the Roman drive to empire, consists of two parts. In the first, the possibility of gaining and maintaining empire is shown to require, in what is only an apparent paradox, the decentering of the state in political life. Machiavelli suggests that the drive to empire in republican political life does not follow from the system of authority and "the vitality of the spirit of foundation, by virtue of which it was possible to augment, to increase and enlarge, the foundations that had been laid down by the ancestors."[27] The augmentation that follows the logic of *potestas* is counter to the augmentation that follows the logic of *auctoritas*. The latter seeks to conserve political form through its amendments; it exhibits an inherently conservative logic. Conversely, the logic of *potestas* is based on the priority of matter over form, which accounts simultaneously for both roots of free political life: the revolutionary changes of political forms and the drive to expansion.

The priority of matter over form in a free political life explains why the republic must emerge from the repeated breaks with the system of authority and its reliance on the symbolic construct of the founder-legislator. As a pure type, the founder-legislator embodies the possibility of an absolute, unresisted imposition of the political form. But this possibility requires an "inert" matter, a people that

---

[26] Ibid., 512-517. Hulliung represents an extreme version of this reading: "Why did Machiavelli favor republics over monarchies? If the answer may be phrased in terms of liberty, it may equally well be phrased in terms of power, for his constant principle is that the greatest triumphs of power politics are the monopoly of free, republican communities.... By no means is imperialism an obscure or occasional topic in Machiavelli's writings. On the contrary, it is a central theme running throughout all his works, from beginning to end." (Hulliung, *Citizen Machiavelli*, 5-6).
[27] Arendt, *On Revolution*, 200.

is broken and enslaved, and for that reason it is a possibility that stands in an antithetical relation to republican political life.

When we look into their [the mythical founders] actions and lives, we will find that *fortune provided nothing for them but an opportunity; that gave them the matter [materia] on which they could impose whatever form [forma] they chose.* Without the opportunity the virtù of their spirit [animo] would have been in vain, and without that virtù the opportunity would have been lost. Hence *it was necessary for Moses to find the children of Israel in Egypt, enslaved and oppressed* by the Egyptians, so that they should be disposed to follow him, in order to escape from that servitude.... *Theseus could never have exercised his virtù if he had not found the Athenians dispersed.*[28]

The virtù of the founder-legislator is inversely proportional to the lack of freedom of the people. This is why the return to the "vitality of the spirit of foundation" (to use Arendt's expression) characteristic of the system of authority signifies a policy designed to deprive the people of their freedom in order to facilitate the imposition of rule, the "augmentation" of the state.

Machiavelli argues that the discord between the people and the Senate, the subsequent institution of the Tribunate, and thus the emergence of the republic, are possible because the previously "inert" matter becomes "alive," i.e., the people become a political subject. The change from an inert to a living matter is symbolically represented by the acephalic political body of the republic:

I judge that it was necessary either that the kings be extinguished in Rome or that Rome in a very short time become weak and of no value. For considering how much corruption those kings had come to, if two or three such had followed in succession, and the corruption that was in them had begun to spread through the members, as soon as the members had been corrupted it would have been impossible ever to reform it. *But since they lost the head when the trunk was sound, they could easily be brought to live free and ordered.*[29]

The people as matter becomes the new "heart" of the political body only because its "head" is cut off, only because the priority of the founder-legislator, and along with it the priority of form, in political life is negated.[30]

Interpreters tend to ascribe to Machiavelli the belief that the free political life becomes corrupt precisely because the people never really become political

---

[28] Machiavelli, *The Prince,* VI. Emphasis mine.

[29] Machiavelli, *Discourses on Livy,* I,17. Emphasis mine.

[30] Nothing could be more mistaken than the following claim: "Throughout his works the Aristotelian pairing of 'matter' with 'form' incessantly recurs, and whenever this leitmotif appears the message is the same: that the people, an undifferentiated mass of matter, are nothing without the form 'stamped' upon them by the elite, the ruling class." (Hulliung, *Citizen Machiavelli,* 44). For a deeper analysis of the form/matter dualism in Machiavelli's thought, see Wendy Brown, *Manhood and Politics* (Totowa, NJ: Rowman & Littlefield, 1988), chs. 5 and 6, where the limitations of interpreting politics "as the process of giving form to matter" in the case of Machiavelli are clearly exposed. At the same time, as will become clear in what follows, if it is true that "Western political man has regarded the body as a trap.... [and] political freedom is rooted in opposition to confinement by the body, by natural needs and desires, by the body politic," (ibid., 180) then my reading of Machiavelli places him much closer to Brown's thesis that "the body is the locus, vehicle, and origin of our freedom rather than the encumbrance to it Western political theory has always claimed the body to be." (Ibid., 196)

subjects due to their dependence on the "vitality" of the political form.[31] This kind of reading turns Machiavelli's actual thesis upside down. It is not because the people are insufficiently in-formed by the "spirit" of the founder-legislator and by the "authority" of the political form, that political life becomes corrupt, but, on the contrary, a free political life happens only because of the resistance of the people, as bearers of the desire for freedom, to the heteronomous imposition of the law and order of the state. Corruption is warded off through the repeated breaks with the attempts to impose the priority of political form on political life, that is, with the attempts to reduce political life to the process of legitimating domination and securing rule. Furthermore, as the symbol of the acephalic political body indicates, it is false to assert that Machiavelli's discourse does not recognize the political subjectivity of the people. For the *Discourses on Livy* shows that the people become political subjects and in so doing offer to the political body a completely new source of life than the one located in the mythical virtù of the founder-legislator and in the institution of civic religion. This new source is constituted by the desire for no-rule, whose political force appears through a break with the system of authority and the instituting of the republican counter-institutions.[32]

The acephalic political body is the symbolic formula for a political life that privileges matter over form. The priority of matter over form means that political life owes its dynamism to the saturation and overflow of the given political form on the part of matter. In the free political life there exists a congenital lack of control of the political form over its matter. Only this situation accounts for the two logics of augmentation that Machiavelli identifies throughout the history of the Roman republic. For the state and its system of authority, augmentation means to sustain or administer (*gerere*) the political form that is originally set in motion (*augere*) by the founder-legislators. In this moment of political life, the "empire of law" internally augments its control over the people and their desire for freedom as no-rule. The augmentation of the legal rule of the state over the people

---

[31] Sasso, for instance, ascribes corruption to the failure of religion and "civic-mindedness" to arise spontaneously from the people, or, what is the same, due to the people's failure to incarnate completely the laws that inculcate a certain civic and religious *ethos* or ethical substance. For Sasso, corruption exhibits the "character of a natural cycle, governed by an internal criterion, which is, precisely, that of the decline and extinguishing of the virtuous energy that, in the beginning, had conferred 'form' to 'matter'." (Sasso, *Niccolò Machiavelli*, 554-8). Machiavelli's discourse purportedly suffers from a "speculative limit: the incapacity... to give life to the internal 'matter' of the state, which, because it depends only on the wise hand of the legislator, was thereby destined to 'decay', to become 'corrupt'." (Ibid.) See also Esposito's more nuanced reading of the relation between form and matter in Machiavelli, which nonetheless also assigns, in the end, priority to the form over matter: "The form unifies the social division, but it does so from a place (the State) which is external in relation to the general movement of its matter. The masses determine power, but power lies outside the capacity of the people to control and condition it. Power orders the masses, even if the masses do not touch power; or, better, whereas power invests subjectively the masses, these can determine power (its strategy) only objectively. It is the same relation as the one found between the head and the multitude, between prince and people, between general and army. The second is necessary to the first, but it is the first that forms the second." (Esposito, *Politica e la Storia*, 86). For similar arguments, see also Skinner, *Machiavelli*, 56-64; and Mansfield, *Machiavelli's Virtue*, 76-77, 237-238.

[32] I discuss the true source of corruption, and the question of the different senses in which the people are said to be political subjects, in the next chapter.

as its subjects is one sense in which Machiavelli understands politics as a kind of war. The vicissitudes of this war are recounted throughout the first book of the *Discourses on Livy* where Machiavelli repeatedly unveils the ideological character of Roman concord and the subterfuges of religion as the instrument of the state that support the rule of laws.[33] This internal, juridical augmentation of "empire" is a form of war because the political form is always already overflowed by a recalcitrant matter. It follows that the possibility of organizing the political body, or ruling over its political life, presupposes the necessity of a change of political form designed to incorporate and at the same time neutralize the people's demands for freedom. In this situation, legislation of necessity becomes a strategic affair, a war of position.

In contrast, the second logic of augmentation features the people and their desire for freedom as a political agency, and it involves primarily the introjection of matter such that it overflows the given form of the state.[34] The introjection of matter into the political form requires external expansion and conquest, and lies at the basis of the logic of popular *potestas*. The republican modality of political life, in a first moment, opens the state to the outside so that un-formed matter may enter into it. In a second moment, the introjected matter re-opens the state from the inside, from a position in which the people have gained *potestas*, that is, have managed to arm their desire for freedom. The whole second book of the *Discourses on Livy* can be read as the analysis of this second understanding of politics as war. It illustrates the way in which the external war for empire is, from the start, turned inwards and employed for the war between the people and the nobles.[35]

My intention is not to offer such an analysis here, but merely to argue that the drive to empire, in the Republican stage of Roman history, is the expression of the fundamental requirement for the preservation of the free political life: that the people must arm their desire for freedom in order to attain the power (*potestas*) with which to counter the authority (*auctoritas*) of the state. There is overwhelming evidence that Machiavelli holds the belief that a free state can find its "foundation" only in the armed people.

Considering thus all these things, one sees that it was necessary for the legislators of Rome to do one of two things if they wished Rome to stay quiet... either not employ the plebs in war, as did the Venetians, or not open the way to foreigners, as did the Spartans. They did both, which gave the plebs strength and increase and infinite opportunities for tumult. But if the Roman state had come to be quieter, this inconvenience would have followed: that it would also have been weaker because it cut

---

[33] See *Discourses on Livy*, I, 12-13, 29, 32, 35, 37, 40, 46-48.

[34] Machiavelli discusses the introjection of matter by the political body in *Discourses on Livy*, II,3 where he interprets the expansionist phenomenon designated by Livy with the formula *crescit interea Roma Albae ruinis* ("Meanwhile Rome grew from the ruins of Alba"). This chapter sets the stage for the whole discussion of external warfare found in the second book of the *Discourses on Livy*.

[35] The most convincing interpretation of the second book of the *Discourses on Livy* remains that of Lefort, for whom "the truth that the phenomenon of war teaches... is the same that one sees in the examination of the internal organization of the city. The discourse on war and the discourse on politics are but one." (Lefort, *Le Travail de l'oeuvre*, 556).

off the way by which it could come to the greatness it achieved, so that if Rome wished to remove the causes of tumults, it removed too the causes of expansion.[36]

The debate between interpreters begins as soon as one has to determine what kind of justification is offered by Machiavelli on behalf of this claim.

One possible interpretation of Machiavelli's justification of conquest, which takes its point of departure from the downplaying of "the enmities that arise between the people and the Senate, taking them as an inconvenience necessary to arrive at Roman greatness,"[37] runs as follows:

> For Machiavelli conquest is a necessity dictated by the things themselves which, being unstable by nature, always in movement and therefore menacing, condemn to ruin those states which choose to live in peace within narrow borders, hoping to withdraw themselves from its law. But since it is impossible to escape this necessity, states must be organized in such a way as to respect it and be able to win against it. Therefore, states "must" conquer. But they can conquer only when all the energies contained in them are expressed in the laws and orders: the social conflicts, the opposed "humors," are to be disciplined, not suppressed. Thus, freedom is a function of conquest, which, in turn, is a function of the vital force and of the security of political existence itself. And the theory of the free republic, which excludes the empire as a political form that is antithetical and incompatible with it, contradicts itself, in this way, through a theory of imperialism which finds its culmination, and also its necessary instrument, in the empire. But if things stand like this, then here lies the fundamental limit of Machiavelli's thought: a limit that is nowhere overcome in his work.[38]

Undoubtedly, Machiavelli's thought would encounter such a "limit" if it were true that his discourse privileges conquest over freedom for the sake of the security of the state (or, better, the security and survival of political life as such, which Sasso identifies with the security of the state) understood as an ultimate value. But the "contradiction" that Sasso perceives between the theory of the "free republic" and the theory of "imperialism" dissolves if one understands that political freedom is not identical, indeed is antithetical, to the security of the state; and therefore that the opposition of a secure or stable state against a "menacing" exteriority is not fundamental.[39] Rather, the openness of the state to this exteriority is sought, through a politics of conquest, in order to provide the conditions of possibility for the instability and insecurity of the state, that is, for the political discord which calls forth, in turn, the changes of the political form that maintain political

---

[36] Machiavelli, *Discourses on Livy*, I,6. See also the long debate against mercenary armies found in *The Prince*, XII-XIII, which Machiavelli concludes by saying that "without having arms of one's own, no principality is secure.... And arms of one's own are those composed either by subjects or by citizens or by vassals [*creati tua*]."

[37] Machiavelli, *Discourses on Livy*, I,6.

[38] Sasso, "Machiavelli e i Detrattori, Antichi e Nuovi, di Roma," in *Machiavelli e gli antichi*, I: 419-420.

[39] Lefort's description of this exteriority is akin to Sasso's in that both see it as being apriori menacing: as "the brute and unsituatable division between the being of a people [*l'etre-peuple*]... and the world of the outside. This division is not the empirical one between states, each with their interests in survival and power... but the division that founds the latter, the division of the being of the political itself [*l'etre meme du politique*] for each society, whose grouping is achieved in the experience of a radical alterity, of the pure indeterminacy of the outside, and in the exposition to death." (Lefort, *Le Travail de l'oeuvre*, 551). I find such a description highly problematic because of the lack of distinction between the relations held by the political body and the political form with respect to their exterior.

freedom alive.[40] Machiavelli does not think that the survival of political life as such is the ultimate goal; only the survival of a free political life counts as such a goal, and even this goal must be understood as being ultimate only in a "finite" way, as I illustrate in the next chapter.

The openness of the political body to the exterior is not a source of danger for the body itself. The political body *qua* body is nothing but such an openness to the exterior, to matter, to events, to the transcendence of freedom carried by the people's desire. Only to the state or political form, which is always already constituted as a closure of the political body to its exterior, must the latter appear as a mortal threat. Likewise, only the assumption that the fundamental threat to the political body emerges from the inside, from the very permanence of law and order that denies the transcendence of political freedom as no-rule, accounts for the priority that Machiavelli assigns to the change of political form over the establishment of such form, to the necessity of political change over and against the defense of the permanence of one form or another, for the sake of keeping political life free.[41]

---

[40] In this sense, Lefort is right to say that "the relation that society entertains with its internal division commands the relation that it entertains with its division of the outside. Only from the first does a history emerge." (Lefort, *Travail de l'oeuvre,* 554). My reading of Machiavelli's understanding of the Roman "war machine" also bears important similarities with the discourse developed by Gilles Deleuze and Félix Guattari, following the intuitions of Pierre Clastres, in their "Treatise on Nomadology – the War Machine." The basic claim made by Deleuze and Guattari is that "the war machine is exterior to the state apparatus": "as Hobbes saw clearly that *the state was against war, so war is against the state*, and makes it impossible." (Gilles Deleuze and Félix Guattari, *A Thousand Plateaus: Capitalism and Schizophrenia* [London: University of Minnesota Press, 1987], 351 and 357).

[41] In Lefort's elegant formulation, Machiavelli employs the Roman "war machine" in order to criticize his age for not taking "the Decision which animated the Romans and gave to their enterprise the quality of a historical work.... [Machiavelli's contemporaries] hide to themselves the fact that political society exists only from its division and has power only by finding in the effects of the division the possibility to relate to the external world; they hide to themselves that the society rests entirely on itself, that its foundation is given in its history, in the movement of temporal difference that accompanies that of the social division; and that they escape before the thought that the world is one, and one only for those who sustain in it the experience of transcendence." (Lefort, *Le Travail de l'oeuvre,* 555). My reading coincides with Lefort's except for the crucial proviso (which he does not acknowledge) that the "transcendence" in question is that of political freedom as no-rule.

CHAPTER 6

THE CORRUPTION OF POLITICAL FREEDOM:
THE MODERN STATE AS CIVIL PRINCE

THE TWO METABOLISMS OF POLITICAL LIFE

The connection between the development of historical consciousness and the metaphorical transposition of concepts borrowed from biology to politics is a well-established feature of the history of historiography. Describing how "the naturally derived 'historically immanent' concept of time" is formulated prior to the rise of philosophies of history in the eighteenth century, Koselleck remarks that the "naturalistic determinants that penetrate all histories," and therefore every conception of historical change, are all connected to the metaphorics of the political body. But Koselleck does not provide specific illustrations of the way in which "historical motion is first recognizable as such" in political discourses that employ "natural, organic categories."[1] In this chapter I endeavor to give just such a specific illustration.[2] So far, my interpretation of the *Discourses on Livy* has centered on the dissolution of the classical ideal of ethical substance in the vision of modern politics put forward by Machiavelli. In what follows I show the ways in which modern political life is thoroughly traversed by historical becoming in the sense that political form emerges as the resultant of two antithetical processes of political change. Relying on Machiavelli's constant use of the term "political life" (*vivere politico*), and on the common derivation of the terms for political revolution (*metabole politeion*) and for the process constitutive of organic life-forms ("metabolism"), I shall call these "revolutionary" political processes of state-formation and state-dissolution the two "metabolisms" of modern political life.

With the dissolution of the ancient concept of the state as ethical substance, and the decentering of political form in political life, due to the entrance into politics of the popular desire for freedom as no-rule, one can begin to speak about modern political life in terms of situation rather than substance, event rather than form. This situation or event of political life is characterized by the dependence of political form on the foundation offered by the people as a potentially revolutionary political subject. It turns out that this popular foundation is responsible for historicizing, in the most thorough manner, the instance of political form: by revealing popular freedom to be an aporetic foundation, a ground that has the

---

[1] "The comparisons of constitutions with the human body, together with its functions and ailments, customary since Antiquity, naturally introduce given constants against which decline or approximation might be measured. Here we have natural constants which, for their part, make possible temporal determinations without, however, involving a purely natural chronology based on biology or astronomy." (Reinhard Koselleck, *Futures Past: On the Semantics of Historical Time* [Cambridge: MIT Press, 1985], 98).
[2] On the historicity of political form and its connection with the metaphors of the body and of life see also part 3, ch.2.

capacity to unground, Machiavelli brings about a reversal of the priority of the form over the event in the conception of politics, and prepares the way for the thesis that political life is entirely dependent on the internal relation between political freedom and history.

The aporetic foundation of political form accounts for the two antithetical and irreducible dynamics of political change that compose the situation of modern political life. The first dynamic is responsible for the life of the state in the situation of modernity. *The Prince* presents the essential elements of the state in this situation through the theoretical construct of the "new" and "civil" principality. The *Discourses on Livy*, ultimately, does not present a different picture of the modern state than the one found in *The Prince*. Rather, the *Discourses on Livy* differs from *The Prince* only because it distinguishes, in a far clearer fashion, the life of the state from political life in the situation of modernity. Modern political life has immanent and imminent possibilities that transcend the life of the modern state: the difference between the two defines Machiavelli's republicanism.[3]

The fundamental thesis advanced by *The Prince* is that the modern state is nothing other than the "civil" or "popular" principality. The state is modern, the prince is civil, if and only if it seeks its foundation or support in a people that is potentially revolutionary, precisely because it is animated by the desire for freedom as no-rule.[4] The prince needs the people for a simple reason: only a self-reliant state can withstand the onslaught of external war; and this means that the prince must have armies of its own, as opposed to mercenary ones. In other words, the prince must arm its people.

Without its own arms no principality is secure; indeed it is wholly obliged to fortune since it does not have virtue to defend itself in adversity.... And one's own arms are those which are composed of either subjects or citizens or your creatures.[5]

Machiavelli predicates modernity of any state that pursues its permanence in history by confronting the "rise and fall" of circumstances on the basis of popular

---

[3] I find myself in general agreement with Mansfield's attempt to circumvent the tradition of interpretation that seeks to determine the theoretical relation between *The Prince* and the *Discourses on Livy* on the basis of hypotheses as to their composition dates. (Mansfield, *Machiavelli's Virtue*, 57-62). Like Mansfield, I believe that "the reference to 'reasoning about republics' in *The Prince* and the references to *The Prince* in the *Discourses* might then be understood as cross references by a writer who has put 'everything he knows' into two books from the two essential points of view." For me the two essential perspectives are given by (the form of) the state and (the event of) the republic, two antagonistic expressions of one and the same modern political situation.

[4] The literature on the origins of the modern state is immense. Only slightly less voluminous is the literature on Machiavelli's conception of the state (*stato*), what it is and whether it can be considered "modern." Another work would be required to treat these questions in depth. For good overall reviews of these questions and bibliography, see Quentin Skinner, "The State," in *Political Innovation and Conceptual Change,* ed. T. Ball, J. Farr, and R. Hanson (Cambridge: Cambridge University Press, 1989), 90-131; and Harvey Mansfield, "Machiavelli's Stato and the Impersonal Modern State," in *Machiavelli's Virtue*. These two interpreters agree that the "modern" state is "impersonal" in that it has an abstract or representative character in relation to the citizens that are its subjects. According to this understanding of the state (which Skinner articulates along Weberian lines, while Mansfield does so according to Straussian ones), Machiavelli's usage of the term *stato* is deemed to be still "personal," and therefore not "modern" in a strict sense, although both authors argue that it does prepare the ground for the advent of the properly "modern" state in Hobbes.

[5] Machiavelli, *The Prince*, XIII.

support.[6] Sparta and Venice are, in this sense, exemplars of an "ancient" state. They are states that attempt to resist the flow of historical events by stabilizing their political form through the exclusion of popular freedom from political life.

In short, the modern state is "civil" because it is founded on the support of the people which it elicits by acting for the sake of its welfare: "Whence it must be noted that, in taking a state, he who occupies it must be capable of securing the people and win them over by providing for their welfare [*nel pigliare uno stato, debbe l'occupatore d'esso assicurare gli uomini e guadagnarseli con benefi-carli*]."[7] Additionally, the modern state is a "principality" because its basic tendency is to occupy the public space of political life by transforming the popular desire for freedom as no-rule into the means of the stability of its laws and orders.[8] The state as civil prince orients political life towards a "civil life" (*vivere civile*), whereas the republican moment of political life orients it towards a "free life" (*vivere libero*).[9]

In the life of the modern state, political action is oriented exclusively toward the goal of making the people serve as the subject-foundation of the political and legal order of the state:

And let nobody pretend to answer me with that trite proverb that "The man who builds on the people builds his house on mud." That may be true when a private citizen plants his foundations [*uno cittadino privato vi fa su fondamento*] amid the people and lets himself think that the people will come to his aid when he is in trouble with his enemies or the magistrates.... But if it is a prince who puts his trust in the people, one who knows how to command, who is a man of courage and does not lose his head in adversity, if he will make the necessary practical preparations and can animate the universal through his spirit and his orders [*e tenga con lo animo e ordini suoi animato lo universale*], he will never find himself betrayed by it, and his foundations [*li suoi fondamenti*] will prove to have been well laid.[10]

This dynamic is internal to the constitution: it intends to give stability to the orders of the state, which it can do only if the people function as the foundation of the state. The dynamic is described in chapters VII-IX of *The Prince*. Starting from the discussion of the new principality, where it is necessary for the prince "to have so much virtù that he quickly prepares himself to preserve what fortuna has showered on them; and the foundations that others have laid before becoming

---

[6] Further justification for this sense of "modernity" is found in the discussion of the conflict between virtù and fortuna as matrix of modern historical consciousness in part 2.

[7] Machiavelli, *The Prince*, VIII. On the "welfare" of the people as purpose of state, see Hobbes, *Leviathan*, II,30 where the end of the Sovereign is said to be "the safety of the people," *Salus populi suprema lex est*. See also Rousseau, *The Social Contract*, III,9 where the criterion for good government is the increase in citizen population; this reflects that the state is performing well its duties in view of the "protection and prosperity of its members." The difference between Hobbes's and Rousseau's definitions of welfare is that for Rousseau, following Machiavelli, "prosperity" means "not peace but freedom.... In ancient times, Greece flourished at the height of the cruellest wars; blood flowed in torrents, but the whole country was thickly populated." (Ibid.).

[8] The identity that I draw between state and civil prince should not surprise: apart from Hobbes (discussed below), also Rousseau, in *The Social Contract*, III,1 defines the state as "prince," whereas he refers to the republic as the "general will," that is, as the people who are self-constituted in and through giving themselves the form of the law.

[9] For the justification of the strong distinction between these two modalities of political life, see part 3, ch.4.

[10] Machiavelli, *The Prince*, IX.

princes, he may be able to lay afterwards,"[11] working through the exemplars of both Cesare Borgia and Agathocles in chapters VII and VIII respectively, and culminating in the discussion of the civil principality, where he demonstrates "that for a prince it is necessary to have the people as friend; otherwise he has no remedy in adversities,"[12] Machiavelli offers the groundwork of the only politics of foundation that is effectively, i.e., not ideologically, present in his discourse.[13] These texts outline the strategies for giving a foundation to a political form that emerges, always already, from a contingent origin. The task of the "new prince" is that of changing the contingency of the advent of the state in the political situation of modernity into its necessity. This task defines the metabolics of the state, what is required for the state to maintain itself alive; it is a task that makes the state into a revolutionary political actor.

The change from contingency to necessity of a political form must accomplish two results: it must give the state a foundation in the people, and at the same time it must assure that the state remains necessary for its foundation: "a wise prince will think of ways to keep his citizens of every sort and under every circumstance dependent on the state and on him; and then they will be trustworthy."[14] Since the people are animated by the desire for freedom as no-rule, the project of state-building calls for an extreme risk: it requires founding the state on a subject that is potentially revolutionary because its desire for freedom has been armed. The modern state must ground itself on what can always subvert it. The horizon of radical historicity that invests the state in the situation of modernity becomes visible through the requirement that the state must not only convert the people into its foundation, but must also "secure" itself of this very foundation. The foundation itself, paradoxically, has become a source of contingency and insecurity for the state.

In *The Prince* Machiavelli offers the strategy of "well" and "badly" used cruelty, exemplified in his famous readings of Cesare Borgia and Agathocles, to cope with this paradox of foundation:

Cruelty is well used (if it is permissible to speak well of what is evil) when it is applied all at once, *out of the necessity to secure oneself* [*per la necessità dello assicurarsi*], and afterwards not to persevere in it, but is turned to the greatest possible advantage of the subjects.... In taking a new state, the one who occupies it should review all the offenses necessary for him to commit and do them all at once, so as not to have to renew them every day, and *by not repeating them, to secure the people* [*assicurare gli uomini*].... Whoever does otherwise... is always required to keep his knife in hand; and will never *be able to found himself on his subjects* [*fondarsi sopra li sua sudditi*], *because his fresh and recurring injuries will not allow them to be secure of him* [*assicurare di lui*].[15]

---

[11] Ibid., VII.

[12] Ibid., IX.

[13] Lefort, once again, has the merit of having placed in its proper perspective Machiavelli's politics of *fondamenti* (Lefort, *Le Travail de l'oeuvre*, 335-380). An important treatment of the topic is also found in Christian Lazzeri, "Machiavel, la guerre interieure et le gouvernement du prince," forthcoming in: *Archives de Philosophie* (May 1999).

[14] Machiavelli, *The Prince*, IX.

[15] Ibid., VIII. Emphasis mine. For a brilliant reading of this and other passages in the context of Machiavelli's argument on the civil prince, see Victoria Kahn, *Machiavellian Rhetoric: From the Counter-Reformation to Milton* (Princeton: Princeton University Press, 1994), ch. 1, passim. Kahn

The modern state or civil prince is a process of interpreting the discord between rule and no-rule in view of securing rule, of making rule a matter of mutual security between those who govern (the civil prince or modern state) and those who are governed (the people). The instituting process that secures a foundation for the modern state is the process of founding security. First, the civil prince must secure itself (*la necessità dello assicurarsi*) against its potential rivals. This moment institutes the monopoly of violence of the modern state. It is symbolically represented by Cesare Borgia's decision "to depend no longer on the arms and fortune of others. And the first thing he did was to weaken the Orsini and Colonna parties in Rome" in order to "eliminate" the heads of the former and "disperse" those of the latter.[16] Second, the civil prince has to secure its subjects (*assicurare gli uomini*), i.e., the people, from the extra- and infra-legal desire for domination present in the nobles. Historically, this entails the destruction, on the part of the modern state, of feudalism (but not the elimination of the noble desire to dominate, which is re-channeled). This moment is symbolically expressed by Cesare Borgia's employment of "Messer Remirro de Orco, a cruel and ready man," who is given the mandate to disband the "impotent lords [*signori impotenti*] who had been readier to despoil their subjects than to correct them," and in so doing to "reduce it [the territory of Borgia's state] to peace and obedience to a kingly arm."[17]

The third and last moment is the decisive one: here the prince has to make the subjects secure of it (*li sua sudditi... assicurare di lui*), so that they will act as the support of the state. Perhaps the most important achievement of Machiavelli's treatise on principalities is the demonstration that this last task is impossible to achieve without deception on the part of the state. The exercise of the monopoly of violence, even when in favor of the people, cannot but give of the state a negative or "bad" image that is anything but reassuring to the people. Therefore, the modern state or civil prince is forced to enter the path of "simulation and dissimulation"[18] in order to construct for itself the appearance of "goodness" (i.e., the legitimacy of its rule) that has a chance of satisfying the subjects.

Then the duke [Cesare Borgia] judged that such excessive authority [the "kingly arm" of Messer de Orco] was not necessary, because he feared that it might become hateful; and he set up a civil court in the middle of the province, with a most excellent judge, where each city had its representative.... [And] to purge the spirits of that people and to gain them entirely to himself, he wished to show that if any cruelty had been committed, this had not come from him but from the harsh nature of his minister. And having seized this opportunity, he had him placed one morning in the piazza at Cesena

---

argues convincingly that the civil principality is articulated, in Machiavelli's discourse, through the exemplarity of both Cesare Borgia and Agathocles.

[16] Machiavelli, *The Prince*, VII.

[17] Ibid.

[18] "There are two ways of fighting, one with laws and the other with force. The first is proper to human beings, the second of animals. But as the first method does not always suffice, you sometimes have to turn to the second. Thus a prince must learn how to use well both the animal and the man.... Since a prince must learn how to use well the animal, he should pick for imitation the fox and the lion.... It is necessary in playing this part [of the fox] to conceal it well, and be a great simulator and dissimulator [*simulatore e dissimulatore*]." (Ibid., XVIII).

in two pieces, with a piece of wood and a bloody knife beside him. The ferocity of this spectacle left the people at once satisfied and stupefied.[19]

The final captivation of the people as foundation for the civil principality requires that the state become an ideological apparatus, to speak with Althusser. *The Prince* shows that the foundation of the modern state is ideological because, in the last instance, it is virtual: it depends on the purely apparent, theatrical, and representative character of the "common good," in direct contrast to the substantial, non-representative, idea of the "common good" in the ancient state.[20] Hence the symbolic importance of Borgia's institution of a civil and supreme court of justice, with all the trappings of modern political representation, at the climactic moment of founding the state.

But why should the people be content with a merely apparent "common good"? Why do the people, in Machiavelli's infamous formulation, let themselves be deceived by "spectacles" that leave them "at once satisfied and stupefied;" indeed, why do they demand such deception on the part of their rulers as a condition of their support?[21] Part of the answer is that Cesare Borgia's spectacle communicates to the people that the goal of mutual security between them and the state shall take the form of right. In the modern state, mutual security is not one right among many, but is the content of all rights; it is the meaning of right.[22] The connection between right and security in the modern state is given an illuminating formulation in Mill:

I have, throughout, treated the idea of a *right* residing in the injured person and violated by injury, not as a separate element in the composition of the idea and sentiment, but as one of the forms in which the other two elements clothe themselves. *These elements are a hurt to some assignable person or persons, on the one hand, and a demand for punishment, on the other.... These two things include all that we mean when we speak of violation of a right.* When we call anything a person's right, we mean that he has a valid claim on society to protect him in the possession of it, either by force of law or by that of education and opinion. If he has what we consider a sufficient claim on whatever account, to have something guaranteed to him by society, we say that he has a right to it.[23]

---

[19] Ibid., VII.

[20] Kahn employs the language of "theatricality" rather than that of "ideology": "the function of the first [example of cruelty well used by De Orco] is primarily destructive and repressive... the function of the second [example of cruelty well used by Borgia on De Orco] is theatrical and cathartic: this, too, pacifies the subjects but by the theatrical display of violence.... The first example reestablishes justice from the perspective of the ruler; the second stages this reestablishment from the perspective of the ruled." (Kahn, *Machiavellian Rhetoric*, 34).

[21] "Men are so simple and so obedient to present necessities that he who deceives will always find someone who will let himself be deceived." (Machiavelli, *The Prince*, XVIII).

[22] This point was clearly perceived by Marx when he writes that "security is the supreme social concept of civil society... the concept that the whole of society is there only to guarantee each of its members the conservation of his person, his rights and his property." (Karl Marx, "On the Jewish Question," in *Early Writings* [New York: Vintage Books, 1975], 230). Security is also inscribed in the very idea of the right of liberty: "Liberty is therefore the right to do and perform everything which does not harm others." (Ibid., 229).

[23] John Stuart Mill, *Utilitarianism* (Indianapolis: Hackett, 1979), 52. Emphasis mine. Mill is simply redescribing an intuition with regard to the form of right that was formulated by Kant, Rousseau and Hobbes. I refer to the discussion found in the conclusion.

It belongs to the very idea of right that society, through the state, must commit violence on whoever harms individuals by violating their persons (their socially recognized identity). Modern right is what it is in virtue of its need to (publicly) coerce those who coerce (privately), to violate those who use violence. This essential relation of right to the violation of violence is what Cesare Borgia "theatricalizes" in his own violation of De Orco's violent "kingly arm." De Orco's severed body, displayed in the public space next to a bloody sword, symbolizes the sense in which violence will be cut off from the civil body politic, a sense that is perhaps best captured by the well-known saying that "those who live by the sword perish by the sword."

What Mill's formulation hides, and what Machiavelli's text shows very clearly, is that the violence of right (the violence that right 'has a right' to exert), which is directed against a pre- and non-rightful violence, itself presupposes the employment of such a pre-rightful violence in order to legitimate and institute itself. Machiavelli's analysis of Cesare Borgia's "well-used" cruelty shows that the pre-rightful violent destruction of feudal relations on the part of the modern state's monopoly of violence (the action carried out by De Orco's "kingly arm") is the condition of possibility for violence to come under right, to be righted, for the sake of the mutual security of state and people. This trace of violence, anterior to the institution of modern right, both can and cannot be sublated in its theatre of well-used cruelty: the simulation and dissimulation of the modern state both works and does not work. The reason why it does not work is that the destruction of the feudal nobility must not entail the destruction of the "noble" desire to dominate. On the contrary, the civil prince requires the permanence of this desire to dominate since without it, the people would no longer require the state's protection against its excesses. One can say that the ideological apparatus of the state succeeds in founding the state on the people, but fails to make this foundation into something substantial, into something that can withstand each and every contingency.

The modern form of the state is not a substance in at least two senses: it is not an ethical substance because in order to become substantial political action needs the "good" to be real, not virtual. Whereas the political action of the modern state destroys its own substantiality when it becomes, as it must, a function of securing the individual rights (to security in the pursuit of "happiness") of its subjects. Furthermore, the modern political form cannot ab-solutize itself from historical becoming, from its situational origin. The ground of the modern state, i.e., the people and their desire for freedom as no-rule, is a ground that can revoke itself and become the un-ground, the abyss of the state. The necessity of the modern state can never overcome the contingency of its radically historical origin which is determined by the event-like withdrawal of its ground. As Lefort says, the aporia of the modern state in Machiavelli's *Prince* is that its "necessary search for something to fasten itself on to passes through the experience of a void that no politics can ever fill in, passes through the recognition of the impossibility of the state to reduce society [with its originary discord] to a unity."[24] Because the

---

[24] Lefort, *Travail de l'oeuvre*, 382.

foundation of the modern state is inherently aporetical and the political form in the modern political situation lacks substance, the politics of *fondamenti* that Machiavelli theorizes in *The Prince* cannot totalize political life, it cannot bridge the abyss opened up by the demand for no-rule.

At this point emerges the second dynamic of modern political life which obtains when the people no longer serve the state as its foundation, as its subject in a passive, foundational sense. The people as political subjects question the orders of the state, contest their validity in the name of the desire not to be dominated, and become the subject-actors of the extra-constitutional re-ordering or metabolism of the political form which I call the "republican event." The event consisting in the subversion of the ground of the state is characterized by the fact that political freedom is no longer a means for the consolidation of political form (for mutual security of state and subjects), as happens in the civil principality, but an end of political action. As such, this action has no proper form and exists in the absence of ground: for these reasons it is most appropiately termed an event. This emancipatory and non-foundational possibility inherent in modern political life, of which I delineate the theory in the third part, is presented by Machiavelli in the same chapter of *The Prince* where he delineates the modern concept of the state:

In every city one finds these two different humors; and it is born from this, that the people desire not to be commanded nor oppressed by the nobles, and the nobles desire to command and oppress the people; and from these two distinct appetites arise in cities one of three effects, either principality, or freedom, or license [*e da questi dua appetiti diversi nasce nelle città uno de' tre effetti, o principato o libertà o licenza*].[25]

Depending on the kind of political interpretation that is given to the discord between the desires of the political body, there results either the state as civil principality, or the republican event of freedom, or license (which Machiavelli connects to tyranny).

Political life in the modern situation is a force field whose two, antinomical poles are the form of the state and the event of the republic. The modern state is always a civil principality, which at most can have two variants: princely democracy or princely aristocracy. Any other state of affairs, be it the absence of the state and of the rule of laws found in license (*licenza*, or anarchy in the traditional sense), or the absence of political freedom as no-rule found in tyranny (*tirannia*, again understood in the traditional sense) are not considered by Machiavelli to be moments of either civil or political life.

At the start of *The Prince*, Machiavelli asserts that "all states, all dominions that ever have ruled and still rule over men were and are either republics or principalities."[26] As Lefort warns, "one must renounce the idea that the introductory chapter contains a plan, but instead admit that it furnishes just a substitute for one."[27] Like in the *Discourses on Livy*, so the initial moves of the *The Prince* turn

---

[25] Machiavelli, *The Prince,* IX.

[26] Ibid., I.

[27] Lefort, *Le Travail de l'oeuvre*, 340. This structural feature of *The Prince* is not often recognized. Among the interpreters who make the point that Machiavelli's discourse constructs through its argument a new concept of the state, and that one should not assume that by this concept Machiavelli

out to be merely a relative starting point for the dialectical unfolding of a discourse that leads to a wholly other order of things. For, the conjoined reading of the *Discourses on Livy* and *The Prince* that I have proposed so far shows, if anything, that the state is not a genus of political life, whose two species are the principality and the republic. *The Prince* begins with the assumption of the term "state" as a necessary convenience in order to construct the concept of the modern state as civil principality in and through the progression of its argument. The effective dualism of political life obtains between the moments of republic and state. As I show in the third part, only this hypothesis makes sense of the puzzling fact that after treating of the corruption of political life in *Discourses on Livy,* II, 16-18 Machiavelli reduces the essential problem of political life to that of effecting transitions from "tyranny" to "freedom" and back. If one adds to this puzzle the explicit reference to *The Prince* contained in these same chapters it becomes clear that by "tyranny" Machiavelli can only be referring to the civil principality or "stable state" (*stato stabile*) whose concepted is constructed in *The Prince*. The civil principality is not a tyranny from the point of view of the state, but it becomes such from the point of view of the republic, understood as that moment of an expanded political life in which there exists a radical opposition to the stability of the given political form. Such a moment is the event of political revolution.

CORRUPTION AS THE LIFE OF THE STATE

The discussion of corruption found in *Discourses on Livy,* I, 16-18 has been understood, not entirely without reason, as marking the end of Machiavelli's exposition of the basic political principles operative in his fundamental work.[28] Part of the reason lies in Machiavelli's claim that to preserve freedom in a corrupt republic "it is necessary to go to the extraordinary [means], such as violence and arms, and before anything else become prince of that city, able to dispose it in one's own mode."[29] This reference to the figure of the "new prince" at the theoretical center of the *Discourses on Livy* has led interpreters to see the problem of the corruption of political freedom as the joint that both separates and holds together Machiavelli "the republican citizen and author of *The Prince*," to use Baron's well-known expression.[30] While I agree that the problem of corruption

---

had in mind what his contemporaries understood by the word, Lefort is still the most penetrating. (Lefort, *Le Travail de l'oeuvre,* 326-340). But see also the important work by Sasso on the state as civil principality. (Sasso, "Principato Civile e Tirannide," in *Machiavelli e gli antichi,* 2:396-423).

[28] Sasso claims that the first eighteen chapters of the *Discourses on Livy* "complete" Machiavelli's political theory, and that the rest of the first book adds nothing essential to it. (Sasso, *Niccolò Machiavelli,* 561-562).

[29] Machiavelli, *Discourses on Livy,* I,18. This passage echoes the one found in *The Prince,* IX where Machiavelli speaks of the transition, on the part of the prince, "from a civil order to an absolute one."

[30] Sasso argues that this passage in *Discourses on Livy,* I,18 contains an explicit reference to the "new prince" delineated by Machiavelli in *The Prince*, and indeed serves as the link between the two texts. (Sasso, *Niccolò Machiavelli,* 562). Mansfield and Tarcov refer to the same text to support their claim that "for Machiavelli... a republic must be both opposed and receptive to tyranny. To preserve its liberty it must stand by its laws and its constitution; to survive, it must be willing to forego them." (Machiavelli, *Discourses on Livy,* Introduction, xxx). These two interpreters go so far as to claim that "his talk of 'corruption' is more an excuse for tyranny than an accusation against it, and it signifies

does indeed serve as such a joint between the arguments developed in the *Discourses on Livy* and *The Prince*, the interpretation that I have presented so far of Machiavelli's conception of political life encourages a new way of thinking about the connection between the problem of corruption and the theory of the state.

Although they approach Machiavelli from vastly different perspectives, interpreters like Skinner, Mansfield and Sasso share the belief that the corruption of political life stands in an antithetical relation to the secure founding of the political and legal order of the state, irrespective of whether this founding requires the fostering of "civic virtues" (Skinner) or the "tyrannical" intervention of a "new prince" (Mansfield, Sasso). In diametrical opposition to this belief, I claim that for Machiavelli the very process of founding the form of the state by giving it the support of the people is the process of corrupting political freedom. To make the people serve as the foundation of the state is equivalent to the process of giving substance or reality to the desire for freedom as no-rule, thereby denying what is most proper to this desire: its capacity to transcend the factical political and legal order and suspend its validity.

Machiavelli typically points out that the corruption of the people is due to their prince, "the sins of peoples are born from princes," and that corruption descends from the "head" to the rest of the (political) body.[31] These assertions do not mean that corruption finds its source in a tyrannical prince. Tyranny is rather the result of corruption; its possibility is disclosed once the desire for freedom as no-rule becomes "excessive" in the sense that it seeks to give form, to realize and substantialize this formless freedom. The project of giving a stable foundation to the state requires that the discord between political freedom as no-rule and political rule come to an end, that political freedom be fixated into a political form. This requirement signals the end of a free political life.

An example of the antithetical relation between the stability of the state and the freedom of political life is found in Machiavelli's interpretation of the experience of the Decemvirate in republican Rome. This experience teaches that the project "to confirm new laws in Rome through which the freedom of the state would be more stabilized" gives way to tyrannical attempts against the republic.[32] Once again, it is only the desire for no-rule of the people, expressed through political discord, that maintains political freedom: the "tumults in Rome and in the armies, which, retiring together with the rest of the Roman plebs, went off to the Sacred Mount, where they laid until the Ten [the Decemvirate] laid down the magistracy. Tribunes and consuls were created, and Rome was brought back to the form of its

---

rather a surrender to necessity than moral resistance to its apparent dictates." (Ibid., xxxii). For the technical aspects of the problem of the relation between the *Discourses on Livy* and *The Prince*, see Hans Baron, "Machiavelli the Republican Citizen and Author of *The Prince*," in *In Search of Florentine Civic Humanism*, 2:101-151. Baron's article polemizes with Sasso's thesis, which in turn expands on Federico Chabod's claim that the first eighteen chapters of the *Discourses on Livy* were written before *The Prince*, and that the latter was conceived as a solution to the problem of corruption. See Federico Chabod, *Machiavelli and the Renaissance* (Cambridge: Harvard University Press, 1958).

[31] Machiavelli, *Discourses on Livy,* III, 29; and I,17.
[32] Ibid., I,40.

ancient freedom."[33] The experience of the Decemvirate appears as the one clear example in Roman history in which the Senate tried to deny, once and for all, the discord between the desire to rule and the desire for no-rule, which is equivalent to the attempt to stabilize the rule of laws and immunize it from contestation. For Machiavelli, it is such an attempt that lies at the root of corruption and leads to tyranny.

Machiavelli's theory of corruption depends on the possibility that one and the same process receives two antithetical readings. From the perspective of the state, the process of securing for itself a foundation by securing the welfare of the people in their private sphere becomes the proper content of a "civil" political life. From the perspective of the republic, the process through which the state achieves integrity amounts to the corruption of a "free" political life. Stability of the state, mutual security of the ruler and the ruled, and welfare of the subjects are the end results of the process of corrupting political freedom.

In order to explain and defend this thesis, it is useful to begin from a general comment on the concept of corruption. Guicciardini, in his notes on the *Discourses on Livy*, makes a biting but deep criticism of Machiavelli's thesis concerning the benefits of discord for freedom: "to praise discord is like praising in a sick man his sickness for the goodness of the medicine which has been given him."[34] I believe that Guicciardini correctly identifies in Machiavelli's conception of the political body the hypochondriac judgment that such a body is constitutively a sick body. Where Guicciardini errs is in his prejudice that the sickness consists in political discord and the medicine in the laws that pacify and cure the state from its afflictions. Machiavelli's political hypochondria is of a completely different character. For him, it is the very ideal of a political body whose health is constituted by the order and harmony produced in it by the imposition of discipline and law that is most responsible for the sickness of the political body, because such an ideal forgets the "open," even "wounded," character of the body which alone makes it a living body rather than the artifact of an external political *techne*.[35] As a consequence, Machiavelli is the first to propose the strange "medicine" against corruption which consists in a momentary suspension of the validity of law and order so as to project in freedom a radical re-organization of the political form, i.e., a return to the originary openness of the political body.

The interpretation of the constitutional history of Rome shows that one and the same event brings life to the political body and allows it to fall sick. The political body is alive only when it is discordant with itself, when it makes space for the people and their desire for freedom in opposition to the desire for domination expressed by the noble elements of the body. Prior to the events that "leave free" the Roman political body in and through the "wounding" of it (by eliminating its "head," the monarchy, and cutting it down the middle in order to add another "heart," the Tribunate), the political body is not alive at all because its "matter,"

---

[33] Ibid.

[34] Francesco Guicciardini, *Considerazioni sui "Discorsi" del Machiavelli,* in *Opere,* ed. Vittorio de Caprariis (Milan: Ricciardi, 1953), 1: 4.

[35] The analogy between a healthy body and soul and the health of a political body is at least as old as Plato *Gorgias* 504c-d. Plato asserts that "order" (*taxis*) and "harmony" (*kosmos*) constitute health, and these are the results of the technical imposition of form on to matter. (Ibid., 503e).

the people, is completely inert. In Machiavelli's discourse the life of the political body coincides with its sickness, but only because this life is animated by the desire for freedom.[36]

In contrast to the life of the mixed political body, the life of the state rests on the following basic presupposition:

> it is necessary to whoever disposes a republic and orders laws in it to presuppose that all men are culprits [rei], and that they always have to use the malignity of their spirit [animo] whenever they have a free opportunity for it. When any malignity remains hidden for a time, this proceeds from a hidden cause, which is not recognized because no contrary experience has been seen. But time, which they say is the father of every truth, exposes it later.[37]

Some interpreters see in this kind of assertion evidence of Machiavelli's deep-seated anthropological pessimism.[38] To do so is to forget that only the life of the state, but not political life as such, requires the presupposition of the apriori culpability of the political "matter" to which the laws and orders are to apply. The law presupposes that individuals are bad or culpable "by nature" as a condition for positing that "the law makes them good."[39] The law, in other words, understands itself as a cure to the originary sickness of the political body qua body.

But it is just this assumption of the "goodness" of the law that allows for the veritable "malignity" to grow undiscovered in time. By indiscriminately negating what lies outside of it as "culpable," the law covers the difference between the desire for freedom and the desire for domination present in the political body, allowing the latter to fester under cover of the law, corrupting the free political life. The formula "time is the father of all truth" (veritas filia temporis) refers to

---

[36] To trace the connection between freedom and sickness (or corruption) in modern political thought would require another work. But among its central episodes one would certainly include Rousseau's *Discourse on the Origin and Foundations of Inequality among Men* where sickness is associated to the passage from the state of nature to civil society, and thus with the first occasions for "perfectibility" and "freedom" to set to work. In discussing the master-slave dialectic in the *Phenomenology of Spirit*, Hegel also argues that freedom first manifests itself (though latently) as "sickness" vis-à-vis mere "animal" life. Spirit is the sickness of the living. In the "Third Essay" of the *Genealogy of Morals* Nietzsche makes the same point, although, against Hegel, he uses it to reassert the point of view of (animal) life over spirit.

[37] Machiavelli, *Discourses on Livy,* I,3. The term employed by Machiavelli, *reo*, can mean both "bad" and "culprit." It does not have the more severe connotations of terms like "wicked" or "evil."

[38] Sfez, on the basis of this text, claims that Machiavelli's importance consists in "thinking the possibility of a common life, of the common good in a given state, under the explicit condition of the radical and irreducible character of general evil.... The realist perspective – to describe men as they are and not as they ought to be – that animates Machiavelli's thought is therefore based on something else: the metaphysical assertion of radical evil." (Sfez, "Machiavel: la raison des humeurs," 11). For one of the best presentations of the case regarding Machiavelli's anthropological pessimism, see Stelio Zeppi, "Il pessimismo antropologico nel Machiavelli del periodo anteriore ai 'Discorsi'," in *Filosofia Politica* 6, no.2 (1992): 193-242.

[39] Machiavelli, *Discourses on Livy*, I,3. The relative value of the presupposition that human beings are naturally bad is a common feature in all theories of modern natural right, from Hobbes onwards. Hegel clearly states the reason for this presupposition: "As immanent and so positive, the determinations of the immediate will are good; thus man is said to be by nature good. But, in so far as these determinations are natural and thus in general opposed to freedom and the concept of mind, and hence negative, they must be uprooted, and so man is said to be by nature evil. At this point a decision in favour of either thesis depends equally on subjective arbitrariness." (Hegel, *Philosophy of Right*, §18). On the relative nature of the distinction between good and evil in modern natural right, see Strauss, *Natural Right and History*.

the constitutive blindness on the part of the rule of laws to the fact of domination (the "hidden cause" of which Machiavelli speaks) that allows for inequalities to grow under its cover, until time brings them to light, but always too late for the same laws to reddress the balance.

The direct link between corruption and the uncontested rule of law and order becomes explicit in the discussion of corruption in *Discourses on Livy*, I, 16-18. These chapters pose the question of how it is possible to maintain political freedom once it has been acquired in the transition from tyranny. In this context, Machiavelli has in mind the transition from the inert political body of the system of authority to the living political body of the republic. This question therefore invests what I take to be the central problem of Machiavelli's discourse: the foundation of freedom in a political form. The problem embraces political life as a whole in its two dynamics: the one constitutive of the state, the other of the republic.

The text of *Discourses on Livy,* I,16 contains two assertions that get to the bottom of the problem of corruption. The first claims that in the transition from tyranny to a free political life, the "matter" of political life is always already corrupt to some extent.[40] Given that a free political life, as I showed previously, is attained through a revolutionary discontinuity in which "matter" (the discordant desires of the people and the nobles) is assigned a priority over "form" (the laws and orders of the state), it follows that the corruption of the "matter" prior to the revolutionary break can only be due to the forceful and heteronomous imposition of "form" on the part of the founder-legislator and the system of authority. The politico-philosophical priority of form over matter reveals itself once again to be the source of corruption; or, put differently, corruption is given with the absence of the desire for freedom as no-rule.

The second important claim concerns the great difficulty in instituting or founding freedom with a "matter" that is already corrupt to some degree:

For a people into which corruption has entered in everything cannot live free, not for a short time or at all, as will be discoursed of below. So our reasonings are about those peoples among whom corruption has not expanded very much and there is more of the good than the spoiled.... So, as is said above, a state that is free and that newly emerges comes to have partisan enemies and not partisan friends. If one wishes to remedy these inconveniences and the disorders that the difficulties written above might bring with them, there is no remedy more powerful, nor more valid, more secure, and more necessary, than to kill the sons of Brutus.[41]

The difficulty consists in this: freedom as no-rule cannot function as a source of political obligation because, unlike the command of the law, it has no authority behind it. It also lacks support from the parts of the political body: from the people who desire it but have not yet been integrated into the state as a recognized political force, and from the nobles who do not want it because it impedes their

---

[40] "Infinite examples read in the remeberances of ancient histories demonstrate how much difficulty there is for a people used to living under a prince to preserve its freedom afterward, if by some accident it acquires it, as Rome acquired it after the expulsion of the Tarquins.... It [the people] finds itself in these difficulties whenever the matter is corrupt." (Machiavelli, *Discourses on Livy*, I,16).
[41] Ibid.

desire to dominate. Machiavelli formulates the republican solution to the question of how political freedom is to be maintained in the disconcerting formula that "there is no remedy... [other] than to kill the sons of Brutus."[42]

But what makes *Discourses on Livy*, I,16 into one of the turning points of the whole first book is that after stating the republican solution to the problem of founding freedom the text undergoes a radical shift of register and begins to speak about the ways in which a prince, rather than a republic, can deal with the awakened desire for freedom in the people.

Although this discourse does not conform to the heading, since it speaks here of a prince and there of a republic, nonetheless, so as not to have to return to this matter, I wish to speak of it briefly. Therefore, if a prince wishes to win over a people that has been an enemy to him... I say that he should examine first what the people desires; and he will always find that it desires two things: one, to be avenged against those who are the cause that it is servile; the other, to recover its freedom. The first desire the prince can satisfy entirely, the second in part.[43]

Interpreters, if they have noticed it at all, explain this remarkable discussion of the relation between the prince and the people's desire for freedom as a shift of topics, from the founding of a republic to the founding of a civil principality. The motivation for this shift being the claim that the people happen to be corrupt and are unable to found a republic.[44] But such an explanation presupposes that a republic (as opposed to a civil principality) could be founded only if the people (the "matter") were not corrupt to begin with. I have shown that this presupposition is inadmissible. As Machiavelli repeatedly indicates, the corruption of the people is not optional. It is not a mere contingency but a constitutive fact of free political life because this life comes into existence precisely by de-centering the political form which has always already been imposed upon the people, and therefore has always already corrupted them to some degree.

The shift in the text toward the princely solution to the problem of founding freedom can only signify that the founding or preserving of political freedom is identical to the process of founding the state on the basis of the people, i.e., is identical to the process of constituting a civil principality. The inescapable corollary is that a republic, as a political form, cannot be founded at all: republican political freedom cannot be reduced to the state-form without thereby corrupting itself. Machiavelli effects a radical caesura between the project of founding freedom in a state and the emergence of a republic. Only in the third book of the *Discourses on Livy* does he return to the republican solution to the problem of the foundation of political freedom, and takes the path that in *Discourses on Livy,* I,16 is merely indicated by explaining what it means to "kill the sons of Brutus."

Only one explanation seems to account for the strange shift in argument that occurs in *Discourses on Livy,* I,16 where Machiavelli poses the problem of founding the desire for freedom as no-rule (awakened in the transition from tyranny to political life), only to proceed to discuss the problem from the

---

[42] I discuss at length this formula for the republican solution to the problem of founding political freedom in part 3, ch.1.
[43] Machiavelli, *Discourses on Livy*, I,16.
[44] This is Sasso's thesis in "Principato Civile e Tirannide," op.cit.

perspective of the prince, that is, of the state. The explanation is that the process of founding this freedom, the process of realizing or giving substance to freedom as no-rule, is identical to the project of providing a popular foundation to the state, of constituting a civil principality. Since *Discourses on Livy,* I,16 sets out to discuss the essence of corruption, one is led to conclude that the very process of stabilizing the state by transforming the people into its subject-foundation is what Machiavelli calls the corruption of political life. The process of corrupting freedom as no-rule just is the process of founding a civil principality, which in turn is the proper content that civil political life must take if it does not transcend itself into the republican event. Machiavelli's remarkable thesis is that corruption simply is the life of the state.

THE FORM OF THE STATE AS REIFIED PUBLIC SPACE

Giving the state a foundation in the people is equivalent to the process of realizing freedom as no-rule. But the desire for no-rule is a desire for the negative: strictly speaking, it cannot be fulfilled by something positive, or, what is the same, it cannot be realized or given substance. To realize such a desire for the negative effectively requires redescribing it as a negative desire for the positive, which Machiavelli thinks under the name of the appetite for possessions.[45] The analysis of the process of corruption in *Discourses on Livy*, I,16-18 shows that the state realizes the desire for freedom as no-rule by transforming it into the desire for security of possession. To effect this change in political desire defines the essence of the political action of the state on the people; it constitutes the life of the modern state.

Performing the shift from the perspective of the republic to that of the civil prince, Machiavelli writes that the prince can easily master the desire for freedom as no-rule awakened in the people by the republican event if only this desire is decomposed into two other desires:

But as to *the other popular desire, to recover freedom, since the prince cannot satisfy it,* he should examine what causes are those that make [peoples] desire to be free. *He will find that a small part of them desires to be free so as to command, but all the others, who are infinite, desire freedom so as to live secure.* For in all republics, ordered in whatever mode, never do even forty or fifty citizens reach the ranks of command; and because this is a small number, it is an easy thing to secure oneself against them, either by getting rid of them or by having them share in so many honors, according to their situations, that they have to be in good part content. *The others, to whom it is enough to live secure, are easily satisfied by making orders and laws in which the universal security is included, together with one's own power. If a prince does this, and the people see that he does not break such laws because of any accident, in a short time he wil begin to live secure and content.*[46]

This passage clearly defines the modern civil prince as that political actor who addresses the demand "not to be commanded or oppressed" and "not to be

---

[45] The strength of this appetite is emphasised by Machiavelli when he states that the prince will avoid the hatred of the subjects "as long as he abstains from the property of his citizens and from their women.... But above all by abstaining from the property of others, because men forget more easily the death of their father than the loss of their patrimony." (Machiavelli, *The Prince*, XVII).

[46] Machiavelli, *Discourses on Livy,* I,16. Emphasis mine.

dominated"[47] by interpreting freedom as no-rule into negative liberty ("desire freedom so as to live secure") and formal equality before the law ("making orders and laws in which the universal security is included, together with one's own power"). The creative misprision of freedom as no-rule into negative liberty founds the modern state: it realizes the desire for freedom as no-rule by corrupting it. The generation of formal equality and negative liberty is the way in which the civil prince captivates the people's desire for no-rule by providing them with a simulacrum of that desire. Through this simulacrum of non-domination, the prince makes the people secure of the state, so that the state may rest secure on them.

In his reading of Machiavelli's theory of corruption, Skinner assumes that the people's desire for negative liberty is a natural given. In reality, negative freedom turns out to be the effect of a political process initiated by the state against the people in order to subsume their desire for freedom as no-rule into its strategy of foundation. The princely creative mis-interpretation of the popular desire turns political freedom from an end into a means of political life in exchange for giving the unformed people the security of a function in civil society that will result in their private welfare.

The integrity of the modern state is symbolically achieved through an interpretation of political freedom as no-rule that neutralizes the discord between political freedom and political order in view of re-uniting the political body.[48] The appetite for possessions is characteristic of all the parts of the political body considered *qua* parts; its presence in the people signals their having become functional to the orders of the state. When the people become a part of the state, its members are integrated into political life as "citizens," i.e., as political actors who maintain and serve the given order of the state; and this order is itself imposed by the (civil) "prince." Emerging with Machiavelli, this state-centered re-interpretation given to the republican desire for freedom as no-rule assumes the liberal form of individual natural rights in Hobbes. As bearers of such rights (which Locke later condenses, appropiately enough, into the right to private property) the people are incorporated into the state as its stable foundation.[49]

---

[47] Machiavelli, *The Prince*, IX; and *Discourses on Livy*, I, 5; respectively.

[48] The Hobbesian construction of the state shows a marked analogy with Machiavelli's concept of the state as civil prince. In Hobbes one finds the identification of the state with the "one person" which is constituted by the integration of a multitude of individuals into a whole in and through their alienation of the kind of freedom that creates a conflict with the instance of pure order: "Since therefore the conspiring of many wills to the same end doth not suffice to preserve peace, and to make a lasting defence, it is requisite that, in those necessary matters which concern peace and self-defence, there be but one will of all men. But this cannot be done, unless every man will so subject his will to some other one, to wit, either man or council, that whatsoever his will is in those things which are necessary for common peace, it be received for the wills of all men in general, and of every one in particular." (Hobbes, *De Cive*, V,6).

[49] In Hobbes one also finds the concept of the state as "civil person" which is at the same time the instance of subjection of individuals, and thus counts as a "civil prince": "Now union thus made is called a city or civil society; and also a civil person. For when there is one will of all men, it is esteemed for one person.... Insomuch as neither any one citizen, nor all of them together (if we except him, whose will stands for the will of all), is to be accounted the city. A city therefore (that we may define it) is one person, whose will, by the compact of many men, is to be received for the will of them all." (Hobbes, *De Cive*, V,9). These passages, as well as analogous ones in *Leviathan*, in my opinion, are sufficient to warrant reconsidering the widespread belief that Machiavelli has a

The discussion of corruption in the *Discourses on Livy* combined with the construction of the civil prince in *The Prince* opens the horizon that will be occupied by all of modern political theory. The state can be founded only on the basis of the security of the people, that is, only on condition that the negativity of freedom as no-rule is neutralized and co-opted by realizing it as a system of negative liberties or rights that is both secured by, and securing for, the political and legal order of domination. The change whereby the desire for freedom as no-rule turns into the appetite for the security of possessions defines the shift from republican public freedom as negation of legal domination into liberal private freedom as negative liberty. Machiavelli's theory of political freedom features both no-rule and negative liberty, and its fecundity consists in allowing one to understand the liberal modality of modern political life as a function of the creation and sustenance of social and political systems of negative liberty (the free labor market, the positive rational-legal order, the recognition of individual natural rights) through which the modern state secures for itself a foundation. But if liberal politics undoubtedly accomplishes the goal of legitimating domination, it inevitably does so by corrupting the desire for freedom as an end, providing freedom only as a means. The final result of such corruption is what Machiavelli calls license, which spells the end of political life proper.

One may recapitulate Machiavelli's theory of political form as follows. The republic emerges in political life through the discord between the desire for freedom as no-rule and the desire for domination, in the antagonism between political freedom and political form. The state, instead, gains in reality the more this desire for freedom as no-rule is corrupted into negative liberty secured by the political form. The desire for freedom as no-rule always manifests itself negatively: its desire is that no one possess the public, or, what amounts to the same, that the public space be the space of plurality. When this desire is alienated by the people in exchange for undisputed possession (*dominium*) over the private sphere, then the civil prince or state is allowed to gain command (*imperium*) in and through its possession of the public sphere. The captivation of the "public thing" (*res publica*) by the state or civil prince has as its necessary condition of possibility the security of the "private thing" (*res*). The public becomes the possession of some one in the sense that political life is reduced to the unity of the state.[50]

The "possession" of the public space by the state or civil prince does not make the state "personal" in a subjective sense of property. Machiavelli plainly argues that the civil prince cannot do as it pleases with the public space that it has captivated, at the cost of losing the necessary support of the people. The captiva-

---

"personal" conception of the state whereas Hobbes has an "impersonal" conception of the same, and that consequently the origin of the modern state is to be found in the latter.

[50] This idea of the state as the political subject that reifies and captivates the public space may provide another explanation for the locutions common in Renaissance political language that refer to the state (*lo stato*) as the "possession" of the prince. See Nicolai Rubinstein, "Notes on the Word 'Stato' in Florence before Machiavelli," in *Florilegium historiale: Essays presented to Wallace K. Ferguson* (Toronto: Toronto University Press, 1971), 313-326; as well as the discussion of the difference between republic and "the state of someone" in Maurizio Viroli, "The Revolution in the Concept of Politics," *Political Theory* 20, no.3 (1992): 473-495.

tion of the public space by the civil prince is an essential aspect of the so-called "impersonality" of the modern state. In the process of captivation, the public thing (*res publica*) is turned into the thing of the state (*stato*). By closing the space of contestation of the process of rule, the political form achieves the integrity, unity and stability that one associates with the modern state-form. In Machiavelli the modern state emerges as the reifying subject of the public space: the realized or reified republic is always a civil principality.

Conversely, the *res publica*, the "public thing," should not be thought as something that can be realized because it is not a thing (*res*) at all, and consequently it cannot become, as such, the (public) thing of some one, i.e., it cannot assume the form of the state.[51] The "reality" of the republic consists in those political events in and through which the desire for freedom as no-rule is reactivated and the people withdraws itself as support for the given orders and laws, radically calling into question the reality of the state, of the political form. To understand corruption as the process through which the legal and political order of the state is founded and political freedom reified was necessary in order to appreciate Machiavelli's thesis that the survival of free political life, beyond the life of the state, requires radical innovations of the state-form. As Machiavelli argues in *Discourses on Livy,* III,1 it becomes needful for citizens to embark upon a "return to beginnings [*riduzione ai principii*]" that consists in a suspension of the ends of the state, an interruption of the order of legal domination, in which the necessity and purpose of any given order is reviewed and contested by drawing it back to its contingent origins. In these events, political action (virtù) emerges in a republican rather than princely guise: it takes its chance and virtualizes the reified orders of the state. These are the revolutionary events in which the republican modality of modern political life insists, in which the people can be said no longer to live in the security provided by the state, but to survive in a freedom that is sovereign with respect to the state. But what can this kind of popular sovereignty mean if it is not reducible to the state-centered sovereignty of the rule of laws? This is the fundamental question raised by the *Discourses on Livy.* And modern republicanism after Machiavelli just is the series of responses given to that question.

---

[51] In this sense, Augustine was more right than he knew in claiming that the Roman Republic was never "real": "Scipio gives a brief definition of the state, or republic, as the property of the people [*res publica est res populi*]. Now if this is a true definition then the Roman republic was never a reality, because the Roman state was never the property of the people." (Augustine *City of God* XIX, 21).

PART 2

MACHIAVELLI'S THEORY OF HISTORY:
MODES OF ENCOUNTER BETWEEN ACTION AND TIME.

The materialist doctrine that men are products of circumstances and upbringing, and that, therefore, changed men are products of other circumstances and changed upbringing, forgets that it is men who change circumstances and that it is essential to educate the educator himself.... The coincidence of the changing of circumstances and of human activity or self-changing can be conceived and rationally understood only as revolutionising practice.

Marx, Theses on Feuerbach, thesis III

Brief habits – I love brief habits and consider them an inestimable means for getting to know many things and states, down to the bottom of their sweetness and bitternesses.... Enduring habits I hate.

Nietzsche, The Gay Science, aphorism 295

MACHIAVELLI AND MODERN HISTORICAL CONSCIOUSNESS

This part begins a long argument designed to advance the thesis that Machiavelli's thought discloses the horizon of modern historical consciousness in virtue of establishing the internal relation between political freedom and history. In Machiavelli one finds the idea that history is constituted by events in which human praxis encounters its circumstances in order to change them. The freedom of human action lies with its capacity to transcend what is given to it by viewing this given as circumstantial. The power of free action to change these circumstances constitutes historical change. This encounter between free human action and its circumstances that is responsible for history expresses one sense of the internal relation between political freedom and history that I take to be characteristic of modern historical consciousness. To understand freedom as the cause of history is to acknowledge the radical contingency of all order, which no longer derives its support from the necessity of foundational instances like Nature or God.

Machiavelli develops his theory of history by providing a new philosophical explanation for the role played by chance or luck (fortuna)[1] in human affairs. This explanation of the phenomenon of the variation of fortuna provides a central guiding thread of Machiavelli's thought: introduced in the *Ghiribizzi al Soderino* (fancies or speculations written to Giovan Battista Soderini in 1506), one of his earliest theoretical writings; it can be found, only barely changed, in *The Prince*, and then again in the *Discourses on Livy*. Although in Machiavelli's corpus one can find many other treatments of fortuna, only this one gives a philosophical

---

[1] In what follows I leave the terms "fortuna" and "virtù" untranslated. Their meaning is best determined by their plurivocal use in Machiavelli's discourse about history, and therefore can only begin to emerge in the understanding of the discourse as a whole. I do not review the well-known territory in the history of the idea of fortuna, except when reference to this history is implied by Machiavelli's own treatment. On these occasions, I offer my own interpretation of this history which often departs significantly from the received views. For these views, see H.R. Patch, "The Tradition of the Goddess Fortune in Medieval Philosophy and Literature," *Smith College Studies in modern languages* 3 (1922); A. Doren, "Fortuna in Mittelalter und in der Renaissance," *Vorträge der Bibliothek Warburg* 2,1 (1922-23); K. Heitmann, *Fortuna und Virtus; eine Studie zu Petrarcas Lebensweisheit* (Köln: Bohlau, 1958); M. Santoro, *Fortuna, ragione e prudenza nella civiltà letteraria del Cinquecento* (Turin: Liguori, 1966); E. Panofsky, "'Good Government' or Fortune," *Gazette des Beaux Arts* 6e serie, LXVIII (1966); T. Flanagan, "The Concept of Fortuna in Machiavelli," in *The Political Calculus: Essays on Machiavelli's Philosophy*, ed. A. Parel (Toronto: Toronto University Press, 1972); F. Kiefer, "The Conflagration of Fortune and Occasion in Renaissance Thought and Iconography," *Journal of Medieval and Renaissance Studies* 9 (1977); J, Leeker, "Fortuna bei Machiavelli – ein Erbe der Tradition?," *Romanische Forschungen* 101 (1989): 407-432; and A. Parel, *The Machiavellian Cosmos* (New Haven: Yale University Press, 1992). Provisionally, fortuna can be rendered as chance or luck, and virtù as free action.

account of fortuna, and for that reason is privileged in my interpretation.[2] In what follows I refer to this account as the "problem of the Ghiribizzi."

With this philosophical theory of fortuna Machiavelli effects a revolution in the way of thinking about the relation between action and time. This revolution consists in subverting the primacy of theory (*vita contemplativa*) over practice (*vita activa*) through which the classical and Christian traditions of political thinking had come to determine the possibilities of action. The primacy of theory is due to the fact that in these traditions chance, or contingency, is considered a derivative phenomenon, a by-product of the natural or divine ground of order, to which human beings accede, if at all, only through theory or contemplation. The presence of chance in the world does indeed open a space for free human action, but at the same time the derivative character of contingency limits the capacities of free action: not only can human action not move against the pre-established, necessary order, but it must to a greater or lesser extent be informed by this order through the human theoretical capacity that cognizes it.

The result is that the classical and Christian conceptions of human action determine the goal of praxis to be that of corresponding to what the circumstances demand. I use the term "correspondence" to designate the theoretical adequation of practice to the requirements of (an ideal) order. This correspondence is articulated, on the one side, by the Greek and Roman aristocratic ethics of prudence which is oriented by the search for the best political order or form of domination. On the other side, this correspondence to the order of the world finds its articulation in the Christian popular ethics of charity which is oriented by the belief in divine providence and in the ultimate goodness of Creation. This ethics, according to Machiavelli, exhibits the deleterious effects of the primacy of contemplation over practice in human affairs:

[Christianity] glorified humble and contemplative more than active men.... [It] asks that you have strength in yourself... to be capable more of suffering than of doing something strong. This mode of life thus seems to have rendered the world weak and given it prey to criminal men, who can manage it securely, seeing that the collectivity of men, so as to go to Paradise, think more of enduring their beatings than avenging them.[3]

Machiavelli's theory of fortuna subverts the primacy of contemplation over practice and provides the conceptual schema for modern revolutionary action. By questioning the derivative role played by contingency in the order of the world, it opens a new horizon for human praxis: instead of making action correspond to the times, action is assigned the task of changing the times. The idea that action has the power to change its circumstances may be taken for granted today, after four centuries of political, social and scientific revolutions,[4] but it constituted a radical break with tradition in Machiavelli's day, and is one of the main reasons

---

[2] For an excellent overview of the different registers under which the topic of fortuna is treated in Machiavelli's corpus, and for the arguments why this topic should also be treated from a feminist theory perspective, see Pitkin, *Fortune is a Woman*, ch.6, passim; and Brown, *Politics and Manhood*, passim.

[3] Machiavelli, *Discourses on Livy*, II,2.

[4] Still, perhaps it is not so self-evident as might appear, if Marx himself thought it necessary to reassert it as a thesis in the *Theses on Feuerbach*.

for advancing the claim that his discourse inaugurates modern historical consciousness.

Given its importance, I shall analyse in detail the texts in which Machiavelli puts forward his philosophical account of fortuna. The first chapter provides a commentary of the *Ghiribizzi al Soderino* where the new theory is first sketched. In the second chapter I elucidate its philosophical significance, concentrating on Machiavelli's critique of the primacy of contemplation in the sphere of human praxis. In the third, and most important, chapter I provide a commentary of the twenty-fifth chapter of *The Prince* where I show that the conflictual relation established by Machiavelli between fortuna and virtù contains the formula of modern historicity. The fourth chapter discusses the political solution to the problem of the Ghiribizzi offered by the *Discourses on Livy*.

CHAPTER 1

THE ENCOUNTER OF ACTION AND TIMES
AS EXPLANATION OF FORTUNA

PRUDENCE AND AUDACITY

The text known as the *Ghiribizzi al Soderino*[1] has been rightly said to contain "the most unique and mature fruit" of Machiavelli's writings during his active political life, prior to the main works.[2] The text addresses the traditional, and all too pertinent, question of the change of fortune in the life of individuals. But from the start Machiavelli makes clear that his perspective on the question differs from the one of the addressee. The "mirror" through which he sees the world is not that of Soderini ("wherein nothing but prudence is visible") but that of "the many, who think that one should judge things in terms of the end to which they are done, and not the means with which they are done." From the perspective of the people, of the "many," actions are judged in view of their consequences. Irrespective of who the real addressee of the *Ghiribizzi* is (whether Machiavelli intended his views to reach Piero Soderini, the political leader, or just stay with his nephew), it is not difficult to see that he is drawing a contrast with the perspective of the traditional civic humanist statesman[3] who judges actions in accordance to the morality of the means that are employed to carry out the end.[4] The distinction between the "prudent" and the "popular" ways of proceeding in politics sets the stage for

---

[1] The *Ghiribizzi* were written by Machiavelli in Perugia in September 1506. They are addressed to a nephew of Piero Soderini, the Gonfaloniere of the Florentine Republic for which Machiavelli served as Secretary. All quotations in this chapter (unless otherwise noted) refer to the text of the *Ghiribizzi al Soderino* found in Niccolò Machiavelli, *Machiavelli and his Friends. Their Personal Correspondence,* ed. James B. Atkinson and David Sices (DeKalb: Northern Illinois University Press, 1996), 134-136. This translation of the text follows the version contained in Niccolò Machiavelli, *Lettere,* ed. Franco Gaeta (Milan: Feltrinelli, 1981). When needed, I have modified the English translation basing myself on the Gaeta edition of the *Ghiribizzi*; I also follow this edition with respect to the glosses that Machiavelli wrote on the margins of the manuscript. They are significant, and so will be subject to commentary.

[2] As Sasso remarks: "on the foundation of a radical philosophy of fortuna, it expounds, in powerful sketches, the outlines of a complete philosophy of politics." (Sasso, *Niccolò Machiavelli,* 226). For the best discussion of the context and meaning of the letter in the secondary literature, see ibid., 226-240.

[3] Piero Soderini the Gonfaloniere might well be taken as an exemplar of this kind of statesman. Indeed, Machiavelli returns more than once to the critique of Soderini's government of the Republic in his later works. I discuss this critique in part 3, ch.3. On Soderini's political position, as well as that of his aristocratic adversaries, at the time of the Republic, see the important articles by Felix Gilbert, "Bernardo Rucellai and the Orti Oricellari: A Study of the Origin of Modern Political Thought," *Journal of the Warburg and Courtauld Institutes* 12 (1949): 101-131; idem, "Florentine Political Assumptions in the Period of Savonarola and Soderini," *Journal of the Warburg and Courtauld Institutes* 20 (1957): 187-214.

[4] Machiavelli makes a similar distinction in *The Prince.* For the thesis about the two perspectives on "political things," see the "Dedicatory Letter," where he writes that "to know well the nature of the people one must be a prince, and to know well the nature of princes, one must be of the people." For the distinction between the "prudent" and the "many," see *The Prince,* XVIII.

Machiavelli's attempt to think the problem of historical change through a critique of the classical republican doctrine of prudence.

Machiavelli's adoption of the "popular" perspective that judges the means of the action in terms of its consequences for the "many" who are affected by it contains an implicit critique of the aristocratic bias in the moral regulation of political action embodied by the ideal of prudence. This aristocratic bias is visible in Aristotle's discussion of the qualities of the political leader of the city: "the good ruler [*ton archonta ton spoudaion*] is a good [*agathon*] and prudent [*phronimon*] man and the statesman [*politikon*] is necessarily prudent, but the citizen need not be prudent."[5] Prudence (*phronesis*) is the only virtue that is "peculiar to the ruler: it would seem that all other virtues must equally belong to ruler and subject. The virtue of the subject is certainly not wisdom, but only true opinion [*doxa alethes*]; he may be compared to the maker of the flute, while his master is like the flute-player or user of the flute."[6] Aristotle models his exemplary portrayal of the prudent leader (*phronimos*) on Pericles, under whose leadership, according to Thucydides's famous gibe, Athens was a democracy only in name.[7] Machiavelli's rejection of the "mirror" of Piero Soderini, the contemporary exemplar of the Periclean leader, contains a polemic against the ideology of civic republicanism which prides itself on its retrieval of the Aristotelian doctrine of prudence.

The "popular" perspective on political action disregards the moral quality of the means in favor of their effectiveness in attaining the ends desired by the "many," namely, the cessation of oppression and domination.[8] It is against this standard for political action that Machiavelli rejects, along with Soderini's way of proceeding, the basic Aristotelian belief in the exceptional capacities for deliberation of the prudent individual (*phronimos*) and, even more crucially, the Aristotelian reliance on the noble and valorous individual (*spoudaios*) as the criterion of ethical judgment, the living standard of value.[9]

What troubles Machiavelli about the ideal of prudence[10] is that the theory of action that it presupposes does not seem to match up with the phenomena he

---

[5] Aristotle *Politics* 1277a15.

[6] Ibid., 1277b25-30.

[7] Aristotle *Nicomachean Ethics* 1140b7. For an excellent analysis of this example in the context of Aristotle's theory of the prudent individual, see Pierre Aubenque, *La prudence chez Aristote* (Paris: PUF, 1963), 51-63. In the following discussion of Aristotle's ethical theory I am thoroughly indebted to Aubenque's interpretation.

[8] On the desire of the people for freedom as non-domination, I refer the reader back to part 1, ch. 4.

[9] Aristotle refers to the *spoudaios* in order to resolve the problem of the criterion of ethical judgment in *Nicomachean Ethics* 1166a12 and 1176a17-20: "But in all such cases it seems that what is really so is what appears so to the excellent person... virtue, i.e., the good person insofar as he is good, is the measure of each thing." Aubenque points out the crucial role of the *spoudaios* as the source of value: "since prudence has no essence in relation to which it can be defined, it can only refer to the existence of a prudent person as foundation of all value.... What permits to distinguish truth from appearance is therefore the decision of the *spoudaios*." (Aubenque, *La prudence chez Aristote*, 45-6). Significantly, in this context Aubenque refers to Nietzsche's "First Essay" of the *Genealogy of Morals* where the Greek origin of the ethical or prudential judgment is to be found in the "pathos of distance" that characterizes the aristocratic nobility with respect to the "people," the *demos*.

[10] Whether Machiavelli breaks with the traditional doctrines of prudence and the extent to which he does is a matter of dispute. For interpretations arguing that Machiavelli offers a new a paradigm of prudence, as opposed to breaking with the discourse of prudence as such, see Rodolfo de Mattei, "Dal

observes in worldly affairs: "Seeing that various ways of governing oneself can bring about the same thing, how by different paths one reaches the same place, and that acting in different ways can bring about the same end." The phenomenon of the heterogeneity of the means for a given end is the starting point for Machiavelli's thinking about fortuna. How is it possible that the same result can be achieved by different means? What does this say about the relation between virtue and situation, action and time?

According to Aristotle the prudent individual deliberates only about means, never ends.[11] The field of deliberation is limited to means for two related reasons: the end is the object of the wish or rational desire (*boulesis*), and it is not "up to us" to decide the end.[12] It follows from the nature of the human wish that it wants the good, unless it happens to be perverted by nature, in which case the individual is considered a "monster," a failure on nature's part to attain the form of man.[13] The rootedness of ends in nature entails their relative transcendence with respect to the given situation of action. Deliberation, instead, is about what means, given the situation, are best in order to attain the predetermined end. One has to deliberate about means because the same end can be reached by different means or the same means can lead to different ends depending on the circumstances in which the means display their causality. Ethical action relies on prudence as the intellectual virtue that purportedly permits to discern what is the right thing to do (what choice of means is the best) in any given circumstance presupposing that the causality of the means is potentially affected by the accident of circumstances.[14]

The phenomenon of the heterogeneity of the means with respect to a given end, i.e., the dependence of human action on its circumstances, leads Machiavelli to propose a series of striking departures from the ideal of prudential action. The first gloss that accompanies Machiavelli's rejection of the aristocratic bias of that ideal is as follows: "Each governs oneself according to one's imagination [*ciascuno secondo la sua fantasia si governa*]."[15] The juxtaposition between prudence and imagination (*fantasia*) as guide for action expresses the need for an irreducible element of individual freedom, associated with imagination, in the choice of

---

primato della sapienza al primato della prudenza nel dottrinarismo politico italiano del cinque e del seicento," *Giornale Critico della Filosofia Italiana* vol.7, fasc.1 (Gennaio-Marzo 1976); Eugene Garver, *Machiavelli and the History of Prudence* (Madison, Wis.: University of Wisconsin Press, 1987); Nancy S. Struever, *Theory as Practice: Ethical Inquiry in the Renaissance* (Chicago: University of Chicago Press, 1992); and Christian Lazzeri, "Prudence, Ethique et Politique de Thomas D'Aquin à Machiavel," in *De la prudence des Anciens à celle des Modernes. Annales littéraires de l'université de Franche-Comté* (1995). For a view that emphasises Machiavelli's break with the tradition of prudence, see Klaus Held, "Civic Prudence in Machiavelli: Toward the Paradigm Transformation in Philosophy in the Transition to Modernity" in *The Ancients and the Moderns*, ed. Reginald Lilly (Bloomington: Indiana University Press, 1996).

[11] On prudence as the capacity to deliberate about what leads to a good life, see Aristotle *Nicomachean Ethics* 1140a31 and 1142b31. On the idea that deliberation is only about means, see ibid., 1112b14; idem, *Rhetoric* 1362a18.

[12] Aristotle *Nicomachean Ethics* 1111b30; idem, *Eudemian Ethics* 1227a29-30.

[13] Aristotle *Nicomachean Ethics* 1111b26-27, 1113a15-25, 1114b5-8, 1114b18ff, and 1099b19.

[14] Aubenque, *Prudence chez Aristote*, 109-110.

[15] This gloss is present in the Gaeta edition, but absent in the Atkinson and Sices edition.

means in an action.[16] The favor accorded to the individual's imagination to govern the choice of means suggests that for Machiavelli the relation between action and circumstances precludes the existence of a right or correct rule (*orthos logos*) to determine the action.[17]

The appeal to imagination points towards a new orientation that Machiavelli wants to give to human praxis; an orientation that repudiates the primacy of the intellectual virtue of prudence in order to make space for another kind of virtue that grants a more practical sense of the autonomy of action. This repudiation of prudence is more visible in the following gloss, which draws the first consequence from the phenomenon of the heterogeneity of means: "Counsel no one and take counsel from no one; except for a piece of general advice: that each man must do what his *animo* prompts him to – and do it with audacity [*audacia*]." Machiavelli again introduces a new term, *animo* (which is to be distinguished from *anima*, "soul," and translates into Italian the Latin *animus* and the Greek *thymos*, "spirit"), in order to problematize the claims of prudence on action.[18] The reliance on *animo* and its quality of audacity shifts the focus of attention from the rightness of the means to their efficacity or strength (*virtù*). This shift to efficacity not only denies that action can be guided by a knowledge that is in possession of someone else (for example, the prudent man as living rule) and can be communicated in the form of counsel, but it also points more generally to the idea of the anteriority of action with respect to that possible rule under which it would be a priori comprehended and determined as being "right" or "correct."

Machiavelli's "general advice" calls for a kind of self-reliance that is required for the experience of extremes and of the transgression of limits, and thus is needed to withstand the perils that attach to what the ancients call *hybris*. The way of proceeding should be unique to the individual (in accordance with one's *daimon*, as Max Weber says in *Science as Vocation*); and above all needs to be followed with audacity.[19] In general, the call for audacity, in Machiavelli as in

---

[16] On Machiavelli's concept of *fantasia*, see K.R. Minogue, "Theatricality and Politics: Machiavelli's Concept of Fantasia," in *The Morality of Politics*, ed. B. Parekh and R.N. Berki (London: Allen and Unwin,1972). For the use of the term after Machiavelli, see Pierre-Francois Moreau, *Spinoza. L'experience et l'éternité* (Paris: PUF, 1989).

[17] Aristotle *Nicomachean Ethics* 1106b36.

[18] On the distinction between soul (*anima*) and spirit (*animo*), see Mansfield, *Machiavelli's Virtue*, 40-41. For the Roman understanding of *animo* (and *ingegno*), see Livy *Ab Urbe condita* 9, 17-19; and the illuminating glosses on these terms given in Vico's *De antiquissima Italorum sapientia*.

[19] For an interesting discussion of Renaissance ethics along the lines adumbrated by Machiavelli's call on self-reliance, see Struever, *Theory as Practice*. Struever views Machiavelli's contribution from the perspective offered by the debate between Gramsci and Croce on the autonomy of politics with respect to morality. One could also say that Machiavelli's polemic against prudence places his discourse uncannily close to themes that would gain ascendancy in late modernity with the existential turn taken by ethics. On the lack of general rules to guide conduct, see the discussion of forlorness in Jean-Paul Sartre, *Existentialism is a Humanism*, in *Essays in Existentialism* (New York: Citadel Press, 1970). For the re-evaluation of *hybris*, see Deleuze's understanding of the "selective character of the eternal return" in Nietzsche: "Only the extreme forms return – those which, large or small, are deployed within the limit and extend to the limit of their power, transforming themselves and changing into one another. Only the extreme, the excessive returns; that which passes into something else and becomes identical... it is in hubris that everyone finds the being which makes him return, along with that sort of crowned anarchy, that overturned hierarchy which, in order to ensure the selection of difference, begins by subordinating the identical to the different." (Gilles Deleuze,

later modern thought, is always made against the appeal to prudence and to all forms of classical "wisdom."[20] There is no doubt that this "general advice" polemizes with the classical doctrine of prudence understood in the widest sense: for Machiavelli, the "good for oneself" is not an object of knowledge, and therefore is also not a good that only the knowledge of the "wise man" or "sage" has access to. From here comes the anti-Platonic move of dismissing the figure of the advisor and thus severing the relation between tyrant and philosopher developed by the Socratic tradition of Plato and Xenophon, which bolsters and illuminates Machiavelli's previous adoption of the point of view of the "many" against that of the "prudent" leaders.[21]

The *Ghiribizzi* gives three new determinants of action (*fantasia, animo, audacia*), all of which stand in opposition to the role played by the specific dianoetic virtues of *nous* and *phronesis* in the Platonic and the Aristotelian ethical discourses.[22] These dianoetic virtues are excluded on the basis of Machiavelli's interpretation of the phenomenon of the heterogeneity of means: there is no "one right way" to attain the given end, or, what amounts to the same, the fact that two opposite means can lead to the same end entails that this end cannot be identified with the "good" or the "just."[23] Instead of the ideal of a correct rule (*orthos logos, recta ratio*), imagination, spirit, and audacity are advanced as determinants of action because the end of action has changed: at stake is no longer the good life but the free life.[24] The principle of conduct is no longer determined by intellect (*nous*) or by prudence (*phronesis*) but shifts into a space of determination shared by the will (understood as autonomous from the intellect) and the imagination. Machiavelli displaces the question of action toward a sphere in which a reliance on the rational identification of moral standards by the few for the many is supplanted by a reliance on the individual responsibility and decision of the many. He opens the space of an ethics that is at once democratically inclined and expressive of the individual and factical character of freedom.

Difference and Repetition, 41). I discuss Machiavelli's theory of the "return to beginnings" and its consequences for political action as transgression in the third part.

[20] Giordano Bruno's *Cena delle ceneri* gives perhaps the most scathing version of the modern topos that the ancients are "prudent" and therefore "ignorant": this idea results in the caricature of Prudenzio. Immanuel Kant's "What is Enlightenment?" and its defense of the motto *sapere aude* contains an implicit democratic charge intended to deny the claims of classical wisdom, accessible only to the few.

[21] On the Platonic "tyrannical teaching," see Strauss, *On Tyranny*, passim.

[22] For examples, see Plato *Laws* 962b-c, and Aristotle *Politics* 1331b26-28.

[23] Compare with Aristotle's definition of virtue as a mean: "There are many ways to be in error, since badness is proper to what is unlimited... and good to what is limited; but there is only one way to be correct. That is why error is easy and correctness hard, since it is easy to miss the target and hard to hit it. And so for this reason also excess and deficiency are proper to vice, the mean to virtue.... Virtue, then, is a state that decides, consisting in a mean, the mean relative to us, which is defined by reference to reason, i.e. to the reason by reference to which the intelligent person [*phronimos*] would define it. It is a mean between two vices, one of excess and one of deficiency." (Aristotle *Nicomachean Ethics* 1106b30-1107a).

[24] In his reading of the *Ghiribizzi*, Parel recognizes the point that the end of action has changed, but he believes that Machiavelli's introduction of the concepts of *ingegno* and *fantasia* as guides for action belong to his purported premodern "astrological anthropology." (Anthony Parel, "The Question of Machiavelli's Modernity," *The Review of Politics* 53, no.2 [1991], 335-337). I discuss various aspects of Parel's astrological interpretation below.

From the perspective of the "people," the absence of the mean is not considered prejudicial to the result of the action. Employing the Polybian topos of the comparison between Hannibal and Scipio, Machiavelli remarks that:

the former kept his armies in Italy united through cruelty, treachery, and impiety and won the admiration of the people, who, in order to follow him, rebelled against the Romans.... The latter achieved the identical result among the people of Spain with compassion, loyalty, and piety.... Lorenzo de' Medici disarmed the people to hold on to Florence, Messer Giovanni Bentivoglio armed them to hold on to Bologna; the Vitelli in Città di Castello and the current duke of Urbino in his territory tore down fortresses in order to hold on to those territories; the count Francesco in Milan and many others constructed fortresses in their territories in order to secure them for themselves.

In all these cases, the end consists either in gaining the support of the people or in securing the state, that is, the end is an unstable composite of freedom and power. Depending on the circumstances in which the political actor finds itself, contrary ways of proceeding may yield the same result. But what consequences are to be drawn from this fact?

The gloss which comments the above passage is fraught with an internal tension, if not contradiction, that betrays more the sense of the problem than that of a possible solution:

To try one's luck [fortuna], because she is the friend of youth, and to change according to the times. But it is impossible both to have fortresses and not to have them; it is impossible to be both cruel and compassionate.

The connectives in this text disclose possibilities that Machiavelli, at this stage in his thinking, has not yet decided upon. As Sasso remarks, there is an obvious tension between the call for audacity and the advice to change according to the circumstances.[25] In the latter case, if it is possible to alternate ways of proceeding to fit with what the circumstances require there is clearly no need to "try one's luck." Conversely, to act with audacity means to take chances in a situation that does not let itself be anticipated; and this seems to entail that luck or fortuna alone decides the outcome of the action.

Yet this way of reading the gloss omits a decisive point by not taking into proper account its last phrase: precisely because there is no middle way that allows both "to have fortresses and not to have them," every action and every choice entails taking chances and trying one's luck. If such a mean were to exist and were a possible object of choice for human action then the dependency of action on its circumstances could be neutralized and it would be possible to "master" the situation in the sense of doing the "right thing at the right time," as the ideal of prudence promises. But in a context of action that is defined by the absence of the mean, the incidence of luck, and as a consequence the need to try one's luck, merely refers to the impossibility of mastering, in a theoretical sense, the situation in which one is to act prior to the action itself. It does not mean, as Sasso implies, that the result of the action is at the mercy of fortuna, i.e., that the end of the action can only be attained thanks to the intervention of luck. In the

[25] Sasso, "Qualche osservazione sui *Ghiribizzi*," in *Machiavelli e gli antichi*, 2: 53.

Ghiribizzi, the incidence of luck is a condition of possibility for the autonomy of action with respect to theory; it does not as such signal the captivation of praxis in a new heteronomy. With this gloss Machiavelli takes cognizance of the risk factor in any action worthy of its name. The gloss expresses the ungrounded character of action, the sense in which every action is a thrown project because it embodies the factical character of freedom and power, in direct contrast to the teleological and normative structure of action, the directedness of action toward the good and the fitting, that one finds in the classical ideal of prudence.

TO MATCH WITH THE TIMES

Having described the phenomenon of the heterogeneity of the means, and alluded to the change in perspective that this phenomenon brings to the context of human action, the text of the *Ghiribizzi* proceeds to formulate the main theoretical question.

We have seen, and continue to see, in all the examples mentioned above [Hannibal and Scipio, etc.]... that kingdoms are conquered, or are subdued, or have fallen, as accidents [*li accidenti*] would have it. Sometimes the way of proceeding that was praised when it led to conquest is vilified when it leads to defeat, and sometimes when defeat comes after long prosperity, people do not blame themselves but rather indict the heavens and the will of the Fates [*il cielo et la dispositione de' fati*]. But what determines that different actions are sometimes equally useful and sometimes equally harmful I do not know – yet I should very much like to; so, in order to learn your view, I shall be presumptuous enough to give you mine.

The problem of the Ghiribizzi refers to the power that circumstances have to affect the outcome of actions. What makes an action succeed in one circumstance and fail in another? How is it possible for opposite actions to have similar results in different circumstances? What is the cause of the change in fortune? In short: how is historical change possible? Machiavelli implicitly discards two traditional answers: the one blames the change of fortune on the actor, while the other blames the heavens and Fates. These two explanations share the characteristic that they each identify only one element of the phenomenon's configuration as the cause of success or failure: this cause is either the actor's way of proceeding (and so at bottom its free will or capacity for choice), or something completely external to the actor's control, i.e., fatality in all of its guises. Both of these purported causes fail to account for the change of fortune, i.e., why the same action now succeeds and then fails. Clearly the way of proceeding cannot, as such, be responsible for the change in its results: what remains the same cannot account for the change. But the appeal to fatality as a viable explanation for changes that occur "according to accidents" is equally static because it presupposes that such an outcome (e.g., the loss of the state or its acquisition) was pre-determined ("written in the stars"). Such an explanation also abstracts from the very concept of a situation, and thus from the role played by circumstance, because it implies the outcome of the action is predetermined no matter what the circumstances are. Neither the internal (free will) nor the external (fate) explanation of the change of fortune takes into account the event-character of the relationship between means and ends: the outcome of the action depends on the kind of encounter that takes place between the means put to work in the action and the circumstances, the situation, in which they are put to work.

The *Ghiribizzi* offers a philosophical explanation of the change of fortune that takes as its starting point the event-character of all human action:

> I believe that just as nature has created men with different faces, so she has created them with different wit [*ingegno*] and imagination [*fantasia*]. As a result, everyone governs themselves according to their wit and imagination. And, on the other hand, because the times are variable [*i tempi sono vari*] and the orders of things are different [*gli ordini delle cose sono diversi*] the one who gets his wishes *ad votum* and is happy is the one who matches [*riscontra*] his way of proceeding with time [*il tempo*]; and the one who is unhappy, conversely, is the one who diverges [*diversifica*] with his actions from time and from the order of things. Hence, it can well be that two people can achieve the same result by acting differently: because each one of them may conform himself to its match [*conformarsi con il suo riscontro*], because the orders of things are as manifold as the number of territories and states. But because the times and the things, both universally and particularly, often change, and because men change neither their imaginations nor their ways of proceeding, it happens that a man has good luck [*buona fortuna*] at one time and bad luck at another. And truly if someone were so wise as to know the times [*i tempi*] and the order of things, and could adapt himself to them, he would always have good luck or would always avoid bad luck; and it would come to be true that the wise man commands the stars and the Fates [*che il savio comandasse alle stella et a' fati*]. But such wise men do not exist: because men are shortsighted, and because they cannot command their nature; thus it follows that fortune [*la fortuna*] varies and commands men, keeping them under her yoke.

This extraordinary text is the first place where Machiavelli formulates his theory of the encounter (*riscontro*) between actions and times as cause of the variations in fortune.[26] The argument rests on two presuppositions: the diversity of "natures" in human beings which is determined by the individual wit (*ingegno*) and imagination (*fantasia*) with which each individual governs its conduct;[27] and the diversity of "the times" (*i tempi*) and of the "orders of things," terms that refer to the historical, political and cultural circumstances surrounding individuals.

The first consequence that follows from the diversity of the modes of action (*modi di procedere*) and the diversity of the times is that the satisfaction of desires

---

[26] The term *riscontro* is semantically very rich. It can be translated as "match," "coincidence," or "encounter," but it also contains the term *scontro*, which means "conflict" or "clash." Machiavelli plays off all of these senses.

[27] According to Fleischer, "the term *ingegno* is employed by Machiavelli to designate wit of a high order.... Render *ingegno* as wits, ingenuity, or cunning, Machiavelli does not use the term in a pejorative sense. It refers to the ability to devise, contrive, or arrange things so that the desired goal is reached.... It focuses on technical ability as sheer technical ability, free of moral overtones." (Martin Fleischer, "A Passion for Politics: The Vital Core of the World of Machiavelli," in *Machiavelli and the Nature of Political Thought* [New York: Atheneum, 1972], 138-9). More deeply, Moreau explains the concept of *ingenium* as follows: "It oscillates between two senses: that of marking the diversity of wits, or the superiority of some among them. It can mean what is 'natural' to a given individual in opposition to others; but it can also indicate the genius, the superior wit that characterizes some over against others. In both cases, the concept clearly shows that the human spirit is not reducible to Reason: the *ingenium* in Vivès is the set of creative capacities beyond the mere faculty of understanding. In Spinoza, this duality loses its sharpness: the first sense becomes the essential one, and the second one is never thought, when it emerges, otherwise than as falling under its jurisdiction. To have talents is just one possible complexion, one possible nature of the individual." (Moreau, *Spinoza,* 397). Machiavelli's understanding of *ingegno* is very close to the one ascribed by Moreau to Spinoza's use of *ingenium*.

depends on the match (*riscontro*) between the action and its circumstances (*il tempo*). If these two factors diverge from one another, the result will be unhappiness and failure. The theory of the *riscontro* accounts for the phenomenon of the heterogeneity of means: two different ways of acting may lead to the same result because each can match their circumstances, or more properly: "because each can conform itself to its match [*perché ciascuno di loro può conformarsi con il riscontro suo*]."

The second consequence of the theory is the explanation of the changes in fortune during the lifetime of a person. In the medieval Christian imaginary, these changes are explained as a function of the "up and down" motion that the individual suffers on being nailed to the "wheel of fortune." As Boethius illustrates this view of the human condition, the inconstancy of Fortuna is, by its very essence, stronger than human action, and cannot be withstood nor, properly speaking, matched.

Change is her normal behavior, her true nature.... Once you have bowed your neck beneath her yoke, you ought to bear with equanimity whatever happens on Fortune's playground. If after freely choosing her as mistress to rule your life you want to draw up a law to control her coming and going, you will be acting without any justification and your impatience will only worsen a lot which you cannot alter. Commit your boat to the winds and you must sail whichever way they blow, not just where you want.... If you are trying to stop her wheel from turning, you are of all men the most obtuse. For if it once begins to stop, it will no longer be the wheel of chance.[28]

Boethius adopts the Stoic attitude towards Fortuna by giving it power over external or worldly goods but not over internal goods,[29] and in this way excludes a priori the idea that human virtue (*virtus*) might engage fortuna in the worldly arena. The specifically medieval illustration of the wheel of fortune in terms of its capacity to "depose once fearful kings/ while trustless still, from low she lifts a conquered head,"[30] expresses the belief that Fortuna has a complete hold on the course of worldly affairs. Only the disengagement of political virtue from the events of the world permits the medieval illustration of the wheel of fortune to cover the four cardinal positions by the words: *regnabo, regno, regnavi, sum sine regno*. There is no better expression for the loss of the political and worldly nature of providence found in the Romans and its replacement by the contemplative, other-worldly nature of providence in Christianity.[31]

In contrast to Boethius, Machiavelli's explanation of the change in fortunes does not refer to the "essence" of Fortuna, to its intrinsic capacity to change itself. The change of fortune is explained by the fact that the times often change whereas individuals keep their "imaginations and their ways of proceeding [*le loro*

---

[28] Boethius *Consolation of Philosophy* II,1. On the image of the wheel of fortune, apart from the sources already cited, see Giorgio Stabile, "La Ruota della Fortuna: Tempo Ciclico e Ricorso Storico," in *Studi Filosofici* II (1979) (Florence: Olshki, 1981), 93-104. On Machiavelli's critique of the Boethian image of fortuna, see Philippe Desan, *La Naissance du Méthode. Machiavel, La Ramée, Bodin, Montaigne, Descartes* (Paris: Nizet, 1987), ch. 2.

[29] Taking up a tenet of Seneca's: "Non fulgetis extrinsecus; bona uestra introrsus observa sunt. Sic mundus exteriora contempsit, spectaculo sui laetus. Intus omne posui bonum; non egere felicitate felicitas uestra est." (Seneca *De providentia* I,6,5).

[30] Boethius, *Consolation of Philosophy* II,1.

[31] I discuss Machiavelli's critique of the Roman concept of providence in ch. 4 below.

fantasie... i loro modi di procedere]" fixed. Thus at one time their action will be adequate to the circumstances while at another time, with a change in circumstances, the same type of action will be inadequate. The cause of the change of fortune is then displaced onto the cause of the change of the times. In one quick reversal Machiavelli undoes the hegemony of the Boethian representation of the goddess Fortuna according to which Fortuna is the personified cause of the change of times.[32] For Machiavelli, it is only the encounter (*riscontro*) between human action and circumstances, i.e., the human determinants of historical happening, that accounts for those phenomena that are hypostatized into something like Fortuna, and not the opposite. As Sasso says, the theory of the *riscontro* finds a "rationalistic solution to the paradoxes of historical and political vicissitudes" because it provides an explanation of Fortuna and of its apparent power over human beings as a result of a process that does not appeal to any mythical force.[33]

The last consequence of the theory of the *riscontro* is the denial of wisdom. According to the *Ghiribizzi*, if one is to always have good luck, and thus to be happy (to be a sage or *savio*), it is necessary to know the times and the orders of things, and to be capable of changing one's nature so as to match their changes. But this kind of knowledge is impossible because individuals are "shortsighted": they lack true foresight (*pronoia, providentia*) to grasp the change of times (*i tempi*) ahead of time (*il tempo*).[34] Likewise, it is impossible for individuals to "command their own nature" and change it at will. Having denied the presuppositions that wisdom requires for its claim to transcend the horizon of the times and

---

[32] "Inconstancy is my very essence; it is the game I never cease to play as *I turn my wheel* in its ever changing circle, filled with joy as *I bring the top to the bottom and the bottom to the top*." (Boethius, *Consolation of Philosophy*, II,2; emphasis mine). I discuss below how Boethius derives the causality of Fortuna from its hidden providential purpose, that is, from its role in establishing a predetermined order. The providential meaning of Fortuna's mutability is that such mutability applies only to the inessential "worldly goods" thereby permitting the individual to become aware of the true goods that lie beyond the range of Fortuna: "bad fortune, I think, is more use to a man than good fortune. Good fortune always seems to bring happiness, but deceives you with her smiles, whereas bad fortune is always truthful because by changing she shows her true fickleness. Good fortune deceives, but bad fortune enlightens." (Ibid., II,4).

[33] Sasso, *Niccolò Machiavelli*, 234. This is said to counteract the kind of interpretations that emphasize fortuna as "the mythical element in Machiavelli's political philosophy." (Cassirer, *Myth of the State*, 156). For Cassirer, Machiavelli's theory of fortuna achieves a "secularization of the symbol of Fortune," (ibid., 160) yet it does not lose its mythical qualities for all that. For Sasso, on the contrary, the explanation of the process that deprives fortuna of its mythical hypostatization exhibits a strong naturalism: the theory of the *riscontro* shows how the sway that chance has over human affairs is rooted in the structure of human "nature," in the structure of the *animo*. This structure is determinable and knowable: "it is thereby possible to have a science of it." (Sasso, *Niccolò Machiavelli*, 234). Sasso does not mean that there is a "science" of fortuna in the sense of a knowledge that would allow one to master it: he does not share Strauss's interpretation of Machiavelli's discourse on fortuna. Rather, Machiavelli merely gives a "scientific," as opposed to "mythological," explanation of the power of fortune in human affairs. I discuss both Sasso's and Strauss's interpretations below. The naturalistic reading of the theory of the *riscontro* in the *Ghiribizzi* is also advocated by Luigi Derla, "Sulla concezione machiavelliana del tempo," in *Ideologia e scrittura nel Cinquecento* (Urbino: Argalia Editore, 1977), 27-28.

[34] The association of prudence with the capacity to see ahead of oneself, to have foresight, is present in both classical and Christian conceptions of prudence. See Cicero's saying that *prudentia* is a contraction for *providentia*, in *De re publica* VI,1; *De natura deorum* II,22,58; and *De legibus* I,23,60. See also Thomas Aquinas's positing of foresight as the main part of prudence, in *Summa teologica* IIa IIae, Qu.49, art.6, concl.

of their immanent change, the text draws its "pessimistic" conclusion: "fortuna varies and commands men, keeping them under her yoke." The Ptolemaic formula for astral wisdom according to which the "wise man commands the stars and the fates" is rejected as false.[35]

But it would be a mistake to terminate the discussion of the *Ghiribizzi al Soderino* with the passage in which Machiavelli expounds his theory of fortuna along with its apparently pessimistic conclusion because the text, and the argument, does not end there. After sounding that pessimistic note Machiavelli immediately returns to the examples he gives at the beginning of the discussion in order to "check this opinion [i.e, the theory of the *riscontro*]... against those examples that I have based it on, and so I should like the one to support the other." This phrase is crucial to the understanding of the status of the whole theory: the hypothesis of the *riscontro* that explains the phenomenon of fortuna is worked out on the basis of certain exemplary actions (e.g., the comparison between Hannibal and Scipio), but it must itself find its match (*riscontro*) with these actions. Machiavelli's argument in the *Ghiribizzi* stages a movement that begins from historical phenomena, elevates itself to the theoretical plane, and then descends to practice (that is, back to the plane of history).

Yet the practical descent does not return to the point from which the theoretical ascent took off, for the *Ghiribizzi* concludes in the following, unexpected manner:

To show cruelty, treachery, and impiety [*irreligione*] is effective in providing reputation to a new ruler [*dominatore nuovo*] in that province where humanity, loyalty, and piety have long been common practice, just as to show humanity, loyalty, and piety is effective where cruelty, treachery, and impiety have reigned for a long time; for just as bitter things irritate the taste and sweet things cloy it [*lo stuccano*], so men become impatient with the good and complain about the bad. These causes, among others, opened Italy up to Hannibal and Spain to Scipio, and in this way each one matched the time and the things according to their way of proceeding [*et cosí ognuno riscontrò il tempo et le cose secondo l'ordine del procedere suo*].

This passage reverses the apparent meaning of the previous formulation of the theory of the *riscontro*. It is no longer the times that come, or do not come, to match the human ways of proceeding, but instead these human ways now come out to engage, and are a match for, the times and the orders of things.[36] The

---

[35] For some of the classical sources of the possible meaning of "commanding the stars and the fates," see Plato *Republic* 617d-e; idem *Epinomis* 982c-e; idem *Laws* 903b; Aristotle *Metaphysics* 1075a19-22; and Plotinus *Enneads* III,4. Boethius recapitulates the topos well: "whatever moves any distance from the primary intelligence becomes enmeshed in ever stronger chains of Fate, and everything is freer from Fate the closer it seeks the center of things. And if it cleaves to the steadfast mind of God, it is free from movement and so escapes the necessity imposed by Fate." (Boethius *Consolation of Philosophy* IV,6). Parel, who is one of the main proponents of the thesis that Machiavelli is still captivated by medieval astrological thinking, acknowledges the "rejection of the astrological formula" in the *Ghiribizzi* but would still like to claim that this "does not mean that he rejected the astrological mode of analysis in terms of times and temperament." (Parel, "Machiavelli's Modernity," 337). I show below that Machiavelli's politico-philosophical discourse on fortuna rejects not only the formula but also the "mode of analysis" of astrology.

[36] This basic shift in the mode of encounter between action and times has passed unnoticed by commentators who tend to see the encounter always in the first mode, where fortuna "from time to time brings 'untimely' sequences" and the human being has a series of possible "phases of conduct" available to respond to "the three stages of the visit" of fortuna. (Robert Orr, "The Time Motif in Machiavelli," in *Machiavelli and the Nature of Political Thought*, 200). Orr does not take into

encounter (*riscontro*) between times and actions assumes a thoroughly polemical character: when the times are "humane," inhumane actions will succeed; when the times are "cruel," humanity and piety will succeed.

The theory of the *riscontro* flows into a theory of innovative action for which the times or circumstances (irrespective of whether individuals are doing "well" or "bad" in them) are immanently open to the action that can change them. The surprising reversal of the meaning given to the encounter (*riscontro*) in the argument of the *Ghiribizzi* performs the very conflict between theory and practice which is the true subject-matter of this text. Machiavelli's text assigns a priority to practice which "finds its own match" only with the possibility that human action can change the times or situations, rather than correspond to them. Fortuna loves the impetuous actor because, far from being the principle of its own change, it requires human action to move against the grain of the times.

account the possibility (clearly stated at the end of the *Ghiribizzi*, and repeated both in *The Prince* and the *Discourses on Livy*) that human action can itself be "untimely" in order to anticipate the "visit" of fortuna in the first place.

CHAPTER 2

FROM ACTION AS CORRESPONDENCE WITH THE TIMES TO ACTION AS CHANGING THE TIMES

THEORY AND PRACTICE OF CHANCE IN THE ANCIENTS

The text of the *Ghiribizzi* is aporetic, if not antinomical. It appears to argue for a pessimistic concept of fate in which fortuna "commands men and keeps them under her yoke;" in which the path provided by classical thought to escape from this yoke, namely, astrological wisdom or the belief that intellect (*nous*) is stronger than necessity (*ananke*), is systematically barred. On the other hand, the text contains passages (like the last analysis of Hannibal and Scipio and the glosses) that give a different picture of the possibilities of human action by arguing that the encounter (*riscontro*) between human modes of action and circumstances has a conflictual meaning that favors innovation and discontinuity rather than adequation (in the sense of an harmonious fitting of action with the demands of the situation at hand).

In the *Ghiribizzi* Machiavelli does not give any indication, with the exception of the last passage, as to what the encounter or *riscontro* between human modes and times really consists in: whether it is cause or effect, whether its sense is that of adequation or conflict, and so on. Likewise, no clue is given as to the provenance of the term and why it is employed in a philosophical discussion of fortuna. Yet the fact that Machiavelli employs this term and not a different one is highly significant because in so doing his theory links up directly with the main formulations of the problem of chance in classical and Christian thought and allows one to determine quite clearly the extent to which it subverts them.

Remarkably, Machiavelli's term *riscontro* translates one of the originary senses of chance (*tyche*): the sense of "fortunate encounter" found in Empedocles and cited by Aristotle in his treatment of chance in the *Physics*.[1] Aristotle's own conception of *tyche* is meant to account for the kind of event that happens neither "of necessity and always... [nor] for the most part."[2] The two species of chance, luck (*tyche*) and automatic processes (*automaton*), are "causes of things for which

---

[1] Commenting and redressing Aristotle's rendition of Empedocles's theory of chance in *Physics* 196a17-20, Bollack states: "The word itself of encounter [*rencontre*] (*tuchein*) does not have the meaning that Aristotle assigns it. Far from designating the accident and the exception, it implies accomplishment [*la réussite*]. The elements [in Empedocles] do not fall by chance one over another [*ne tombent pas au hasard l'un sur l'autre*], but they find and obtain each other, they enter into the mould that favors them. The One accomplishes itself progressively through the encounter [*la rencontre*]. Every approach is beautiful, subject to the universal end which is creative of order." (Jean Bollack, *Empedocle*, vol.1, *Introduction à l'ancienne physique* [Paris: Edition de Minuit,1965], 68). Empedocles's idea of chance as the encounter that makes and unmakes the order of the world is in many senses closer to Machiavelli's theory than the Aristotelian treatment of chance. This unsuspected connection between Machiavelli and the pre-Socratics merits further investigation.
[2] Aristotle *Physics* 196b12.

149

mind [*nous*] or nature [*physis*] might be responsible, when something comes to be responsible for these same things by virtue of concurrence [*kata symbebekos*]," that is, by accident or by coincidence.[3] As Sorabji comments, "each accident involves a relation between two items which have come together (etymologically, the expression *ta symbebekota* meant having come together), when things of this kind do not come together always or for the most part."[4] In Aristotle, just like in Empedocles, the concept of chance entails the concept of an encounter between two elements which do not have an internal relation, that is, whose relation is purely external.[5]

The exteriority of the encounter signals the uncaused character of the event that happens "by chance." The event does not contain a reference to something other than itself, and that is why it is pure exteriority: it happens "because" it happens. This tautological "because" is the real content of Aristotle's definition of *tyche*:

> luck is a cause by virtue of concurrence in connection with those among things for something which are objects of choice. Hence thought [*dianoia*] and luck [*tyche*] have the same field, for choice [*proairesis*] involves thought [*dianoias*]. Necessarily, then, the causes from which an outcome of luck might come to be are indeterminate [*aorista*]. That is why luck is thought to be an indeterminate sort of thing and inscrutable to men, and at the same time there is a way in which it might be thought that nothing comes to be as the outcome of luck. For all these things are rightly said, as might be expected. There is a way in which things come to be as the outcome of luck: they come to be by virtue of concurrence, and luck is a concurrent cause [*aition ou symbebekos*]. But simply, it is the cause of nothing.[6]

For Aristotle, accidental events or coincidences do not have causes except by accident in the following sense: to say that something happened "by chance" or "by accident" is exactly the same as saying that something happened "because it happened."[7] The conclusion to be drawn from the Aristotelian analysis of chance

---

[3] Ibid., 198a5-12. But see also the additional definition of chance: "Anything which might be done as an outcome of thought or nature is for something. Whenever something like this comes to be by virtue of concurrence [*kata symbebekos*], we say that it is the outcome of luck." (Ibid., 196b23).

[4] Richard Sorabji, *Necessity, Cause, and Blame* (Ithaca: Cornell University Press, 1980), 4.

[5] Hence Aristotle's famous example of the man who goes to the market with some purpose in mind and encounters someone who owes him money, as if he had gone to market for the express purpose of getting his money back: such an encounter is said to be "by chance." Luck represents an encounter between a real causal series, which has a purpose, and an imaginary purpose that was not effectively pursued but which can be reconstructed retrospectively after the event. As Aubenque says, "chance is in this sense a retrospective illusion, the projection of a human purpose on a causal relation that is, in itself, completely foreign to that purpose." (Aubenque, *Prudence chez Aristote*, 76).

[6] Aristotle *Physics* 197a5-15.

[7] Sorabji (*Necessity, Cause, Blame,* 7-9) and Diano (*Forma ed Evento,* 35) both give definitive arguments, based on the refutation of determinism given by Aristotle in *Metaphysics* 1027a30-b10, for the thesis that coincidences or accidents do not have causes, and thus that chance is not a cause except in the "accidental" sense of the term. Likewise Aubenque, who understands chance as an effect: "From this point of view, chance, as the encounter of a real series with a purpose that was not effectively pursued, appears as a fact that is exceptional and without causes: in this sense, chance belongs to the domain of the indeterminate." (Aubenque, *Prudence chez Aristote,* 77). Dorothea Frede's discussion of the critique of determinism in Alexander of Aphrodisias's *De fato* makes the point that "for Alexander just as for Aristotle there is a limit to what nature can and does predetermine [*Physics* 196b28ff]. The interference from 'without' [i.e., the instance of exteriority] is accidental because there is no natural principle which coordinates chance happenings. Coincidences, then, have no causes contained *in rerum natura*; and once this is established for cases where there normally is a natural law to the contrary, the accidental determination for the disorderly class of

is that every state of affairs that can be explained by an exhaustive and sufficient causal account will not be an event in which a theoretically indeterminate encounter takes place (indeed, will not be an event as such), but rather will belong to the order of substances (forms, essences) and their modifications. "Chance only appears in a world where the accident – what advenes, *symbainei*, to a thing – does not let itself be brought back to the essence, in a world where not everything is deducible."[8]

The space of chance as contingency is the space of causal indeterminacy. It functions as the cosmological underpinning of Aristotle's understanding of ethical or prudential action. Not only do all virtues, as dispositions to act in certain ways, have an internal reference to certain situations,[9] but the determination of the right thing at the right time requires prudence, which is itself situated by a wider horizon that any of the other virtues, namely, the domain of the contingent, of that which can be otherwise than it is.[10]

For Aristotle, human activity, whether it be action (*praxis*) or production (*poiesis*), consists in bringing into being what can either be or not be. The root of this contingency is matter as indeterminate potential for contraries, and human activity consists in giving a form to this matter from the outside, i.e., to bring into existence things whose principle resides in the actor or producer. This possibility of giving form from the outside depends on a certain indeterminacy or lack of completion in nature (*physis*), which is the cause of things from the inside, that is, of things which have their principle of motion in themselves. Action and production are both constituted as complements to nature: "In general, art [*techne*] either imitates the works of nature or completes that which nature is unable to bring to completion."[11] And this complementary status of action with respect to natural order corresponds to the residual status of contingency in Aristotelian cosmology: "since nothing which is by virtue of concurrence is prior to that which is by itself, it is clear that no cause by virtue of concurrence is prior to that which is by itself a cause. Hence the automatic and luck are posterior to both mind and nature."[12] Thus if the world were completely rational and everything would follow from the teleology or necessity of nature, there would be no logical space for action or production. It is only because there is chance in the (sublunar) world that the individual has the chance to operate in it: from here Agathon's saying, cited by Aristotle, that "*techne* loves *tyche* and *tyche* loves *techne*."[13]

---

contingent events can be seen as established too. This seems to be the reason why Alexander can pass so lightly from chance happenings to the contigent [*endechomena*] in general." (Dorothea Frede, "The Dramatization of Determinism: Alexander of Aphrodisias's *De fato*," *Phronesis* 27, no.3 [1982], 281).

[8] Aubenque, *Prudence chez Aristote,* 77.

[9] Aristotle *Nicomachean Ethics* 1109a25-30.

[10] "Phronesis is about human concerns, about what is open to deliberation. For we say that deliberating well is the function of the prudent person [*phronimos*] more than anyone else; but no one deliberates about what cannot be otherwise, or about what lacks a goal that is a good achievable in action." (Ibid., 1141b10-13).

[11] Aristotle *Physics* 199a15.

[12] Ibid., 198a7-11.

[13] Aristotle *Nicomachean Ethics* 1140a20.

But the residual space that is left for contingency in Aristotelian cosmology also determines the theoretical overdetermination of practice in its theory of action, i.e., the need for action to bring about order where nature has left things unfinished. Diverging from the main tendency in classical thought, and then in Christianity, Aristotle rejects providence as a factor in his explanation of human action: happiness or the state of acting virtuously requires external goods (above all: situations in which to act with virtue) that are not dependent on the actor alone but on chance. This partial dependence of virtue on chance signals a separation in Aristotle between the sphere of God and that of human action which no providence can bridge. Aristotle's God is indifferent and impotent with respect to the events of the sublunary world.[14] Contingency signals not the absence of the law but the distance that separates its generality from being realized in the particular, in matter, which as indeterminate potential for contraries is the limit to the determination of the law.[15] Matter is the condition for the possibility of movement, and the more distant this movement is from the immobility of the divine, the more the matter which underlies resists its determination by the actuality of what is divine: "Aristotelian contingency... is less a positive reality, a principle of disorder, than an impotence of the form, of Nature, that is, in the last analysis, of God."[16] But just such an indeterminacy of universal reason opens the space for the "reasonable action of man.... Aristotle counts on reasonable desire to finish ordering the world, taking over from a withering providence."[17]

The residual, but still relatively autonomous, status of contingency in Aristotle that allows for human intervention in the world for the sake of perfecting its order is rejected in the Boethian interpretation of chance. Boethius denies the possibility of events "produced by random motion without any causal nexus.... If God imposes order upon all things, there is no opportunity for random events."[18] In this sense, he denies the Aristotelian possibility of an event that happens as a coincidence without having itself a cause. Boethius's definition of chance depends on the Aristotelian one but changes it slightly and decisively: what happens by chance is determined as having a cause, i.e., the "unforeseen and unexpected conjunction of which have clearly effected the chance event." Chance is a result of the "conjunction" or "coincidence" of "opposite causes": it is this conjunction that acts as cause of what happens by chance, rather than being the causeless chance event itself. Boethius's definition of chance,

as an unexpected event due to the conjunction of its causes [*ex confluentibus causis*] with action which is done for some purpose. The conjunction and coincidence of the causes is effected by that order which proceeds by the inescapable nexus of causation, descending from the fount of Providence and ordering all things in their own time and place,[19]

---

[14] Aristotle *Metaphysics* 1074b27-32.
[15] Ibid., 1039b29 and 1032a22; idem *De caelo* 283b13.
[16] Aubenque, *Prudence chez Aristote*, 88.
[17] Ibid.
[18] Boethius *Consolation of Philosophy* V,1.
[19] Ibid., V,1.

inscribes the event of chance (*casus*) into the divine order (*ordo*), rather than seeing it, as was the case in Aristotle, as the impotence on the part of the divine intellect to determine the domain of events.

The hypostatization of chance into the providential entity of Fortuna turns on the doubling of the event that is the conjunction of causes: for Boethius, this conjunction is both the event of chance and the cause of chance. It is in this sense that he speaks of the conjunction of causes as being itself caused, rather than being precisely that event which has no prior cause and so is pure chance. Once the conjunction is understood as caused it becomes possible to place chance under teleological control. In this way, Boethius manages to subject fortuna to the system of divine order while keeping its pagan connotations, thereby undoing the either/or between chance and God that had structured the classical discourse on chance since Anaxagoras.[20] God becomes invested in the contingency of the world in an attempt to exorcise the cosmological source of disorder that functions as the opening for the Aristotelian concept of practical freedom.

From Boethius onwards the source of contingency is to be found solely in the individual's freedom of will, which, although autonomous from the necessity of the world, is not autonomous from the necessity of divine providence:

All things, therefore, whose future occurrence is known to God do without doubt happen, but some of them are the result of free will. In spite of the fact that they do happen, their existence does not deprive them of their true nature, in virtue of which the possibility of their non-occurrence existed before they happened.[21]

The internalization of contingency into the sphere of human free will allows Boethius to introduce divine providence in such a way that it can resolve the new problem of evil. The presence of Fortuna in the world is held responsible for the fact that "good men are oppressed by punishments reserved for crime and bad men can snatch the rewards that belong to virtue." Therefore the power of Fortuna arouses the suspicion that if God is indeed the "ruling power of the universe," and "sometimes He is pleasant to the good and unpleasant to the bad, and other times He grants the bad their wishes and denies the good... since he often varies between these two alternatives, what grounds are there for distinguishing between God and the haphazards of chance?"[22] Boethius's elimination of the uncaused character of chance provides the basis to overcome the alternative between chance and God. Divine providence assures human beings that everything in the universe that is or happens belongs to the divine order and is, consequently, for some good.

The Boethian world has a tripartite division. Divine providence stands highest: "The generation of all things, the whole progress of things subject to change and whatever moves in any way, receive their causes, their due order and their form from the unchanging mind of God... the mind of God has setup a plan for the multitude of events."[23] The divine plan, which is present all at once (*totum simul*) in God's mind, receives the name of Fate when it is "unfolded in the course of

---

[20] I refer to my discussion in part 1, ch.1.
[21] Ibid., V,6.
[22] Ibid., IV,5.
[23] Ibid., IV,6.

time." Fate is the "planned order inherent in things subject to change through the medium of which Providence binds everything in its allotted place."[24] No events can escape from the grasp of "the unchanging order of causes" which is Fate: the appearance of confusion or disorder or chance is therefore due to a failure of the human mind to attain the contemplation of divine providence.

And so sovereign Providence has often produced a remarkable effect – evil men making other evil men good.... It is only the power of God to which evils may also be good, when by their proper use He elicits some good result. For a certain order embraces all things, and anything which departs from the order planned and assigned to it, only falls back into order, albeit a different order, so as not to allow anything to chance in the realm of Providence.[25]

It is at this point that Boethius reveals the complete providential nature of pagan Fortune: "all fortune whether pleasant or adverse is meant either to reward or discipline the good or to punish or correct the bad. We agree, therefore, on the justice or usefulness of fortune, and so all fortune is good."[26] The practical implications of the Boethian discourse on chance are easily seen: the absolute priority of contemplation or wisdom over practice or politics. If all fortune is good, there is no point in engaging in a struggle with it in order to master or change it. If there is any purpose to this confrontation with fortune it lies in the opportunity it offers to strengthen wisdom, that is, to contemplate ever more clearly the providential ways of God and thereby to see that evil has no real existence.[27]

FORTUNA AND DETERMINISM: MACHIAVELLI'S CRITIQUE OF *VITA CONTEMPLATIVA*

The employment of the term "encounter" (*riscontro*) in the theory of fortuna indicates the appropiation of the Aristotelian insight that the logical space of events is a space of theoretical indeterminacy in view of extra-theoretical encounters. But the unprincipled and ungrounded character of the encounter or event between human praxis and its circumstances offers the opportunity to think a radical emancipation of praxis from the theoretical imperative, present in both Aristotle and Boethius, to recognize the goodness of order and bring about its presence wherever it is lacking. In Machiavelli action is freed for a completely different purpose: that of engaging the times in order to bring about their change. The world of human things becomes a function of the contingency of every order found in it.

To demonstrate this far-reaching thesis requires an analysis of the kind of relation between action and times that composes their encounter or *riscontro*. The *Ghiribizzi* text seems, at first sight, to indicate that such a relation is one of identity or homology. After all Machiavelli writes that any mode of proceeding "is unhappy which diverges [*si diversifica*] with its actions from time [*tempo*] and

---

[24] Ibid.
[25] Ibid.
[26] Ibid., IV,7.
[27] Ibid., IV,7 and IV,3.

the order of things." It is standard for interpreters to read Machiavelli's theory of fortuna as calling for actions that are adequate to the circumstances in the sense that they follow along with what the times demand. The theory of the *riscontro* would thus be nothing but a call for opportunism.[28] Except, of course, for the fact that Machiavelli asserts repeatedly that thoroughgoing opportunism is impossible because one cannot change one's way of proceeding in the world according to the change of circumstances.[29] This impossibility explains why all human affairs exhibit a motion with "ups and downs" and why everyone seems to be nailed to the wheel of fortune.[30]

But there is a completely different reason for rejecting the interpretation of the concept of *riscontro* in terms of the correspondence between action and times. The last passage of the *Ghiribizzi* offers a glimpse of it. In light of this passage, the sense of the encounter (*riscontro*) appears to be the opposite of what has been understood traditionally: the encounter refers to the event in which a given situation is changed in virtue of the collision between action and times. The meaning of the encounter is that of a transformation of, rather than a correspondence to, what is given. In other words, the match or *riscontro* should not be conceived analogously to the correspondence between thought and reality, subject and object, in the theoretical sense, but to an opposition between action and situation that seeks to transcend and change it in a practical sense. The most proper content of the *riscontro* expresses a discordance between human modes and times such that the action which has a "happy" result[31] is precisely that which brushes against the grain of time, the action that innovates or revolutionizes the

---

[28] Skinner, for instance, understands the theory of the *riscontro* as if it advocates the ideal of the "wise man": "The moral is obvious: if a man wishes 'always to enjoy good Fortune,' he must 'be wise enough to accommodate himself to the times.'…. [Machiavelli] endorses the conventional assumption that virtù is the name of that congeries of qualities which enables a prince to ally with Fortune to obtain honour, glory and fame. But he divorces the meaning of the term from any necessary connection with the cardinal and princely virtues. He argues instead that the defining characteristic of a truly *virtuoso* prince will be a willingness to do whatever is dictated by necessity… in order to attain his highest ends. So virtù comes to denote the requisite quality of moral flexibility in a prince." (Skinner, *Machiavelli*, 39-40).

[29] Pitkin's treatment of fortuna in Machiavelli's corpus is admirable for showing the diversity of beliefs Machiavelli associates with fortuna on different occasions, and for highlighting the undeniable tensions, if not contradictions, between these beliefs. But Pitkin also gives up on the possibility of giving a philosophical sense to the one, constant explanation of fortuna Machiavelli offers with the theory of the *riscontro*. According to Pitkin, Machiavelli's discourse "leads repeatedly to the teaching that success depends on suiting one's style of action to the times; which, in turn, is soon followed by the observation that men are unable to change their style of action. There is, moreover, a third layer of ambiguity about the units of analysis to be employed: whose fortune is at stake, and how are the fortunes and virtù of some related to those of others? Both the second and third layer of ambiguity tend to push Machiavelli back toward the assumption he initially most wanted to challenge: that fortune's power might be total and absolute; yet he cannot rest content with that as a conclusion; so a final layer of ambiguity concerns the limits of fortune's power, and the whole meditation repeatedly starts over." (Pitkin, *Fortune is a woman*, 155-156). The "ambiguities" of which Pitkin speaks are more than anything indicative of the contrasting, and always partial, readings offered by interpreters. This and the following chapters demonstrate that all these so-called "ambiguities" have a reason for existing as moments of Machiavelli's argument, which is both unitary and cogent.

[30] Machiavelli, *Discourses on Livy*, II, preface; idem, *The Golden Ass*, ch. 5; idem, *Della Fortuna*.

[31] Machiavelli uses the term "felice," happy, to qualify the person who finds their match with the times, but this sense of happiness is neither that of classical *eudaimonia* nor Christian blessedness: it refers to the feeling of having been a match for the situation and come out of it unvanquished.

situation.[32] This idea of the *riscontro* alone fits with all the other texts where a positive value is given to radical political change, to the *mutazione di stato*, and to those texts that advocate the conflict between political virtù and fortuna.[33]

If my interpretation of the sense of the *riscontro* is correct, what can one make of the pessimistic note sounded in the *Ghiribizzi*? Sasso claims that this text betrays the radical pessimism of Machiavelli with regard to the capacity of the individual's virtù to withstand fortuna because the coincidence (*riscontro*) of the human mode of proceeding and the situation (the times) ultimately depends on fortuna and not on human virtù. According to Sasso, Machiavelli renounces the idea that there exists "good" and "bad" virtù, an effective virtù which is able to defeat fortuna and a weak virtù which succumbs to it.[34] If the mode of proceeding is going to succeed, it will need its *riscontro*, independently of the quality of the virtù, and the *riscontro* depends on chance (*il caso*).

Sasso's interpretation implicitly falls into the Boethian trap of doubling the sense of fortuna: the *riscontro* accounts for varying fortunes and allows fortuna to be seen as a result; but the *riscontro* is itself a product of fortuna, which then is seen as cause.[35] Machiavelli's innovation would consist in the reason for positing fortuna as cause: not because it is a mythical and providential force but because human virtù exhibits intrinsic "limits" that can be identified with the idea of an unchanging and fixed human "nature" advanced in the *Ghiribizzi*. Fortuna is no longer a goddess, the hypostatized cause of chance found in the Roman and Christian traditions, but the consequence of an intrinsic limit of human nature, and is thus unconquerable.[36] Because fortuna is still identified as the hegemonic force of historical change Sasso denies that Machiavelli's discourse exhibits a modern concept of history.

---

[32] It is much too little to say, for example, that for Machiavelli the human being is "a turner of events. Whatever the precise shape of his response... he can turn events in only one of two ways: either right side up or wrong side up, to his advantage or disadvantage." (Orr, "Time motif in Machiavelli," 192).
[33] I discuss the former texts part 3, ch.3 and the latter in part 2, ch. 3.
[34] Sasso, *Niccolò Machiavelli*, 230-240. For a useful review of the debate on whether virtù can govern fortuna, and vice versa, see O. Balaban, "The Human Origins of Fortuna in Machiavelli's Thought," *History of Political Thought*, XI, no.1 (1990): 21-36; and Brown, *Manhood and Politics*, ch.5. Sasso, Balaban and Brown share the view that fortuna is a by-product of the character of human action. As Brown says: "[fortuna] is thus the amalgamated consequences, a reified expression of the effects of man's rigidity and subjectivity in a world that moves more quickly and divergently than his own understanding and capacity to adapt to it." (Ibid., 114). As I discuss below, I agree with this formulation but differ on what exactly this "rigid" human character is.
[35] Sasso's reading is not without textual support. For example, in *Discourses on Livy*, III,8 Machiavelli asserts that "fortuna varies because she varies the times and he does not vary his ways." In his commentary to the *Discourses on Livy*, Giorgio Inglese writes that "the fortuna [as effect] of an individual varies, because Fortuna [as cause] changes the quality of the times and the individual does not change his ways.... The logical position of fortuna presents itself as doubled. On the one hand, 'being lucky' is explained in the happy or unhappy *riscontro* of one's way of proceeding with the quality of the time or context; on the other hand, Fortuna (as a substantive) is identified with the cause of the change of times, that is, as the mutability of the world itself." (Niccolò Machiavelli, *Discorsi*, ed. Giorgio Inglese [Milan: Rizzoli, 1984], 601).
[36] Lefort coincides with Sasso's interpretation of the *riscontro*: "Happiness and misfortune are not only our work, they are the fruits of an encounter. Even though it is up to us to cease the occasion, the encounter is a gift; and of this gift there is nothing to be said, its origin is unknowable." (Lefort, *Travail de l'oeuvre*, 442). For all that, fortuna does not become a mythical principle that governs worldly affairs. (Ibid., 443).

Although I am in agreement with Sasso's general point that Machiavelli destroys the mythical conception of fortuna by explaining historical change through the theory of the *riscontro*, I consider the further claim that Machiavelli's thinking about history derives from an ahistorical set of assumptions about human "nature" to be false. Attributing a wholesale naturalism to Machiavelli is perhaps the central obstacle to understanding how it discloses the horizon of modern historical consciousness. Sasso's reading of the *Ghiribizzi* is simply one-sided: by assuming as a given that the times change by themselves it hands over to fortuna, conceived as cause, the very possibility of the encounter (*riscontro*) between action and times that constitutes historical change. In this way, Sasso forecloses the possibility that free political action is the agent of the change of times, thereby separating Machiavelli's concept of politics from its internal relation to history, leaving it imprisoned within the strictures of a pessimistic and naturalistic anthropology, i.e., a discourse on the "limits" of human "nature."

I propose to consider the pessimistic aspects of Machiavelli's theory of fortuna as elements in the critique of the priority of *vita contemplativa*, of the claims made by wisdom (understood in the wide acceptation of *sophia* and *phronesis*) regarding the possibilities of human action in the central traditions of classical and Christian philosophy. In other words, I suggest that Machiavelli's seemingly pessimistic understanding of fortuna is one of the inaugural instances of the critique of the classical notion of wisdom and the consequent revolution in the relation between theory and practice that one associates with the modern thought of Bruno, Hobbes or Descartes. The argument consists of two parts. Machiavelli assigns a privilege to fortuna over prudence only in order to show the non-derivative character of contingency in the order of things. Seen from the perspective of contemplation or theory, contingency appears to be primordial with respect to necessity. But viewed from the practical perspective the primacy of contingency gives an enlarged scope to the power of action, which can change and revolutionize the orders of things because these are no longer rooted in purportedly necessary structures accessible only to contemplation.

The classical notion of contemplation (*theorein*) expresses the possibility of a conformity (*homologia*) between knower and known, thinking and being, in accordance to the ancient saying that "like knows like," of which an exemplary instance is found in the *Republic*:

Neither sight itself nor that in which it comes to be – what we call the eye – is the sun... but I suppose it is the most sun-formed of the organs.... Say that the sun is the offspring of the good I mean – an offspring the good begot in proportion with itself: as the good is in the intelligible region with respect to intelligence and what is intellected, so the sun is in the visible region with respect to sight and what is seen.[37]

By positing the Good as the highest Idea, *epekeina tes ousias*, Plato establishes a circular relation between the ideality of the Good and the goodness of Ideality. The Idea or Form (*eidos*) provides a model or standard for human action which lies beyond the domain of events (the horizon of circumstances) and is accessible

---

[37] Plato *Republic* 508b.

only theoretically. The Idea is good because it allows human action to confront its circumstances by shaping itself in such a way that it will always correspond to them, i.e., by letting itself be in-formed by the theoretical knowledge of the Idea. It is in this sense alone that the action is "fitting" or "good." Conversely, the possibility of a permanent correspondence (*homologia*) of actions to times is kept open only if the Good does not fall into the purview of the circumstances themselves, only if it can never be found in the here and now, in actuality. In other words, the possibility of correspondence between action and times presupposes the ideality of the Good.

For Plato the belief in the possibility of a correspondence between action and times has two basic political variants. In the first, found in the *Republic*, the search for the continuous fit between action and times leads to the tyranny of the philosopher because no laws, obeyed by all, can express such a fit or embody such a knowledge. In the second variant, found in the *Statesman* and in the *Laws*, the ideal of a correspondence between action and times is given up as something that cannot be realized, even by a philosopher-king. A second-best solution is found in the establishment of a code of laws that is completely fixed and, in this sense, impervious to circumstances: this solution amounts to mimicking (providing a simulacrum) at the political level the relation between the domain of the Ideas (form) and that of circumstances (event).

The ancient presupposition of homology that establishes the rights of contemplation in political life is absent in the argument of the *Ghiribizzi*. This text insists on the fundamental disconformity between human "nature" and what stands against it, namely "the times" and "the orders of things." This disconformity is thematized most pointedly by the assertions concerning the fixity of human "nature" and the mutability of times and orders. Conformity (*homologia*) between these two spheres is impossible. Indeed, the text never states that human modes and times simply conform; rather, it says that the success of action depends on "conforming oneself with one's *riscontro*." The conformity is secondary with respect to the *riscontro*, that is, to the conflict between modes and times.[38] The theory of the *riscontro* calls for a conformity to the facticity of the difference, in opposition to the Platonic ideality of the identity, between action and circumstances. The facticity of the situated character of human action is primary with respect to every attempt to transcend this situation. There is no providential underpinning to the confrontation between action and circumstances, no order or form that precedes and sublates their conflict.

Machiavelli rejects the primacy of *homologia* presupposed by the claims of contemplation on two grounds. He denies that there can be a cognition of the *logos* by which times change (and this, in turn, because times do not change according to a *logos* but to a *praxis*). Furthermore, he denies that human "nature" can change, under rational motivation, such that it could correspond to the changes in the times. Given these new conditions, it is no longer possible to achieve a correspondence between action and circumstances based on the primacy of the conditions of the contemplative attitude.

---

[38] The word for "match" or "encounter" in Italian, *riscontro*, contains within itself the term for "conflict" or "clash": *scontro*.

The idea that the "pessimistic" conclusion of the *Ghiribizzi* is exclusively directed against the presuppositions of every discourse that maintains the priority of the *vita contemplativa* over the *vita activa*, of theory over praxis, confronts two possible objections. First, how does one square the rigidity of human "nature," taken in conjunction with the assertion of the contingency of the times, with a critique of the contemplative attitude? Second, what function does the pessimism of Machiavelli's critique of wisdom, i.e., the idea that fortuna controls the destiny of individuals, have in relation to his positive theory of praxis?

The mutability of times and circumstances is a crucial factor in the critique of wisdom because it implies that there is no *logos* to the change of times. Machiavelli would have adhered to the Shakespearian formula "time is out of joint," i.e., to the idea that the link between the order of time and the order of the cosmos is broken. The *Ghiribizzi* nowhere asserts or implies that the "times" are predetermined by an order that is knowable theoretically, e.g., by the cyclical processes of the *kosmos*, however construed.[39] Seen from the perspective of contemplation, this entails that the times and their changes are radically contingent and unpredictable: Machiavelli eliminates the possibility for any dianoetic virtue (including Aristotelian *phronesis*) to grasp the "right time" (*kairos*) in which it is possible to do the "right thing."[40] That fortuna exerts ultimate control over human existence is a valid proposition only in relation to the claims of wisdom because "there are no such wise men" who can "command the stars and the fates." It is crucial that the validity of the proposition is relative to the point of view of contemplation: it does not mean that, in absolute terms, there is such a thing as fatality and that the motions of the stars determine the course of history; nor that there exists a divine providence (identified with an intellect standing higher than the stars). As I argue in the next chapter, these are imaginary constructs that are brought into play in an attempt to explain, under the theoretical register, what is devoid of such an explanation in reality, namely, the possibility that the times or circumstances can only be changed by the polemical encounter with human action. This polemical encounter may happen or may not happen (in this sense it is radically contingent and inaccessible to *theorein*), but either way it does not admit of an antecedent cause, of a determination that is accessible, always already, through contemplation. For Machiavelli, it is impossible to match

---

[39] For example, Machiavelli nowhere links the change of times with the ordered, and therefore intelligible motions of the heavens, pace Parel. This interpreter argues, erroneously as I show below, that Machiavelli's discourse is based on "premodern cosmological assumptions," above all the idea that "everything that happens in history, then, happens according to the laws of cosmic motion. Strictly speaking history is a conjoint product of cosmic and human motions, in which the one plays the superior, and the other, the subordinate role." (Parel, "Machiavelli's Modernity," 322).

[40] Aristotle employs the expression: "the goal of an action reflects the occasion [*to de telos tes praxeus kata ton kairon estin*]." (Aristotle *Nicomachean Ethics* 1110a14). For Aristotle's discussion of the "right time" or *kairos*, see *Nicomachean Ethics* 1096a25-35, where he speaks of the "science of the opportune moment," and ibid., 1106b15-25, where the very definition of virtue includes an internal relation to the "right time" and, in general, to the right circumstances. Aubenque claims that already in Pindar (*Nemean Odes* III ,74-5) one finds the concept of a faculty or sense, termed *phronein*, that allows human beings to "do what is good in time." (Aubenque, *Prudence chez Aristote*, 105). In any case, it is a mistake to identify Aristotelian *kairos* with Machiavellian *occasione*, as in Held, "Civic prudence in Machiavelli," 123-124.

actions with the times on the basis of a principle (*arche*) that is itself independent
of circumstances; the match (*riscontro*) is not an object of wisdom or prudence.

To the radical indeterminacy of the times (but, again, an indeterminacy which
is relative to the contemplative attitude alone) there corresponds an equal and
opposite radical determinacy of human modes of conduct, of human "nature." I
suggest that this deterministic thesis also has validity only in so far as it serves to
counter the claims of wisdom. In classical thought the Protean capacity to change
or elect one's nature is an expression of the priority assigned to the contemplative
perspective, in accord with the Platonic-Aristotelian re-elaboration of the
Heraclitean notion that "the soul, in a certain way, is all things."[41] Although the
belief that one's nature is changeable seems to pertain to practice, in reality it
belongs wholly within the discursive requirements of the primacy of theory over
practice. The mutability of the soul is a function of its knowledge: for the soul, in
order that it may know something, must "become" (like) it, must receive the form
of the thing. Hence the change of the soul (i.e., its Protean capacity) is actually a
sign of its passivity in relation to "that which is" (given to it).[42]

Machiavelli's discourse employs determinism to attack the classical idea of the
mutability of the soul because it ultimately wants to reject the underlying passivity
of the contemplative attitude. This capital point can be illustrated by considering
Pico's *Oration on the Dignity of Man*, which is exemplary of the Renaissance
attempt to achieve a syncretistic vision of the Neo-Platonic and the Christian
conceptions of the soul. In all probability Machiavelli knew Pico's text; in any
case the argument of the *Ghiribizzi* questions its central assumptions.[43] According
to the myth of creation recounted by Pico, human beings were fashioned by God
without an archetype or form because this was His last creation and all the
archetypes had been used up. Thus "the best of artisans ordained that the creature
to whom He had been able to give nothing proper to himself should have joint
possession of whatever had been peculiar to each of the different kinds of
beings."[44] The human being is a "creature of indeterminate nature," i.e., which
does not have a proper essence. It lacks a "fixed abode," a proper "form" and "any
function peculiar to thyself" but this lack is in turn the support for an excess: the

---

[41] Aristotle *De anima* 431b21. In Plato, the possibility of choosing one's "nature" or character of soul
is discussed in the Myth of Er: "A demon will not select you, but you will choose a demon... to which
he will be bound by necessity. Virtue is without a master; as he honors or dishonors her, each will
have more or less of her. The blame belongs to him who chooses; god is blameless." (Plato *Republic*
616e). Aristotle interprets Heraclitus's *ethos anthropon daimon* (fr.119 DK) in a less predetermined
fashion: character (*ethos*) is a product of habits (*ethe*) that are acquired through actions (as opposed
to once and for all, as in Plato's myth) and which, in turn, determine the capacity to act in different
ways. (Aristotle *Nicomachean Ethics* II,1).

[42] This point is elegantly made by Brague's analysis of perception and intellection in Aristotle, where
he comments on Aristotle's use of the phrase "the soul, in a certain way, is all things": "Presence
comports two inseparable aspects: things are there, and we are there – we are the there of things [nous
sommes le là des choses]. Things are there for us and affect us: we are, in this sense, passive; but they
are there because we are there to let ourselves be affected by them, and in this sense we are active."
(Remi Brague, *Aristote et la question du monde*, [Paris: PUF, 1988], 355). But this activity, of course,
is that of the soul in so far as it contemplates (in perception or intellection), not in so far as it acts.

[43] Sasso acknowledges the opposition between Pico's *Oration* and Machiavelli's *Ghiribizzi*, but does
not delve into its details. (Sasso, *Niccolò Machiavelli*, 236).

[44] Pico della Mirandola, *Oration on the Dignity of Man*, in *The Renaissance Philosophy of Man*, ed.
E. Cassirer, P.O. Kristeller, and J.H. Randall (Chicago: University of Chicago Press, 1948), 244.

individual is allowed "with thine own free will" to set "limits" to its nature, that is, to take the place, form and function that it judges best. In short, the human being gives itself a limit, unlike all other creatures whose limits are prescribed by the laws of God. "We have made thee neither of heaven nor of earth, neither mortal nor immortal, so that with freedom of choice and with honor, as though the maker and molder of thyself, thou mayest fashion thyself in whatever shape thou shalt prefer."[45] The only essential attribute of the human being is its freedom of choice to make itself into whatever it desires. It seems that Pico asserts that in the case of the human being not only is there a priority of existence over essence, as it were, but also of freedom over nature: "To him it is granted to have whatever he chooses, to be whatever he wills."[46]

The apparent modernity of Pico's vision of human freedom is tempered if one considers the cosmological structure within which the individual is given this freedom by the "supreme generosity of God the Father." It is true that for Pico the human being is unlike both lower and higher beings in the chain of Being because its essence is not determined prior to what it makes of itself. But the possibilities for such self-fashioning are already given: "On man when he came into life the Father conferred the seeds of all kinds and the germs of every way of life. Whatever seeds each man cultivates will grow to maturity and bear in him their own fruit."[47] These seeds range from the vegetative, through the intellectual (in which the human being is angel and son of God), all the way to the unification with God, in which the individual transcends its state of creatureliness and becomes one with the Maker. "Who would not admire this our chameleon? It is man who Asclepius of Athens, arguing from his mutability of character and from his self-transforming nature, on just grounds was symbolized by Proteus in the mysteries."[48] The human being as "Proteus" and as "chameleon" stands in stark contrast with both the Aristotelian and Machiavellian conceptions of humanity. Aristotle criticizes the chameleon-like indeterminacy of the individual as a sign of instability of character and thus of lack of virtue.[49] For different reasons, having to do with a polemic with Pico on the character of human freedom rather than on ethical virtue, Machiavelli in the *Ghiribizzi* equally wants to deny to the individual its chameleon-like indeterminacy.

The freedom that Pico ascribes to human beings is of a peculiar kind: it is the freedom to move up and down the chain of Being, taking up for itself the forms

---

[45] Ibid., 225.

[46] Ibid. See the classic interpretation of Pico offered by Ernst Cassirer in *The Individual and the Cosmos in Renaissance Philosophy* (Philadelphia: University of Pennsylvania Press, 1963), ch.3. In contrast to my interpretation, Cassirer believes that Pico and Machiavelli share a common horizon: "both Machiavelli and Alberti [in positing an opposition between virtù and fortuna] are voicing the sentiments of their Florentine circle," i.e., of the Platonic Academy of Ficino and Pico. (Ibid., 77). In any case, Cassirer assigns a more radical idea of human freedom to Pico than to Machiavelli: "The Renaissance was, in its feelings and its thoughts, under the strong pressure of astrology. With the sole exception of Pico della Mirandola no Renaissance thinker could avoid or overcome this pressure. The life of such a great and noble mind as Ficino was still filled with superstitious astrological fears. Even Machiavelli could not entirely free himself from astrological conceptions." (Cassirer, *Myth of the State*, 158-159).

[47] Pico, *Oration*, 225.

[48] Ibid.

[49] Aristotle *Nicomachean Ethics* 1100b6-7.

that are available therein (or, at best, the "form" of He who gives form, namely God). The individual is not free to create itself ex nihilo but merely free to actualize any of the given, infinite, potentialities it is granted when first made. Pico explicitly says that human freedom is expressed in terms of the capacity for metamorphosis; but this means that the freedom in question is one of adaptation to given forms, not to create new forms or to change the order of the cosmos in any way. The picture that Pico gives is at bottom a contemplative one: it is based on the fundamental assumption that, through knowledge, one becomes like the thing that is known. Put another way, the human being becomes what it is only relative to the kind of function (vegetative, sensitive, rational, divine) that it chooses to develop.

In short, for Pico the soul changes form, but only in relation to a cosmic order (or chain of Being) which is fixed for all time. In Machiavelli, instead, the order of things is radically contingent and mutable, at least within the world of human things, and the world of eternal things, if there is such a thing for him, is never mentioned as being pertinent to the conduct of human life. The only eternity that Machiavelli conceives of is that of "the world," and this ultimately resolves into the eternity of becoming.[50] The world of Machiavelli, with its lack of teleology, has less in common with the cosmos of Pico and Ficino, and their transpositions of the Platonic and Aristotelian cosmologies, than with the concepts of world that Bruno, Descartes and Spinoza develop later.[51]

But there is more to Machiavelli's strategic adoption of the fixity of human "nature" than the role it fulfills in a critique of the theoretical picture of the soul presupposed by the paradigms of classical and Christian wisdom. The *Ghiribizzi* characterize human "nature" through the radical individuality of its faculties of *ingegno* and *fantasia*. To speak of these faculties is already to refer to the capacity of self-invention that bespeaks the non-existence of something like a human "nature" understood in an essentialist sense. The uniqueness of *ingegno* and *fantasia* in each *animo* (as the trait that makes of this human being an individual) constitutes a denial of the picture of the soul (*psyche*) whose highest faculty is the active intellect in its Aristotelian, and then Averroistic, sense of an intellect (*nous*) that is detached, in principle, from the body and its individualizing function: a picture of the soul that is reprised in Pico's *Oration*. The analogy made in the *Ghiribizzi* between the diversity of human spirits (*animi*) and that of human faces

---

[50] "Human things are always in motion, either they ascend or they descend.... I judge the world always to have been in the same mode and there to have been as much good as wicked in it. But the wicked and the good vary from province to province, as is seen by one who has knowledge of those ancient kingdoms, which varied from one to another because of the variations of customs, though the world remained the same." (Machiavelli, *Discourses on Livy*, II, preface). See also the discussion of the eternity of the world in *Discourses on Livy*, II,5. Another work would have to be dedicated to a thorough exploration of Machiavelli's understanding of the world and its relation to historical becoming. For the best discussion of Machiavelli's approach to the problem of the eternity of the world, see Sasso, *Machiavelli e gli antichi*, 1:177-399.

[51] The conception of "world" in early modern thought is too vast a topic to engage here. Nonetheless, as the work of Duhem, Koyré, Popper, Blumenberg et al. shows, modern cosmology and positive natural science require the concept of the radical contingency of "orders of things" as a condition of possibility for the mathematization of the world. From this perspective one could begin to develop another argument that would see in Machiavelli's insistence on the contingency of the "times" and "orders of things" a sign of the modernity of his discourse.

(*volti*) stands in radical contrast to the metamorphosis of the individual into other creatures hailed by Pico. Machiavelli's analogy illustrates the non-transcendable status of the finite individual.

At this point the real problem of interpretation emerges: what leads Machiavelli to ascribe the fixed and immutable character of these radically individualizing faculties of *ingegno* and *fantasia*? After all, both of these faculties are characterized by a capacity of invention that seems to belie any fixity in human "nature." The paradox can be resolved by understanding this fixity as an assumption that serves Machiavelli's purpose of warding off the claims of wisdom as to the possibility of an a priori conformity or correspondence (*homoiosis, homologia*) between human "nature" and the "orders of things," so as to emancipate (from its theoretical overdetermination) the human capacity to cope through invention, ingenuity and imagination with the contingency of the world as such.

This reconstruction of the argument in the *Ghiribizzi* gives it a pragmatic stamp because it presupposes that the ability to cope successfully with the world not only expresses a priority of practice over theory, but depends on the reiterated experience of the fundamental discontinuity between the self and the world.[52] For if there were to exist a predetermined continuity (*homoiosis*) between them, no coping would be needed in the first place, and the contemplative attitude would be necessary and sufficient for happiness, and indeed would have to be taken as the standard for all human praxis, as occurs in Plato and Aristotle, through Boethius and Dante, all the way to Pico and Ficino. If the world were like the contemplative attitude sees it, there would exist no need or possibility for projects which acquire their "thrown" character precisely because nothing about the world or about the self assures these projects of a fundamental "correspondence" or "harmony" with reality.

The apparent privilege of the power of fortuna over human action in the *Ghiribizzi* is only the first move in a complex argument that intends to break with the captivity of the possibilities of action by its dependency on theory. One can say that Machiavelli's privilege of chance (*tyche*) indicates an impotence of intellect (*nous*) in view of unleashing the capacities withheld by will, imagination and ingenuity (*metis*). Far from giving too much power to *tyche*/fortuna, Machiavelli instead prepares the ground for the modern re-elaboration of the internal

---

[52] Blumenberg argues for a similar understanding of the relation between theory and practice at the origin of modernity: "Thus 'self-assertion' here does not mean the naked biological or economic preservation of the human organism by the means naturally available to it. It means an existential program, according to which man posits his existence in a historical situation and indicates to himself how he is going to deal with the reality surrounding him and what use he will make of the possibilities that are open to him." (Blumenberg, *The Legitimacy of the Modern Age*, 138). It is interesting to note that Blumenberg identifies in Nietzsche the highest exponent of this modern attitude which privileges practice over contemplation because of the idea that "the destruction of trust in the world made him [the individual] for the first time a creatively active being, freed him from a disastrous lulling of his activity." (Ibid., 138). Lastly, Blumenberg expresses what I take to be the basic intuition behind Machiavelli's critique of the classical world-view in the *Ghiribizzi*: "The cosmos of the ancient world and of the metaphysical tradition – in other words: the belief that one is confronted throughout reality with what is already 'finished', that all one can really do is either adapt oneself to this order or violate it, determining thereby nothing but one's happiness or unhappiness – this cosmos proves in retrospect to be precisely what Nietzsche was to call 'the most crippling belief for hand and reason'." (Ibid., 220).

relation between *techne* and *tyche* that perhaps is already envisaged in the Greek understanding of *metis*[53] but was kept in abeyance by classical thought after Plato thanks to its insistence on the priority of the contemplative life.[54]

Machiavelli's strategic adherence to a belief in the fixity of human "nature," the belief that human beings cannot "command their own nature," by no means signals acquiescence to a deterministic naturalism. On the contrary, this fixity is the presupposition that allows his discourse to posit the primordiality of the conflict (*riscontro*) between human modes of factical existence and the "orders of things" that accounts for their historical constructibility and deconstructibility. The constructivist approach to the problem of order is simply not possible without the destruction of the classical *harmonia praestabilita* between subject and object established on the basis of a priority of the contemplative attitude.[55]

A similar interpretation can be given to the other reason adduced by Machiavelli to deny the claims of wisdom through the appeal to the fixity of human "nature," namely, the lack of foresight in human beings. To read this thesis as a simple affirmation of determinism is to misunderstand the strategic role it plays in the overall argument. The lack of foresight in human beings expresses the unsurpassable horizon of circumstances for the sphere of human praxis. It means that human beings do not have a faculty that allows them to transcend the historically situated character of their action, i.e., the event-like encounter between the action and the circumstances that surround it. They do not have a noetic capacity (which is also a pro-vidential capacity = *pro-noia*) to perceive what is going to happen before it happens. The belief that the intellect (*nous*) can be raised, beyond the unconditioned eventness of the situation of action (*tyche*), to the plane of form (*eidos, ousia*) is a fundamental belief common to classical and Christian thought. The rejection of this belief in the *Ghiribizzi* confirms Machiavelli's essential innovation: in human affairs the domain of the form falls within the horizon of the domain of the event because all forms emerge and disappear as a result of the conflictual encounter between the interiority of human action (rooted in the desires of the *animo*) and the exteriority of historical circumstances.

In conclusion, the idea that human beings "cannot command their nature" should be read as an indication of Machiavelli's attention to the facticity of human existence rather than as a sign of a deterministic and naturalistic anthropology. For what cannot be commanded or regulated (at least not by theoretical reason) is precisely the "fact" that the freedom of action is for the individual its "nature." More exactly, as I showed in part one, what cannot be commanded is the interplay between the two fundamental drives or desires in human beings: the desire to dominate and the desire for freedom. My reading of the role played by the assumption that human "nature" is fixed fits with Machiavelli's ascription of the "opinion" expressed by the *Ghiribizzi* to the perspective of the "many," to their

---

[53] The saying "art loves luck and luck loves art" comes from the logical space of *metis* rather than *nous* or *phronesis*.

[54] For indications in this sense, see Detienne and Vernant, *Les Ruses de l'Intelligence*.

[55] Machiavelli's use of the terms *ingegno, fantasia, animo* to carry out the critique of wisdom is repeated by all the major thinkers of early modernity. It is sufficient to think of Descartes's and Gracián's elaboration of *ingenium*, or Spinoza's and Hobbes's redescription of Machiavelli's *animo* into *conatus*, or, finally, Vico's elaboration of *fantasia* as the basic human symbolical capacity.

desire for freedom, to how this desire is the subject-matter of political action, and to how this desire stands counter both to the idea of an end-state of things (natural teleology) and to the irrational belief in the omnipotence of fortuna. Themes which I am now in a position to take up in more detail and from the perspective opened up by the problem of the Ghiribizzi.

CHAPTER 3

HISTORY AS EFFECT OF FREE ACTION:
FORTUNA AND VIRTÙ IN *THE PRINCE*

THE CONFLICT BETWEEN VIRTÙ AND FORTUNA AS MODERN HORIZON OF HISTORY

The conflict between virtù and fortuna is identified by Cassirer as the "ultimate root, to which we must always return if we would comprehend in their true depth the philosophical doctrines of the Renaissance concerning the relationship between freedom and necessity."[1] Notoriously, at the close of *The Prince* Machiavelli proposes his version of this conflict by asserting that "fortuna is a woman," and "if one desires to keep her down" it becomes "necessary to beat her."[2] In this chapter I argue that Machiavelli's formula gives expression to a modern conception of history as effect of free human action.

Of all the interpreters of Machiavelli, perhaps no one has made a stronger case for the importance of the question of chance in political philosophy than Leo Strauss.[3] According to Strauss, the belief that "fortuna is a woman who can be controlled by the use of force" is the inaugural formula of modernity.[4] He contrasts this belief with that of classical political philosophy according to which "the establishment of the best regime depends necessarily on uncontrollable, elusive fortuna or chance."[5] The reason why the ancients maintain that the best regime depends on chance is that the standard for the best regime is ideal and there is a radical separation (*chorismos*) between ideal and real. There is no "reason" (*logos*) that can bridge the *chorismos* between the ideality of the good (the domain of form) and the facticity of the real (the domain of matter and of events): the ideal can realize itself in the real only "by chance." Strauss interprets Machiavelli's formula to mean that chance can be "controlled by the use of force," and as such understands it as the rejection of the belief, held by classical political philosophy, that "man's power is limited," that "the limitations of his nature" cannot be overcome, and finally that "this limitation shows itself in particular in the ineluctible power of chance."[6] For the ancients the limitation of human beings corresponds to the fact that these beings belong in the teleological order of nature:

---

[1] Cassirer, *Individual and the Cosmos,* 75.
[2] Machiavelli, *The Prince,* XXV.
[3] For further discussion of the question of chance in contemporary political theory, I refer to the literature cited in the Afterword.
[4] Strauss, "Three Waves of Modernity," 84.
[5] Ibid., 85.
[6] Ibid., 86.

there is a specific perfection which belongs to each specific nature.... Nature supplies the standard, a standard wholly independent of man's will; this implies that nature is good.... The good life is the life according to nature, which means to stay within certain limits: virtue is essentially moderation.[7]

Moderation here stands for *sophrosyne*, which Aristotle renders as what "saves prudence [*sozousan ten phronesin*]."[8] Strauss's reading confirms the analysis of the fundamental correspondence found in classical thought between prudence (virtue oriented toward the good) and the respect of chance that I gave in the first part.

For Strauss, Machiavelli's thesis "rejects the whole philosophic and theological tradition" in the sense that both classical ("Athens") and Judeo-Christian ("Jerusalem") thought are in agreement with regard to the secondary or derivative place held by human beings in the order of things: for the latter, righteousness is compliance with the "divinely established order;" for the former, justice "is compliance with the natural order."[9] To "the recognition of elusive chance" which follows from the conception of justice of "Athens," there corresponds "the recognition of inscrutable providence" which follows that of "Jerusalem."[10] Strauss concludes that modern political philosophy emerges as a function of Machiavelli's rejection of both the divine and the natural foundations of political order.

The assertion of the conflict between human virtù and "elusive chance" entails a rejection of the classical belief that the scope of human action is limited by a predetermined, fixed and immutable order. But this interpretation raises the following question: does Machiavelli's critique of an ideal order, and of the ideal of order, intend to provide a new foundation to political order which would be neither divine nor natural; or does it provide a vision of political life that questions the very project of giving stable foundations to political order, i.e., that problematizes all attempts to secure and stabilize political order? Strauss's reading of Machiavelli's formulation of the conflict between virtù and fortuna upholds the first alternative. His claim is that Machiavelli's apparent "lowering" of the "standards" of virtue (from how one "ought" to live to "how men do live"), i.e., the rejection of an absolute difference between ideal and real, coupled with a privilege of the "technical" domination of chance in opposition to the "prudent" acceptance of its power over human beings, "guarantee for the solution of the political problem.... [because it] becomes a technical problem."[11] The reduction of politics to a technique for establishing, as effectively and securely as possible, political order would thus be Machiavelli's legacy.

Far from implying a technical conception of politics, I read the conflict between virtù and fortuna in light of the second alternative according to which the very project of giving stable foundations to political order is called into question. When Machiavelli establishes the ineluctible conflict between human action (virtù) and its circumstances (fortuna), he thereby discloses the possibility that political order

---

[7] Ibid., 85.
[8] Aristotle *Nicomachean Ethics* 1140b12.
[9] Strauss, "Three Waves of Modernity," 86-87.
[10] Ibid.
[11] Ibid., 87

emerges and is revoked in these encounters (events) between action and circumstances. The necessity of a given order can convert into its contingency, and, conversely, the contingent emergence of an order can acquire the traits of necessity, depending on the kind of relation established between human praxis and the times. Machiavelli's fundamental thesis that human action has the power to change its circumstances, the orders of the times, and not simply correspond to them, reverses the relation between form and event that one finds in classical political philosophy. The form is subject to the events in which human actions change the times: political form is historicized.

To support this interpretation I provide a detailed commentary of the twenty-fifth chapter of *The Prince*. Although it is one of the most cited topics, the discourse of fortuna in *The Prince* remains understudied: rarely does one find a close reading of the whole chapter in the secondary literature, and as a consequence there is a general tendency to ignore or miss its intricate rhetorical and argumentative structure.[12] The common procedure is to cite from different parts of the text without working through Machiavelli's discourse. This way of proceeding is full of perils because it disregards the dialectical style in which the text is written. One runs the risk of mistaking what is only the thesis or the antithesis of Machiavelli's actual point. It is equally fundamental to reconstruct the philosophical sources that the discourse implicitly refers to. Without keeping track of these references, it is more difficult to determine the structure of the argument, which is intimately tied to Machiavelli's engagement with, and sublation of, the tradition of politico-philosophical discussions of the question of chance.

An important justification for offering this commentary lies with my reconstruction of the historico-philosophical context of Machiavelli's argument. Only once it is situated in this context does the argument disclose its profound significance for modern historical consciousness. The main guiding-thread for the reconstruction of this context is my claim that Machiavelli's theory of fortuna constitutes a response to the ancient aporia of the Master Argument of Diodorus Cronus. The Master Argument constitutes the primary topos where the question of determinism and freedom is discussed from Aristotle to the early Renaissance. I argue that Machiavelli's discourse on fortuna begins the process of breaking away from the fundamental presupposition accepted by every solution to the Diodorean aporia in classical and Christian thought. All of these solutions share the presupposition that the modal difference between necessity and contingency is rooted in an ontology of substance or form (be it of natural or divine origin). This ontology sets a limit to human freedom because it makes the possibility of practical freedom depend upon the existence of contingent events, and gives to the latter a derivative, accidental status within the general ontological and cosmological framework. The result is dual: on the one hand, practical freedom cannot truly aim at "conquering" contingency, i.e., at changing the order of the times. On the

---

[12] An important exception is the recent commentary of *The Prince* by Gérald Sfez, *Machiavel, le prince sans qualités* (Paris: Kimé, 1998), ch.4, passim.

other hand, human freedom is ultimately understood to realize itself fully only in the contemplative life.[13]

Machiavelli rejects the above presupposition by rooting the modal difference between necessity and contingency in the domain of the event, rather than that of atemporal form, in view of emancipating human freedom from its ancient limits. The domain of the event consists in the change of times brought about by the collision between action and circumstances. The change of times is no longer an object of theoretical determination but a practical result that determines what is necessary and what is contingent on a temporal basis alone. The overturning of the classical priority of form over event goes hand in hand with the overturning of the priority of theory over practice, and leads to a definition of human freedom in terms of the capacity to transform what is contingent into what is necessary and conversely. In short, it allows human freedom to assert itself in and through the negation of every transcendent source of order. In this sense Machiavelli's theory of fortuna can be said to inaugurate modernity and its historical consciousness.

The twenty-fifth chapter of *The Prince* can be broken into three parts: the "optimistic" thesis in which there is a reference to the Master Argument and its solution offered by the classical theory of prudence; the "pessimistic" thesis in which the theory of the *riscontro* is rehearsed and the prudential solution criticized; and the synthesis in which both positions are sublated, and the new historico-philosophical horizon of the question of chance is articulated in terms of the internal relation between freedom and history that privileges practice over theory.

THE MASTER ARGUMENT AND THE OPTIMISTIC THESIS

Machiavelli begins his treatment of fortuna by voicing the opinion, that "has been and is held by many," according to which "things in the world are governed by fortuna and by God, that men with their prudence cannot correct them... and that because of this they could judge that it is not worth working up a sweat about things, but it is better to let oneself be governed by chance."[14] He admits to having been often "inclined" towards this fatalistic position himself. The formulation of this position sets apart, on one side, two transcendent causes of events, fortuna and God, and, on the other, human prudence. This division is meant to expose the powerlessness of human prudence against such causes, leading to the conclusion that it is better or easier to leave the conduct of one's life up to chance (*la sorte*). The coupling of fortuna and God in the government of the course of the world refers, first, to the idea that it makes no difference to the fatalistic attitude whether the course of the world is ultimately controlled by chance (fortuna) or necessity (God) because either one controls it absolutely. By coupling fortuna and God as the two transcendent causes of events the text is also calling forth the idea of

---

[13] This is the case even in Aristotle: see *Nicomachean Ethics* X,8; and *Metaphysics* 1075a19-22, where Aristotle compares the cosmos to a household in which free individuals are like the stars, moving in a fixed and rational order, whereas it is only for "slavish" natures to act "by chance" or in virtue of it.

[14] Machiavelli, *The Prince*, XXV. All further quotations in this chapter, unless otherwise noted, refer to this text.

providence. The reference is generic enough to contain both its classical and the Christian versions.

The implicit point is that every providential understanding of the domain of events always already sublates the grammar of prudence: if providence exists, then the difference between leading one's life in accordance with prudence or in accordance with chance is not a critical difference, precisely because prudence cannot break with providence. On the contrary, prudence presupposes one of the central traits of providence, namely, the idea that there exists an order in the world that is fixed independently of human action and that plays a determinant role in human affairs. Depending on how strong the conception of providence is, then the possibility of acting against chance by trying to master it may even be antithetical to prudent, moderate or virtuous behavior because it entails going against the divine order.[15]

This fatalistic beginning of the twenty-fifth chapter contains a reference to the so-called Lazy or Idle Argument (*argos logos, ratio ignava*) first introduced by Aristotle in *De Interpretatione* IX in the context of his refutation of Diodorus Cronus's Master Argument (*kurieon logos*). This reference, which has to my knowledge yet to be noted, is extremely significant because both the Master and Idle Arguments are central topics in the ancient debate on determinism, choice and the problem of future contingents.[16] The Idle Argument is present in Cicero's *De Fato* XII 28 – XIII 30 as well as in Boethius's *Consolation of Philosophy* VI, from where it spreads throughout medieval literature on divine providence and predetermination and reaches up to Florentine Neo-Platonic circles, i.e., up to the philosophical contemporaries of Machiavelli.[17]

The Master Argument emerges out of an aporia concerning modalities whose resolution by Diodorus amounts to an argument for determinism. The aporia consists in the demonstration of the incompatibility of the following premises: A) whatever is past and true is necessary, or: the past is irrevocable; B) the impossible does not follow from the possible; C) there are possibles that will never be actualized, or: possible is what is not true or will never be true; D) what is cannot not be during the time that it is, or: the principle of conditional necessity. Diodorus's Master Argument shows that premise C) must be rejected because it is contradictory that such a possible exist. In other words, the acceptance of A), B) and D) leads to the incompatibility of C).[18] Thus the Master Argument serves Diodorus to define the possible as what is true or what will be true, and therefore

---

[15] I refer to part 1, ch.1 and part 2, ch.2 for the discussion of providence in the classical and Christian traditions, and the internal relation between prudence and the "respect" for chance.

[16] It is remarkable that the secondary literature does not mention the Idle Argument in reference to the treatment of fortuna in *The Prince* XXV given the well-known opposition that Machiavelli's discourse makes between virtù and idleness (*ozio*), where the latter is seen as harbinger of ruin in a world where nothing stands still and becoming is eternal. (Machiavelli, *Discourses on Livy*, I,6 and idem, *Florentine Histories*, V,1).

[17] For the best historico-philosophical treatments of the Master Argument see Jules Vuillemin, *Nécessité ou contingence. L'aporie de Diodore et les systèmes philosophiques* (Paris: Les Editions de Minuit, 1984); Pierre-Maxime Schuhl, *Le Dominateur et les possibles* (Paris: PUF, 1960); and Richard Sorabji, *Necessity, Cause, and Blame*.

[18] I rely on the masterful discussion of the aporia given by Vuillemin, *Nécessité ou contingence*, ch. 2.

to imply that whatever happens does so of necessity. Diodorus's logical fatalism is closely related to the doctrines of the ancient Megarians that deny becoming on the ground that each essence (form) is a complete and self-enclosed universe that contains, since all eternity, everything that it will be or will happen to it. As Sorabji recapitulates the main issue: "Diodorus may have wanted to infect the future with the necessity which belongs to the past."[19] In short, the Master Argument is one of the most radical expressions of the priority of the form over the event in ancient thought.

From the Master Argument follows the Idle Argument: if everything that happens is necessary then there would be no need to deliberate or take trouble in the mistaken belief that if one does such and such, this will happen, but if one does not, it will not.[20] Aristotle's refutation of the Master Argument in *De Interpretatione* IX repeats the deterministic and "idle" consequences that follow from Diodorus's conception of the possible as what is or will be true:

These and others like them are the absurdities that follow if it is necessary, for every affirmation and negation either about universals spoken of universally or about particulars, that one of the opposites be true and the other false, and that nothing of what happens is as chance has it, but everything is and happens of necessity. So there would be no need to deliberate or take trouble (thinking that if we do this, this will happen, but if we do not, it will not).[21]

Aristotle's famous response to these "absurd" consequences is to assert their impossibility by appealing to the evidence of human "free will," that is, to the belief that certain events are "up to us" (*ep' hemin*), and therefore that the human capacity to deliberate and decide makes the individual capable of self-determination and responsible for its actions. "We see that what will be has an origin (*arche*) both in deliberation and in action, and that, in general, in things that are not always actual there is the possibility of being and of not being; here both possibilities are open, both being and not being, and, consequently, both coming to be and not coming to be."[22] For Aristotle, human deliberation depends on the independent existence of future contingents: "not everything is or happens of necessity: some things happen as chance has it, and of the affirmation and the negation neither is true rather than the other."[23] Only the "ontological status of genuine contingent events in the future"[24] explains the final form taken by Aristotle's solution to the deterministic argument of Diodorus:

---

[19] Sorabji, *Necessity, Cause, and Blame*, 105.

[20] This conception of determinism is expressed by Ammonius in the Mower Argument: "If you are going to mow, it is not that you will perhaps mow, perhaps not mow, but that you are going to mow in any case [*modis omnibus*]; as a consequence it is necessary that either you are going to mow or you are not going to mow." From this argument to the Idle Argument the step is simple because the Mower Argument eliminates the "perhaps" itself, the natural contingency of the future, which alone opens the possibility that the event is an effect of the human choice to mow or not to mow. (Vuillemin, *Nécessité ou contingence*, 84-85).

[21] Aristotle *De Interpretatione* 18b26-18b33.

[22] Ibid., 19a7-12.

[23] Ibid., 19a18-20.

[24] Dorothea Frede, "The Sea-Battle Reconsidered: A Defense of the Traditional Interpretation," *Oxford Studies in Ancient Philosophy*, vol.3 (Oxford: Clarendon Press, 1985), 75.

Since statements are true according to how the actual things are, it is clear that wherever these are such as to allow of contraries as chance has it, the same necessarily holds for the contradictories also. This happens with things that are not always so or not always not so. With these it is necessary for one of the other of the contradictories to be true or false – not, however, this one or that one, but as chance has it; or for one to be true rather than the other, yet not already true or false.[25]

This solution requires future contingents to have an autonomous status with respect to the human capacity to deliberate, and this contingency depends in turn on the natural existence of chance.[26]

Machiavelli opens the discourse on fortuna in *The Prince*, XXV with a reference to the Idle Argument because he intends to refute not just this argument, but the whole conceptual paradigm that makes it possible. This argument stands for an understanding of "worldly things" (*le cose del mondo*) that tends towards idleness, that has not given sufficient space to the power and freedom of human praxis. Behind Machiavelli's treatment of the question of chance lies the project of disclosing a new understanding of what it means to act in the world, or, better, of what a worldly, as opposed to other-worldly, approach to action looks like. That human beings cannot "correct" with their prudence the government of things by fortuna and God, therefore, is clearly not an argument that Machiavelli adduces in order to criticize the possibility of human action as such, but only a certain narrow understanding of the same. As a consequence, Machiavelli's refutation of the Idle Argument should not be understood as an argument in favor of prudence. On the contrary, Machiavelli's rhetorical set-up at the beginning of the chapter entails that if one horn of the dualism falls (i.e., the heteronomy through fortuna and God) then also the other horn falls (i.e., prudence as guide for action). In contrast to the classical tradition begun by Aristotle in his refutation of the Master Argument, Machiavelli's rejection of the separation of the "worldly things" into the spheres of fortuna/God and human prudence implies that the grammar of prudence is part and parcel of the Idle Argument. The classical tradition of prudence is still part of a generally idle or contemplative approach to the world, and not an effective solution to the Idle Argument.

Machiavelli's text proceeds to claim that the opinion concerning the omnipotence of fortuna gathers more support "in our times" because everyone is witness "every day" to the "great variation of things... outside of any human conjecture."

---

[25] Aristotle *De Interpretatione* 19a32-9.

[26] This is not the case with Boethius's theory of contingency, for example. As Kretzmann shows, Boethius conceives of three modes of contingency: chance, free choice, or possibility of nature. But unlike Aristotle, for Boethius chance depends on free choice: "chance is any unintended outcome of an action arising from free choice." (Norman Kretzmann, "Nos Ipsi Principia Sumus: Boethius and the Basis of Contingency," in *Divine Omniscience and Omnipotence in Medieval Philosophy*, ed. T. Rudavsky [Leiden: Reidel, 1985], 35). As Kretzmann reiterates: "Boethian chance is not an independent source of real randomness in nature; it is not a third kind of agency, alongside free choice and natural necessitation (or nature)... for Boethius 'chance' is simply a designation for one sort of outcome of free choice operating on real potentiality." (Ibid., 36). Incidentally, this shows that Balaban does not grasp the specificity of Machiavelli's theory of fortuna when she claims that "in Machiavelli's view men create fortuna, although only indirectly and unintentionally", i.e., as a by-product of human teleological activity, because this view is at least as old as Boethius. (Balaban, "Fortuna in Machiavelli's thought," 30-31). In fact, the sense in which fortuna is a human creation in Machiavelli has more to do with the reification of human action than with its unintended consequences, as I argue below.

The chaotic and unexplained series of events that have occurred in Italy during Machiavelli's times is said to give rise to the opinion that events follow an order that transcends the horizon of human affairs.[27] The explanation of fortuna that the text offers will count therefore as one "human conjecture" that can give an account of the phenomenon of historical change which, if left unexplained, serves to foster superstitious beliefs in a mythical Fortuna.[28] The superstitious belief in Fortuna as a transcendent power can be displaced only by an immanent explanation of historical becoming.

A more difficult question concerns the status of such a theoretical attempt to undermine all claims that ascribe the government of "worldly things" to other-worldly, transcendent and mythical causes. Does Machiavelli offer a "conjecture" that intends to "save the appearances" of fortuna, much like Aristotle's theory of chance does; or does he intend to "reduce" the phenomenon of fortuna to its "real" causes thereby revealing it as an ideological construct, mere superstition and illusion, anticipating the Cartesian project that one finds also in Spinoza; or, finally, does Machiavelli's theory have an entirely different status?

The argument begins by positing a thesis that raises an objection to the Idle Argument: "Nonetheless, so that our free will is not extinguished, I judge that it could be true that fortuna governs half of our actions, but that she also lets us govern the other half, more or less."[29] This objection turns on the existence of "our free will" (libero arbitrio), which is assumed only ex hypothesi. The argument of the thesis is merely de dicto and not de re: it follows analytically from the definition of free will that fortuna cannot be omnipotent, thus if one is to be ascribed a free will, then it must be conjectured that fortuna governs "about half" of human actions and leaves "up to us" the government of the other half.

The hypothetical status of this new partition of the government of "worldly things" into human free will, on one side, and fortuna, on the other, is a good indication that Machiavelli may not, as such, endorse the thesis he is expounding.[30] Indeed, the thesis merely gives voice to the traditional attempts to refute the

---

[27] For two divergent but equally stimulating analyses of the relation between the historical events during Machiavelli's life and the development of his political thought, see Sasso, *Niccolò Machiavelli* and Negri, *Le pouvoir constituante*.

[28] Spinoza explains the belief in Fortune in similar terms: as the expression of superstition caused by a failure to master chance through political freedom; this failure is exploited by religion and despotism alike. "If men were able to exercise complete control over all their circumstances, or if continuous good fortune were always their lot, they would never be prey to superstition. But since they are often reduced to such straits as to be without any resource... the wretched victims of alternating hopes and fears, the result is that, for the most part, their credulity knows no bounds.... Only while fear persists do men fall prey to superstition... the supreme mystery of despotism, its prop and stay, is to keep men in a state of deception, and with the specious title of religion cloak the fear by which they must be kept in check, so that they will fight for their servitude as if for salvation.... To invest with prejudice or in any way coerce the citizen's free judgment is altogether incompatible with the freedom of the people." (Spinoza, Preface, *Tractatus Theologico-politicus*).

[29] The thesis is reiterated in *The Prince*, XXVI: "God does not want to do everything so as not to take away our free will and part of the glory that belongs to us." Notice the replacement of fortuna by God, which reinforces the idea, expressed at the start of *The Prince*, XXV, that they are interchangeable sources of heteronomy.

[30] Sfez sees that "Machiavelli posits the existence of free will but never demonstrates it," yet he continues his interpretation assuming the absolute validity of the thesis. (Sfez, *Le prince sans qualités*, 313-314). Negri notices the problematic and untenable character of the thesis but provides no arguments as to why it must be overcome. (Negri, *Le pouvoir constituante*, 79-80). Sasso

Idle Argument for the sake of upholding a degree of human freedom, of which Aristotle for classical thought and Boethius for Christian thought represent the paradigms. Machiavelli's text plays off both Aristotle's unproblematical or self-evident assumption of the existence of future contingents as well as of the existence of free will (i.e., things that are "up to us"); and Boethius's equally unproblematic assumption of the personification of chance into a goddess that governs the course of the world in the attempt to "save" human free will.

The consequences of the partition of the world into fortuna and free will are illustrated by the analogy of Fortuna as a river that can be controlled by human actions designed to channel its force.

I compare her [fortuna] to one of those torrential streams which, when they overflow, flood the plains.... everyone flees before them, everyone yields to their force, unable to stand up to them in any way.... Yet this does not mean that men cannot take countermeasures while the weather is still fine [*quando sono i tempi quieti*], shoring up dikes and dams, so that when the waters rise again, either they are carried off in a channel or their force is not so licentious and harmful. So with fortuna; who demonstrates her power where there is no orderly virtù [*ordinata virtù*] to resist it; and she turns her impetuousness where it knows that no dikes and restraining dams have been built in order to contain her.

This analogy seems to fit the prudential scheme of worldly action in view of containing the power of Fortuna. With the thesis, Machiavelli appears to overturn, at least partially, the Idle Argument in favor of an "active" relation of resistance to fortuna posed by "orderly virtù." The continuation of the text makes clear that the variations of fortune are so great in places like Italy, which is compared to a "countryside without dikes and without any restraining dams." In other places, like Spain and France, where there is "proper virtù" (*conveniente virtù*), fortuna is not allowed to wreak its devastation to the extent that it does in Italy.

Interpreters have called this thesis an "optimistic" one because Machiavelli links explicitly the existence of a great variation of fortuna with the absence of virtù, thereby implying that it is possible for a strong enough virtù to prevent fortuna from causing its devastating effects.[31] Machiavelli's image of Fortuna as a river that can be controlled by virtù is by no means original to him. Already Leon Battista Alberti said that "the current of Fortuna will not drag away a man who, trusting his own virtù, makes his way in the current as an able swimmer."[32] But Alberti's "agonistic" conception of virtù expresses a defensive attitude towards fortuna whose "mutability" cannot be changed but must be withstood:

---

questions the coherence of Machiavelli's discourse by opposing this thesis with other assertions made later in the text, but he does not as such question the validity of the thesis. To my knowledge these are among the few exceptions in the secondary literature to the generalized practice of taking at face value the validity of the thesis instead of considering the possibility that it may be simply a thetic starting point which is to be negated and possibly sublated as part and parcel of the dialectical structure of the overall argument.

[31] See for example Mario Santoro who speaks of the "optimistic faith in the winning chances of virtù against the dangers and difficulties of fortuna." (Santoro, *Fortuna, ragione e prudenza*, 51).

[32] Leon Battista Alberti, *Della tranquillità dell'animo*, in *Leon Battista Alberti: the Complete Works*, ed. Franco Borsi (Milan: Rizzoli, Electa, 1989), I, 113.

With respect to things having to do with fortuna, one must prepare one's *animo* and foreclose any opportunity that she may have in time to perturb you.... Remember that fortuna was always voluble and inconstant.... The practical man at sea prepares with many anchors, ropes, and armaments more for adverse events than for securing the ease of his navigation. Similarly, during the course of life we have to prepare ourselves so that the instability of the times can cause the least damage possible.[33]

The image of the river that needs to be contained in a prudent fashion presents itself again in Bernardo Rucellai's *De Bello Italico* and in the letters of Pontano: "when the heavens does not find a resistance below it, it draws things its own way, like a river which suddenly floods over because of rain and which finds no dikes or dams."[34] But in both Pontano and Rucellai it is once again the virtù of the "prudent individual" that keeps up with the changes of the times thanks to its central quality of *versatilitas*, the capacity to change the modes of proceeding in accord with the changing of the times.[35] In short, Machiavelli's optimistic thesis remains well within the traditional understanding of the relation between virtù as prudential action and fortuna. If only for this reason one may raise a suspicion that it represents a point of arrival, or even of support, for his discourse on fortuna, and its effective function in the overall argument should be carefully reconsidered.

Indeed, it is probably because the treatment of fortuna has not at this stage overcome the "common" and "received" topoi that Machiavelli ends his presentation of the prudential thesis on fortuna by asserting that such a thesis contains only an account of what it means to "oppose oneself to fortuna in universals [*opporsi alla fortuna in universali*]." This statement marks a caesura in the discourse between the "optimistic" thesis and the subsequent presentation of the "pessimistic" theory of the *riscontro*. The received interpretations of this text, if they even perceive its antinomical structure, irremediably fall along these two lines, as if the text presented a choice between the "optimistic" and the "pessimistic" positions. Some interpreters emphasize the ability of virtù to check fortuna, if not to abolish it as an independent factor; other interpreters highlight the ineluctible hold that fortuna has on human projects.[36] No one has yet proposed a solution that aspires to transcend both positions by seeing them as opposite but equal theses whose dialectical relation is intended to show the insufficiency of each, and in so doing destroy the paradigms of human praxis that make them possible.

Consideration of the structure of Machiavelli's argument suggests that this last possibility is the most promising one: as the argument passes from thesis to antithesis, it also moves from a "universal" treatment of the opposition between virtù and fortuna toward a "particular" treatment of the same. What is the significance of the fact that the transition from the universal to the particular point of view implies a reversal of the "optimistic" thesis that virtù can control fortuna?

---

[33] Idem, *De Iciarchia*, II.

[34] Cited in Santoro, *Fortuna, ragione e prudenza*, 168.

[35] See Santoro's discussion of Pontano's conception of prudence and especially *versatilitas*. (Ibid., 58ff). Santoro does not hesitate to speak of the "modernity" of "Pontano's investigation of prudence," without for all that giving sufficient grounds to separate this investigation from the classical understandings of prudence. (Ibid., 56).

[36] For example, choosing at random from interpretations already cited, those of Santoro, Cassirer, Strauss, and Desan uphold versions of the optimistic position; those of Sasso and Parel uphold versions of the pessimistic position.

One possibility is that Machiavelli is simply referring to the different spheres in which fortuna plays itself out. To speak about fortuna "in universals" would mean to speak about it in the sphere of international politics; whereas speaking about it "in particulars" would refer to its role in the sphere of individual life. But this possibility is contradicted by the fact that the twenty-fifth chapter is a prelude to the last chapter of *The Prince* in which Machiavelli calls for the entrance of an individual into the sphere of international politics, who will assume the role of prince, and carry out the task of liberating and unifying Italy. If the direction from a universal treatment of fortuna to a particular one corresponds to a passage from optimism to pessimism, then one could not explain why it is in the sphere of the particular that Machiavelli seems to find hope in a form of action that provides the very condition of possibility for the optimism of the thesis, i.e., the transformation of Italy into a national state that can put into practice the "prudential" logic of confrontation with fortuna.[37]

Another possible reading is that the difference between treating of fortuna in universals as opposed to in particulars betrays a veiled reference to certain astrological conceptions commonly held in Machiavelli's time.[38] This interpretative hypothesis holds that the descent from universals to particulars leads to the pessimistic antithesis because it expresses the control that the order of nature, which can be "known" through universals and has itself universal scope, has over the sphere of particulars.[39] For Parel, the theory of the *riscontro* that characterizes the treatment of fortuna "in particulars" entails that,

it is one's fortune, not free will or choice, that sees to it that one's times and one's temperament harmonize. That is to say, the chances of mastering fortune depends on fortune itself.... The point is that humans, not having control over the quality of their times, nor over the humor with which they

---

[37] According to Sasso, Machiavelli's "theoretical" pessimism with regard to the capacities of virtù, as this is reflected in the twenty-fifth chapter of *The Prince*, is overcome, in a purely "utopian" fashion, by the "practical" optimism of its last chapter. Sasso thinks that the last chapter of *The Prince* is merely wish-fulfilment, an "affective outburst" that has nothing to do with the "reality-principle" that Machiavelli sets out in his treatment of fortuna. (Sasso, *Niccolò Machiavelli*, 440; idem, *Machiavelli e gli Antichi*, 2:52). This reading, in turn, takes off from Gramsci's understanding of *The Prince* as a "revolutionary utopian manifesto." For a different understanding of Gramsci's characterization of *The Prince*, see Althusser, *Écrits philosophiques et politiques*. For a commentary on *The Prince*, XXVI that takes up and responds to Sasso's reading, see Mario Martelli, "La logica provvidenzialistica e il capitolo XXVI del Principe," *Interpres* IV (1981-82): 262-384.

[38] See Parel, *The Machiavellian Cosmos*; idem, "The Question of Machiavelli's Modernity." Parel claims that the distinction between "universal" and "particular" treatments of fortuna is taken from Ptolemy's manual of astrological wisdom (*Tetrabiblios* II,1). This quotation from Ptolemy is one of the few pieces of textual evidence that Parel provides for his sweeping claim that Machiavelli's "treatment of fortune is based on premodern cosmology." (Parel, "Machiavelli's Modernity," 333). The idea of situating Machiavelli's treatment of fortuna within the debate on astrology in the Renaissance is at least as old as the work of Cassirer and Garin. Viroli's most recent attempt to sketch Machiavelli's "philosophy of life" heavily relies on the astrological reading of Machiavelli's thought proposed by Parel.

[39] Parel claims that for Machiavelli, "the motions of the heaven and the planets... affect all human motions, collective as well as individual. The 'order' that human history follows – of rise and fall, corruption and renewal – and the 'power' which makes such 'order' possible, are received from the motions of heavens and the planets." (Parel, *Machiavellian Cosmos*, 28).

are born, are dependent on fortune, who (or which) controls both the times and the temperament. This is the pessimistic conclusion that Machiavelli reaches.[40]

Since Parel assumes that fortuna in Machiavelli symbolizes "the power of heavenly bodies," the pessimism at issue would reflect the astrological determinism that emerges from the possibility of a thoroughgoing determination of the particular historical event by the universal cosmological order. "Everything that happens in history, then, happens according to the laws of cosmic motion. Strictly speaking history is a conjoint product of cosmic and human motions, in which the one plays the superior, and the other, the subordinate role."[41]

The interpretative hypothesis that I propose stands in contrast to any such astrological interpretation. The reason why the passage from a universal treatment of fortuna to a particular one leads to pessimism is due to Machiavelli's belief that the "universal" treatment of fortuna means a "theoretical" treatment of fortuna, in two related senses. First, the prudential form taken by the opposition to fortuna betrays a priority of theory over praxis; second, this priority has as a consequence the *merely* theoretical, i.e., non-effective, opposition to fortuna. It is precisely because there is no "science" of the particular event that the "theoretical" or "prudential" approach to fortuna must ultimately fail, and this failure is expressed by the pessimistic antithesis. If it were possible for the universal order to determine the particular event, then this determination could be known in advance and the human being could make the necessary adjustments that the prudential thesis speaks about. The continuation of the argument shows that such knowledge is impossible, hence the apparent pessimism, which is solely aimed against the theoretical pretension. More importantly, the impossibility of a "science" of events expresses Machiavelli's destruction of the deterministic antithesis that posits the domain of events as being completely determined a priori by the domain of form, by the universal cosmological order. The symptom of the emancipation of praxis from theory is a pessimism with respect to the claims of the "theoretical" and "prudential" logic of control of fortuna. Conversely, this emancipation of praxis from theory is expressed by the unheard of possibility that not only is there no predetermination of events by universal structures or orders, but the order of "worldly things" is determined by the relation that human action has with its circumstances: nature dissolves into history.

THE CRITIQUE OF PRUDENCE AND THE PESSIMISTIC ANTITHESIS

To consider the role played by fortuna "in particulars," i.e., in reference to individual destiny, Machiavelli's argument returns to the problem of the Ghiribizzi: "one sees today this prince be successful, and tomorrow fall into ruin, without having noticed in him any change in nature or quality." What causes an individual to incurr a change of fortunes, if it is not the change in its "nature" or "qualities"? Is good or bad fortune in an individual's life (i.e., the success of its actions) completely independent of what the individual is and does? Machiavelli

---

[40] Parel, "Machiavelli's Modernity," 332.
[41] Ibid., 322.

gives two explanations for the change of fortune in an individual's life. The first concerns the unreliability of fortuna as a foundation for power: "that prince who supports himself completely on fortuna will fall into ruin, as soon as she varies." Machiavelli leaves open the possibility that a prince can find a better foundation for the state than fortuna, implying that it can rest on his virtù. As shown previously, Machiavelli holds that the foundation of the modern state must be the people's desire for freedom. But in *The Prince* it is left undetermined what kind of relation obtains between the project of opposing fortuna and the people, and whether this project can really be carried out by princely virtù.

The second explanation is given by the theory of the *riscontro*: "I also believe that he is happy who can match [*riscontra*] his way of proceeding with the qualities of the times, and likewise he is unhappy whose ways of proceeding are discordant with the times [*discordano e' tempi*]." This theory is set alongside the first explanation but they are clearly not compatible, at least at first sight, because the latter opens the possibility of stabilizing and controlling fortuna through virtù, while the former seems to reduce to indifference the import of different ways of proceeding (be they with or without virtù) and leaves success up to the encounter or match (*riscontro*) of these ways with the "quality of times." This explanation seems to leave the success of the action up to an encounter which has no other determination than chance itself, the chance of the "appropiate time." The changes of fortune are explained by the theory of the *riscontro*, but only at the price of bringing back fortuna as a cause. It would seem that fortuna has the last word in determining the success of the action, and thus constitutes an inextirpable and fatalistic dimension of human praxis.

But whether fortuna is truly inextirpable from human action, and above all what this apparent limit of human virtù means, can be decided only by determining what Machiavelli's theory of the *riscontro* is trying to establish:

Because one sees men proceed variously in those things that lead them to the end which everyone has before them, that is, glories and riches;[42] one proceeds with respect, the other with impetus; one with violence, the other with skill; one with patience, the other with its opposite: and each of them with these diverse ways can attain the end. One also sees two respectful persons, one attains his plan, the other does not; and likewise one sees two persons equally attain success with two different ways, one being respectful and the other impetuous: and this is caused by nothing other than the quality of times, which either conform themselves or do not conform to their way of proceeding. From here arises what I said, that two persons, acting in different ways, attain the same effect; and of two who act in the same way, one will attain his end and the other will not.

According to this explanation of the change of fortunes, individuals proceed towards their common goals in different ways and with different means. Contrary ways and means can lead equally to the same result, just as similar ways can lead to contrary results. What decides the outcome of a certain action is the conformity

---

[42] The belief that the "end" of all human action is composed of "glories and riches" does not correspond to Machiavelli's last word. As I show below, in the *Discourses on Livy* there is a critique of the idea that ambition is the sole cause of the change of fortune. But in this context of *The Prince*, XXV Machiavelli is playing on the terrain disclosed by Boethius's theory of Fortuna, according to which Fortuna alone has control of human destiny in so far as the latter attaches itself merely to worldly ends like glories and riches, which only the goddess has the power to bestow and withdraw.

(or lack thereof) between the "quality of the times" (*qualità de' tempi*) and the ways of proceeding, the "quality of the action." Accounting for human action in this way takes away the very premises of a theory of prudence as explanation of human action because it rejects the idea that prudential deliberation about the means can determine the achievement of the desired end. What escapes the reach of prudence is the very "quality of the times."

But the real basis of this critique of prudence is another one: the theory of the *riscontro* accounts first and foremost for the fact that human beings have such different ways of proceeding and acting. The circumstances of human action, the "quality of the times," favor different means at different times, allowing for a variety of ways of acting to succeed and continue their development. The point is that human ways of proceeding in the world are constituted or selected in virtue of their adaptability to circumstances. The variety of human "habits" or "natures" are a consequence of a process of historical selection which is radically anti-teleological, in at least two senses: it is not because someone has a certain nature or function that they can cope with the circumstances, but, on the contrary, it is the fact that certain actions cope with the circumstances that accounts for their becoming the functions or habits or natures which characterize the individual. In a second sense, the sphere of human action is anti-teleological because this fact of coping with the circumstances, or of "matching" the quality of one's actions with the qualities of the times, is itself historically variable in the sense that it has no a priori determinable final end: human nature is entirely given over to historical becoming. As it turns out, this anti-teleological understanding of the basis of human praxis is also the ground for a new theory of human freedom that Machiavelli develops.

But before reaching the formulation of the theory of freedom, Machiavelli discusses the "pessimistic" consequences that follow from the theory of the *riscontro*:

> From this also depends the variation of the good; because, if one governs himself with respect and patience, and the times and the things turn in such a way that his conduct is good, he will be successful; but if the times and the things change, he falls into ruin, because he does not change his way of proceeding. Nor can one find any man so prudent as to know how to accomodate himself to this; both because one cannot deviate from that to which nature inclines one, and also because having always prospered by walking on one way, one cannot be persuaded to leave it. But the man who is respectful does not know how to change when it is time to become impetuous, from which results his ruin: because if he were to change nature with the times and with the things, he would not change in fortune.

The critique of the prudential logic presented by the "optimistic" thesis could not be stronger. One after the other, all the pillars of the classical doctrine of prudence fall to the ground. To begin with, only the encounter (*riscontro*) with the times and circumstances grants to the means their value: the means are "good" (in the sense of adequate) if the encounter is favorable, they are "bad" otherwise. The implication is that the "good" varies with the times and according to situations; it cannot be determined theoretically, that is, ahead of time and in reference to a rule that is independent of the situation.

The second consequence of the theory of *riscontro* is the rejection of the possibility of changing means and ways of proceeding in accordance with the change of times. The text thoroughly rejects the *versatilitas* that Pontano sees as the primary quality of the prudent individual. Two reasons are given for this rejection of the correspondence theory of action on the basis of the fixity of human "nature." The first is that one cannot go against what one's "nature" inclines one to do.[43] The second is that no one can persuade someone who has prospered by doing things in a certain way to change these ways that have been, to date, successful. The possibility of maintaining always good fortune, by means of a change of nature that would correspond to that of the times, is thus categorically excluded for human affairs.

But what do these consequences amount to, what dialectic between the optimistic thesis and the pessimistic antithesis is Machiavelli setting up? According to Sasso's interpretation of the twenty-fifth chapter, Machiavelli's optimistic thesis is simply inconsistent: the partition of "worldly things" into free will and fortuna cannot be maintained if Machiavelli truly believes that there is fortuna only when virtù is absent or when it is of a "bad" character. Sasso claims that Machiavelli holds onto the thesis because of "moralistic" reasons, intended to allow him to castigate the lack of virtù found in Italian princes. But in so doing he ignores the problem of the Ghiribizzi which is only re-established with the antithesis, in the second part of the twenty-fifth chapter.

For Sasso, the "pessimistic" antithesis ascribes the limit of virtù to human "nature," no longer to the purported ignorance or incompetence (i.e., lack of prudence) of the political actor. Fortuna as the limitation of human virtù is no longer the mythical cause described by pagans and Christians but "coincides... with the same human nature, with that obscure and non-virtuous area of character, which every man, even the most prudent and virtuous one, necessarily holds within himself."[44] It is human "nature" that prevents individuals from understanding or knowing certain aspects of reality (i.e., from grasping the situation), and thus leaves them powerless when faced with the changes of times. Machiavelli's theory of the *riscontro* explains fortuna by referring the intelligence of the events to the structure of the human "spirit," *animo*:

It is in the latter, and in nothing else, that such explanation finds its criterion; and consequently this intelligence of events assumes a strong rationalistic character. Of course, the criterion that this second conception brings into play itself suffers from the intrinsic poverty of the schematization of the animo into two alternative and non-communicating characters. But what interests us here is not the naturalistic schematization, but its implicit rationalistic richness. By virtue of this idea, fortuna is transformed into a criterion of judgment: it is no longer a myth but tends toward a *logos*.[45]

---

[43] The Hobbesian and Spinozist tone of this passage is remarkable; when Machiavelli states that "one cannot deviate from what nature inclines one towards" he refers to what will become the modern theory of the conatus. Parel, on the other hand, interprets this phrase to mean that "the Machiavellian personality is incapable of going against its natural inclination set by its humor and temperament" and this limitation has its origin "in astrological anthropology." (Parel, "Machiavelli's Modernity," 337).

[44] Sasso, *Niccolò Machiavelli*, 436.

[45] Ibid., 437.

The innovative aspect of Sasso's interpretation consists in understanding the variability of fortuna as an effect caused by the limits of human nature. Against the Straussian interpretation, Sasso argues that virtù never commands fortuna (the change of times). One can act either with impetus or with respect, but not with both at the same time; hence virtù is limited and depends, for its efficacity, on the favor of the circumstances. The explanation of the phenomenon of the change of fortune is itself dependent on the presence or absence of an "encounter" between action and times which is due to chance: in this sense, fortuna is an ineluctible aspect of the horizon of human action.

The weakness of Sasso's interpretation consists in misunderstanding the strategic role, and limited scope, of Machiavelli's naturalism. Sasso can claim that fortuna causes the encounter (*riscontro*) between action and times only because of a naturalistic reading of virtù which reduces it to human "nature" and its limits. This reduction has two problems: it is in itself inconsistent, and it does not correspond to the sense of Machiavelli's text. Sasso claims that there is a distinction between "that obscure and non-virtuous part" of human nature (*animo*) which is counter to virtù, which fixes the individual to a determined course and does not allow it to change "nature." But he also claims that virtù itself cannot change; thereby he does away with the specific difference between the parts of the human *animo* that is presupposed by his argument.

The reason for this inconsistency lies with Sasso's presupposition that human "nature" is a given in Machiavelli. But, on my reading of it, the theory of *riscontro* shows that human "nature" is a function of habits of action acquired thanks to the favor bestowed by circumstances on a given way of proceeding, i.e., thanks to the adaptation of these ways to the times. Human "nature" in Machia-velli is a function of custom, it is always "second nature."[46] If human "nature" is not something given, but a result of a certain adaptation between actions and circumstances, it is possible to conceive of a mode of action that is not "natural" or "customary," a mode of action that Machiavelli calls "extra-ordinary virtù" (*istraordinaria virtù*) precisely because it goes counter to customary activity. This kind of action goes against customary activity in the sense that it coincides (*riscontro*) with the active changing of the times, whereas customary activity is constituted by the very prohibition of such a coincidence, by remaining always in a position of passivity with respect to the possibility of such changes of time.[47]

Sasso's interpretation never countenances the possibility that human action may itself change the times, and in this way take the place of fortuna as the cause of such a change of times.[48] Sasso, who is joined by most interpreters on this

---

[46] This point is perceived by Mansfield and Tarcov, but it is neither properly developed nor is it brought back to its original context, i.e., the theory of the *riscontro*. (Machiavelli, *Discourses on Livy*, Introduction, xl).

[47] Held's belief that Machiavelli proposes a positive role for habits in terms of their capacity to "run counter to the activity of the will," and therefore to curb free action, is exactly the opposite of what Machiavelli argues. (Held, "Civic prudence in Machiavelli," 125). In spite of this error of evaluation, Held is one of the few interpreters to have thematized the decisive role played by habits in Machiavelli's discourse on freedom.

[48] This possibility is countenanced by Negri: "there is no circle that contains in itself virtù and fortuna; there is only one possibility: virtù occupying the place of fortuna, this and nothing else. Virtù must win or perish: this is the alternative that constitutes it and its dignity. Virtù is freedom." (Negri,

count, never questions the content of the encounter (*riscontro*) between action and times, and therefore cannot see that fortuna exists only as a symptom of the non-coincidence of actions and times, that is, as a symptom that human virtù has given up the goal of changing the times. Fortuna is stripped of its status as cause of the change of times precisely in so far as virtù itself changes the times, rather than merely "corresponding" or "adapting" itself to them. Were virtù only to adapt itself to the times, then their change would be always already left up to fortuna as cause. Sasso's naturalistic reading of the theory of *riscontro* must assume that this is necessarily the case, but such assumption is false, and its falsity coincides with the disclosure of the horizon of human freedom.

In sum, Sasso's interpretation of the "pessimistic" antithesis is correct when it argues that fortuna emerges from a limitation of human action; but it fails to see that this limitation is the source of human "nature" as reified action, and as a consequence is a transcendable limitation. The transcendence of human "nature" is identical with the action that coincides (that finds its *riscontro*) with the times in and through its changing of the times, thereby denying fortuna as heteronomous cause of the same change. The theory of the *riscontro* is a vehement attack on the reduction of action to behavior, to the type of human action that is predictable and controllable because it follows a pattern; in short, behavior as habitual action.[49] This sort of activity is destined to depend upon the favor or disfavor of the circumstances: behavior has the capacity to turn success into the cause of failure precisely because success strengthens the pattern, making it more encroached and harder to break with, thereby rendering the human being that falls under its sway more vulnerable to the change of circumstances.

The possibility of turning action into behavior, of habituating action, is immanent to every way of proceeding. Even though Machiavelli illustrates the "pessimistic" theory of the *riscontro* by thematizing the fragility of the ways of the "respectful" individual, his argument applies also to the "impetuous" individual, as shown by his subsequent analysis in the twenty-fifth chapter of the way of proceeding characteristic of Julius II. Machiavelli does not shirk from the conclusion that if Julius II had lived long enough to make a habit out of his capacity of extraordinary and impetuous action, then only the favor of the times, and not his virtù, would have allowed him to attain his ends, "because, if times had come in which one would have had to proceed with respect, his ruin would have followed; because he would have never deviated from his mode of proceeding, to which his nature inclined him."

Le pouvoir constituante, 104). But it is not worked out in relation to all the pertinent texts in Machiavelli's discourse; and, paradoxically, Negri rejects as worthless ("the discourse becomes hesitant, then is taken over by routine, banality and fashion") the very text *(The Prince*, XXV) that supports the possibility at issue. (Ibid., 81).

[49] On the difference between action and behavior, apart from the classical analysis found in Hannah Arendt, *The Human Condition*; see also the treatment given in Ermanno Bencivenga, *Oltre la tolleranza* (Milan: Feltrinelli, 1992); and idem, *Freedom: a Dialogue* (Indianapolis: Hackett, 1997).

FORTUNA IS A WOMAN: THE SYNTHESIS OF HISTORY

Machiavelli resolves the dialectic between "optimistic" thesis and "pessimistic" antithesis in the final synthetic formula for the opposition of virtù to fortuna.[50]

> I conclude, therefore, that, given the change of fortuna and the fact that men remain in their obstinate ways, they are happy when these are concordant [*mentre concordano insieme*], and unhappy, when they are discordant [*discordano*]. I judge as good the following: that it is better to be impetuous [*impetuoso*] than respectful [*respettivo*]; because fortuna is a woman: and it is necessary, if one wishes to keep her down, to beat her and collide with her [*batterla e urtarla*]. And one sees that she lets herself be won [*si lascia più vincere*] more by the impetuous than by those who proceed coldly; and always, like a woman, she is the friend of youth, because they are less respectful, more ferocious, and have more audacity to command her.

The prudential formula for the opposition between virtù and fortuna contained in the thesis reveals its "idleness" when it is negated by the antithesis that posits the power of fortuna over reified human action. In turn, the theoretical explanation of fortuna contained in the "pessimistic" theory of the *riscontro* gives way to the practical synthesis in which human action transcends its naturalization or reification and opens up the horizon of human freedom characterized by the "effective" opposition of virtù to fortuna, beyond the antinomy of free will and determinism.

That one is confronted with a synthesis is evident from the caesura present at the heart of the above, concluding passage. The text restates the theory of the *riscontro* according to which the "quality of the times" is indifferent toward the ways of proceeding of human action, now favoring one, then another of these; only to leap violently on to the side of audacity and impetuosity because fortuna, or the mutability of the "quality of times," is a "woman" who can be "kept down" and "commanded" by "less respectful," more audacious and ferocious youth.[51] Rhetorically, the violence of the leap with which the discourse reneges the antithesis and leaps to the synthesis performs the very violence that is expressed in the synthetic formula.[52]

---

[50] I speak of a "formula" in the sense that Aby Warburg uses the term *Pathosformeln* to designate the plastic expression that brings together "irreconcilable and bizarre opposites… understood as the organic polarity of the wide capacity for oscillation in a cultivated man of the early Renaissance, who aspires to a characteristic reconciliation in the age of the metamorphosis of energetic self-consciousness." (Aby Warburg, "Francesco Sassettis Letztwillige Verfügung," in *Ausgewählte Schriften und Wurdigungen* [Baden-Baden: Verlag Koerner, 1980], 145).

[51] Machiavelli's choice of the "young" over the "elders" echoes the Socratic topos found in Plato's call for a youthful tyrant in the *Laws* 709ff. Machiavelli's conjuring up of the audacious prince has been interpreted with reference to Plato by Edgar Wind, "Platonic Tyranny and Renaissance Fortuna: on Ficino's Reading of the *Laws*, IV, 709a-712b," in *Essays in Honor of Erwin Panofsky*, ed. M. Meiss (New York: New York University Press, 1961). But in reality the content of Machiavelli's call is anti-Platonic since it entails an opening on the part of the modern prince to the people. Machiavelli's choice in favor of youth, though, must be primarily understood in opposition to the doctrine of prudence: Aristotle remarks that prudence necessarily requires a certain experience of the world, and is consequently associated with older people. (Aristotle *Nicomachean Ethics* VI,5). See also J. de Romilly, "Alcibiade et le mélange entre jeunes et vieux: politique et médecine," *Wiener Studien* 10 (1976): 93-105.

[52] Feminist interpretations of Machiavelli have read the formula for the relation between virtù and fortuna by reconstructing the content of the gender difference inscribed in it. Once this step is taken, and depending on the reconstruction given to the meaning of the gender difference, the "violent"

Generally speaking, Machiavelli shows a marked preference to treat any given topos according to the method of division by dichotomy which originates with the *dissoi logoi* of the Sophists, supremely enacted in the dialogue pieces of Thucydides, and is appropiated and innovated by Plato's employment of *diaresis*. This method "seeks to define and classify a subject by dividing in two, supposedly along the line which distiguishes an essential element in the genus and hence significant differentia in the two species," permitting the presentation of the topoi in terms of "clear-cut alternative or antithetical principles of action."[53] Usually, Machiavelli announces to the reader when he is about to decide the question and choose sides between the antinomical positions, and he generally gives reasons for his choice.[54] In this case, though, the dialectical structure of the discourse is well camouflaged; and there is no rhetorical flourish that prefaces a decision on the part of Machiavelli in favor of one position or another. All the more brutal does the synthetic formula appear, in form as in content.

The formula with which Machiavelli closes his discourse on fortuna is unprecedented in the history of political thought. No one before thought that the conflict between virtue and fortune should be irreconcilable and certainly not of such dramatic proportions.[55] The formula is a synthesis of the two positions uncovered in *The Prince* XXV: it brings together aspects of both positions while at the same time destroying their claims to an autonomous standing. The formula sublates the thesis to the extent that it reproposes the ability of virtù to be a match for fortuna, but on a basis that is completely anti-prudential, as the priority assigned to audacity makes clear. The formula also sublates the antithesis to the extent that it affirms the theory of the encounter (*riscontro*) between action and times, but it gives a completely different content to this encounter: the violence with which virtù is called to confront fortuna assigns a distinctly polemical,

---

nature of the "match" between virtù and fortuna could be seen as betraying a basic misogyny in Machiavelli's political thought. For some readings along these lines, see Brown, *Manhood and Politics*; Pitkin, *Fortuna is a Woman*; and R. Claire Snyder, *Citizen-Soldiers and Manly Warriors. Military Service and Gender in the Civic Republican Tradition* (New York: Rowman &Littlefield, 1999).
[53] Martin Fleischer, "The Ways of Machiavelli and the Ways of Politics," *History of Political Thought* XVI, no.3 (1995), 346. Fleischer rightly comments that "the procedure of dichotomizing and the accompanying grammatical structure of 'either... or...' is so native to Machiavelli's style that it is a puzzle why commentators have generally chosen to ignore it. Machiavelli's thought is so marked by this tendency that it may be taken as basic to its modo di procedere." (Ibid.).
[54] For examples of typical rhetorical pointers to the method of division, see *Discourses on Livy*, I,5: "And truly, he who discourses well on the one thing and the other could remain doubtful as to which should be chosen by him.... In the end, he who subtly examines the whole will draw this conclusion from it." See also *The Prince*, XX: "Thus fortresses may be useful or otherwise, according to circumstances.... The prince who fears his own people more than he does foreigners ought to build fortresses, but a prince who is more afraid of foreigners than of his own people can neglect them.... Actually, the best fortress of all consists in not being hated by your people. However many fortresses you hold, if the people hate you, the fortress will not save you."
[55] Interpreters commonly miss the degree to which Machiavelli breaks with the previous treatments of the dualism virtù-fortuna, which in no way can be reduced to its Greek or Roman or Christian or humanist counterparts, as I have shown repeatedly. See the typical discussion of this question in Leeker, who claims that "Machiavellis Fortuna-Konzeption in nicht unerheblichem Masse auf traditionellen, d.h. antiken, mittelalterlichen und humanistischen Elementen beruht und dass ihre Originalität vor allem in bestimmten Neubewertungen sowie in Erweiterungen ihres Geltungsbereichs besteht." (Leeker, "Fortuna bei Machiavelli," 407).

conflictual content to the encounter between actions and times. There is no sense that the concordance (*concordano/discordano*) between ways and times takes the form of a correspondence, as it did in the formulation of the antithesis.

The twenty-fifth chapter of *The Prince* is structured by the opposition between a prudential conception of virtue that, in seeking to correspond to the times, remains at the mercy of fortuna; and an "audacious" conception of virtù that is capable of "beating" fortuna because it seeks to change the times. The synthetic formula proposed by the discourse entails thinking the possibility of a concordance or co-incidence between the action and the times that is at once a conflict between these. Machiavelli advances the idea that what the times call for, or favor, is precisely to act against the times. Indeed, audacity designates the quality of an action that goes "against the current" of the times, that does what is completely unexpected because it breaks with longstanding habits. In general, a call for audacity is always a call to change the current situation. The encounter between action and times is conceived as a coincidence of opposites (*coincidentia oppositorum*), in the sense that what is "favored" by fortuna ("who is a woman"), what allows for the action and the times to find their concordance, is precisely the opposition or conflict between them.[56]

There is another sense in which Machiavelli's formula points to the figure of a coincidence of opposites: what coincides in this case is virtù and fortuna as opposite causes of change of times. When Machiavelli states that fortuna favors those who beat "her," this means that the action in question has managed to change the times by taking the place of fortuna as cause of the change of times, and this exchange of positions is favored by fortuna because the change of times occurs in any case, except that fortuna lets "herself" be changed rather than changes "herself" by "herself." One can say that the "violence" done to fortuna is no violence at all: the clash between virtù and fortuna does not "master" or "extinguish" or even "control" chance, but, in changing the situation in an unforeseeable way, makes for more of it, and is consequently "favored" by fortuna.

The theory of the *riscontro* presupposes that it is possible for opposites to coincide because the identity of unchanging human "nature" and the difference of the changing quality of times can "match" each other, their encounter can be "timely." The synthetic formula claims that such a timely encounter requires that the action be untimely. How are these two positions to be reconciled? The timely and the untimely are only opposed in appearance. In reality, when action is in accordance to what is customary, the aspect of time and timeliness, as such, does not enter into the frame of reference at all. The reason is that one is doing what has already been done before: custom is a way of fixing the mutability of times, of neutralizing the timeliness of time itself. Conversely, the timeliness of time enters the frame of reference only within the context of an action that desires to

---

[56] One interpreter who has identified the problem of the coincidence of opposites in Machiavelli's theory of virtù, and is therefore able to approximate the polemical and revolutionary nature of the encounter between action and circumstances that is expressed in this theory is Raffaello Ramat, "Il momento dinamico nel pensiero del Machiavelli," *Saggi sul Rinascimento* (Florence: La Nuova Italia, 1969): 148-168.

change the times, i.e., in the context of an action that is to bring something radically new to light. In this case, the question as to the timely or untimely nature of an action can effectively be posed.[57] Machiavelli gives a new turn to the grammar of time and action by making use of the idea that when something is done in a timely fashion one means that it is done in a non-habitual way.[58] The grammar of action done according to custom leaves no logical space for considerations of the right or wrong time because it has no need for them. Likewise, it is part of the grammar of what is timely to predicate it of an action that "turns things around just in time," to prevent a disaster or to save the day. Therefore, the passage from antithesis to synthesis allows Machiavelli to frame the problem of the conformity or disconformity of action to the times within the context of the more originary question: when must things be turned around, when must one change what is in the mode of having always already been (i.e., in the mode of *stato* or *hexis*)?

Likewise, the determinism about human nature expressed by the antithesis, and the correlate pessimism with respect to the possibility for the individual to free itself from the yoke of fortuna, must be understood from the perspective of the synthesis, where it assumes its full significance. Only in relation to every thing that has been constituted into a "nature" does it come to be true that a change of times, a caesura in the order of time, is potentially disastrous. The reason is that this "nature" is constituted in and through the synthesis of continuous time: as a custom or habit (*ethos/hexis*). The crucial point about the theory of *riscontro* is that the "nature" of the individual is so constituted that a "change of times" can destroy it. In other words, for Machiavelli human "nature" is not given extra- or supra-temporally, but must be constructed intra-temporally, as custom or habit. Only habit gives to the activity of beings that form[59] which can also be destroyed if the times change. Machiavelli discovers that habit or custom is the "passive synthesis" of continuous time: the continuity of this time is due to its apparent circularity, itself an effect of the fact that customs tend to build-in the evanescence of (their) beginnings.[60]

If it is accepted that human "nature" as custom or habit stands in a negative relation with the change of times, then it is evident that only an action which goes against custom can change the times: such an encounter between action and times

---

[57] The coincidence of the timely and the untimely in the change of times parallels that of novelty and repetition in the event that constitutes the change of times, i.e., in the event that allows the contingent to pass into the necessary and vice versa. I discuss this point in part 3, ch.3.

[58] A crucial question is whether, at bottom, one can say the same for the Aristotelian theory of action. Aristotle states that there is a need for *phronesis* precisely because the issue is not just what to do but when to do it (i.e., there is always a temporal index to the "right action," namely the index of the *kairos*, the "right time"). Furthermore, *phronesis* is also required because the right thing to do may often not coincide with what is habitual or natural. Granted these points, one can still argue that for Aristotle action is essentially a question of character-formation (*hexis*) and concerns the ways in which character can "trump" time and contingency if only it becomes "upright." Indeed, all ethical failings for Aristotle in the end boil down to the lack of character itself. See Aristotle *Nicomachean Ethics* 1100b15-20, and the discussion of *akrasia*.

[59] Machiavelli refers to this form as *natura* or *stato*: both terms can stand for habit (*hexis*).

[60] On the passive synthesis of custom, I refer to the discussion found in Gilles Deleuze, *Difference and Repetition*, ch. 2. On the relation between circular and linear time in the ancients as a function of the question of action versus custom, see my discussion in part 3, ch.2.

is an event in which the continuity of time is broken, in which there is a change of times that comports the destruction of form. One can say that forms emerge as the reification, or passive synthesis, of the event into the continuity of time which founds customs. But likewise forms are revoked into the domain of the event when there is a de-reification of this domain in and through counter-habitual action that changes the times. Only because this action de-reifies the event can one speak of it as being timely in the highest sense, namely, as effecting a discontinuity in continuous time such that one course of events is closed and a new one is opened, thereby reversing at once the passive synthesis of time. The new coincides with the revolutionary reversal of time.[61]

It is now possible to bring together the "optimistic" and the "pessimistic" theses. The "pessimistic" antithesis is taken into account by showing that human "nature" as custom and habit is inherently vulnerable to changes of circumstances. If one governs one's action according to custom, then one's fortune, i.e., the result of action, will be dependent solely on fortuna, on heteronomous chance as cause of change of times. In other words, Fortuna (the personification of a change of times that finds its cause outside of the scope of human action) is merely the mythical representation of one of the effects of reified action, an effect that, in this "upside-down world" of ideological representation, appears as a cause.[62]

The "optimistic" thesis is incorporated into the concept of revolutionary action that transcends the sphere of custom and habit. For Machiavelli, action becomes political when it breaks with the customary and innovates orders and laws. Only for this kind of action is there a real question as to its timeliness, i.e., as to whether it will be a match for (*riscontro*) the circumstances. And the question, carefully considered, is simply whether the times are ready to be changed or not; that is, whether the events let themselves be given a new course or not (in analogy with virtù giving a new course to fortuna). In this context, it is clear why the synthesis asserts that it is absurd to be "respectful" (*respettivo*) or "prudent" (*prudente*): when the question is whether the times or circumstances allow for their change, the answer can only be provided through action that is characterized by audacity (*audacia*) and impetuousness (*impeto*). In the grammar of action that seeks to "change the times," that is revolutionary, it is senseless to advocate that the actor be respectful: a gamble is a gamble, whether one is betting much or little. One cannot, in this sense, truly be *respettivo* and at the same time a gambler. This, perhaps, is the most proper meaning that can be given to Machiavelli's assertion that Fortuna is a woman who loves youth: chance loves those who take their chances against her, and conversely, there is chance only because there are those who take chances.

Machiavelli's synthetic formula opens the modern historical horizon because it states that the encounter or coincidence of human virtù (as free action) with the

---

[61] The closing and opening of new courses of time through counter-habitual action sublates that aspect of the optimistic thesis in which fortuna is compared to a river whose course can be controlled by means of sluices and gates.

[62] Analogously, in Marx the "invisible hand" of the market is the mythical representation of one of the effects of alienated labor. Its mythical quality is defined by the fact that this effect appears as a cause: hence the "magical" working of the "invisible hand" that establishes equilibrium in market dynamics.

times can only be conceived as the revolutionary changing of these times.[63] Modern historicity is disclosed when fortuna as sole cause of change of events is replaced by political action that goes against what is customary, by political action as revolutionary action.

THE PRINCELY ENCOUNTER WITH THE TIMES

Now the task is to understand what constitutes an action that changes the times in virtue of moving against custom. The synthetic formula must be given a more distinctly political reading. Put in terms of this formula, the question is why does fortuna favor those who take their chances against "her"? What makes for the "timeliness" of the untimely character of revolutionary action? The argument of *The Prince* contains a clue to this question. The prince inevitably loses the state if the latter is founded on chance (*The Prince*, VII). The foundation of the state must therefore be pursued by virtuous action that goes against fortuna (*The Prince*, VII and XXV). Furthermore, the stability of the state depends on the ability of the new prince to seek the foundation of the state in the people and their desire for freedom (*The Prince*, IX). It follows that a counter-customary action that goes against fortuna will be "timely" (in the sense that it will be able to change the times) only if it is "timely" in another, looser sense of encountering the people's desire for freedom. This is the sense of Machiavelli's frequent allusions to the quasi-identity between the "quality of the times" and the "quality of the people."[64] But, as I showed in the first part, there are two ways in which revolutionary, historically-effective action can encounter the desire of the people: the way of the civil prince and the way of the republic. In what follows I discuss the way in which the civil prince can "beat" Fortuna (the capricious goddess) by acting in such a way as to make the people, rather than chance, serve as a foundation of the state. In the next chapter I discuss the other encounter with the desire of the people in the republican event.

The idea that free political action has the power to move against the times allows Machiavelli to reject classical and Christian theories of providence and replace them by a modern theory of history. The formula "Fortuna is a woman: and it is necessary... to beat her" is the synthetic expression of Machiavelli's rejection of the providential reconciliation between virtue and fortune, whether this takes a worldly (Greek and Roman) or an other-worldly (Christian) shape.[65]

---

[63] Machiavelli's basic intuition is echoed by the third of Marx's *Theses on Feuerbach*, if only one operates the following substitutions: "The materialist doctrine that men are products of circumstances and upbringing, and that, therefore, changed men are products of other circumstances and changed upbringing, forgets that it is men who change circumstances and that it is essential to educate the educator himself.... The coincidence [*riscontro*] of the changing of circumstances [*fortuna*] and of human activity or self-changing [*virtù*] can be conceived and rationally understood only as revolutionising practice."

[64] For the people as foundation that resists fortuna: see Machiavelli, *Discourses on Livy*, II,30; and *The Prince*, VIII-IX, especially chapter IX and the reference to the people as true "subject" (*soggetto*, sub-ject, foundation) of the state's power. In that text Machiavelli hints at the quasi-identity between the people as "subject-foundation" and the "quality of the times," a thesis that he proposes in *Discourses on Livy*, III,8. I discuss this thesis in the following chapter.

[65] I refer to my discussions of this reconciliation in Greek thought (part 1, ch.1), Christian thought (part 2, ch.2), and Roman thought (part 2, ch.4).

But the formula also contains an explicit political meaning that becomes apparent when it is contrasted with the politico-philosophical assumptions of those contemporaries of Machiavelli who were not prepared to jettison the providential understanding of history.

Among these, certainly the figure of Ficino, whose Neo-Platonic circle found the sympathy of the Medici, stands out. Ficino responds to the Renaissance problematization of the conflict between fortuna and virtù by sublating it into the Platonic understanding of their reconciliation. Responding to a query posed to him by Giovanni Rucellai[66] as to whether "human reason and practical cleverness can do something against the contingencies of Fate or Fortuna," Ficino answers:

You ask me what is fortuna and how to counter her: To the first question I answer that fortuna is what happens outside of the order that we usually know and desire but nonetheless happens according to the order that is known and seen by what moves and wills above our nature; so that what is called luck and chance [fortuna e caso] in relation to us, can be called fate [fatto (scil. fato)] in relation to universal nature and prudence in relation to the intellectual principle and rule in relation to the highest good. To the second question I answer that the way to govern oneself well in those things that happen by the fatal and legal order of chance [ordine fortuito fatale e legale] is taught by that which is equally the principle of this order and this knowledge is also taught by this order so that it does not impede or remove but follows and completes the universal government. Keeping these things in mind, we will approach to the secret and divine mind of our Plato, prince of philosophers, and we will end the letter with this moral sentence: that it is good to combat fortuna with the weapons of prudence, patience, and magnanimity. Better still is to flee such a war from which very few come out victorious and those few with intellectual effort and extreme exertion. The best of all is to make peace with her by conforming our will with hers and willingly go where she points to so that she will not drag us there by force. We will do all this if in us there is harmony between patience, wisdom, and will. Finis. Amen.[67]

Ficino recommends that one ought to govern oneself with regard to the conflict between virtù and fortuna by disengaging oneself from this conflict at the practical level and engage it only at the intellectual level, if at all. His recommendation explicitly presupposes the Platonic, and later Boethian idea that chance is a manifestation of divine providence. As a consequence any attempt to change the course of affairs which is determined ("known and seen") by this order would in the end be an impious attitude that sets the individual against the divinely established, "fatal and legal" order of things.

Ficino's advice to prudently adapt the individual's way of proceeding to the ways of fortuna is followed by Giovanni Rucellai to the letter: Rucellai apparently conceived of the marriage between his son, Bernardo, and Piero de' Medici's daughter Nannina as an instance of a successful adaptation to fortuna. This marriage is represented in a print in which Bernardo Rucellai is depicted naked, in the position of a mast, holding the sails of a boat guided by Nannina, with the inscription: "I let myself be guided by fortuna hoping in the end to have good

---

[66] Giovanni Rucellai was the main aristocratic supporter of the Medici in Florence during Machiavelli's youth. On his politico-philosophical position, see Felix Gilbert, "Bernardo Rucellai and the Orti Oricellari: A Study on the Origin of Modern Political Thought"; idem, "Florentine Political Assumptions in the Period of Savonarola and Soderini".

[67] Ficino, letter to Giovanni Rucellai. Quoted in Warburg, Ausgewählte Schriften, 149. Emphasis mine.

fortune [*Io mi lascio portare alla fortuna sperando alfin davvero buona ventura*]."[68] As Aby Warburg points out, this print testifies to the willingness on the part of the Rucellai family to let itself be governed by the fortunes of the Medici family, with Nannina representing the mythical Fortuna herself.

The document is symptomatic of a deeper ideological phenomenon: during this period in Renaissance Florence a passive, or at best "contemplative," attitude towards Fortuna is directly associated with an active support for the Medici and, more generally, for an aristocratic, if not tyrannical, understanding of politics.[69] Ficino explicitly places his solution to the question of fortuna under the figure of Plato, and if one recalls that Plato's appreciation of *tyche* grows out of the attempt to bring about an absolute government of laws through tyranny, then it is not surprising that the analogous position that accepts the primacy of fortuna over virtù is the philosophical pendant to an anti-republican political position.[70]

Bernardo Rucellai, an important political and intellectual figure on his own account,[71] was the closest disciple of Ficino and became the supporter of Giovanni Pontano, the Neapolitan philosopher who took Ficino's place as the leading intellectual guide of the Florentine aristocracy. It was Rucellai and the circle of the Orti Oricellari who placed Ficino's and Pontano's respective appropiations of the Platonic and Aristotelian variants of the classical approach to the question of fortuna at the service of a modern aristocratic, or elitist, understanding of politics.

Machiavelli, by contrast, inaugurates the most radical version of the modern approach to the question of fortuna: his break with the classical paradigm closely corresponds to the modernity of his republican political thinking. It is well known that Machiavelli's personal career as Secretary of the Florentine Republic crossed paths with the plans of Bernardo Rucellai who was the leader of the aristocratic party in Florence and intended to bring back the Medici, or, at the very least, undermine the Republic headed by Soderini. Considered under this light, the synthetic formula that "Fortuna is a woman: it is necessary, if one wants to keep her under, to beat and hit her," acquires its direct political significance as a provocative invitation to Lorenzo de' Medici, to whom *The Prince* is dedicated, to cast away the traditional Medicean assumption that the power of the prince had

---

[68] Warburg refers to the print found in the Bibiloteca Nazionale of Florence, Manuscript II. III. 97, apparently one of the prints made by Baccio Baldini in the series "Imprese amorose." I follow Warburg's brilliant reading of the understanding of Fortuna in the aristocratic circles of Renaissance Florence, and in particular his famous interpretation of this document. (Ibid., 138-141).

[69] On Florentine political assumptions in the early Renaissance, see the classical works by Felix Gilbert, "Florentine Political Assumptions;" Nicolai Rubinstein, "Politics and Constitutions in Florence at the End of the Fifteenth Century," in *Italian Renaissance Studies*, ed. E.F. Jacob (London: 1960); and Rudolf von Albertini, *Firenze dalla repubblica al principato* (Turin: Einaudi, 1995).

[70] On this topic, see Wind, "Platonic Tyranny and Renaissance Fortuna;" and Alison Brown, "Platonism in Fifteenth-Century Florence and Its Contribution to Early Modern Thought," *Journal of Modern History* 58 (1986): 383-413. On the Medici's appropiation of Platonic themes to legitimate their domination, Brown writes: "The quality necessary to transform the power of wealth into a political asset was wisdom.... Bartolomeo Scala in his letters, Cristoforo Landino in his *Camaldulensian Disputations*, and Marsilio Ficino on the preface to his *Platonic Theology* all encouraged Lorenzo de'Medici to combine philosophy with supreme public authority – as Ficino put it, 'as Plato above all wanted to happen in great men'. Sapientia/potentia, wisdom combined with power, becomes again the crucial formula to justify Lorenzo's status in Florence." (Ibid., 394).

[71] On Bernardo Rucellai, see Felix Gilbert, "Bernardo Rucellai and the Orti Oricellari;" and Mario Santoro, *Fortuna, ragione e prudenza*, passim.

to rest with the support of the aristocracy. A support which, in turn, depended on the guidance of Bernardo Rucellai, leader of the pro-Medici faction in virtue of his marriage to Nannina de' Medici alias Fortuna.

In contrast to the Neo-Platonic political thought of the Renaissance which favors an aristocratic support for the state, and thus views Venice as the ideal republic,[72] Machiavelli inaugurates the modern republican understanding of fortuna by arguing that only the state which finds its support in "the people that desires not to be commanded or oppressed by the nobles"[73] can engage success-fully in the conflict with fortuna, and manage to impress a new course to the events. As Machiavelli makes clear when he advocates that form of the state called a civil principality, "for a prince it is necessary to have the people as friend; otherwise he has no remedies in adversities."[74] And such a civil principality is the model of the modern state. Modernity is predicated of any state that pursues its permanence in history by confronting the "ups and downs" of the times on the basis of popular support.[75] In this sense, Venice exemplifies an ancient state because it attempts to resist the flow of historical events by stabilizing its orders through the exclusion of the principle of popular freedom and relies, instead, on the classical, aristocratic prejudice in favor of the prudence of lawgivers and patricians.

But the encounter of political action with the desire for freedom of the people cannot just take the princely form described in *The Prince*. As I argue in the next part, the *Discourses on Livy* shows that the inclusion of the people in political life need not be reduced to turning the people into the subject-foundation of the state. On the contrary, this inclusion necessarily opens the possibility for the people to become the subject-actor of periodical renewals of the constitutional framework of the state. It is the real possibility of such renewals that gives political life its "republican" character. The desire for freedom as no-rule embodied in the people can never be satisfied by a fixed political form, that is, by a determinate order of political and legal domination. As a consequence, this desire tends to be either excluded or domesticated by the process of state-rule and stands in conflict with it. For this reason, modern political life, if it is to counter fortuna, must open the state to revolutionary changes of its political form made on behalf of the excluded claims to freedom.

Machiavelli reverses the priority of form over event by showing that the change of political forms, in revolutionary political events intended to give political expression to popular freedom, accounts for historical becoming and provides the unsurpassable horizon in which the modern state must construct its unity and struggle for its permanence in time. In *Discourses on Livy*, III,1 he conceives of the revolutionary event in which orders and laws are changed in order to give expression to political freedom as no-rule through the figure of a "return to

---

[72] An excellent discussion of the Neo-Platonic philosophers and their influence on Rucellai and the group of the Orti Oricellari is found in Sasso, "Machiavelli e i detrattori, antichi e nuovi, di Roma." It is no coincidence that Plato's *Laws* influenced Bernardo Rucellai through the translation produced in Venetian intellectual circles, as Sasso remarks.

[73] Machiavelli, *The Prince*, IX.

[74] Ibid.

[75] Machiavelli, *Discourses on Livy*, I,6.

beginnings" (which literally translates the Latin *revolutio*). This return to beginnings indicates an encounter between action and times in which innovation and repetition coincide. The modern concept of revolution, far from entailing a return to the purity of archaic origins, to the "Golden Age," as was the case in classical thought,[76] expresses a movement that goes against the grain of the times in order to bring something new to light. The figure of the return to beginnings plays a decisive role for the republican tradition in modernity because it corresponds to the modern experience of revolutionary events in which the necessity of a given legal and political order is brought back to the contingency of its emergence, and therefore lets itself be overthrown; while, conversely, the contingency of new orders are given the appearance of necessity. In Machiavelli freedom and history, rather than Nature or God, become the terms in which the difference between necessity and contingency is framed for the first time in modernity.

---

[76] Paradigmatic examples are found in the myth of Kronos expounded in Plato's *Statesman*, and in Vergil's *Fourth Eclogue*. I refer to my discussion of this myth in part 3, ch. 2.

CHAPTER 4

THE PEOPLE AS SUBJECT MATTER OF HISTORY:
FORTUNA AND VIRTÙ IN THE *DISCOURSES ON LIVY*

HISTORY AS EFFECT OF AMBITION:
THE ARISTOCRATIC CONCEPTION OF HISTORY.

The problem of the Ghiribizzi reappears in the *Discourses on Livy*, where it is a question of the people's encounter (*riscontro*) with the times. The theory of the *riscontro* between action and circumstances receives an explicit political articulation afforded by the idea that there is an analogy between the circumstances as the "subject" of action and the people as the "matter" of political life.

Again, Strauss is one of the few interpreters who has paid attention to this analogy between the sphere of chance and the people as basis of political form.[1] He claims that for the ancients "the establishment of the best regime depends necessarily on uncontrollable, elusive fortuna or chance" in the sense that it depends on the chance of finding the people "fit for the best regime; whether or not that matter is available depends in no way on the art of the founder, but on chance."[2] For Machiavelli, instead, "chance can be conquered"[3] and it is not impossible but only very difficult "to transform a corrupt matter into a good matter; that obstacle to the establishment of the best regime which is man as matter, the human material, can be overcome because the matter can be transformed... by an outstanding man who uses extraordinary means."[4]

Undoubtedly, the *Discourses on Livy* expands the potentialities of political action such that action can change the times (even though, *pace* Strauss, this does not amount to "conquering chance"), and that the people as "matter" can pass from a state of "corruption" to its opposite. But these two potentialities, far from indicating Machiavelli's adherence to the project of realizing and securing the state by any means necessary, i.e., by disregarding morality and denying the transcendence of the good, as Strauss claims, instead open a wholly distinct horizon: that of historical becoming as the result of revolutionary changes of state pursued on the basis of the people's desire for freedom.

Machiavelli's idea that history is the result of changes of times caused by the polemical encounter between political action and its circumstances, therefore, depends on giving the concept of circumstance an immediate political character by associating it with the people as the "subject matter" of political action. In turn, political action confronts a situation characterized by the dualism of desires found

---

[1] For another viewpoint on this topic, see J.G.A. Pocock, "Custom and Grace, Form and Matter: An Approach to Machiavelli's Concept of Innovation," in *Machiavelli and the Nature of Political Thought*, 153-174.
[2] Strauss, "Three Waves of Modernity" 85.
[3] Ibid., 86.
[4] Ibid., 85.

in political subjects: the desire to be free as non-domination and the desire to dominate. Machiavelli associates the former desire with "the people" and the latter with "the nobles." As a consequence, it is possible to conceive of history not only as the result of the encounter between action and the "popular" desire for freedom, but also as the result of the encounter with the "noble" desire for domination. The latter case envisages the classical topos of history as the result of human ambition, or what can also be called the aristocratic conception of history. Machiavelli's discourse, therefore, not only offers a deduction of such a conception of history but also gives grounds to judge its relative validity with respect to the conception of history as the result of human freedom. I begin by treating the former in order to clear the way for the latter, which constitutes Machiavelli's effective innovation in political thought.

The account of the noble conception of history in the *Discourses on Livy* starts from the following premise:

It is a saying of ancient writers that men tend to grieve with the bad and to get bored with the good [*affligersi nel male e stuccarsi nel bene*], and that from both of these two passions result the same effects. Because whenever one takes away from men the occasion to engage in conflict out of necessity, they will engage in conflict out of ambition; the latter is so powerful in human hearts, that it never abandons them, no matter how high they rise.[5]

There are a number of indications in this passage that one finds oneself amidst the problem of the Ghiribizzi. Since the *Ghiribizzi al Soderino*, Machiavelli has brought attention to the tendency in individuals to remain captivated in a given state (be it a "bad" or a "good" one).[6] Similarly, the phenomenon that two distinct behaviors may lead to the same result, first analyzed in the *Ghiribizzi al Soderino*, is used to engage the problem of fortuna, for it denotes the dependence of human ways of acting on intermediary and heteronomous causes in order to attain their result. The underlying principle of the analysis of fortuna remains unvaried: the fixity of human "nature" opens the individual to the sphere of fortuna.

The second part of the passage posits a connection between the disclosure of the sphere of fortuna and the fact that individuals engage in conflict either out of necessity or out of ambition.[7] Human beings are always dissatisfied with their situation and attempt to change it through conflict.[8] In particular, the conflict arising out of ambition is responsible for the kind of change of times that allows fortuna to hold sway over the life of individuals.

---

[5] Machiavelli, *Discourses on Livy*, I,37.

[6] In the *Discourses on Livy*, Machiavelli refers to this dictum once again (III,21) and even gives advice about it (III,31). I discuss these texts in part 3, ch.4 in the context of his theory of political action.

[7] Interpreters have yet to identify the source of Machiavelli's "saying of ancient writers." On this problem, see the comments by Inglese and Mansfield/Tarcov in their respective editions of the *Discourses on Livy*. The difficulty may very well be due to the fact that no such source exists. Machiavelli may simply be giving his rendition of the operative presupposition in the classical conception of history, i.e., history as the result of conflicts due to unchecked ambition. In general, Machiavelli tends to associate the "noble" or "aristocratic" perspective on worldly affairs to that of the "ancient authors": they reflect, in other words, the noble prejudice.

[8] In any case, the two reasons given for conflict here are matched by assertions made to this effect in *The Prince*, XV and XVIII.

Nature has created men so that they are able to desire everything and are unable to attain every thing.... From this arises the variability of their fortune; for since some men desire to have more, and some fear to lose what has been acquired, they come to enmities and to war, from which arise the ruin of one province and the exaltation of another.[9]

This famous account of historical change needs to be situated within Machiavelli's discourse as a whole. The passage occurs in the context of showing how the conflicts around the Agrarian Laws were the cause of the Roman civil wars that led to the end of the Republic. Machiavelli explains these events in terms of the hegemony of the desire for "all things," for "substances," in the political actors.[10] But this desire is not identical to the desire "not to be dominated" that is ascribed to the people: if the desire for substances explains the conflict out of ambition, then the desire for freedom accounts for the conflict out of necessity. The logic of ambition can explain the events of the civil war only because the people have become corrupt to the extent that the desire for possessions has taken over from their desire for freedom, that is, because the people have become "ennobled." In this sense, the conflict around the Agrarian Laws is the struggle between nobles and plebeians over property, as opposed to freedom. This kind of conflict has the potential to degenerate into a civil war because it is a war between homogeneous, "noble" desires for domination.[11]

The importance of situating Machiavelli's various pronouncements on human "nature" within his complex discourse on history cannot be overestimated. In the passages under analysis, one can see how Machiavelli anticipates the Hobbesian theory of desire that characterizes human beings in the "state of nature." But if Machiavelli, just like Hobbes, agrees that the unbridled conflict between desires to dominate cannot but lead to civil war or the "war of all against all," he also shows why this war is a result of a historical process of corruption of the desire for freedom as non-domination. Unlike Hobbes, Machiavelli does not locate the "war of all against all" in the ahistorical "state of nature," so that he is not forced to claim, as Hobbes does, that the passage from nature to history depends on the institution of the "absolute dominion" of the state.[12] On the contrary, because for Machiavelli the passage to the "state of nature" (civil war) is determined by the corruption of freedom, and this civil war can only be ended by the absolutization of the state (as occurred in Rome with the emergence of the Empire), then, conversely, civil war will be avoided only if freedom is historicized, that is, de-

---

[9] Machiavelli, *Discourses on Livy,* I,37.

[10] In *Discourses on Livy,* I,37 he reiterates that individuals desire possessions more than honors.

[11] Machiavelli's analysis in this case supports Arendt's controversial claim made in *On Revolution* that social conflict, which turns on the question of poverty, as opposed to political conflict, which turns on the question of freedom, has no solution. I leave aside, in this context, a detailed discussion of Machiavelli's analysis of the nobility. Suffice it to say that Machiavelli is one of the first political thinkers to identify the noble desire with the unbridled desire to possess. In so doing he contradicts the widespread belief in classical political thought that only the nobleman (*spoudaios*) can separate himself from the sphere of the *oikos* and of property in order to aim for the "good life." Ultimately, Machiavelli attacks the ideal of magnanimity in the aristocracy that is theorized both by Aristotle and Cicero. This allows Machiavelli to show the ideological character of the attachment to the "public good" in the nobility, something that Cicero's impassioned defense of private property in *De Officiis* reveals quite clearly.

[12] Hobbes, *De Cive,* V,11 and VI,13.

naturalized. This can only happen if its polemical relation with the possibility of "absolute dominion" is reinstated, something that happens in what I call republican or revolutionary events.

The historical situatedness of the logic of ambition, its secondary character with respect to the logic of freedom, is reiterated in *Discourses on Livy,* I,46. Discussing the civil conflict between patricians and plebeians, this chapter attempts to explain why "the desire to defend freedom caused each party, as soon as it prevailed, to oppress the other party... as if it were necessary either to offend or to be offended."[13] This passage, more than asserting a thesis held by Machiavelli himself, raises the question whether the desire that is connected with ambition is the same as the desire to defend freedom: does ambition exhibit a universal scope, belonging both to the nobles and to the people? The question serves as one of the principal dividing lines between liberal and republican thinkers in early modern political theory: if the answer is assumed to be affirmative, then one sides with Hobbes's "negative" anthropology; if it is negative, then one sides with Rousseau's "positive" anthropology.[14]

As becomes clear from the development of the argument, Machiavelli does not share the thesis he considers in the passage under analysis: the merely hypothetical character of the assertion ("*as if* it were necessary either to offend or to be offended") must be taken seriously. The point is precisely that it is not necessary either to offend or to be offended, but that this is the opinion of those who live ambitiously in a republic, those who want to live "above the law." Necessity and

---

[13] Machiavelli, *Discourses on Livy,* I, 46. It is crucial to notice that Hobbes assumes as unconditionally valid what in Machiavelli is merely a hypothetical assertion: "All men in the state of nature desire and will to hurt, but not proceeding from the same cause, neither equally to be condemned.... This man's will to hurt ariseth from vain glory, and the false esteem he hath of his own strength; the other's from the necessity of defending himself, his liberty, and his goods, against this man's violence." (Hobbes, *De Cive,* I,4).

[14] For Hobbes, "vain glory" or ambition is a fundamental passion of human beings in the state of nature: "Now whatsoever seems good, is pleasant, and relates either to the sense or to the mind. But all the mind's pleasure is glory (or to have a good opinion of one's self), or refers to glory in the end; the rest are sensual, or conducing to sensuality, which may be all comprehended under the word conveniences. All society therefore is either for gain, or for glory; that is, not so much for love of our fellows, as for the love of ourselves. But no society can be great or lasting, which begins from vain glory.... I hope no body will doubt, but that men would much more greedily be carried by nature, if all fear were removed, to obtain dominion, than to gain society. We must therefore resolve, that the original of all great and lasting societies consisted not in the mutual good will men had towards each other, but in the mutual fear they had of each other." (Hobbes, *De Cive,* I,2).

In contrast, Rousseau holds that neither "vain glory" (*amour propre*), nor ambition or the desire for possession are natural or universal human dispositions: "N'allons pas surtout conclure avec Hobbes que pour n'avoir aucune idée de la bonté, l'homme soit naturellement méchant... ni qu'en vertu du droit qu'il s'attribue avec raison aux choses dont il a besoin, il s'imagine follement etre le seul propriétaire de tout l'Univers.... En raisonnant sur les principes qu'il établit, cet Auteur devoit dire que l'état de Nature étant celui où le soin de notre conservation est le moins préjudiciable à celle d'autrui, cet état étoit par conséquent le plus propre à la Paix, et le plus convenable au Genre-humain. Il dit précisément le contraire, pour avoir fait entrer mal à propos dans le soin de conservation de l'homme Sauvage, le besoin de satisfaire une multitude passions qui sont l'ouvrage de la Société, et qui ont rendu les Loix nécessaires." (J.-J. Rousseau, *Discours sur l'origine et les fondements de l'inégalité parmi les hommes* [Paris: Gallimard, 1985], 83). As is well known, apart from the desire for self-conservation, the only other passion that Rousseau attributes to the human being in the state of nature is "natural pity," "vertu d'autant plus universelle et d'autant plus utile à l'homme, qu'elle précède en lui l'usage de toute réflexion." (Ibid., 84). For Rousseau, it is "la raison qui engendre l'amour propre, et c'est la réflexion qui le fortifie." (Ibid., 86).

ambition are confirmed as two equiprimordial but distinct sources of political conflict. There is no "necessity" of ambition. To believe otherwise is to adopt the perspective of Callicles, who sees in the law merely a tool in the hand of the people to oppress those who are "stronger" or "nobler."[15] The grammar of "offend or be offended" characterizes only those who speak and act from the subject-position of the nobility, with its substantive interests and above all with its desire to dominate. To think exclusively in terms of "offenses" is therefore an essential feature of the concept of what is noble or aristocratic. This concept expresses the idea of being superior to others in the specific sense of being exempt from things (such as the equality of all before the law) that are considered to be "offensive," in principle, to the ideas of privilege and status (whether they be determined by Nature or by God). By maintaining the crucial difference between necessity and ambition Machiavelli can argue that the only kind of conflict which effectively counters fortuna is the one that arises out of necessity. Furthermore, the sense in which a conflict is said to be "necessary" can only be determined in relation to the idea of political freedom as no-rule.

To support these two claims I turn to the last text in Machiavelli's long analysis of the role of ambition in politics. The forty-ninth chapter of the *Discourses on Livy* makes two remarkable points: first, a free city often requires new laws to deal with new threats to its freedom, and, as a consequence, no legislator can have the necessary foresight to establish once and for all a set of laws sufficient to assure the future good of the community. Machiavelli says that the capacity to frequently change laws is due to the "free beginning" (*principio libero*) of the free city. It is in the context of elaborating the significance of free beginnings that Machiavelli clearly demonstrates the compatibility between necessity and freedom: the free beginning allows the city to deal better with the condition that "new necessities in governing were always discovered, and it became necessary to create new orders.... Provisions that helped keep Rome free for the time its lived in freedom."[16] Having a free beginning allows the city to re-order itself according to necessity: freedom necessitates renewal of orders.

Machiavelli remarks that the principal reason for the necessity of such renewals of orders is due precisely to the ambition of the nobility. Rome was able to deal better than other cities with the problem posed by ambition because the power to punish, in the sense of the power to maintain the equality of all before the law, was vested with the people and its desire for no-rule.[17] This remark confirms the interpretation I give in the first part as to what Machiavelli means by the expression "free beginning": it does not just mean that the city has an autarchic foundation (e.g., that it is not a colony), but more basically that the principle (*principio*) of the city is that of freedom, which locates the beginning (*principio*)

---

[15] Machiavelli's implicit reference to Plato's *Gorgias*, 507-509 is quite striking, although it is not often remarked upon.

[16] Machiavelli, *Discourses on Livy*, I,49.

[17] In Hobbes, the power of the sovereign or state is constituted by the "sword of punishment." In order to achieve this power, the contract of association that creates it must at the same time be a pact of subjection of every individual to the sovereign. (Hobbes, *De Cive*, V,6 and VI,5-6). The decisive premise that allows Hobbes to construe a univocal relation of command between the state and the people is the universality of ambition.

of the free city with the repeated emergence of popular power (in the sense of *potestas in populo*).[18]

The relation between freedom, necessity and renewal unveiled here expresses Machiavelli's belief that political freedom emerges when political orders are renewed according to necessity, and therefore not once and for all. Far from being a concept with an intrinsic relation to an ahistorical concept of nature, necessity connotes the kind of heteronomy that is equivalent to an openness to the change of historical situations, an openness to the emergence of the new.[19] Similarly, by making necessity the criterion for the renewal of orders, Machiavelli rejects the idea that these orders are to emerge from the mind's theoretical grasp (*theorein*) of universal, ahistorical orders or forms. Machiavelli continues the polemic against the Platonic privilege of mind (*nous*) over necessity (*ananke*) by linking necessity to freedom. The assignment of a privilege to necessity over mind (or prudence) with respect to the establishment and change of political form is to be explained by the changed finality of this form which is no longer the "good life" (that would require the priority of *nous*) but the "free life." In sum, only the perspective of freedom allows one to discern what is necessary, in both of its manifestations: as the equivalent of the realization of freedom through the imposition and grounding of political form; and as the criterion of the occasion to renew this form itself. For Machiavelli freedom is both the criterion of itself and of its contrary.

THE UN-HISTORICAL READING OF NECESSITY: THE ASTROLOGICAL CONCEPTION OF HISTORY.

Those interpreters who read Machiavelli's use of the concept of necessity as an indication that he lacks a modern historical sense often find recourse in a treatment of the problem of fortuna that occurs in *Discourses on Livy,* II, 29-30.[20] In the course of discussing the theme of unexpected threats to the freedom of cities, Machiavelli seems to advocate an understanding of historical events that betrays an adherence to providential beliefs as well as to astral determinism: "many times one will notice the emergence of things and the happening of accidents for which the heavens [*i cieli*] have simply not wanted people to provide

---

[18] The implications for political freedom of this interpretation of the problem of beginnings is discussed at length in part 3.

[19] "Every day new causes emerged for which it [Rome] had to make new orders in favor of a free way of life." (Machiavelli, *Discourses on Livy*, I, 49).

[20] See Parel's discussion of the "tradition of astrological natural science" that he claims dominates Machiavelli's historical discourse: "Machiavelli sometimes appears to attribute to heaven a naturalistic providence or pronoia over humankind.... There is no suggestion in Machiavelli that the universe is run by 'blind' forces. At the same time, the motion that runs the universe does not emanate from a wholly transcendent Good or, for that matter, from a wholly transcendent Mind.... The motion from heaven has both physical and non-physical occult attributes: so much so that one could almost speak of a quasi-providence." (Parel, *Machiavellian Cosmos,* 37). One of the central examples adduced by Parel to support his claim that "even to act virtuously, one needs the 'providential' assistance of heaven" is *Discourses on Livy,* II, 29: "the analysis of the Gallic War is premised on the theory of naturalistic providence." (Ibid., 40). Eugenio Garin also tends to interpret Machiavelli's conception of history as heavily influenced by astral determinism, see Garin, *Machiavelli fra politica e storia*; idem, *Rinascite e Rivoluzioni* (Rome: Laterza, 1976).

for."[21] Such occurrences even happened in Rome, in spite of "so much virtue, so much religion, and so much order." It would seem that these accidents demonstrate "the power of the heavens [*cielo*] over human things."[22]

The example that Machiavelli has in mind is the invasion of Italy by the Goths and the consequent sack of Rome. After listing all the uncharacteristic mistakes that the Romans committed in order to find themselves in such a weak position, he refers to Livy's explanation of how such unusual behavior could have come about: "to such an extent does Fortune blind spirits where it does not want its impetus to be stemmed."[23] Then Machiavelli continues:

Nor can this conclusion [Livy's saying] be more true; from which it follows that men who live customarily [*ordinariamente*], in great adversity or prosperity deserve neither praise nor blame. For most often it will be seen that they have been brought to ruin or to greatness by a great favor that the heavens made them, giving or taking away from them the opportunity [*occasione*] to operate virtuously. Fortuna does this well, since when she wants to lead to great things she elects a man of so much spirit [*spirito*] and so much virtù that he recognizes those opportunities that she proffers him. Likewise, when she wants to lead to great ruin, she advances men who will aid in that ruin. As can be seen very well from this text [*questo testo*], when, in order to make Rome greater and lead it to the greatness it came to, fortuna judged it was necessary to beat it... but still did not want to ruin it altogether.... In ordering this, she prepared everything in view of Rome's recovery.... I affirm it anew to be very true, according to what all the histories tell us, that men can second fortuna but not oppose her; they can weave her plot [*orditi*] but not break it. They should indeed never give up for, since they do not know her purpose, and because she moves on tortuous and unknown paths, they have always to hope and, in hoping, not to give up, no matter what fortuna and what trouble they find themselves in.[24]

It is not hard to see why this passage appeals to those interpreters who see Machiavelli's discourse caught in the astrological web of beliefs prevalent in its times, asserting not only the omnipotence of Fortuna but also "her" providential character.[25] But a slightly more careful reading reveals both the ironical sense in which Livy's saying is cited (Machiavelli argues exactly the opposite point both in *The Prince* and elsewhere in the *Discourses on Livy*), and the parodic intention behind the adoption of the language of providential Fortuna found in many Roman historians. That *Discourses on Livy,* II,29 cannot be taken at face value is also suggested by the fact that this text presents perhaps the strongest version of the Idle Argument, which Machiavelli destroys in the numerous treatments of the problem of the Ghiribizzi. The achievement of the above passage therefore lies in its great rhetorical ability to condense, strictly for purposes of parody, the

---

[21] Machiavelli, *Discourses on Livy,* II,29.

[22] Ibid.

[23] "Adeo obcaecat animos fortuna, cum vim suam ingruentem refringi non vult." (Livy *Ab Urbe condita* 5,39). Notice that the image of fortuna as an irrepressible force is rejected by Machiavelli in *The Prince*, XXV.

[24] Machiavelli, *Discourses on Livy,* II,29.

[25] Parel cites two other instances of Machiavelli's belief in astrological determinism of this providential kind: *Discourses on Livy,* III,1 and I,56. In the third part, I argue at length that *Discourses on Livy,* III,1 is the text that gives strongest support to the claim that in Machiavelli one finds a modern conception of history. As to what regards the text of *Discourses on Livy,* I,56 one can provide the same deconstruction of its "apparent" astrological meaning as I provide for *Discourses on Livy,* II,29.

essential traits of the providential treatment of Fortuna found in much Roman historiography in order to dismantle them in the very next chapter.

The force of Machiavelli's parody becomes apparent if one reviews some basic assumptions of Roman historiography. Polybius's *Histories* raises the question of the causes of Rome's greatness and resolves it by understanding the development of Roman history in terms of a synthesis or reconciliation between virtue and fortune.[26] The general form taken by Polybius's solution plays a determinant role in the Roman historico-philosophical understanding of fortuna in its relation to politics. In Livy, the topos of whether fortuna or virtue (*virtus*) lies at the root of Rome's greatness is discussed in the famous counterfactual excursus on the possible results of an encounter between Rome and Alexander the Great.[27] Livy begins by stating that "it seems that the most important elements in war are the number and the courage of soldiers, the talents of the commanders, and luck, which is a powerful influence on all the affairs of men and particularly in warfare."[28] Fortuna is understood as the force which changes circumstances unpredictably, for Livy asserts that Alexander, though undoubtedly a prodigious commander, was also lucky to die young and not live to see fortuna change on him.

However impressive we find the great reputation of this man, the fact remains that it is the great reputation of a single individual built up from the successes [*felicitate*] of little more than ten years, and those who sing its praises on the grounds that the Romans have been defeated in many battles, even if they have never lost a war, whereas Alexander's good fortune never failed him in a single battle [*nullius pugnae non secunda fortuna fuerit*], do not understand that they are comparing one man's achievements – and those of a younger man too – with the exploits of a nation now in its eighth century of warfare. Should it be surprising, then, if on one side more generations are counted up than years on the other, that there have been more vicissitudes of fortune over so long a period of time than in the space of thirteen years?[29]

Livy clearly implies that the virtue of the Roman people was tested by the change of fortune, whereas Alexander's was not, since he always had fortune on his side, albeit for a brief time.

The opposition between the history of the Roman people and the biography of a single individual, no matter how great, reminds one of the Periclean belief that adverse chance can affect individuals but not the *ethos* of an entire city or of a people, since this *ethos* is fashioned in time and by resisting just those changes of fortune. This is why Livy's concluding argument, after comparing the merits of the Roman armies with those of Alexander, is decisive for his conception of fortuna:

For arrows, impassable defiles, regions with no roads to carry supplies can well cause fear amongst heavily armed troops, but Rome has driven back a thousand armies more dangerous than those of

---

[26] I refer to the discussion of Polybius in part 1, ch.1.

[27] Livy *Ab Urbe condita* 9,17-19. In what follows I rely on Sasso's impeccable scholarship in "Machiavelli e i detrattori, antichi e nuovi, di Roma," which contains the most extended references to Roman texts on the topos of the causes of Roman greatness. But my interpretations of the single authors and of the significance of their discourses differs markedly from those given by him.

[28] Livy *Ab Urbe condita* 9,17.

[29] Ibid., 9,18.

Alexander and Macedon, and this she will do, provided that the love of peace which rules our lives and our care for civil concord [*pacis amor et civilis concordiae*] continue unbroken.[30]

Livy identifies in civil concord (*civilis concordia*) the element present in the Roman people that allows them to withstand, with their virtue, the changes of fortune, so that, as a result, it appears as if Roman history acquires its providential sense (*providentia*). Livy's idea of providence is the result of the conciliatory encounter between chance and virtue: "And it seemed that the effort of the siege would last as long as in Veii, if luck [*fortuna*], and the proof that a Roman captain gave of his known loyalty in leading military campaigns, had not given them a rapid victory."[31] In these cases, fortuna acquires its providential sense because it becomes a sign of the Roman virtue which is elected to succeed. As Livy states elsewhere: "but the result demonstrated that luck helps the strong [*sed euentus docuit fortes fortunam iuuare*]."[32]

Vergil's *Aeneid* echoes the Livian belief that the apparent opposition of virtue and fortuna gives way to their effective reconciliation. Vergil grants the omnipotence of fortuna, which is identified with *fatum* or the ordainment of things in accord with the will of Jupiter.[33] But fate or fortune is, in a first moment, counterbalanced by human strength and striving: "let us follow where our fates may lead, or lead us back. Whatever comes, all Fortuna can be mastered by endurance [*Quidquid erit; superanda omnis fortuna ferendo est*]."[34] In a second moment, it is fortuna itself that comes to the aid of the virtuous in a providential way: "Fortune favors men who dare [*Audentis Fortuna iuuat*]."[35] The more that Roman virtue acquires the traits of an ethical substance, as opposed to the traits of mere military prowess, the more fortuna takes on the semblance of providence: the unity of virtue and chance in providence finds its ground in the idea of an ethical substance characterized by the *concordia civium* that Livy saw in the origins of Rome, describes in its decay and final exhaustion in the civil wars of Caesar, and experiences together with Vergil in its recomposition under Augustus.[36]

The explicit theorization of the providential synthesis of fortune and virtue is found in Plutarch's *De Fortuna Romanorum*, which only apparently seems to argue that the cause of Rome's greatness lies with its fortuna. In fact, for Plutarch the opposite is the case: from the beginning of this text, which has been handed down incomplete, the author insists that the opposition between virtue (*arete*) and fortuna (*tyche*) is overcome in the case of Rome's development into an empire. Plutarch argues that only the reconciliation between these two powers gives as a result the providential pattern of Roman history:

---

[30] Ibid., 9,19.
[31] Ibid., 5,26. Another example of the providential encounter between virtue and chance: "To the Gauls that were leaving the City luck herself [*fortuna ipsa*] wanted to give a testimony of Roman valor [*virtutem*] by pushing them to Ardea, where Camillus lived in exile." (Ibid., 5,43).
[32] Ibid., 8,29.
[33] "Fortuna omnipotens et ineluctabile fatum." (Vergil *Aeneid* VIII,334).
[34] Ibid., V,710.
[35] Ibid., X,284.
[36] For all these motifs, see Cochrane, *Christianity and Classical Culture*, part 1, passim.

However much Fortune and Virtue perpetually contend and struggle with each other, the probability is that, in order to form such a mighty power and empire, they made a truce, and collaborated in the execution and completion of this noblest of human works.... Time, who, with God's help, laid her foundations, yoked Fortune and Virtue together, so as to use the special powers of both in creating for all mankind a hearth truly "holy and wealth-giving," a secure "mooring-cable," an abiding element, an "anchor in the surge and drift" of this shifting world.[37]

The reconciliation of virtue and fortune which constitutes providence depends on giving virtue the specific meaning of actions that have as their end the civic concord that Roman authors, whether historians or philosophers, inevitably locate at the origin of the Roman republic. Cicero gives a clear formulation of this interpretation of political virtue:

Thus, before our own time, the customs of our ancestors called to the government of the state the most excellent men, and eminent men preserved our ancient customs and the institutions of their forefathers. But though the republic, when it came to us, was like a beautiful painting, whose colors, however, were already fading with age, our own time not only has neglected to freshen it by renewing the original colors, but has not even taken the trouble to preserve its configuration and, so to speak, its general outlines. For what is left of the "ancient customs" on which the poet said "the commonwealth of Rome" was "founded firm"? They have been, as we see, so completely buried in oblivion that they are not only no longer practised, but are already unknown.... For it is through our own faults, not by accident, that we retain only the semblance of the republic, but have long since lost its substance.[38]

The "ancient virtues" to which Cicero refers belonged to the aristocratic elements of the city,[39] which employed their *auctoritas* in order to keep all political conflict, stemming from the demands of the plebeians for wider participation and land reform, within the bounds of moderation and in so doing produced that concord to which the greatness of the early republic was attributed. One may conclude that fortuna acquires its providential traits only from the perspective of the aristocratic reading of Roman virtue.

Once the ancient civic concord, together with the ancient virtue, is understood to have disappeared, then the representation of fortuna changes character and becomes the fickle force of circumstances that has the best of the Roman state and undoes its providential development. Sallust's *De Coniuratione Catilinae* offers the most famous description of this meaning-shift in the history of the concept of fortuna. Sallust argues that fortuna brought about the decadence of ancient virtue and thereby the discord of the civil wars which are no longer distinguished by that moderation shown by the conflicts of the early Republic, a moderation that was made possible by the control that the nobility had over political life. This concept of omnipotent fortuna is opposed to the connection between virtue-as-concord and providence-as-chance of which Polybius, Livy, Vergil and Plutarch speak.[40] The meaning-shift demonstrates, retrospectively as it were, not only that Roman

---

[37] Plutarch *De Fortuna Romanorum* 316-317.

[38] Cicero *De re publica* V,1.

[39] The *aristoi* and *sophrones* of whom Posidonius speaks in *Athen.* 6, 273a-b (=265 Edelstein-Kidd; fr.59 Jacoby).

[40] "Sed profecto fortuna in omni re dominatur; ea res cunctas ex lubidine magis quam ex vero celebrat obscuratque." (Sallust *De coniuratione* 8).

greatness was not a matter of mere chance but also that authentic virtue always calls upon itself the favor of fortune.[41]

The text of *Discourses on Livy,* II,29 cited above appropiates a number of the motifs found in the Roman elaboration of the theory of fortuna. For example, Machiavelli's assertion that "in order to make Rome greater and lead it to the greatness it came to, fortuna judged it was necessary to beat it... but still did not want to ruin it altogether.... In ordering this, she prepared everything in view of Rome's recovery," reflects the providential understanding of fortuna established in the passages cited from Livy. Likewise, when Machiavelli states that "this is very true, according to what all the histories tell us, that men can second fortuna but not oppose her; they may weave her web but not break it," he is faithfully recapturing the assumption, found in Vergil and Plutarch, that fortuna is destiny which has to be endured with *virtus.*

But Machiavelli's text also betrays its parodic intention. To begin with, it repeatedly emphasizes that the providential concept of fortuna exists only as a discursive regularity: the traits of fortuna "can be seen very well *from this text* [of Livy];" and "I affirm again that this [feature of fortuna] is very true, *according to what all the histories tell us.*"[42] By pointing out the discursive status of the Roman providential idea of fortuna, Machiavelli implies that such an idea is ideological, a fictional construct which does not correspond to the *verità effettuale* of historical becoming. Secondly, in *Discourses on Livy,* II, 29 it is clearly stated that the power of "the heavens" (*i cieli*) or "fortune" (*la fortuna*) (they are used as synonyms here) is greatest when "men live customarily" (*ordinariamente*). The text purposefully excludes from consideration that "extraordinary virtù" (*virtù istraordinaria*), i.e., that kind of action which goes counter to what is customarily done, and, instead of seconding fortuna in "her" plot, opposes and beats "her."

Machiavelli's irony with respect to the providential discourse on fortuna is again visible when he speaks about those "chosen" individuals who accomplish great things: here it becomes clear that the "opportunity" (*occasione*) furnished to them by fortuna is nothing short of unexpected disasters that permit the emergence of those who do have extraordinary virtù: "without that opportunity the virtù in their spirit [*la virtù dello animo loro*] would have extinguished itself, and without that virtù the opportunity would have come around in vain."[43] The resolutely worldly appreciation for the "opportunities" offered by bad fortune plays off and with the Boethian understanding of providence for which all fortune, and especially bad fortune, is ultimately good because it gives occasion for the

---

[41] "Because the greatness of the Roman people is certainly not due to chance [*non fortuito*], but to its wisdom and to its discipline in so far as it was not hindered by an adverse fortuna [*nec tamen adversante fortuna*]." (Cicero *De re publica* 2,XVI).

[42] Machiavelli, *Discourses on Livy,* II, 29. Emphasis mine.

[43] Machiavelli, *The Prince,* VI. In *The Prince,* VI and XXVI, Machiavelli points out that all founders were "fortunate" precisely to the extent that there was misfortune all around them. In particular, they were "fortunate" enough to find peoples who were completely disbanded or enslaved, so that "one can say that they [the founders] received from fortuna only the occasion [*non avessino altro dalla fortuna cha la occasione*]; which gave them the matter [*materia*] into which they could introduce whatever form they pleased [*quella forma parse loro*]." (Ibid., VI).

mind to leave worldly affairs to their fated course and elevate itself to the contemplation of the divine source of this fate.[44]

Machiavelli also undermines the strong claims on behalf of fortuna apparently made by *Discourses on Livy*, II, 29 when he discusses the role of fortuna in the case of political disasters. These are purportedly caused by fortuna having "elected" incompetent individuals to lead their cities: the irony here is that this way of positing the agency of fortuna at the same time undermines it. Fortuna becomes the effect of the tautology that if incompetent individuals are put in charge then the result will be disastrous: obviously it does not take fortuna as a heteronomous cause of events to make it so. In the end, Machiavelli's ironical descriptions of fortuna's providential character make the same point that Spinoza would famously make about the presence of teleology in nature: both are anthropomorphic constructions of the imagination.

The parody of the use of providential constructs by Roman historians is intended as a warning to their future readers: the analyses of actions contained in these histories are as vitiated and prejudiced in proportion to their reliance on mythical constructs such as providence or fortuna. Nonetheless, for Machiavelli the fact that these constructs are purely discursive does not deprive them of a certain effective reality, but only as ideological expressions of particular political positions. For instance, if a political subject acts in accordance to the belief that "men can only second fortuna but not oppose her; they can weave her web, but not break it," then it will turn out to be true that fortuna has power over the actions of individuals, and that the best one can do is to maintain one's hope in something that is completely undecipherable and capricious.[45] The ideological force of the Roman belief in providence consists in reinforcing the perspective of the aristocracy on the dynamics of Roman history and of its political and social conflicts.

That Machiavelli's parody intends to expose the ideological constructs of the "aristocratic" reading of Roman history is confirmed as clearly as possible in the chapter which immediately follows upon it. In fact, *Discourses on Livy*, II, 30 operates a glaring reversal of the literal meaning of *Discourses on Livy*, II,29. Read together, these two chapters constitute one of the most elegant examples of Machiavelli's art of writing which allows the text to perform what it cannot say, namely, the way in which it should be read. This lesson in reading offers at the same time one of Machiavelli's basic lessons in political thinking. It is as if his discourse were to say: "think about politics like you read this text of mine: paying attention to the contexts in which statements are made, varying your perspectives on any given utterance, understanding the effect that is sought by those who proffer it at this time, in this place, and so on." Time and again, Machiavelli proves to be acutely aware of the textuality of his discourse, of the dialogism and heteroglossia that characterizes its text.

---

[44] Boethius *Consolation of Philosophy* II,8 and IV,7.

[45] The advice to maintain one's composure in all circumstances reappears in *Discourses on Livy*, II,27 and III,41; but the context is rather different and not ironical, unlike in the passage under consideration.

Returning to *Discourses on Livy,* II,30 one sees that it takes back everything that the preceding chapter asserts as "true" concerning the omnipotence of fortuna. It explicitly argues that fortuna has such great power to determine events (or, better, is posited as having such power) only because of the political mistakes made by the Romans. But in direct contrast to Livy's account, Machiavelli identifies the fundamental mistake in the attempt by the nobles to disarm the people: "*the heart and the vital parts of a body are to be kept armed, and not the extremities of the body... because the foundation of its state [il fondamento dello stato suo] was the people of Rome.*"[46] Livy is unmasked as maximizing the role of fortuna in proportion to his minimizing the political importance of "the people of Rome." In so doing Livy gives an ideological rendition of the *verità effettuale* of the events, not so much because he shares the aristocratic reading of Roman history present also in the likes of Cicero and Sallust, but because the appeal to providence or fortuna as an explanation of the course of human events dispenses with the need to thematize the political and social conflicts that effectively determine these events. The formula of a reconciliation between fortuna and virtue is the sublimated image of the Roman aristocratic wish-fulfilment: a version of Roman greatness in which the disempowerment of the people and their desire for freedom, in which the neutralization of the irreconcilable discord that this desire engages with the dominating "virtue" of the aristocracy, is complemented by the empowerment of a mythical agency, fortuna, which favors the "virtues" of the aristocracy.

By identifying the armed people as the "foundation" of the Roman state, Machiavelli gives an entirely different sense to the conflict of virtù and fortuna.

Because, where men have little virtù, there fortuna indeed shows its power; and because she is varied, so do republics and states vary frequently, and they will always vary until someone emerges that is so great a lover of the ancients [*della antichità tanto amatore*] as to be capable of regulating them in such a way that fortuna may not have cause to show, with every rotation of the sun, how much she can do.[47]

In conjunction with the previous passage that ascribed fortuna's empowerment to the disempowerment of the people, Machiavelli makes clear that there is only one political solution to the problem of the change of fortuna, and it consists in arming the people as foundation of the *stato*. For Machiavelli, it is *il popolo* and its desire for freedom that must be armed, and thereby granted *potestas*, if the wheel of fortune is to be arrested and stripped of its providential and divine hypostatization. In a brief formula: the pursuit of political freedom alone guarantees the elimination of all mythical and theological foundations of political domination. It also follows, as a corollary, that if the texts of *Discourses on Livy,* II,29 and II,30 are read together they refute in a startling fashion those interpretations which claim that Machiavelli's conception of history, far from being modern, is captivated by

---

[46] Machiavelli, *Discourses on Livy,* II,30. Emphasis mine.
[47] Ibid.

all sorts of pre-modern beliefs, ranging from astral determinism to divine providence.[48]

The above quoted passage from *Discourses on Livy,* II,30 does not say what kind of virtuous "regulation" of the state is required to give the people the power that arrests the revolutions of fortuna. Nevertheless, Machiavelli's association of the revolutions of the wheel of fortune to the solar revolution indicates, by way of contrast, what kind of political movement would arrest and counteract the revolutions of fortuna. As I discuss in the next part, this movement takes the form of "untimely" and "counter-natural" revolutions of the orders of the state. This revolutionary political action receives the metaphorical name of "return to beginnings." It is this name that explains the sense in which this passage intimates that Livy was not a "great lover of the ancients" because of his underappreciation of the political role of the people. The "antiquity" that Machiavelli has in mind refers to that political action which goes "against the course of time," i.e., returns to the beginnings, by renewing the orders of the state in order to empower the people's desire for freedom. Thus, in so far as Livy privileges the "ancient virtues" of the aristocratic hegemony, he proves to be, paradoxically, not a "true lover of the ancients."

THE PEOPLE AS SUBJECT MATTER OF HISTORY

Machiavelli's critique of the aristocratic or noble interpretation of history prepares the way for the third major treatment of the problem of the Ghiribizzi, found in *Discourses on Livy,* III, 8-9 where the people and their desire for freedom constitute the "subject matter" of the encounter (*riscontro*) between political action and the times.[49] In *Discourses on Livy,* III, 8 the problem of the encounter between action and times is situated in the context of a discussion on the conditions for changing a republic into a tyranny. Reflecting on the early attempts to set up tyrannies in the Roman republic, Machiavelli argues that the Roman people (considered as "the subject [*suggetto*]" of the "mode of life of the city [*modo del vivere della città*]") rejected the "bad form" (*trista forma*) on account of their uncorrupt character.[50] In both cases analysed, that of Spurius Cassius and Manlius Capitolinus, Machiavelli points out that the nobility and the people surmount their discord for the sake of eliminating the danger of tyranny. The ambition of Spurius "was exposed by the Fathers and brought under so much suspicion that when he spoke to the people and offered to give them money… they refused him altogether, since it appeared to them that Spurius wished to give

---

[48] This reading also serves to reconfirm the break effected by Machiavelli with respect to Roman political and historiographical discourses, which is all too often denied. One wonders how carefully interpreters read texts when they are led to make claims such as this: "[Machiavelli] shows not the slightest interest in demythologizing the past, not the slightest intention of challenging the conventions of a rhetorical – and necessarily inaccurate – retelling of ancient deeds. Not for a moment did Machiavelli stray from the conventions of Latin historiography, which perpetuated Roman myths and used them to arouse the young." (Hulliung, *Citizen Machiavelli,* 166).

[49] The specific theory of political action that derives from this situation is analyzed in part 3, ch.4 in relation to *Discourses on Livy,* III,21-22.

[50] Machiavelli, *Discourses on Livy,* III,8.

them the price of their freedom."[51] Likewise, in the case of Manlius, "none of the nobility moved to favor him, although they had been very fierce defenders of one another.... Although the people of Rome, very desirous of its own utility and a lover of things that went against the nobility, did very many favors to Manlius, nonetheless, as the tribunes summoned him and delivered his cause to the judgment of the people, that people, from defender having become judge, without any respect condemned him to death."[52] From which it is easy to see that when Machiavelli refers to the "perfection of that city and the goodness of its matter [*la bontà della materia sua*]"[53] he means the "matter" of the political body considered as united in its discord between the people and the nobility.

It is the discord between popular and noble desires that tyranny attempts to negate, now favoring one desire, now another. The lack of corruption in the subject matter of the city does not at all mean that the nobles and the people find themselves in harmony, undivided, but, on the contrary, it means that they are able to unite in order to preserve their discord, which animates the free political life. One can say more: although Machiavelli points out that it is the nobility or its organ (the Senate) that picks out the tyrants (as a direct threat to their own exercise of legitimate domination), it is always and only the people that decides their fate, that rejects them (because of the logical impossibility of uniting the desire for no-rule with the desire for uncontested rule). In this sense, there is a clear priority assigned to the people over the nobility as ground of the uncorrupt character of the political matter.

The idea that the success or failure of political change depends on the "quality" of the subject (*suggetto*) matter (*materia*) of political life rather than on the kind of political form that is being imposed constitutes a major innovation in the tradition of political thought because it makes political change dependent on the desires of those who are ruled rather than on those who want to rule, i.e., who want to impose a given form. By way of contrast, a fundamental presupposition of classical political thought is that all political change is initiated by the desire to rule, or better: by the conflict that the various and heterogeneous claims to rule give rise to.[54]

The new priority of matter over form permits Machiavelli to deduce the following two consequences:

the first, that one must seek glory in other ways in a corrupt city than in one which still lives politically [*viva politicamente*]; the other (which is nearly the same as the first), that men in their ways of proceeding and even more in great actions must consider the times and accomodate themselves to them. And those who through a bad choice or through natural inclination are discordant

---

[51] Ibid.
[52] Ibid.
[53] Ibid.
[54] See Plato *Laws* 690a-691d; idem, *Republic* 434a4-6 and 545d1-3: "change in every regime comes from that part of it which holds the ruling offices – when faction arises in it." Also Aristotle, in this sense, follows Plato: see *Politics* 1301a35-39 and 1302a23-27. For a general overview of classical theories of political revolution, see Lucio Bertelli, "Metabole Politeion," *Filosofia Politica* 2 (1989): 275-326.

with the times [*si discordano dai tempi*] live for the most part unhappily and their actions have bad results; the opposite happens to those who are concordant with time [*si concordano col tempo*].[55]

Two aspects strike me as decisive in this passage. The first being that the distinction between a city that is "corrupt" and one that "lives politically" depends on the kind of matter which is present in the city, as opposed to the kind of form which it exhibits. If the matter is "alive" then the city itself is considered to be politically alive and will not allow the imposition of tyranny. The condition of possibility of radical political change (from republic to tyranny or from tyranny to republic) depends on the degree of passivity shown by the people as "subject matter" of political life. To use Hegelian terminology, one can say that for Machiavelli everything turns on understanding the people not just "as substance" but also "as subject."[56]

The second decisive aspect of the passage concerns Machiavelli's remark that there is an identity of sorts between the first thesis (according to which the success of political action depends on the quality of the people) and the second one (according to which the action is successful if it "concords" with the times). Machiavelli speaks of the second thesis as being "nearly the same as the first [*che è quasi quel medesimo*]." In other words, he just about (*quasi*) identifies the (quality of the) times (*i tempi*) with the (quality of the) people.[57] Political action, and particularly those "great actions" consisting in the change of state (*mutazione di stato*), depends for its result on both the subject upon which it acts and the times in which it is carried out. This ambiguous quasi-identity posited between the times and the people sheds new light on the meaning of Machiavelli's theory of *riscontro* which holds that if the action is discordant with the times, then it will fail; if it is concordant with them, then it will succeed.

But the same text contains a further complication in that it posits quite another sort of relation between matter and time, which has to be equally taken into account in order to elucidate the political significance of the theory of the *riscontro* as it is presented in the *Discourses on Livy*. Continuing the discussion of the conditions for political change, Machiavelli asserts:

---

[55] Machiavelli, *Discourses on Livy,* III,8.

[56] I discuss the double possibility expressed in the idea of the people as subject matter of political form in part 3, ch.1.

[57] The analogy between times or circumstances and the political "subject matter" is also found in Aristotle: "government too is the subject of a single science, which has to consider what government is best... to be most in accordance with our aspirations, if there were no external impediment, and also what kind of government is adapted to particular states. For the best is often unattainable, and therefore the true legislator and statesman ought to be acquainted, not only with that which is best as such [*haplos*], but also with that which is best relatively to circumstances [*ek ton hypokeimenon*]." (Aristotle *Politics* 1288b21-28). As it turns out, by "circumstances" (*hypokeimenon* is better translated as subject matter, Machiavelli's *suggetto* or *materia*) Aristotle refers to the "elements" contained in each state, in accordance to which the best form of government is determined. These "elements" are composed of the families and the multitude of citizens considered according to "differences of wealth... and differences of rank and merit" which determine their respective claims to rule. (Ibid., 1289b30-1290a1). Elsewhere, Aristotle distinguishes between the "necessary elements" for the "mere existence" of the state, like wealth and freedom, and those elements, like justice and courage [*polemikes arete*], without which the state cannot "exist well." (Ibid., 1283a20-23).

But it is necessary, if one wants to take authority in a republic and put in it a bad form [*trista forma*], to find the matter disordered by time [*la materia disordinata dal tempo*], and which little by little, from generation to generation has brought itself into disorder; into which condition the matter is led by necessity, unless it be, as we wrote above,[58] frequently refreshed by good examples and with new laws brought back to its beginnings [*ritirata verso i principii suoi*].[59]

Whereas previously Machiavelli emphasizes the quasi-identity between matter and time, here he introduces a great difference between matter and time. The passage of time, of itself, is said to corrupt the matter and brings it into a state of disorder. This process happens "out of necessity" unless there is a "return to beginnings."

The reversal of the classical conception of matter expressed here is quite extraordinary: from being the primary source of corruption and disorder, matter has passed to be its primary object. For the moment, though, the pressing questions concern the way in which the passage of time brings disorder into the subject matter of the city, and what kind of disorder is at issue. If one understands how time dis-orders the subject matter, and thus can be said to be "discordant" with this matter, one can understand, conversely, what it means to act in a "concordant" way with the times (and with the matter). In fact, the meaning of acting in "concord" with the times is determined by two elements: that time dis-cords or dis-orders the matter; and that there is a quasi-identity between the times and the subject matter. Therefore, to act in concord with the times will mean to act against whatever causes time to dis-cord the matter and, by virtue of their quasi-identity, also the times.

Upon reflection, it is clear that the disorder (*disordine*) of the subject matter refers to its corruption, which in turn permits the imposition of the *trista forma* of tyranny on the city. Thus by corruption Machiavelli means the loss of the desire for freedom in the people.[60] The "beginning" (*principio*) to which the subject matter must be lead back (*ritirata verso i principii suoi*) if it is to counteract this process of corruption can only refer to the event in which the subject matter first came to "life," i.e., when the people passed from being merely the inert matter of the founder's creative act to become the "heart" of the republic, the principle that accounts for the city being "politically alive." This event is symbolized by the withdrawal or "retreat"[61] of the Roman plebeians to the Aventine hill, and the subsequent creation of the Tribunate of the people whose function was to protect the republic from the danger of tyranny exerted by the aristocracy.

If this is the case, then the dis-order of the people qua subject matter must be due to their loss of that very principle (*principio*) which kept the people together and ordered, not as such, but in the event, and throughout the event, when they expressed their fundamental discord with the nobles. This principle is the desire not to be dominated or oppressed. In other words, the fundamental "discordance"

---

[58] Machiavelli refers to his discussion of the "return to beginnings" in *Discourses on Livy,* III,1. I analyze this aspect of his theory in the next part.

[59] Machiavelli, *Discourses on Livy,* III,8.

[60] I refer to my discussion of the concept of corruption in part 1, ch.6.

[61] In Italian the term *ritirata* has both meanings: to draw something back, and to "retreat" in the military sense.

between time and matter that leads to the disorder of the latter, paradoxically, is caused by the loss on the part of the matter of its principle of discord. Conversely, this entails that the only action which can be in "concordance" with the times and with the matter (so that their quasi-identity is re-established) is that action which returns the matter to its originary discordance and simultaneously "goes against the times" (i.e., against what dis-orders and corrupts the subject matter). The action which is a match (*riscontro*) for the times is revolutionary action.

This dense chapter ends with the claim that the relation between political action, the subject matter, and the times, is addressed through the question of those political actions that are "in favor of freedom or in favor of tyranny."[62] Both types of action must "concord" with the times and the subject matter if they are to succeed. In this case, Machiavelli returns to the quasi-identity between times and subject matter and thinks this quasi-identity in terms of the desires of the people: "because it is as difficult and dangerous to want to free a people that wants to live enslaved, as it is to want to enslave a people that wants to live freely."[63] This passage supports my contention that the corruption or dis-order of the subject matter refers to its desire to live slavishly; whereas the problem of the return to beginnings is precisely that of awakening or responding to its desire to live freely.

Once again, the significance of these formulas consists in the overturning of the traditional sense of what it means to act "in accord" with the times. Machiavelli opens the possibility of a "difficult and dangerous" but not impossible type of action which consists in changing the times, and not simply being "adequate" or "in accord" with them, in and through awakening the principle of discordance carried by the people as subject matter of a free political life. This possibility for political action is disclosed once the idea that time is corruptive of the matter has been introduced, for then it becomes necessary to think a "return to beginnings" as the formula for an action which "goes against time," i.e., an action which consists in "freeing a people that wants to life slavishly." At this point the problem of the Ghiribizzi culminates in the problem of revolutionary action, which I discuss in the next and last part of the book.

THE REPUBLICAN ENCOUNTER WITH THE TIMES

The topic of *Discourses on Livy*, III, 9 is a reprise of the problem of the Ghiribizzi from a republican perspective. Or, better, this problem sets the stage for the central question of the third book of the *Discourses on Livy*: what is a revolutionary event? What kind of encounter between the action and the times is required in order to effect the passage from slavery to freedom? Here I briefly review the stage, and notice some changes in its set-up, before passing on to the discussion of the above questions.

Echoing his treatments of the problem in the *Ghiribizzi al Soderino* and *The Prince*, Machiavelli remarks that he has,

---

[62] Machiavelli, *Discourses on Livy*, III,8.
[63] Ibid.

often considered that the cause of the bad and of the good fortune of men is the matching [*riscontrare*] of their mode of proceeding with the times. For one sees that some men proceed in their actions with impetuosity, some with respect and caution. And because in both of these modes suitable limits are passed, since one cannot observe the true way, in both one errs. But he comes to err less and to have prosperous fortune who matches the time with his mode [*riscontra... con il suo modo il tempo*], as I said, and always proceeds as nature forces you [*e sempre mai si procede secondo ti sforza la natura*].[64]

With respect to the other versions of the theory of the *riscontro*, Machiavelli only adds two variants. The first consists in the clarity with which the ideal of prudence is eliminated: irrespective of the "way of proceeding," the individual will err and transgress the "suitable limits" in any case, being unable "to observe the true way [*non potendo osservare la vera via*]." No action seems to be able to embody the mean. The reason for this failure lies with human "nature" which makes it impossible to adopt "the middle way [*via del mezzo*]" between different "ways of life [*modi di vivere*]": one cannot both be impetuous and cautious, gentle and cruel.[65] At best, the individual can at times be one and at times be the other, thus leaving open the success of a mode of action to the "match" that it may have with the times in question. From the proposition that the "best" way, the middle way, is unachievable it follows analytically that every way of life or *ethos* has its inconveniences, every *ethos* is a kind of extremity, a form of erring. Machiavelli situates action within a logical space in which only considerations of the "less bad," or of "erring less" apply, rather than those of "the best" or "the good."

Only those actions which are performed according to a given *ethos* forego the possibility of hitting the "middle way" between extremes. These actions proceed from an *ethos* that has become "second nature" to the individual: one "always proceeds as nature forces you [*e sempre mai si procede secondo ti sforza la natura*]." Given this naturalization of action, assuming that all of these habits are fallible, then "to err less and have a prosperous fortune" depends on whether or not the *ethos* "matches" the times. And this is equivalent to letting chance be the guide: it is "good fortune that made this way of proceeding match well with the times [*la buona fortuna fece che questo suo modo riscontrò bene con i tempi*]."[66]

For Machiavelli an *ethos* or "way of life" is not an object of choice: this is another way of saying that an *ethos* functions in the individual as its "nature." There are two reasons why it is impossible for the individual to change "nature" with the times:

The first is that we cannot oppose ourselves to what nature inclines us; the other is that, when someone prospers greatly with one way of proceeding, it is not possible to persuade them that they may do better by changing their ways; which causes the changes in the fortune of one man, because she changes the times and he does not change his ways.[67]

---

[64] Machiavelli, *Discourses on Livy*, III,9.
[65] Ibid., III,21
[66] Ibid., III,9.
[67] Ibid.

These two reasons directly contradict the Aristotelian belief that "men do many things against habit and nature, if reason persuades them that they ought."[68] The object of the polemic against Aristotelian, and in general classical, conceptions of prudence is double: in the first place, it is not "reason" (*logos*) that allows the individual to act against "habit and nature." This is why, once the reification or naturalization of action into habit, into behavior, has taken place, it follows that the presence or absence of the "match" (*riscontro*) between the *ethos* and the times is determined by fortuna conceived as the heteronomous cause of the change of times and not by a rational principle.

But the second object of the polemic follows from the exclusion of the dimension of choice (*elezione*): this is another way of saying that no *ethos*, as such, can claim to be "the best," since there is no virtue without prudence and no prudence where there is nothing to elect. Not surprisingly, the exclusion of the aristocratic ideal of the "best" form of life, along with the teleological understanding of political action, proposed by the theory of the *riscontro* turns into an argument in favor of republics as against principalities. Republics have many available "natures" and "humors" to match against the times, and thus a higher possibility of success. The republic

can accomodate itself better than a prince to the diversity of times due to the diversity of the citizens that are found in it. Because a man who is accustomed to proceed in one way, will never change, as I said, and therefore it is necessary that he fall into ruin when the times change into disformity with his way of proceeding.[69]

At first sight it seems true that the mixture of diverse "natures" or *ethoi* is most likely to persist in time than any single "nature" or *ethos* because it has more chances to match the right "nature" to the given time. But this argument poses the problem of what determines which individual, which "nature," is in charge of the republic at any given time. If this determinant is not to be heteronomous fortuna, then the only other possibility consists in the kind of political action that keeps the republic from adopting one hegemonic *ethos* and thereby keeps it from becoming-individual, or becoming-one. But in order to maintain the openness of the republic to a plurality of *ethoi*, in order to make the republic into the open space of the "many," the political action has to be of a revolutionary sort, that is, it has to bring about the change, rather than the fixation, of its political orders.

To avoid "the ruin of cities... caused by the fact that the orders of the republic do not change with the times," political action has to move against the becoming-individual of the republic in order to spare it the heteronomy that characterizes the individual *ethos*.[70] If it is true that every *ethos* and every *natura*, in its fixity, succumbs to the changes of times, then it seems that political action as virtù, if it is not to participate in the becoming-one of the republic, has to become anti-natural and ethically-contradictory (in the sense of moving against an *ethos*).

---

[68] Aristotle *Politics* 1332b5.
[69] Machiavelli, *Discourses on Livy,* III,9.
[70] Ibid.

These two features of political action are the focus of the third part of my interpretation. In it I discuss a theory of political action which transcends the sphere of human nature and opens the dimension of human historicity. At the same time, the historicity of political action serves to illuminate the thorny topic of the conflict between politics and morality in Machiavelli, the problem of ethically-contradictory action.

PART 3

THE EVENT OF THE REPUBLIC – THE RETURN TO BEGINNINGS

Returning is the being of that which becomes.

Gilles Deleuze, *Nietzsche and Philosophy*

La république est par constitution attentive à l'évenement.

Jean Francois Lyotard, *Le Postmoderne expliqué aux enfants*

RETURN TO BEGINNINGS AS FORMULA FOR THE HISTORICITY OF FREEDOM

Interpreters have for the most part paid scant attention to the theory of "return to beginnings [*riduzione verso il principio*]" introduced at the start of the third book of the *Discourses on Livy*.[1] And yet it is difficult to exaggerate its importance for Machiavelli's entire discourse. By articulating his theory of political freedom through a discourse on historical repetition (i.e., the theory of return to beginnings) Machiavelli posits an internal link between freedom and historical becoming as well as the anti-foundational character of freedom. Political freedom exhibits such an internal link to history because it exists only in a repetition (return to) that coincides with an innovation (beginning). In political theory, there exists only one phenomenon that combines repetition and innovation in what I shall call the event of originary repetition: this is the phenomenon of modern political revolutions. The theory of the return to beginnings therefore inaugurates modern revolutionary thinking.

Situating political freedom in the context of the return to beginnings makes of this freedom the experience of the non-integrity of origin. Freedom comes into existence (beginning) only by breaking with the primacy of foundations and of principles in an event of originary repetition (return to). Freedom is anti-foundational in the sense that it begins as a return, hence as what lacks principle and origin (*arche, principium, principio*). Such an unprincipled or anarchic conception of political freedom entails the effective negation of an essential or "natural" difference between who commands (*princeps*, prince) and who obeys (*civis*, citizen). This difference, though it may be legitimately drawn, nonetheless lacks a substantial a priori ground. The legitimacy of the division between ruler and ruled, always already, depends on the possibility of its delegitimacy, on the

---

[1] Sasso, for instance, holds the opinion that in the theory of return to beginnings nothing new is contained with respect to the previous concepts, arguments and topics introduced in the first eighteen chapters of the *Discourses on Livy*. "The necessity of the 'return' to 'beginnings'... is nothing but the formula which recapitulates his thought on constitutions – on the relation that must establish itself between laws and the changing reality of things which forms these constitutions." (Sasso, *Niccolò Machiavelli*, 507). For Sasso the "historicity of states" forms part of Machiavelli's political theory, but he does not draw an essential link between this historicity and the return to beginnings. In general, Sasso is surprisingly cavalier about the third book of the *Discourses on Livy*, which he believes to lack a unifying theme, unlike the other books. (Ibid., 613). Mansfield either misreads or minimizes the theory of return to beginnings. (Mansfield, *Machiavelli's Virtue*, 118 and 75, respectively). In his commentary of the *Discourses on Livy*, the return to beginnings is treated without any historico-philosophical contextualization which sets his reading from the start on a false footing. (Mansfield, *Machiavelli's New Modes and Orders*, 299-304). Viroli speaks about the problem of "restoration of liberty" as the restoration of the rule of law by "founders or redeemers," without analysing the structure of return to beginnings that is constitutive of such a "restoration." (Viroli, *Machiavelli*, 143-147). Strauss, Lefort and Pitkin are among the most significant interpreters who pay somewhat more attention to the theory. They are each treated in the appropiate context.

possibility of returning politics to a site where the division is inapplicable. With the theory of return to beginnings Machiavelli introduces the idea that a free political life requires the transgression of those political forms that tend to fixate the division between ruler and ruled. Machiavelli calls for citizens who are capable of reversing their roles as political subjects and become political actors in revolutionary events that open spaces of isonomy and no-rule in political life.

This third part of my interpretation defends the claim that the theory of the return to beginnings completes Machiavelli's discourse on political freedom.[2] The first chapter situates the emergence of this theory of historical repetition within the context of the problem of giving political freedom a foundation. The second chapter provides a commentary of the text in which Machiavelli introduces the return to beginnings (*Discourses on Livy*, III,1). This close reading is needed not only because of the importance I assign to the theory, but also because to date there exists no extended discussion of this text, and its historico-philosophical context, in the secondary literature. The third chapter contains an argument for understanding the event-character of the return to beginnings as the first formulation of the concept of revolution in modernity. Finally, the fourth chapter offers a new interpretation of Machiavelli's critique of morality in light of the new conceptions of political action and citizenship that grow out of the anti-foundational understanding of political freedom.

---

[2] Negri also considers the "beginning and the conclusion" of the third book of the *Discourses on Livy* "as the crowning aspect of the constitutive movement of Machiavelli's thought." (Negri, *Le pouvoir constituante*, 90). The return to beginnings is deemed important (ibid., 102) yet no in-depth analysis is given of it. Negri fails to recognize that the theory of return to beginnings is nothing short of a theory of revolutions, and he fails to situate it in the context of the problem of historical repetition in modern historical consciousness. An attempt to provide a close reading of the return to beginnings is found in Thomas Berns, "Le retour à l'origine de l'état," *Archives de philosophie* 59 (1996): 219-248. Berns argues that Machiavelli theorizes the "historicity of the law.... Outside of every morality and of all pre-science of politics, events and their exigencies are the only secure, and even possible, basis for the law." (Ibid., 226) Unfortunately, Berns's analysis does not offer a theory of such events, nor does it link the return to beginnings, or originary repetition, to such a theory. Furthermore, it misses the role of the theory of return to beginnings in establishing the internal relation between history and freedom which alone determines the emergence and dehiscence of all political and legal form. As a consequence Berns remains caught in the interpretative scheme proposed by Strauss which identifies the topic of return to beginnings solely with that of law-constituting violence rather than law-transcending freedom. (Ibid., 219 and 243).

CHAPTER 1

THE APORETIC FOUNDATION OF POLITICAL FREEDOM

THE FREE STATE AND ISONOMY: ON THE SYMBOLIC VALUE OF BRUTUS

The theory of the return to beginnings addresses the problem of whether and how political freedom can be given a foundation. As Arendt demonstrates, this problem is that of modern revolution: "where the liberation from oppression aims at least at the constitution of freedom can we speak of revolution."[1] The constitution or foundation of freedom (*constitutio libertatis*) is synonymous with the "constitution of a republic."[2] Machiavelli offers the first modern discussion of the project of founding political freedom, of constituting the republic as a political form, and concludes that such a project is aporetic. Political freedom has an antinomical relation to the possibility of its own founding.[3] The theory of return to beginnings expresses this antinomy of political freedom: to return to a beginning is, in a strict sense, an impossible project because were such a return to occur, there would be no sense to the action of beginning. Analogously, the project of giving freedom a foundation is an impossible one in the sense that if such a foundation were possible, it would condition the possibility of freedom itself and thus negate it as free. As it functions in Machiavelli, the return to beginnings should rather be understood as figuring the experience of a radical loss of origin, the experience that nothing predetermines becoming. At the same time, this experience coincides with the emergence of effective renewals. Analogously, only the groundlessness of political freedom makes both for its radical finitude and ensures its existence and survival in and through its historical repetitions.

The aporia of the foundation of freedom is already visible in Machiavelli's discussion of the emergence of freedom after the expulsion of the kings in Rome by Brutus (*Discourses on Livy,* I,16-18). Political freedom is internally related to the entrance of the people into political life: the problem of the republic is the problem of the passage from a people as mere "matter" (that is given a "form" by the founder-legislator and the system of authority) to the people as a political "subject" animated by a counter-institutional desire for no-rule. The articulation

---

[1] Arendt, *On Revolution,* 35.
[2] Ibid.
[3] Negri identifies the centrality of the project of *constitutio libertatis* in Machiavelli, but not its aporetic character: "The *Discourses on Livy* have from now on [starting in book three] as their purpose the demonstration that the sole content of the constituting form [*forme constituante*] is the people, that the sole constitution of the Prince is democracy. The discussion turns toward the *institutio populi*." (Negri, *Le pouvoir constituante*, 90). I diverge from Negri's reading of Machiavelli because I argue that "the people," as bearer of a desire for freedom as no-rule, cannot possibly give itself a constitutional form of rule without negating this desire, and thereby themselves as "*pouvoir constituante*." In this sense, the power of the people is not a power that has as its final end a constitution of political form. The *institutio populi* is not a form of government, much the less of "absolute government," as Negri claims, but rather an event of political freedom in which any and every political form of government can be called into question and changed.

of this passage is symbolized by the figure and the actions of Brutus. There are two actions that Machiavelli associates with the symbol of Brutus: the expulsion of the kings, and the killing of his sons.

To identify the event in which the monarchy is expelled and the possibility of the republic (defined provisionally as "political life without kings") is established, Machiavelli employs the locution "the state becomes free [*lo stato che diventa libero*]."[4] But the opposition between the "free state" (*stato libero*) and the "tyrannical state" (*stato tirannico*) denotes, in the last instance, the locus of a problem: does the republic consist in a state of freedom (i.e., in a political form of domination which is free), or does it insist in events of no-rule, in those moments in which political life is free of the state-form?

From the start, Machiavelli discusses the possibility of the "free state" in terms of the difficulty to maintain it. This difficulty points to the precarious nature of the event of freedom, but not necessarily to the precarious nature of the state. *Discourses on Livy*, I,16 advances the thesis that political freedom, upon its emergence, lacks support: in becoming free, the state encounters the enmity of the nobility (favored by the preceding monarchy), and it does not meet the favor of the people because the "free life" (*vivere libero*) gives out honors only in proportion to merit and does not "offend" the sphere of private liberty (i.e., does not imperil the "security" of possessions), and "no one will ever confess to have an obligation to those who do not offend one."[5] Freedom as no-rule is difficult to maintain precisely because one of its characteristics is that it does not create obligations, and therefore it has a congenital problem with its own stabilization. The task is to find a political "subject" that functions as support for freedom and allows for its maintenance.

At this point, the text introduces the other aspect of the action of Brutus: to maintain the newly gained freedom it is necessary to "kill the sons of Brutus." The "sons of Brutus" represent the nobility, for whom "the freedom of the people seemed to have become their slavery."[6] Machiavelli justifies Brutus as follows: "Whoever takes up the governing of a multitude, either by way of freedom or by way of principality, and does not secure himself against those who are enemies to that new order makes a state of short life."[7] The action of Brutus therefore brings into the state the variable of the people's desire for freedom: only this variable grants the state access to freedom. But the freedom of the state does not designate the property of a unity, of a substance: it points to the problem of governing the people (*governare una moltitudine*). This problem receives two solutions: the people can be governed "either by way of freedom or by way of principality [*o per via di libertà o per via di principato*]."[8] As I showed in part one, the text of *Discourses on Livy,* I,16 leaves aside the first way (which becomes the explicit topic of book three where a republican theory of citizenship is developed), and proceeds to theorize the dynamics of the new principality. This

---

[4] Machiavelli, *Discourses on Livy,* I,16.
[5] Ibid.
[6] Ibid.
[7] Ibid.
[8] Ibid.

principality is "new" because it is not based on the nobility (as the "tyrannical state" prior to the symbolical act of Brutus), but seeks its support with the people. The task of the new principality becomes that of securing popular support by transmuting the people's desire for freedom as no-rule into a desire for security or negative liberty. From this unexpected development of *Discourses on Livy*, I,16 one can only surmise that the "free state" (*stato libero*) contains an antinomy: if the state is to persist (and that means: find a ground in the people), then it must negate the people's desire for freedom as absence of domination and transform it into negative liberty, thereby ceasing to be a state of freedom in the full sense of the term. In this sense, political freedom as no-rule is ungroundable: the freedom of the state denotes a political event that exceeds the political form as such.

Machiavelli implies as much by leaving open the possibility of governing the multitude "by way of freedom," as opposed to the government of the many that the "new" prince (or modern state) imposes. Hence there is an irreducible difference between "freedom" (republic) and "principality" (state). Although the prince can provide security to the people, it cannot satisfy the "popular desire to regain its freedom [*popolare desiderio di riavere la sua libertà*]."[9] The prince or state cannot give a foundation to freedom, but it can "govern" freedom by making it into a means for satisfying other desires of the many: in part to command, but mostly to live in security. This means that the "way of freedom," and the effective republic, has yet to be discussed after the first sixteen chapters of the *Discourses on Livy*. My claim is that the whole of the third book of the *Discourses on Livy*, which turns on the theory of the return to beginnings, offers just such a discussion. Only in the last book of the *Discourses on Livy*, and not before, does Machiavelli reveal the sense he assigns to the concept of republic.

Corruption is the other face of the event-character of political freedom. The treatment of corruption in these chapters (*Discourses on Livy*, I,16-18) is intended to locate the emergence of freedom, symbolized by Brutus, as an event that cannot be maintained within the form of the state. By bringing together the emergence of freedom and the growth of corruption in such close proximity, Machiavelli makes the point that freedom is something that must be returned to, that it is not a beginning in and for itself, something that emerges at once and integrally: only the return to beginnings forestalls corruption. The symbolic significance of Brutus consists in pointing to the non-coincidence of freedom and origin. Brutus names both the emergence of freedom in an event that breaks with the dynamic of state-formation (as I showed in the first part), and the non-integral character of every such emergence of freedom. Brutus denotes the kind of political event that must be repeated in order for it to be what it is, i.e., the event of the emergence of freedom. In short, Brutus is symbolic of a beginning which is not one; of an origin that remains what it is only by ceasing to be original and integral, and becoming something repeatable, something that requires its supplementation.

A good example of this double denotation of Brutus is found in *Discourses on Livy*, I,17 where the corruption of the political body is said to descend always from the head to the rest of the body. Rome would have been lost had it not rid

---

[9] Ibid.

itself of its king: "But since they [the Roman people] lost the head when the trunk was sound, they could easily be brought to live freely and ordered."[10] The emergence of freedom associated with Brutus shows its lack of integrity in that it consists in a symbolic break with the beginning of the Roman state, that is, with the system of authority that posits as absolute its beginning, the founding act of Romulus.[11] Brutus initiates political freedom by effecting a discontinuity with the beginning of the state, symbolized by the decapitation of the monarchic head. Here appears for the first time in the *Discourses on Livy* that peculiar character of political freedom that is explicitly thematized with the theory of the return to beginnings: freedom "begins" by cutting itself off from the ab-soluteness of beginning, from the foundation itself. The political body augments (its freedom) by reducing (its rule), i.e., by getting rid of its head.

After Machiavelli, the idea that a "free life" is attained in and through the "reduction" of the political body into an acephalic body comes to symbolize every revolution. The decapitation of the monarch in the French Revolution, for instance, was not a mere contingency: it also functioned as a sign that, also in this respect, the French were repeating the Romans, i.e., were "returning to begin-nings" in the new Machiavellian sense. By theorizing this kind of "reduction" of the political body, Machiavelli attacks all of the medieval representations of sovereignty and of the political body. Simply put, Christian political philosophy

---

[10] Machiavelli, *Discourses on Livy*, I,17.

[11] Berns does not distinguish the break that Brutus (event of political freedom) effects with respect to Romulus (system of authority) but flattens the former onto the latter: "What revives with Brutus... and which consists in reviving the initial leap of Romulus, is the moment of complete antagonism between a presence of the legislator – he kills, isolates himself in power, decides and wants something precise – and its effacement, its retreat – Romulus creates a senate in order to let history make itself, Brutus restores freedom and obeys the law.... These are the antagonisms, the circles that make the birth of the law something 'mystical' and inexpressible, otherwise than as a pure imposition and violence occurring in a memorable instant; [these antagonisms] make of the birth of the state, in a first moment, a simple *'augumento'*... which one must understand as the (first) movement of growth, the (first) vigor, the (first) power." (Berns, "Retour à l'origine de l'état," 245-6). The only sense of "beginning" that Berns accepts is the beginning of the state as posited by the system of authority; there is no sense that the "beginning" of the republic (in opposition to the state) may well correspond to a movement in which the event of repetition is originary, productive in and through its break with origins.

A similar elision of the break effected by Brutus with respect to the religious system of authority set up by Romulus, Numa and the Senate is found in the recent reading of archaic Roman politics and law given by Giorgio Agamben, *Homo Sacer. Sovereign Power and Bare Life* (Stanford: Stanford University Press, 1998). It is significant that Agamben's reading of the *homo sacer* ("one whom the people have judged on account of a crime. It is not permitted to sacrifice this man, yet he who kills him will not be condemned for homicide") completely avoids discussing the political context in which such a function of *sacratio* first emerges, namely, in the context of the plebeian secession from the Roman state and provides the content of the first tribunitian law. Agamben, instead, reads the *sacratio* solely in terms of establishing the "sovereignty" of the state law and as the *arcanum* of political domination, thereby abstracting from it all of its potentially emancipatory connotations. (Ibid., 81-2, 88) Whereas it could be argued that, if the function of "sacrifice" belongs to the system of authority of Roman state religion, then the first tribunitian law, "if someone kills the one who is sacred according to the plebiscite, it will not be considered homicide," can be seen as giving the right to violently resist the religious authority of the state and the persons embodying it – something like the first articulation of the 'legitimacy' of tyrannicide. This right, obviously, could not be inscribed within the religious system of authority that controls the meaning of both sacred "sacrifice" and profane "homicide" because it articulates a resistance to such a system, not its foundational instance (Agamben, *Homo Sacer*, 71).

cannot conceive of a political body as being alive without having a head that commands the whole in an organic and teleological fashion.[12] The decapitated political body symbolizes the attainment of the role of active political subjects by the people, previously considered as inert "matter." Henceforth their desire for freedom is the principle that animates political life.

But the "reduction" associated with Brutus is not just the elimination of an absolute instance of command imposed heteronomously on the people by a founder legislator. Brutus is also responsible for a second "reduction," namely, the killing of his sons. This reduction is not aimed at the absolute role played by the founder-legislator in the system of authority, but at the hegemony of the "nobility" in that system. Aristocratic hegemony refers to the exclusive recognition awarded by the system of authority to the desire of individuals and groups to dominate. Through its dual reduction the action of Brutus opens the space of the public (which is the laceration maintained by the discord between the desire for freedom and that for domination) as a space that cannot be occupied by some one as opposed to any other. This is the political space of plurality, of the multitude. The reduction is dual because it counters both the univocity of command (the mon- archical status of rule) and those who profit from it, the nobility, symbolized by the sons of Brutus. These sons stand for all those who grow to have privileges (and thus become "noble") under a given political and legal form of rule.

All political and legal orders privilege some as opposed to others: every order and every law fosters some inequality and is productive of some form of "nobility." Machiavelli does not discover this characteristic of political form. Classical political thought explicitly thematizes the problem and offers two general strategies to resolve it: the transcendence of justice (*epieikeia*) with respect to the law in the Socratic tradition; and the pre-Socratic idea of *isonomia*, which should not be restricted to the idea that everybody is equal before the law, but, much more interestingly, includes the possibility that everybody can equally make the law before which they are to be equal.[13] The idea of isonomy, in contrast to the idea of justice developed by classical natural right, entails that the law needs to be made and re-made precisely because the law cannot produce, as such and once and for all, effective political equality.

In Machiavelli the action undertaken by Brutus against his sons is symbolic of a new elaboration of the idea of isonomy according to which, in the space of the public or *res publica*, there is to be no privileged individual. In a "free life" orders and laws emerge from such a space of freedom as the space in which everyone can equally make the orders and laws before which they are to be equal. Machia- velli's republican understanding of isonomy entails that all political forms emerge from this space and are reducible to it (Lat. *reducere*: a leading-back) whenever

---

[12] See for example the metaphor of the political body in John of Salisbury, *Policraticus*. For its status as the paradigmatic discourse on the structure of the Christian body politic, see Ernst Kantorowicz, *The King's Two Bodies* (Princeton: Princeton University Press, 1975). For an excellent overview of the changing ideas of the political body in the history of political thought, see Adriana Cavarero, "Il corpo politico come organismo," *Filosofia Politica* 3 (December 1993).

[13] On the history of the term *isonomia* in early Greek political thought, see *Isonomia. Studien zur Gleichheitsvorstellung im griechischer Denken*, eds. J. Mau and E.G. Schmidt (Berlin: Akademie Verlag, 1964).

the privilege or inequality that the given political form establishes begins to corrupt those that grow under this form and are favored by it. Time brings out the inequality implicit in the application of any political form and legal order: *veritas filia temporis*. This is why the re-duction to the equality and freedom of the public space can only occur in an event that "returns to beginnings," i.e., that re-volutionizes the political form whose permanence in time constitutes the corruption in the first place.

The action of Brutus cuts open a political space-time in which neither the founder-legislator nor the nobility (the two subject-positions operative in the system of authority) are present: the clearing of this space-time is the purpose of actions that "reduce to freedom" the political body and its form. One can say that Brutus is symbolic of the emergence of freedom in an event that reduces the political body to its principle (*riduzione verso il principio*)[14] only in the sense of reducing (diminishing, cutting down) the principle of the nobility, i.e., the desire to dominate, thereby disclosing a space and a time of radical political equality. Only such republican and revolutionary events counteract the process of corruption in the political body which results from the reification of inequality in and through the fixation and perdurance of any given form of domination. The theory of the return to beginnings thematizes the re-duction of the political body to its freedom, in accordance with the symbolic force of the event of Brutus.

In recent reconstructions of modern republicanism, all of which agree that Machiavelli's thought constitutes an essential moment of this family of political doctrines, the relation between isonomy and rule of laws posited by his discourse is all too often misconstrued. Viroli, for instance, argues that freedom as no-rule, or non-domination, requires the priority of the rule of laws: "Like the liberty of the city, the individual citizen's liberty is also described as independence from the will of other men, which can exist only in so far as the laws and not men rule."[15] In a second moment, he claims that not any rule of laws will do, but only one that is isonomic:

To be able to protect the liberty of citizens, the laws must be fair – that is, aim at the common good – and not further the particular interest of the prince or of a faction or of a social group. According to republican theorists, this goal can be attained, and therefore *true liberty properly secured, only if sovereign power – that is, power to pass laws and to appoint magistrates – belongs to the citizens....* *The consequence of this conception of political liberty was that equality before the law must be accompanied by the liberty to participate in equal terms to the government of the republic.*[16]

Although Viroli still equivocates on whether "the liberty to participate in equal terms to the government of the republic" is merely an "accompaniment" of the principle of "equality before the law," it is obvious that modern republicanism cannot possibly support the rule of laws unless the latter depends on democratic participation. Only such participation prevents this rule from being heteronomous; and without such condition the rule of laws cannot possibly claim to defend freedom as non-domination. Hence the question of isonomy, the question of who

---

[14] Machiavelli, *Discourses on Livy*, III,1.

[15] Viroli, *Machiavelli*, 119.

[16] Ibid., 120. Emphasis mine.

makes the law and whether it is made "on equal terms," is more fundamental to the principle of equality before the law which Viroli posits as having priority. As a consequence of this conceptual confusion, Viroli's interpretation of Machiavelli does not even pose the question around which all of Machiavelli's re-elaboration of isonomy turns: what decides who is to be counted as a law-making citizen, if by definition this cannot be a decision that falls within the purview of the rule of laws since the latter is instituted by the citizens themselves?

Pettit's reconstruction of modern republicanism falls prey to a similar confusion with regard to the theoretical location of the question of isonomy. Pettit wants to separate republicanism from democracy, broadly understood as popular participation in determining who is to rule:

> the important point to notice, then, is that the writers at whom we have been looking, the writers who identify with a broad republican tradition of thinking, take liberty to be defined by a status in which the evils associated with interference are avoided rather than by access to the instruments of democratic control, participatory or representative. Democratic control is certainly important in the tradition, but its importance comes, not from any definitional connection with liberty, but from the fact that it is a means of furthering liberty.[17]

For Pettit the idea of freedom as non-domination is primary in republicanism, and the question of democratic participation is a secondary matter, designed merely to "further" such freedom, but having no essential link to it. In other words, contrary to Machiavelli's intuition, Pettit separates at the root freedom as no-rule from the question of isonomy, i.e., from the idea of equal access to making the laws before which everyone is to be equal. For this reason he can collapse freedom as no-rule on to the rule of law: "the laws of a suitable state, in particular the laws of a republic, create the freedom enjoyed by citizens."[18] But this only begs the question: what is a "suitable state" such that its laws "create the freedom enjoyed by its citizens"? It turns out that Pettit defines "the properly constituted law" as "the law that answers systematically to people's general interests and ideas."[19] This is clearly a reference to the need for democratic participation in the law-making process: for how else is Pettit going to ascertain that the law "answers systematically" to the citizens, unless it is these citizens themselves who make it? In other words, Pettit presupposes some sort of Rousseauian "general will" as expression of the "people's general interests and ideas," and is forced back on to the sort of "democratic self-rule" that he simultaneously wishes to attack as "populist."[20] Perhaps Pettit's discourse encounters such a tension because it prejudicially flattens republican freedom as no-rule or non-domination onto a discourse of justice (to which expressions like "the laws of a suitable state" or "the properly constituted law" refer), rather than articulating republican freedom through a discourse of isonomy, in the Machiavellian understanding of the term. The appeal to justice forces Pettit to assume, without prior question, that there exists something like "people's general interests and ideas," instead of thematiz-

---

[17] Pettit, *Republicanism*, 30.
[18] Ibid., 36.
[19] Ibid., 35.
[20] Ibid., 30.

ing the political, yet extra-legal, situations that determine the emergence of any given rule of laws, as well as the kind of legitimacy it can aspire to acquire for itself.[21]

CORRUPTION AND POLITICAL REVOLUTION: THE DANGERS OF FREEDOM

Whether freedom can be maintained depends on the degree of corruption that has affected the matter, i.e., the people, of the political body:

> where the matter is not corrupt, tumults and other scandals do not hurt; where it is corrupt, well-ordered laws do not help unless they have been put in motion by one individual who with an extreme force ensures their observance so that the matter becomes good. I do not know whether this has ever occurred or whether it is possible.[22]

Matter acquires an intrinsically positive value: it is the standard that determines, in accordance with its "quality" (corrupt/not-corrupt), the relative value of order and disorder. Where matter is not corrupt, disorder is not an evil; where matter is corrupt, the best order is not a good. This means that matter is not corrupt or corrupting "by nature" but becomes corrupt through time. The cause of corruption is not to be found in matter, then, but in the perdurance of a given order or form in time; for such perdurance is itself a sign that the desire for freedom, manifest in discord, is being extinguished.

From the perspective of classical political thought, it is inconceivable that a good law cannot redress corruption, and, conversely, that disorder not be taken as a sure sign of corruption. These beliefs follow from the Platonic and Aristotelian assumption that corruption is caused by matter that is un- or mis-formed. Machiavelli, instead, endows matter with freedom: matter is a subject that has the power to transcend any given form. This striking revaluation of matter finds its first effective metaphysical exposition with Giordano Bruno:

---

[21] In Skinner one finds an analogous confusion with regard to the priority of isonomy and rule of laws. Skinner posits that "free states, like free persons, are thus defined by their capacity for self-government." (Skinner, *Liberty before liberalism*, 26). From this he deduces some "constitutional implications.... One is that, if a state or commonwealth is to count as free, the laws that govern it... must be enacted with the consent of all its citizens, the members of the body politic as a whole." (Ibid., 27). Notice that the question of isonomy, i.e., of the equality of access to law-making, is reduced to the level of a "constitutional implication" of the idea of "self-government" under laws rather than as its condition of possibility. Furthermore, in clarifying what is meant by "consent of all its citizens," Skinner adds: "when they speak of the will of the people, they mean nothing more than the sum of the wills of each individual citizen.... When we speak about the will of the people, we must in effect be referring to the will of the majority." (Ibid., 28-29). Willy-nilly, the republicanism sketched by Skinner seems to lead straight into the highly contested territory of democratic theory, where every term and every reduction employed by Skinner is up for grabs because once the equality before the law is acceptable only if it presupposes equality to make the law, the latter equality cannot possibly be pre-determined by the law itself. Therefore, one is lead into the territory of the problem of *constitutio libertatis* as revolutionary praxis: a territory that Machiavelli is the first to explore, and yet which is systematically shunned by those contemporary theorists of republicanism who claim to draw much of their thought from the bases provided by his discourse.

[22] Machiavelli, *Discourses on Livy,* I,17.

When one gives the cause of corruption, one should not say that the form escapes matter or leaves matter behind, but rather that the matter rejects that form in order to take another one. In this case, we have no more reason to say that matter desires the form, but on the contrary it hates forms.... Indeed, *matter hates forms with more power than it desires them, given that it eternally rejects that numeral form which it kept for a brief time.*[23]

For Bruno, as for Machiavelli, corruption is nothing but the result of the perdurance of a given order or form. The incapacity of matter to reject a given form becomes the symptom of matter's corruption, for in this case matter merely functions as a passive support (*hypokeimenon*) of the form, rather than as the active subject (*suggetto*) of freedom. Only because the duration of political and legal form is the cause of corruption does it make sense for Machiavelli to assert that good laws are incapable of stopping the spread of corruption. This surprising proposition leads directly to the positive valuation of revolutions given in the discussion of the return to beginnings.

A reference to what can be called revolutionary action is already present in *Discourses on Livy,* I,17. To counteract corruption, the text opens the possibility that "one individual who with an extreme force ensures their [the laws] observance so that the matter becomes good," and later states that "such corruption and slight aptitude for free life arise from an inequality that is in that city, and if one wishes to reduce it to equality [*ridurre equale*] it is necessary to use the greatest extraordinary means [*usare grandissimi straordinari*] which few know how or wish to use."[24] These texts suggest a peculiar, extra-ordinary action that "equalizes" conditions in the city and makes the matter once again "good." I discuss at length the sort of action that Machiavelli has in mind in chapter three below. For now it is sufficient to point out that corruption entails inequality, which is itself a consequence of the growth of the desire to possess that is co-implicated in the stability of political form, as I showed in part one. Political freedom, on the other hand, is associated with equality: not of possessions (Machiavelli is very clear in *Discourses on Livy,* I,17 that the complete corruption of the Roman people which led to the formation of the Marian faction and to Ceasarism is due to the ennobled desire for possessions that takes over the Roman people), but of access to the space of the public. The two are intimately linked because the "equality" of political access is subverted by the "inequality" of possessions. Hence the need for a moment of radical "equalization" as a condition of possibility of political freedom. This "equalization" in effect implies a radical "purification" of the matter by rejecting its political form and revolutionizing its orders.[25]

The last chapter composing the tryptich on corruption (*Discourses on Livy,* I,18) has long been acknowledged as a decisive moment in Machiavelli's discourse. Interpreters are tempted to see in its argument the prefiguration of the "new prince," the modern state, that is found in *The Prince*.[26] I suggest that this

---

[23] Giordano Bruno, *De la causa, principio e uno,* ed. A. Guzzo (Milan: Mursia, 1985), IV. Emphasis mine. In this context, Bruno also speaks of the spontaneity of matter as "a divine being in things [*uno esser divino nelle cose*]." (Ibid.).

[24] Machiavelli, *Discourses on Livy,* I,17.

[25] As an analysis of *Discourses on Livy,* I,25-26 can corroborate.

[26] I refer to my discussion in part 1, ch.6.

chapter, in an equal and opposite manner, prefigures the theory of the return to beginnings as the linchpin of Machiavelli's conception of the modern republic.[27] *Discourses on Livy*, I,18 first poses the problem, without resolving it, of how a "free state" can be created or maintained in a political body that is corrupt. Machiavelli claims that the project of establishing or maintaining a "free state" in a corrupt city is of extreme difficulty. I take the difficulty to consist in the extra-constitutional or revolutionary action required for the renewal of freedom in a state; the need for such action follows from the assumption, established in *Discourses on Livy*, I,16-17, that the source of corruption is nothing other than the fixity of the constituted order with the inequality that it generates.

The argument begins by presupposing that in a corrupt city neither its laws nor its orders are sufficient to arrest the spread of corruption. The laws and orders that were made in

a republic at its birth, when men were good, are no longer to the purpose later, when they have become wicked. If laws vary according to the accidents in a city, its orders never vary, or rarely; this makes new laws insufficient because the orders which remain fixed, corrupt them.[28]

The stability of orders, far from making men "good," account for their becoming "bad" or "wicked" in the passage of time. If Machiavelli now says that at the "birth" of the state men are "good," earlier (in *Discourses on Livy,* I,3) he argues that all lawgivers presuppose men to be culpable "by nature". How can these claims be reconciled? The two claims do not contradict each other only if Machiavelli considers human "nature" from two incommensurate perspectives: that of law (rule), and that of freedom (no-rule). Considered from the perspective of the law, or political form in general, individuals start "bad" and are made "good" by laws. (This is the point of view expressed in *Discourses on Livy*, I,3). From the perspective of freedom, at the "birth" of a free state (i.e., at the "birth" of a mixed political body) the people are "good" in the sense that their desire for freedom as no-rule remains strong, but they become "bad" precisely through the fixity of laws and orders. (This is the point of view expressed in *Discourses on Livy*, I,18). The logic of the foundation of the state discussed in the first part confirms this interpretative solution. According to this logic, the people must be brought, as a functional organ of the political form, under the empire of law; this can only be done if the desire for freedom as no-rule is changed into the desire for security of possession (negative liberty). But the latter desire is inseparable from the desire to dominate, and this desire is what makes the people potentially transgressive with respect to the law, even though it is the very dynamic of

---

[27] To this extent my interpretation coincides with that of Negri, who understands the relation between *The Prince* and the *Discourses on Livy* as moving from the former discourse to the latter one, unlike Sasso and other theorists who see in *The Prince* Machiavelli's ultimate theoretical point of arrival. For Negri, the discourse of *The Prince* is designed to resolve the quandary of *Discourses on Livy*, I,18 (i.e., how to maintain freedom once it is conquered) by joining together with book three of the *Discourses on Livy* in the thesis that democracy is the new prince. Here I depart from Negri because his reading undermines the distinction between republic and state (i.e., new prince) in the modern political condition and reiterates the belief that the republic is a political form rather than a political event.
[28] Machiavelli, *Discourses on Livy*, I,18.

establishing the rule of laws that requires the people to exhibit the potentially transgressive desire.

Through the distinction between law and order, Machiavelli can theorize the difference between reform and revolution:

> But by holding steady [*tenendo fermi*] the orders of the state, which in corruption were no longer good, the laws that were renewed were no longer enough to keep men good; but they would indeed have helped if the orders had been changed [*rimutati gli ordini*] together with the innovation [*innovazione*] in laws.[29]

The language shows a marked distinction between renewal (*innovazione*) of laws and revolution (*ri-mutazione*) of orders. An essential aspect of the "life" of the state consists in making room for a change of laws in accordance to the advent of "accidents," i.e., in accordance to the necessity for the state to in-form as much matter as possible in order to minimize the impact of circumstances on its stability. This kind of "metabolism" of matter is governed by the constitutional order: the permanence of the political form depends on the capacity of forming citizens in accordance with the laws. Yet this very permanence, the "holding steady" of the orders of the state, is what corrupts the matter. Therefore, the only possibility for the state to transcend its "life," which is intrinsically a process of corruption, does not lie with the reform of laws but with the radical change of orders, that is, with a political movement that can only be termed revolutionary. In this revolutionary movement (or metabolism) the free political body "survives," over and above the "life" of the state. In brief, only a revolution at the level of the state itself, and not just a reform of the laws of the state, can stem the spread of corruption.[30]

Machiavelli articulates the event of revolution by arguing the priority of matter over form. Such a priority is closely linked to the concept of revolution, since at issue in a revolution is the possibility of "expelling" a given form from the matter, to use the language of Bruno. The priority of matter is presented as follows:

> It was necessary, in order to maintain Rome free in its corruption, that just as it had made new laws during the process of its life, it would have made new orders; because other orders and forms of life

---

[29] Ibid.

[30] I return to discuss the rest of *Discourses on Livy*, I,18 in chapter four below. Suffice to say that Machiavelli links the origin of corruption to the closure of the state onto itself that is made possible once its "liberty" is assured through the gaining of empire. It is the closure of the state towards the "exterior," i.e., towards the influx of un-formed matter characterized by a desire for freedom, that allows the state to favor the criterion of power (*potenza*) rather than virtù when deciding to fill the magistracies. *Potenza* is, here, a function of possession: one needs to have possessions (and so power) to gain access to the positions of influence and rule, and one desires these positions in order to acquire more possessions, which in turn is the only way of securing them. Such is the logic of the "nobility" as it appears in *Discourses on Livy*, I,18. The process of corruption can be formulated simply as the process whereby the "people" are en-nobled. It is interesting to note that here Machiavelli's criterion for "good" citizens is their proposal of laws "for the public or common freedom [*per la comune libertà*]"; whereas "bad" citizens do so "for their own power [*per la potenza loro*]." (Ibid., I,18).

have to be ordained in a bad subject than in a good one, nor can the form be the same in a matter that is wholly contrary.[31]

The survival of political freedom requires the mutation of order and form, and not simply its reform through new laws. This passage strongly supports the view that freedom and order are contradictories: the death of order is required for the survival of freedom. I use the term "survival" in a peculiar acceptation: it refers to that surplus of political life which manifests itself in and through the change of forms of life, rather than through the mere augmentation of life in a given form by repeated amendments of that form. In order for freedom to survive in a corrupt state what needs to be countered is the "life-process" (*processo di vivere*) of the state; the process whereby the state secures and augments its foundation. The return to beginnings is simply a name for those re-volutionary events in which the state, *in toto*, is countered. And if the only way to counter the process of corruption is to be found in a radical re-ordering of the state, that is, in the ungrounding of the given political order, then it must be the case that corruption is the *processo di vivere* through which the state attempts to fix and ground its orders. The source of corruption lies in the foundationalist strategy that characterizes the life of the state.

The maintainance of freedom calls for the repeated attempt to re-assert the priority of matter over form in political life by showing how the permanence of any given form ruins the quality of the matter (i.e., the degree to which the desire for freedom is present in the people). But what does Machiavelli mean when he speaks of changing the matter from "bad" to "good"? How to bring back the "love of freedom" in the people and so eliminate the "fear" that the powerful (*potenti*) use in order to control the "public thing"?[32] The task of renewing free political life by way of a re-ordering of the constitution of the state is "nearly impossible" (*quasi impossibile*): for if the renewal is to occur "little by little," it is necessary that a "prudent" individual exist who is capable of seeing the "evils" as soon as they emerge, and this is difficult enough. But even if such a person were to exist, it would be difficult to convince fellow citizens of the necessity of changing their customs, laws, orders and forms of life precisely because they do not see the emerging "evil" in their ways of proceeding. Conversely, to renew the orders "suddenly," when everyone realizes that they are not good, is equally difficult because it requires extra-ordinary action, since "it is not sufficient to use ordinary [*ordinari*] means, because the customary ways [*modi ordinari*] are bad."[33] In other words, it is impossible to renew an order in and through the kind of laws permitted by such an order. And since "there are two ways to fight: with laws or

---

[31] Machiavelli, *Discourses on Livy*, I,18.

[32] Machiavelli argues that "when the citizens have become bad, such an order [whereby any citizen or tribune could propose laws] becomes the worst, for only the powerful propose laws, not for the common freedom but for their own power; and for fear of them nobody can speak against them. So the people came to be either deceived or coerced to decide its own ruin." (Ibid.). One of the most important signs of corruption is the fear of speaking out against those who are powerful: absence of *libertas philosophandi*, of the "public use of reason," as Spinoza and Kant will say.

[33] Machiavelli, *Discourses on Livy*, I,38.

with force,"[34] it seems that extra-constitutional action is highly dangerous because it requires both violence and arms.

Yet revolutionary action faces a deeper problem than the necessity of violence. For the radical re-ordering of political life to freedom requires a prior transformation of the political actor: from law-abiding citizen the actor has to become

first of all the prince of this city so as to be able to dispose of it as he likes. And since the reordering of a city to political life presupposes a good man, and the becoming prince of a republic through violence presupposes a bad man, for this reason it will rarely come to pass that a good man, through bad ways, even if the end were good, would want to become prince; and that a bad [reo] man, having become prince, would want to do good and get the idea to make good use of that authority that he has acquired badly.[35]

The definition of revolutionary action is stringent. It is a case of changing political orders for the sake of counteracting corruption and freeing political life, which can only happen through a peculiar transformation of the political actor: either "a good man, through bad ways, even if the end were good, would want to become a prince," or "a bad man, having become prince, would want to do good." The reason why the prior transformation of citizen into prince, or prince into citizen, is more important than the mere fact of the use of violence ("through bad ways") is spelled out in *The Prince*. There is a "good" and a "bad" employment of violence or cruelty: the former use of cruelty entails the limited employment of violence always in view of gaining the support of the people. "Well used cruelties (if one may speak well of evil) are those that are done all at once, when it is necessary to secure oneself, and in which one does not persist, but are converted into the greatest possible advantage of the subjects."[36] Whether violence is limited or not is decided by the style with which the transition from citizen to prince, or from prince to citizen, is performed. The agreement between the text of the *Discourses on Livy* and *The Prince* suggests that the problem of how to sustain and shape the conflict between morality and politics is more fundamental in Machiavelli than the theoretical consideration of the uses of violence in political life, to which his thought has all too often been reduced. It is no surprise that interpreters see in the eighteenth chapter of *Discourses on Livy* the privileged locus of the "passage" from the *Discourses on Livy* to *The Prince*, and conversely.

I call ethically contradictory that political action which, because of its extra-constitutional character, requires a "good man" to become "bad" (enter the "path of evil," as Machiavelli says in *The Prince*) or for a "bad man" to become "good." At this stage of the argument, though, the meaning of the terms "good" and "bad" is unclear, and thus also the sense of the ethical contradiction that Machiavelli uncovers as an essential element of his theory of political freedom. To approximate the meaning of the ethical contradiction it is necessary to ask what is meant by the phrase "to reorder a city to the political life (*riordinare una città al vivere politico*)." Is it simply a question of changing from one state or political form to another, a matter of imposing one *ethos* over another *ethos*? If this is the case,

---

[34] Machiavelli, *The Prince*, XVIII.
[35] Machiavelli, *Discourses on Livy*, I,18.
[36] Machiavelli, *The Prince*, VIII.

then the political actor is merely involved in an ethical contradiction of the sort that has been associated with Robespierre and every form of Jacobinism since then.[37] Machiavelli is not unaware that this type of contradiction (something akin to the Hegelian dialectic of absolute freedom and terror) may very well emerge out of the revolutionary moment, since he claims that such a "renewal" of political life in a republic seems to negate the republic rather than renew it, because "it would be necessary to reduce it more to the monarchic state [*stato regio*] than to the popular state [*stato popolare*]."[38] But this is only to say that if revolutionary change amounts to the change from one form of state to another form of state, then such a change is not only ethically contradictory (in that the "good" end presupposes "bad" means for its realization) but also politically contradictory, in so far as the action that intends to renew a republic that is corrupt seems of necessity to realize the opposite of a free political life, i.e., a "monarchic state."

But it is possible to interpret otherwise the ethical contradiction carried by any extra-constitutional action having in view the renewal of political life. To think the ethical contradiction without political contradiction, one should conceive the ethically-contradictory action in terms of a political action that is the vehicle for a counter-diction of the "ethical voice," understood as the voice of the *ethos* (the *Sittlichkeit*) imposed and adopted by citizens in so far as they are functional to the life of the state. Extra-constitutional action can be thought as a carrier of the voice of the desire for freedom as no-rule, which indeed stands counter to the desire for domination that is embodied in the orders and laws that make up a given *ethos*. This is the possibility that I shall examine in what follows.

To recapitulate the problem: there exists a structural ambivalence in Machiavelli's call to re-order the state in view of maintaining (its) freedom. The extra-constitutional and ethically-contradictory sort of action that political freedom requires opens the way both to the new, civil prince and to the renewal of the republic. It is as if one and the same revolutionary action (symbolized by the return to beginnings of Brutus) could trigger two radically opposed dynamics. So far I have argued that one should read the possibility of revolutionary action as a symptom of the impossibility of reducing political freedom to the form of the state. What this symptom reveals is the existence of an elective affinity between republican freedom (i.e., political freedom in so far as it exceeds political form) and "tyranny," where tyranny is now carefully distinguished from the state as civil prince, i.e., from the state as political and legal order founded on the support of the people. It is as if Machiavelli's republican freedom, by going against the process that founds and maintains the civil life assured by the modern state, necessarily acquires some of the traits of tyranny: political freedom becomes tyrannical, not against itself, but in being too much itself.

Two questions need to be explored systematically in order to resolve, if it is at all possible or even desirable, the paradox of the "tyrannical" character of republican freedom. The first question refers to the content of the revolution of political form. When the state is "reduced" to freedom in the return to beginnings,

---

[37] Beginning with Hegel's analysis of the Terror in the *Phenomenology of Spirit* all the way to Arendt's deconstruction of the Jacobin mentality and its "hypocrisy" in *On Revolution*.
[38] Machiavelli, *Discourses on Livy*, I,18.

does it merely assume another political form or is there a transcendence of political form as such in a republican event? This question is treated in the third chapter. The second question concerns the meaning of the ethical contradiction, or the conflict between morality and political life. I show that such a conflict is possible only on the basis of the concept of revolutionary action, because a true conflict between politics and morality is impossible in a theory for which the establishment and maintenance of political form (understood in its widest sense) is at once the source of ethical value, as in ancient political thought. But why does Machiavelli believe that the action whose end is political freedom (the restoration of free political life) calls for a repudiation and contradiction of the ethical sphere? Is there an incommensurability between the discourse of freedom and that of justice in the modern political situation? I treat this question in chapter four. It is now time to provide the detailed analysis of the theory of return to beginnings in the third book of the *Discourses on Livy* that contains the answers to these questions.

CHAPTER 2

THE THEORY OF RETURN TO BEGINNINGS

THE POLITICAL SIGNIFICANCE OF HISTORICAL REPETITION

The theory of return to beginnings is a theory of historical repetition. By historical repetition I do not refer to the belief that historical events repeat themselves, but rather to the claim that the possibilities of historical becoming are determined by logics of repetition. As I discuss below, the content of the events that are classed as "return to beginnings" is the renewal or reordering of political forms, in the widest sense of the term (it remains to be seen how varied this content is, i.e., how radical these changes are). With the theory of return to beginnings Machiavelli introduces into political and, more generally, philosophical thought the idea that "return" or "repetition" is the proper modality for "beginning" or "innovation." Furthermore, since political freedom is inseparable from the event of changing political form, and this event appears to have the character of a historical repetition, the theory of return to beginnings establishes the historicity of political freedom and thereby seals the mutual interdependence between freedom and history.

But how can something like repetition or return coincide with something like innovation or beginning? In this chapter I answer this question in two ways. First, I review different sets of possible variations in which a coincidence of repetition and innovation can be thought. Each of these variations is represented by some aspect of the complex and overdetermined discourse on the relation between event and form found in Machiavelli. In a second moment, I argue that there are two paradigmatic philosophical elaborations of historical repetition out of which the above variations emerge. The first elaboration is found in Plato's myth of Kronos, and it reflects the general priority granted to form over event in the ancients. The second elaboration is Machiavelli's, and it explicitly overturns the Platonic idea of historical repetition and sets the basis for the priority assigned to event over form in the moderns.

The first set of variants argues that the link between repetition and innovation is the expression of an impossible wish-fulfillment: the return to beginnings means "a going forward by moving backwards, a pointing toward the future by going back to the past.... Renewal as return. It is the extreme chance to arrest becoming: to nail it to origins."[1] According to one such variant, described in Mircea Eliade's analysis of cyclical conceptions of history, "archaic humanity... defended itself, to the utmost of its powers, against all the novelty and irreversibility which history entails" precisely by "the abolition of time through the

---

[1] Esposito, *Ordine e Conflitto,* 31.

imitation of archetypes and the repetition of archetypical gestures."[2] Here repetition coincides with beginning only in the sense that repetition keeps a beginning in absolute separation from historical becoming. The logic is as follows: if history amounts strictly to repetition of the same events, then there exists no innovation, and as a consequence it is possible to remain, forever, at the beginning (of history).[3] This variant of the logic of historical repetition corresponds to what Lovejoy and Boas call "primitivism," to the ideal of Arcadia, first voiced in Hesiod.[4] In Machiavelli's discourse, it corresponds to the natural origin of the political form, in which there is an absolute priority of the form or archetype over the event.

Another variant, thematizing the problem contained in the possibility of imitating archetypes, concedes that the relation between repetition and innovation is possible although paradoxical, but in any case is bound to be self-defeating:

But the imitation of character as a means to autonomy is inherently paradoxical; it means copying those who copy no one. It implies both sameness and radical difference between model and imitator. Insofar as the stress falls on the sameness, on the model's merely human fallibility, the hope of rescue and radical transformation is lost. Insofar as the stress falls on difference, on the model's extraordinary greatness, imitation will seem impossible, will degenerate into playacting, will be a false piety disguising secret resentment, or will even imply identification with the oppressor and destruction of the self that he was to rescue. The imitation of radical difference cannot result in the mutuality that practical, human, political autonomy requires. So long as the point of imitation remains rescue, it blocks rather than serves autonomy.[5]

For Pitkin, repetition (or imitation) is contrary to the aspirations of freedom and innovation: it always comes too short of what it wants to be, either because it fails to meet its mark (the archetype) or because it meets the mark only to reveal the archetype as a false one. In Machiavelli's discourse this variant corresponds to the religious origin of political form, to the system of authority. This system turns on the paradox of the routinization of charisma (i.e., of the repetition of an absolute beginning) that both posits and negates the absolute or charismatic archetype. Both Eliade's and Pitkin's variants understand repetition as possible on condition that there exists something, the archetype, which is not itself repetition, something which is truly "first" or "original," and on which imitation and repetition depend as their unconditioned condition. Repetition here exhibits an external relation to innovation and beginning: it is always the repetition of something that remains outside of it. In this sense, these variants privilege form over event, archetype over repetition.

---

[2] Mircea Eliade, *The Myth of the Eternal Return* (Princeton: Princeton University Press, 1974), 48 and 34.
[3] For Eliade, "what predominates in all these cosmico-mythological lunar conceptions is the cyclical recurrence of what has been before, in a word, eternal return.... This eternal return reveals an ontology uncontaminated by time and becoming.... In a certain sense, it is even possible to say that nothing new happens in the world, for everything is but a repetition of the same primordial archetypes; this repetition, by actualizing the mythical moment when the archetypical gesture was revealed, constantly maintains the world in the same auroral instant of the beginnings." (Ibid., 89-90).
[4] See Arthur O. Lovejoy and George Boas, *Primitivism and Related Ideas in Antiquity* (Baltimore, 1935).
[5] Pitkin, *Fortune is a Woman,* 273.

A second set of variants rejects the belief that repetition is itself "secondary," dependent on the "firstness" or "priority" of the form (archetype). Instead, the originary character of repetition is thematized: the beginning insists in the event of returning. In this case, there exists no beginning to return to because what begins is this very return. Here the repetition exhibits an internal relation to beginning, and the dimension of form emerges from that of event. In Machiavelli's discourse, this set of variants covers those modes of political life that emerge from the free origin of political form.

In his study of the concept of imitation in modernity, Lacoue-Labarthe shows that such a concept can only be understood in light of the originary status assigned to repetition by the moderns, particularly in Nietzsche's reflections on history and imitation.

In the last instance – and in a certain sense this instance has always been there, for Nietzsche is neither the first nor the last to assume it in its extreme form – he enjoins to imitate the Greeks without imitating them, or, more exactly, to imitate the Greeks upto the point where they cease to be inimitable and become responsible for the *imitatio* of the ancients… this is the perfect structure of "double bind."[6]

The imitation of what is inimitable means, as Lacoue-Labarthe adds, that the action of repetition must enjoin a rupture with the past. The political actors who can make this break, who are able to imitate the very condition that there is nothing to imitate, are the "disinherited, those who are themselves nothing because the weight of their heritage is so enormous, those who have absolutely nothing of their own, they can find in this extreme alienation and dispossession the force to be born: the force to find the greatness of a beginning."[7] That one should imitate only what is inimitable; and that this carries the consequence that such imitation must break with everything that is assumed as tradition, as custom, as result of the passive synthesis or repetition of time, corresponds to the interpretation I offer of Machiavelli as effecting a decisive break with the ancients in and through repeating their "inimitability," i.e., what is contained "in them" prior to and beyond what they themselves were able to recognize and thematize as a pattern to be followed by all generations. That such a break is effected politically in virtue of a theory of return to beginnings as schema for revolutionary action on behalf of the people, the bearers of the desire for freedom as no-rule, once again matches Lacoue-Labarthe's acute remark that it is only the "disinherited," those "who have absolutely nothing of their own," who are motivated by the idea that repetition is originary, i.e., by the idea that all hierarchies derived from archetypes are ideological effects.

That originary repetition is the modern possibility is already proposed by Derrida in his interpretation of Rousseau's "return to nature," a quintessential example of the modern return to beginnings or origins.

L'essence est la présence. Comme vie, c'est-à-dire comme présence à soi, elle est naissance. Et comme le présent ne sort de lui-meme que pour y rentrer, une re-naissance est possible qui permet

---

[6] Philippe Lacoue-Labarthe, *L'imitation des modernes* (Paris: Galilée, 1986), 105.
[7] Ibid.

seule, d'ailleurs, toutes les répétitions d'origine. Le discours et les questions de Rousseau ne sont possibles qu'à anticiper une re-naissance ou une réactivation de l'origine. La re-naissance, la résurrection ou le reveil se réapproprient toujours, dans leur fugitive instance, la plénitude de la présence revenant à soi. Ce retour à la présence de l'origine se produit après chaque catastrophe dans la mesure du moins où elle renverse l'ordre de la vie sans le détruire. Après qu'un doigt divin eut renversé l'ordre du monde en inclinant l'axe du globe sur l'axe de l'univers et eut ainsi voulu que "l'homme fut sociable", la fete autour du point d'eau est possible et le plaisir est immédiatement présent au désir.[8]

Derrida places Rousseau's cosmological account of renewal under the shadow of the Platonic version of the myth of Kronos, to which the text clearly alludes when speaking of the "divine finger that reverses the order of the world," while linking its discourse on re-birth to the problem of the Renaissance and, more generally, to the birth of modernity. Countering the reading that sees in Rousseau's "return to nature" a continuation of the tradition of ancient "primitivism," Derrida employs Rousseau's idea of historical repetition to mark the discontinuity between ancients and moderns. Derrida claims that the "return to nature" can only be understood as an attempt to repair the effects of the catastrophe constituted by modernity: "in all of its orders, the possibility of what represents overtakes the represented presence, just as evil does with good, history with origin. The catastrophe is the signifier, what represents. Likewise, the signifier is always in itself 'new,' irrespective of the epoch in which it appears. It is the essence of modernity."[9] Rousseau's seemingly anti-modern "return to nature" as a re-birth of presence or origin is only understandable as a reaction against the "modernity" of representation or repetition, which is thereby essentially linked to the advent of the "new," of historicity itself.

Derrida's reading of Rousseau uncovers a double meaning in the modern variant of historical repetition or return to beginnings:

Rousseau articule lui-meme cette chaine de significations (essence, origine, présence, naissance, renaissance) sur la métaphysique classique de l'étant comme energie.... "Je me disais qu'en effet nous ne faisons jamais que commencer, et qu'il n'y a point d'autre liaison dans notre existence qu'une succession de moments présents dont le premier est toujours celui qui est en acte. Nous naissons et nous mourons à chaque instant de notre vie." Il s'ensuit – mais c'est une liaison que Rousseau fait tout pour élider – que l'essence meme de la présence, si elle doit toujours se répéter dans une autre présence, ouvre originairement, dans la présence meme, la structure de la représentation. Et si l'essence est la présence, il n'y a pas d'essence de la présence ni de présence de l'essence. Il y a un jeu de la représentation.... La représentation ne survient pas à la présence; elle l'habite comme la condition meme de son expérience.[10]

Rousseau's elaboration of "re-naissance," of re-birth as repetition of the origin, is understood by Derrida as an admission (which nonetheless he claims Rousseau at the same time wants to "elide") that the experience of presence and origin is always contaminated, as regards its condition of possibility, by what should be secondary to it, by the order of representation and repetition. And only because a re-presentation is always already at issue in any presentation or presence,

---

[8] Derrida, *De la Grammatologie*, 437ff.
[9] Ibid., 418.
[10] Ibid., 439.

Derrida goes on to claim that the order of representation is not an order at all, but rather "play [*jeu*]." An "order of representation" would obtain only on condition that presence (origin) could be grasped apart from its representation (repetition) and as a standard for putting in order representations. Derrida calls the "play" between representation and presence the "logic of supplementarity."

The logic of the supplement depends on the duplicity inherent in the possibility of a "return to beginnings" or "return to origins." This return or repetition can be understood as the way in which an origin (repeatedly) establishes its presence and, conversely, as the way in which an origin never attains presence (and, by the same token, presence never becomes originary). Derrida's logic of the supplement maintains both possibilities in play: his variant on the concept of originary repetition is characterized by the claim that repetition is both the condition of possibility and the condition of impossibility for the presence of origin.

Et il y a une nécessité fatale, inscrite dans le fonctionnement meme du signe, à ce que le substitut fasse oublier sa fonction de vicariance et se fasse passer pour la plénitude d'une parole dont il ne fait que suppléer la carence et l'infirmité. Car le concept de supplément... abrite en lui deux significations dont la cohabitation est aussi étrange que nécessaire. Le supplément s'ajoute, il est un surplus, une plénitude enrichissant une autre plénitude.... Il cumule et accumule la présence.... Mais le supplément supplée. Il ne s'ajoute que pour remplacer. Il intervient ou s'insinue à-la-place-de; s'il comble, c'est comme on comble un vide.... Suppléant et vicaire, le supplément est un adjoint, une instance subalterne qui tient-lieu. En tant que substitut, il ne s'ajoute pas simplement à la positivité d'une présence, il ne produit aucun relief, sa place est assignée dans la structure par la marque d'un vide. Quelque part, quelque chose ne peut se remplir de soi-meme, ne peut s'accomplir qu'en se laissant combler par signe et procuration. Le signe est toujours le supplément de la chose meme.[11]

The supplement or repetition conditions the possibility of an origin because there is no experience of origin or birth other than as a re-birth, as Rousseau shows. In this case, the supplement serves to "cumulate and accumulate presence" to the origin. But the supplement or repetition is also the condition of impossibility of the origin because it shows that its presence is inhabited by a lack at the very moment that it affirms itself as full. To say that "the sign is always the supplement of the thing itself" means nothing other than that the sign "is" the thing itself, the repetition "is" the origin, for in Derrida "to be" means "to supplement," in both of its constitutive and irreducible senses. The duplicitous mode in which repetition enters into relation with origin, to subvert it by establishing it and to establish it by subverting it, in the Derridean variant of historical repetition sheds important light on the theory of return to beginnings in Machiavelli's formulation. More explicitly than in Rousseau, Machiavelli's return to beginnings lets itself be interpreted in terms of the logic of the supplement because the latter accounts for the peculiar claim that a return to beginnings is operative both in the attempt to stabilize the state and in the attempt to subvert it. In other words, Derrida's variant of historical repetition offers a possible account of Machiavelli's paradoxical thesis that the revolutionary event, denoted by the return to beginnings, is both the

---

[11] Ibid., 208.

condition of possibility and the condition of impossibility of the political form in the situation of modernity.[12]

A third variant of originary repetition is introduced by Deleuze in *Difference and Repetition*, a work that is contemporary to Derrida's *Of Grammatology*. Like Lacoue-Labarthe after him, Deleuze offers an account of the coincidence of repetition and innovation on the basis of a new reading of Nietzsche's theory of historical repetition (doctrine of the eternal return of the same). Like Derrida, Deleuze uses the originary status of repetition to establish the crucial trait of the situation of modernity. But unlike the previous two variants, the theory of originary historical repetition in Deleuze is explicitly linked from the beginning to a theory of political revolution. The possibility of repetition is conceived in opposition to the possibility of the law:

> If repetition is possible, it is due to miracle rather than to law. It is against the law: against the similar form and the equivalent content of law. If repetition can be found, even in nature, it is in the name of a power which affirms itself against the law.... In every respect, repetition is a transgression. It puts law into question, it denounces its nominal or general character in favour of a more profound and more artistic reality.[13]

Laws are constitutive of patterns and generalities; if it is possible to break with such patterns, it must be in virtue of carrying a difference that stands outside the "orders of laws," and can be termed both a "miracle" and a "transgression." It remains to be seen why Deleuze imputes such a difference that does not fall under a previous identity, such a difference without concept, to repetition.

Another reason for linking repetition to revolutionary action lies with Deleuze's identification of habit as the essence of morality, which entails the extra-moral character of freedom understood as the power to innovate, to break from habit.[14] Again, it is repetition, understood as an action, that figures "such a novelty; that is, a freedom and a task of freedom."[15] By the same token, the action of repetition stands in opposition to the institution of morality, "to the point where it becomes the suspension of ethics, a thought beyond good and evil."[16] Given that in

---

[12] One of the most suggestive applications of Derrida's discourse on originary repetition to the problem of the foundation of political freedom is found in Bonnie Honig, *Political Theory and the Displacement of Politics* (Ithaca: Cornell University Press, 1993), ch. 4. Moving beyond Pitkin's reading of the problem of repetition in Machiavelli, Honig argues that Machiavelli "sees that a beginning too firmly rooted in the past is in danger of becoming reified and foundational. Our commitment to augmentation and amendment may derive from our reverence for a beginning that is in the past; but our practices of augmentation and amendment make the beginning our own, not merely our legacy but our construction and our performative." (Ibid., 115) For Honig, the foundation of freedom is effectively politicized only in and through its repetition (as augmentation or amendment of the foundation), or, what is the same, there is a politics of foundation only as historical repetition. My interpretation of Machiavelli differs from Honig in that it attempts to think a dimension of political freedom that exists without foundation rather than one that exists through the renewal of foundations. The logics of repetition, and in particular the Derridean one, can be used not only to repoliticize foundational instances, as Honig suggests, but also to break the bind between political freedom and foundationalism.

[13] Deleuze, *Difference and Repetition*, 2-3.

[14] For Deleuze, the moral law, in its application, exhibits the generality of "habit as a second nature.... It is the form of habit... which is essentially moral or has the form of the good." (Ibid., 4.).

[15] Ibid., 6.

[16] Ibid.

Machiavelli revolutionary action is an ethically-contradictory action whose character is that of historical repetition or return to beginnings, Deleuze's variant of originary repetition provides a possible schema through which to think political freedom beyond the institution of morality.

Deleuze's conception of repetition follows from his interpretation of Nietzsche's doctrine of the eternal return of the same, in particular from a new understanding of the "return" itself, which can be helpfully applied to Machiavelli's own idea of return (to beginnings).

Eternal return cannot mean the return of the Identical because it presupposes a world (that of the will to power) in which all previous identities have been abolished and dissolved. *Returning is being, but only the being of becoming. The eternal return does not bring back "the same," but returning constitutes the only Same of that which becomes. Returning is the becoming-identical of becoming itself. Returning is thus the only identity, but identity as a secondary power; the identity of difference, the identical which belongs to the different, or turns around the different. Such an identity, produced by difference, is determined a "repetition."*[17]

The return is the instance of repetition, "the being of becoming." Only what becomes also thereby returns; or, better, it returns to the extent that it becomes; it acquires an identity only to the extent that it differs. The possibility of return, or repetition, is like a filter through which passes all becoming. The filter maintains (by assigning it "being" or "identity") only the kind of becoming which makes a difference.

The Deleuzian interpretation of the (eternal) return as criterion for the "identity of the different" matches another aspect of the Machiavellian return to beginnings as symbolized in the actions of Brutus. The action through which Brutus returns Roman political life to its "beginnings," giving rise to a republican revolutionary event, as I discuss below in more detail, exemplifies the double sense of the formula "the identity of the different" found in Deleuze. In the republican revolutionary event "identity" refers to the equality before freedom (isonomy) and not to the equality before the law: it is those who are "different," and as "different," who are granted equal access to the space of the public. The equality before the law applies to those who are "different" only with respect to that aspect which makes them "identical" to each other. Whereas the equality before the law applies only within such spaces, as their reification, isonomic equality is the kind of equality or identity that is needed to disclose new public spaces, spaces of freedom as no-rule. Isonomic equality is the condition of possibility of citizenship; the equality before the law is the equality of already constituted citizens. The second sense of the Deleuzian formula for repetition as "the identity of the different" is that "identity" is assigned only on condition that a radical change and subversion of previous identities occurs. In Machiavelli's theory of return to beginnings, this second sense of repetition corresponds to the change in the political actor that defines the revolutionary event: the becoming-princes of citizens and the becoming-citizen of princes.

---

[17] Ibid., 41. Emphasis mine.

Deleuze's concept of repetition allows for a subversive reconfiguration of the relation between identity and difference, being and becoming, only because it also offers a schema through which to think the event in which radical novelty emerges. Radical innovation occurs only if it is possible to change the times in an event that is not predetermined by any form of change; indeed, such a change of times must contain in itself the possibility of emergence and dehiscence of every form as such. Deleuze speaks of the event of the change of times as containing time "as a totality," in its past, present, and futural dimensions.

The idea of a totality of time must be understood as follows: the caesura, of whatever kind, must be determined in the image of a unique and tremendous event, an act which is adequate to time as a whole. This image itself is divided, torn into two unequal parts. Nevertheless, it thereby draws together the totality of time. It must be called a symbol by virtue of the unequal parts which it subsumes and draws together, but draws together as unequal parts. Such a symbol adequate to the totality of time may be expressed in many ways: to throw time out of joint, to make the sun explode, to throw oneself into the volcano, to kill God or the father. *This symbolic image constitutes the totality of time to the extent that it draws together the caesura, the before and the after.... In effect, there is always a time at which the imagined act is supposed "too big for me." This defines a priori the past or the before.... The second time, which relates to the caesura itself, is thus the present of metamorphosis, a becoming-equal to the act and a doubling of the self, and the projection of an ideal self in the image of the act.... As for the third time in which the future appears, this signifies that the event and the act possess a secret coherence which excludes that of the self; that they turn back against the self which has become their equal and smash it to pieces, as though the bearer of the new world were carried away and dispersed by the shock of the multiplicity to which it gives birth: what the self has become equal to is the unequal in itself.*[18]

The three moments of time that the event of historical repetition, or event of revolution, holds together match, to an uncanny degree, the modes of experiencing historical distance in Machiavelli's theory of return to beginnings. When conceived as a repetition constitutive of the past, the return to beginnings describes (Roman) history as a function of an unrepeatable origin, of founding acts which are "supposed [to be] 'too big for me'," and that serve to model political action as an action of maintenance of forms and habits that are, always already, given and must be passed down in time. This is the mode of experiencing historical distance that corresponds to the system of authority, with its dependence on the temporal continuity constructed by tradition.

When conceived as a repetition constitutive of the present, the return to beginnings describes (Roman) history as a function of breaks with the tradition, of events in which political life transcends the process of maintaining political form and aims at radically changing such forms. This is the mode of experiencing historical distance that corresponds to the symbolic value of Brutus and the emergence of the republic in a "present of metamorphosis, a becoming-equal to the act and a doubling of the self," in which the very division between founders and citizens, those who initiate and those who maintain, falls away.

Lastly, when conceived as a repetition constitutive of the future, the return to beginnings describes (Roman) history as a function of the event-like, revolutionary character of both the process of founding political form and the process of

---

[18] Ibid., 89. Emphasis mine.

subverting these foundations. In this mode of experiencing historical distance, history itself, the difference between past and present, is reoriented towards the dimension of the future as future, toward that event which opens historical becoming from the outside and keeps history openended or without end. In the political terms through which Machiavelli articulates this futural mode of repetition, one can say that history has a future only on condition that every political position can be indiscriminately occupied, or, in Machiavelli's formula, only on condition that citizens become princes and princes citizens. This is the sense of historical repetition "in which the future appears, this signifies that the event and the act possess a secret coherence which excludes that of the self; that they turn back against the self which has become their equal and smash it to pieces, as though the bearer of the new world were carried away and dispersed by the shock of the multiplicity to which it gives birth."[19]

The link between historical repetition and political revolution is already made in antiquity. The expression "return to beginnings" is synonymous with that of "revolution," understood in its astronomical sense. In the central myth of the *Statesman* Plato illustrates the possible directions, temporal and countertemporal, of the revolutions (return to beginnings) of the cosmos. I suggest that this myth should be read as an allegory of political revolution. My hypothesis is that Machiavelli develops the terminology and the problematic of the return to beginnings directly from its origin in this Platonic text.[20] Plato's theory of repetition stands to the ancients as Machiavelli's stands to the moderns.[21]

---

[19] Lefort's analysis of the return to beginnings, although it identifies the coincidence of innovation and repetition, does not thematize the logic(s) which account for such a coincidence, and is therefore less useful for the understanding of Machiavelli's theory of historical repetition than the texts discussed above. Lefort states that "the creation of the tribunes [as example of return to beginnings] is an innovation that supposes a break with the principles valid since the early times of Rome. It permits the established legality to relive by modifying it profoundly.... Such is the truth of the return to beginning: not return to the past, but, in the present, analogous response to that which was given in the past.... The maintenance of the law implies always the possibility of a renewal of the law and, in the long run, requires it.... Because it is one and the same thing to recognize that the 'principio' is not determinable from an empirical point of view, or according to our terminology, that the law transcends all the institutions in which it is figured, and to discover the place of the political subject." (Lefort, *Travail de l'oeuvre*, 601). For Lefort the return to beginnings is essentially a function of the establishment of the legal order through its repeated renewal; whereas for me the return thematizes a critique of this same order, which is not itself dependent on the idea of the transcendence of the law. Lefort's conjunction of return to beginnings with the legal dynamic is what prevents him from identifying the concept of the return to beginnings as the locus of a theory of revolutionary action.

[20] It is not known whether Machiavelli read Plato's *Statesman*, but he could have had access to it through Ficino's translation. According to Eugenio Garin, "the Italian Platonists of the fifteenth century like to insist on the fatal decay of 'republics' and debate the possibility of its renewal, of a return to beginnings: of a resurrection of dead things, as Machiavelli will say." (Eugenio Garin, *Lo Zodiaco della vita* [Rome: Laterza, 1976], 21). Garin here is mistaken: the treatment of the "return to beginning" in Ficino and Machiavelli are completely different. For Ficino the myth of Kronos found in the *Statesman* and the *Laws* refers, primarily, to the "eternal recurrence" of the motion of the world-soul. The circularity of this motion is due to the "fatal law" [*fatali lege*] that rules over all motions of souls in conjunction with their innate appetite. (Marsilio Ficino, *Theologia Platonica de immortalitate animorum* [Hildesheim: Olms, 1995], IV,2). In the introduction to his translation of the *Statesman*, Ficino gives an allegorical reading of the myth of Kronos in which he compares the reign of Kronos to the contemplative life and the reign of Zeus to the active life. He goes on to argue that individuals can regenerate themselves only if they "return to the beginning" symbolized by the reign of Kronos, i.e., if they live in accordance to the intellect rather than to the senses. (Ficino,

The problem of revolutions, in the Platonic-Aristotelian tradition, is concerned with the question of the rotation or circulation of power, in the sense that it seeks to establish a circular relation between ruler and ruled as the just or best form of domination. Plato and Aristotle choose two different strategies to solve the problem of distributing an inequality (in this case: who is to rule and who is to obey) among equals, but both seek the solution in the theory of the "mean" (which is found both in Plato's *Statesman* and in Aristotle's *Politics*). This is why justice has a place only in the polis; where there is a "natural" distinction between ruler and ruled, i.e., where there exists a "natural" inequality, one speaks of justice only in a derivative sense. The difference between Plato and Aristotle is that for the latter it is possible to achieve a political form in which the rotation of rulers is "internalized" so that it would not have to decay into the vicious cycle of constitutions, whereas for the former the political form must be immunized from every such rotation in order to avoid, for as long as possible, falling into that cycle.

In Machiavelli, the axis of political conflict is no longer drawn between ruler and ruled, but between the sphere of rule (determined by the dualism, to rule/to be ruled) and the sphere of no-rule (freedom as absence of domination). Since rule and no-rule refer to incommensurable dimensions of political life there can be no "mean" for them. A mean can only be found, in principle, within the duality to rule/to be ruled: this is the fundamental intuition behind the classical conceptions of justice. But freedom as no-rule exceeds the sphere(s) of justice; at least if one understands justice in relation to the mean, i.e., to that which contains in itself the extremes in such a way that it is not itself an extreme.[22] For Machiavelli, there is no mean for the extremes of freedom and tyranny. This is the reason why his discussion of political rotation or revolution breaks with the classical tradition in a decisive fashion and rejects the assumption that the rotation of rule must have as its end the maintenance of a political form. For Machiavelli, the rotation or return to beginnings is excentric with respect to the form: the return to beginnings marks a circular movement that has no center, or no beginning to return to in the first place. The return to beginnings names the event of historical transcendence of the form. Politically speaking, the consequence of such transcendence is that every given form needs to historicize itself if it is to maintain itself in time; which is to say that revolution becomes a constitutive element of the form of the state in the modern political situation. There can hardly be a more striking break with the tradition of ancient political thought.

Additionally, Machiavelli raises the interesting question (which modern political thought has not ceased to try to answer) of whether this revolution of political forms, understood as an essential component of modern political life, remains within the purview of political form, or whether it expresses a mode of

---

"Epitome," *In librum Platonis de regno, vel civilem*). For another aspect of Ficino's adoption of Plato's myth, see Marsilio Ficino, *Sopra Lo Amore, ovvero Convito di Platone*, V.12; VI. 3.

[21] By far the most complete treatment of the myth of the Golden Age in early modernity, from Dante to Vico, is found in Gustavo Costa, *La leggenda del secoli d'oro nella letteratura italiana* (Bari: Laterza, 1972). Although Costa identifies the presence of the myth of Kronos in Machiavelli, he does not attribute to it the importance I do, and offers no political interpretation of it. (Ibid., 82-84).

[22] For another discussion of the tension between freedom and justice in Machiavelli, see now Vatter, *Machiavelli's 'The Prince': A Reader's Guide* (London: Bloomsbury, 2013).

political life that transcends, if only finitely, the very instance of political form. For Machiavelli every effective revolution is a "change of state" (*mutazione di stato*) from "tyranny" to "freedom" and vice versa. The question is whether such a change of state consists in effecting a transition from one form (of state) to another, or consists in a shift of political life from the dimension of form (state) to the dimension of event (republic) and vice versa. Do political changes presuppose an ontological priority of the form (that is, presuppose the permanence of some ethical substance), or do they transcend such priority by introducing a concept of political change as a radical discontinuity and innovation with respect to what is traditional and customary? I propose the latter hypothesis. My claim, in very general terms, is that the theory of the mean (under which I subsume all Platonic-Aristotelian political ethics) is inapplicable to political action once it has been defined in terms of effecting transitions from tyranny to freedom and conversely, as occurs in Machiavelli. All political action, in this sense, becomes revolutionary. Modern political freedom knows no mean.

The most dramatic evidence of the revolutionary content of the theory of return to beginnings consists in the new theory of citizenship that it elicits. If I am correct in thinking that the discourse on historical repetition exorcises the very idea that political life consists in the foundation of rule, i.e., in the idea that what or who is "first," "authentic," or "original" (by nature or by convention) ought to rule, and that rule is the "first" of things, then Machiavelli's theory of return to beginnings is an attempt to think political life as the simulacrum of rule. If every instance of beginning or origin is understood from the possibility of the return to beginnings or historical repetition, then it is impossible to institute the difference (of Platonic origin) between what is original (one) and what is a copy (many), and as a consequence also the distinction between copy (many) and simulacra (plurality without form).[23] The theory of return to beginnings subverts the ultimate foundational schema that holds together every system of authority: that one (founder) must begin to rule by setting up the form, and that many (citizens) must augment the beginning and support the form by carrying out its orders.[24] I argue that in the third book of the *Discourses on Livy* Machiavelli offers a theory of citizenship that systematically undoes any principled difference between princes and subjects, founders and citizens, members of a political community and the unnameable plurality of those who stand outside it. In the new political situation that is traced out by his discourse, the difference between who rules and who obeys is a simulacrum. In this situation, the "new" prince is the political subject that (dis)simulates itself into the position of the citizen, that acts like citizens would act if they were in its place, which is that of the state needing to ground itself on the people. Conversely, the "new" citizen is the political subject that emerges in the republican events, that (dis)simulates itself into the position of the prince: like a prince in its disregard for established law and custom, unlike a prince in that its transcendence and transgression of the established political form is performed in the name of freedom from rule.

---

[23] On the concept of the simulacrum, I refer to the discussion in Gilles Deleuze, *Logic of Sense* (New York: Columbia University Press, 1990).
[24] I refer to the discussion of authority in part 1, ch.3.

RETURN TO BEGINNINGS AND THE MYTH OF KRONOS

The third book of the *Discourses on Livy*, unlike the other two, contains no preface but begins with a long chapter, entitled "If one wishes a sect or republic to live long, it is necessary to revoke it often towards its beginning [*a volere che una sètta o una republica viva lungamente, è necessario ritirarla spesso verso il suo principio*]," that presents the theory of return to beginnings. Although the text refers to cosmological and naturalistic considerations in its argument, I argue that the theory, far from betraying Machiavelli's naturalism, discloses the thorough-going historical character of political life.   A careful reading of the text reveals the anti-naturalism implicit in Machiavelli's theory from the first lines:

It is a very true thing that all the things of the world have an end to their life; but generally those that run through the whole course that is ordered for them by heaven [*ordinato dal cielo*] are those things that do not disorder their body [*disordinano il loro corpo*] but maintain it in an orderly way so that either it does not alter or, if does alter, it is for the sake of its health and not to its harm. And because I am speaking about mixed bodies, such as republics and sects, I say that those alterations are for the sake of health that return them to their beginnings [*le riducano inverso i principii loro*]. But the mixed bodies which are better ordered and have a longer life are those that can renew themselves frequently by means of their orders, or indeed that through some accident outside the said order come to the said renewal. And it is a thing clearer than light that these bodies do not last if they do not renew themselves.[25]

This passage carries out a radical reversal of perspective during its course, as if it were performing the very motion (the return to beginnings) about which it speaks. The text starts with a generic statement that all worldly things are finite and mortal. It then presents the view that every thing has its course, and that such a course is ordained by the heavens (*ordinato dal cielo*).[26] According to this view, the course that is ordained by the heavens is followed through by those things that do not disorder their bodies, and that do not alter themselves, or, if they alter, that do so towards their health and not against it. So far the text formulates a generic appeal to maintain the stability of the body so that it may follow the course that is preordained to it by the heavens, conceived as the highest (or universal) cause of its natural motion. The passage may be read as an expression of acquiescence

---

[25] Machiavelli, *Discourses on Livy,* III,1.

[26] I leave the task of presenting the text of *Discourses on Livy*, III, 1 from a *Wirkungsgeschichte* perspective for another work. In the case of this crucial chapter the reconstruction of the sources remains to be done nearly completely. According to Inglese's commentary, the specific view on the mortality of worldly things seems to derive from Lucretius *De rerum natura* 2,1173-74; and 5, 92-96, 306-315. In my view, the belief that the heavens prescribe a course to worldly things, including mixed political bodies, probably derives from Ficino, in particular his *Commentarius in locum Platonis ex octavo libro de Repub. de Mutatione Reipub. per numerum fatalem*. In this text, Ficino gives a numerological account of cycles and revolutions of bodies in the cosmos, both natural and political. These cycles are determined by the behavior of numbers which constitute the "fatal law [*legem fatalis*]" which has its political equivalent in the various theories of *anacyclosis* that I discuss in part 1, ch.2. Ficino claims that worldly motions of generation and corruption, fertility and sterility, are ruled by the law that moves heavenly bodies, and this law acts like "fate." (Ficino, *Opera Omnia*, 3:1414ff). In all probability it is to this kind of discourse that Machiavelli refers when he speaks about the "course" set by the heavens; but it is likewise against this kind of determinism that he advances the theory of the return to beginnings.

on the part of Machiavelli to some sort of astrological fatalism or naturalistic determinism.

Yet a completely different reading can be given of the passage: if a body remains bound to its order and does not change it, then its life will be "ordained" by the heavens and natural motions, and it will indeed follow a pre-ordained course that will bring it, "naturally," to its end or death. On the other hand, and this is where the textual conversion occurs, there are mixed bodies (political and social institutions, thus not strictly "natural" entities) for which frequent "alterations" and "renewals" are essential if they are to "last," that is, if they are to survive. Thus the very change of order that is "bad" for bodies that fall under the ordainment of the heavens is "good" for mixed bodies.[27] In other words, only a body that changes itself, that incorporates its own negation, is able to break with every determinism, with every naturalistic heteronomy, and with every ordainment on the part of the heavens, and therefore break with "nature" as such. Frequent alterations are the content of political life which in this case is clearly opposed to the requirements of "natural" life.

The kind of alterations that Machiavelli has in mind are those that revoke mixed bodies back to their beginnings and/or principles (*le riducano inverso i principii loro*). The movement that returns something to its beginning is a revolution. The question is how to understand the sense of this revolution or return to beginning. The starting point is the idea that such a revolution is counter-natural, in the sense that it intends to counter the course that natural motion, ruled by the ordainment of the heavens, imparts to finite bodies. The natural course moves natural bodies from youth to old age, from vigor to weakness, in general through the course of birth, growth, acme, and decadence. Counter to this course, there is the return to beginnings which amounts to an alteration that Machiavelli appropiately calls a *rinnovazione*: a becoming new again, a renewal, a re-birth of sorts. Thus the revolutionary motion that is at stake here is one that "goes against time," where time refers to natural time or the aionic life-span.

The concept of such a counter-natural revolution is first introduced in the myth of the Golden Age (the age of Kronos or Saturn) in Plato's *Statesman*:

The god himself at times joins in conducting this all and making it circle as it goes along, and at times he just lets go, whenever the circuits have obtained the measure of the time appropiate to the all, *and it then gets to turn around spontaneously in the contrary direction* since it is an animal and has obtained a lot of intelligence from him who at the beginning fitted it altogether.... *Of all the revolutions that occur in heaven, one must believe that this alteration was the biggest and most complete revolution....* Many different circumstances, marvelous and strange, coincide, *but here is*

---

[27] In his interpretation of this passage, Parel claims that "the crucial point to be noted here is that these bodies [mixed bodies], no less than natural bodies, are subject to the laws 'ordained for them by heaven'.... The point that ought not to be overlooked here is that Machiavelli ties his very theory of renewal, to the premodern notion of going back to the origin of the entity that is to be renewed. In other words, Machiavellian renewal is not something that looks forward but rather it is something that looks backward." (Parel, "Machiavelli's Modernity," 328-329). Parel simply fails to perceive the radical distinction between natural and mixed bodies advanced by the text. In general, Parel's reading of the return to beginnings suffers from a simple yet deep flaw: neither in the above article nor in *The Machiavellian Cosmos*, does he give an account of Machiavelli's complex theory of the "origin(s)" of political form, which makes it by definition impossible for him to perceive the complex structure of the "return" to such origin(s).

the greatest one and a consequence of the unwinding at that time of the all whenever it goes into the
turn that's contrary to the one which obtains at present.... First of all, the age, which each and every
animal had, came to a halt, and everything that was mortal stopped its advance toward looking older,
but, in altering, each genus grew back in the contrary direction, younger as it were and suppler....
And from that point on they began to wither away and vanish utterly and completely.[28]

The "biggest and most complete revolution" is the one that returns the cosmos to
its beginning ("it then gets to turn around spontaneously in the contrary direction"). The primary consequence of such return is the interruption and then
inversion of the passage of time so that things originate as old and move forwards
into youth. There can be no doubt that Machiavelli's formulation of the return to
beginnings "cites" from Plato's myth. I suggest that Machiavelli also re-writes
and subverts the political sense of Plato's theory of cosmic revolutions.

Plato thinks the possibility of re-birth and renewal, in a rather transparent
allegory of radical political change, in terms of the backwards motion of time.
Indeed, a possible interpretation of re-birth is to think of it as a process of moving
from old age back to infancy, and even of coming back from the dead. "The elders
go into the nature of the child and, on the other hand, it is from the dead, who lie
in the earth, that they get put together there once more and live again."[29] But for
Plato this kind of re-birth has completely negative consequences: it occurs when
the god (Kronos) who oversees everything suddenly lets go of control. The risk
of this counter-temporal (i.e., counter-Kronos) motion is that all order will "be
dissolved and sink into the sea, which is limitless, of dissimilarity."[30] For this
reason, Kronos "once more takes his seat at its rudder, and by twisting round of
the things diseased and sprung in the former circuit by itself, he makes it a cosmos
and in correcting it, works it up into something deathless and ageless."[31] Thus for
Plato the revolutionary motion in which order is brought to its degree-zero (and
thereby the possibility of a complete renewal of the given orders is disclosed) is
itself the manifestation of the "sickness" of the cosmos, by the well-known
identity between health and order that Plato sets up since the *Gorgias.*

For Machiavelli, instead, the revolutionary and counter-temporal motion has
a positive value: without it, no mixed body could survive the "ups and downs" of
historical becoming. The return to beginnings expresses the revolutionary
movement that becomes necessary once political life gives up on the Platonic
dream of a "divine shephard" that demonically rules over everything, that is, gives
up on the ideal of politics according to which "ruling is everything," and that
leaves no space for the expression of the desire for "no-rule" represented by the

---

[28] Plato *Statesman* 269d-270e. Emphasis mine. On the general significance of the myth of Kronos,
see Pierre Vidal-Naquet, "Plato's Myth of the Statesman, the Ambiguities of the Golden Age and of
History," *The Journal of Hellenic Studies* XCVIII (1978): 132-141; Pierre-Maxim Schuhl, *La
fabulation platonicienne* (Paris: Vrin, 1974), ch.3; and Friedrich Solmsen, "Hesiodic Motifs in Plato,"
in *Hesiode et son influence* (Geneva: Fondation Hardt, 1962). A detailed commentary of the
cosmological aspects of the myth is found in Luc Brisson, *Le Même et l'Autre dans la structure
ontologique du Timée de Platon* (Paris: Vrin, 1974), 478-513. For a recent politico-philosophical
interpretation of the *Statesman*, see Stanley Rosen, *Plato's Statesman: the Web of Politics* (New
Haven: Yale University Press, 1995).
[29] Plato *Statesman* 271b-c.
[30] Ibid., 274d.
[31] Ibid., 273d-e.

people.[32] For Machiavelli this movement goes against the grain of the times in order to bring something radically new to light: not unlike in Plato's account, where time "eats itself up" and thus makes the "elders" into "children," Machiavelli's return to beginnings denotes the event when innovation and repetition coincide. In this sense, the return to beginnings expresses the formula for the concept of modern revolution, if it is true that "to Robespierre ancient Rome was a past charged with the time of the now [*Jetztzeit*] which he blasted out of the continuum of history. The French Revolution viewed itself as the return of Rome. It quoted ancient Rome exactly in the way that fashion quotes a costume of the past."[33]

   That political action needs the power to move against the times is also the conclusion of my discussion of virtù and fortuna. In that context, action is defined as a modality of existence that goes counter to the sphere of activity as habit (*ethos*). Action brings forth the radically new; consequently, it cannot arise out of the sphere of habit and the normative scaffolding that is an outgrowth of it. That is why Machiavelli repeatedly asserts that innovations, as such, always find favorable terrain. The radically new is also the radically untimely. Action is untimely in the sense that it goes "counter to the times," and this is why it does not stand nailed to the wheel of fortuna (as all *ethoi* must stand nailed). Action is revolutionary in the sense that it changes the times as opposed to waiting for the times to change and attempting to correspond to them. There is here something like a "Copernican turn" in the history of praxis: up to Machiavelli, human praxis is not assigned the power to change the times because it is always thought to depend on them, to some degree or another, for its success.[34] Machiavelli makes human praxis conscious of its own historicity precisely to the degree that it discloses the possibility of changing the times, i.e., of revolution. Plato's cosmic revolution illustrates the moment when the cosmos, and along with it time, is "out of joint." Machiavelli's theory of historical repetition turns "time is out of joint" into the motto for modern revolutionary situations.[35]

   In the myth of the *Statesman* Plato situates the possibility of revolution (understood in the above sense of a change of times) as the mythic event that signals the end of the Golden Age (the age of Kronos) and the transition to the age of human beings (the age of Zeus). The latter is an age in which action no longer can correspond or encounter what the times demand because humans have lost their divine guidance, the *daimones* or "divine shepards," of which the myth speaks.[36] It is because of this loss that human beings, after the revolution which brings an end to the age of Kronos, must supplement this lack of truly "political"

---

[32] For the expression of the "divine shephard", see Plato, *Statesman*, 275c. On the use of *daimones* to rule over all living things, see ibid., 271d-e. In this sense, Machiavelli does not think of revolutions as a process that will bring the world back to the purity of archaic origins, to the "Golden Age" of Kronos, as is often thought in the interpretations of this myth in the context of modern revolutions. See Hannah Arendt, *On Revolution*, for an instance of this kind of reading of the myth.

[33] Benjamin, *Über den Begriff der Geschichte*, XIV.

[34] This is also the case for Stoicism, since its "withdrawal" from the slings of fortune is no less a validation of the general framework of the dependence of virtuous action on circumstances.

[35] On a philosophical interpretation of the formula "Time is out of joint," see Deleuze, *Difference and Repetition*, 88-89.

[36] Plato *Statesman* 271d-e.

activity (which accounted for the state of peace and plenty found in the Golden Age of Kronos) by the activity of legislation, by the empire of the law.[37] In Plato the law stands as a frail, "human all too human" attempt to contrast the over-whelming power of time over individuals in the age of Zeus.

Machiavelli is fully aware that the law, and in general the fixity of any political form, cannot withstand the change of times: and that is why he brings back into history the possibility of changing the times, of revolutionary action, that Plato had both opened and closed by placing it at the gate of the mythical Golden Age. At the start of *Discourses on Livy,* III,1 Machiavelli makes the point that without change of political form, no political life can hope to survive in time. Revolution-ary change is essential to the political body; it is not an inconvenient, something intrinsically negative, as it is for classical political philosophy. Machiavelli's thesis marks the beginning of modern political thought: political life is constituted in and through an essential relation to its historicity. Political bodies do not have natural life-spans.

THE SIGNATURE(S) OF THE RETURN

The next issue addressed by *Discourses on Livy,* III,1 is the character of the change that permits political bodies to survive in time.

The way in which they are to be renewed is, as already said, by returning them towards their beginnings. Because all beginnings, those of sects, republics and kingdoms, must have some good, through which they can regain their first reputation and their first augmentation. And because in the process of time that goodness is corrupted, if there is nothing that intervenes and reduces it to the sign [*la riduca al segno*], it will necessarily kill that body. And these doctors of medicine say, speaking of human bodies, "that each day something is deposited (in the body), such that in the end a cure becomes necessary". This reduction toward the beginning, speaking about republics, is done either by extrinsic accident or by intrinsic prudence.[38]

All renewals of the orders of the political body are returns to beginnings. How can innovation emerge from repetition, i.e., out of a revolution as return to begin-nings? To what does a revolution really return, such that it itself is the emergence of the new, such that it itself innovates the political body? The answer seems to be that one returns to the *principio* (principle, beginning) and all beginnings (*principii*) of states or mixed bodies have some "good" in them.

But here Machiavelli's text becomes ambiguous. Either the *principio* is also the chronological beginning of the political body, i.e., the time of its "first reputation and its first augmentation," or the *principio* is something other than the chrono-logical beginning, something that was there "at first" and something that can be returned to in order to gain back this "first reputation and first augmentation." The latter reading seems to be more correct because otherwise the return to the *principio* would not qualify as the means to regain (*ripigliare*) the "first" growth but would simply be a return to the first growth itself, since the *principio* would refer to this "first growth" and it would make no sense for Machiavelli to speak

---

[37] Ibid., 292a-302b4.
[38] Machiavelli, *Discourses on Livy,* III,1.

of gaining again (*ri-pigliare*) the "first growth," as if there could have been a first gain.

Even so, the ambiguity is not dispelled for it is unclear at this stage what "beginning" is referred to by the text. If one takes "Rome" as the paradigmatic political body, then the *Discourses on Livy* has shown that "Rome" could be said to have at least two beginnings: the state "begins" with Romulus, the republic with Brutus. If the content of the return to beginnings is a radical moment of renewal, then it would seem that only the event symbolized by Brutus qualifies as the "beginning" to which the political body is to "return" if it wants to survive. But if this is the case, then the return to beginnings does not aim for the beginning at all since the event of Brutus signals a discontinuity with the system of authority that upholds the primacy of origins and the integrity of the beginning. Conversely, if the reference it to a beginning like the founding of Rome by Romulus, then the formula "return to beginnings" is nothing but a translation of the system of authority whereby every action is legitimate if it is bound back (*re-ligio*) to the beginning in the process of augmenting it. In this case, the return to beginnings excludes a radical break with the past, with origins, with the whole system of authority: all renewal comes under the purview of a stronger and deeper attachment to what is traditional. Here the old adage would be true: "to change everything so that nothing really changes." I shall discuss at length both possible readings below.

Irrespective of the kind of return at issue, a return is necessary: the political body would die "if something does not intervene that leads it back to the sign [*se non interviene cosa che la riduca al segno*]."[39] In his commentary, Inglese renders this curious expression as "to bring back the life of the state to its initial conditions."[40] But this does not mean much unless the "initial conditions" are specified. Do they refer to the conditions at the beginning of political life? Or do they refer to the conditions to begin political life in a given mode, or to something else entirely? Machiavelli uses the locution "to reduce or lead back to the sign" as synonymous to that of "to return to beginnings," as if "in the beginning" there stands a sign, something that refers to something else (to something original) which nonetheless it also defers, and hence must be repeated, returned to, renewed. Perhaps this internal link between repetition and sign is itself already indicative that the conditions to begin something new are not to be identified with the initial conditions of anything in particular.

Similarly, the text asserts that the beginnings to which the political body must return always contain some "good." Whether the beginning refers to Romulus or Brutus, though, it is difficult to perceive what Machiavelli has in mind by using this term. After all, the "goodness" at issue is always an action that is transgressive: for example, the killing of Remus by Romulus, or the killing of the sons of Brutus by Brutus himself.[41] In neither case is the beginning "good" in a moral sense, and in both cases the predicate of "goodness" applied to the action (to the beginning) seems to depend on its "effects," that is, on what comes later. Once

---

[39] Ibid.

[40] Machiavelli, *Discorsi*, 575.

[41] Machiavelli, *Discourses on Livy*, I,9 and III,3, respectively.

again, the beginning is affected by a strange duplicity: the return to the beginnings is a return to some action whose value or meaning is deferred to something else, just like a sign.

In the case of republics, the return to beginnings is either done "by extrinsic accident or by intrinsic prudence."[42] Either the renewal and reduction is prescribed by the constitutional order, or it is necessitated by what is not under the control of this order, and so may require an action that is also thereby extra-constitutional. The text moves on to discuss examples of a renewal by "extrinsic accident": "One sees how it was necessary for Rome to be taken by the Gauls in order that it could be reborn and, by being reborn, regain new life and new virtù, and regain the observance of religion and justice, which were beginning to wither in the city."[43] The return to beginnings is more than a simple renewal: it is a re-birth (*rinascita*). The accident of the Gallic invasion is interesting because it unites the motif of survival (from the invasion) with that of re-birth (of political life): surviving means to be born anew. The return to beginnings concerns always a political re-birth.

The re-birth or survival of political life is here coupled with a renewal of observance of religion and justice. But do religion and justice experience a re-definition in the return to beginnings such that they can be newly observed, or is the return to beginnings simply synonymous with a renewed imposition on political life of its old re-ligious character, that keeps it mindful of the ancient orders whose augmentation it has to ensure? The text leaves room for both readings.

> *It ought to be easily presupposed that they were beginning to take less account of other good institutions ordered by Romulus and by the other prudent princes* than was reasonable and necessary to maintain their free way of life [*vivere libero*]. Thus came this external beating, so that *all the orders of the city might be regained and that it might be shown to that people that it was necessary not only to maintain religion and justice but also to esteem its good citizens* and to take more into account of their virtue than of those advantages that it appeared to them they lacked through their works. *This one sees succeeded exactly; for as soon as Rome was retaken, they renewed all the orders of their ancient religion,* they punished the Fabii who had engaged in combat "against the law of nations," and next they so much esteemed the virtue and goodness of Camillus that they put aside all envy – the Senate and the others – and they again placed all the weight of that republic on him.[44]

Machiavelli at first seems to follow Livy's judgment that Roman mores had begun to decay before the accident of the Gallic invasion because no religious obser-vances were made when the army was pulled out against the Gauls, when the Tribunes were created with consular power, and when the Fabii were given the Tribunate in spite of having fought against the *ius gentium*. In so doing, the text gives the impression that the return to beginnings consists in a return to ancient orders. Yet this impression is mistaken because the actual events constituting the return to beginnings (in this case: the punishment of the noble family of the Fabii and the creation of the Dictatorship) entails the radical renewal of the Roman

---

[42] Ibid., III,1.
[43] Ibid.
[44] Ibid. Emphasis mine.

orders: "all the orders of their ancient religion were renewed." Most significantly, the renewal is made in favor of the plebeians, of the people, rather than of the nobility and the heretofore ruling classes. As Machiavelli makes clear in *Discourses on Livy*, II,30 this particular re-ordering of the constitution was a response to the perception that precisely the nobility's monopoly of the political life had led Rome to its ruin on the eve of the Gallic invasions. In this case, the return to beginnings is an event that comes under the sign of Brutus, rather than of Romulus. But if so, why does Machiavelli also claim that such renewal was an attempt to revive the ancestral constitution given by Romulus "and the other princes"? Does the event of transgression of the old orders and the projection of new ones (which I call the republican event) in the end function to consolidate the hold that the state has over political life, and therefore can be said to fall under the sign of Romulus, always already inscribed within the task of augmenting the foundations of the state?

A decisive feature of the theory of return to beginnings is that the renewal of political form can be performed both under the sign of Brutus and under that of Romulus. The duplicity of "signatures" of the return to beginnings reveals its two modalities. In general, the purpose of such return to beginnings is so

that men who live together in any given order must frequently recognize each other either through these extrinsic accidents or through intrinsic ones. As to the latter, it must arise either from a law that frequently reviews the accounts [*rivegga il conto*] of men who are in that body or indeed from a good man who arises among them, who with his examples and his virtuous works produces the same effect as the order.[45]

Machiavelli is now speaking of those events in which the state is re-ordered as internal "accidents," and no longer as changes caused by the political form itself. In other words, whether the changes have internal or external causes, in no case does the political and legal order control their advent: the return to beginnings is something that "happens" to the state and the state has no control over these events. This point is often ignored by those interpreters who downplay the significance of the theory of return to beginnings. According to Viroli, for instance, Machiavelli's main point is that republics need to "have constitutional procedures to face situations of emergency.... [they must] predispose legal procedures to face situations of emergency."[46] Only when such constitutional arrangements are lacking should the republic's "leaders take upon themselves the burden of violating the laws and use extraordinary powers."[47] Finally, citing *Discourses on Livy*, I,18, Viroli identifies "an even more prohibitive and almost impossible achievement [which] is to redeem a corrupt republic and to restore in it a political life."[48] This kind of reading suggests that Machiavelli considers "situations of emergency" or "situations of necessity" to be rare situations, nothing but exceptionx to the rule according to which a political form can, for the

---

[45] Ibid.
[46] Viroli, *Machiavelli*, 143.
[47] Ibid., 144.
[48] Ibid.

most part, fashion itself so as to avoid such situations or deal with them in constitutional ways.

Yet Machiavelli clearly believes that the "situation of emergency" is not accidental to political life, for if there is anything that texts like *Discourses on Livy*, I,18 show, it is precisely that the "ordinary," constitutional life of the state always fashions the conditions for the corruption of political life and therefore leads political life, in a "constitutional" way, to a situation of emergency or necessity.[49] Furthermore, and this is the decisive point of the passage of *Discourses on Livy*, III,1 under analysis, Machiavelli argues that the constitutional procedures which are set up to face the situation of emergency (in this case the Roman institution of the Dictatorship handed to Camillus after the invasion of the Gauls) themselves emerge only from events or situations of return to beginnings that are extra-constitutional, that befall the political form from a dimension of political life which it does not control, irrespective of whether the motivation for the return to beginnings is an internal or an external political occurrence. Therefore the problem of the extra-legal origin of the rule of laws, the problem of the *pouvoir constituante* that is figured by the theory of the return to beginnings, is inescapable.

The motivation for the "internal" yet extra-constitutional change of political orders is the need for the members of the political body (in the widest sense of the term "member") to "recognize" each other. The text specifies that what is at issue in this moment of recognition is political, isonomic equality. The return to beginnings is an event of equalization in which these members, suspending the distinction between who rules and who is ruled, determine who has been advantaged by the given political and legal order (hence the locution "to review the accounts of men"), and project a new order as a consequence. Examples of the orders that emerged from the various, internally motivated, return to beginnings in Roman republican history are "the Tribunes of the plebs, the Censors, and all the other laws that were made against the ambition and the insolence of men."[50] What meaning does "beginning" (*principio*) have in these cases, when it is clearly no longer a question of returning Rome to an ancestral constitution, but rather of changing the balance of political power in favor of the people, and against the aristocracy set up by the orders of Romulus and Numa? There seems to be a different principle at stake when the return to beginnings has to do with a return to the ancient order of Romulus "and the other princes" (as in the case of externally motivated returns discussed above), than when it has to do with the internally motivated returns on the basis of new orders "that led back the Roman Republic to its principle."[51]

Having reviewed the duplicity of the return to beginnings, I put forward an interpretative hypothesis to account for it. Only externally motivated return to beginnings, precisely because they consist in accidents that imperil the state from the outside, call for a return to beginnings under the sign of Romulus. This modality of return is intended to restore the religious value, and thus to stabilize

---

[49] I refer to my arguments in part 1, ch.5 and 6.
[50] Machiavelli, *Discourses on Livy*, III,1.
[51] Ibid.

the given political form, as a defensive reaction against the external threat. Even these conservative returns involve a moment of renewal (as Machiavelli claims the religious orders were all renewed with Camillus); but such a renewal will always be functional to the stability of political form. Conversely, the internally motivated return to beginnings imperils the stability of the state because the greatest threat to a free political life is understood to be this very stability of political and legal orders of domination and the inequality that they fashion and protect. In this case, the new orders emerge from the discord between the people and the nobles, between the demands of freedom and those of order. This return to beginnings is a reduction of the political body to the sign of Brutus, rather than to the sign of Romulus.

RETURN TO BEGINNINGS AND THE TRANSGRESSION OF THE LAW

The orders that emerge out of the internally caused return to beginnings are motivated by the desire for freedom as no-rule and express themselves in demands for isonomic equality. Since these in turn reflect a resistance against the previous orders of the state, they lack the support of those political subjects who were "ennobled" in and through the previous orders. Machiavelli identifies in this situation the need for a certain law-making violence.[52]

Such orders have to be brought to life by the virtù [fatti vivi dalla virtù] of a citizen who rushes spiritedly [animosamente concorra] to execute them against the power of those who transgress them. Notable among such executions, before the taking of Rome by the French, were the deaths of the sons of Brutus, the death of the ten citizens... after the taking of Rome it was the death of Manlius Capitolinus, the death of the son of Manlius Torquatus.... *Because they were excessive and notable [eccessive e notabili], such things made men draw back toward the sign [facevano gli uomini ritirare verso il segno] whenever one of them arose; and when they began to be more rare, they also began to give more space to men to corrupt themselves....* For one should not wish ten years at most to pass from one to another of such executions; for when this time is past, men begin to vary in their customs and to transgress the laws and unless something arises by which punishment is brought back to their memory and fear is renewed in their spirits, soon so many delinquents join together that they can no longer be punished without danger.[53]

This passage remarks on the fragility of the political order instituted by laws. In particular, it shows that neither laws nor orders, in themselves, exhibit or give rise to political life, since such orders must be "*brought to life* by the virtù of a citizen." If these orders are to be followed, an exemplary action must be attached to them; and this action is nothing other than a punishment for the transgression of the orders in question. These punishments "made men draw back toward the sign," where by "sign" is meant a limit beyond which one is trangressing and will be punished, in a peculiarly "excessive" fashion, in order to instill in the possible transgressor the fear of the state and its orders.

---

[52] On the idea of law-making violence, see Walter Benjamin, "Critique of Violence," in *Selected Writings. Volume 1: 1913-1926*, eds. Marcus Bullock and Michael W. Jennings (Cambridge: Harvard University Press, 1996).

[53] Machiavelli, *Discourses on Livy*, III, 1. Emphasis mine.

On the basis of such texts, Strauss reads the return to the beginnings as a return to the primordial terror involved in the establishment of the law and the state:

The renovation of mixed bodies consists of the renewal of fear in the minds of their members or of putting in men that terror and that fear which the original founders had put into their partisans. This, and not the return to the old modes and orders, is the essence of the return to the beginning. Return to the beginning means in all cases introducing new orders.... Ordinary return to the beginning means return to the terror accompanying the foundation. Machiavelli's return to the beginning means return to the primeval or original terror which precedes every man-made terror, which explains why the founder must use terror and which enables him to use terror. Machiavelli's return to the beginning means return to the terror inherent in man's situation, to man's essential unprotectedness. In the beginning there was terror.[54]

Strauss sees in the human response to "the primeval or original terror" the source of legitimacy of the founding political violence ("the terror acompanying the foundation"). I suggest that the recourse to fear and violence in Machiavelli has other grounds. The new orders have an inherent lack of authority only because they emerge out of a moment of radical freedom vis-à-vis the authority of the factical legal system. They are unable to extract authority from the "religious" mechanism that authorizes the orders of the state only because they emerge from a break with the "spirit" of foundations (with the spirit of the actions performed "under the sign of Romulus"). In short, the new or revolutionary orders lack the "force of the law," and pose the problem of how they can be established. The pessimistic solution consists in having recourse to "excessive and notable" violence, as if the realization of freedom in a political and legal order inevitably calls for violence. Once again, there is something "tyrannical" in the very dynamic of freedom that counters tyranny. The order that brings a new equality to the political body, and which emerges in an event of freedom, that is, in a revolution-ary event, calls for its establishment through violence directed against those "powerful ones who transgress them [*contro alla potenza di quegli che gli trapassano*]."

It is symptomatic of this paradox in the realization of freedom that after discussing republican return to beginnings and the need for violence to establish the new orders, the text of *Discourses on Livy*, III,1 proceeds to illustrate the need for periodic returns to beginnings with the anti-republican example of how the Medici governed Florence.

Those who governed the state of Florence [*governato lo stato di Firenze*] from 1434 upto 1494 used to say, to this purpose, that it was necessary to regain the state every five years; otherwise, it was difficult to maintain it. They called regaining the state [*ripigliare lo stato*] putting that terror and that fear in men that they had put when first taking it, since at that time they had beaten those who, according to that mode of living, acted badly [*male operato*]. But as the memory of that beating fades, men began to dare to try new things and to speak bad things; and so it is necessary to provide for it, returning the state to its beginnings.[55]

---

[54] Strauss, *Thoughts on Machiavelli*, 167.
[55] Machiavelli, *Discourses on Livy*, III,1.

What is the point of this perplexing reference to the regime of the Medici? The text seems to harbor a contradiction: whereas Machiavelli previously claims that the movement of return to beginnings is revolutionary and creative of new orders that maintain the freedom of political life, now the same formula of the return to beginnings is employed to signify the opposite, i.e., the way in which the prince maintains its state by terrorizing the people, just as was done when first acquiring it. Here the return to beginnings is clearly intended to return political life to the situation of the beginning of the state as locus of a certain terror, as Strauss's reading suggests.

But the contradiction vanishes as soon as one realizes that Machiavelli has set in place two antinomical yet irreducible conceptions of the content of the return to beginnings. Under one understanding of the term, which I call the republican one, the new orders that emerge from the return to beginnings are all orders that, minimally, attempt to inscribe into the state a kind of negativity or resistance with respect to the state's capacity to dominate. In this context, Machiavelli refers to the emergence of institutions like the Tribunate, the Censors, and so on. Under the other understanding, which I call the princely one, the content of the return to beginnings is purely and solely the maintenance of the state without effecting any real changes to it: it consists in the attempt to terrorize the opponents of the state, and thus to dissuade every attempt to counteract the personal ownership of the public space, as occurred with the Medici.

But why bring up the example of the Medici now, immediately after discussing the need for violence to establish new orders (i.e., after a discussion of the republican event)? By conjuring the "conservative" or "anti-republican" interpretation of the return to beginnings, Machiavelli emphasizes the point that, from the perspective of the new prince, represented by Cosimo and Lorenzo de' Medici, there is ultimately no difference between the activity of acquiring the state [pigliare lo stato] and that of maintaining it. The new prince, the civil prince, must deny the difference between the "founder" who institutes the state and the "citizen" who maintains its orders. For maintenance of the order implies the same sort of violence as the institution of the order. In other words, Machiavelli criticizes the belief that it is ever possible to establish a political order in a legitimate way that does not rely, at some level, on violence.

But if there is a transgression, on the part of the "new" prince, of the "ancient" distinction between founder and citizen, it is also true (and I think this is the point of the example of Cosimo de'Medici) that there is an inverse transgression of such a distinction on the part of the "new" citizen who emerges in the republican return to beginnings. For the example of the Medici's understanding of the return to beginnings is meant to convey that the practice of maintaining a given order (by returning to terror as the Medici do) is no more "legitimate" than the practice of radically re-ordering it, that is, subverting it and creating a new one (as the republican return to beginnings does).[56] The example of the Medici's interpreta-

---

[56] Notice that Machiavelli emphasizes the "weakness" of the "beating" (battitura) that a princely-aristocratic regime can give to its opponents: the memory of the punishment and terror is never enough to discourage citizens from the attempt to revolutionize the political order for the sake of political freedom.

tion of the need for the state to return to beginnings, just like the example of Camillus, should not lead to the mistaken conclusion that all return to beginnings are actions that "conserve" or "maintain" the integrity of the state; as if there were no properly revolutionary, that is, republican content to the return to beginnings corresponding to the project of a radical re-ordering of the state itself, which draws its origin from the discord between the desire for freedom and the desire to rule or command.

RETURN TO BEGINNINGS AND THE EVENT OF THE REPUBLIC

The analysis of the return to beginnings in *Discourses on Livy*, III,1 reveals that Machiavelli often mixes together, sometimes in a disturbingly indiscriminate fashion, considerations that seem to favor both princely and republican regimes. There seem to be two radically different conceptions of the return to beginnings, which I designate under the signatures of Romulus and Brutus (each referring to a different kind of "beginning"), and Machiavelli seems to speak about them as if they were, at times, indistinguishable. It is time to ask why he does this.

As I discuss in detail in the next chapter, the reason for this ambiguity concerning the content of the return to beginnings is that such a return, in that it figures the very possibility of political change, can be undertaken, as it were, in two opposite directions: from tyranny to freedom, and from freedom to tyranny. In the event of the return to beginnings there are only two possible transitions; and that is why there exist two, radically different senses and signatures for it. But the issue at hand is still more complicated. Machiavelli asserts, as I have shown, that in order to survive a political body requires frequent return to beginnings or revolutions. There are two kinds of returns: one that brings the people back to a beginning of terror and that serves to re-instate the authority of the state (this is the return "under the sign of Romulus"), and the other is the kind of return that subverts the state, and causes its radical re-ordering (this is the republican event, the return "under the sign of Brutus"). In the first kind of return, there is a passage from freedom to tyranny; in the second type of return, the passage leads from tyranny to freedom.

Two very different, yet both warranted, readings can be given of this dualism. The first reading assumes that there exist two types of modern states, republics and principalities. Because they are both modern political forms, their state-form is constituted out of revolutionary events (i.e., return to beginnings), that have different characteristics according to the different type of states. Principalities return to the past, that is, to the conditions (of terror) that are present when their state is initiated by princes and founders; republics return to the future (so to speak), that is, they renew their orders in accord with the demands for freedom coming from the people. If a republic is a form of state, then the return to beginnings, the revolutionary event, is always already functional to the telos of the state's self-preservation: a "republic" (as form of state) would simply have a different way of maintaining itself than a principality. Both require returns to beginnings, but for the republic they are innovative, whereas for the principality they are conservative in nature. According to this reading, all negations of the state, all revolutionary events, are always already inscribed within the life-process of the state and in fact constitute this life.

In modern political thought, Hegel is the figure who thinks this hypothesis through to its extreme consequences. If the events of return to beginnings are only relative discontinuities within a process that lives in and through their sublation (*aufhebung*), then it is possible to conceive of a notion of "organic history" having as its culmination the universal state, that is, the state that is capable of absorbing and expressing all political differences and conflicts.[57] Such a universal state is the existing identity of identity and difference, the historical unity of universal and particular. This universal state is the telos of an "organic history," i.e., a process-history, that can also "end" once it has produced such a state. The "end of history" would be the perpetual present in which the emergence of differences (i.e., of claims to freedom) no longer also mark discontinuities and leaps in history that defer its "end" in virtue of their constituting, always, "beginnings."

This Hegelian reading of Machiavelli's theory of historical repetition ultimately falls short of the deepest intuitions of Machiavelli concerning the political and ontological status of the republic or free political life in modernity. Another interpretative option stands open, and it is the one that I have tried to pursue all along. For Machiavelli, the modern political situation does not give rise to two forms or species of state (republics and principalities), but rather is characterized by two dynamics: one that is constitutive of the form of the state, the other that is subversive of it, which I call the event of the republic. Since Machiavelli delineates the modern political situation as one in which the political form entertains an essential relation to its own historicity, it is not surprising that the state should constitute itself through repeated return to beginnings, understood as standing "under the sign of Romulus." The state, in the situation of modernity, must continuously re-start itself: it has lost the ancient, reassuring difference between the founding of the state and its maintenance. Indeed, the state is in a situation of modernity precisely because it must maintain itself by initiating itself repeatedly; its legitimacy is never assured by a system of authority of the Roman type, i.e., through civil religion and the worship of foundations. But since the purpose of the modern state is to provide security for the people, the way it re-starts itself is precisely by making the people feel, periodically, that "terror" of the

---

[57] By "organic history" I refer to the analogy that Hegel draws so often between history and the life-process: one can call it his "Aristotelian" bias. But it is not just that Hegel, with apparently heavy-handed applications of Aristotelian philosophemes, reads characteristics of "life" into the historical process (e.g., history as unfolding of the in-itself). Much more radically, he reads characteristics of historical processes (of historical negations, if one prefers) into the category of "life." The "life" of Hegel is above all subjectivity, which he defines, in contrast to the category of "life" in Aristotle, against the notion of "substance," precisely because subjectivity (but not substance) endures in and through its own radical negation. So, the "life" that Hegel speaks about is the "life" of spirit, not of nature (as in Aristotle). And this means that it is a "life" that is thoroughly imbued with freedom. At this point the real question poses itself whether the "life of the spirit" in Hegel, and its historicity, does justice to the phenomenon of political freedom, or, on the contrary, whether the very identity between freedom and life (of spirit) posited by Hegel, in the end denies a more radical conception of freedom, one that emerges precisely with a transcendence of the sphere of life as such (even of the sphere of the life of spirit). This transcendence would emerge through a concept of (historical) discontinuity that cannot be sutured or bridged, and which is, crucially, linked to a radical concept of repetition.

beginnings which made them seek the protection of the state to begin with. The Straussian reading of the terror that begins the state, although anticipated in Machiavelli's text, is ultimately much more applicable to Hobbes's theory of the state than to Machiavelli's.[58] For Hobbes, the civil state both takes away and maintains the "terror" of the state of nature: this terror is always potentially associated with the Leviathan. If it were not, so Hobbes argues, there could never be an "exit" from the state of nature, because men would lack the only true incentive to keep their compacts: fear. The reason why I call such a return to beginnings of the modern state a return "under the sign of Romulus" is not because the modern state requires a founder-myth, but because the mechanism by which the state re-starts itself turns on a certain usage of fear to which one can associate a mythical ground for the authority of its orders that are analogous to the analysis of the political function of religion given by Machiavelli in the context of his discussion of Romulus.

At the other pole of modern political life stands the republican event. The republic is an event, not a state. It is constituted, it exists, only in the return to beginnings effected "under the sign of Brutus." This means, simply put, that its purpose is freedom as no-rule, and not the establishment of a political form that brings security. The difference between the two types of return to beginnings is simple and yet decisive. In the return that assures the life of the state, in order to maintain the state, there has to be a return to "beginning." Whereas for the republican return, its maintenance consists only in that it begins, it renews. The goal of the republican return is in no case that of maintenance: that is why it assumes itself and lives itself as a radically finite event. This is also why it must be counterposed to the return to beginnings "under the sign of Romulus." Machiavelli is clear that Romulus above all else wanted to maintain his product: the city.[59] The purpose of the republican event is to effect an authentic discontinuity: time is interrupted in its linear flow. But there is not a return to a "past," as in the returns that characterize the life of the state; rather, the discontinuity is the advent of a future: the past is "telescoped" into the present, so that the new may emerge.

There is one last aspect of this complicated discussion of the theory of historical repetition with which I also deal at length in the next chapter: the peculiar simulacra that emerge in the two types of return to beginnings. The necessity of a return to beginnings for the maintenance of the state is continuously manifesting itself in the impossibility of preserving the division between founder and citizens for the state. What emerges, instead, is the figure of the "new" prince, a figure which in a sense hovers between the poles of the founder and the citizen. Always already cast at an infinite distance from the mythical beginning of foundation, and yet equally distant from the possibility of expressing fully the desire for freedom of the people, the new prince, in order to maintain the unity of

---

[58] Indeed, Strauss first developed this reading of terror in relation to Hobbes. See Leo Strauss, *The Political Philosophy of Hobbes* (Chicago: University of Chicago Press, 1963). On this Straussian reading of Hobbes, see also J. P. McCormick, "Fear, Technology and the State. Carl Schmitt, Leo Strauss and the Revival of Hobbes in Weimar and National Socialist Germany," *Political Theory* 4 (1994): 619-652.

[59] Machiavelli, *Discourses on Livy,* I,9.

the state, must engage the game of simulation and dissimulation, must enter the sphere of the simulacrum.

But if the new prince is the simulacrum of the founder, the "new" citizen that emerges from the republican return to beginnings is likewise the simulacrum of the counterpart to the mythical founder: the mythical citizen. The "ancient" citizen is characterized above all by the respect of the laws of the state (whether in ruling or in obeying), by the care for the "common good," by the possession of "civic virtue," and so on.[60] For Machiavelli, this picture of the citizen represents the political actor manqué. The citizen that emerges, or should emerge, in the republican event is by definition transgressive: but of the orders of the state as such. This citizen acts and exists, during those events, in a space of no-rule, a space beyond the confines of the law, a space and a time in which, to all effects, legality is suspended. This is why Machiavelli sometimes calls this citizen a "prince," playing off the "ancient" sense of the prince or emperor as the political actor who is *legibus solutus*. Yet the crucial difference between the revolutionary citizen and this "ancient" prince is that the dis-solution of the law's grasp over the action of the citizen occurs on condition that this action is emancipatory rather than dominating or tyrannical, as was the case in the actions of the "ancient" prince or emperor. Machiavelli allows and requires action that is dissolute from the law (without principles, he will say), but only because freedom cannot have a law, because freedom as no-rule transcends the sphere of legal domination.

In conclusion, the central role of the return to beginnings in Machiavelli signals a vision of political life, in its totality, as un-foundable: in the end, every political order finds its ground in the domain of the event where grounds are absent, in the throw of the dice. Machiavelli poses the problem of what to do about this radical contingency of politics, and illustrates two possible outcomes, each necessary in its own way. One possibility consists in the attempt to stabilize this throw, turn it into a "state," master chance and negativity, realize freedom: these "impossible" goals name the anxiety of the modern state as "new" prince. The new prince comes to terms with this anxiety through a certain repetition, a certain return to beginnings, in which the magic of foundations is rehearsed, in which authority is religiously produced, but always as simulacra. Another possibility consists in exploiting the contingency of order in a call for renewal; it attempts to deal with chance in another sense, through another repetition, with other forms of transgressions: not law-preserving ones, as the new prince does, but rather law-suspending ones, for the sake of events of no-rule in which the free project of new orders is made possible.

---

[60] For a good discussion of these classical attributes of the citizen, see Viroli, *From Politics to Reason of State*, chs. 1-3.

CHAPTER 3

THE REVOLUTIONARY EVENT:
THEORY OF POLITICAL CHANGE

MODERN REVOLUTION AND ITS APORIAS

Having established that the return to beginnings designates a revolutionary event, in this chapter I explore the specific content of Machiavelli's theory of political change. The content of the revolutionary event is treated through the analysis of "the killing of the sons of Brutus" as the sort of exemplary action that "maintains" a newly gained freedom.[1] In *Discourses on Livy*, III,1 the emergence of the republic in and through the action of Brutus illustrates the theory of return to beginnings. Brutus's action, that "rare example in the memory of things,"[2] equally refers back to *Discourses on Livy*, I,16 where the possibility of "maintaining" freedom after the moment of liberation (after the expulsion of the kings) without instituting a civil principality is opened but not pursued. This possibility is given the label of "killing the sons of Brutus."

Only *Discourses on Livy*, III,3 explicitly discusses such a revolutionary possibility:

This will always be known by those who read of ancient things: that after a change of state, either from republic to tyranny or from tyranny to republic [*una mutazione di stato o da republica in tirannide o da tirannide in republica*] a memorable execution against the present conditions is necessary. *Whoever takes up a tyranny and does not kill Brutus, and whoever takes a free state and does not kill the sons of Brutus, maintains himself for little time.*[3]

In a sense, all of modern revolutionary theory is contained in this striking passage, which offers what may be called a logic of revolutionary action. Indeed, the two possibilities (to kill Brutus or to kill his sons) only apply in case of a revolutionary "change of state" (*mutazione di stato*). Furthermore, the very possibility of such a *mutazione* falls, always already, under the sign of Brutus. The sort of action that attempts to effect a change of state is revolutionary in the sense that it tends toward political freedom; and for this reason is symbolized in the figure of Brutus. Machiavelli asserts this explicitly: to act like Brutus (also in the sense of killing his sons) is to "make a free state [*fare uno stato libero*]," or, better, to free a state.[4] The other *mutazione*, i.e., the change from republic to tyranny, is not on a par with the first change from tyranny to republic. It is not a revolutionary action but a counter-revolutionary one; a change that presupposes the existence of Brutus, and thus of revolutionary change. Although the text appears to treat both actions with

---

[1] Machiavelli, *Discourses on Livy*, III,3.
[2] Ibid.
[3] Ibid. Emphasis mine.
[4] Ibid.

equanimity, the use of the signifier "Brutus" makes it so that the two sorts of action are not on a par: one is active, the other is reactive. Effective political change always comes under the sign of Brutus: to kill him is to kill change. To kill change is itself a change, but an essentially "reactive" or "reactionary" one.

The asymmetry between revolutionary and counterrevolutionary change is significant because it calls into question a widespread assumption that Machiavelli's idea of *mutazione di stato* is still premodern, belonging to the conceptual baggage of classical political thought.[5] Only those "who read of ancient things" in the peculiar fashion taught by the *Discourses on Livy* will find support for this new concept of revolution for the simple reason that the ancients themselves never understand political change as something originarily positive. The ancients never think about the *mutazione di stato* or *metabole politeion* principally in terms of a passage from tyranny to republic, from slavery to freedom. In all the records of "the ancient things" (in all the theories of constitutional cycles, for example) one never finds precisely this change: that from tyranny to republic, from slavery to freedom. In spite of the way in which Machiavelli couches his thought, his concept of revolutionary change is not simply circular or reversible as it is for the ancients. In the latter, political change is circular because natural: the change of forms of government is analogous to the change of seasons. The change that leads from winter to summer is not qualitatively different from that leading from summer to winter. It is meaningless to assert that one change is active and the other reactive. But that is exactly the kind of intensity that should be predicated of Machiavelli's concept of change from tyranny to freedom and conversely. The change towards freedom is always active; it is primary. The reason is that without the transcendence of political freedom with respect to political form there is no political change in the "effective truth" of the term.

The understanding of political change offered in the third book of the *Discourses on Livy* breaks with the tradition of classical political thought because it has in view primarily the freedom of the people. Political change is not between forms of government or of state (in a narrow political sense), as it is for the ancients, but rather involves a change of "state" in the widest possible sense: from the state of slavery (which Machiavelli calls "tyranny") to that of freedom (which he calls "republic").[6] The change of "state" at issue here is not a change between political forms given by citizens to themselves. Machiavelli's change of state envisages the transition into citizenship (i.e., political recognition) by political

---

[5] Arendt oscillates on this point: in "What is Authority?" she claims that Machiavelli, though he never used the word, was the first to conceive of a revolution." (Arendt, *Between Past and Future,* 136). In a later text she denies this claim: "the specific revolutionary pathos of the absolutely new... was entirely alien to him." (Arendt, *On Revolution,* 37). On the history of the concept of revolution in early modernity, see Karl Griewank, "Staatsumwälzung und Revolution in der Auffassung der Renaissance und Barockzeit," *Wissenschaftliche Zeitschrift der Friedrich-Schiller-Universität Jena* Heft 1 (1952/1953): 11-23; and O. Brunner, W. Conze, and R. Koselleck eds., *Geschichtliche Grundbegriffe* (Stuttgart: Klett, 1972), s.v. "Revolution, Rebellion, Aufruhr, Bürgerkrieg." Both of these articles question the attribution of a modern concept of revolution to Machiavelli.
[6] Only such changes of "state" fall under the category of revolution. In this sense, the modern doctrine of natural right is also a revolutionary doctrine. It contains at its center the problem of how to effect a change from the "state of nature" to "civil society" (and back) which is always conceived in terms of a passage from slavery to freedom, even though the number of changes, its modes, and so on, vary in thinkers as different as Hobbes and Locke, Spinoza and Rousseau.

subjects who are excluded in principle from the political sphere, namely, those subjects who are enslaved or otherwise politically disenfranchised by the given political form. The passages from republic to tyranny and tyranny to republic consist in events in which political life itself is disclosed and closed. These events are events of freedom because they consist in the advent of political subjects to a political status that grants them the isonomic capacity to make the law, and not just to be subject to it, and, conversely, also the possibility of being stripped of such a "right" to a political life. The symbol of Brutus gathers its enormous significance in the *Discourses on Livy* as a whole because Machiavelli makes it the symbol for political action that transforms political form as a function of opening political life to emancipatory claims, and shaping it through the struggle for freedom as absence of domination. The revolutionary change that Machiavelli theorizes does not occur within the sphere of civil life (*vita civile*) but outside of it, on a political terrain that is always exterior to the political and legal order of that sphere. This terrain is the political but "uncivil" and "inhuman" site of enslavement. Machiavelli grants to political life a purpose that had previously been constrained to the domain of myth: that of effecting the passage of people from slavery into freedom, from a "state" in which the division of master and slave is in place, to one in which it has been abolished.

The *Discourses on Livy* is the first text in modern political thought where one finds a dialectic of master and slave. Machiavelli considers the abolition of the division between master and slave as the political task of the moderns: this accounts for the radical thesis that political action is essentially revolutionary action, and revolution is carried out under the sign of political freedom as no-rule, as something inherently positive. Conversely, it "will always be known by those who read of ancient things," that for the ancients it is impossible to conceive of politics without the support that the master-slave relation provides to political action. For the ancients political action, by definition, cannot be oriented toward the abolition of that relation, and consequently revolutionary action can only be thought of as inherently negative, as a sign that it has not been possible for equals to come to an agreement about what form of government to give themselves.

One can say that Machiavelli proposes the following division between ancients and moderns. For the ancients the task of politics requires and has as its end justice, because political life is understood as the process of establishing inequality (between ruler and ruled) among equals (citizens). For the moderns, the task of political life is political freedom, understood as the process of establishing equality (no-rule) among unequals (masters and slaves). Machiavelli's position is simple and radical: there is no question of justice (understood in the above sense) when it comes to political freedom. There is no "just" freedom because there is no "unjust" freedom. Freedom knows no mean; it is inherently excessive because transcendent. Modern freedom is essentially revolutionary. When Arendt says that the idea behind modern revolutions is that "freedom, and neither justice nor greatness, is the highest criterion for judging the constitutions of political bodies" she is thoroughly Machiavellian.[7] Likewise, the incommensurability of

---

[7] Arendt, *On Revolution*, 29.

the discourse of political freedom with that of justice accounts for the foundation of justice on political freedom in modernity.[8]

Further evidence of the modern and revolutionary sense of the expression *mutazione di stato* is the fact that Machiavelli names the two "states" between which this change occurs "republic" and "tyranny." Once again, Arendt's profound analysis of modern revolutions offers the key to understand Machiavelli's terminology. As Arendt shows, the term "tyranny," when it is proffered in the revolutionary event, does not denote only an "unconstitutional" government. Its denotation includes a constitutional government that exercises a monopoly over political life.

Under no circumstance could monarchy, one-man rule, be identified with tyranny; yet it was precisely this identification to which the revolutions quickly were to be driven. *Tyranny, as the revolutions came to understand it, was a form of government in which the ruler, even though he ruled according to the laws of the realm, had monopolized for himself the right of action, banished the citizens from the public realm into the privacy of their households, and demanded of them that they mind their own, private business.* Tyranny, in other words, deprived of public happiness, though not necessarily of private well-being, while a republic granted to every citizen the right to become "a participator in the government of affairs", the right to be seen in action.[9]

In Machiavelli, if possible, the distinction between tyranny and republic is even more radical: the republic exists or happens where there is a creation of citizens, a disclosure of spaces of freedom as no-rule and action beyond the reach of laws. A "government of laws" is still "tyrannical" in a revolutionary or republican event because it is still a government, i.e., an imposition of rule over the demand by the desire of freedom to live in a "state" of no-rule. Viewed from the perspective of the republican event, the state itself (irrespective of the constitutional form it takes) is tyrannical vis-à-vis the republic, because the state has an inherent tendency to captivate the public space of the many and imposing upon it a *reductio ad unum.*[10]

The *mutazione di stato* from tyranny to republic, and conversely, does not mean that there is a change from one form of state to another, but rather the change is from the state as form (which is termed "tyranny") to the republic as event (formless political existence) and conversely. But it is only in the republican event, that is, in the revolutionary moment, that the state, no matter how constitutional it may be understood to be by its subjects, assumes the semblance of a tyranny. It is only when passing from the state to the republic that, on looking back on the state, it appears as having changed in "status," as having assumed a tyrannical appearance. The difficult questions are reached only at this point: how can freedom or the republic be a political "state of being" and at the same time a formless event? How can the republic be anything but a state or political form? How is it possible to have a change from a "state of being" which is the state as

---

[8] For a further discussion of this point, see Vatter, "Resistance and Legality: Arendt and Negri on Constituent Power" in *The Philosophy of Toni Negri. Vol. 2. Revolution in Theory*, ed. Tim Murphy and Abdul-Karim Mustapha (London: Pluto Press, 2007), 52–86.

[9] Arendt, *On Revolution*, 130. Emphasis mine.

[10] For an acute reading of this reductive tendency in the history of political thought, see Roberto Esposito, *Nove Pensieri sulla Politica,* (Bologna: Il Mulino, 1993).

political form to a "state of being" which is the republic as political event? What can it mean to "maintain" the event of political freedom?

Before engaging these questions it is advisable to take a step back and read the same passage of *Discourses on Livy*, III,3 from another, more standard perspective according to which the *mutazione di stato* refers to a change between two forms of the political state, the tyrannical and the republican. Why open this possibility of interpretation? Simply because Machiavelli's text is ambiguous, and ambiguous precisely on the crucial issue: can the genus of the state qua political form contain two species, that of tyranny (or "regal state," *stato regio*) and that of republic (or "free state," *stato libero*)? Is a state of freedom possible? Or should one surrender to the other evidence, and, as suggested above, recognize that political freedom, in its modern republican dimension, requires transcending the political form of the state as such, with the consequence that political freedom remains an iterable event, something impossible to "maintain" or "stabilize"?

Whether the republic is a form or an event is a question that already haunts *Discourses on Livy*, I,16: the "killing of the sons of Brutus" (who symbolize the nobility) remains an option for both the "republic" and the "civil prince" (the new prince who founds its state on the people, in contrast to the "old" prince, the traditional figure of the tyrant). But by *Discourses on Livy*, III,3 the same action has become the signature of a "republic," whereas it is now the "killing of Brutus" that represents the signature of "tyranny." Where does the civil prince hide amidst these options? I suggest that the new or civil prince hides in the republican event, but as the political subject who brings this event to a close. The civil prince requires the people as support (as "subjects"), but is also conscious of the fact that the state cannot satisfy their desire for freedom, awakened in the republican event. The civil prince names the process of realizing freedom, the process of changing the republic into a state: this reification can only occur in and through ideology. The ideological foundation of the modern state consists precisely in its claim that it realizes freedom. The reality of the state becomes ideological in proportion to the extent to which it realizes freedom.

Machiavelli illustrates the overdetermined character of the relation between republic and state by analyzing the case of Soderini, the Gonfaloniere of the Florentine Republic in which our author served as Secretary. Soderini is charged by Machiavelli with failing to act like Brutus and thus with undermining the republic itself. Machiavelli points out that Soderini did not "kill the sons of Brutus," that is, the enemies of the republic, because he did not want to act like a tyrant:

He judged (and often vouched for it with his friends) that if he wished to strike his opponents vigorously and to beat down his adversaries, he would have needed to take up extraordinary authority and break, along with the laws, civil equality [*istraordinaria autorità e rompere, con le leggi, la civile equalità*]. Even though afterward it would not be used tyrannically by him, this thing would have so terrified the collectivity [*l'universale*] that it would never after join together, after his death, to remake a gonfalonier for life; which order, he judged, it would be good to augment and maintain.[11]

---

[11] Machiavelli, *Discourses on Livy*, III,3.

Soderini objects, *ante litteram*, to Machiavelli's revolutionary logic on the grounds that "killing the sons of Brutus" is no less a tyrannical act than "killing Brutus." Here, then, is one of the decisive nodes in which the conflict between morality and politics emerges. I discuss this conflict in more detail in the next chapter. For the moment I analyse Machiavelli's response insofar as it touches upon the current problem, namely, whether the transition from tyranny to republic (the "maintenance of freedom") is a transition from one kind of state to another kind, and thus presupposes the kind of violence associated with the "founding" or "beginning" of a state, or whether it is a different kind of transition altogether. At stake in this problem is the very meaning of revolutionary action, perhaps even its condition of possibility: because if Soderini is right, and "killing the sons of Brutus" is the same as "killing Brutus," then there is no real difference, ultimately, between the transition from tyranny to freedom and freedom to tyranny, and so revolutionary action loses all reason for existing. Political change would be reduced to the mere process of reform.

Machiavelli's answer to Soderini's moral scruples is exemplary of his style of political thinking:

[Soderini's] respect was wise and good; and yet one must never let an evil pass with respect to a good, when that good can be easily oppressed by that evil. He should have believed that, since his actions and his intentions were going to be judged by their end, and if he would have had luck and life on his side, that he could have shown everyone that what he had done was for the health of the country (*patria*) and not for his own ambition; and he could have ordered things in such a way that his successor could not do for evil what he had done for good. But he was tricked by his first belief, not knowing that malignity is not tamed by time nor placated by any gifts. So much so, that in order not to be like Brutus, he lost together with his country (*patria*) also the state and reputation.[12]

For Machiavelli the non-tyrannical character of the action would have emerged "in the end," because it would have maintained the freedom of the people (*per salute della patria*) and not the rule of Soderini himself (*per ambizione sua*). Such a result could have been further secured if only Soderini would also have re-ordered the state in such a way that his extra-constitutional action would not have set a precedent for tyranny such that his successor could have used "for evil." There is a certain ambiguity in this dialogue *post res perdita* between Machiavelli and Soderini. Machiavelli counsels Soderini to act "like Brutus," but in effect he also seems to be describing the way in which Romulus proceeds: first there occurs a tyrannical act (the murder of Remus) which then gets redeemed by its result (in this case: the anti-tyrannical institution of the Senate by Romulus).[13] Machiavelli calls for an action (to kill the enemies of republican freedom) that requires Soderini to transgress the respect for the rule of laws and civil equality, and in this sense the action would be "tyrannical," but at the same time this action has freedom as its "end." The proof that such action has in view freedom would be in

---

[12] Ibid. According to Machiavelli, Soderini was fooled by the opinion that "with patience and with goodness to be capable of extinguishing evil humors, and with honors given to someone, to be able to consume their enmity." (Ibid.).

[13] For the analysis of Romulus's institution of the Senate in *Discourses on Livy,* III, 9, I refer to part 1, ch.3.

Soderini's later reform of the very institution that he so dangerously wants to maintain: the gonfalonier for life.

The ambiguity of Machiavelli's proposal, which oscillates between tyranny and freedom, can be resolved, or at least moderated, by the following argument: the action that comes under the name of "killing the sons of Brutus" is indeed "tyrannical" in so far as it calls for a transgression of the law and of civic equality. In a formal sense, it is just as "tyrannical" as the action associated with Romulus's killing of Remus in the founding of the state. But, on the other hand, the end of the transgression is indeed political freedom, because the action breaks with the univocity of rule and the occupation of the public space by the state (under the guise of the order of the gonfalonier for life). In a substantial sense, the transgression that Machiavelli favors is one carried out under the signature of Brutus, and not of Romulus, because what Machiavelli questions in Soderini's approach is precisely the desire to "maintain" himself and his state, namely, the political form of the gonfalonier for life. A desire for domination is operative behind Soderini's manifest respect for the rule of laws and civic equality, and it is the same desire for the stability of the state that Soderini shares with Romulus. This desire is questioned by actions carried under the signature of Brutus, at least in the interpretation that Machiavelli gives of them.[14]

GOVERNING THE REVOLUTION: THE *ARCANUM* OF THE MODERN STATE

The discourse on political change that Machiavelli carries out in *Discourses on Livy,* III, 3 is put into a clearer light by the antithetical chapters that follow it (*Discourses on Livy,* III, 4-5). These discuss the ways in which to save a "regal state" (*salvarne uno regio*) rather than a "free state" (*stato libero*).[15] What does a "regal state" (*stato regio*) mean? Two interpretative options are open: either one understands the *stato libero* as synonymous to *republica*, which (in this specific context) entails determining the *stato regio* as a synonym of *principato* and *tirannide*; or one can understand the term *stato regio* to mean the state in the position of the monarch. Everything depends on the interpretative stance that is assumed: if one neglects the role played by extra-constitutional changes (return to beginnings) as condition of possibility of the modern state, then one assumes that the content of the return to beginnings, i.e., the change of state itself, is merely a transition between two forms of state, from the free state to the regal state. But the other interpretative stance argues that in the return to beginnings the state is "free" because it is shown to exist without a ground or foundation. In the return to beginnings, the very instance and authority of the legal order, as a whole, is relativized; its principles are no longer the sole ones to have validity. In short, in the return to beginnings the state (the political form) is no longer "monarchical" (*regio*) with respect to political life as a whole. If one adopts this interpretative

---

[14] By way of contrast, a decisive theoretical divergence between Vico's and Machiavelli's interpretation of Roman history consists in Vico's denial that the symbol of Brutus signifies a desire for freedom which is "universal," i.e., which belongs to the many, to the *popolo*. For Vico, Brutus only represents "aristocratic freedom." (Giambattista Vico, *Scienza Nuova,* IV,12,2).

[15] Machiavelli, *Discourses on Livy,* III,4.

possibility, then one can understand the kind of political action that seeks to "save the regal state" (*salvare lo stato regio*) as an action that wants to legitimate the state given its origin in a revolutionary event. I suggest that this kind of action is the theme of *Discourses on Livy,* III,4-5.

In presenting the various ways in which a *stato regio* can maintain itself, these texts immediately re-introduce the classical distinction between a prince and a tyrant, in order to counsel the prince to take as his example the "life of the good princes" and never break the laws of the state: "Because when men are well governed [*governati bene*], they neither look for nor desire other freedom."[16] The locution *stato regio* cannot simply refer to a tyranny (*tirannide*) because the logical space of the term *stato regio* is determined by the distinction between "prince" and "tyrant." To understand the meaning of the passage, the term *stato regio* must be taken to refer to the object of a counter-revolutionary action which intends to maintain the state as such (to make the state "monarchical" in the sense of making it the sole occupant of the public space). With respect to the republican event, the state as such is tyrannical; but from the perspective of the state, its tyranny is rendered more secure and stable when it becomes legal, i.e., when it changes its status vis-à-vis the people from "tyrannical" to "civil," when it becomes the civil prince.

According to this interpretation, the formula "when men are well governed, they do not desire other freedom," expresses the *arcanum* of the modern state. The formula that Machiavelli puts in the mouth of the modern state as civil prince is the first appearance of the concept of governmentality.[17] The formula expresses the relation between the state and the people in view of securing the stability of the former: this stability, as I showed in the first part, requires the neutralization of the desire for freedom as no-rule, as desire not to be oppressed, that is active in the republican event. The formula itself presupposes that there exists a desire for freedom that is embodied by the people and that can be reactivated if the people are not "well governed." Governing well refers to the action of securing the state from the source that contests its orders, namely, the desire for freedom as desire not to be dominated.

Two conclusions can be drawn from the argument in *Discourses on Livy,* III, 3-5. First, in modern political life the possibility of a change of state in view of political freedom is primordial with respect to the possibility of establishing a state. Second, viewed from the revolutionary perspective of a change of state in view of political freedom, the project to stabilize the state is a "tyrannical" project. Part of the tyranny of the state consists in employing the distinction between "prince" and "tyrant" in order to justify its domination by claiming a "civil" status for itself. Or, more acurately, the civil prince becomes the political actor who can undermine that distinction, and in so doing preserve its state. The concept of the civil prince understood as a subversion and simulacrum of the distinction between

---

[16] Ibid., III,5.

[17] The concept of governmentality, as I employ it here, is taken from Michel Foucault's analysis and deconstruction of the doctrines of "reason of state." See Michel Foucault, "La Gouvernamentalité," in *Dits et Ecrits,* 3:635-57; and idem, "Qu'est-ce que les Lumières?" in *Dits et Ecrits,* 4:679-88. See also Michel Senellart, *Les Arts de gouverner: du regimen médiéval au concept de gouvernement* (Paris: Ed. du Seuil, 1995).

prince and tyrant proves that the return to beginnings is operative in both the logic of the state/prince and in that of the republic/citizens. If the state wants to maintain itself, the civil prince needs to undermine, or use to its own advantage, the difference between prince and tyrant: the concept of governmentality, of civil domination, issues from this need. Conversely, the republican event occurs once the citizen undermines the distinction between citizen and prince, as I show in the next chapter.

Machiavelli views political life from a perspective that assigns priority to change over stability, such that the state as political form is not taken for granted, is not naturalized, but rather is understood as a historical construction that requires certain specific practices in order to generate its stability, to give itself a foundation. Free political action (or political action directed to freedom) is understood as the subversion of the stability of every state and status, in the disclosure of situations of no-rule or radical isonomy. If citizens must "resemble Brutus" in order to "save the free state,"[18] then the republican event requires citizens who are capable of transgressing the given legal and political order. Exactly the opposite possibility is required to "save the royal state" (*salvare lo stato regio*): if the state wants to maintain itself, then it needs to be as law-abiding as possible. Rather than seeking renewal and innovation (as a republic must, since it only exists as the event of political renewal), the state that emerges in and through the real possibility of the "change of state" always attempts to make itself ancient, traditional. This shows all the more clearly its historical and contingent origin: if the form of the state has lost every claim to being originary or natural, then its proper anxiety consists in seeking stability by appearing as ancient as possible, which it does, according to Machiavelli, by upkeeping its legality.[19] Since the republic depends on the periodic renewal of political form, the republican citizen must "habituate" itself to counter-act and transgress laws, orders, and habits that imperil its freedom. Machiavelli redefines the citizen as that political actor who learns to contest command: this is the mark of citizenship under the signature of Brutus, to which the republic, if it is to survive, must repeatedly return. In opposition to this return, it is in the state's highest interest (as civil prince) to maintain legality and governmentality. For the state stabilizes itself only on the basis of that negative liberty (i.e., non-transgressive freedom) that grows within the empire of the law and requires its protection.

POLITICAL FREEDOM AS STATE AND AS EVENT

The opening chapters of the third book are wholly dedicated to the "changes from freedom to slavery and from slavery to freedom."[20] Slavery (*servitù*) is associated with the tyrannical life (*vita tirannica*) and contrasted with the free life (*vita libera*). The problem of political action is distilled to the problem of how to pass from one form of life to another, from one condition to another. By identifying political action with the passage from slavery to freedom in the sense of a

---

[18] Machiavelli, *Discourses on Livy,* III,4.
[19] Machiavelli, *Discourses on Livy,* I, 25; I, 58; III, 22.
[20] Ibid., III,7.

transcendence of the master-slave relation, Machiavelli makes political emancipation the end of political action. Political life as a whole is displaced from the
preoccupation of knowing how to rule and be ruled toward a center of gravity that
exceeds this dualism because it considers that action as political which brings
those who are excluded from the order of the state into political or "free" life: an
action that requires the radical change of the orders of the state. Whereas in
Machiavelli the problem of constitutional change becomes the essential content
of political life, for the ancients the same problem spells the end of political
activity proper and the beginning of civil war (*stasis*).

The fundamental reason for this radical difference between the ancients and the
moderns is that for Machiavelli the condition of possibility of the state consists in
its changes (*mutazioni*): the change or transition comes first, the state later.
Politics becomes a function, the highest function, of becoming. Modern political
life is about the "state" or "being" of becoming, and this is why it turns around the
possibility of originary historical repetition (return to beginnings) which signifies
that the domain of form is no longer originary or natural. Whereas in classical
political philosophy the passage from a better to a worse form of state coincides
with a passage from a more stable to a less stable political form, in Machiavelli
the possibility of political change is not conceived as a consequence of the
impossibility of realizing the perfect form of state but rather as a condition of the
possibility of political life itself, whether in its modality of *vita libera* or of *vita
tirannica*. But now tyrannical life comes to mean that fixation of the state, that
occupation by political form of the political space, which the ancients considered
the sign of the "good life." Such a negative valuation of stability is possible
because of the primordial status given to the changes of political form: a free life
is a political life that maintains itself in the open possibility of change and
becoming. By way of contrast, a tyrannical life is political life in so far as it
naturalizes what is contingent, makes fate out of what is chance, gives a ground
to what is groundless.

The last text to shed light on the return to beginnings conceived as the event of
the change from slavery to freedom, and conversely, is *Discourses on Livy*, III, 8.
In this chapter Machiavelli makes the following two points: the people as "matter"
must be "disordered by time" (*disordinata dal tempo*) if the change from republic
to tyranny is going to succeed. Conversely, to maintain freedom the matter must
be "often refreshed by good examples or with new laws returned to its beginnings."[21] Secondly, political action has only two possible senses: "the citizens that
act in republics, either in favor of freedom or in favor of tyranny, must consider
their subjects, and judge from there the difficulty of their actions. Because it is
just as difficult and dangerous to want to emancipate a people that wants to live
enslaved, as it is to want to enslave a people that wants to live freely."[22] Taken in
conjunction, these two points support the idea that the return to beginnings denote
the kind of actions that are "in favor of freedom," i.e., actions that tend to "make
a people free." In fact, the passage from republic to tyranny is only possible if the
matter is "disordered by time," that is to say: only if no return to beginnings

---

[21] Ibid., III,8.
[22] Ibid.

occurs such that the given form which is corrupting the matter by the very fact of its permanence in time is not revolutionized.

Machiavelli complicates the traditional schema of form and matter by using it to elucidate the dialectic between freedom and slavery. What poses a problem here is the seeming equanimity with which Machiavelli considers the struggle for freedom (i.e., making a people free) in relation to the struggle for domination (i.e., making a people enslaved). The text merely speaks of the "difficulty" that political action encounters when it has to change the matter, either to make it free when it wants to be enslaved, or to make it enslaved when it wants to be free. There is no normative judgment as to which transition is better or more just. In a sense, equanimity is to be expected given Machiavelli's point that there exists no question of justice where the transition is one from freedom to slavery or conversely.

But in the end this troubling equanimity suggests the need to question not just why there exists domination and tyranny to begin with, but whether there exists a common root to the actions done "in favor of freedom" and those done "in favor of slavery." The balance between the transition to freedom and the transition to slavery indicates that the change toward freedom cannot be effected once and for all. It is a change that inherently calls for its comprehension within a theory of originary historical repetition. Ultimately, what pushes Machiavelli towards all the ambiguities present in such a theory is the following aporia: if freedom and command, if the people and the prince, are not identical, then how is it possible to "command" anything in favor of freedom? How can freedom be "realized" (in a given political form of domination) and still remain itself? Implicit in freedom seems to be, always already, the dimension of its negation, of slavery. Whether the goal is to liberate or enslave a people, if it is done against their choice, an element of tyranny attaches to that action. Any change of state undergone by matter implies a violent action, a tyrannical moment. And yet there is no question of remaining in a "state of freedom," since freedom consists precisely in the radical possibility of changing states.

Machiavelli's concept of revolutionary action (*mutazione di stato*) poses the following dilemma. One position maintains that there exist two "states" of political life, the free one and the tyrannical one, and that it is possible to change from one to the other. This change never happens "without difficulty" if it is a real change, because actions that are accomplished "with ease" entail their match or correspondence (*riscontro*) with the "state of being" or quality of the people as matter. For example, if a people is already corrupt, then it is easy for a tyrant to emerge; but then the tyrant will not have effectively changed one state (of being) into another: this change will have happened "before" the action itself. In which case, any change of state on the part of the actor has to be tyrannical, forcible and go counter to the matter and its state of being. According to this schema there is a transition or mediation into and out of freedom because freedom is assumed to be a "state of being."

The other position maintains that it is illusory to think about freedom and slavery as two states of being, equal and opposite, for there exists no "state" of freedom. Instead, freedom should be thought in terms of (the) change (of state) and slavery in terms of (the) fixity (of state). In which case, there is always something tyrannical and transgressive about freedom, and conversely there is always something free about slavery and tyranny, i.e., the "free" persistence of the form in time which leads to corruption and license. According to this schema, there is no transition or passage into the event of change from a previous state: the event of change happens as a discontinuity. Freedom has the character of an event, not of a state of being.

Why does Machiavelli always formulate the return to beginnings in terms of a double transition, from slavery to freedom and from freedom to slavery? On the basis of the second schema, the double transition refers to the event-character of freedom itself. It reflects the inherent finitude of political freedom. Freedom can only transcend reality as the negation of reality, i.e., of every state of being, hence only as event. Yet this carries the logical consequence that the event of freedom cannot persist, as event, without negating itself. Or, what is the same, freedom encounters the necessity to realize itself, to give itself a form and disappear as event. Under the operation of this necessity, freedom undergoes a reflux into slavery. Slavery or tyranny, in this context, refer to the dimension of the state that emerges out of the republican event. The state emerges out of a republic for two possible reasons: either because the republican event projects a new political order or standard for action which immediately becomes part of the new form of the state.[23] Or because the state reacts against the republican event of no-rule and the imperative of legal domination reappears as primary.

The dual nature of political change (from freedom to slavery and from slavery to freedom) confirms that Machiavelli conceives of political action primarily as a change of state and this change is formulated in terms of historical repetition as return to beginnings. My interpretation suggests that both transitions belong to the features of the return to beginnings as framework of political action, where action is conceived in terms of a change of state/order. It is not as if one transition (from slavery to freedom) belongs to the republican event, and the other (from freedom to tyranny) belongs to the form of the state: the transition from freedom to slavery equally belongs to the event of a return to beginnings, but as seal of the finitude of this event of freedom which always falls back into the process of re-establishing the state.

---

[23] This possibility accounts for the presence of a moment of "slavery" in the republican return to beginnings, i.e., for the idea that all republican or revolutionary events tend to negate themselves, expressed by the famous saying that "the revolution eats its children." The political moment signified by the expression of "killing Brutus" might thus refer not so much to a re-action by the state against the republic but rather to a reaction that emerges amidst the republican event, but against it.

CHAPTER 4

THEORY OF CITIZENSHIP AND ETHICALLY-CONTRADICTORY ACTION

ON THE DIFFERENCE BETWEEN CIVIL PRINCE AND TYRANT

The theory of citizenship advanced in the third book of the *Discourses on Livy* should be understood from within the conflict between politics and morality, what Croce identified as the phenomenon of the "autonomy of politics," and not independently of it. One does the latter if one links Machiavelli's discourse on citizenship to a prior tradition which did not consider such a conflict as a primary and ineluctible trait of political life, or if one links it to a posterior attempt to transcend or pacify this conflict. The reason is briefly stated: *Discourses on Livy* argues that political freedom depends on the capacity to renew the political and legal orders of the state from the outside, i.e., to open these to the claims of freedom as no-rule voiced by those who are excluded or oppressed by any given political form. Such a renewal of the state implies extra-constitutional action, and this action is inevitably seen as counter-ethical. Machiavelli effects a major redefinition of the citizen: citizen is that political subject who is able to trangress the laws and orders of the state for the sake of political freedom. Stated otherwise, the citizen is a political actor who undermines the distinction between citizen and prince in favor of the republic. Conversely, the prince is a political actor who undermines the same distinction, but in favor of the state. These two actors are defined by two antithetical and irreducible projects. The prince is defined by the project to stabilize a transgression, or to make necessary (i.e., to give a ground to) an order that is contingent. The citizen is defined by the project of transgressing a stability, or rendering contingent (i.e., withdrawing the ground of) an order which has acquired the traits of necessity.

So far I have shown that Machiavelli links political freedom to the possibility of a radical renewal or revolution of the orders of the state. When the political body is corrupt, such a renewal requires a type of action that is ethically-contradictory in the sense that a "good man" needs to perform a "bad action," or, conversely, a "bad man" needs to perform a "good action." It is first necessary to analyze the structure of this sort of action, one which establishes the conflict between morality and politics as essential to political freedom. Subsequently, one needs to understand what role it plays in the theory of citizenship.

In *Discourses on Livy,* I,25 Machiavelli treats the following topic: "whoever wants to reform an antiquated state (*stato anticato*) into a free city, must at least maintain the shadow of the old ways (*modi antichi*)." The historical example under analysis is the passage from monarchy to republic in Rome, when the monarchy is replaced by the institution of the consulate. This replacement exemplifies the idea that the new order should resemble, as much as possible, the old order. The resemblance of the new to the old identifies the political change as a reform rather than a revolution: the new order is just as much a preservation of the old order as its destruction or radical change. The text leaves no doubt that such an action is a reform;[1] that its success presupposes the lack of corruption of the city; and, lastly, that it excludes the involvement of the people as bearers of desire for freedom (in fact, according to Machiavelli's reconstruction of Roman history, in the transition from king to consul the people still had not entered the political life of the Roman state). The maxim according to which the new should resemble to the old as much as possible describes cases of political change in which "a political life" (*vivere libero*) is instituted "either by way of republic or by way of monarchy."[2] This kind of change is internal to political life (*vivere politico*) in the sense that it belongs to the dynamic of state-consolidation: this is why it counts as reform. In this context, "republic" and "monarchy" identify two forms of state. Reform is the kind of change that a state can deal with and even encourages: the very idea of making the "new" appear "old" gives the formula for the dynamic of the state, which essentially consists in excluding all radical innovation.

At the same time, this text immediately adds that if one wants to "make an absolute power (*potestà assoluta*), which is called a tyranny by the authors, one must renew everything."[3] Here "absolute power" is contrasted with the two forms of state, i.e., "republic" and "monarchy," and is associated with radical political change. The text gives the impression that a change which "renews everything" can only be tyrannical. Yet, the reference should be weighed carefully: in *Discourses on Livy,* I,18 tyranny is associated with the attempt to preserve freedom in a corrupt state; and in *Discourses on Livy,* III,3-5 it is associated with the kind of change that leads from slavery to freedom or from freedom to slavery, i.e., with a republican or revolutionary concept of change. This last reference gives the requisite clue to understand the new way in which Machiavelli employs the term "tyranny." It is not uncommon for him to introduce a new usage of concepts by referring to the classical "authors" and their use of the word from which he implicitly diverges.

In this case, Machiavelli questions the pejorative interpretation given by classical political thought to the idea of a power that is ab-solved from law, i.e., a power that "the authors" call tyranny. For Machiavelli, instead, tyranny or *potestà assoluta* stands in contrast to *vivere politico* and its two forms of state, "republic" and "principality," because it does not refer to another kind of state but to the transition from one form of state to another, which transition, as I showed above, has two possibilities: from slavery to freedom or from freedom to slavery. Absolute power, then, becomes characteristic of the change of state, not of the state as such. Indeed, if the state is to last in time (and thus not undergo a radical change), whatever tyrannical traits were present in the beginning must quickly transform themselves to match the traits of a civil principality that will gain the

---

[1] Machiavelli speaks of "reforming the state of a city [*riformare uno stato d'una città*]." (Machiavelli, *Discourses on Livy*, I,25).
[2] Ibid.
[3] Ibid.

support of the people by asserting their political and legal security.[4] Therefore a *potestà* that is "absolute" simply means a power that is ab-solved from political and legal order. This is exactly the sort of power needed for a revolutionary (as opposed to reformist) change of order since no order, as such, can suspend itself as a whole, as required by revolutionary action.

This reading of the term *potestà assoluta* explains why "tyranny" is associated in this chapter with the kind of action that has to "renew everything [*rinnovare ogni cosa*]" and not simply "reform a state [*riformare uno stato*]."[5] It is important to realize the shift in the meaning of tyranny in order to determine the sense in which Machiavelli repudiates the classical distinction between prince and tyrant, as both Sasso and Strauss, among others, point out.[6] But whereas Strauss believes that for Machiavelli every principality is at bottom tyrannical, Sasso identifies in the denial of the difference between prince and tyrant "the opposite argument: it is not that principalities resolve themselves into tyrannies but the latter... resolve themselves into the former."[7] According to my interpretation, the distinction made by the ancients between prince and tyrant is possible only on condition that tyranny is understood as a kind of state that is also anti-political, whereas for Machiavelli, in this context, tyranny is a function of the radical change of state, and such change comes to be seen as the central political problem. Sasso is correct to argue that for Machiavelli no state can be tyrannical if it wishes to endure through history: to last, and thus to persist in its statehood, the state must become a civil principality. But this does not mean that there is, as such, no difference between prince and tyrant. Sasso's claim is true only from within the logic of the state and its maintenance (in which the tyrant must become prince); but it is false from within the logic of the change of state (which calls for an act of transgression of the established political order, and thus requires that either the citizens or the prince become "tyrant" in the new sense attributed to this term in Machiavelli's theory of political change.)

THE CONCEPT OF ETHICALLY-CONTRADICTORY ACTION

That Machiavelli is interested in giving a new interpretation of "absolute power" is made clear by the two chapters that follow the introduction of this term and that explicate its new sense. In *Discourses on Livy*, I,26 Machiavelli considers the "new prince" (*principe nuovo*) who must "renew everything in that state" if its "foundations" are weak and if it does not want to maintain the principality "by turning to civil life either through kingdom or republic."[8] The prince is "new" precisely because it lacks support for its actions from the traditional orders and forces. This situation describes moments of radical changes of state (from

---

[4] I refer to my discussion in part 1, chs. 5 and 6. See also Sasso, "Principato civile e tirannide," for other arguments to the effect that in Machiavelli tyranny is always understood in contrast to the logic of establishing a stable state.

[5] Machiavelli, *Discourses on Livy*, I,25.

[6] On Machiavelli's critique of the distinction between prince and tyrant, see Sasso, *Machiavelli e gli antichi*, 2: 481-2; and Strauss, *On Tyranny*, 24ff.; idem, *Thoughts on Machiavelli*, 43.

[7] Sasso, *Machiavelli e gli antichi*, 2: 482.

[8] Machiavelli, *Discourses on Livy*, I,26.

corruption or slavery to freedom, and vice versa) where no support is to be found for the extra-constitutional actions, which are consequently defined as "uncivil."

In the context of a radical change or revolution, when the political actor must "make the rich poor, and the poor rich, as David did when he became king,"[9] the ethical contradiction appears in all of its force. Passages such as these have "shocked" readers not least because of the Biblical references used by Machiavelli as evidence of such "radical innovations," i.e., literal re-volutions of social and political orders. Strauss, in particular, feels that Machiavelli's attempt to use the Bible in a discourse that encourages wrong-doing is a kind of "blasphemy."[10] Machiavelli's complex political critique of religion is discussed shortly. For now I merely suggest that by placing this peculiar Biblical quotation side by side with the discussion of revolutions, Machiavelli's discourse gives an ironical pointer to the fact that revolutionary action involves a "teleological suspension of the ethical," or, put more simply, that all revolutionary action is necessarily ethically-contradictory. This would account for why the text, while offering some Biblical "sources" of revolutionary action, also indicates that these actions are "enemies of every form of life, not just Christian but also human" because they do not belong to civil life (*vivere civile*).[11] There is hardly a better testimony of the un-civil character of revolutions than the fact that the new prince must attack the institution of private property. For any such attack, on Machiavelli's own terms, cannot possibly serve to maintain a state because the latter requires the prince to become civil, i.e., to protect and secure its subjects and above all their property, as I showed earlier. The revolutionizing of property relations is symbolic of the action that destroys an old order and initiates a new one. In short, Machiavelli here reproposes the distinction between civil and political life that is structured by the polarities of order and freedom, security and insecurity, civil power and absolute power.

The ethical contradiction appears at this point. After stating the extreme cruelty of these actions, and advising the reader that it is better to remain a private person rather than become a prince if such ruin is to befall men, Machiavelli presses on to his point: "nonetheless he who does not want to take that path of goodness [i.e., the private life], and wants to maintain himself, must enter into this evil [*conviene che entri in questo male*]."[12] The distinction between the "path of goodness [*via del bene*]" and that of "evil" overlaps the difference between the private and the public. To stay on the former path it is necessary to remain a "private person," a citizen, and not assume absolute power (*potestà assoluta*). Every radical innovation of the state understood as a new creation of public space, though, seems to require embarking on the path of "evil." Or, more correctly, the text states that the worst possibility, the one that is "most harmful," is to take the "middle way [*certe vie del mezzo*]." Yet this is precisely the way most often taken

---

[9] Ibid. Machiavelli cites from *Luke* 1,53 ("qui esurientes implevit bonis, et divites dimisit inanes"), where these actions are attributed to God. The reference to David comes from *Psalms* 33,11 and 106,9.

[10] Strauss, *Thoughts on Machiavelli*, 48-49.

[11] Machiavelli, *Discourses on Livy*, I,26.

[12] Ibid.

by individuals, because "they know not how to be either wholly bad or wholly good [*perché non sanno essere né tutti cattivi né tutti buoni*]."[13]

By proposing a political discourse on evil, Machiavelli attacks, this time on the front of ethical discourse, the most basic intuitions of both classical and Christian political thought. At issue is both the classical conjunction of public life and good life, and the negation of this conjunction in Christian thought, which understands the good as private and devalues all public action that does not follow private morality. Christianity is attacked precisely because it teaches that one can accede to the public through private ways: this is the "middle way" whereby individuals are neither "wholly good" (because they do not stay in the private) nor "wholly bad" (because they attain the public but operate "morally" or "privately" in it).

Assuming that Machiavelli is proposing the idea that all radical change implies a suspension of the ethical, it remains to determine the possible content of such a suspension. Does revolutionary action call for political actors to be both good and evil (in the sense that "good" persons are called upon to become "bad," and vice versa), or beyond good and evil, or are these two options, ultimately, the same? In *Discourses on Livy,* I, 26 the choice seems to be that one is either good (and remains in the private) or one is evil (and moves to the public). But in *Discourses on Livy,* I,18, as elsewhere, another possibility is envisaged: the new prince has to be both good and evil, so as to use tyranny for the sake of freedom. The difficulty of ethically-contradictory actions is explicitly discussed in *Discourses on Livy,* I, 27 where Machiavelli claims that it is rare to find individuals who are "altogether bad or altogether good." The example to be avoided is represented by Giovampagolo Baglioni, the tyrant of Perugia and a thoroughly immoral individual in the private sphere, who, because of misplaced moral scruples, was unable to kill his political enemy Pope Julius II when the latter presented himself unarmed. The new possibile relation between good and evil that Machiavelli wishes to add to the repertory of political action is glimpsed at by contrast to this example. The new modality of action is such that only those who, unlike Baglioni, are "honorably bad [*onorevolmente cattivi*]" can accomplish it. It is an action that must "leave of itself an eternal memory... and would have done *something whose greatness would have surpassed any infamy, any danger that could have arisen from it.*"[14] Baglioni is incapable of such an action because he is incapable of engaging in "*a malice that has in it greatness or is in any part generous.*"[15] These striking formulas disclose a new type of action that is political and yet inhuman and uncivil; they express, with the utmost precision, the breach that Machiavelli opens between political and civil life.[16] This action is "bad [*cattiva*]," an "infamy [*infamia*]" a "malice [*malizia*];" but it is also "honorable," exhibits "greatness," is "generous," and gains for itself "eternal memory."[17]

---

[13] Ibid.

[14] Ibid., I,27. Emphasis mine.

[15] Ibid. Emphasis mine.

[16] The image of the Centaur in *The Prince,* XVIII, elevated to the rank of model for the (new) prince, is both political and inhuman (in so far as it is intended to conjure a particular kind of "animality" in political action). In Machiavelli's discourse "humanity" is a political issue rather than politics being a congenital possibility of "human" nature, as the ancients held.

[17] Machiavelli, *Discourses on Livy,* I,27.

Before attempting an interpretation of such a coincidence of opposites, which I take to be essential for the proper understanding of Machiavelli's theory of citizenship, it is useful to review the other texts in which this new concept of political action is delineated.

The first text that returns to this concept is *Discourses on Livy,* I,30: "men do not know how to be altogether bad or altogether good." Here goodness means "comporting oneself modestly [*portarsi modestamente*]," and being "altogether bad" means "to use violent terms which have in them the honorable [*usare termini violenti e che abbiano in sé l'onorevole*]."[18] Machiavelli offers a peculiar gloss to the terms "altogether good" and "altogether bad": the first term means to act like a decent human being, and the accent on "modesty" refers to the sphere in which one can unproblematically do so, i.e., the private, non-political sphere. The second term, though, is different from both the classical and the Christian understandings of evil. The text suggests as much because it presents a third possibility as the "worst" course of action, much worse than being "altogether bad," namely, the course that attempts to find a middle way between private goodness and public badness. Therefore it is a mistake to think that Machiavelli is simply taking a traditional concept of evil and claiming that it is justified because it has acquired a political significance. Instead he is inventing a new sense for the concept of being "altogether bad," one which is both political and not entirely negative since it contains "in itself something honorable."[19]

The analogous idea is found in a passage where Machiavelli refers to "executions" that "have something great and generous [*hanno il grande ed il generoso*]."[20] The claim is that "the princes of our time" cannot carry out such actions anymore because "the weakness of present men, caused by their weak education and by lack of knowledge about things, makes it possible to judge ancient judgments partly as inhuman, and partly as impossible [*si giudicano i giudicii antichi parte inumani, parte impossibili*]."[21] The humanism developed by Christianity is unable to account for actions that are violent and cruel yet contain "something great and generous." Towards the end of the *Discourses on Livy* Machiavelli proffers the famous praise of un-principled action:

Because where one deliberates completely about the health of the country [*salute della patria*], there can be no consideration neither of what is just or unjust, neither of pity nor of cruelty, neither of praiseworthiness nor of ignominy; indeed, one must set aside all respect, and follow through with that action that will save its life and preserve its freedom.[22]

There exists no more explicit formulation of his extra-moral conception of political freedom.

---

[18] Ibid., I,30.

[19] Another reason why the concept of "altogether bad" is not reducible to traditional conceptions of evil is that Machiavelli explicitly and repeatedly states that a public actor may have to "enter the path of evil" in order to stop the spread of evil or corruption. I refer to the discussion of Soderini in the previous chapter.

[20] Machiavelli, *Discourses on Livy*, III,27.

[21] Ibid.

[22] Ibid., III,41.

These texts describe actions that are contrary to ethical behavior and yet exhibit a "greatness" or "honor" in themselves (*in sé*). The ipseity of such actions reveals something about the context in which they are performed: the context is such that they appear "great" or "honorable" not because they favor someone or something else and are recognized as being "great" by others, but because their "greatness" lies "in themselves." These actions, then, exist in and for themselves: they exhibit a certain type of sovereignty that does not correspond to the criteria of moral action because, in the last instance, they respond to a transgression of the normative sphere itself on the part of political freedom. In other words, these actions indicate a different concatenation of power and freedom than the one envisaged by the institution of morality.

THE CRITIQUE OF CHRISTIANITY

The problem of conceiving an action that is both "bad" and "honorable" culminates with the critique of Christianity found in *Discourses on Livy*, II, 2. The texts considered above suggest that Machiavelli blames the incapacity of his contemporaries to understand the practice of ethically-contradictory action squarely upon the ideal of education provided by Christianity. In what follows I show how the new theory of political action first moves through the critique of Christianity in order to attain its veritable goal: the critique of every form of religious determination of politics, and the consequent theorization of the separation of religion and politics.

The argument of *Discourses on Livy,* II, 2 offers the most extended treatment of the crucial relation between freedom and power (*grandezza*) along with the longest discussion of the connection between "badness" and "honorableness." The text begins by praising political freedom (defined as a political life without princes or kings) as the necessary condition for a city's increase in dominion and wealth.

Experience shows that cities never increase their dominion nor their wealth unless they live in freedom.... The reason is easily determined, because what makes cities great is not the particular but the common good. And there is no doubt that this common good is only observed in republics.... The contrary happens when there is a prince, where most of the time what is good for himself offends the city, and what is good for the city offends him.[23]

The republic here stands for the priority of the "common good" over any "particular good," and this priority accounts for the "greatness" (*grandezza*) of the city. By setting up an antithesis between prince and city (the greatness of one is the weakness of the other), this passage rehearses a motif of civic republicanism, without betraying any of the internal critiques that Machiavelli develops elsewhere. It simply establishes in traditional terms the link between common good, freedom and greatness.[24] But in so doing there seems to be no point to the

---

[23] Ibid., II,2.
[24] The motif of the link between freedom and greatness is found in *Discourses on Livy,* I, 5-6; and it is also criticized vigorously in Machiavelli's discussion of the Agrarian laws (*Discourses on Livy,* I, 55) as well as toward the end of *Discourses on Livy,* II, 2. For opposite ways of reading the

theory of ethically-contradictory action, since this theory posits a conflict between the pursuit of the (common) good and the exercise of freedom as power or greatness. In fact, this beginning of *Discourses on Livy,* II,2 merely prepares the demonstration of the ideological character of the tradition of civic republicanism. The chapter intends to show that the identity between morality (i.e., the pursuit of the common good) and freedom (i.e., the pursuit of power) advanced by civic republicanism shares the same assumptions and problems of Christian political thought: both miss the essential autonomy of political life from the institution of morality, and the necessity of their separation if political freedom is to survive.[25]

The argumentative strategy adopted by this text becomes apparent upon proceeding to its second topic: the explanation of why the "love of freedom" has decayed in "modern" times. The reason for this decadence,

> I believe is the same as the reason that makes men less strong [*forti*], which I believe is the difference between our education and that of the ancients, which is in turn based on the difference between our religion and that of the ancients. Because, having our religion shown us the truth and the true path, it makes us care less about the honor of the world [*l'onore del mondo*]; whereas the Gentiles, caring much about it and having placed in it the highest good [*sommo bene*], were in their actions more ferocious.[26]

One can say, without much exaggeration, that this passage sets the basis for the modern critique of Christianity. The core of the critique consists in exposing the "ascetic" character of Christianity: its belief in an "other world" necessarily devalues "this world," to put the point in Nietzschean vocabulary. Machiavelli charges Christianity with placing the "highest good" outside of the world, in the salvation of the immortal soul. The ancients, instead, place the highest good in what Machiavelli calls *l'onore del mondo,* worldly honor, or, as he says later in the chapter, in "worldly glory [*gloria mondana*]." But what relation does the pagan assumption of worldly glory as the highest good have with the common good (*bene comune*) and the freedom or greatness of republics? In what sense

---

connection of freedom and greatness, see Viroli, *From Politics to Reason of State,* ch.3, passim; and Hulliung, *Citizen Machiavelli,* 168-189. Viroli understands the link between freedom and greatness in terms of Machiavelli's adherence to the brand of republicanism theorized by civic humanism, with its idealization of *vita activa* as dedication to the common good and "civic virtue." Hulliung understands the same link in terms of Machiavelli's repudiation of this tradition and his adherence to a republicanism that is dedicated exclusively to the pursuit of "power politics."

[25] There are two other ways in which one can try to dissolve the cognitive dissonance between Machiavelli's seeming agreement with the tenets of traditional civic republicanism and his theory of ethically-contradictory action. One can argue that the identity between common good and freedom/greatness is established only once a republic is in place and is not corrupt, but that this identity does not apply when thinking the transition into (or out of) a republic. The objection to this solution is that in Machiavelli the "republic" ultimately does not refer to a state but to an event in which the orders of the state are renewed, and thus "republic" denotes only the passage from corruption to freedom. The other possibility is that Machiavelli identifies the "common good" with "greatness," and thus defines the "good" in a way that is "beyond good and evil." This is the core of Hulliung's interpretation. To this one can object, along with Viroli and others, that what Machiavelli understands by the "common good" is not different from what is found in the civic republican tradition: precedence of laws over men, equality in public, security in private, and so on. In my view, what separates Machiavelli so decisively from this tradition is, rather, the non-identity that his discourse establishes between political freedom and the idea of the "common good."

[26] Machiavelli, *Discourses on Livy,* II,2.

does the pursuit of worldly honor give political action more "ferocity"? Is Machiavelli simply proposing a return to pagan ethics in opposition to Christian ethics? These questions need to be answered before attempting to make sense of the concept of action that is "honorably bad." After all the prime example of such an action is symbolized, or would have been symbolized, by a tyrant killing a Pope (Giovampagolo Baglioni and Julius II): a symbol that is an attack on Christian ethics (and perhaps on all religious ethics) for the sake of a new understanding of politics.

In his critique of Christianity Machiavelli insists on the idea that this religion is responsible for a loss of "ferocity" in human beings. From a perspective that uncannily anticipates the Nietzschean analyses of pagan religion, Machiavelli argues that the sacrificial practices of pagan religion, as opposed to those of Christianity, have the purpose of rendering human beings "more similar" to animals, i.e., more ferocious and *terribili*.[27] One understands little of Machiavelli's thought here unless one realizes that ferocity is internally linked to the love of freedom.[28] This love needs to be "ferocious" and so, according to the Christian system of values, in-human or non-human. But why must this be the case? What is this ferocity and animality (or, better, brutality) turned against? The paradoxical answer is that this animality turns all of its ferocity against the sphere of "mere life," of animal or biological life, so to speak, for the sake of an experience of human freedom as the transcendence of such life. For all that, it would be a mistake to believe that Machiavelli returns to pagan ethics, because for Machiavelli animality (now understood as a quality of human freedom) equally transcends the sphere of the "good life." In classical political thought, human freedom is conceived in terms of the capacity for the political animal to transcend the sphere of mere life for the sake of the good life (irrespective of whether such life can be actually lived as a citizen, or whether it requires other extra-political virtues). In Machiavelli, the "political animal" additionally transcends the sphere of the good life for the sake of a free life. As a consequence, its animality is revealed in a form which is "beyond good and evil." In the critique of Christianity Machiavelli does not return to classical political thought: the appeal to the "ferocity" of the love of freedom in the "ancients" does not sit well with the thought of an Aristotle or a Cicero, who are also, not coincidentally, the founding figures of the civic humanist tradition of republicanism. In effect, Machiavelli's

---

[27] Describing pagan sacrifices, Machiavelli points out "the action of sacrificing full of blood and ferocity, where a multitude of animals were killed; which aspect of the sacrifice, being terrible, made men similar to it." (Ibid.). Only the reference to Nietzsche sheds light on Machiavelli's objective behind this often misunderstood praise of ferocity and its re-valuation of animality: it is the problem of the genealogy of morals, or of how the human animal is "domesticated" by giving it a moral conscience. This old problem takes one back to Plato's *Statesman* which culminates with the question of how to domesticate the political animal. I have to postpone a full treatment of this theme for another work.

[28] Not to the love of domination, as Hulliung contends in *Citizen Machiavelli*. After all, Machiavelli's theme in this chapter is the greater love of freedom in the ancients than in the moderns, which he then connects to these remarks about their ferocity. Hulliung, unlike many other interpreters, correctly appreciates the Nietzschean dimension of Machiavelli's critique of Christianity, only to eviscerate both thinkers of any preoccupation with freedom, and in so doing reduces them to thinkers of power politics, no better or subtler than a Callicles or Thrasymachus.

understanding of freedom is here clearly antihumanist. I discuss the sense of this antihumanism shortly.

Christianity is also criticized for its devaluation of the *vita activa* expressed by the privilege that it assigns to the virtue of humility. The Christian religion glorifies the "humble and contemplative ones;" whereas pagan religion glorifies the "active" ones, those who gain *mondana gloria*.[29] Again, it would be a reductive reading to conclude that Machiavelli simply praises pagan religion and calls for its imitation. Instead, what is notable in this analysis is that both religions are compared on the basis of their capacity to generate glory, so that the conflict between paganism and Christianity boils down to the different "ways of life" (contemplative versus active) that are so praised. Machiavelli's analysis of religion shows a tendency to equate all religions in order to understand them from a radically secular perspective, as purveyors of "glory" or "meaning" (if one were to speak with Max Weber), rather than accept, and if need be advocate, the "intrinsic truth" of one religion or another.

By focusing on how glory (meaning) is differently constituted and apportioned in the different religions, Machiavelli leaves open the possibility that the concept of an action which is "honorably bad" and gains "eternal memory" for itself may fall under no concept of religion (neither pagan nor Christian).[30] In short, political glory may be something entirely different from religious glory, be it pagan or Christian. This point is crucial for deciding the effective relation of Machiavelli with the ancients. If it is the case that the ancients make a religion out of politics (and, one could add, Christians make a politics out of religion), does Machiavelli seek to recover this classical unity of religion and politics? Or does he not rather think about political life, for the first time, as a wordly space and time in which meaning is not constituted religiously but politically? Can one say, then, that Machiavelli offers the first attempt to separate church and state in modernity, and, more radically still, attacks every religious foundation of politics? To this question, which is perhaps the essential question of political modernity, I believe one should answer in the affirmative.

The received understandings of Machiavelli heavily favor the first option. Machiavelli is believed to advocate a return to the "religion of politics" that can be found in the ancients, and he is identified as one of the central proponents of civic religion in modernity.[31] I argue that Machiavelli breaks with the ideal of unifying the political and religious dimensions of social life as shown by his critique of the political uses of religion, of the attempt by the state to ground its orders in a quasi-religious fashion, discussed at length in the first part. Further evidence that indicates the rejection of any "religion of politics" is shown by the relation established between political freedom and antihumanism that I have been analysing under the rubric of ethically-contradictory action. The antithesis

---

[29] Machiavelli, *Discourses on Livy*, II, 2.

[30] In this sense, I find myself in broad agreement with Sullivan's claim in *Machiavelli's Three Romes* that Machiavelli offers a generalized critique of religion, not just of Christianity. I differ from Sullivan only on the grounds and finalities of such a critique.

[31] For the secondary literature I refer to the discussion of the political use of religion in part 1, ch.3.

between political freedom and the institution of morality suffices to cast doubt on every attempt to link Machiavelli's discourse to the ideal of a civic religion.

At this point I can elucidate the meaning of Machiavelli's antihumanism, by which I understand the peculiar connection established between a radical concept of political freedom and a re-evaluation of animality. Christianity is charged with placing "the highest good in humility, abjection, and in the contempt of human things; that other religion placed the highest good in the greatness of spirit [animo], in the strength [fortezza] of the body and in all other things that tend to make men exceedingly strong [fortissimi]."[32] Machiavelli attempts to turn around the burden of inhumanity against Christianity itself: it is "our religion" that is inhuman to the extent that it has "contempt of human things." Grandezza and fortezza have now become predicates of humanity, and the attempt by Christianity to transcend this humanity, which is intimately linked to ferocity and animality, is judged to be non- or in-human. The strategy of Machiavelli's critique is, once again, uncannily similar to the antihumanistic humanism of Nietzsche. For Nietzsche, the attempt made by Christianity to accomplish the ascetic ideal results in the "brutalization" of the human being: "this insane, pathetic beast – man! What ideas he has, what unnaturalness, what paroxysms of nonsense, what *bestiality of thought erupts as soon as he is prevented just a little from being a beast in deed.*"[33] Nietzsche and Machiavelli coincide in their claim that the contemplative life is a brutalizing mode of existence in so far as it denies or attempts to control the mainspring of the *vita activa*: what Nietzsche calls "will to power" or "instinct for freedom,"[34] and Machiavelli calls the "desire not to be commanded." The critique of Christianity reaches its first conclusion with the assertion that this religion "made the world weaker and allowed it to become the prey of disgraceful [scelerati] men."[35] Machiavelli's thesis is clear: in the name of saving their souls, Christians have given over the political sphere of "human things" to men who are disgraceful because they enslave others, and who have "weakened the world" because they have made it less free. The true disgrace, the true fall from grace, is the blindness of religion to the positive relation that holds between freedom and power.

THE SEPARATION OF POLITICS FROM RELIGION

By turning the charge of inhumanity against Christian humanism the first part of Machiavelli's critique of religion is in place. The second part begins with the surprising claim that it is not "our religion" as such that is to blame for the fact that "the world has become effeminate and Heaven has been disarmed," but rather only those "who have interpreted [interpretato] our religion according to idleness [ozio] and not according to virtù."[36] Christianity is open to another interpretation that "permits the exaltation and the defense of the country [patria],"[37] and thus

---

[32] Machiavelli, *Discourses on Livy*, II, 2.
[33] Friedrich Nietzsche, *Genealogy of Morals*, "Second Essay," §22. Emphasis mine.
[34] Ibid., §12.
[35] Machiavelli, *Discourses on Livy*, II,2.
[36] Ibid.
[37] Ibid.

grants the *fortezza* which is required for its defense (i.e., for the defense of freedom). In general, religions or sects, like other mixed bodies, are open to different interpretations, and such re-interpretations of sects are necessary to keep them alive.[38] The thesis that Christianity can be given another interpretation, one "according to virtù" rather than idleness, finds an echo in the peculiar reading of the Ancient Testament that Machiavelli offers in *Discourses on Livy,* I,26 (King David) and III,30 (Moses).[39] But that Christianity, properly re-interpreted, can serve as a basis for the primacy of *vita activa,* i.e., that Christianity need not be interpreted from the perspective of the *vita contemplativa* (the life of idleness or *ozio*) is one of the most striking and mysterious theses found in Machiavelli.

Interpreters have paid scant attention to this thesis and its role in Machiavelli's overall understanding of religion.[40] What is the significance of this last "turn of the screw" given to the critique of Christianity? To answer this question some light must be shed on Machiavelli's curious formulations. The effect of Christianity is said to be that "the world became effeminate and Heaven was disarmed [*si sia effeminato il mondo e disarmato il Cielo*]."[41] But when and how was Heaven ever "armed"? Machiavelli uses the term *il Cielo,* rather than the usual *i cieli,* to refer to the sphere of the divine and not just of the heavens, which may or may not be divine. It seems that Machiavelli is speaking about religions in which a god or gods are armed because they are warriors, or, at the very least, manifest their divinity through violence, as the god of Moses and David does. In the context of a discourse that intends to open the way for a "re-interpretation" of Christianity, the distinction between armed and disarmed divinity in all probability refers to the transition from the Old to the New Testament. How does Machiavelli's rejection of the "disarmed" Christian God, along with the suggestion that Christianity can be re-interpreted in a "political" or "armed" sense, compare with the political philosophy of Christianity, first delineated by Paul, but properly elaborated in Augustine's *City of God* and its central idea of the *respublica christiana* as a force that resists (*kat-echon*) the advent of evil? In which direction does Machiavelli wish to overturn the complex Christian conceptualization of the relation between politics and evil?[42]

---

[38] Ibid., III,1. In this text, Machiavelli adduces the examples of the Dominican and Franciscan movements, although these remain re-interpretations of Christianity "according to *ozio.*"

[39] "Whoever reads the Bible in a sensible way [*sensatamente*] will see that Moses is forced to kill an infinity of men in his effort to institute his laws and orders; these men opposed his designs because they were moved by nothing other than envy." (Ibid., III,30). According to Inglese, the references to Moses's killing of his political and religious opponents come from *Exodus* 32 and *Numbers* 16.

[40] Viroli seems to understand the possibility of giving an interpretation of Christianity according to virtù in terms of a discourse on patriotism, as the core of a civic religion. (Viroli, *Machiavelli,* ch.5, passim). But this reading does not take into account the fact that this re-interpretation of Christianity takes place within a discourse in which religion as a whole is criticized. What must be accounted for is the potential role of a re-interpreted Christianity in a historico-political situation in which politics is separated from religion, not joined with it, as occurs in the idea of civic religion and, possibly, also of patriotism. Sullivan's analysis of Machiavelli's critique of Christianity also suffers from not seeing the background of such a critique, namely, the separation of church and state, and the concurrent need to give a positive political role to (what the church considers as) "evil." (Sullivan, *Machiavelli's Three Romes,* ch.4, passim).

[41] Machiavelli, *Discourses on Livy,* II,2.

[42] The classic work on the relation between politics and evil in Christianity and early modernity is Carl Schmitt, *Der Nomos der Erde im Volkerrecht des jus publicum Europaeum* (Berlin: Duncker

Against Christian political thought, Machiavelli advances the claim that "evil" can play a "positive," rather than a purely "negative," role in the historical constitution of political form. This claim is adapted and adopted throughout modern political thought: one only needs to think of the positive value given to the conflict of egoistic passions from Hobbes and Locke to Mill, or to Kant's provocative assertion that even a "race of devils" can constitute a republican government, or to the Hegelian and Marxist tenets of philosophy of history. The problem here is to determine the specific sense of Machiavelli's subversion of the political role assigned to "evil" in Christian political thought.

I suggest that Machiavelli's call for a re-interpretation of Christianity in accordance with virtù is best understood as assigning to political action the task of realizing "the kingdom of God on earth." This task stands completely at odds with the Augustinian belief according to which politics has the task of keeping separate the divine city from the worldly city until the Last Judgment when such a division will be reconciled by God, rather than man. This reading qualifies as a "re-interpretation" of Christianity because the kingdom of God is maintained as the *telos* of action (just like in the Augustinian doctrine), but political action now consists in uniting this kingdom with the worldly kingdom, rather than effecting their separation in the sense of the *kat-echon*.[43] But such a re-interpretation of Christianity for the sake of the *vita activa* also secularizes Christianity, and the result of this secularization is none other than the modern natural right tradition, which begins with Hobbes's idea of the Leviathan as earthly God and culminates with Hegel's idea of the state as the presence of God in history.

---

and Humboldt, 1988). But see also G. Ritter, *The Corrupting Influence of Power* (Westport, CT: Hyperion Press, 1979); O. Cullmann, *Christus und die Zeit*; and W. Carr, *Angels and Principalities. The Background, Meaning and Development of the Pauline Phrase hai archai kai hai exousiai* (New York: Cambridge University Press, 1974). For an excellent formulation of modern politics and its relation to Christianity see Esposito, *Nove Pensieri sulla Politica*, ch.1; and, of course, Strauss, *Thoughts on Machiavelli*, whose extremely complicated subtext (or "esoteric teaching") would require a treatment of its own.

[43]In this context I cannot investigate further the hypothesis that the Augustinian conception of the state as *katechon*, and the relation of mutual exclusion between politics and evil, is in effect constructed in order to avoid, or contrast, the link between freedom and power (expansion) that characterizes Roman imperial politics (and thus also the concurrent notion of extra-moral political action). In other words, it may very well be that the theory of the *katechon* is not designed, primarily, to "prevent" or "halt" the take-over of the worldly city by the forces of "evil" or by the Antichrist, but rather to counter the relation between the principles of freedom and expansion as these were exemplified by the growth of the Roman republic into an empire (well before the advent of the Roman Empire). According to this hypothesis, under the code word of "evil" or Antichrist, what Augustine wants to exclude is really that extra-moral virtù that connects freedom and power, recovered by Machiavelli's discourse. This hypothesis would find some confirmation in the return in modernity of the connection (ever so republican: see Spinoza for the Dutch and Harrington for the English republican experiences) between freedom and expansion that characterizes the modern nation-state and its "empire" (colonialism) required precisely by the downfall of the *respublica christiana* and its ideal of the *katechon*, as Schmitt's *Der Nomos der Erde* convincingly demonstrates.

If I am correct in understanding Machiavelli's call for a re-interpretation of Christianity to political ends as the first manifestation of modern secularism, then one can argue that such a re-interpretation of Christianity comprises Machiavelli's hypothetical solution to the modern state's need for a new ideological grounding after the dissolution of classical and Christian ethical substance. This ideological grounding would be provided by the re-interpretation of Christianity in political and secular terms such that a new, strictly modern, configuration of politics and religion emerges according to which the separation of church and state functions as the religious underpinning of the legitimacy of the modern state. From this point of view, the separation between church and state should be understood as a result of a (Machiavellian) re-interpretation of Christianity, rather than as its rejection.[44]

But there is another possible sense to the autonomy of politics in Machiavelli. One gains access to it by understanding the autonomy not as something that satisfies the foundational needs of the modern state, but rather as characterizing the kind of politics that emerges in revolutionary or republican events. In this second sense, the autonomy of politics with respect to morality does not refer to the position of the state in relation to religion and civil society, but it refers to the position of the republican event in relation to the form of the state itself. Here Machiavelli attains an atheological conception of political life in which politics is absolved from religion. In this sense one can say that Machiavelli's republicanism leaps over the whole modern liberal theologico-political interpretation of the secularization thesis, whose roots are nevertheless also found in Machiavelli's thought to the degree that this thought thematizes the constitution of the modern state, but not in so far as it theorizes the republican event. The complexity of Machiavelli's discourse is determined by the presence of these two very distinct senses of the autonomy of politics. In the first sense, the formula of autonomy designates the secularized, but still religious, way in which the modern state receives a religious foundation in the modern political situation. In the second sense, the formula of autonomy designates the anti-foundational sense of modern political life, embodied by the event of the republic.

---

[44] The profound analysis of modern natural right and the ideological character of the division of church and state in liberal democracy offered by Marx in *On the Jewish Question* shows one sense in which the secular modern state is still essentially religious, that is, Judeo-Christian. Marx and Nietzsche (and then Weber and Freud) have much to say about the ways in which modernity (and in particular the modern state) joins elements of Judaism to elements of Christianity in ways prefigured by Machiavelli's idea that Christianity could be re-interpreted according to the virtù manifested by Moses and David (in his particular reading of these figures). One of the great failures of Marxist thought is precisely the lack of attunement to the problem of religion in Marx. It took Weber and then Schmitt, paradoxically, to shed retrospective light on the depth of that aspect of Marx's thought. Marx and Nietzsche, for example, show how the very term "Judeo-Christian" has a referent only in modernity; prior to modernity one still can and must think these names without the hyphen. The great depth of Marx's and Nietzsche's critiques of religion lies precisely in showing that the agent of the unification (by way of a *trait d'union* which is also a *traître d'union*) of these religions in modernity is the "secular" state. This thesis forms the necessary presupposition of the work of Rosenzweig and Benjamin, who attempt to overcome it.

From this perspective, the terms in which Croce and Berlin frame the debate on the meaning of the autonomy of politics in Machiavelli are misleading.[45] Croce, who speaks of the autonomy of politics with respect to morality in Machiavelli, and sees in it an anti-Christian pathos, does not realize that this autonomy can have two distinct senses. If it is interpreted in terms of the separation of state and religion, as I suggest above, then the autonomy of politics, far from being anti-Christian, is actually the content of the re-interpretation of Christianity according to virtù. But from this perspective, Berlin's interpretation of the autonomy of politics (diametrically opposite to that of Croce) is no less flawed. According to Berlin, Machiavelli's critique of Christianity issues from a relativist and proto-liberal discourse that opens up two incommensurable notions of the good (the classical versus the Christian), and argues for a political society in which such incommensurable conceptions of the good can be maintained without leading to civil war. For Berlin, Machiavelli himself sides with the ancient idea of the good, but this is simply a matter of "private" preference.

I propose that Machiavelli's critique of Christianity needs to be understood as genealogical: by thematizing the different possible relations between religion and politics Machiavelli presents the phenomenon of religion as a whole from a radically secular perspective, rather than from a "relatively" secular perspective, as the one of modern liberalism. From the genealogical perspective, religion is in a first moment the instrument of the state in the specific sense that it serves to provide political life with a source of authority, and thus permits the foundation of political form as classical ethical substance. In a second moment, the seculari- zation of religion permits the religious separation of church and state that is characteristic of the birth of political modernity in its liberal trajectory.

Machiavelli's discourse on Christianity offers the key to a reading of history in terms of a series of theologico-political epochs. According to this narrative, there are three epochs (the classical, the Christian, and the modern) that corre- spond to three types of theologico-political frameworks: the classical religion of politics (action ruled by ethics of prudence); the Christian articulation of religion and politics as two separate "cities" (action ruled by ethics of charity, i.e., humility); and finally the modern articulation of religion and politics in which the secular re-interpretation of Christianity results in "one city" in which church and state are separate (action ruled by ethics of moral autonomy [Moralität]). These three epochs exhaust Machiavelli's philosophy of history constructed in the theologico-political key. But this interpretation of history is itself an effective- historical narrative and serves a genealogical purpose: it discloses the possibility of overcoming the theologico-political foundation of political form in an atheological concept of the republican event, where action is not ruled by morality because it is not oriented by the requirement to provide a religious foundation to the practice of political rule.

Corroboration for this interpretative hypothesis comes from the last, and crucial, displacement of the extremely dense argumentation of *Discourses on Livy,* II, 2.

---

[45] See Berlin, "The Originality of Machiavelli," and Benedetto Croce, "Machiavelli e Vico. La politica e l'etica," in *Elementi di Politica* (Bari: Laterza, 1925).

These forms of education ["that have interpreted our religion according to idleness and not according to virtù"] and false interpretations [*false interpretazioni*] are responsible for the fact that in the world one no longer sees as many republics as in ancient times; nor, as a consequence, does one see in peoples so much love of freedom as then [*ne' popoli tanto amore alla libertà*].[46]

The "false interpretations" are not the ultimate cause for the decadence of political freedom. The text ends by turning the tables around on the ancients: the contemplative or idle interpretations of Christianity are ultimately caused by "the Roman Empire with its weapons and its greatness extinguished all the republics and all the forms of civil life [*tutti e vivere civili*]."[47] Through this last thesis Machiavelli's discourse presents a grand narrative that is nothing short of a philosophy of world history. By positing an internal link between the creation of the Roman Empire and the emergence of the *respublica christiana*, this philosophy of history gives a purely political (rather than religious) logic to the rise of Christianity and the decadence of political freedom because both this rise and this decadence originate from the development and inner logic of ancient republics themselves. The claim that Christianity emerges out of the extinction of political freedom on the part of the Roman Empire is perhaps the most striking example of the thesis that every political form contains the germs of its own downfall (*veritas filia temporis*). But the same example confirms the more basic thesis that the realization of political freedom negates this freedom itself, hence the need for a return to beginnings.[48]

Collecting all the partial conclusions, the discussion in *Discourses on Livy* II, 2 winds towards its final goal. Given that the Roman Empire is responsible for Christianity, and Christianity causes the decay of the love of political freedom, it must be inferred that the Roman expansion could not have been caused by the weakness of other ancient republics but, on the contrary, these were "extremely well armed and extremely obstinate in defense of their freedom."[49] Machiavelli infers that under these conditions the expansion of Rome could only have been caused by the "rare and extreme virtù" of the "Roman people."[50] Why does Machiavelli lead the reader through such an intricate argument in order to arrive at the recognition that the expansion of Rome is due to the *estrema virtù* of the people of Rome? What made the virtù of this "people" so "extreme" that the freedom of the Etruscan republics was extinguished in spite of their ferocity in defending it? The answer is given by the very terms that Machiavelli employs: the

---

[46] Machiavelli, *Discourses on Livy*, II,2.

[47] Ibid.

[48] Machiavelli points out in the first book of the *Discourses on Livy* that the Roman republic, precisely because of its "virtuous" character, contains the seeds of its downfall into idleness (*ozio*) and, eventually, into Christianity. In that context he introduces the following dialectic: freedom leads to greatness, greatness to empire, empire to the tyranny of the emperors, and finally the Empire to the *respublica christiana*. Machiavelli, in his own way, validates Augustine's argument in the *City of God* to the effect that the rise of Christianity is not to be blamed for the "fall" of Rome. The difference between Augustine and Machiavelli is that the former sees in this lack of connection a "proof" of sorts that the fate of the two "cities" were separate, whereas Machiavelli understands the same phenomenon as showing the inseparability of religion and the state (as well as the nefarious consequences for politics and freedom that emerge out of such inseparability).

[49] Machiavelli, *Discourses on Livy,* II, 2.

[50] Ibid.

"secret" of Rome's expansion is its reliance on the "people" and their *estrema virtù*. The virtù is "extreme" because it is based on the desire for freedom as no-rule characteristic of the people, and on the empowerment of this desire for freedom (*potestas in populo*).

Extreme virtù is constituted by the empowerment of the desire for freedom. The freedom of the people entails two things: first, security of private property and ability to produce wealth; secondly, and decisively, that "*everyone realizes not only that their children are born free and not slaves, but also that they can become princes through their virtù.*"[51] This last point is essential: what makes the virtù of the Romans extreme with respect to that of other peoples is precisely its republican character. Republican freedom means that citizens can become princes, that freedom is not only negative liberty (i.e., the knowledge that one is born free and not a slave) but also isonomy, understood as the equal freedom to make and unmake laws, and not simply as the equality of everyone before these laws. That citizens can become princes explains the sense in which virtù becomes extreme because, as I show next, the passage of citizens to the status of princes requires a certain positive relation to the transgression of laws, a positive relation to the possibility of revolution, and thus the capacity to act in extra-moral, ethically-contradictory ways.[52]

POLITICAL FREEDOM IN THE EXTRA-MORAL SENSE

At this point I am in a position to bring to a close my interpretation of Machiavelli's theory of political freedom by broaching the apex of the *Discourses on Livy*: its theory of citizenship. I have shown that Machiavelli's concept of republican freedom is linked to the concept of *estrema virtù*, which in turn is related to the possibility of "citizens becoming princes." The detour through the critique of Christianity was necessary because Machiavelli's theory of political action presupposes the autonomy of politics from the institution of morality. This autonomy, in the two senses outlined above, can only be explained through the complex discourse on Christianity. In short, the discussion of citizenship in the third book of the *Discourses on Livy* follows from the two senses of the autonomy of politics. The first sense concerns the action of the civil prince who behaves like

---

[51] Ibid. Emphasis mine.

[52] The depth of Machiavelli's grasp of the fundamental dynamics of Roman history never ceases to surprise: only recently has the most advanced historiography of the early Roman Republic shown conclusively that Rome's expansion (the acquisition of *estrema virtù*) is due to the abandonment of the system of rule of other Etruscan states and its adoption of a republican system of power. Central to this new system is the expulsion of the figure of the monarch. See the central works on archaic Roman history by Arnaldo Momigliano, *Roma arcaica* (Florence: Sansoni, 1989), and Santo Mazzarino, *Dalla monarchia allo stato repubblicano* (Milan: Rizzoli, 1992). How "Machiavellian" the latter text is can be seen by its conclusion: "The history of the Roman state differs in this from Greece: in Greece the republic came from the aristocracies, in Rome it came from the plebians who owned property.... The old Indoeuropean 'marginal' people had created 'its' democracy. And yet there remained the curias as well as the centurias: in Rome there flowed together, at once, both evolution and revolution. This was really the Roman 'miracle'. This is also a teaching for us. History is not the history of destructions that do not reconstruct, of conservations that do not renew. Just like the Roman state, history has two faces: revolution and continuity; the eternal renewal and the eternal duration." (Mazzarino, *Dalla monarchia allo stato repubblicano*, 209-210).

a citizen. This princely action is to be understood in terms of the autonomy of the state in relation to religion, an autonomy which is still "Christian," but a Christianity re-interpreted "according to virtù." The sense in which the modern state (civil prince) is both Christian and secular is given very exactly in *The Prince*'s famous discussion of "the way in which princes should keep their word": "a prince should take great care never to drop a word that does not seem imbued with the five good qualities noted above; *to anyone who hears him, he should appear all compassion, all honor, all humanity, all integrity, all religion. Nothing is more necessary than to seem to have this last virtue.*"[53] The second sense of the autonomy of politics from morality concerns the action of the citizen who acts like a prince. Citizen action is to be understood in terms of the autonomy of the republic in relation to the state, an autonomy which is irreligious and revolutionary. Prior to the discussion of the critique of Christianity, I established that only revolutionary actions exhibit the trait of being ethically-contradictory; such actions occur in the event of return to beginnings as a remedy to the corruption of the political body. I now return to the theme of the ethically-contradictory or "honorably bad" action as it is developed in the third book of the *Discourses on Livy* in order to show that this theory of action is integral to Machiavelli's new theory of citizenship.

Machiavelli understands the event of the return to beginnings in terms of the need for "for men who live together in any given order to recognize each other frequently."[54] The context makes clear that the stake of this recognition is equality. The question is what equality? The equality before the law is an insufficient answer given that the equality at stake must arise out of a return to beginnings that denotes an event in which laws and orders are radically changed. The recognition between citizens (the equality at issue) must be understood as a function of the revolutionary change of political form, whose possibility derives from the principle of republican freedom as no-rule: a concept of political freedom which is transgressive of the political and legal order of domination in virtue of its an-archism.

The first time that Machiavelli speaks about extra-moral action in the discussion of return to beginnings is in the context of establishing a new order: "these orders need to be made alive by the virtù of a citizen who will execute them with animosity [*animosamente*] against the power of those that trangress them."[55] The "animosity" required to establish an order through violence presupposes the radical novelty of the order in question: if the order were not new, then the old customs would suffice to elicit obedience for it. The permanence of customs and orders creates inequalities; the criterion for the emergence of something radically new will then be that of equality. A corollary of Machiavelli's thesis is that the "old" is always a sign for "inequality," and the "new" always a sign for "equality." Moments of equality occur in the interruptions of temporal continuity.

In the case of radically new laws and orders legitimacy cannot come from the previous political form and the customs that it has made possible (indeed, the very

---

[53] Machiavelli, *The Prince*, XVIII. Emphasis mine.
[54] Machiavelli, *Discourses on Livy*, III,1.
[55] Ibid.

fact of the renewal presupposes that both orders and customs were corrupt). This is why these new orders "need to be made alive by the virtù of a citizen." The point is that such a virtù cannot possibly be customary, it cannot be a function of the old *ethos*. Hence the virtù that establishes (gives "life" to) the new order will be anti-ethical or ethically-contradictory in the strict sense of the term. This is why Machiavelli calls such virtù *animosa*, and the actions that arise from it are termed "excessive and remarkable [*eccessive e notabili*]." These are the actions that Machiavelli elsewhere calls "honorably bad." Machiavelli accepts the Aristotelian idea that ethical virtue allows one to "find the mean" or consists in such a "mean." Machiavelli proposes counter-ethical actions, actions that change *ethoi* and therefore cannot follow the mean and for that reason are termed excessive. The real question concerns the principle which is expressed in these counter-ethical actions. I suggest that Machiavelli identifies this principle in revolutionary terms: freedom as absence of domination, as no-rule or isonomy, understood as equality to make the law that applies to everyone equally. Such isonomic equality, by definition, cannot fall under the empire of the law, and consequently always needs to be regained through a re-ordering of orders, and thus through some sort of transgressive action.

The texts dedicated to the return to beginnings (*Discourses on Livy*, III,1-4) speak of the "fear" that makes those who are "powerful" obey the new laws. Strauss interprets these passages in terms of the respect for the law that fear is supposed to elicit by the very fact of returning human beings to the "state of nature" and its terror. For Lefort, by way of contrast, the transgression of orders and laws in the return to beginnings is always already comprised under the "transcendental" dimension of the law: for it is the law that "transcends all the institutions in which it assumes a certain form."[56] According to my reading, Strauss equivocates on the origin of the fear, while Lefort equivocates on the origin of the transgression. The element of fear reflects the fact that every law, in so far as it emerges out of a return to beginnings, must arise from the law-transcending principles of freedom and (isonomic) equality. The fear is elicited by these principles, and not by (the state of) nature. In Machiavelli the principles of freedom and equality are revolutionary in the strict sense that they do not stand under the rule of laws and the respect of the law. According to my interpretation, the principle of freedom and equality are only lost, or reified, once they are realized in any factical political and legal form: consequently they exist only in their active repetition. Whereas I agree with Strauss that what Machiavelli is thinking about here is the necessity of the extra-legal foundation of the law, I disagree with him about the description of the instance that is extra-legal with respect to the empire of the law. For Strauss this instance is the "state of nature" as "state of exception." For me, this instance is the principle of freedom as no-rule: it is a principle that transgresses the rule of laws without leading back to a "state of nature" that negates the rule of laws, but rather allows for the transcendence of the law in a republican event of non-domination and isonomic equality. For Machiavelli, the extra-legal instance is not foundational of the sphere of legal

---

[56] Lefort, *Travail de l'oeuvre*, 601-615.

domination, as Strauss believes; rather, this extra-legal instance withdraws, if only momentarily, its grounds.

Perhaps no chapters are more important than *Discourses on Livy*, III, 21-22 to illustrate the relation that obtains between the ethically-contradictory action found in the theory of the return to beginnings and the theory of citizenship. The account of the ethically-contradictory action culminates in these strange and difficult texts. Machiavelli frames the discussion of these chapters with two references to Xenophon's *Cyropaedia* (in *Discourses on Livy*, III,20 and 22 respectively). Following the antihumanist sense of his discourse, Machiavelli criticizes Xenophon for advancing the thesis that "humanity" in a captain or prince leads to glory and obedience. Machiavelli takes apart this claim in *Discourses on Livy*, III,21-22, except that he uses Scipio rather than Cyrus as the exemplar of a "humane" commander, and Hannibal as the counter-exemplar.

Discourses on Livy, III, 21 poses the formal question of how two contrary ways of acting (the humanity of Scipio versus the inhumanity of Hannibal) can lead to the same results (i.e., glory and obedience). The question is treated along two distinct paths. In the first, there are two general reasons, common to both Scipio and Hannibal, that explain their success: individuals "always desire new things," and they "are moved by two main things, either by love or by fear; so that they can be commanded both by he who makes himself loved, as by he who makes himself feared."[57] The first reason requires some explanation. Machiavelli says that,

in most cases, novelty is desired both by those that are well off as by those that are badly off; because, as I said before and it is true, men become satiated of the good [*gli uomini si stuccano nel bene*], and are afflicted by the bad. This desire therefore opens the door to anyone who becomes head of an innovation in the province.[58]

This can mean either that those who are well off in a given condition become bored by it, and open themselves to new things, or that their good condition leads them into idleness (*ozio*) and weakness, preventing them from counteracting the arrival of novelty if it is supported by force. The explanation given as to why antithetical ways of proceeding can be successful offers two reasons that are operative irrespective of the way of proceeding, as long as this way innovates.

Since this explanation abstracts from the type of *ethos* of the commander, it cannot be said to account fully for the phenomenon at issue; any valid account needs to take into consideration, rather than abstract from, these contrary *ethoi*. Thus Machiavelli proceeds along the second path: what counts is not the *ethos* of the commander but the fact that "he is a virtuous man and that this virtù makes him reputed between men. Because when this virtù is great... it cancels all those errors that one makes from wanting to be loved too much or for wanting to be

---

[57] Machiavelli, *Discourses on Livy*, III,21.

[58] Ibid. Inglese gives as a possible source for this idea the following citation from Plutarch: "most men receive well an innovator, because of the satiety and the boredom occasioned by the customary life [*sic enim ordientem plerique consuetorum satietate ac taedio promptus excipiunt*]." (Plutarch *Praec. ger. rei* 804d).

feared too much."[59] Both Scipio and Hannibal fall into these "errors" because they exceed in their *ethoi*: Scipio becomes "contemptible" and Hannibal "hated." Their authentic virtù, therefore, appears in relation to this possibility of error:

> And to maintain the middle way is not possible precisely because our nature does not permit it; but it is necessary to mitigate these excessive things with an excessive virtù [*eccessiva virtù*], as did Hannibal and Scipio.... It is not very important in which way a captain proceeds, as long as there is in it a great virtù that supplements [*condisca*] well both forms of life [*modi di vivere*]. Because, as I said, in both forms there is a defect and a danger, when it is not corrected by an extraordinary virtù [*virtù istraordinaria*].[60]

What is the sense of the terms "excessive virtù" (*eccessiva virtù*) and "extraordinary virtù" (*virtù istraordinaria*). These texts are especially paradoxical, self-effacing, and duplicitous; so much so that one cannot fully understand this chapter apart from its counterpart (*Discourses on Livy*, III, 22). I have had occasion to analyse this typical strategy of Machiavelli's art of writing previously: it consists in the juxtaposition of two versions of the same topic with the result that the thesis that appears to be defended at the outset is overturned by the end of the argument.

The above text posits two contrary, mutually exclusive forms of life or *ethoi* (*modi di vivere*): the actor can proceed "humanely" or "cruelly." The middle way (*via del mezzo*) is excluded: it is not possible to be both humane and cruel (inhumane). But on what grounds is the mean excluded? It is unclear from the text whether the exclusion is performed from a logical point of view (i.e., there is no middle to contradictories) or, as the text also asserts, from an anthropological point of view (i.e., our nature does not "permit" such a middle). In fact, the status of the latter premise is ambiguous: although Machiavelli frequently employs the thesis that individuals cannot change their form of life (*modo di vivere*), in this particular chapter this change is clearly allowed for, since Scipio, for one, will use cruelty in order to regain from his soldiers the reputation that he loses in virtue of "exceeding" in his humaneness. Therefore the thesis of the fixity of "our nature" seems to reduce itself to the mutually exclusive character of *ethoi*: if cruel, then not humane, and vice versa.

The mutual exclusion of the *ethoi* means that they are as such excessive in relation to the absent mean. The excess that is necessarily figured by every ordinary *ethos* is, in turn, "mitigated" or "corrected" by extra-ordinary and excessive virtù. This is where the paradoxical element enters because it is as if a new "mean" is established by supplementing the excessive *ethos* with an excessive virtù. The point is that no *ethos* by itself leads to glory or power or greatness: virtù is not reducible to any form of life, any "nature" of individuals, but is what exceeds every form and nature. Virtù is anti-nature precisely because extra-ordinary and excessive virtù leads to innovation (here the "new" is set up against the "customary" character of every *ethos*), and such innovative force of virtù transcends the domain of *ethos*, in which the ethical (good/bad) distinction has absolute validity, since both those who are "in the good" as well as those who are "in the bad" are open to innovation, as Machiavelli points out repeatedly. Yet

---

[59] Machiavelli, *Discourses on Livy*, III,21.
[60] Ibid.

the relation between innovation and extra-ethical virtù remains obscure until one determines what sort of innovation Machiavelli has in mind, and in particular why such innovation always meets with success. What is the significance of Machiavelli's idea that the ethical sphere cannot contain the "mean" because its *ethoi* are inherently "excessive," whereas this very "mean" or "equilibrium" can be attained in the sphere of "excessive" virtù, i.e., in the sphere of the autonomy of politics from morals? The answer comes with the theory of citizenship that culminates in *Discourses on Livy,* III,22.

Ostensibly, *Discourses on Livy,* III,22 covers the same ground of the chapter that preceeds it. Here Machiavelli sets out to discuss "how the severity [*durezza*] of Manlius Torquatus and the humanity [*comità*] of Valerius Corvinus gained each of them the same glory."[61] The text poses four questions: "first, what caused Manlius to proceed so rigidly; second, what caused Valerius to proceed so humanely; third, what was the reason for these different ways to produce the same effect; and, lastly, which of them is better and more useful to imitate."[62] The text begins by treating the "nature" of Manlius, "a very strong man [*uomo fortissimo*], pious toward his father and toward his country [*patria*] and full of reverence for his commanders [*a' suoi maggiori*]."[63] It proceeds to claim that the reason for Manlius's cruelty and harshness in commanding his troops is that such a type of man

desires to find all men like himself, and his strong spirit [*l'animo suo forte*] makes him command things that are strong [*gli fa comandare cose forti*] and the same spirit, once the things are commanded, wants them to be observed.[64]

From which it follows that when commanding harsh things, obedience must be enforced harshly. But what are the "strong" or "harsh" things that Manlius is said to command? It would be a mistake simply to refer to Livy's historical account of Manlius's deeds in order to answer the question, just like it is misleading to employ Livy's account of the actions of Brutus to understand the symbolic significance that Machiavelli ascribes to them. Analogously to Brutus, Manlius represents the ideal-type of a kind of political action and of the requisite character of the command (*impero*): both elements must be determined starting from the presupposition (which I have demonstrated above) that Machiavelli is elaborating a theory of action in the context of the return to beginnings, i.e., in the context of the revolutionary event. If the discussion of Manlius is read in this way, the first thesis advanced by *Discourses on Livy,* III,22 is that only those actions that effect a return to beginnings by commanding what is extra-ordinary or extra-constitutional (*straordinari suoi imperi, imperi istraordinari*) require the "force" or "strength" (*fortezza*) exemplified by Manlius.

To command strong things [*cose forti*] one must be strong; and whoever has this strength, and commands these things, cannot then make them be observed with docility. But whoever does not

---

[61] Ibid., III,22.
[62] Ibid.
[63] Ibid.
[64] Ibid.

have this strength of spirit [*fortezza d'animo*] must stay away from extraordinary commands [*imperi istraordinari*], and can use his humanity [*umanità*] in ordinary commands.[65]

In other words, the problem of ethically-contradictory (of "inhumane") action should be situated in the context of the transgression of orders and customs that is performed in view of their re-ordering, i.e., that takes place within a logical space defined by the political opposition of freedom versus slavery rather than by the moral opposition of good versus bad. Likewise, Machiavelli's critique of "humanity" in political action is meaningful only if situated in the context of revolutionary action: a political actor can be "humane" in its command when the latter executes what is customary, what is taken as good. Only if the authority of the orders is not questioned by those who have to obey them, can the command of the order afford to be "humane." But if what is commanded is intended to transgress customary laws and orders, and thereby is a command that is not authorized, that lacks authority, then another "force" is called for to make the command be obeyed: this is the *fortezza* of Manlius.

That these are the real issues at stake in this chapter is suggested by the gnomic excursus about command inserted in the middle of the discussion of Manlius's *fortezza*:

Whence it must be noted that, if one wants to be obeyed, it is necessary to know how to command; and those know how to command who compare their qualities with those of whoever has to obey, and if they see proportion [*proporzione*] there, then they command, and when they see disproportion then they abstain from commanding. But a prudent man used to say that to hold a republic with violence, it was necessary for there to be proportion between who is forcing [*sforzava*] and who is forced [*sforzato*]. And any time that such a proportion existed, then one could suppose that this violence would be lasting [*fusse durabile*]; but when what is violated [*il violentato*] is stronger than what violates [*il violentante*], one could suppose that the violence might cease any day.[66]

What is meant by the "proportion" between the "qualities" of those who command and those who obey? Is it simply that the commander has to be at least as strong as those who are to be commanded, otherwise the commander should not command at all? What is Machiavelli actually referring to in such elliptical terms? Why does he swerve into a discussion about "keeping a republic through violence" in the context of discussing exemplary citizens?

On a first reading, the passage begins by claiming that in order to command "strong things" it is not just necessary for obedience to be elicited "harshly," but those that carry out the commands must be equally or proportionately "strong." But this claim also reveals a deeper meaning: whoever commands and whoever obeys "strong" things must be of equal strength because the "strong" thing that is commanded here is precisely the overcoming of the division between command and obey, rule and being ruled. What is commanded here is the kind of action that effects isonomy, in its radical sense of no-rule.

The second part of the passage is even more obscure. The text ascribes to an unidentified "prudent man" a suggestion as to how one can maintain a republic

---

[65] Ibid.
[66] Ibid.

through violence. If whoever commits the violence is equally strong as those who suffer it, then the violence will be lasting; otherwise the one who inflicts the violence is forced to stop by those who have suffered it. It is unclear whether those who are "violated" are those that must obey the commands or whether they are those that are opposed to the commands. The obscurity is lifted by the text that follows the excursus:

One must be strong to command strong things; and whoever has this strength, and commands these things, cannot afterwards make them be obeyed with meekness. But whoever does not have this strength of spirit [*fortezza d'animo*] must keep away from extraordinary commands [*imperi istraordinari*], and may use humanity in ordinary commands; because ordinary punishments are not imputed to the prince, but to the laws and to those orders. *One must believe then that Manlius was constrained to proceed so rigidly by the extraordinary nature of his commands [straordinari suoi imperi], to which he was inclined by his own nature; and these commands are useful to a republic because they return its orders to their beginning [principio] and to their ancient virtue [antica virtù]. And if a republic were to be so fortunate that it often had, as we said above, those people who through their example renew its laws, and not only kept it back from running to its ruin but actually brought it back [la ritirasse indietro], the republic would be perpetual.*[67]

At stake is the kind of command exercized in extra-ordinary political situations (*imperi istraordinari*, *straordinari suoi imperi*) when the command goes against the established political orders: in short, revolutionary command. That is why Machiavelli reveals in this context that the command is designed to make the republic return to beginnings ("reduce its orders to their beginning"). But, at the same time, the text masks the revolutionary character of the command by saying that in the case of Manlius the return to beginnings consists in a return to the "ancient virtue." For the same reason, Machiavelli is keen to point out that Manlius is a "patriot," that he respects the ancestors, his father, and so on. In this way, the revolutionary command of Manlius appears "conservative" or "reactionary" in nature, belonging to the system of authority, and oriented toward the ancestral order. But the lure is easily uncovered by recalling Machiavelli's earlier thesis according to which the republic emerges in a repeated break from the given "ancestral orders" and "natural ways" of political life. Under cover of a return to origins and ancient ways, Machiavelli speaks about the return to beginnings in the sense of the revolution of old orders and the imposition of new ones. The beginning (*principio*) that the republic returns to with Manlius, in Machiavelli's interpretation, cannot coincide with the ancestral order; and that is the point of the reference to the "perpetual republic": the republic "perpetuates" itself only in and through the counter-temporal innovations of, and counter-traditional discontinuities with, the old orders.

In these passages Machiavelli gives the first theoretical description of the phenomenon discussed by the likes of Marx and Benjamin much later: in the course of modern revolutions, for instance the French Revolution, the destruction of the old order ("ancien régime") assumes the configuration of a return of and to the past. The modern revolution dresses itself in Roman garbs designed and cut in the workshop of the *Discourses on Livy*. This does not mean that the modern

---

[67] Ibid. Emphasis mine.

revolution is "conservative" or "reactionary," or that it really aspires to return to the past. Revolutionary action dresses itself in Roman garbs because of the reconstruction and reinvention of Roman political experience in the *Discourses on Livy* which presents Rome as the first "revolutionary" political society (i.e., Rome exhibits a political life that is born and constituted out of revolutions); and presents all revolutionary action as requiring the degree of discipline and "ferocious" love of freedom instilled into the Roman popular militia by Manlius and the *Manliana imperia*.[68]

At this point I can propose an explanation of the different ways of proceeding of Manlius and Valerius. Manlius wants to re-order or revolutionize an established order, and so needs a certain kind of cruel and ferocious command. In contrast, for Valerius "it was enough that men observed the ordinary things that are observed in Roman armies" and, consequently, because he does not change the orders but follows them, Valerius can proceed and command in a more "humane" way.[69] Valerius can do this because he does not have to confront the possibility of soldiers disobeying his commands, since these are designed to preserve an old order, and even if there were to be transgression, the punishment could be ascribed to the orders and laws themselves "and not to the cruelty of the prince," i.e. to Valerius's character.[70] But in the case of Manlius, where the command is designed to overthrow an old order, then transgression and disobedience is more likely to occur, and the responsibility for the punishment inflicted by Manlius falls squarely upon his shoulders (and he will be termed a "cruel prince") because it is impossible for an old order to punish those who do not want to change it (and who disobey the new commands coming from the revolutionary commander).

The analysis of Manlius offers the last formulation of the problem of establishing new orders with the "authority" needed to make political subjects comply with them and, in so doing, transgress the established political orders and laws. Lefort stands alone among interpreters in having seen the problem that occupies Machiavelli in these texts: how to command without having the support of the authority of the established political order?[71] But Lefort does not perceive the antinomy of revolutionary action in all of its severity: the real problem consists in thinking the possibility of "commanding" the transgression of the very principle of command, and thus of authority. In the end, the problem posed by Machiavelli is how to command political freedom, when political freedom means the absence of the relation of command and obedience.

For Lefort the antinomy of freedom and command is not so stark: he believes that the revolutionary action of transgressing factical legal orders is performed in the name of the ideal (validity) of the law. It is always the instance of the law, the transcendental purity of its ideal validity, that "authorizes" the political actor to trangress factical laws in attempting to approximate the law in its ideality. One can say that Lefort offers a Rousseauian reading of Machiavelli's republicanism:

---

[68] This is also why Machiavelli reminds the reader that Manlius "maintained military discipline in Rome through the harshness of his command." (Ibid.)

[69] Ibid.

[70] Ibid.

[71] Lefort, *Travail de l'oeuvre*, 602-640.

just like in Rousseau's theory of the formulation of the *volonté générale* in the popular assembly, for Lefort the legal orders of the state can be suspended or transgressed only for the sake of the people giving themselves the law. According to my interpretation, the problem of revolutionary action is how to "command" the transcendence of the desire for freedom as no-rule, over and against the desire to dominate and to command that is operative in every law (be it factical or transcendental, empirical or pure). In other words: what kind of command allows the political actor to "command" against all command? The importance of Machiavelli's theory of revolution lies in having posed this question, which was sublated (both assumed and negated) in the revolutionary legacy of modern natural right.

There is one more issue that needs to be addressed in this context. Machiavelli claims that Manlius acts "inhumanly" because he is "constrained by his nature, and after by his desire that men observe that which his natural appetite had made him order."[72] This explanation appears to clash with the one I just gave of the Manlian command. Does Manlius act with cruelty because of the revolutionary circumstances, i.e., because he wants to overthrow or reform established orders and authorities, or is it his cruel and strong "nature" that forces him, necessitates in him, to act in transgressive or revolutionary ways? The problem is complicated because it involves Machiavelli's idea of human "nature." Is the revolutionary impetus (in Manlius, for example) just as "natural" to certain individuals, as the conservative impetus (in Valerius, for example) is "natural" in others? Or are revolutions anti-nature in a significant sense?

The first task is to determine what "natural appetite" is operative in Manlius. In Machiavelli's discourse there exist two basic political desires: the desire for freedom and the desire for domination. Nothing speaks against the possibility that Manlius's cruelty and inhumanity is determined by the "ferocity" with which he follows the desire for freedom, rather than that for domination. It is interesting to note that Valerius's "humanity" is not natural in the same sense as Manlius's "inhumanity" since the former is conditioned by the fact that Valerius wants to command only what is authorized by law and custom. Machiavelli's reference to Manlius's "nature" in this context is clearly designed to recall the Sophist's use of the distinction between nature (*physis*) and convention (*nomos*), where the transgression of customary law is ascribed to nature. But Machiavelli's use of the concept of "nature" departs from the Sophistic use because what is natural does not refer to the pre-legal, pre-political sphere of physical force but is immediately political.[73] To transcend and transgress customary law is "natural" in a second-order, not pre-legal sense, i.e., in the sense that freedom (as desire not be ruled) belongs to the "nature" of man as a political animal. In other words, Machiavelli posits the "naturality" of human freedom, by which I mean the factical character of freedom's transcendence of the given. The paradox, of course, is that in

---

[72] Machiavelli, *Discourses on Livy*, III,22.

[73] A similar use of "nature" is found in *The Prince,* XVIII where Machiavelli speaks of the Centaur-like character of the political animal who needs to act beyond the domain of the law. On the classical distinction between *physis* and *nomos*, see Plato's reading of Pindar's *nomos basileus* as expressed by Callicles in the *Gorgias*; as well as Thucydides's Melian dialogue: "it is a general and necessary law of nature to rule whatever one can." (Thucydides *Peloponnesian War* §89, §105).

contrast to the modern natural right tradition (including Rousseau and Kant), Machiavelli does not give a "humanist" or moral reading of the "fact" that the "nature" of human beings is freedom, but rather forces the reader to think the ways in which this facticity of freedom posits the individual in an antinomical relation with respect to the instance of the law and to the institution of morality in general. The autonomy of politics is one expression of this antinomical structure.[74]

THE SIMULACRUM OF THE CITIZEN

Machiavelli's theory of the republican citizen culminates with a discussion of whether the "humanity" of Valerius or the "inhumanity" of Manlius is most praiseworthy. According to Machiavelli, "those who write about how a prince ought to govern himself favor more Valerius than Manlius; and Xenophon, previously mentioned by me, giving many examples of the humanity of Cyrus, conforms very well with what Livy says of Valerius."[75] The reference to the classical topic of the "mirror of princes" subtly signals that the issue consists in the way of acting of the citizen as prince. The question becomes: which is better, the law-observing prince (Valerius) or the law-transgressing, the revolutionary, prince (Manlius)? The text situates this question by joining the names of Xenophon and Livy under the proposition that a prince should be humane and law-abiding, i.e., non-revolutionary. To understand how Machiavelli employs this proposition one must keep in mind both that the *Discourses on Livy* systematically subverts Livy's aristocratic prejudices,[76] and that the Xenophontic corpus advocates a tyrannical politics.[77] The point of these references is to indicate that the arguments in favor of the law-abidingness of the commanders, although at first sight they seem to favor freedom because of the classical topos that freedom exists when no one, and especially not the prince or the commander, is above the law, are effectively anti-republican. The anti-republican significance of the praise of "humanity" and "law-abidingness" in princes follows directly from Machiavelli's central thesis that a republic requires repeated transgressions of old orders on the part of its citizens, as much as the state requires the preservation of law-abidingness in its subjects. Paradoxically, in defending the "cruel prince" in the ideal-typical figure of Manlius, Machiavelli is actually defending the republican attitude towards political order which requires the repeated revolutions of such order in order to preserve freedom. In contrast, by defending the law-abiding prince, Livy and Xenophon prove themselves partisans of the established orders of political and legal domination.

That the text also remarks on Livy's appreciation of the "severity" of Manlius's actions (e.g., the killing of his son for disobedience) should not mislead into thinking that Machiavelli and Livy share a common standpoint. Livy's divided

---

[74] On the factical character of political freedom in the Machiavellian legacy, see also Vatter, "Pettit and Modern Republican Political Thought," in *NOMOS XLVI: Political Exclusion and Domination*, ed. Melissa S. Williams and Stephen Macedo (New York: New York University Press, 2005), 118–63.
[75] Machiavelli, *Discourses on Livy*, III,22.
[76] I refer to the discussion in part 2, ch.4.
[77] On Xenophon's tyrannical teaching, see Strauss, *On Tyranny*, passim.

judgment on Manlius and Valerius merely offers the occasion for Machiavelli to establish his style of argumentation. Whenever a question has to be resolved in one or another way, Machiavelli always begins by making the case for both, and then, in a sudden move, decides the question and reveals his own preference.[78]

Nonetheless, in order not to leave this part undecided, I say that in a citizen who lives under the laws of a republic, I believe that it is more praiseworthy and less dangerous the way of proceeding of Manlius: because this way is wholly in favor of the public, and takes no consideration of private ambition; because, in this way of proceeding, one cannot acquire partisans, showing oneself always harsh towards everybody and loving only the common good; because whoever acts like this does not acquire particular friends which we call, as said above, partisans.... But in the way of proceeding of Valerius the contrary is true: because in spite of the fact that with regard to the public one attains the same effects, nonetheless there emerge many doubts, for the particular benevolence that this person acquires with his soldiers, such that in a long lasting command it causes bad effects against freedom.[79]

The crucial insight of Machiavelli's theory of citizenship, thanks to which the relation between principality and republic, and the commanders in each, receive their final, systematic arrangement is found in this passage. Machiavelli's conclusion is that for a republic it is better to have commanders like Manlius than ones like Valerius, because whoever acts like Manlius toward the soldiers (popular militia) under their command cannot produce partisans and cannot further their own ambition as commanders. The "Manlian command" therefore acts in a way that is "wholly in favor of the public, and takes no consideration of private ambition." But Manlius's command is also favored, in a more subversive sense, because it commands revolutionary actions that maintain the republic by renewing its orders in view of isonomy, i.e., the political equality that comes from maintaining the political space from becoming the possession of any "one." Manlius represents a form of transgression that is constitutive of the *res publica* itself. The republic comes into existence when citizens become princes in the exemplary sense of Manlius. Valerius does not fit these criteria of republican citizenship for two reasons: his actions are not revolutionary but conservative; and they make for (potential) partisans, i.e., for a partition of the public space in view of owning it for the sake of particular interests.

The long meditation on citizenship is by no means finished, for the text proceeds to treat the same issue (whether it is better to proceed in the way of Manlius or of Valerius) from the opposite perspective, i.e., from the point of view of what is good for a principality as opposed to a republic.

But if we have to consider a prince, as Xenophon does, we will favor wholly the example of Valerius, and will leave aside that of Manlius; because a prince must seek in his soldiers and his subjects obedience and love.... Because being a prince who is particularly well loved, and having the army as his partisan, agrees with all the other parts of his state; but in a citizen who has the army as his partisan, this part does not agree with the other parts which have to live under laws and obey the magistrates.... I conclude therefore that the way of proceeding of Valerius is useful in a prince but pernicious in a citizen, not only for country but for oneself: for country, because those ways prepare for tyranny; for oneself, because his own city will suspect his way of proceeding and is forced to

---

[78] I refer to the discussion of Machiavelli's style of argumentation in part 1, ch.4 and part 2, ch.3.
[79] Machiavelli, *Discourses on Livy*, III,22.

assure itself at his expense. And so contrariwise I assert that the way of proceeding of Manlius is harmful in a prince, but useful in a citizen, and most useful to country; and rarely will you offend, if only this hatred that your severity brings upon you is not increased by the suspicion aroused by your other virtues, due to their great reputation, bring you; as we will see in the case of Camillus.[80]

Machiavelli's innovative introduction of perspectivism into political thinking is nowhere better represented than in this text. The dialectical procedure characteristic of Machiavelli's discourse (i.e., given two contrary types of action, which one to choose) is resolved and dissolved by adopting two different and opposite perspectives that render account of the different logics of republics and principalities. To understand the solution adopted by Machiavelli one must note the seemingly strange fact that he maintains a tri-partite division of regimes (republic, principality, and tyranny) while operating with a bi-partite division of political actors (citizen, prince). This peculiarity is comprehensible only if one understands these actors, as one must always do in Machiavelli, in functional rather than substantial terms, i.e., as positions held by possible political subjects (subject positions).

Given this premise, Machiavelli offers the following paradoxical solutions. A republic needs citizens who act under the sign of Manlius. These citizens are "princes" because their actions are revolutionary and transgress the rule of laws without creating partisans, since they disclose spaces accessible only to the public, to the multitude as such, without distinction between the few and the many, the rich and the poor, the rulers and the ruled. These Manlian citizens have a conflictual relation of command and obedience with respect to their equals (i.e., the people). Because in the republican event political action commands isonomic equality (and commands it to equals), the command must be self-conflicted, in the sense that it is turned against the relation of command and obedience. This peculiar situation explains the "severity" of Manlius with respect to his own soldiers. But the same Manlian citizen, now no longer considered as acting in a republic (in the name of the desire for freedom as no-rule) but in a principality and as a prince, i.e., in view of owning the public space and turning it into a state, would immediately become a tyrant. In a principality, the prince needs the support of both the people and the army. A principality needs a prince who must act as a "citizen" would act if placed in that position, i.e., act under the sign of Valerius. Conversely, if the same citizen were to act like Valerius in a republic, this way of acting would pose a threat to freedom because the cultivation of the love of the army sets the citizen in potential opposition to the magistrates who uphold the equality of all before the law.

The paradoxical nature of Machiavelli's theory of citizenship follows directly from the loss of origins (of archetypes or forms) suffered by political life once this life is conceived from the originary situation of the return to beginnings. The priority assigned to the change of form over the form itself entails that all political actors are effective only in so far as they become simulacra and abandon their "original" positions in order to take over opposite ones: in a republic, citizens should be princes; in a principality, princes should be citizens. Or, more precisely,

---

[80] Ibid.

in Machiavelli's discourse the republic is defined as the event in which citizens become princes because they trangress the political form in the name of freedom as no-rule. The principality, conversely, is defined as the modality of political life in which princes become citizens because they stabilize the form of the state by gaining the support of the (armed) people. But for a citizen to act in a republic like a prince acts in a state is equivalent to preparing the way for the end of political freedom. Only if read with this combination of perspectives, from this logic of simulacra, does Machiavelli's discourse reveal the guiding thread that permits an unravelling of the perplexing, contradictory and continuously shifting meaning of the terms "citizen" and "prince," "republic" and "principality" that reaches a peak in the third book of the *Discourses on Livy*. In the last instance, the varied and contrary interpretations of Machiavelli owe their existence to the misreading of such semantic shifts, all of which obey a logic of simulacra that follows from a vision of politics without foundations.

If there is a conclusion to be drawn from Machiavelli's complex theory of citizenship it is that the "effective truth" of tyranny, in the modern political situation, consists in the practice and theory of the purity or integrity of political form. When a prince is "only" princely, when a citizen is "only" a citizen, then political life is truly no longer free. The fundamental reason behind Machiavelli's critique of political foundationalism is that political form and political freedom can only be combined in an antinomical, and thus radically unstable, configuration. In the end, Machiavelli argues that tyranny is always a tyranny of form; and political freedom is always a subversion of form. The subversion of political form can itself have two manifestations according to the two senses of the autonomy of politics: autonomy of the state as civil prince with respect to morality; and autonomy of the republican event with respect to the form of the state. That the autonomy of politics has itself a plural sense is evidence that Machiavelli's discourse establishes the inescapability of conflict, plurality, subversion, and perspectivism as the traits of modern political life and modern political freedom. These anti-metaphysical traits attach to the concept of citizenship because the latter emerges from the originary character of historical repetition, the key to Machiavelli's entire political discourse. That is also why its political categories (e.g., citizen, prince, republic, principality) should be read according to a logic of simulacra. The emancipation of politics from foundationalism comes at this price. For Machiavelli, in modern politics the only true corruption is the pursuit of purity and integrity, which translates into the project of providing both mythically and metaphysically secured foundations to political forms of domination. Modern political life, in its two modes of state and republic, is animated by the art of trangressions. The only anti-political act, the only truly tyrannical act, is taking exception to transgression, the "abolition" of the logic of transgression.

AFTERWORD
TO THE PAPERBACK EDITION

POLITICAL FREEDOM: NONDOMINATION OR NO-RULE?

During the past fifteen years, many debates in contemporary continental political theory have registered the fact that the political life of a free people is sooner found in the disruptions or "tumults" of streets and public squares than in the horse-trading carried out in the corridors of constituted power, be these the forum or the market. However, the reemergence of the street as a global public square appears to have exacerbated the chasm between those who want to reduce a free political life to social movements, seeing the rule of law as merely a tool of the dominant classes, and those who wish to grant the people their political freedom only on the condition of tying their hands by pre-commitment to constitutional norms of which they are also supposed to be the author. Through a reading of Machiavelli, *Between Form and Event* set out to conceptualize a relation between "plebeian" social conflicts and republican rule of law in order to move beyond the anarchy of the first option and the statism of the second option and break through what Arendt called the "vicious circle" between constituent and constituted powers.

Written in the late 1990s, *Between Form and Event* intervened in the nascent debate on the republican meaning of freedom initiated by Quentin Skinner and pursued by Philip Pettit. It seemed to me then that Skinner's intuition to read Machiavelli as the crucial modern representative of the republican ideal of political freedom was an important one, and this for at least a couple of reasons. First, the new genealogy of liberty relativized the liberal conception of negative freedom and its rhetorical crushing of Aristotelian positive freedom at the hands of Isaiah Berlin, which had had the unfortunate result of discrediting all political ideas of freedom, not just neo-Aristotelian ones. After Skinner and Pettit reminded political theorists why the negative freedom of an individual could not be separated from the freedom of a people and of their political life, it became easier to speak in the Anglophone world of a people's freedom and a people's power without being accused of uttering sheer nonsense. Additionally, Skinner's reconstruction of Machiavelli as a theorist of neo-Roman liberty helped to make sense of Machiavelli's predilection for Roman political and rhetorical thought and its differences with Greek political thinking, thus bringing to the table the difficult and still open question as to whether Machiavelli's conception of the republic owes more to the Greek democratic experience or to the Roman republican experience.[1]

---

[1] Recent work on the importance of the Greek influence on Machiavelli is found in Eric Nelson, *The Greek Tradition in Republican Thought* (New York: Cambridge University Press, 2004), and now Gabriele Pedullà, *Machiavelli in tumulto. Conquista, cittadinanza e conflitto nei "Discorsi sopra la prima deca di Tito Livio"* (Rome: Bulzoni Editore, 2011). Pocock's Aristotelian insights retain their interest, judging from Pasquale Pasquino, "Machiavelli and Aristotle: The anatomies of the city" in *History of European Ideas* 35 (2009): 397–407, even though Bruni's neo-Aristotelian civic humanism as a whole has convincingly been shown to mask elitist aristocratic ideology; see James Hankins (ed.), *Renaissance Civic Humanism: Reappraisals and Reflections* (Cambridge: Cambridge University Press, 2004).

I remain of the opinion that the republican concept of freedom in Machiavelli is a species of negative liberty in the neo-Roman sense of *libertas* as a *sui iuris* status and so can helpfully be distinguished both from Hobbes's idea of negative liberty as absence of impediments and from Aristotelian positive freedom.[2] Likewise, I think Skinner and Pettit have successfully parried the attacks coming from the front of pre-political liberalism, according to which the only concept of negative liberty is the Hobbesian one.[3] However, in *Between Form and Event* I argued that Skinner's and Pettit's conceptions of republican freedom as nondomination could not explain all the characteristics of Machiavelli's idea of political freedom unless one enlarged the notion of nondomination in the direction of the Arendtian idea of political freedom as no-rule (isonomy). Arendt defines no-rule as "a form of political organization in which the citizens lived together under conditions of no-rule, without a division between rulers and ruled. . . . This notion of no-rule was expressed by the word isonomy, whose outstanding characteristic among the forms of government . . . was that the notion of rule (the "archy" from *archein* in monarchy and oligarchy, or the "cracy" from *kratein* in democracy) was entirely absent from it."[4] A republican conception of freedom, Arendt goes on to say, puts an end to relations of rule between human beings thanks to a rule of law based on the (constituent) power of the people.[5]

I proposed to extend the range of what a republican concept of freedom needs to negate, from freedom as *non*domination to freedom as *no*-rule, because at the time I thought Skinner and Pettit painted much too sanguine a picture of the *imperium* (rule) of the state as the sole agent capable of checking arbitrary or personal *dominium* (dominion) over others, proposing a much too timid picture of resistance to governmental powers when compared with Machiavelli's understanding of the conditions for the rule of law. Their construal of nondomination did not help an understanding of two fundamental points made by Machiavelli: first, that it was entirely possible for a state to exercise forms of structural or impersonal (as opposed to arbitrary and personal) domination; and, second, that the only rule of law capable of checking domination was the one *based* on the productive character of social conflict. It seemed to me, then, that the only effective check upon the legal or structural domination exerted by a constituted power could come from the extraconstitutional constituent power of a people's desiring of isonomy or no-rule. The people's

---

[2] See here Chaim Wirszubski's masterwork *Libertas as a Political Ideal at Rome During the Late Republic and the Early Principate* (Cambridge: Cambridge University Press, 1950), which I regret not consulting at the time of writing my book; I relied, somewhat naïvely, on Skinner's partial use of Wirszubski's theses.

[3] For different stages of this debate, see Quentin Skinner, "A Third Concept of Liberty," in *Proceedings of the British Academy*, 117 (2002), 237–68; and Philip Pettit, *On the People's Terms: A Republican Theory and Model of Democracy* (New York: Cambridge University Press, 2012), as well as the essays in C. Leborde and J. Manor (eds.), *Republicanism and Political Theory* (Oxford: Blackwell, 2008).

[4] Hannah Arendt, *On Revolution* (New York: Penguin, 1990), 30; cited in *Between Form and Event*, 87.

[5] I developed a reading of Arendt as a thinker of no-rule (*an-arche*, absence of rule or command) back in the mid-1990s in my Ph.D. dissertation at the New School, first under the direction of Reiner Schürmann and then, after his untimely death, with Agnes Heller. Schürmann's antifoundationalist understanding of *an-arche* influenced my use of no-rule in *Between Form and Event*, and his work is duly noted therein. The first published record of my reading of no-rule is found in "La fondazione della libertà" in Simona Forti (ed.), *Hannah Arendt* (Milan: Bruno Mondadori, 1999), 107–35.

power as negation of the state's legal power: This is what I called the dimension of no-rule that needed to be added to the current accounts of republicanism, and that I tied back to a theory of the primacy of social conflict in Machiavelli, following and amplifying the insights found in previous interpretations proposed by Claude Lefort, Louis Althusser, Roberto Esposito, and Antonio Negri.[6]

There is no civil life without a state or form of government, without an instance of public rule; but a *free* political life entails a state, and a rule of law, that is open to, yet not identical with, events in which social and political orders and laws are generated from a situation of no-rule and that inscribe in the constitution of the state this resistance to command. That form of state which is constitutionally open to its event of reconstitution is what I call a "republic." Hence, a republican conception of the rule of law requires the kind of "dualist" reading of constitutionalism first theorized by Arendt and later picked up both by Ackerman and Rawls, according to which a constitution is such only if it makes possible *both* the power of the people *and* a limited government. Because the people's political freedom can never be identified with the state's public command, a republican rule of law must make it possible for the people to act as a constituent power and not merely as the subjects of a constituted power. Only the interplay between these two forms of power makes it possible for a society to live politically and free.[7]

Rephrasing my thesis in this book in terms borrowed from Canguilhem's analysis of complex life-forms, for Machiavelli a political life-form can be sustained either in a normal or in a pathological way, with normal and pathological being the two necessary modalities of any life-form. To the first corresponds a republic, wherein state and *imperium* belong to the many; to the second corresponds a principality, wherein state and *imperium* belong to one, following the typology of states found in the first chapter of *The Prince*. The only way in which a principality can ally itself with popular freedom as no-rule is by transforming the desire for no-rule into a desire for liberal freedom from interference or for security. This transformation is the function Machiavelli assigns the civil principality, the central conceptual invention of *The Prince*. I see in Hobbes's concept of sovereignty his debt to Machiavelli and this idea of a principality oriented toward the preservation of the security of its subjects. In this idea of the civil prince I also see the condition of possibility for the neo-Straussian reading of Machiavelli's teaching as a "liberal republicanism," advocated by Rahe, Sullivan, and others.[8] Last, the problem of the civil principality

---

[6] My critique of Pettit's state-centred republicanism is found in "Pettit and Modern Republican Political Thought," in *NOMOS XLVI: Political Exclusion and Domination*, ed. Melissa S. Williams and Stephen Macedo (New York: New York University Press, 2005), 118–63.

[7] I have discussed dualist constitutionalism through a comparison of Rawls's and Schmitt's doctrines in "The Idea of Public Reason and the Reason of State: Schmitt and Rawls on the Political" in *Political Theory* 36:2 (2008): 239–71; and in relation to the Habermasian critique of Rawls, in "Il potere del popolo e la rappresentanza in Rawls e nel repubblicanesimo civico" in *Filosofia Politica*, 24:2 (2010): 263–84. See also my response to Negri's use of Machiavelli in his critique of dualist constitutionalism, in "Resistance and Legality: Arendt and Negri on Constituent Power" in *Kairos. Revue de philosophie de l'Université de Toulouse* 20, (2002): 191–230, now reprinted in *The Philosophy of Toni Negri. Vol. 2. Revolution in Theory*, ed. Tim Murphy and Abdul-Karim Mustapha (London: Pluto Press, 2007), 52–86.

[8] See Paul Rahe, *Against Throne and Altar: Machiavelli and Political Theory under the English Republic* (Cambridge: Cambridge University Press, 2009); Vickie B. Sullivan, *Machiavelli, Hobbes, and the Formation of a Liberal Republicanism in England* (Cambridge: Cambridge University Press, 2004); and Paul Rahe (ed.), *Machiavelli's Liberal Republican Legacy* (Cambridge: Cambridge

is the point at which I disagree with Skinner's and Stacey's readings of *The Prince* as being an ironical critique of princes, as if Machiavelli thought that the modern principality he was constructing in thought merely designated an enslaved form of civil life. For me, the civil principality denotes a state of civil liberty, but not a condition of full-fledged political liberty. However, this does not make the civil prince simply a state of unfreedom or slavery.[9]

Compared with a republican political life, a civil principality is pathological because its laws and orders arise not out of the empowerment of the many, out of the conflict between those who do not want to be oppressed (the people) and those who want to oppress (the nobles or great) but out of the commands of one sovereign and representative government. The "normality" of republican political life requires the transgression and re-creation of new laws and orders, or what Canguilhem calls "normativity," made possible by the social struggle for empowerment by those excluded from political life, and the creation of new, equal rights reflecting the new alliances established during the course of these conflicts. Left to its own devices, and without a return to social conflict as a source of normativity, the civil principality (which I associated with proto-liberalism) ends up in what chapter 9 of *The Prince* calls "license" and is the radical opposite of what Arendt understands by isonomy or absence of domination (*an-arche*). License (akin to libertarianism) is the condition in which anyone feels free to overpower whomever they please, with neither the state nor the people having enough power to defend its members from this domination.

MACHIAVELLI AND THE PEOPLE: REPUBLICANISM OR POPULISM?

In order to counteract the rule or *arche* of those who wish to control the state and exercise *imperium* in order to increase their *dominium*, the "great" or "nobles" characterized by a desire to oppress others, Machiavelli consistently argues that political life needs to open itself to the participation of the people as bearers of a desire not to be dominated. Since my thematizing and radicalizing the political significance of this popular desire for no-rule in *Between Form and Event*, a lively debate has taken place on what this opening to the people could have meant for Machiavelli and, more widely, what it should mean for contemporary democratic political theory.

Machiavelli was keenly aware that the desire to rule over others is an inextirpable fact of the human condition, but his aim was to think the conditions that would establish a republic and prevent it from decaying into either a form of populist

University Press, 2006). These texts emphasize the continuity between modern republicanism and liberalism and among Machiavelli and Hobbes and Locke and thus *de facto* deny the difference between the two conceptions of negative liberty uncovered by Skinner and Pettit.

[9] See the essays in Quentin Skinner, *Visions of Politics. Volume 2: Renaissance Virtues* (Cambridge: Cambridge University Press, 2002); and Peter Stacey, *Roman Monarchy and the Renaissance Prince* (New York: Cambridge University Press, 2007). Skinner and Stacey argue that *The Prince* is a work about unfree states or principalities and that the *Discourses on Livy* is a treatise on free states or republics. I indicate in the last part of *Between Form and Event* the main problem with this kind of reading, namely that the entire third book of the *Discourses on Livy* treats of the necessity of citizens to become "princes" of the republic by returning the republican order to its revolutionary beginnings and thus fighting against the corruption of republican freedom by acting in an extraconstitutional fashion.

government or a form of elitist government. Like many proponents of a revolutionary brand of republicanism after him—from Spinoza, Milton, and Rousseau to Jefferson, Kant, and Hegel—Machiavelli distinguishes a modern republic from the
Greek conception of direct democracy. According to this early modern view, Greek
democracy refers to the regime in which one part of the potential citizenship, called
the *demos*, characterized by its numbers (the many) and by certain capacities (its
liberty, the fact of their not being slaves), attains power (*kratos*) and rules over other
parts of the city (the few, the rich, the wise, the well-bred, etc.). Democracy is the
antithesis of aristocracy (or, more realistically, of oligarchy), but both are forms of
rule as *krattein*.[10] In comparison, modern republicanism does not seek to establish a
state in which one part rules over another, what Kant called a despotic form of
government, but rather seeks to establish a state in which political life supports
conditions of no-rule between the parts of the polity leading to equal law, what Kant
called a republican form of government.

Some Machiavelli scholars have argued that the no-rule variant of republicanism
is too utopian and have instead proposed a more "realistic" interpretation of Machiavelli's "populist" turn. John McCormick's work defends one form of populist
interpretation, according to which Machiavelli teaches that the part of the people
must accede to the control of the state and "ferociously" oppress the nobles if they
wish to avoid being oppressed by the nobles in turn.[11] On this view, a free political
life is characterized by the struggle between proponents of populist democracy and
proponents of elitist oligarchy. Conversely, the neo-Straussian interpretations of
Machiavelli developed by Paul Rahe and Vickie Sullivan defend the claim that
Machiavelli teaches that the control of the state is always in the hands of an elite
because all government is *a priori* oligarchic and always needs to exclude the people
from attaining rule. For that reason, the elites need to keep the people satisfied and
in awe, mostly by the clever combination of instrumental uses of religion and by
projects of military expansion. Both standpoints share the belief that taking effective
hold of the state, either by the people or by the greats, in order to check the respective "class" enemies is the key to a free political life. By way of contrast, I argue
that the key to a free political life is constructing a state that is open to contestation
from social forces animated by the principle of no-rule and which alone can give
rise to laws and orders keeping under check both the domination of the state and of
those with power in society.

---

[10] For a deconstruction of the Greek concept of democracy, where the *demos* now comes to mean
that "part" of those who have no part in rule, see Jacques Rancière, *Hatred of Democracy* (London:
Verso, 2009): "the anarchic title, the title specific to those who have no more title for governing than
they have for being governed. This is what of all things democracy means. Democracy is not a type
of constitution, nor a form of society. . . . It is simply the power peculiar to those who have no more
entitlements to govern than to submit" (46). To judge from such formulations, Rancière's idea of
democracy has moved considerably closer to the position of no-rule. For a discussion of Greek and
Roman conceptions of popular participation in light of the contemporary debate in continental
political theory, see my "Quarrel between Populism and Republicanism: Machiavelli and the Antin-
omies of Plebeian Politics" in *Contemporary Political Theory* 11:3 (2012): 242–63, where I also
discuss Joshua Ober's recent hypotheses concerning the meaning of *kratos* in the Greek democratic
understanding of the term, which may require modifying in part Arendt's identification of *kratein*
with *archein*. In general, though, both Rancière and Ober conduct their deconstruction and reconstruction of the Greek democratic experience under the horizon of what Arendt designates as no-rule.
[11] John McCormick, *Machiavellian Democracy* (New York: Cambridge University Press, 2011).

Machiavelli's texts make room for all three interpretations, and, in fact, all three were already thematized in *Between Form and Event*. As the most acute of observers of political reality, Machiavelli was all too aware that the elites who run governments often trick the people and usually employ religion and military conquest for that purpose. And he was also aware that some members of the people harbor ambitions to be like the nobles and desire to acquire the state in order to oppress their political enemies and secure particular advantages for themselves. But this awareness does not invalidate the republican core of his political proposals. The argument I have with the advocates of the view that either the people or the oligarchs "must" rule has both a normative and a historical side. Normatively, the question at stake is whether the form of a modern republic, characterized by the equal liberty of all its members and aiming toward a roughly egalitarian condition of wealth in all of its members, requires a reference to the principle of no-rule as isonomy or whether it can do merely with the principle of hegemony. I shall deal with the normative side in the next section.

The historical side of the debate boils down to the question of how Roman republican institutions really worked, and how Machiavelli interpreted them: Were these legal and political orders always instrumentalized by the elites? Or did they successfully elevate the people to positions of control and empire? Or did they manage to establish conditions of no-rule that were the object of continual social struggle? Again, depending on which Roman or Greek historian of Rome one favors, and which nineteenth- or twentieth-century meta-theory of Roman institutions one follows, it is possible to find in Machiavelli's text corroboration for all three positions: the elitist, the populist, and the no-rule variants of Roman republicanism. In *Between Form and Event* I tried to argue that the standpoint of no-rule comes into view through the Roman, plebeian "creative translation" of Greek democracy in a series of Roman institutional inventions that I call "counter-institutions," something absent from the Greek *polis*. By counter-institutions I mean those laws and orders that set the *imperium* of the state *against* itself, thus effectively establishing the division of powers and "guarding freedom," as Machiavelli says in the first book of the *Discourses on Livy*. I take it as a given that one of the main distinctions between modern republicanism and the Greek conception of direct democracy is the fundamental principle of the division of powers, which is absent in the latter conception. In this book, I have considered the institution of the Tribunate as exemplary of this Roman innovation—that is, as an institution which permits the accusation to the people's judgment of any governmental attempt to shift away from no-rule (or equal liberty, *aequum ius*, *isonomia*) toward the rule by one part over another part (domination).[12]

---

[12] I find support for the no-rule perspective in the institutional analyses of the Roman so-called mixed constitution found in such classics as Arnaldo Momigliano, *Roma arcaica* (Florence: Sansoni, 1989); Santo Mazzarino, *Dalla monarchia allo stato repubblicano: Ricerche di storia romana arcaica* (Milan: Rizzoli, 1992), and Kurt von Fritz, *The Theory of Mixed Constitution in Antiquity* (New York: Columbia University Press, 1994); von Fritz sees in the Roman republic "an excess of negative powers the like of which can hardly be found in any other state in history" (cited herein on p. 104). See also the work of Wilfried Nippel in this context. In my opinion, their analyses have not been surpassed by newer perspectives, for example those collected in Kurt Raaflaub (ed.), *Social Struggles in Archaic Rome: New Perspectives on the Conflict of Orders* (London: Wiley-Blackwell, 2006). See also the more recent work of Machiavelli scholars like Pedullà (*op. cit.*) and now Fabio Raimondi, *L'ordinamento della libertà. Machiavelli e Firenze* (Verona: ombre corte, 2013) on Machiavelli's thinking about Roman orders, as well as in other recent discussions of plebeian politics like the one found in Martin Breaugh, *L'expérience plébéienne. Une histoire discontinue de la liberté politique*

THE BASIS OF REPUBLICAN RULE OF LAW:
SOCIAL CONFLICT OR POLITICAL CONCORD?

Between Form and Event was perhaps the first book in English on Machiavelli to address the question of the productivity of social conflict and division, which the interpretations of Machiavelli put forward by Lefort, Althusser, Negri, and Esposito had previously thematized. The novelty of my reading was that I identified the primary conflict as one between a desire to rule and a desire for no-rule, and the upsurge of this conflict as a real division of powers that limited the state's legal domination and allowed for the opening of a free sphere of popular opinion and consent as the sole basis for the creation of equal law.[13] I opposed this view of social conflict to the view that conflict is always part and parcel of a struggle for hegemony and, thus, for the control of state power. But I also rejected the Ciceronian view that the rule of law depends on the primacy of political concord. I remain of the opinion that a productive relation among social conflict, people's power, and rule of law can be had only on the condition that social conflict remain a conflict between rule and no-rule, rather than one between homogeneous desires to rule.

The normative argument for no-rule can be stated along the following lines: State rule or command is required for the consequent and sustained pursuit of social interests, be these individual or group interests. If the rule of law is subsumed under state rule, rather than grounding itself on no-rule, then the rule of law becomes instrumental to the unimpaired pursuit of interests. In that case, the rule of law ceases to be what it ought to be—namely, an impartial or disinterested or fair regulation and judgment of such interested pursuits. The demand and condition of possibility for such a disinterested judgment, evidently, can come only from a desire for no-rule, which in turn stands in conflict with the demand for rule that is intrinsic to the sustained pursuits of interests supplied by state power. This conflict between no-rule and state-rule is one that a free political life cannot afford to institutionalize or neutralize in the name of concord. On the contrary, this is the one form of social conflict to which a free political life must continuously return in its struggle against the slide into liberal, neo-liberal, and libertarian regimes. Further, the conflict between rule and no-rule need not take the form of armed state repression against nonviolent forms of resistance; quite to the contrary, Machiavelli offers a complicated critique of violence in order to make sense of the structure and logic of this all-important conflict, which is outlined in detail in the third and concluding part of *Between Form and Event*.

In later essays, I have tried to find alternative ways to formulate the co-originality of social division and rule of law, and to see the latter not only as an integrative moment of political life but also as an instrument of critique to state sovereignty, to

---

(Paris: Payot, 2007) and Isabell Lorey, *Figuren des Immunen. Elemente einer politischen Theorie* (Berlin: diaphanes, 2012).

[13] Since then, there has been a veritable explosion in the secondary literature on the nature of social conflict in Machiavelli, of which I here cite only some of the most important examples: Marie Gaille-Nikodimov, *Conflit civil et liberté. La politique machiavelienne entre histoire et medicine* (Paris: Honoré Champion, 2004); Marco Geuna, "Machiavelli ed il ruolo dei conflitti nella vita politica," in Alessandro Arienzo and Dario Caruso (eds.), *Conflitti* (Naples: Dante&Descartes, 2005), 19–57; Filippo del Lucchese, Luca Sartorello, and Stefano Visentin (eds.), *Machiavelli: immaginazione e contingenza* (Pisa: ETS, 2006); and Filippo del Lucchese, *Conflict, Power and Multitude in Machiavelli and Spinoza* (London: Continuum, 2011).

governmentality, and to legal domination. I believe that when the republican meaning of "rule of law" is properly articulated, there is no opposition between the rule
of law and political freedom as no-rule. The problem, in my view, is that neither the
republicanism developed by Skinner and Pettit nor the neo-Straussian liberalism and
the populist democracy of McCormick have as yet developed an adequate conception of what the "rule of law" means for republicanism. A proper republican theory
of law remains a desideratum, and in order to pursue it, I consider taking up Spinoza's, Rousseau's, Kant's, and Hegel's contributions to republicanism unavoidable.
Perhaps this is another point where my current work parts ways with Skinner's and
Pettit's republicanism, for they tend to see these thinkers as trapped within the
scheme of the Hobbesian theory of sovereignty.[14]

An important objection to my standpoint in *Between Form and Event* is that it
privileges too much the constituent moment of no-rule and of institutional renewal
over the constituted moment of state-rule and of the rule of law, within the process
of a free political life.[15] More precisely, the objection is that I tend to conflate the
form of state (or *imperium*) with the rule of law. In *Between Form and Event* I have
maintained a fundamental distinction between what classical republicanism called
"rule by laws," which I tried to capture through an account of charismatic foundings
and the system of *auctoritas*, and what modern republicanism calls "rule of law,"
which is tied to a public use of reason on the part of a free people. Whereas the
principle of no-rule stands in conflict with the legal system of *auctoritas*, it serves
as basis for republican rule of law and the public use of reason. Having said that, I
agree that, in hindsight, some formulations of *Between Form and Event* sound too
antinomian, and one can easily be forgiven for understanding the "rule" that is
negated by no-rule to refer not only to *imperium* and *dominium*—that is, to forms
of command and ownership—but also to the juridical idea of a "rule" of law, which
in reality has nothing to do with either command or ownership. I have since argued
for the fundamental mutual implication of no-rule and republican rule of law, while
maintaining the basic conflictual relation between no-rule and state-rule.

The principle of no-rule as I understand it remains republican, not anarchist, if
by anarchism one understands the tradition of social and political thinking started
in the nineteenth century and that attempts to organize society without a state. Anarchists believe in the possibility of a society in which domination and coercion are
eradicated, and thus where the state is no longer necessary. Instead, republicans
believe only that domination can be checked, not eradicated, and that to this end a
state of a certain kind is needed. Republicans and anarchists both have sovereignty
as their sworn enemy, but their relationship to the rule of law is different. As I
understand it, the anarchist position is tendentially antinomian, whereas republicans
think that no-rule requires a rule of law based on the power of the people.[16]

---

[14] For Kant as a neo-Roman republican thinker, see my "People Shall Be Judge: Reflective Judgment
and Constituent Power in Kant's Philosophy of Law," in *Political Theory* 39:6 (2011): 749–76.

[15] See the early review by Mary Dietz in *Political Theory*, 31 (2003), 742–46; and more recently
James Muldoon in *Theory & Event*, 16.2 (2013).

[16] For a contemporary return to anarchism, see the work of Todd May, *The Political Philosophy of
Poststructuralist Anarchism* (University Park: Pennsylvania State University Press, 1994) and
Contemporary Political Movements and the Thought of Jacques Rancière: Creating Equality (Edin-
burgh: Edinburgh University Press, 2009); Saul Newman, *The Politics of Postanarchism* (Edinburgh:
Edinburgh University Press, 2011); Jimmy Klausen and James Martel (eds.), *How Not to Be
Governed So Much: Readings and Interpretations from a Critical Anarchist Left* (Lanham, MD:
Rowman & Littlefield, 2011).

MACHIAVELLI'S PHILOSOPHY AND THE CULTURE
OF THE FLORENTINE RENAISSANCE

Between Form and Event takes a strong position on Machiavelli's ontological or philosophical standpoint by arguing that undergirding his entire political thought is the overturning of the classical, metaphysical priority given to form over event. In so doing, the book seeks to radicalize Baron's and Pocock's insights on how the Florentine Renaissance gave rise to a new concept of republican freedom because it adopted a historicist horizon illuminating the fundamental contingency and historicity of political forms. This historicist horizon is what Pocock calls the "Machiavellian moment" as opposed to the previous grounding of political form on a providential account of history. *Between Form and Event* rejected Pocock's neo-Aristotelian reading of Machiavelli's politics but adopted Pocock's insights into the emergence of modern historical consciousness. By bringing attention to Machiavelli's sustained attempts at putting forward what I call a theory of the event, *Between Form and Event* criticized the all-too-frequent association of his historical thinking with astrological determinism.[17] It offered a new interpretation of Machiavelli's account of *fortuna* as the "encounter" (*riscontro*) between actions and times first delineated in the *Ghiribizzi al Soderino* based on the reception of the Idle Argument via Aristotle and the medieval debate on future contingents.[18] Last, this perspective on the ontology and logic of events permitted an explanation of the fundamental political teaching of the Platonic myth of Saturn in Machiavelli's Florence and its importance for Machiavelli's theory of the "return to beginnings."[19]

Thus, along with the inscription of no-rule, the account of the event I develop here is the second innovation of my antifoundationalist reading of Machiavelli and, by extension, of the radical democratic political theory proposed by this book. At the time of writing, Althusser's posthumous "aleatory materialism" had barely registered in Machiavelli studies and in political theory. Furthermore, it must be said, Althusser himself was unable to connect his recovery of Lucretian themes to a proper discussion of Machiavelli's theory of the *riscontro*. Similarly, Sheldon Wolin's fundamental suggestion that a free political life was not reducible to a question of political form because of its "fleeting," eventlike character had received scant notice, and nowhere else, as far as I can tell, was it accorded the importance I assigned it in *Between Form and Event*.[20] My antifoundationalist reading of the event based itself, with respect to the Machiavellian text, on the primacy of the so-called return to beginnings, introduced in the third part of his *Discourses*. In order

---

[17] Argued by Anthony Parel, *The Machiavellian Cosmos* (New Haven, CT: Yale University Press, 1992) and still prevalent in much secondary literature. See now the interesting discussion of necessity and contingency in Miguel Saralegui, *Maquiavelo y la contradicción* (Pamplona: Ediciones Universidad de Navarra, 2012).

[18] or a contrasting hypothesis, see now Carlo Ginzburg, "Diventare Machiavelli. Per una nuova lettura dei 'Ghiribizzi al Soderini'" in *Quaderni storici* 41 (2006): 151–64.

[19] For a fascinating interpretation of the crucial neo-Platonic politico-theological context against which Machiavelli reacted, see Fabián Ludueña Romandini, *Homo oeconomicus. Marsilio Ficino, la teología y los misterios paganos* (Buenos Aires: Miño y Dávila, 2006).

[20] The situation is now different thanks also to the important work by Vittorio Morfino, *Il tempo e l'occasione. L'incontro Spinoza-Machiavelli* (Milan: LED, 2002), who follows the indications of Althusser's aleatory materialism. I treat Althusser's reading of Machiavelli and aleatory materialism in "Machiavelli after Marx: The Self-Overcoming of Marxism in the Late Althusser" in *Theory and Event* 7.4 (2004).

to elucidate what was at stake in this formula, I deployed the theory of historical repetition and of historical discontinuity found in Foucault, Deleuze, and Derrida. My goal in so doing was not only to offer a theoretical schema that could shed light on what was entailed by Machiavelli's theory of historical repetition but also, conversely, to place this poststructuralist theory of repetition in its proper political and revolutionary context. I now regret, of course, not having discussed in this context, and in the context of my account of Machiavelli's theory of action in Part III of this book, Alain Badiou's early formulations of his theory of the event and its implications for a theory of revolutionary action. I have since attempted to show the opposition I see between the standpoint of historical repetition I favor and the "messianic," Pauline conception of the event employed by Badiou and others.[21]

The attempt to understand Machiavelli's contribution to political thought within any philosophical horizon has been contested in the recent Italian Machiavelli scholarship of Mario Martelli and Francesco Bausi.[22] These scholars argue, on philological and historico-political grounds, that Machiavelli did not have the "culture" necessary to know, much less to oppose and overturn on theoretical grounds, the classical tradition, as Strauss, Berlin, Lefort, and Althusser have variously claimed. Furthermore, radicalizing the contextual approach found in Gilbert, Rubinstein, and Skinner but overturning its political meaning, they attempt to show that after the fall of the republican regime, Machiavelli was always motivated by philo-Medicean, philo-monarchic positions and was never tempted by civic republican ideology. In *Between Form and Event*, I did not pay due attention to the problem of Machiavelli's "culture." I now believe that this problem and, indeed, the problem of the "culture" of the Florentine circles in which he moved (e.g., Orti Oricellari) or in those circles about which he could have known (Medicean and Savonarolan circles) is a fundamental one, even though I do not share the answers given to this problem by Martelli or Bausi. Thus, for example, I would now give far more importance to the reception of Roman rhetorical theory by Machiavelli as well as to the reception of Lucretius' *De rerum natura* in Machiavelli's cosmology.[23]

And yet, I maintain that the recovery neither of Cicero, nor of Quintillian, nor of Lucretius, by themselves or in some combination accounts for what is truly innovative in Machiavelli's political theory, although they undeniably offered Machiavelli important pieces of his puzzle. Rather, far more important politically and philosophically, so it seems to me today, remains another part of his "culture" and of the "culture" of the Florentine circles associated with the reception of Platonism via the arrival of Byzantine thought and teachers of Greek to Florence, Rome, and Venice in the decades before Machiavelli's birth. In my mind, Machiavelli remains a thinker who is profoundly influenced by and struggles with Florentine Platonism, and, in

---

[21] See my *Constitución y Resistencia* (Santiago: Editorial Universidad Diego Portales, 2011) and *The Republic of the Living: Biopolitics and the Critique of Civil Society* (New York: Fordham University Press, forthcoming 2014).

[22] Francesco Bausi, *Machiavelli* (Roma: Salerno editrice, 2005); Mario Martelli, *Otto studi machiavelliani* (Roma: Salerno editrice, 2008).

[23] On rhetoric, see Peter Godman, *From Poliziano to Machiavelli: Florentine Humanism in the High Renaissance* (Princeton, NJ: Princeton University Press, 1998), as well as the previously cited Skinner and Stacey; on Lucretius and Machiavelli, see Allison Brown, *The Return of Lucretius to Renaissance Florence* (Cambridge, MA: Harvard University Press, 2010).

this sense, Strauss was right to insist on the importance for Machiavelli of Xeno-phon, translated by Bracciolini, over Aristotle, translated by Bruni.[24] Along with Byzantine Platonism, the other crucial admixture to Machiavelli's "culture" was that provided by medieval Arabic and Jewish philosophical conceptions of the rela-tion between revealed law and political regimes, which relativize to a certain extent the opposition between historicist and providentialist visions of history that I employ in this book.[25] This project of re-contextualizing Machiavelli's political lan-guage beyond the neo-Roman and Christian civic humanist constellations also requires a rethinking of late medieval doctrines on law, which is still in its infancy with respect to Machiavelli's vocabulary[26] and leads toward a radical rethinking of the bases of a republican "rule of law" with and against the late medieval treatment of the divine *nomoi*.

---

[24] A point admirably made by Felix Gilbert back in 1939, "The Humanist Concept of the Prince and the *Prince* of Machiavelli," in *The Journal of Modern History* 11, 4 (1939): 449–83. See also on the reception of Platonism in Florence Patricia Springborg's *Western Republicanism and the Oriental Prince* (Austin: University of Texas Press, 1992), which unfortunately I did not know of at the time; and recently Giovanni Georgini, "The Place of the Tyrant in Machiavelli's Political Thought and the Literary Genre of *The Prince*" in *History of Political Thought* 29 (2) (2008): 230–56.

[25] I have discussed Byzantine Platonism in Florence and its importance for Machiavelli in "La política del gran azar: providencia y legislación en Platón y el Renacimiento," in Miguel Ruiz Stull and Miguel Vatter (eds.), *Política y acontecimiento* (Santiago: Fondo de Cultura Económica, 2011), 23–56. The question of divine providence and of Averroism in Machiavelli raised by Martelli and Rahe, respectively, is treated in "Machiavelli and the Republican Conception of Providence," in *Review of Politics* 75 (4) (2013): 605–23. The groundwork for re-positioning Machiavelli anew within late medieval thought in a cross-cultural perspective between Byzantine neo-Platonism and Spanish Averroism and the reception of Jewish medieval thought (mainly Maimonides) in Florence has been advanced by Vasileios Syros, *Marsilius of Padua at the Intersection of Ancient and Medieval Tradi-tions of Political Thought* (Toronto: University of Toronto Press, 2012); Abraham Melamed, *The Philosopher-King in Medieval and Renaissance Jewish Thought* (Albany: State University of New York Press, 2003); Fabrizio Lelli, "Jews, Humanists, and the Reappraisal of Pagan Wisdom, Asso-ciated with the Conception of Dignitas Hominis," in Allison P. Coudert and Jeffrey S. Shoulson (eds.), *Hebraica Veritas? Christian Hebraists and the Study of Judaism in Early Modern Europe* (Philadelphia: University of Pennsylvania Press, 2004), 49–70.

[26] See now Diego Quaglioni, *Machiavelli e la lingua della giurisprudenza* (Bologna: Il Mulino, 2011), which is centered on the reception of Roman law.

BIBLIOGRAPHY

Abensour, Miguel. *La démocratie contre l'Etat: Marx et le moment Machiavéllien.* Paris: PUF, 1997.
____. "Démocratie sauvage et principe d'anarchie." *Cahiers de philosophie* (Lille) 18, *Les choses politiques* (Winter 1994-5): 125-149.
Agamben, Giorgio. *Homo Sacer. Sovereign Power and Bare Life.* Stanford: Stanford University Press, 1998.
Alberti, Leon Battista. *The Complete Works.* Edited by Franco Borsi. Milan: Rizzoli, 1989.
Althusser, Louis. "Machiavel et nous." In *Ecrits philosophiques et politiques.* (Paris: Stock/IMEC, 1995).
Apel, Karl-Otto. "Sinnkonstitution und Geltungsrechtfertigung. Heidegger und das Problem der Transzendentalphilosophie." In *Martin Heidegger: Innen- und Aussenansichten.* Frankfurt: Suhrkamp, 1989.
Arendt, Hannah. *Between Past and Future. Eight Exercises in Political Thought.* New York: Penguin, 1977.
____. *On Revolution.* New York: Penguin, 1990.
____. *The Human Condition.* Chicago: University of Chicago Press, 1958.
____. *The Life of the Mind.* New York: Harcourt Brace, 1978.
____. "Karl Marx e la tradizione del pensiero politico occidentale." Translated and edited by Simona Forti. *Micromega* 5 (1995).
____. *Lectures on Kant's Political Philosophy.* Chicago: University of Chicago Press, 1982.
____. *Crises of the Republic.* New York: Harcourt Brace, 1972.
____. *The Origins of Totalitarianism.* New York: Harcourt Brace Jovanovich, 1975.
Aristotle. *The Politics.* Edited by Stephen Everson. New York: Cambridge University Press, 1988.
____. *Nicomachean Ethics.* Translated by Stephen Irwin. Indianapolis: Hackett, 1985.
____. *The Complete Works of Aristotle. The Revised Oxford Translation.* Edited by Jonathan Barnes. Princeton: Princeton University Press, 1984.
Aron, Raymond. *Machiavel et les tyrannies modernes.* Paris: Éditions de Fallois, 1993.
Ascoli, A. and Kahn, V., eds. *Machiavelli and the Discourse of Literature.* Ithaca, NY: Cornell University Press, 1993.
Augustine, Saint. *Concerning the City of God against the Pagans.* Edited by John O'Meara. New York: Penguin, 1984.
Aubenque, Pierre. *La prudence chez Aristote.* Paris: PUF, 1963.
Balaban, O. "The Human Origins of Fortuna in Machiavelli's Thought." *History of Political Thought* 11 (Spring 1990): 21-36.
Baron, Hans. *In Search of Florentine Civic Humanism.* Princeton: Princeton University Press, 1988.
____. *The Crisis of the Early Italian Renaissance.* Princeton: Princeton University Press, 1966.
____. "The *Querelle* of the Ancients and the Moderns as a Problem for Renaissance Scholarship." *The Journal of History of Ideas* 20 (1959): 3-22.
Bencivenga, Ermanno. *Oltre la tolleranza.* Milan: Feltrinelli, 1992.
____. *Freedom: a Dialogue.* Indianapolis: Hackett, 1997.
Benjamin, Walter. *Illuminations.* New York: Schocken, 1968.
____. *Reflections.* New York: Harcourt Brace Jovanovich, 1978.
____. *Gesammelte Schriften.* Edited by Rolf Tiedemann. Frankfurt: Suhrkamp, 1979-89.
____. *The Correspondence of Walter Benjamin and Gerschom Scholem 1932-1940.* Cambridge: Harvard University Press, 1992.
____. *Charles Baudelaire. Un poète lyrique à l'apogée du capitalisme.* Paris: Payot, 1982.
____. *Walter Benjamin. Sul concetto di storia.* Edited by G. Bonola and M. Ranchetti. Turin: Einaudi, 1997.

____. *Selected Writings. Volume 1: 1913-1926*. Edited by Marcus Bullock and Michael W. Jennings. Cambridge: Harvard University Press, 1996.

Benveniste, Émile. *Le vocabulaire des institutions indo-européennes*. Paris: Minuit, 1969.

Berlin, Isaiah. *Four Essays on Liberty*. Oxford: Oxford University Press, 1982.

____. "The Originality of Machiavelli". *Against the Current. Essays in the History of Ideas*. New York: Penguin, 1980.

Berman, H.J. *Law and Revolution: The Formation of the Western Legal Tradition*. Cambridge: Harvard University Press, 1983.

Berns,Thomas. "Le retour à l'origine de l'état." *Archives de philosophie* 59 (1996): 219-248.

Bernstein, Richard. "Foucault: critique as philosophical ethos." In *Philosophical Interventions in the Unfinished Project of the Enlightenment*. A. Honneth, T.McCarthy, C. Offe, and A. Wellmer, eds. Cambridge: MIT Press, 1992.

Bertelli, Lucio. "Metabole Politeion." *Filosofia Politica* 2 (December 1989): 275-326.

Black, R. "Ancients and Moderns in the Renaissance." *The Journal of History of Ideas* 43 (1982): 3-32.

Blumenberg, Hans. *The Legitimacy of the Modern Age*. Cambridge: MIT Press, 1983.

____. *Die Genesis der kopernikanischen Welt*. Frankfurt: Suhrkamp, 1975.

Blythe James M. *Ideal government and the Mixed Constitution in the Middle Ages*. Princeton: Princeton University Press, 1992.

Bobbio, Norberto. *Liberalism and Democracy*. London: Verso, 1990.

Bock, Gisela, Maurizio Viroli, and Quentin Skinner, eds. *Machiavelli and Republicanism*. Cambridge: Cambridge University Press, 1991.

Boethius. *Consolation of Philosophy*. London: Penguin, 1969.

Bollack, Jean. *Empedocle. Introduction à l'ancienne physique*. Paris: Edition de Minuit, 1965.

Bonadeo, A. *Corruption, Conflict and Power in the Works and Times of Niccolò Machiavelli*. Berkeley: University of California, 1973.

Bondanella, Peter. *Machiavelli and the Art of Renaissance History*. Detroit: Wayne State University Press, 1973.

Brague, Remi. *Aristote et la question du monde*. Paris: PUF, 1988.

Brisson, Luc. *Le Meme et l'Autre dans la structure ontologique du Timée de Platon*. Paris: Vrin, 1974.

Brown, Alison, "Platonism in Fifteenth-Century Florence and Its Contribution to Early Modern Thought." *Journal of Modern History* 58 (June 1986): 383-413.

Brown, Wendy. *Manhood and Politics*. Totowa, NJ: Rowman & Littlefield, 1988.

Bruni, Leonardo. "Laudatio of the City of Florence." In *The Humanism of Leonardo Bruni*. Edited by Gordon Griffiths, James Hankins, David Thompson. Binghamton: Medieval and Renaissance Texts and Studies in conjunction with the Renaissance Society of America, 1987.

Bruno, Giordano. *Cena delle ceneri*. Edited by Christian Bartholomess. Bologna: A. Forni, 1974.

____. *De la causa, principio e uno*. Edited by Augusto Guzzo. Milan: Mursia, 1985.

____. *Opere*. Milan: Ricciardi, 1956.

Brunner, O., Conze, W., and Koselleck, R., eds. *Geschichtliche Grundbegriffe*. Stuttgart: Klett, 1972.

Buck, August. "Des Geschichtsdenken der Renaissance." In *Schriften und Vorträge des Petrarca-Instituts Köln* IX. Krefeld: Sherpe, 1957.

Burke, Peter. *The Renaissance Sense of the Past*. New York: St. Martin's Press, 1970.

Carr, Wesley. *Angels and Principalities. The Background, Meaning and Development of the Pauline Phrase hai archai kai hai exousiai*. New York: Cambridge University Press, 1981.

Cassirer, Ernst. *The Myth of the State*. New Haven: Yale University Press, 1974.

____. *The Individual and the Cosmos in Renaissance Philosophy*. Philadelphia: University of Pennsylvania Press, 1963.

Cavarero, Adriana. "Il corpo politico come organismo." *Filosofia Politica* 3 (December 1993).

Chabod, Federico. *Machiavelli and the Renaissance*. Cambridge: Harvard University Press, 1958.

____. *Opere*. Turin: Einaudi, 1979.

Châtelet, Francois. *La naissance de l'histoire: la formation de la pensée historienne en Grèce*. Paris: Union générale d'éditions, 1974.

Cicero, Marcus Tullius. *Works*. Lipsia: Teubner, 1931.

Cioffari, Vincent. "Fortune, Fate and Chance." In *Dictionary of the History of Ideas*. New York: Scribner, 1973.

Clastres, Pierre. *Society against the State*. New York: Zone Books, 1987.

Clavero, Bernardo. "Institución politica y derecho: acerca del concepto historiografico de 'estado moderno'." *Revista de estudios politicos* 19 (1981).

_____. *Tantas personas como estados. Por una antropologia politica de la historia europea*. Madrid: Tecnos, 1986.

Cochrane, Charles N. *Christianity and Classical Culture*. New York: Oxford University Press, 1980.

Cochrane, Eric. *Historians and Historiography in the Italian Renaissance*. Chicago: University of Chicago Press, 1981.

Colish, Marcia L. "The Idea of Liberty in Machiavelli." In *Renaissance Essays II*. Edited by William J. Connell. Rochester, NY: University of Rochester Press, 1993.

Collingwood, R. G. *The Idea of History*. London: Oxford University Press, 1973.

Costa, Gustavo. *La leggenda dei secoli d'oro nella letteratura italiana*. Bari: Laterza, 1972.

Croce, Benedetto. *Elementi di politica*. Bari: Laterza, 1925.

_____. "Una questione che forse non si chiuderà mai: la questione del Machiavelli." In *Indagini su Hegel e schiarimenti filosofici*. Bari: Laterza, 1952.

_____. *Teoria e storia della storiografia*. Milan: Adelphi, 1989.

Cullmann, Oscar. *Christus und die Zeit*. Zollikon-Zürich: Evangelischer Verlag, 1946.

De Grazia, Sebastian. *Machiavelli in Hell*. Princeton: Princeton University Press, 1989.

De Mattei, Rodolfo. "Dal primato della sapienza al primato della prudenza nel dottrinarismo politico italiano del cinque e del seicento." *Giornale Critico della Filosofia Italiana* 7, no. 1 (1976).

Deleuze, Gilles. *Difference and Repetition*. New York: Columbia University Press, 1994.

_____. *The Logic of Sense*. New York: Columbia University Press, 1990.

Deleuze, Gilles and Guattari, Felix. *A Thousand Plateaus: Capitalism and Schizophrenia*. Minneapolis: University of Minnesota Press, 1987.

Derla, Luigi. "La concezione machiavelliana del tempo." In *Ideologia e Scrittura nel Cinquecento*. Urbino: Argalia Editore, 1977.

Derrida, Jacques. "Force of Law: The 'Mystical Foundation of Authority.'" In *Deconstruction and the Possibility of Justice, Cardozo Law Review* 2, no. 5-6 (July-August 1990).

_____. *Limited Inc*. Paris: Galilée, 1990.

_____. *De la Grammatologie*. Paris: Editions de Minuit, 1967.

_____. *Specters of Marx*. London: Routledge, 1994.

_____. *The Gift of Death*. Chicago: University of Chicago Press, 1995.

Desan, Philippe. *La Naissance du Méthode. Machiavel, La Ramée, Bodin, Montaigne, Descartes*. Paris: Nizet, 1987.

Detienne, Marcel and Vernant, Jean-Pierre. *Les Ruses de l'Intelligence. La Mètis des Grecs*. Paris: Flammarion, 1974.

Diano, Carlo. *Forma ed Evento. Principi per una interpretazione del mondo greco*. Venezia: Marsilio, 1993.

_____. *Saggezza e poetiche degli antichi*. Vicenza: Neri Pozza, 1968.

Di Napoli, Giorgio. "Machiavelli e l'aristotelismo del Rinascimento." *Giornale di Metafisica* (1990): 215-264.

Dionisotti, Carlo. *Machiavellerie*. Torino: Einaudi, 1980.

Doerrie, H. "Pronoia." *Freiburger Zeitschrift für Theologie und Philosophie* 26 (1977).

Doren, A. "Fortuna in Mittelalter und in der Renaissance." *Vorträge der Bibliothek Warburg* 2, no.1 (1922-23).

Edelstein, Ludwig. *The Idea of Progress in Classical Antiquity*. Baltimore: Johns Hopkins Press, 1967.

Edmunds, Lowell. *Chance and Intelligence in Thucydides*. Cambridge: Harvard University Press, 1975.

Eliade, Mircea. *The Myth of the Eternal Return*. Princeton: Princeton University Press, 1974.

Ercole, Francesco. *Dal Comune al Principato: saggi sulla storia del diritto pubblico del Rinascimento italiano*. Florence: Vallechi, 1929.

Esposito, Roberto. *La Politica e la Storia. Machiavelli e Vico*. Naples: Liguori, 1980.

____. *Ordine e Conflitto*. Naples: Liguori, 1984.

____. *Nove Pensieri sulla Politica*. Bologna: Il Mulino, 1993.

Ferry, Luc. *Political Philosophy 1. Rights: the new quarrel between the Ancients and the Moderns*. Chicago: University of Chicago Press, 1992.

____. *Political Philosophy 2. The System of Philosophies of History*. Chicago: University of Chicago Press, 1992.

____. *Rejouer le politique*. Paris: Galilée, 1981.

Ficino, Marsilio. *Theologia Platonica de immortalitate animorum*. Hildesheim: Olms, 1995.

____. *Opera Omnia*. Turin: Bottega D'Erasmo, 1962.

Flanagan, Thomas. "The Concept of Fortuna in Machiavelli." In *The Political Calculus: Essays on Machiavelli's Philosophy*. Edited by Anthony Parel. Toronto: Toronto University Press, 1972.

Fleischer, Martin. "A Passion for Politics: The Vital Core of the World of Machiavelli." In *Machiavelli and the Nature of Political Thought*. New York: Atheneum, 1972.

____. "The Ways of Machiavelli and the Ways of Politics," *History of Political Thought* XVI, no.3 (1995).

Fontana, Biancamaria ed. *The Invention of the Modern Republic*. Cambridge: Cambridge University Press, 1994.

Foucault, Michel. *Dits et Ecrits: 1954-1988*. Paris: Gallimard, 1994.

____. *L'Archeologie du savoir*. Paris: Gallimard, 1969.

____. *The Foucault Reader*. New York: Penguin, 1991.

____. *Power/Knowledge*. New York: Pantheon, 1980.

____. *L'ordre du discours*. Paris: Gallimard, 1971.

____. *The Politics of Truth*. Edited by Sylvère Lotringer. New York: Semiotext(e), 1997.

Franklin, Julian H. *Jean Bodin and the Sixteenth Century Revolution in Methodology of Law and History*. New York: Columbia University Press, 1963.

Frede, Dorothea, "The Dramatization of Determinism: Alexander of Aphrodisias's *De Fato*." *Phronesis* 27, no.3 (1982).

____. "The Sea-Battle Reconsidered: A Defense of the Traditional Interpretation." In *Oxford Studies in Ancient Philosophy* 3. Oxford: Clarendon Press, 1985.

Fritz von, Karl. *The Theory of the Mixed Constitution in Antiquity*. New York: Columbia University Press, 1954.

____. *Schriften zur griechischen u. römischen Verfassungsgeschichte*. Berlin: de Gruyter, 1976.

Fueter, Eduard. *Geschichte der neueren historiographie*. Berlin: Oldenburg, 1936.

Funkenstein, A. "Periodization and Self-understanding in the Middle Ages and Early Modern Times", *Mediaevalia et Humanistica* 5 (1976).

Gaiser, Konrad. *Platon und die Geschichte*. Stuttgart: Frommann Verlag, 1961.

Garin, Eugenio. *Machiavelli fra politica e storia*. Turin: Einaudi, 1993.

____. *Dal Rinascimento all'Illuminismo*. Pisa: Nistri-Lischi, 1970.

____. *Rinascite e Rivoluzioni*. Rome: Laterza, 1976.

____. *Lo Zodiaco della Vita*. Rome: Laterza, 1976.

____. *Medioevo e Rinascimento*. Rome: Laterza, 1973.

Garver, Eugene. *Machiavelli and the History of Prudence*. Madison, Wis.: University of Wisconsin Press, 1987.

Gentile, Giovanni. *Giordano Bruno e il pensiero del Rinascimento*. Florence: Le Lettere, 1991.

Gerschmann, K.-H. "Über Machiavellis Modernität", *Archiv für Begriffgeschichte* 17 (1973).

Geuna, Marco. "La tradizione repubblicana e i suoi interpreti: famiglie teoriche e discontinuità concettuali", *Filosofia Politica* XII,1 (1998): 101-32.

Geuss, Raymond. "Auffassungen der Freiheit", *Zeitschrift für philosophische Forschung* 49, no.1 (1995): 1-14.

Gigante, Marcello. *Nomos basileus*. Naples: Bibliopolis, 1993.

Gilbert, Felix. *Machiavelli and Guicciardini. Politics and History in Sixteenth Century Florence*. Princeton: Princeton University Press, 1965.

____. "Bernardo Rucellai and the Orti Oricellari: A Study of the Origin of Modern Political Thought." *Journal of the Warburg and Courtauld Institutes* 12 (1949): 101-131 .

____. "Florentine Political Assumptions in the Period of Savonarola and Soderini." *Journal of the Warburg and Courtauld Institutes* 20 (1957): 187-214.

____. "The Composition and Structure of Machiavelli's *Discorsi*." *The Journal of History of Ideas* 14 (1953): 136-156.

____. "The Humanist Concept of the Prince and *The Prince* of Machiavelli." *Journal of Modern History* 11 (1939): 449-83.

Gmelin H. von "Das Prinzip der Imitatio in den romanischen Literaturen der Renaissance." *Romanische Forschungen* 46 (1972).

Grauhan, Rolf-Richard. "Der 'Staat' des Machiavelli und der moderne Begriff des 'Politischen' - Hypothesen für eine erneute Überprüfung." In *Res Publica. Studien zum Verfassungswesen*. Edited by Peter Haungs. München: Wilhelm Fink, 1977.

Gravelle, S. S. "Humanist Attitudes to Convention and Innovation in the 15th century." *Journal of Medieval and Renaissance Studies* 11 (1981).

Green, Louis. *Chronicle into History: an Essay on the Interpretation of History in Florentine Fourteenth Century Chronicles*. Cambridge: Cambridge University Press, 1972.

Greene, T.M. *The Light in Troy: Imitation and Discovery in Renaissance Poetry*. New Haven: Yale University Press, 1982.

Griewank, Karl. "Staatsumwälzung und Revolution in der Auffassung der Renaissance und Barockzeit." *Wissenschaftliche Zeitschrift der Friedrich-Schiller-Universität Jena* 1 (1952/53): 11-23.

____. *Der neuzeitliche Revolutionsbegriff*. Frankfurt: Suhrkamp, 1973.

Guicciardini, Francesco. *Opere*. Edited by Vittorio de Caprariis. Milan: Ricciardi, 1953.

Guillemain, Bernard. *Machiavel: L'Anthropologie politique*. Geneva: Librairie Droz, 1977.

____. "Machiavel lecteur d'Aristote." In *Platon et Aristote à la Renaissance: XVI Colloque Internationale de Tours*. Paris: Vrin, 1976.

Gunnell, John G. *Political Philosophy and Time*. Middletown, CT: Wesleyan University Press, 1968.

Habermas, Jürgen. *Between Facts and Norms*. Cambridge: MIT Press, 1996.

____. *The Philosophical Discourse of Modernity*. Cambridge: MIT Press, 1987.

____. *Theory and Practice*. Boston: Beacon Press, 1973.

____. "Law and Morality". In *The Tanner Lectures on Human Values VIII, 1988*. Cambridge: Cambridge University Press, 1990.

Hampshire, Stuart. *Innocence and Experience*. Cambridge: Harvard University Press, 1989.

Hariman, Robert. "Composing Modernity in Machiavelli's *Prince*." *The Journal of the History of Ideas* 50, no.1 (January-March 1989): 3-29.

Hegel, Georg Wilhelm Friedrich. *Phenomenology of Spirit*. New York: Oxford University Press, 1977.

____. *Philosophy of Right*. Oxford: Oxford University Press, 1942.

Heidegger, Martin. *Ontologie: Hermeneutik der Faktizität*. Frankfurt: V. Klostermann, 1995.

Heitemann, Klaus. *Fortuna und Virtus: eine Studie zu Petrarcas Lebensweisheit*. Köln: Bohlam,1958.

Held, Klaus. "Civic Prudence in Machiavelli: Toward the Paradigm Transformation in Philosophy in the Transition to Modernity." In *The Ancients and the Moderns*. Edited by Reginald Lilly. Bloomington: Indiana University Press, 1996.

Heller, Agnes, *Renaissance Man*. London: Routledge, 1978.

Hexter, J.H. *Reappraisals in History: New Views on History and Society in Early Modern Europe*. Chicago: University of Chicago Press, 1979.

Hobbes, Thomas. *Leviathan*. New York: Penguin, 1981.

____. *De Cive*. In *Man and Citizen*. Cambridge: Hackett, 1991.

Honig, Bonnie. *Political Theory and the Displacement of Politics*. Ithaca: Cornell University Press, 1993.

Horkheimer, Max. *Anfänge der bürgerlichen Geschichtsphilosophie*. Frankfurt: Fischer, 1970.

Hulliung, Mark. *Citizen Machiavelli*. Princeton: Princeton University Press, 1983.

Jacks, Philip. *The Antiquarian and the Myth of Antiquity. The Origins of Rome in Renaissance Thought*. Cambridge: Cambridge University Press, 1993.

Jamme, Christoph. "Gangrene and Lavender Water: Hegel as an Advocate of Machiavelli." *Philosophical Studies* 33 (1992): 93-106.

Kahn, Victoria. "Virtù and the Example of Agathocles in Machiavelli's *Prince*." *Representations* 13 (Winter 1986): 63-83.

____. *Machiavellian Rhetoric. From the Counter-Reformation to Milton*. Princeton: Princeton University Press, 1994.

Kant, Immanuel. *Grounding for the Metaphysics of Morals*. Indianapolis: Hackett, 1983.

____. *Political Writings*. Edited by Hans Reiss. New York: Cambridge University Press, 1991.

____. *Metaphysics of Morals*. New York: Cambridge University Press, 1991.

Kantorowicz, Ernst. *The King's Two Bodies: a Study in Medieval Political Theology*. Princeton: Princeton University Press, 1957.

Kelley, D.R. "The Theory of History." In *Cambridge History of Renaissance Philosophy*. New York: Cambridge University Press, 1988.

Kiefer, F. "The Conflagration of Fortune and Occasion in Renaissance Thought and Iconography." *Journal of Medieval and Renaissance Studies* 9 (1977).

Koselleck, Reinhard. *Futures Past. On the Semantics of Historical Time*. Cambridge: MIT Press, 1985.

____. *Geschichtliche Grundbegriffe*. O. Brunner, W. Conze, R. Koselleck eds. Stuttgart: Klett, 1972-.

____. "Time and Revolutionary Language." *The Public Realm: Essays on Discursive Types in Political Philosophy*. Edited by R. Schürmann. Albany, NY: State University Press of New York, 1989.

____. *Critique and Crisis: Enlightenment and the Parthogenesis of Modern Society*. New York: Berg, 1988.

Koyré, Alexandre. *Etudes d'histoire de la pensée philosophique*. Paris: Gallimard, 1971.

Krantz, F. "Between Bruni and Machiavelli: History, Law, and Historicism in Poggio Bracciolini." In *Politics and Culture in Early Modern Europe*. Edited by P. Mack and M. Jacobs. Cambridge: Cambridge University Press, 1987.

Kretzmann, Norman. "Nos Ipsi Principia Sumus: Boethius and the Basis of Contingency." In *Divine Omniscience and Omnipotence in Medieval Philosophy*. Edited by T. Rudavsky. Utrecht: Reidel, 1985.

Kucharski, Pierre. "Le concept du kairos." *Revue Philosophique* 18 (1963).

Lacoue-Labarthe, Philippe. *L'imitation des modernes*. Paris: Galilée, 1986.

Lazzeri, Christian. "Prudence, Ethique et Politique de Thomas D'Aquin à Machiavel." In *De la prudence des Anciens à celle des Modernes. Annales littéraires de l'université de Franche-Comté* (1995).

____. "Machiavel, la guerre interieure et le gouvernement du prince." Forthcoming: *Archives de Philosophie* (May 1999).

Leeker, Joachim. "Fortuna bei Machiavelli - ein Erbe der Tradition?" *Romanische Forschungen* 101 (1989): 407-432.

Lefort, Claude. *Le Travail de L'oeuvre Machiavel*. Paris: Gallimard, 1972.

____. *Ecrire. A l'épreuve du politique*. Paris: Calmann-Levy, 1992.

Levinas, Emanuel. *Nouvelles Lectures Talmudiques*. Paris: Minuit, 1996.

Livy. *Ab urbe condita*. Cambridge: Harvard University Press, 1974.

Lovejoy, Arthur O. and Boas, George. *Primitivism and Related Ideas in Antiquity*. Baltimore, 1935.

Löwith, Karl. *Meaning in History*. Chicago: University of Chicago Press, 1949.

Lukes, Steven ed. *Power*. New York: Blackwell, 1986.

Lyotard, Jean-Francois. *L'enthousiasme. La critique kantienne de l'histoire*. Paris: Galilée, 1986.

____. *Le Postmoderne expliqué aux enfants*. Paris: Galilée, 1986.

Machiavelli, Niccolò. *Tutte le opere*. Edited by M. Martelli. Florence: Sansoni, 1974.

____. *Discorsi sopra la Prima Deca di Tito Livio*. Edited by Giorgio Inglese. Milan: Rizzoli, 1984.

____. *Discourses on Livy*. Translated by Harvey C. Mansfield and Nathan Tarcov. Chicago: University of Chicago Press, 1996.

____. *Il Principe*. Edited by Giorgio Inglese. Turin: Einaudi, 1995.

____. *The Prince*. Translated by Harvey C. Mansfield. Chicago: University of Chicago Press, 1998.

____. *The Prince*. Translated by Robert M. Adams. New York: W.W. Norton, ____1992.

____. *Lettere*. Edited by Franco Gaeta. Milan: Feltrinelli, 1981.

____. *Machiavelli and His Friends. Their Personal Correspondence*. Edited by James B. Atkinson and David Sices. DeKalb, Ill.: Northern Illinois University Press, 1996.

Mansfield, Harvey. *Machiavelli's Virtue*. Chicago: University of Chicago Press, 1996.

____. *Machiavelli's New Modes and Orders*. Ithaca, NY: Cornell University Press 1979.

Manuel, Frank. *Shapes of Philosophical History*. Stanford: Stanford University Press, 1965.

Marongiu, A. "La parola 'stato' nel carteggio Machiavelli- Guicciardini-Vettori." *Storia e Politica* 14 (1975).

Martelli, Mario. "La logica providenzialistica e il capitolo XXVI del 'Principe'." *Interpres* 4 (1981-2).

Marx, Karl. *The Marx-Engels Reader*. New York: W.W. Norton and Company, 1978.

____. *Early Writings*. New York: Vintage Books, 1975.

Masters, Roger D. *Machiavelli, Leonardo and the Science of Power*. Notre Dame: University of Notre Dame Press, 1996.

Mau, J. and Schmidt, E.G., eds. *Isonomia. Studien zur Gleichheitsvorstellung im griechischen Denken*. Berlin: Akademie Verlag, 1971.

Mazzarino, Santo. *La Fine del Mondo Antico*. Milan: Rizzoli, 1995.

____. *Dalla Monarchia allo Stato Repubblicano: Ricerche di Storia Romana Arcaica*. Milan: Rizzoli, 1992.

____. *Storia romana e storiografia moderna*. Napoli: Conte, 1954.

____. *Il pensiero storico classico*. Bari: Laterza, 1983.

McCormick, J. P. "Fear, Technology and the State. Carl Schmitt, Leo Strauss and the Revival of Hobbes in Weimar and National Socialist Germany." *Political Theory* 4 (1994).

McIlwain, Charles. *Constitutionalism : ancient and modern*. Ithaca, NY: Great Seal Books, 1961.

Meier, Christian. *The Greek Discovery of Politics*. Cambridge: Harvard University Press, 1990.

Meinecke, Friedrich. *Machiavellism: the Doctrine of Raison d'Etat and its Place in Modern History*. New Brunswick: Transaction Publishers, 1998.

____. *Historism: the Rise of a New Historical Outlook*. London: Routledge, 1972.

Meyer, Eduard W. *Machiavellis Geschichtsauffassung und sein Begriff virtu. Studien zu seiner Historik*. Berlin: R. Oldenburg, 1912.

Mill, John Stuart. *Utilitarianism*. Indianapolis: Hackett, 1979.

Minogue, K.R. "Theatricality and Politics: Machiavelli's Concept of Fantasia." In *The Morality of Politics*. Edited by B. Parekh and R.N. Berki. London: Allen and Unwin, 1972.

Momigliano, Arnaldo. "History between Medicine and Rhetoric." In *Ottavo contributo alla storia degli studi classici e del mondo antico*. Rome: Edizioni di storia e letteratura, 1987.

____. "Sulla Religione Romana". In *Ottavo contributo alla storia degli studi classici e del mondo antico*. Rome: Edizioni di storia e letteratura, 1987.

____. *Roma Arcaica*. Florence: Sansoni, 1989.

____. *Essays in Ancient and Modern Historiography*. Oxford: Oxford University Press, 1977.

____. *The Classical Foundations of Modern Historiography*. Berkeley: University of California Press, 1990.

____. "The Origins of the Roman Republic." In *Quinto Contributo alla storia degli studi classici e del mondo antico*. Rome: Edizioni di storia e letteratura, 1975.

____. "Prolegomena a ogni futura metafisica sulla plebe romana." In *Sesto Contributo alla storia degli studi classici e del mondo antico*. Rome: Edizioni di storia e letteratura, 1980.

____. "Ricerche sulle magistrature romane." In *Quarto Contributo alla storia degli studi classici e del mondo antico*. Rome: Edizioni di storia e letteratura, 1969.

____. *La storiografia greca*. Turin: Einaudi, 1982.

Mommsen, Theodor. *The History of Rome*. London: J.M. Dent, 1969.

____. *Römisches Staatsrecht*. Tübingen: Wissenschaftliche Buchgemeinschaft, 1952.

Mommsen, Theodor E. "St. Augustine and the Christian Idea of Progress." *The Journal of the History of Ideas* 12, no.3 (1951).

Moreau, Pierre-Francois. *Spinoza. L'expérience et l'éternité*. Paris: PUF, 1994.

Münckler, Herfried. *Machiavelli. Die Begründung des politischen Denkens der Neuzeit aus der Krise der Republik Florenz*. Frankfurt: Fischer, 1984.

Nadel, G. "Philosophy of History before Historicism." In *Studies in the Philosophy of History*. Edited by G. Nadel. New York: Harper and Row, 1965.

Nancy, Jean-Luc. *L'experience de la liberté*. Paris: Galilée, 1988.

Negri, Antonio. *Le pouvoir constituante. Essai sur les alternatives de la modernité*. Paris: PUF, 1995.

Nietzsche, Friedrich. *On the Genealogy of Morals*. New York: Vintage Books, 1989.

Nippel, Wilfried. *Mischverfassungstheorie und Verfassungsrealität in Antike und Früher Neuzeit*. Stuttgart: Klett-Cotta, 1980.

Nussbaum, Martha. "Shame, Separateness, and Political Unity: Aristotle's Criticism of Plato." In *Essays on Aristotle's Ethics*. Edited by Amelie Rorty. Berkeley: University of California Press, 1980.

____. *The Fragility of Goodness: Luck and Ethics in Greek Tragedy and Philosophy*. New York: Cambridge University Press, 1986.

Orr, Robert. "The Time Motif in Machiavelli." In *Machiavelli and the Nature of Political Thought*. Edited by Martin Fleischer. New York: Atheneum, 1972.

Ortega y Gasset, José. *Del Imperio Romano*. Madrid: Alianza, 1985.

Ostwald, Martin. *From Popular Sovereignty to the Sovereignty of Law: Law, Society and Politics in Fifth-Century Athens*. Berkeley: University of California Press, 1986.

Parel, Anthony. *The Machiavellian Cosmos*. New Haven: Yale University Press, 1992.

____. "The Question of Machiavelli's Modernity." *The Review of Politics* 53, no.2 (1991).

Panofsky, Erwin. "'Good Government' or Fortune." *Gazette des Beaux Arts* 68 (1966).

Patch, H.R. "The Tradition of the Goddess Fortune in Medieval Philosophy and Literature." *Smith College Studies in Modern Literature* 3 (1922).

Pennington, Kenneth. *The Prince and the Law, 1200-1600: Sovereignty and Rights in the Western Legal Tradition*. Berkeley: University of California Press, 1993.

Pennock, J., Roland, J., and Chapman, John W. eds. *Authority revisited*. New York: New York University Press, 1987).

Pettit, Phillip. *Republicanism. A Theory of Freedom and Government*. New York: Oxford University Press, 1997.

Pico della Mirandola. "Oration on the Dignity of Man." In *The Renaissance Philosophy of Man*. Edited by E. Cassirer, P.O. Kristeller, and J.H. Randall. Chicago: University of Chicago Press, 1948.

Pigman, G.W. "Versions of Imitation in the Renaissance." *Renaissance Quarterly* 33, no.1 (1980): 1-32.

Pitkin, Hannah. *Fortune is a Woman*. Berkeley: University of California Press, 1987.

Plato. *The Collected Dialogues of Plato*. Edited by Edith Hamilton and Huntington Cairns. New York: Pantheon Books, 1961.

____. *The Laws of Plato*. Translated by Thomas Pangle. New York: Basic Books, 1980.

____. *The Republic*. Translated by Allan Bloom. New York: Basic Books, 1968.

____. *Plato's Statesman*. Translated by Seth Benardete. Chicago: University of Chicago Press, 1986.

Plutarch. *Moralia*. Paris: Belles Lettres, 1990.

Pocock, John G.A. *The Machiavellian Moment. Florentine Political Thought and the Atlantic Republican Tradition*. Princeton: Princeton University Press, 1975.

____. "Custom and Grace, Form and Matter: An Approach to Machiavelli's Concept of Innovation." In *Machiavelli and the Nature of Political Thought*. Edited by Martin Fleischer. New York: Atheneum, 1972.

Pöggeler, Otto. "Hegel et Machiavel. Renaissance Italienne et Idéalisme Allemand." *Archives de Philosophie* 41 (1978): 435-467.

Polin, Raymond. "Les Régimes Politiques et l'imitation des Anciens chez Machiavel." In *Platon et Aristote à la Renaissance*. Paris: Vrin, 1976.

Polybius. *The Histories*. London: Penguin, 1979.

Poppi, A. "Fate, Fortune, Providence and Human Freedom." In *Cambridge History of Renaissance Philosophy*. New York: Cambridge University Press, 1988.

Puech, Henri-Charles. *En quete de la Gnose*. Paris: Gallimard, 1978.

Rahe, Paul A. *Republics Ancient and Modern: Classical Republicanism and the American Revolution*. Chapel Hill, NC: University of North Carolina Press, 1992.

Ramat, Raffaello. *Saggi sul Rinascimento*. Florence: La Nuova Italia, 1969.

Rancière, Jacques. *Dis-agreement: Politics and Philosophy*. Minneapolis: University of Minnesota Press, 1999.

Ranke, L. von. *Über die Epoche der neueren Geschichte. Vorträge dem Könige Maximilian II. Von Bayern gehalten*. Darmstadt: 1982.

Rawls, John. *Political Liberalism*. New York: Columbia University Press, 1993.

Raz, Joseph ed. *Authority*. Oxford: Blackwell, 1990.

Reinhardt, Karl. "Thucydides und Machiavel." In *Vermächtnis der Antike: Gesammelte Essays zur Philosophie und Geschichtsschreibung*. Göttingen: Vandenhoek and Ruprecht,1966.

Renaut, Alain. "Kant et l'humanisme." *Revue de philosophie politique* 2. Paris: PUF, 1992.

Richardson, Brian. "The Structure of Machiavelli's *Discorsi*." *Italica* 49, no.4 (1972): 460-471.

Ritter, Gerhard. *The Corrupting Influence of Power*. Westport, CT: Hyperion Press, 1979.

Ritter, Joachim. "Politik und Ethik in der praktischen Philosophie des Aristoteles." *Philosophisches Jahrbuch* 74 (1967).

____. *Metaphysik und Politik: Studien zu Aristoteles und Hegel*. Frankfurt: Suhrkamp, 1977.

Rogozinksi, Jacob, ed. *Le Retrait du Politique*. Paris: Galilée, 1983.

Romilly, Jacqueline de. "Le classement des constitutions d'Hérodote à Aristote." *Revue des études grecques* 72, 1959.

____. *La loi dans la pensée grecque des origines à Aristote*. Paris: Les Belles Lettres, 1971.

____. "Alcibiade et le mélange entre jeunes et vieux: politique et médecine." *Wiener Studien* 10 (1976): 93-105.

Rorty, Richard. *Contingency, Irony, and Solidarity*. Cambridge: Cambridge University Press, 1995.

____. *Truth and Progress. Philosophical Papers 3*. Cambridge: Cambridge University Press, 1998.

Richard Rorty, Jerome B. Schneewind, Quentin Skinner, eds. *Philosophy in History: Essays on the Historiography of Philosophy*. Cambridge: Cambridge University Press, 1984.

Rosen, Stanley. *Plato's Statesman: the Web of Politics*. New Haven: Yale University Press, 1995.

Rousseau, Jean-Jacques. *The Social Contract*. Translated by Maurice Cranston. Harmondsworth: Penguin, 1968.

____. *Discours sur l'origine et les fondements de l'inégalité parmi les hommes*. Paris: Gallimard, 1985.

Rubinstein, Nicolai. "Notes on the Word Stato in Florence before Machiavelli." *Florilegium Historiale: Essays presented to Wallace K. Ferguson*. Toronto: Toronto University Press, 1971.

____. "The History of the Word 'Politicus' in Early-Modern Europe." In *The Languages of Political Theory in Early-Modern Europe*. New York: Cambridge University Press, 1987.

____. "Politics and Constitutions in Florence at the End of the 15th Century." In *Italian Renaissance Studies*. Edited by E.F. Jacob. New York: Barnes and Noble, 1960.

____. "Stato and Regime in 15th Century Florence" In *Per Federico Chabod* (Annali della Facoltà di Scienza Politiche). Perugia: Olschki, 1980-1.

____. "Florentine Constitutionalism and Medici Ascendancy in the 15th Century." In *Florentine Studies. Politics and Society in Renaissance Florence*. Edited by N. Rubinstein. Evanston, Ill: Northwestern University Press, 1968.

Ryffel, H. *Metabole Politeion. Der Wandel der Staatsverfassungen*. New York: Arno Press, 1973.

Sallust. *Works*. New York: G.P. Putnam's sons, 1931.

Santoro, Mario. *Fortuna, ragione e prudenza nella civiltà letteraria del Cinquecento*. Napoli: Liguori, 1966.

Sartre, Jean-Paul. "Existentialism is a Humanism." In *Essays in Existentialism*. Edited by W. Baskin. New York: Citadel Press, 1970.

Sasso, Gennaro. *Studi su Machiavelli*. Naples: Morano, 1967.

____. *Machiavelli e gli antichi e altri saggi*. Milan: Ricciardi, 1987.

____. *Niccolò Machiavelli*. Bologna: Il Mulino, 1993.

Saxl, Fritz. "Veritas Filia Temporis." In *Philosophy and History. Essays presented to Ernst Cassirer*. Gloucester, MA: Peter Smith, 1975.

Schmitt, Carl. *Der Nomos der Erde im Volkerrecht des jus publicum Europaeum*. Berlin: Duncker and Humblot, 1988.

Schuhl, Pierre-Maxime. *La fabulation platonicienne*. Paris: Vrin, 1968.

_____. *Le Dominateur et les possibles*. Paris: PUF, 1960.

Schürmann, Reiner. *Heidegger on Being and Acting: From Principles to Anarchy*. Bloomington: Indiana University Press, 1987.

Seneca, *Dialogi*. Paris: Les Belles Lettres, 1922-1927.

Senellart, Michel. *Machiavélisme et raison d'état XIIe-XVIIIe siècle*. Paris: PUF, 1989.

_____. *Les Arts de gouverner: du regimen médiéval au concept de gouvernement*. Paris: Ed. du Seuil, 1995.

Serres, Michel. *Rome: the Book of Foundations*. Stanford: Stanford University Press, 1991.

Sfez, Gérald. "Machiavel: la raison des humeurs." *Rue Descartes* 12 (1995): 11-37.

_____. *Machiavel, le prince sans qualités*. Paris: Kimé, 1998.

Shklar, Judith. "Subversive Genealogies." *Daedalus* 101 (1972).

Skinner, Quentin. *The Renaissance*, vol.1 of *The Foundations of Modern Political Thought*. Cambridge: Cambridge University Press, 1978.

_____. "Machiavelli on the Maintenance of Liberty." *Politics* 18, no.2 (1983): 3-15.

_____. *Machiavelli*. New York: Hill and Nang, 1981.

_____. "The Idea of Negative Liberty: Philosophical and Historical Perspectives." In *Philosophy in History*. R. Rorty, J.B. Schneewind, and Q. Skinner, eds. Cambridge: Cambridge University Press, 1984.

_____. "The Paradoxes of Political Liberty." In *The Idea of Freedom*. Edited by A. Ryan. Oxford: Oxford University Press, 1979.

_____. "The Republican Ideal of Political Liberty." In *Machiavelli and Republicanism*. New York: Cambridge University Press, 1990.

_____. "The State." In *Political Innovation and Conceptual Change*. Edited by T.Ball, J. Farr, and R. Hanson. New York: Cambridge University Press, 1989.

Smith, Bruce James. *Politics and Rememberance. Republican Themes in Machiavelli, Burke, and Tocqueville*. Princeton: Princeton University Press, 1985.

Snyder, Claire R. *Citizen-Soldiers and Manly Warriors. Military Service and Gender in the Civic Republican Tradition*. New York: Rowman & Littlefield, 1999.

Solmsen, F. "Hesiodic Motifs in Plato." In *Hésiode et son influence. Entretiens sur l'Antiquité Classique VII*. Geneva: Fondation Hardt, 1962.

Sorabji, Richard. *Necessity, Cause, and Blame. Perspectives on Aristotle's Theory*. Ithaca, NY: Cornell University Press, 1980.

Spinoza, Baruch. *Tractatus theologico-politicus*. Translated by S. Shirley. New York: E.J. Brill, 1989.

Spitz, Jean-Fabien. *La Liberté politique*. Paris: PUF, 1995.

Stabile, Giorgio. "La Ruota della Fortuna: Tempo Ciclico e Ricorso Storico." In *Studi Filosofici. Istituto Universitario Orientale, Annali II, 1979*. Firenze: Olshki, 1981.

Strauss, Leo. *On Tyranny*. New York: Free Press, 1991.

_____. *An Introduction to Political Philosophy*. Detroit: Wayne State University Press, 1989.

_____. *Natural Right and History*. Chicago: University of Chicago Press, 1953.

_____. *What is Political Philosophy?* Chicago: University of Chicago Press, 1988.

_____. *Thoughts on Machiavelli*. Chicago: University of Chicago Press, 1984.

_____. *The Political Philosophy of Hobbes*. Chicago: University of Chicago Press, 1963.

Struever, Nancy. *The Language of History in the Renaissance: Rhetoric and Historical Consciousness in Florentine Humanism*. Princeton: Princeton University Press, 1970.

_____. *Theory as Practice: Ethical Inquiry in the Renaissance*. Chicago: University of Chicago Press, 1992.

Sullivan, Vickie. "Machiavelli's Momentary 'Machiavellian Moment': A Reconsideration of Pocock's Treatment of the *Discourses*." *Political Theory* 20 (1992): 309-318.

_____. *Machiavelli's Three Romes*. Ithaca: Cornell University Press, 1997.

Taylor, Charles. "What's Wrong with Negative Liberty". In *The Idea of Freedom*. Edited by A Ryan. Oxford: Oxford University Press, 1979.

_____. *Multiculturalism: Examining the Politics of Recognition*. Princeton: Princeton University Press, 1994.

Tenenti, Alberto. *Stato: un'idea, una logica*. Bologna: Il Mulino, 1987.

Thucydides. *History of the Peloponnesian War*. Translated by R. Crawley. London: Dent, 1993.

Trinkaus, Charles. "Antiquitas versus Modernitas: An Italian Humanist Polemic and its Resonance." *The Journal of the History of Ideas* 48, no.1 (1987): 11-21.

Veyne, Paul. *Les Grecs ont-ils cru à leurs mythes?* Paris: Seuil, 1983.

____. *Comment on ecrit l'histoire, suivi de Foucault revolutionne l'histoire*. Paris: Seuil, 1978.

Vico, Giambattista. *On the Most Ancient Wisdom of the Italians*. Ithaca, NY: Cornell University Press, 1988.

____. *The New Science*. Ithaca, NY: Cornell University Press, 1986.

Vidal-Naquet, Pierre. "Plato's Myth of the Statesman, the Ambiguities of the Golden Age and of History." *Journal of Hellenic Studies* 98 (1978): 132-141.

Vidal-Naquet, Pierre and Vernant, J.-P. *La Grèce ancienne. L'espace et le temps*. Paris: Seuil, 1991.

Virgil. *Vergil's Eclogues*. Chapel Hill, NC: University of North Carolina Press, 1997.

____. *Aeneid*. Translated by Robert Fitzgerald. New York: Random House, 1983.

Viroli, Maurizio. *From Politics to Reason of State*. New York: Cambridge University Press, 1992.

____. "The Revolution in the Concept of Politics." *Political Theory* 20, no.3 (1992): 473-495.

____. "Machiavelli and the Republican Idea of Politics." In *Machiavelli and Republicanism*. New York: Cambridge University Press, 1990.

____. *Machiavelli*. New York: Oxford University Press, 1998.

Von Albertini, Rudolf. *Firenze dalla repubblica al principato*. Turin: Einaudi, 1995.

Vries, H. de. *Essai sur la terminologie constitutionnelle chez Machiavel ('Il Principe')*. The Hague: Kluwer, 1957.

Vuillemin, Jules. *Nécessité ou contingence. L'aporie de Diodore et les systèmes philosophiques*. Paris: Editions de Minuit, 1984.

Walbank, F.W. *A Historical Commentary on Polybius*. Oxford: Clarendon Press, 1970.

Walsh, W.H. "Plato and Philosophy of History." *History and Theory* 2, no.1 (1962).

Walzer, Michael. *Thick and Thin: Moral Argument at Home and Abroad*. Notre Dame: University of Notre Dame Press, 1984.

Warburg, Aby. *Ausgewählte Schriften und Würdingungen*. Baden-Baden: Verlag Koerner, 1980.

Weber, Max. *Economy and Society*. Edited by G. Roth and C. Wittich. Berkeley: University of California Press, 1978.

Weisinger, H. "Ideas of History during the Renaissance." *The Journal of History of Ideas* 6 (1945).

Wilcox, Donald J. *The Development of Florentine Humanist Historiography in the Fifteenth Century*. Cambridge: Harvard University Press, 1969.

Wind, Edgar. "Platonic Tyranny and Renaissance Fortuna: on Ficino's Reading of *Laws*, IV, 709a-712b." In *Essays in Honor of Erwin Panofsky*. Edited by M. Meiss. New York: New York University Press, 1961.

Wolin, Sheldon. "Norm and Form: The Constitutionalizing of Democracy." In *Athenian Political Thought and the Reconstruction of American Democracy*. Edited by J. Peter Euben, John R. Wallach, Josiah Ober. Ithaca: Cornell University Press, 1994.

____. "Fugitive Democracy." In *Democracy and Difference. Contesting the Boundaries of the Political*. Edited by S. Benhabib. Princeton: Princeton University Press, 1996.

Zeppi, Stelio. "Il pessimismo antropologico nel Machiavelli del periodo anteriore ai 'Discorsi'." *Filosofia Politica* 6, no.2 (1992): 193-242.

NAME INDEX

Abensour, Miguel, 6n, 97n
Aeneas, 68
Agamben, Giorgio, 224n
Agathocles, 116–19
Agathon, 41, 151
Alberti, Leon Battista, 161n, 175–6, 175n
Albertini, Rudolf von, 191n
Alexander the Great, 202–3
Althusser, Louis, 2n, 22–23, 118, 177n
Anaxagoras, 39–40, 153
Anaximander, 38
Aquinas, Saint, 84, 96n, 146n
Arendt, Hannah, 5n, 12n, 14n, 41n, 51n, 63–6,
  71n, 75n, 76n, 80, 87n, 99, 107n, 108, 183n,
  197n, 221, 234n, 251n, 266n, 267n, 268n,
  308n
Aristotle, 20–1, 27n, 44–7, 50, 99–100, 138–41,
  147n, 150–2, 160–1, 168, 170–4, 184n, 187n,
  209n, 210n, 214, 218–19, 246, 261n, 285
Aron, Raymond, 13n
Aubenque, Pierre, 138n, 150–2, 150n, 159n
Augustine, Saint, 57–58, 130n, 289, 292n

Balaban, O., 156n, 173n
Baldini, Baccio, 191n
Baron, Hans, 13n, 17n, 19n, 122n
Bausi, Francesco, 316, 316n
Bencivenga, Ermanno, 183n
Benjamin, Walter, 3n, 20n, 31n, 251n, 257n, 290n
Benveniste, Emile, 77n
Berlin, Isaiah, 2, 3n, 84, 84n, 291, 291n
Berns, Thomas, 220n, 224n
Bertelli, Lucio, 209n
Blumenberg, Hans, 7n, 11n, 12n, 19n, 58n, 163n
Blythe, James M., 101n
Boas, George, 238n
Bobbio, Norberto, 84n
Boethius, 145–7, 145n, 146n, 152–4, 171, 173n,
  175, 179n, 206n
Bollack, Jean, 149n
Bondanella, Peter, 17n
Borgia, Cesare, 116–19
Brague, Remi, 160n
Brisson, Luc, 250n
Brown, Alison, 191n, 316n
Brown, Wendy, 108n, 134n, 156n, 185n
Bruni, Leonardo, 19, 103n
Brunner, Otto, 266n
Bruno, Giordano, 141n, 157, 228–9, 229n, 231

Brutus, 88–95, 99, 102, 126, 221–6, 243, 265–7,
  298
Buck, August, 17n
Burke, Peter, 17n

Callicles, 75, 199, 285, 302n
Camillus, 256–7, 260
Carr, Wesley, 289n
Cassirer, Ernst, 9n, 146n, 161n, 167, 176–7, 176n
Cavarero, Adriana, 225n
Chabod, Federico, 122n
Cicero, 50, 72, 76, 89n, 146n, 171, 197n, 204–7,
  205n, 235, 319
Clastres, Pierre, 14n, 97n, 132n
Cochrane, Charles, 27n, 38n
Cochrane, Eric, 17n
Collingwood, Robin George, 7n
Costa, Gustavo, 246n
Croce, Benedetto, 9n, 277, 291n
Cullmann, Oscar, 58n, 289n

David, 209n, 280, 288
De Grazia, Sebastian, 2n
De Mattei, Rodolfo, 139n
Deleuze, Gilles, 10n, 97, 112n, 140n, 187n,
  242–5, 247n
Derla, Lucio, 146n
Derrida, Jacques, 10n, 239–42
Desan, Philippe, 145n, 176n
Descartes, 157, 162n, 164n
Detienne, Marcel, 39n, 164n
Diano, Carlo, 37–8, 40n, 150n
Dietz, Mary, 314n
Doren, A., 133n

Edelstein, Ludwig, 40n
Edmunds, Lowell, 40–1
Eliade, Mircea, 237–8
Empedocles, 149
Esposito, Roberto, 93n, 101n, 109n, 237n, 268n,
  289n
Euripides, 40

Fichte, 21
Ficino, 161n, 163, 190–1, 245n, 246n, 248n
Flanagan, Thomas, 133n
Fleischer, Martin, 144n, 185n
Foucault, Michel, 3n, 14, 272n
Frede, Dorothea, 150n, 172n
Freud, Sigmund, 290n
Fritz, Kurt von, 47n, 48, 54–55n, 64n, 104n, 312n

331

334 NAME INDEX

Vuillemin, Jules, 171n, 172n

Walbank, Frank W., 47n
Warburg, Aby, 184n, 191
Weber, Max, 65, 67n, 140, 286, 290n
Weil, Simone, 39n
Weisinger, Hans, 17n

Wind, Edgar, 184n, 191n
Wirszubski, Chaim, 308n
Wolin, Sheldon, 5n, 16n, 99n

Xenophon, 141, 296, 303, 317

Zeppi, Stelio, 124n

SUBJECT INDEX

COMMONALITIES
Timothy C. Campbell, *series editor*

Roberto Esposito, *Terms of the Political: Community, Immunity, Biopolitics.* Translated by Rhiannon Noel Welch. Introduction by Vanessa Lemm.

Maurizio Ferraris, *Documentality: Why It Is Necessary to Leave Traces.* Translated by Richard Davies.

Dimitris Vardoulakis, *Sovereignty and Its Other: Toward the Dejustification of Violence.*

Anne Emmanuelle Berger, *The Queer Turn in Feminism: Identities, Sexualities, and the Theater of Gender.* Translated by Catherine Porter.

James D. Lilley, *Common Things: Romance and the Aesthetics of Belonging in Atlantic Modernity.*

Jean-Luc Nancy, *Identity: Fragments, Frankness.* Translated by François Raffoul.

Miguel Vatter, *Between Form and Event: Machiavelli's Theory of Political Freedom.*

Miguel Vatter, *The Republic of the Living: Biopolitics and the Critique of Civil Society.*

Maurizio Ferraris, *Where Are You? An Ontology of the Cell Phone.* Translated by Sarah De Sanctis.